THE BIBLE IN AMERICAN LIFE

The Bible in American Life

Edited by

Philip Goff

Arthur E. Farnsley II

Peter J. Thuesen

OXFORD UNIVERSITY PRESS

2017

OXFORD
UNIVERSITY PRESS

Oxford University Press is a department of the University of Oxford.
It furthers the University's objective of excellence in research, scholarship,
and education by publishing worldwide. Oxford is a registered trade mark of
Oxford University Press in the UK and in certain other countries.

Published in the United States of America by Oxford University Press
198 Madison Avenue, New York, NY 10016, United States of America.

Library of Congress Cataloging-in-Publication Data
Names: Goff, Philip, 1964– editor. | Farnsley, Arthur Emery, editor. |
   Thuesen, Peter Johannes, 1971– editor.
Title: The Bible in American life / edited by Philip Goff, Arthur E. Farnsley II,
   Peter J. Thuesen.
Description: New York, NY : Oxford University Press, 2016.
Identifiers: LCCN 2016026845 (print) | LCCN 2016032236 (ebook) |
   ISBN 9780190468910 (hardcover : alk. paper) | ISBN 9780190468927 (pbk. : alk. paper) |
   ISBN 9780190468934 (updf) | ISBN 9780190468941 (epub)
Subjects: LCSH: Bible—Criticism, interpretation, etc.—United States. |
   Bible—Study and teaching—United States. | Bible—Reading—United States.
   | Bible—Publication and distribution—United States. | Bible—Influence.
   | Religion and culture—United States. | Religion and politics—United
   States. | United States—Religion.
Classification: LCC BS540 .B44533 2016 (print) | LCC BS540 (ebook) |
   DDC 220.0973—dc23
LC record available at https://lccn.loc.gov/2016026845

9 8 7 6 5 4 3 2 1

Paperback printed by Webcom Inc., Canada
Hardback printed by Bridgeport National Bindery, Inc., United States of America

Contents

Acknowledgments

A BOOK SUCH as this one, with so many authors from so many disciplines, is a team effort. That is just as true behind the scenes. We are grateful for Nathaniel Wynne's hard work and attention to detail in putting together the manuscript from start to finish. Becky Vasko's expertise and commitment to excellence appeared throughout the Bible in American Life Project, including the 2014 conference. Finally, we want to thank Lilly Endowment, especially Christopher Coble, for having faith in this study and offering advice at crucial moments.

Contributors

Bryan Bibb is the Dorothy and B. H. Pearce, Jr. Associate Professor of Hebrew Bible at Furman University in Greenville, South Carolina. He is currently researching the rhetorical and theological context of contemporary biblical translation in America. His longer term project is a monograph, *Translation as Reception*, which examines English biblical translation from a historical and theoretical perspective. He has taught broadly in the biblical canon as well as an advanced seminar on the history of biblical reception. He is the author of *Ritual Words and Narrative Worlds in the Book of Leviticus* (2009) and *God's Servants, the Prophets* (2015).

James S. Bielo is Assistant Professor of Anthropology at Miami University, where he has taught since 2008. Bielo is the author of *Words upon the Word: An Ethnography of Evangelical Bible Study* (New York University Press, 2009), *Emerging Evangelicals: Faith, Modernity, and the Desire for Authenticity* (New York University Press, 2011), *Anthropology of Religion: The Basics* (Routledge, 2015), and editor of *The Social Life of Scriptures: Cross-cultural Perspectives on Biblicism* (Rutgers University Press, 2009). As a teacher-scholar at Miami, he primarily teaches courses in cultural and linguistic anthropology, ethnography, religion, American communities, and transnationalism.

Robert E. Brown is Associate Professor and Associate Head of the Department of Philosophy and Religion at James Madison University, where he teaches courses on religion in America. He is the author of *Jonathan Edwards and the Bible*, a study of Edwards's engagement with early modern biblical criticism. He is the editor of the ninth volume of Cotton Mather's *Biblia Americana* (forthcoming), Mather's encyclopedic commentary on the Bible. Brown recently walked the entire length of Hadrian's Wall.

Christopher D. Cantwell is Assistant Professor of Public History and Religious Studies at the University of Missouri-Kansas City, where he teaches courses on religious history, public history, and digital history. His work focuses on the relationships between evangelical Protestantism and industrial capitalism in America, particularly the role that class plays in shaping Protestant communities. His book manuscript, *The Bible Class Teacher: Piety and Politics in the Age of Fundamentalism*, is a microhistory of a self-identifying fundamentalist who also ran for political office as a member of the Socialist Party. He is also an editor of *The Pew and the Picket Line: Christianity and the American Working Class* (University of Illinois Press, 2016). Before joining UMKC, Cantwell was the Assistant Director of the Dr. William M. Scholl Center for American History and Culture at the Newberry Library in Chicago, where he oversaw a number of digital humanities projects and exhibits.

Russell W. Dalton is Professor of Religious Education at Brite Divinity School in Fort Worth, Texas. His current research examines children's Bibles from throughout America's history. He has presented papers on children's Bibles at the annual meetings of the American Academy of Religion, the Religious Education Association, and the Society of Biblical Literature and has published two articles on the topic. He is the author of *Children's Bibles in America: A Reception History of the Story of Noah's Ark in US Children's Bibles* (Bloomsbury T & T Clark, 2015). His other publications include *Marvelous Myths: Marvel Superheroes and Everyday Faith; Faith Journey through Fantasy Lands: A Christian Dialogue with Harry Potter, Star Wars and The Lord of the Rings*, and other books, essays, and articles. Dalton has led national and regional conferences on topics related to religion and popular culture and religious education. He is an ordained minister of the American Baptist Churches USA.

Amy Easton-Flake is Assistant Professor of Ancient Scripture at Brigham Young University. Her research focuses on nineteenth-century women's reform literature and biblical hermeneutics. Currently, she is looking at how women from different religious backgrounds in the late nineteenth century interpreted the Bible and the exegetical works they produced for public consumption. Her work may be found in the *New England Quarterly, Symbiosis: A Journal of Transatlantic Literary and Cultural Relations, Journal of Mormon History, Journal of Book of Mormon Studies, Religious Educator*, and multiple collected volumes. She currently serves on the steering committee of the Recovering Women Interpreters of Scripture group at the Society of Biblical Literature.

Arthur E. Farnsley II is Research Professor of Religious Studies at Indiana University-Purdue University Indianapolis, Associate Director of the Center for the Study of Religion and American Culture, and Executive Officer of the Society for the Scientific Study of Religion. His books include *Flea Market Jesus; Sacred Circles, Public Squares: The Multicentering of American Religion; Rising Expectations: Urban Congregations, Welfare Reform, and Civic Life;* and *Southern Baptist Politics: Authority and Power in the Restructuring of an American Denomination.* He edits an Indiana University Press series on urban religion and was research director for the video series *Faith and Community: The Public Role of Religion.*

Linford D. Fisher, Associate Professor of History at Brown University, is a historian who writes and teaches on religion, Native Americans, and slavery in colonial America. He received his doctorate from Harvard University in 2008. He is the author of *The Indian Great Awakening: Religion and the Shaping of Native Cultures in Early America* (Oxford, 2012) and the coauthor, with J. Stanley Lemons and Lucas Mason-Brown, of *Decoding Roger Williams: The Lost Essay of Rhode Island's Founding Father* (Baylor, 2014). He is currently working on a book-length project on Indian and African enslavement in colonial New England and the English Atlantic. Fisher is also the author of ten additional essays and book chapters. His research has been supported by the National Endowment for the Humanities, the Massachusetts Historical Society, the American Antiquarian Society, the Newberry Library, the American Philosophical Society, Harvard University, and Brown University.

Amanda Friesen is Assistant Professor of Political Science and Faculty Research Fellow with the Center for the Study of Religion and American Culture at Indiana University-Purdue University Indianapolis. Her research interests include religion and politics, women and politics, political psychology, and biology and politics. She has published in *Political Behavior, Politics & Religion, Journal of Women, Politics & Policy, Social Science Quarterly, Forum,* and *PS: Political Science and Politics.*

Philip Goff is Chancellor's Professor of American Studies and Religious Studies, Director of the Center for the Study of Religion and American Culture at Indiana University-Purdue University Indianapolis, and coeditor of *Religion and American Culture: A Journal of Interpretation.* A historian of religion in North America, he is author or editor of more than forty books or journal issues. He is author of more than 150 articles, chapters, papers, and reviews on religion in the United States.

Paul C. Gutjahr is Ruth Halls Professor of English at Indiana University. His main field of research is American religious publishing. He has published numerous books and articles, including *An American Bible: A History of the Good Book in the United States* (Stanford University Press, 1999), *Charles Hodge: Guardian of American Orthodoxy* (Oxford University Press, 2011), and *The Book of Mormon: A Biography* (Princeton University Press, 2012).

Paul Harvey is Professor of History and Presidential Teaching Scholar at the University of Colorado. He received his PhD from the University of California, Berkeley, in 1992. He is the author and editor of eight books in American religious history and is the creator and "blogmeister" of the nationally known professional scholarly blog *Religion in American History,* as well as a contributor to the online journal *Religion Dispatches.* He also serves on the Board of Editors for the *Journal of Southern History* and *American Nineteenth Century History,* as well as *Religion Compass.* Harvey's recent book, coauthored with Edward J. Blum, *The Color of Christ: The Son of God and the Saga of Race in*

America, was named by *Choice* in 2013 to "Top 25 Outstanding Academic Titles," an award selected from among the several thousand academic books published in the previous year.

Jason A. Hentschel earned his MDiv at Baylor's Truett Theological Seminary and his doctoral degree in historical theology at the University of Dayton. Besides the theological and cultural foundations of local KJV-only congregations, his research interests lie in the function of biblical inerrancy for twentieth-century American evangelicals. Hentschel's recent publications have appeared in the *Journal of Theological Interpretation* and T & T Clark's *Companion to Reformation Theology*.

Sylvester A. Johnson is Associate Professor of African American Studies and Religious Studies at Northwestern University. His research examines religion, race, and empire in Atlantic geographies. Johnson recently published a postcolonial study of Black religion titled *African American Religions, 1500-2000: Colonialism, Democracy, and Freedom* (New York: Cambridge University Press, 2015). His first book, *The Myth of Ham in Nineteenth-Century American Christianity* (Palgrave, 2004), received the American Academy of Religion's Best First Book Award. He is a founding coeditor of the *Journal of Africana Religions*. Among his current research projects are a study of U.S. empire, a coedited volume on religion and the FBI, and a digital scholarly edition of Samuel Purchas's *Purchas His Pilgrimage* (1626).

John F. Kutsko is Executive Director of the Society of Biblical Literature and Affiliate Professor of Biblical Studies at Emory University. He earned a PhD in Near Eastern languages and civilizations from Harvard University. In 2012, he received a grant to explore forming a learned society for scholars of the Qur'an, which in 2014 became the International Qur'anic Studies Association, and serves as its consultant. He also serves on the editorial advisory board for the *Journal of General Education* and is guest editing an issue on religion in liberal arts and general education. He is a contributing editor of *The SBL Handbook of Style* (1999) and directed its 2014 revision. He is author of *Between Heaven and Earth: Divine Presence and Absence in the Book of Ezekiel* (2000) and coeditor of *The King James Version at 400: Assessing Its Genius as Bible Translation and Its Literary Influence* (2013).

J. Derrick Lemons is Assistant Professor of Religion at the University of Georgia. His teaching and research are guided by his interest in how religion in American culture changes over time and space. Currently, he is doing research on the effects of the Missional church movement in evangelical denominations in America and how millennials' theological, social, and religious community orientations influence their religiosity, and he is developing an anthropologically informed reflexive theological structure to aid research in the anthropology of Christianity. His most recent publications include a forthcoming chapter for Oxford University Press entitled "'Us-Them' Dilemma: The Need for Reflexivity While Teaching Interreligious Encounters," and an article in *CBE-Life Sciences Education*: "Questions for Assessing Higher-Order Cognitive Skills: It Is Not Just Bloom's."

Mark A. Noll is Francis A. McAnaney Professor of History Emeritus at the University of Notre Dame. His books include *In the Beginning Was the Word: The Bible in American Public Life, 1492–1783* (Oxford University Press, 2015), *Protestantism: A Very Short Introduction* (Oxford University Press, 2011), *God and Race in American Politics: A Short History* (Princeton University Press, 2008), *The Civil War as a Theological Crisis* (University of North Carolina Press, 2006), *America's God: From Jonathan Edwards to Abraham Lincoln* (Oxford University Press, 2002), and, as coeditor, *The Bible in America: Essays in Cultural History* (Oxford University Press, 1982). Recent essays have treated the Bible in the United States and Canada, the three-hundredth anniversary celebrations for the King James Version, and Bishop James Gibbons and the Bible.

Sara M. Patterson is Associate Professor of Theological Studies at Hanover College where she teaches courses in American religion and the history of Christianity. She is currently completing a book manuscript on Salvation Mountain, a work of outsider religious art in the California desert. Patterson received a Luce Fellowship from the Society of Arts in Religious and Theological Studies for this project.

B. M. Pietsch is Assistant Professor of Religious Studies at Nazarbayev University in Astana, Kazakhstan. He received a PhD in 2011 from Duke University in American religious history. His revised dissertation manuscript, *Dispensational Modernism*, examines the taxonomic impulses of American Protestant fundamentalism and is under contract with Oxford University Press. He is currently researching the early twentieth-century sciences of the family and the development of ecumenical family values.

Emerson B. Powery is Professor of Biblical Studies and Coordinator of Ethnic and Area Studies at Messiah College and an adjunct instructor in Bible at Lancaster Theological Seminary. In 2012, he was a visiting scholar at Princeton Theological Seminary. Most of his research, writing, and editing relates to the New Testament, hermeneutics, and the function of the Bible in underrepresented communities, including *Jesus Reads Scripture* (Brill), *True to Our Native Land: An African American NT Commentary* (Fortress/Augsburg), and "Philemon" in *The New Interpreter's One-Volume Commentary* (Abingdon). His current research is on the function of the Bible in the nineteenth-century African American "slave narrative" tradition, including one published essay, "'Rise Up Ye Women': Harriet Jacobs and the Bible," for *Postscripts: The Journal of Sacred Texts and Contemporary Worlds*. Powery served on the editorial board of the *Journal of Biblical Literature* (2005-2013) and the editorial board of the *Common English Bible*. He was the 2006–2007 President of the Society of Biblical Literature (SE Region).

Beth Barton Schweiger teaches early American social and cultural history at the University of Arkansas, Fayetteville. She is the author of *The Gospel Working Up: Progress and the Pulpit in Nineteenth-Century Virginia* (Oxford, 2000) and coeditor of *Religion in the American South* (North Carolina, 2004). She is completing a study of print and vernacular culture in the early South that has received support from the National Endowment for Humanities, Yale University, the American Antiquarian Society, the Library Company of Philadelphia, and the Huntington Library.

Claudia Setzer is Professor of Religious Studies at Manhattan College in Riverdale, New York. Her books include *The Bible and American Culture: A Sourcebook* (Routledge, 2011, with David Shefferman), *Resurrection of the Body in Early Judaism and Early Christianity* (Brill, 2004), and *Jewish Responses to Early Christians* (Augsburg Fortress, 1994). She studies early Jewish-Christian relations, women in the Greco-Roman era, nineteenth-century women interpreters of Scripture, and the Bible in American culture. She serves on the editorial board of the *Journal of Biblical Literature* and the steering committee of the Recovering Women Interpreters of Scripture group at the Society of Biblical Literature. In 2006 she founded the Columbia University Seminar on the New Testament and has chaired the Early Jewish-Christian Relations group at the Society of Biblical Literature.

Daniel Silliman teaches American religion and culture at the University of Heidelberg. His research interests include American evangelicals and Pentecostals, book history, atheism, and secularity. His recent publications include "The Possibility of Secularity and the Material History of Fiction" (*Claremont Journal of Religion*), and "Der Heidelberger Katechismus in Nordamerica: Vom Bürgerkrieg bis Heute" (*Evangelische Theologie*). Silliman has a BA in philosophy from Hillsdale College and an MA in American studies from the University of Tübingen. In Heidelberg, he is currently writing his doctoral dissertation on the representations of belief in contemporary evangelical fiction. He has lived in Germany with his wife since 2008. Before that he worked as a newspaper reporter in metro Atlanta.

Corwin E. Smidt is Professor Emeritus of Political Science and a Research Fellow of the Henry Institute at Calvin College. He is the author, editor, or coauthor/coeditor of sixteen books and has published in a variety of sociology and political science journals. His most recently completed volumes are *Pastors and Public Life: The Changing Face of American Protestant Clergy* (Oxford University Press, 2016), *American Evangelicals Today* (Rowman & Littlefield 2013), *The Disappearing God Gap? Religion in the 2008 Presidential Election* (Oxford University Press, 2010), *The Oxford Handbook of Religion and American Politics* (Oxford University Press, 2009), and *Pews, Prayers, and Participation: The Role of Religion in Fostering Civic Responsibility* (Georgetown University Press, 2008). Smidt was a founding member of the Religion and Politics section of the American Political Science Association, serving several terms on the section's executive council and once as its Executive Director. He has also served on the governing council of the Society for the Scientific Study of Religion and has recently served as its President.

Garrett Spivey teaches for the Department of History at Auburn University. His research interests include the confluence of religion, culture, and politics in twentieth-century American history. His dissertation is on the history of the Evangelical Orthodox Church, a group of evangelical Protestants who converted to Eastern Orthodox Christianity over the period of two decades beginning in the early 1970s. Led by former regional directors of Campus Crusade for Christ, this large group of converts subsequently began developing evangelization materials and strategies for further converting Protestants to Orthodox Christianity. Spivey has taught courses at Auburn University on American religious history and world history with a focus on religion.

Jan Stievermann is Professor of the History of Christianity in North America at the University of Heidelberg. He has written on a broad range of topics in the fields of American religious history and American literature, including articles for *Early American Literature, William and Mary Quarterly*, and *Church History*. His book *Der Sündenfall der Nachahmung: Zum Problem der Mittelbarkeit im Werk Ralph Waldo Emersons* (Schöningh, 2007; trans. *The Original Fall of Imitation: The Problem of Mediacy in the Works of Ralph Waldo Emerson*) is a comprehensive study of the coevolution of Emerson's religious and aesthetic thought. Together with Reiner Smolinski, he edited *Cotton Mather and Biblia Americana—America's First Bible Commentary* (Mohr Siebeck and Baker Academic, 2010). Most recently, he published, with Oliver Scheiding, *A Peculiar Mixture: German-Language Cultures and Identities in Eighteenth-Century North America* (Pennsylvania State University Press, 2013). Currently, he leads a team transcribing and editing vol. 5 of Cotton Mather's hitherto unpublished *Biblia Americana*, the first comprehensive Bible commentary produced in British North America. For the *Biblia* project as a whole (10 vols.) he also serves as the executive editor.

Matthew Avery Sutton is the Edward R. Meyer Distinguished Professor of History at Washington State University. He is the author of *American Apocalypse: A History of Modern Evangelicalism* (Harvard University Press, 2014), *Jerry Falwell and the Rise of the Religious Right: A Brief History with Documents* (Bedford/St. Martin's, 2012), and *Aimee Semple McPherson and the Resurrection of Christian America* (Harvard University Press, 2007). He has published articles in diverse venues ranging from the *Journal of American History* to the *New York Times* and has received fellowships from the National Endowment for the Humanities, the U.S. Fulbright Commission, and the Woodrow Wilson Fellowship Foundation.

Peter J. Thuesen is Professor of Religious Studies at Indiana University-Purdue University Indianapolis, where he also serves as coeditor of *Religion and American Culture: A Journal of Interpretation*. A historian of American religion and of the Christian tradition, he is the author of *Predestination: The American Career of a Contentious Doctrine*, which received the 2010 *Christianity Today* Book Award for History/Biography, and *In Discordance with the Scriptures: American Protestant Battles over Translating the Bible*, which received the Frank S. and Elizabeth D. Brewer Prize of the American Society of Church History. He is also the editor of a major critical edition, *The Works of Jonathan Edwards, Vol. 26, Catalogues of Books*.

Daniel Vaca is Assistant Professor of Religious Studies at Brown University. A historian of religion in North America, he specializes in the cultural and intellectual history of the nineteenth- and twentieth-century United States. Focusing much of his writing and teaching on the relationship between religious life, economic activity, and media, he currently is revising a book manuscript, *Book People: Commercial Media and the Making of American Evangelicalism*, which traces the history of the evangelical book industry and its audience from the end of the nineteenth century to the present. He received his PhD from Columbia University and held a postdoctoral appointment at Princeton University's Center for the Study of Religion.

John B. Weaver is the Dean of Library Services and Educational Technology at Abilene Christian University, providing leadership for the university's academic information technology and for a consortium of libraries in West Texas. His academic research and writing has focused on the literature of early Christianity and the contemporary role of the Bible in modern society. Weaver is currently writing a book on spiritual disciplines in digital culture.

Introduction

Philip Goff, Arthur E. Farnsley II, Peter J. Thuesen

THERE IS A paradox in American Christianity. According to Gallup, nearly eight in ten Americans regard the Bible as either the literal word of God or as inspired by God. At the same time, surveys have revealed—and recent books have analyzed—surprising gaps in Americans' biblical literacy. These discrepancies reveal American Christians' complex relationship to Holy Writ, a subject that is widely acknowledged but rarely investigated.

This lack of understanding of how, where, when, and why Americans use the Bible is frustrating for a variety of people. Clergy devoted to teaching parishioners often find an audience quick to revere the Bible but slow to read it for themselves—at least in a fashion beyond eisegesis. Seminary professors struggle to help the next generation of ministers convey the Bible's relevance and meaning in a world where online sources compete with the traditional authority of the church. Other scholars attempt to reconcile people's professed respect for the Bible with their general practice of ignoring it. All three of these—clergy, seminary faculty, and other scholars—struggle with the dearth of research on Bible reading as an aspect of lived religion.

This book provides the first large-scale investigation, past and present, of the Bible in daily American life, outside services. First, we added questions to an annual national survey of American social characteristics and attitudes, as well as questions on a study of congregations. After making public our findings of how the Bible is used in daily life, we asked scholars from a variety of disciplines—sociology, history, and theology, among others—to help us provide historical, cultural, and social background for interpreting the survey data. Together, these deeper analyses of key questions asked of the data provide a foundation for scholars and ministers to better understand the Bible's role in Americans' daily lives.

The project has been driven by the recognition that though the Bible has been central to Christian practice throughout American history, many important questions remain unanswered in scholarship, including how people have read the Bible for themselves outside worship, how denominational and parachurch publications have influenced interpretation and application, and how clergy and congregations have influenced individual understandings of scripture. These questions are even more pressing today, as denominations are losing much of their traditional authority, technology is changing people's reading and cognitive habits, and subjective experience is continuing to eclipse textual authority as the mark of true religion.

Despite the Bible's tremendous influence in American culture, there is a remarkable dearth of recent overviews of the subject. Indeed, the last landmark attempts to synthesize the Bible's role in the culture are now some three decades old. In 1982, amid the Reagan presidency and the rise of the Christian Right, Nathan O. Hatch and Mark A. Noll edited *The Bible in America: Essays in Cultural History*, which included chapters on, among other topics, the Bible in colonial New England, the Bible and science in the nineteenth century, the Bible in Protestant fundamentalism, and the Bible in American Catholicism.[1] The same year, the Society of Biblical Literature (SBL) released the first installment in a six-volume collection, *The Bible in American Culture* (Scholars Press, 1982–88), overseen by general editors Edwin S. Gaustad and Walter J. Harrelson.[2] Since then, the SBL has produced several more focused studies, including *The Bible in the Public Square: Its Enduring Influence in American Life* (2014).[3] Yet not since the 1980s has there been any truly synthetic attempt to understand the Bible's relationship to the multiple facets of American culture.

There have been, of course, both monographs and edited volumes on particular aspects of the Bible in the culture. On Bible versions—the scriptures as continually retranslated, reformatted, and republished—a pair of monographs appeared in 1999: Paul C. Gutjahr's *An American Bible: A History of the Good Book in the United States, 1777–1880* and Peter J. Thuesen's *In Discordance with the Scriptures: American Protestant Battles over Translating the Bible*.[4] The four-hundredth anniversary of the King James Bible in 2011 also prompted a spate of publications, including Hannibal Hamlin and Norman W. Jones, eds., *The King James Bible after 400 Years: Literary, Linguistic, and Cultural Influences*. Other books have examined the Bible's role for particular communities. Vincent L. Wimbush's edited volume *African Americans and the Bible: Sacred Texts and Social Textures* is a wide-ranging collection. And for primary source documents for classroom use, Claudia Setzer and David A. Shefferman's edited volume is a useful resource. But there currently exists no comparable recent collection of secondary studies, a gap we hope this volume will fill.[5]

Finally, this project differs from all others in that it contains both historical and recent social scientific studies, all focused on the Bible in American life. Part I (chapter 1) contains the analysis of questions placed on the General Social Survey and the National Congregations Study III by the Center for the Study of Religion and American Culture at Indiana University-Purdue University Indianapolis (IUPUI). This chapter gives a good overview of the survey materials and some historical contexts for those findings.

Part II contains historical studies of how Americans have used the Bible in their daily lives. Part III offers eleven chapters on contemporary uses of the Bible by an interdisciplinary group of scholars. The final part, containing a concluding chapter by Mark Noll, ties together the approaches. In all, the chapters and parts complement one another in approach and periods covered, with some themes running through both.

This book is the culmination of a four-year study by the Center for the Study of Religion and American Culture at Indiana University-Purdue University Indianapolis. Sponsored by Lilly Endowment, the interdisciplinary project's goal was to gain insight for scholars and clergy on Bible-reading as religious practice. We were particularly interested in how people use the Bible in their personal lives and how other influences, including religious communities and the internet, shape individuals' comprehension of scripture. Employing both quantitative methods and qualitative research, the project provided an unprecedented perspective on the Bible's role outside worship, in the lived religion of a broad cross-section of Americans both now and in the past.

This book is therefore a collection of the social scientific and historical findings of that project. The chapters were among those presented at the national conference about the project that was held in Indianapolis in August 2014.[6] Our goal was a more complete understanding of the many ways Americans engage the Bible in their everyday lives, with a special emphasis on biblical engagement outside the traditional worship setting. For that reason, we hope this book will find readership among various audiences.

THE BIBLE IN AMERICAN LIFE

PART ONE

Overview

1

The Bible in American Life Today

Philip Goff, Arthur E. Farnsley II, and Peter J. Thuesen

THERE ARE MANY scriptures in such a religiously diverse country as the United States. The most ubiquitous and influential is the Bible. But there are many translations of the Bible employed by Americans. On top of that, there are many resources Americans consult to better understand what they read—and many reasons they turn to the Bible in the first place. So while the United States may appear to be a Bible-dominated country, there is incredible variety within that description.

The purpose of this chapter is to get at how and why Americans use the Bible in their daily lives. How many people read it? What are their feelings about the text? Which versions are most often used? Do people memorize it? Are there favorite shared books or passages? Why do people turn to the Bible on their own? What sources do they consult if they need assistance in understanding it? How do they read their Bibles—as a book, online, on e-devices? And what role do religious traditions play in the practice of scripture reading? Across the board, as one would expect, American social structures and cultural differences appear in people's responses to these questions, including, most notably, race, gender, education, and income levels.

We got answers to many of these questions through two national surveys. The first, the 2012 General Social Survey (GSS), included two dozen questions on individual Bible use alongside the hundreds of others that usually appear on the GSS. This enabled us to put the responses to our questions into much larger data sets, thus revealing how various social structures and cultural differences are tied to the levels and types of Bible reading. We also included questions on the National Congregations Study III (NCS), an excellent longitudinal study by Mark Chaves that reveals much about congregational life. Our concerns in those questions centered on how the Bible is used in congregations and how congregational life might shape Bible usage outside services. (Both surveys' questions are in the appendices at the end of the chapter.)

Throughout this chapter, we attempt to explain in a deeper fashion some of the contexts for the results revealed in the surveys. We had help in this endeavor. Our project advisors, Ronald Allen, Mark Chaves, Thomas J. Davis, Sylvester A. Johnson, and Amy Plantinga Pauw—all top scholars in their fields—offered helpful analysis, and many of their incisive comments are sprinkled throughout.[1]

1. A NATION DIVIDED
Scripture Reading in the United States

There are many ways to read or use scripture, but we were especially interested in learning how many people read scripture on their own outside worship services. This is not to discount the use of scripture in worship—which we also examined— or to ignore references to scripture in law, literature, or popular media. But we wanted to know "Who reads scripture and how often do they do it?" As one might expect, scripture reading in America is overwhelmingly Bible reading, so we began by asking about all scripture and then turned quickly to the Bible because of its dominant position.

1. The first question to individuals—the question on which all other results depended—was simply this: "Within the last year, have you read the Bible, Torah, Koran, or other religious scriptures, not counting any reading that happened during a worship service?" The nation is divided almost equally between those who read any scripture in the past year and those who did not (see fig. 1.1).

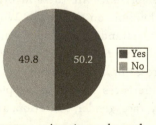

FIGURE 1.1 Americans who read scripture in past year

2. Among most faiths and denominations in the United States, women constitute the greater portion of congregants and attend- ees. This gender difference can also be seen among those who read scripture individu- ally, outside formal services: 56 percent of women and 39 percent of men said they read scripture individually in the past year.

3. There are also differences in age. For all scriptures, older people read more than younger people do (see fig. 1.2).

4. Regional differences appear. The regional demographics of scripture readers closely align with the regional distribution of race and religious traditions, both of which are discussed later in this chapter (see fig. 1.3).

Bible Reading in the United States

While it is important to know about all types of scripture reading in the United States, most of this chapter concerns those who identified the Bible as the scripture they read within the past twelve months, which is 48 percent of the total U.S. population.

This split on Bible reading is fascinating because we can look at so many characteristics of people on two roughly equal sides. For instance, the United States is frequently portrayed as a land of conservative, even fundamentalist, beliefs about the Bible, so one might reasonably assume that the half who have read the Bible in the past year are the religious conservatives or fundamentalists. But it might be better simply to say they are *more* religiously conservative than the population as a whole. In fact, 15 percent of those who have *not* read *any* scripture in the past year still think the Bible is the "inerrant Word of God," and another 50 percent of those who have not read scripture think of the Bible as the "divinely inspired Word of God." In other words, two-thirds of Americans who do not read any scripture still have a very high view of the Bible.

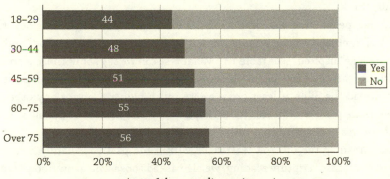

FIGURE 1.2 Ages of those reading scripture in past year

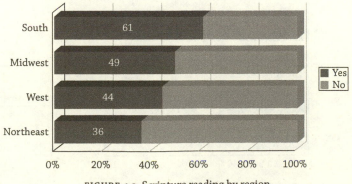

FIGURE 1.3 Scripture reading by region

TABLE 1.1

	Feelings about the Bible			
In the past year, have you read the Bible outside a worship service?	Inerrant word of God	Inspired word of God	Book of fables	Other
Yes	45%	46%	9%	1%
No	15%	50%	33%	2%

This reinforces what religion scholars knew already: *Americans have a very high view of the Bible—they think of it as inerrant or at least divinely inspired—whether they read it or not.* As Paul C. Gutjahr, one the advisors of the study, said, "there is an interesting connection here between the fact that one need not necessarily read the Word of God regularly to deem it divinely inspired. There is a separation here between belief and practice. A strong belief in the status of the Bible does not necessarily dictate regular reading of that same Bible. In that sense, the Bible takes on a sort of sacred totemic value that might be less instrumental in terms of reading practices than one might originally think."

Of course, people who *have* read the Bible in the past year hold views of it that are higher still. Among them, 45 percent think it is the "inerrant Word of God" and 46 percent think it is "inspired" (see table 1.1). What else can we say about those who did read the Bible at least once in the past year? Most important, 70 percent of black people said they read the Bible at least once, a rate much higher than for any other group. Meanwhile, 44 percent of whites (non-Hispanic) and 46 percent of people who identified themselves as Hispanic said they had read it (see fig. 1.4).

Because reading the Bible at least once within the past year hardly constitutes a standard of intense scripture reading, we also asked those who answered yes to tell us about their scripture reading in the past 30 days. While these frequencies apply to all

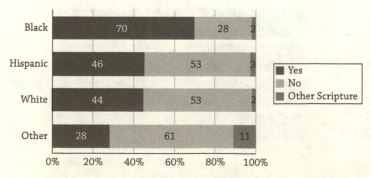

FIGURE 1.4 Read the Bible at least once in past year

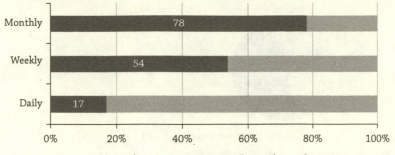

FIGURE 1.5 Bible reading frequency among those who read in past year

scripture readers, the frequencies for "Bible readers" are essentially the same. The number of people who read other scriptures is too small to make meaningful comparisons even in a very good sample such as this (see fig. 1.5).

In summary, roughly half of Americans have read scripture outside worship in the past year. For 95 percent of those, the Bible is the scripture they read. Most of those people read at least monthly, and a substantial number—9 percent of all Americans—read every day. Women were more likely to read than men, older people were more likely to read than younger, southerners were more likely to read than those of any other region, and black people were more likely to read than those of any other race. Even Americans who do not read the Bible tend to have a high view of it, but, not surprisingly, those who do read it have a higher view still—or put another way, those with a higher view are even more likely to read it.

2. WHICH VERSION OF THE BIBLE?

Most Americans who use the Bible in their everyday lives read it in translation from the original Hebrew and Greek. Since the earliest English-speaking settlements in America, the Protestant King James Bible (1611) has had a special place in the culture. Yet huge advances in biblical scholarship led to an explosion of new Bible versions by the twentieth century. These included the Revised Standard Version (1952) and its successor, the New Revised Standard Version (1990), both sponsored by the National Council of Churches (an ecumenical coalition of Protestant denominations that share a moderate to liberal stance on social issues), and the New International Version (1978), published by Zondervan (a conservative evangelical press).[2] The NIV quickly became so popular among evangelicals that in 1986 it overtook the King James Bible as the best-selling translation.[3] Since then, the NIV has been published in a variety of study editions catering to different niche markets, including the NIV Women's Devotional Bible (1990), the NIV Men's Devotional Bible (1993), the NIV Teen Study Bible (2004), the NIV Couples' Devotional Bible (1994), and the NIV Engaged Couples Bible (2012).

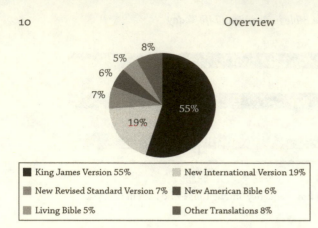

FIGURE 1.6 Bible translation
used by readers

Though the NIV's best-selling status has been driven in part by the multimillion-dollar evangelical publishing industry, we wondered whether Americans actually choose to read the NIV more than other Bibles. On the GSS, therefore, we asked the self-identified Bible readers: "What translation of the Bible do you most often read? Is it the King James Version, New International Version, New American Bible, New Revised Standard Version, Living Bible, or some other version?" Surprisingly, the KJV remained the most widely read (see fig. 1.6).

FIGURE 1.7 Congregations that
encourage use of the NIV

On the NCS, we asked: "Does your congregation encourage people to use the New International Version of the Bible rather than other translations?"

As these figures show, about one-fifth of both individual respondents and congregations either use or encourage the use of the NIV. Among congregations, approximately 40 percent report using the KJV in worship and 10 percent the New Revised Standard Version (the translation adopted for use in some mainline Protestant lectionaries). The percentages for other translations are all in the single digits.

Clearly, then, the King James Bible is far from dead, since more than half of individual respondents and two-fifths of congregations still prefer it. The percentage of KJV readers among black respondents on the GSS is even higher, 79 percent, compared to 51 percent of white respondents, including 58 percent of white Protestants in traditionally conservative denominations. The GSS also revealed that 69 percent of respondents who make less than $25,000 read the KJV, compared to 44 percent of those making $75,000 or more. Similarly, 72 percent of respondents with less than a high school education read the KJV, compared to 33 percent of those with a graduate degree.

The full reasons for the KJV's enduring popularity remain to be investigated by scholars. Is the version's appeal mostly aesthetic—a preference for the way familiar passages sound? The archaic diction of the KJV lends a certain grandeur to favorite texts ("behold,

I bring you good tidings of great joy," KJV) that may be missing from modern versions ("see—I am bringing you good news of great joy," NRSV). Or do particular denominational cultures account for much of the KJV's popularity—its venerable status in black churches, for example? Some groups' attachment to the KJV may be theologically motivated; witness the "King James Only" movement, which claims that the KJV alone corresponds to the literal words of God.[4] Interestingly, of KJV readers, 53 percent responded that the Bible is the literal word of God, while only 39 percent of NIV readers agreed with this statement. At the same time, the GSS revealed that people who read the NIV are more likely to have read the Bible individually at least weekly (four days or more in the past 30 days). Of NIV readers, 70 percent read weekly, compared to 54 percent of KJV readers. This may be related in part to the aforementioned heavy marketing of the NIV in niche devotional Bibles designed to encourage daily use.

Yet the continued prevalence of the KJV, despite the welter of up-to-date competitors, is a major finding, according to project advisor Mark A. Noll. "Although the bookstores are now crowded with alternative versions, and although several different translations are now widely used in church services and for preaching, the large presence of the KJV testifies to the extraordinary power of this one classic English text," Professor Noll commented. "It also raises most interesting questions about the role of religious and linguistic tradition in the make-up of contemporary American culture." Project advisor Sylvester A. Johnson also remarked on the peculiar cultural power of the King James Bible, noting that its language seems to function for many Americans as "a type of lingua sacra or sacred dialect."

3. BIBLE MEMORIZATION AND VIEWS OF SCRIPTURE

In the Protestant-dominated culture of nineteenth-century America, the memorization of Bible verses was commonplace. Mark Twain satirized the practice in *The Adventures of Tom Sawyer* (1876), recounting the fate of a boy who recited three thousand verses without stopping: "the strain upon his mental faculties was too great, and he was little better than an idiot from that day forth."[5] Bible memorization was theologically important for Protestants because of their adherence to the dictum of "scripture alone," which meant that the book, not the church, was the preeminent religious authority. Memorized verses also furnished a ready source of comfort in affliction. The American Bible Society distributed by the thousands a little tract entitled *Where to Look in the Bible*. It suggested chapters and verses for a variety of life situations, including starting a new job, facing temptation, lapsing in faith, or fearing death.

Yet with some other polls showing that Americans have little knowledge of the Bible, we wondered if individuals or congregations still memorize scripture passages. A highly publicized Gallup poll in 2005, for example, revealed that fewer than half of the American teenagers surveyed knew that Jesus turned water into wine at the Cana wedding, nearly two-thirds could not identify a quotation from Jesus's Sermon on the Mount, and about one in ten thought Moses was one of Jesus's twelve disciples.[6]

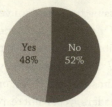

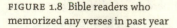

FIGURE 1.8 Bible readers who memorized any verses in past year

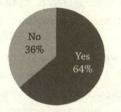

FIGURE 1.9 Congregations with Bible memorization events for children

On the GSS we asked the self-identified Bible readers: "In the past year, have you memorized any Bible verses?"

On the NCS, we focused the question on children: "In the past 12 months, have there been any events during which children from your congregation recited scripture from memory?"

The percentage of verse memorizers among Bible readers (48 percent) equates to roughly a fourth of the American population as a whole, or about 80 million people. Memorization is roughly equal among men and women and is highest among black respondents (69 percent). Among white respondents, 51 percent of conservative Protestants said they memorized verses, while 31 percent of moderate/liberal Protestants said they did. Similarly, the NCS revealed that 73 percent of white evangelical congregations hold memorization events while 46 percent of white moderate/liberal congregations do. The inverse relationship between income/education and use of the KJV is repeated here, as respondents of higher income and education show lower rates of scripture memorization. Among individuals with less than a high school education, 57 percent commit scripture passages to memory, compared to only 30 percent of persons with a graduate degree.

Rates of Bible memorization are one measure of the Bible's authority for individuals and congregations. Another classic barometer, included on both the NCS and GSS, was some form of the question whether respondents consider the Bible the literal word of God. On the NCS, in answer to the question, "Does your congregation consider the Bible to be the literal and inerrant word of God?" fully 83 percent responded yes. On the GSS we found that 77 percent of all participants regard the Bible as either the literal, inerrant word of God (29 percent) or the inspired word of God (48 percent). Views of scripture were highest among black respondents on the GSS, with 50 percent regarding the Bible as the literal word of God, compared with 45 percent of Hispanic respondents and 23 percent of white respondents. On income and education, 42 percent of individuals living in households making less than $25,000 regard the Bible as inerrant, while only 20 percent of people living in households making $75,000 or more do. Of individuals with less than a high school education, 52 percent are inerrantists; only 10 percent of those with a graduate degree are.

As reported earlier, high views of the Bible are not confined to persons who actually read it. Of the 50 percent of Americans who have not read scripture at all in the past year, 15 percent consider the Bible to be the literal, inerrant word of God and 50 percent consider it to be the inspired word of God. In other words, fully two-thirds of non–Bible readers (65 percent) have a high view of scriptural truth and authority. This suggests that the Bible's outsized status in the culture transcends (and is separable from) any theologically defined fundamentalism since a genuine biblical fundamentalist would presumably revere the Bible and read it too.[7]

4. FAVORITE BOOKS OR STORIES

We asked the 48 percent of people who had read the Bible at least once outside worship in the past year whether they had a favorite verse or story. Just over half of those—or roughly a quarter of the total population—said they did.

Verses from the book of Psalms, or Psalms in its entirety, were named much more often than anything else (about a quarter of those with a favorite said this). Not surprisingly, Psalm 23—which begins "the Lord is my shepherd"—was the most popular. It is possible this passage was named most often simply because it is so frequently memorized or quoted. But it is worth noting that this soothing chapter, which for centuries has been read aloud across Christian cultures at funerals and in other times of trouble, fits well with another of our findings: more people read the Bible for personal prayer and devotion than for any other reason. (See section 6 of this chapter.) It comes as little surprise, then, that they take solace in this extremely well known passage from Hebrew scripture.

Historian Mark A. Noll did not find this surprising. "The Bible has historically been a source of great comfort and consolation for those who read it regularly, or who turn to it in times of crisis. This historical usage of scripture seems to have continued, and with surprising strength, into the present." Project advisor Thomas Davis reminds us: "Historically, this may be explained for Protestants, anyway, by Luther, Calvin, and other early reformers, all of whom held the Psalms up as special—indeed, elevating it practically to the status of Gospel."

After Psalms, the most cited response was the book of John, especially John 3:16. Again, this passage is often repeated in popular culture. Those of a certain age will remember seeing signs that read "John 3:16" at sporting events all over America, and might even associate them with (Rock'n') Rollen Stewart and his multicolored wig. It is a famous verse, but it also fits the pattern of finding comfort and consolation, in addition to being a tool for evangelism. The verse, "For God so loved the world, that he gave his only begotten Son, that whosoever believeth in him should not perish, but have everlasting life" (KJV), is an assurance. It offers people a promise that many find supportive when the going gets hard.

The pattern seems clear. Philippians 4:13, "I can do all things through Christ who strengthens me," is mentioned frequently, as is the story of David and Goliath, another place where God helps someone overcome disadvantage.

On the other hand, well-known stories that are not about gaining support or consolation are mentioned much less frequently. The story of Jesus's birth, for instance, plays as large a role in American popular culture as any, but it was only cited by a handful of people. Paul's letters are mentioned only infrequently despite their importance (especially his Letter to the Romans) in American evangelicalism. The book of Revelation is mentioned infrequently despite the popular imagery surrounding the apocalypse. In fact, the book of Ruth—another example of consolation and hope, especially for women—is mentioned more often than the book of Revelation. Perhaps consolation is not the only concern. As Thomas Davis helpfully reminds us, "In much of the literature, it is also about a type of active perseverance and love that may be at odds with 'consolation and hope,' especially as those two words together evoke a sort of passivity, a patient waiting, that may not be at the heart of Ruth."

The connections are suggestive and strong: Poorer people read the Bible on their own more frequently than richer ones. Black people read it on their own more than white people. Women read it on their own more than men. And among all people, personal prayer and devotion is the reason given by the most people for reading scripture. None of these *proves* these same people are reading the Bible to gain inspiration, hope, consolation, and perseverance, but since the abovementioned passages are, by far, the ones most often cited, the connection between readers and what is most often read seems clear enough.

Early twentieth-century theories of religion, often influenced by Freud and Marx, viewed all religious activity as an otherworldly response to present-world deprivation. That reductive view of religion has largely been discounted. However, it is possible, even likely, that *some* religious activity is geared toward spiritual and emotional comfort, and individual Bible reading seems to be one such activity.

Similarly, contemporary American religion is often described as "therapeutic." One need not reduce all religious ideas and activities to "therapy" to acknowledge that *some* religious ideas and activities are therapeutic, and again, it would not be surprising to find that this is especially true at the level of individual activity. As project advisor Amy Plantinga Pauw says, "evangelical Bible study is often very individually and therapeutically oriented. 'What does this verse mean to me?' Scripture is a companion in the journey of faith, providing strength and consolation in difficult moments." If others use the Bible less for this purpose, Pauw explains, "perhaps it is because seeking external therapeutic help for troubled relationships is more socially acceptable to liberal Protestants, Catholics, and those with no religious affiliation."

5. RACE

Throughout this chapter, many different factors are apparent that are positively associated with Bible reading outside worship. Older people are more likely to have read the Bible in the past year. Protestants are more likely than Catholics. People who make less than $75,000 are more likely than those who make more. Southerners are more likely than people from any other region.

But the strongest correlation with Bible reading is race. Specifically, black people read the Bible at a higher rate than people of other races, and by a considerable margin. As we mentioned in section 1, 70 percent of all African Americans said they had read the Bible outside worship at least once in the last year, compared to 44 percent for whites, 46 percent for Hispanics, and 28 percent for all other races.

While the role of race and the Bible reading practices of African Americans are discussed throughout this chapter, several general findings must be underscored here. Of those who have read scripture in the past year, 69 percent of black people have memorized some passage, compared to 40 percent for whites and 55 percent for Hispanics. Most clearly, black people take a more conservative view of the Bible as they read it. Out of all respondents, 50 percent of blacks view the Bible as the "inerrant word of God." This is more than twice the rate for white people.

These results at the individual level mirror what we found at the congregational level. If all black congregations—those in which at least 80 percent of the attendees are black—are counted together as a group, they are as biblically conservative as white conservative Protestants. Approximately 98 percent of all black congregations report that their members regard the Bible as inerrant. Three-fourths (75 percent) of all black congregations held an event in the past year where children were encouraged to recite scripture from memory.

The subset of white congregations categorized as conservative/fundamentalist has numbers approaching black congregations' level of confidence in biblical authority, but it is worth noting that this similarity is between the most biblically conservative set of white congregations on the one hand and *all* black congregations on the other. Nowhere else in our data is there such a clear linkage between one descriptive variable—self-identification by race—and such a high level of interaction with the Bible.

Black Christians read the Bible outside worship at rates as high as or higher than conservative/fundamentalist white Protestants, and higher than any other religious tradition, but there are significant differences in *why* black Christians read. On some of these—personal relationships, wealth, and learning about the future—it is worth noting that Hispanics (both Catholic and Protestant) read the scripture for reasons similar to black Protestants. But this comparison to Hispanics, like the earlier comparison to white conservative Protestants, helps make the point. On most individual measures, black people are the most literal and most engaged Bible readers across the board. On some measures, black Christians as a whole are as religiously conservative as the most conservative white Protestants. On other measures, black Christians read scripture to learn about life issues at the same high rate as Hispanic Protestants. But there are *no* measures, individually or in congregations, where "black" is not strongly correlated with the most conservative, most active, most involved level of scriptural engagement, no matter which other group comes closest. If one wanted to predict whether someone had read the Bible, believed it to be the literal or inspired Word of God, and used it to learn about many practical aspects of life, knowing whether or not that person was black is the single best piece of information one could have.

Scholars will not find this surprising. Sociologically speaking, we know from previous surveys that African Americans are more likely to report a formal religious affiliation. Even those who are not members of congregations are still religious at much higher rates than others. Black congregations remained the "center" of the African American community longer than religious congregations did for whites. The Civil Rights Movement was led by pastors. And, until recently, political leadership in the African American community still came out of the so-called black church. Historically speaking, it is important to remember that, as project advisor Sylvester A. Johnson put it, "African American Christianity (in its denominational formation) is almost singularly the product of missionary theology, which is deeply rooted in Biblicist, fundamentalist theology."[8] White Protestants evangelized first the slaves and later the freed blacks with a theologically conservative message built on a high view of the Bible's authority. Generally speaking, the Bible remains important in the black community because it has for centuries been identified with the African American narrative in U.S. history (moving from slavery to freedom just as ancient Israel in the Old Testament, and moving to freedom in Christ in the New Testament). Simply put, black Christians since the eighteenth century have been able to read their experience into the Bible more easily than other groups.

On the other hand, while the finding that African Americans use the Bible more across the board is not surprising, the level of difference with other groups is striking. This finding has important consequences for the ways scholars, pundits, and all Americans think about race in America. As Mark A. Noll says, "the significantly higher proportion of black Americans who read the Bible regularly reveals a significant fact about African American religious life as well as a significant fact about public life in general. Approaches to the nation's continuing racial disparities and problems that leave scripture completely out of the picture seem to be missing a vital element in black culture."

6. INDIVIDUALS' REASONS FOR READING THE BIBLE

Despite the coverage popular media gives to people claiming biblical mandates on social issues, individuals are actually far more likely to read the Bible for personal edification and growth than to shape their views of culture war issues.[9] Indeed, Bible readers consult scripture for personal prayer and devotion three times more than they do to learn about abortion, homosexuality, poverty, or war (see fig. 1.10).

Several key facts about the reasons people read the Bible emerged from those surveyed.

1. Women read the Bible more than men for reasons of personal prayer and devotion, as well as to make decisions about relationships with spouses, parents, children, and friends (see fig. 1.11). This roughly corresponds to the gender difference in church attendance and membership.
2. There was a fairly consistent difference in age among stated reasons for reading the Bible, with the youngest (18–29) and oldest (75 and over) reading scripture

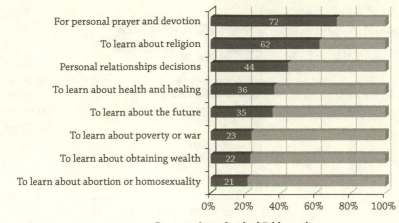

FIGURE 1.10 Reasons for individual Bible reading

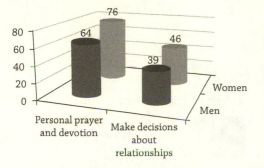
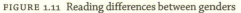

FIGURE 1.11 Reading differences between genders

the least for specific purposes (see fig. 1.12). This difference was especially pronounced on such culture war issues as abortion and homosexuality, where 15 percent of those under 45 and 12 percent of those 75 and older consulted scripture, compared to 25 percent of those 45–74 years old. Meanwhile, those between 40 and 60 years old more often consult the Bible on health, money, and personal decisions about relationships. Recent work on the "sandwich generation"—who are simultaneously raising children and caring for aging parents—might conceivably explain why this age group moves to the front on these particular issues. It is a question worth further exploration.

3. Income differences appeared among those who read the Bible for specific purposes, with lower income readers ($25,000) consulting scripture more often than higher income readers (above $75,000). Usually the percentage of difference was in the double digits. For instance, those with lower income read the Bible to learn about their religion more often than those with higher incomes, 67 percent to 54 percent. The difference continued even among those making less than $50,000 and those making over $75,000: lower income Bible readers consulted scripture more often to make decisions about personal relationships (49 percent to 36 percent) and to learn about the future (42 percent to 28 percent). The two starkest examples of reading practices among those with different incomes appeared in the areas where lower income individuals are most at risk: health and accumulation of wealth. In those cases, Bible readers with lower incomes were about twice as likely to consult scripture (see fig. 1.13).

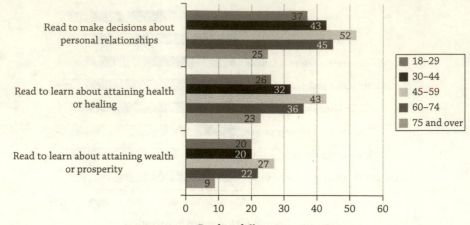

FIGURE 1.12 Reading differences among ages

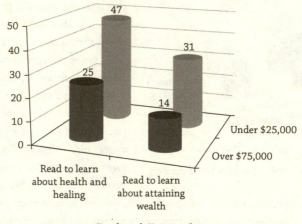

FIGURE 1.13 Reading differences between incomes

4. The level of education, often linked to other social and economic factors, consistently separated Bible readers who turned to scripture for a specific purpose (see fig. 1.14). Those with a high school diploma or less generally read the Bible more, and at several key points they did so at least twice as much. For instance, 48 percent of Bible readers with less than a high school diploma and 39 percent of those with only a high school diploma consulted scripture to learn about obtaining health or healing, compared to only 25 percent of those with a bachelor's degree. This difference in reading also appeared when it came to learning about the future, homosexuality and abortion, poverty and war, and attaining wealth. In other words, those with less education read the Bible at twice the rate of those with college degrees for the purposes of learning about culture war issues, health and wealth, and what the future holds.

5. Reading the Bible with a specific purpose is closely aligned to individuals' frequency of consulting scripture. Those reading it weekly more often affirm one or more of the eight purposes for reading scripture than those who consult the Bible less often. The trend is generally clear for four of the stated purposes for reading the Bible (see fig. 1.15).

Even more striking was the relationship between those who read the Bible often and the four other stated reasons for doing so—making decisions about personal relationships, learning about poverty and war, attaining wealth, and learning about abortion or homosexuality. In those cases, more frequent Bible readers consulted scripture twice (in some cases, nearly three times) as often (see fig. 1.16).

6. Meanwhile, how one feels about the nature of the Bible—is it the Word of God, an inspired document, or a book of fables?—corresponds to the reasons why one reads it. Literalists, those who believe the Bible is the literal word of God, are, not surprisingly, the most likely to read scripture in all eight categories. Those with more complicated views of the Bible, who believe it is inspired but

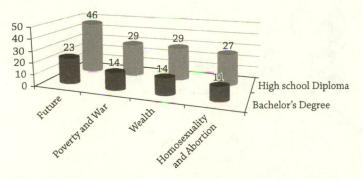

FIGURE 1.14 Reasons for reading and differences in education levels

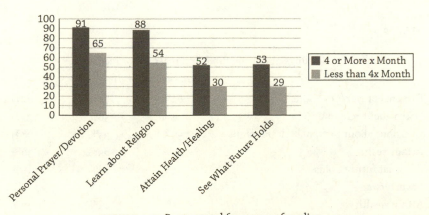

FIGURE 1.15 Purpose and frequency of reading

not necessarily literally God's word, tend to consult it more often than those who believe the Bible is a book of fables (see table 1.2). Overall, the traditions that hold to literalist views of the Bible—black Protestants, Hispanic Protestants, and white conservative Protestants—read at higher rates that correspond to feelings about the nature of scripture.

In summary, Bible readers rated the extent to which they consulted the Bible on a number of issues. Grouping readers who said they did so "to a moderate extent," "to a considerable extent," and "to a great extent," we found that respondents overwhelmingly turned to scripture for personal growth and to learn about the faith as compared to other reasons. Overall, culture war issues rated about one-third as popular as devotional reasons for reading scripture. As project advisor and seminary professor Ronald Allen says, "this is hugely important for the minister or teacher in a typical congregation who may think that the (usually) small number of parishioners who are loudest on social issues and the Bible represent the congregation as a whole."

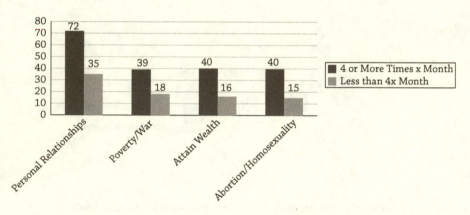

FIGURE 1.16 Purpose and frequency of reading—at least twice the effect

TABLE 1.2

Feelings about the Bible and reasons for reading			
	Word of God	Inspired	Book of fables
Personal prayer/devotions	81%	71%	42%
Learn about religion	74%	58%	35%
Decisions about personal relationships	59%	35%	28%
Attain health	49%	25%	30%
See what future holds	53%	23%	16%
Poverty/war	36%	15%	9%
Attain wealth	35%	11%	17%
Abortion/homosexuality	34%	12%	13%

Even with a clearer picture of the more personal reasons individuals read the Bible, the situation remains complicated. Frequent readers consulted the Bible three times more often about abortion, homosexuality, poverty, and war, as well as to attain wealth and seek guidance on decisions about personal relationships. The Bible, as advisor Sylvester A. Johnson points out, is "not just a book to be read. It is also a cultural symbol." As such, in public life "the Bible's use in culture wars is more likely rooted in its power as a cultural symbol of moral authority than in reading its specific content." Mark A. Noll concurs but is hopeful these findings can affect the conversation. "Religion has been a major subject of popular American journalism since the Civil Rights Movement, and even more since the rise of the Religious Right. Such journalism has often reported accurately on how the Bible has been brought into public life. What it has often missed, however," he reminds us, "is that political uses of the Bible have never been their most important uses. These IUPUI surveys should bring sanity back into journalists' reporting on religion, at least to the extent that they show how important non-political use of scripture continues to be in modern American life."

7. SOURCES OF HELP IN UNDERSTANDING AND INTERPRETING THE BIBLE

On the GSS we asked those who had read the Bible in the past year whether they had turned to people, books, or other sources for help in interpreting it. The majority had not (see fig. 1.17).

Among those who did seek help in understanding and interpreting the Bible, a number of key facts emerged.

1. Those with more education seek help in understanding and interpreting the Bible at a higher rate. Those with a bachelor's degree (53 percent) or graduate degree (49 percent) did so more than respondents with less than a high school diploma (38 percent) or a high school diploma (41 percent).
2. Clergy remain the top source for individuals looking for assistance in understanding or interpreting the Bible. Indeed, by nearly a two-to-one margin, respondents turned to clergy over the Internet, although, as we will show, seeking help on the Internet appeals to certain populations (see fig. 1.18).
3. Education is a factor between those who seek help from clergy and those who do not. Although less educated people seek help understanding the Bible at a lower rate than more educated people, those with the least education sought help from clergy more than from other sources of assistance (see fig. 1.19).
4. Differences in age and income appear prominently among those who read Bible commentaries as books, CDs, or DVDs. Older

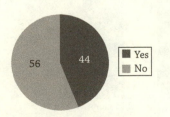

FIGURE 1.17 Bible readers seeking help in understanding/ interpreting

respondents (60–75) consulted published sources nearly twice as often as younger people (18–20), 65 percent to 33 percent. Those making over $75,000 seek help understanding and interpreting the Bible from published sources more often than those making less than $50,000, 63 percent to 39 percent.

5. Several differences appeared among those who turn to mass media for help in understanding the Bible. Black people, who read the Bible at higher rates than other racial groups, also turn to radio or television more than others. Indeed, 54 percent of African American Bible readers consult mass media compared to 34 percent of Hispanics and 32 percent of whites. Meanwhile, these older forms of media appeal to those 45–59 years old (47 percent) and 60–74 years old (40 percent) more than they do to those 18–29 years old (28 percent). Finally, differences in education levels again appeared. Although radio and television preachers are portrayed in popular culture as preying on the least educated, that group actually tunes in less than those with high school diplomas or some college (see fig. 1.20). One should keep in mind, as we have just noted, that those without a high school degree turn to their clergy at a much higher rate than others.

6. Two striking differences appeared among respondents who sought help understanding and interpreting the Bible on the Internet: gender and education. First, while females make up the majority of congregation members and read the Bible at higher rates than men (56 percent to 39 percent), among those

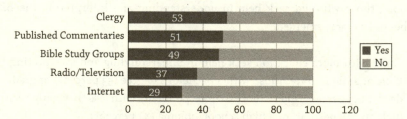

FIGURE 1.18 Sources for help in understanding the Bible

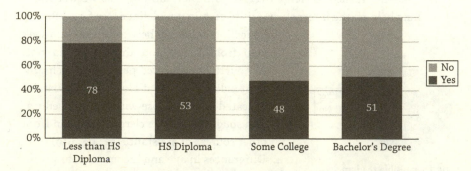

FIGURE 1.19 Education differences among those seeking help understanding/interpreting Bible from clergy

seeking help in understanding it, men turn to the Internet at a higher rate (36 percent to 24 percent). Second, while education has appeared as an important variable in a number of ways, it shows a clear distinction among those seeking help from the Internet (see fig. 1.21). Economic situations tied to education levels may be behind these differences, as well as familiarity with using the Internet to research topics. Whatever the reason, many ministries hoping to provide help in understanding and interpreting the Bible on the Internet will find these differences important to their work. Project advisor Ronald Allen, a seminary professor, noted that very point: "As a biblical scholar, I have to say the quality of resources on the Internet is uneven. Indeed, much of the material on the Internet can generously be described as appalling. However, the rates of Internet use suggest that congregations, judicatories, and schools should provide more high quality interpretive materials in that venue."

8. READING THE BIBLE ON THE INTERNET AND E-DEVICES

Recent claims by e-device applications such as YouVersion place the number of subscribers in the hundreds of millions.[10] Given the changing reading habits of Americans, we wondered how many people actually use the Internet and e-devices such as iPads,

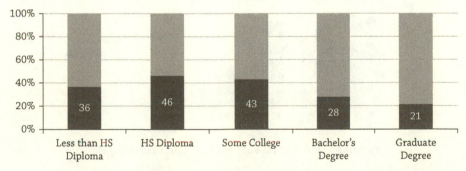

FIGURE 1.20 Education differences among those seeking help from radio/television

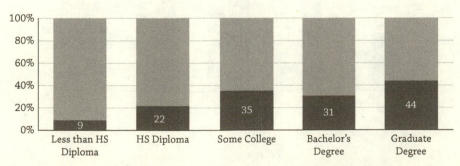

FIGURE 1.21 Education differences among those seeking help from Internet

smartphones, and Kindles as their sources for Bible reading.[11] In all, we found that among those who had read the Bible in the past year, 31 percent read it on the Internet, while 22 percent employed e-devices.

Among those who read the Bible on the Internet or e-devices, we found differences when it comes to age, income, and education level.

1. Reading the Bible on the Internet is fairly popular for those under 60 years of age, but those over 60 do so much less than others. Not surprisingly, younger people read the Bible on an e-device more often than other age groups (see fig. 1.22).
2. According to a recent study by the U.S. Department of Commerce, lower income and less educated households experience computer ownership and broadband adoption rates well below the national average (see fig. 1.23).[12] This likely helps to explain our findings. Respondents with higher incomes and more education read the Bible on the Internet or on an e-device more than those with low incomes and less education. The difference of use among education levels was particularly striking (see fig. 1.24).

In all, numerous categories that affect socioeconomic differences are significant for ownership and use of technology. That may be driving some of the differences we see here. Generational differences in one's relation to technology could also be at play.

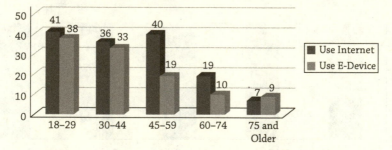

FIGURE 1.22 Age and use of Internet/e-devices to read Bible

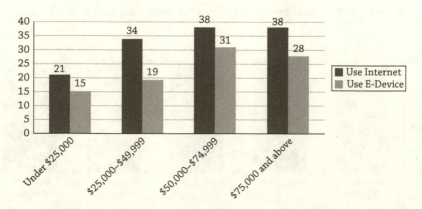

FIGURE 1.23 Income and use of Internet/e-device to read Bible

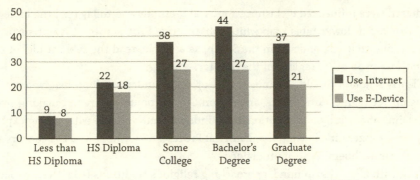

FIGURE 1.24 Education and use of Internet/e-device to read Bible

What we can say, however, is that younger people, those with higher salaries, and most dramatically, those with more education among the respondents read the Bible on the Internet or an e-device at higher rates.[13]

9. RELIGIOUS TRADITIONS

Beginning with our very first pass at the survey results, we followed with keen interest the differences among religious traditions in reading the Bible outside formal services. Among our respondents, there was a clear difference among traditions.

However, as we queried the data over several months from various angles, it became clear that religious traditions were inextricably tied to race and region. For instance, black people as a whole read the Bible at similar rates to black Protestants. Here, race seemed to be as important, or more so, than religious tradition. Similarly, we know from multiple previous studies that region complicates our understandings of religious traditions. For example, a midwestern Methodist couple who migrate to the South often do not remain Methodist. Rather, they join a Southern Baptist church and thereby align with the dominant religious culture. On an institutional level, it appears that individual congregations in moderate/liberal Protestant denominations often reflect their local surroundings rather than holding to the official teachings of headquarters. This is not always the case, of course, but the dominant role of this sort of "hard shell" regionalism that persists in religion in the United States makes it difficult to argue for religious tradition as an independent variable to be applied across the board.

That is not to say that religious tradition plays no part in rates of reading the Bible outside services. The historical differences between Protestants and Catholics and between white conservative Protestants and white moderate/liberal Protestants clearly contribute to regional differences. Black Protestants and white conservative Protestants, both of whom place great emphasis on biblical authority, have higher concentrations in the South. Catholics, who historically elevate the church over scriptural authority, dominate the Northeast and many sections of the Midwest and West. White moderate/liberal Protestant denominations, with strongholds in the Northeast and

Midwest, were influenced by historical-critical methods and today read the Bible out-side worship at lower rates than white conservative Protestants. It is not surprising then to find that respondents in the South, as a whole, read the Bible at higher rates than those in all other regions of the country.

Clearly scholars should continue to work toward understanding this dynamic rela-tionship between tradition, race, and region. At this point, we are not making sweep-ing claims about religious tradition as an independent variable with strong explana-tory power extending beyond the historical Protestant/Catholic and the conservative and moderate/liberal Protestant divides.

Still, with all of this in mind, approaching religious traditions from the perspective of Bible reading revealed findings that contradict the stereotypes of specific traditions. We note them here (see fig. 1.25).

1. Although the survey showed the historic difference between Protestants and Catholics in individuals' Bible use, we found several cases where a less familiar story has developed. "What seems to be taking place for a minority of Catholics," said historian Mark A. Noll, "is a somewhat more Protestant use of the Bible (personally read for personal purposes), though historical Catholic-Protestant differences remain obviously important."

    Indeed, when asked about the two topics that ended up being the top rea-sons why people read the Bible—for personal prayer and devotion and to learn about their religion—Catholics read at higher rates than one might anticipate. While the difference between Catholic and Protestant traditions is still notice-able, those who think Catholics only read scripture in services are missing an important point: over one-third of Catholics consult scripture outside formal services, and among those readers, about half do so for their personal devo-tions and to learn more about their faith.

2. Figures 1.25 and 1.26 indicate another important observation: "Nones"—that growing demographic of people who do not identify with any religion—read scripture, at least from time to time. In fact, we discovered that in certain

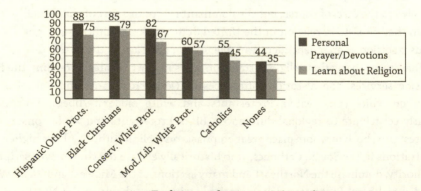

FIGURE 1.25 Traditions and top reasons for reading

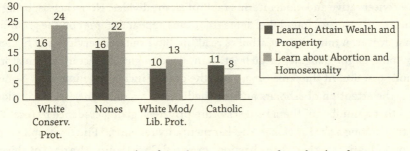

FIGURE 1.26 Nones' reading of scripture compared to others' reading

situations they consult scripture more than adherents of some Christian traditions do. For instance, they read it more than white moderate and liberal Protestants do to learn about attaining health or healing (21 percent to 15 percent) and about the same as moderate to liberal white Protestants and Catholics to learn about poverty or war (15 percent to 13 percent each). When it comes to reading in order to attain wealth and prosperity and to learn about abortion and homosexuality, they rival the reading levels of white conservative Protestants (see fig. 1.26). The important point here is not to compare the rates of reading; rather it is to point out that Nones, who eschew religious identity, read scripture at times as often as those who identify with specific traditions.

3. With race playing a major role in this study, it makes sense to return to it one final time in the context of religious traditions. As Sylvester A. Johnson pointed out, there persists "the radical disconnect between the dominant reality of biblical fundamentalism in Black churches on the one hand and the symbolism, on the other, that governs popular ideas about African American churches." Because of their struggle against slavery in the nineteenth century and for civil rights in the twentieth century, Black churches are generally perceived as centers of a socially progressive Christianity that left behind conservative theology. In fact, there were major debates on this very issue within the Southern Christian Leadership Conference, culminating in 1961 when members of the National Baptist Convention separated to found the Progressive National Baptist Convention. Today, black Protestantism exists in the public imagination as the Civil Rights Movement's legacy. However, as Johnson points out, "it is especially ironic and significant that fundamentalism actually defines, in the main, the theological disposition of most Black churches today. In this sense, the data from this study offer incisive and starkly important insight into the legacy and present reality of Black churches."

In summary, while the different Bible and scripture reading practices of various religious traditions are on a certain level interesting, they rarely provide an independent variable separate from race and region beyond the predictable Protestant/Catholic and white conservative and moderate/liberal Protestant divides. Nonetheless, using Bible reading as a prism, we found that some traditions appear different on the ground than from a flyover. A minority of Catholics read the Bible outside services at a higher rate than some might imagine, or at least than some might characterize as historically Catholic practice. At the same time, while the quickly increasing number of Nones has drawn the attention of scholars and the media as signs of further secularization, we found that a number of them read scripture privately, giving credence to recent findings that among a slice of Nones a seeker mentality remains.[14] Finally, despite the perception of black churches as the bastions of social Christianity, the data of this study make clear that the vast majority of black congregations and believers also hold to highly conservative views of the Bible and consult it on more topics than do members of any other tradition. As discussed in section 5, there are a number of historical and sociological reasons for this. Despite popular notions of black Protestantism as highly influenced by the Social Gospel, it is also, in certain respects, as biblically conservative as white conservative Protestantism. As advisor Mark A. Noll notes, "I hope one of the survey's major results will be to reduce the hyper-politicized treatment of religion that has prevailed since the early years of the Civil Rights Movement. The ideal result would not be to deny such uses, but to realize that such uses are only the tip of a very large iceberg, with the vast majority of its bulk hidden away out of the political public eye."

9. CONCLUSION

Americans approach the Bible outside church from assorted perspectives, with different needs, and with various frequencies. Learning more about those facts—and placing them in their historical and cultural contexts—we can offer this summary of findings:

- There is a 50/50 split among Americans who read any form of scripture in the past year and those who did not. Among those who did, women outnumbered men, older people outnumbered younger people, and Southerners exceeded those from other parts of the country.
- Among those who read any form of scripture in the past year, 95 percent named the Bible as the scripture they read. All told, this means that 48 percent of Americans read the Bible at some point in the past year. Most of those people read at least monthly, and a substantial number—9 percent of all Americans— read the Bible daily.
- Despite the proliferation of Bible translations, the KJV is the top choice, and by a wide margin, of Bible readers.
- The strongest correlation with Bible reading is race, with African Americans reading the Bible at considerably higher rates than others.
- Half of those who read the Bible in the past year also committed scripture to memory. About two-thirds of congregations in America hold events for children to memorize verses from the Bible.

- Among Bible readers, about half had a favorite book, verse, or story. Psalm 23, which begins "The Lord is my shepherd...," was most often cited, followed by John 3:16.
- Bible readers consult scripture for personal prayer and devotion three times more than to learn about culture war issues such as abortion, homosexuality, war, or poverty.
- There are clear differences among Bible readers consulting scripture for specific reasons. Age, income, and education are key factors.
- Those reading the Bible frequently consult it on culture war issues at more than twice the rate of those who read it less frequently.
- Less than half of those who read the Bible in the past year sought help in understanding it. Among those who did, clergy were their top source; the Internet was the least cited source.
- Among Bible readers, 31 percent read it on the Internet and 22 percent use e-devices.
- Bible reading differences among religious traditions followed predictably the historic divides between Protestants and Catholics, and between white conservative and white moderate/liberal Protestants. However, reading practices defy some stereotypes about certain groups.

Appendix A

QUESTIONS ON THE 2012 GENERAL SOCIAL SURVEY

We are interested in whether or not people read the Bible, Torah, or other religious scriptures such as the Koran or any others, *in addition to* the reading that often happens in worship services.

Within the last year, have you read the Bible, Torah, Koran, or other religious scriptures, not counting any reading that happened during a worship service?

In the past year, which scripture have you read most often, the Bible, Torah,. Koran, or some other scripture?

If you most often read a scripture other than the Bible or Koran, please name it:

In the past year, have you read the {NAME OF SCRIPTURE} on the Internet?

In the past year, have you read the {NAME OF SCRIPTURE} on an e-device such as iPad, Kindle, etc.?

In the past year, have you made an intentional effort to commit any parts of {NAME OF SCRIPTURE} to memory?

The {NAME OF SCRIPTURE} is used in many ways. In the past year, to what extent have you used the {NAME OF SCRIPTURE} in the following ways? Please use a scale of 1–5 with (1) being "not at all," (2) being "to a small extent," (3) being "to a moderate extent," (4) being "to a considerable extent," and (5) being "to a great extent."

To what extent did you read {NAME OF SCRIPTURE} to learn about your religion?

To what extent did you read {NAME OF SCRIPTURE} to prepare to teach or participate in a study group?

To what extent did you read {NAME OF SCRIPTURE} to make decisions about your relationship with your spouse, parents, children or friends?

To what extent did you read {NAME OF SCRIPTURE} to learn about attaining wealth or prosperity?

To what extent did you read {NAME OF SCRIPTURE} to learn about attaining health or healing?

To what extent did you read {NAME OF SCRIPTURE} to learn about what the future holds?

To what extent did you read {NAME OF SCRIPTURE} to learn about issues like abortion or homosexuality?

To what extent did you read {NAME OF SCRIPTURE} to learn about issues like poverty or war?

When reading the {NAME OF SCRIPTURE} in the past 30 days, have you turned to other people, books, or other sources for help in interpreting and understanding what you read?

In the past 30 days, have you received help in interpreting and understanding scripture from....

a. Your pastor, priest, or other clergy?
b. Study group leader or members?
c. Published commentary in a book, CD, or DVD?
d. Internet site?
e. Television or radio program?

What translation of the Bible do you most often read? Is it the King James Version, New International Version, New American Bible, New Revised Standard Version, Living Bible, or some OTHER version?

King James Version	1
New International Version	2
New American Bible	3
New Revised Standard Version	4
Living Bible	5
Other	6
DON'T KNOW	DK

NO ANSWER
Do you have a favorite book of the Bible? (PLEASE NAME)
Do you have a favorite Bible story, verse, or passage? (PLEASE NAME)

Appendix B

QUESTIONS ON THE NATIONAL CONGREGATIONS STUDY III

Does your congregation encourage people to use the New International Version of the Bible rather than other translations?
YES
NO

Does your congregation consider the Bible to be the literal and inerrant word of God?
YES
NO

Are there Bibles in the pews or chairs for people to use during worship services?
YES
NO [GO TO Q68]
What translation?

Are people encouraged to bring their own Bibles to worship services?
YES
NO

Does your congregation follow a lectionary or some other schedule of scripture readings when it comes to what passages are read in worship services?
YES
NO

In the past 12 months, have there been any events during which children from your congregation recited scripture from memory?
YES
NO

An earlier version of this chapter appeared as "The Bible in American Life" (2014) on the website of the Center for the Study of Religion and American Culture, http://www.raac.iupui.edu.

PART TWO
Past

2

America's First Bible

NATIVE USES, ABUSES, AND REUSES OF THE INDIAN

BIBLE OF 1663

Linford D. Fisher

IN 1663, THE fledgling printing press in Cambridge, Massachusetts, made history. Over the course of a year, more than 1,298,000 pages poured off the press housed in the Indian College at Harvard and were eventually bound into approximately eleven hundred volumes containing 1,180 pages each. The final product was the first complete Bible printed anywhere in the Americas.[1] More significant, however, it was an ambitious translation of the entire Bible into Wôpanâak, an Indian language.[2] John Eliot, the Roxbury, Massachusetts, minister and missionary to New England's Natives, eagerly distributed the Bibles to Native towns, churches, schools, and villages around southeastern New England, in addition to sending a shipment of twenty to his missionary sponsors in London, including one to King Charles II himself.[3]

Eliot surely must have patted himself on the back as he held the thick volume in his hands in 1663. But who in fact could read it? What did Natives do with this literary gift? The publication of the Indian Bible in 1663 is an important window into the history of the Bible in the Americas, by virtue of it being the first to be published there. But it is also a rare look at the reception of and interaction with the Bible by a people group who rarely figure into histories of the Bible in American history, namely, American Indians. Scholars now increasingly recognize what a complicated book it is—simultaneously a product of settler colonialism, of the "invasion within," as James Axtell famously put it,[4] and a thoroughly indigenized creation in which Natives greatly aided in the translation, typesetting, and printing and, to some degree, adopted it as their own in Indian communities in southeastern New England.

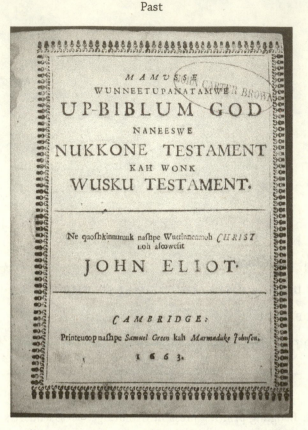

FIGURE 2.1 *Mamusse wunneetupanatamwe Up-Biblum God* title page, 1663 ed. Photograph by
Linford D. Fisher. Courtesy of the John Carter Brown Library at Brown University, Providence, RI.

In some ways, the fact that there is an Indian Bible at all is somewhat surprising.
Whatever the professions of New England colonists were regarding Native evangelization, the reality was quite different, at least for the first few decades. Despite the idealized 1629 Massachusetts Bay seal, in which an Indian cries out "Come Over and Help
Us!," early Indian-settler relations were more marked by warfare and trade than evangelization. When John Eliot and Thomas Mayhew Jr. first began learning local Indian
languages in the early 1640s with an eye toward evangelization in Roxbury and on
Martha's Vineyard (for Mayhew), the Pequot War—it is important to realize—was
fresh in Native minds. This bloody war of extermination culminated in a May 1637
massacre at Mystic Fort in southeastern Connecticut when English forces systematically slaughtered approximately five hundred Indian men, women, and children. After
the war, English leaders even tried to obliterate the very name of the Pequots.[5]
Furthermore, the regional Wampanoag sachems west of Boston had already formally
submitted to the English government in Boston, in 1644, prior to Eliot's first sermon
attempts in 1646.[6] In other words, it is impossible to extricate the evangelization process from the violence of colonization, at least as experienced by Natives.

Although Eliot's early preaching attempts to local Massachusett Indians in 1646 were halting at best, he threw himself into a more full-blown study of Wôpanâak, aided by a Native servant/slave named Cockenoe, who had been taken as a captive in the Pequot War. Being the good Protestant that he was, Eliot soon turned, first, to self-promotion (in the form of a dozen promotional tracts over time), and second, to the translation and printing of the Bible, all significantly aided by the formation of a missionary society in London in 1649 (rechartered in 1662 and usually referred to by historians as the New England Company).[7] Notably, the New England Company chose as its seal a spinoff of the 1629 Massachusetts Bay seal, with a significant addition: a printed book, likely the Bible.

Even as early as the late 1640s, Eliot dreamed of publishing the entire Bible in Wôpanâak. Although he started the translation work on the Bible in the early 1650s, the first Indian-language book to emerge from the press in Cambridge was *The Indian Primer*, published in 1654.[8] Eliot sent a few sections of the Bible to press as he worked, including the books of Genesis and Matthew in 1655 and Psalms in 1658. By December 1658, Eliot reported to the New England Company that the translation of the entire Bible was complete: "the whole book of God is translated into their own language, it wanteth but revising, transcribing, and printing."[9] While Eliot and his Native linguists were translating the Bible, Eliot was also slowly building a network of "praying towns," or Christian Indian villages, that by 1674 consisted of fourteen towns stretching from northeastern

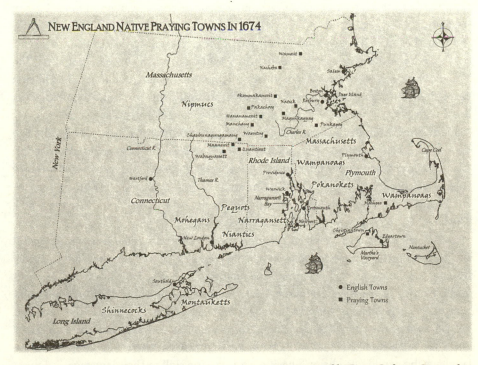

FIGURE 2.2 New England native praying towns in 1674. Map created by Lynn Carlson, Geographic Information System Professional, Brown University. Copyright Linford D. Fisher, 2016.

Connecticut to northern Massachusetts. (This was in addition to the Christian Indian towns on Cape Cod and Martha's Vineyard, under different oversight.)[10]

Nonetheless, the Wôpanâak New Testament did not appear in print until 1661, and the entire Bible not until 1663. The reasons for this seeming delay were partly logistical and partly political. The Indian Bible was translated in fairly uncertain times, so far as England was concerned. Between the completion of the translation of the Bible in 1658 and its publication in 1663, the political and ecclesiastical structure of England was changed, once again, from a puritan-led overthrow to a restored monarchy, with Charles II on the throne. Much of what had been created during the interregnum—like the 1649 missionary society—was called into question and simply dissolved. By 1660, much time, labor, and money had been invested in the Indian Bible, but no one really knew to what end. When the printing of the New Testament was completed in the spring of 1661, for example, the first two hundred unbound copies just sat on the floor of the printing press room in Cambridge for six months. A new charter for the missionary society was not approved until February 1662.[11] But the delay between translation and printing also happened in part because to typeset and print such a large volume required an enormous amount of physical type and labor: the tiny metallic letters had to be arranged, backward, individually, in a newly phoneticized language, into a press form.[12] Since the Cambridge printers—Marmaduke Johnson, Samuel Green, and James Printer (an Indian)—planned to set up the type of both the Old and New Testament concurrently, at four pages each, this meant roughly 32,000 pieces of type were potentially in operation at any one given time—a huge number by any measure.[13]

When the entire Bible was finally finished in 1663, it was a significant book, the likes of which the printing presses in the Americas would not again see for a long time. The Indian Bible itself is noteworthy for its careful preparation and production. In addition to a painstaking translation by Indian translators and Eliot, the text of the Bible was lined with printed marginal cross-references, which were a popular feature of early modern English Bibles, such as the Geneva Bible and the King James Bible. The full text of the Bible—Old and New Testaments—was followed by a version of the metrical psalms, not uncommon for Bibles printed in this time period. But included at the very back was a short listing of "Rules for Christian Living" designed for Natives that included questions like "How can I walk all the day long with God?" and "What should a Christian do, to keep perfectly holy the Sabbath Day?"[14]

One of the key questions when thinking about the Indian Bible is *who* actually did the translation? Past generations have so venerated Eliot that they have blindly insisted that the work was solely his. "The history of the first Bible printed in America is the history of the devotion and persistence chiefly of one man," thundered John Wright in *Early Bibles of America* in 1894.[15] But Eliot himself admitted his own linguistic weaknesses from the beginning. In 1649, Eliot wrote to Edward Winslow a letter in which he noted that while he desired to translate a primer into the Native language, he would need help: "I having yet but little skill in their language.... I must have some Indians, and it may be other help continually about me to try and examine

Translations."[16] Eliot's own vision for this process was a team of Native and English linguists, translators, and fact-checkers. Central to this process was, first, Cockenoe, and later, John Sassamon and Job Nesutan. Nesutan, as described by Eliot's contemporary Daniel Gookin, was "a very good linguist in the English tongue, and was Mr. Eliot's assistant and interpreter in his translations of the Bible, and other books of the Indian language."[17] Eliot repeatedly admitted to leaning heavily on Indian linguists. In 1651, he noted in a letter that "it hath pleased God this winter much to inlarge the abilitie of him whose help I use in translating the Scriptures," and in 1654 he noted again his Indian interpreter, "whom I have used in Translating a good part of the Holy Scriptures."[18]

In fact, Eliot was so busy with his own ministerial duties at Roxbury that, at times, he seemed to think that the translation of the Bible could not be accomplished in his lifetime. On June 18, 1653, Eliot confided to the English minister Thomas Thorowgood, speaking of the translation of the Bible: "I fear it will not be obtained in my dayes. I cannot stick to the work, because of my necessary attendance to my ministerie in Roxbury, and among the Indians, at sundry places."[19] It was only because of the Native linguists that the Indian Bible was completed at all. In addition to Native translators and linguists, to get the Bible actually printed required at least three printers, including an Indian named Wowaus, who quickly became known as James Printer for his adeptness at setting type and churning out pages of accurate text, and who likely provided input regarding the translation process.[20]

Beyond Eliot's own admissions, there are other hints that the Indian Bible might, if read closely enough, evince clear stamps of Native translation work. Some seem to be simple mistakes. In 2 Kings 2:23, for example, the young boys who jeer Elisha for his bald head, in the Indian Bible, say, "Go on up, ball head!" The word that should be "bald" (no hair) is instead rendered as a ball to play with.[21] But others reflect a greater level of indigenization. Perhaps the most interesting such example has been recently pointed out by the Wampanoag linguist Jessie Little Doe Baird. According to Baird, Native languages did not have a word for "hell." Instead, one can imagine Eliot trying to explain to his Native translators that he needed a word that summed up the worst possible experience known to Natives. In response, his Native translators gave him a long phrase, *chepiohkomukqut*, which can be translated as "a house of heads without a brain," or "the house of empty skulls." For Natives, the soul resided in the brain, and the worst possible thing that could happen in the afterlife was for an individual to be consigned to an eternity of wandering without a soul, aimlessly, separated from his or her kin. There is no traditional Christian fiery hell in the Indian Bible but simply a terrifying, soulless existence.[22] Less significant, there are many words throughout for which no translational approximation was attempted. English words are scattered throughout the Indian Bible, for example most proper names (including Jesus), *salt*, and *amen*.

This is all very interesting, of course, to historians and bibliophiles, but the question still remains: who could actually read the Indian Bible? And, relatedly, what did Natives do with it? In 1660, Eliot estimated that approximately one hundred Natives in Massachusetts alone could read the phoneticized version of Wôpanâak, with dozens more in Plymouth Colony, particularly on Martha's Vineyard, under the tutelage of the Mayhews.[23] Even so, it was an optimistic translation and printing enterprise, with the vast majority of New England's sizeable Indian population uninterested in either European religion or learning to read and write. Even a decade after the printing of the Indian Bible, in 1674, only 30 percent of Christian Indians in Plymouth Colony could read in Wôpanâak; literacy rates among the much larger non-Christian Indian population were basically at zero.[24] Although Eliot was optimistic about the possibility of successful translation of key Christian concepts and ideas, he had his critics, to be sure.[25] Roger Williams, in Rhode Island, repeatedly questioned whether Eliot or anyone knew the Indian languages well enough to adequately communicate Christian doctrine. Williams implied that Eliot had a hard time communicating with Natives about objects of everyday life, like clothing, let along deep theological truths, like salvation.[26]

It is certainly possible that there was more conceptual ambiguity than Eliot or his sponsors wanted to admit. This was due in part to the translation process itself, in trying to put into Native language concepts that were mostly foreign to Native lifeworlds.[27] Even New England Company commissioners and missionaries admitted as much in the early eighteenth century, sixty years into the evangelization process. After one New England Company missionary toured Native villages in the early eighteenth century, he reported back: "There are many words of Mr. Elliott's forming which they never understood.... Such a knowledge in their Bibles, as our English ordinarily have in ours, they seldom any of them have."[28] And there are little bits of evidence of this confusion from Natives themselves, in their own handwriting, written in the margins of the Indian Bible itself: one Native who was struggling through the Old Testament wrote in the margins of the book of Numbers: "I am forever a pitiful person in the world. I am not able clearly to read this, this book."[29]

Nonetheless, some Native peoples did engage this Indian Bible from the moment it was printed. From the surviving evidence, it seems that there were a range of responses to the Indian Bible, from apparent acceptance, readership, and use on the one side to full-out rejection on the other end of the spectrum. In between were a variety of other responses, such as indifference and even unorthodox political uses and appropriations.

One of the most fascinating pieces of evidence we have of Native engagement with the Indian Bible are the notes in Native languages that are contained in the margins of some extant Indian Bibles. Marginal notations in Wôpanâak began early. Although most marginal entries are not dated, the earliest found so far is from July 17, 1670, only seven years after the publication of the Indian Bible.[30] The marginalia reveal the excitement of owning a book and having open spaces in which to write. For some Natives, at least, these Bibles were a big deal. There is clear evidence of tender ownership, of thoughtful engagement with the ideas in the book, of honest frustration. The Indian Bibles were loaned out to friends, used to write sermons, written in as journals and for writing practice, and passed down to successive generations.

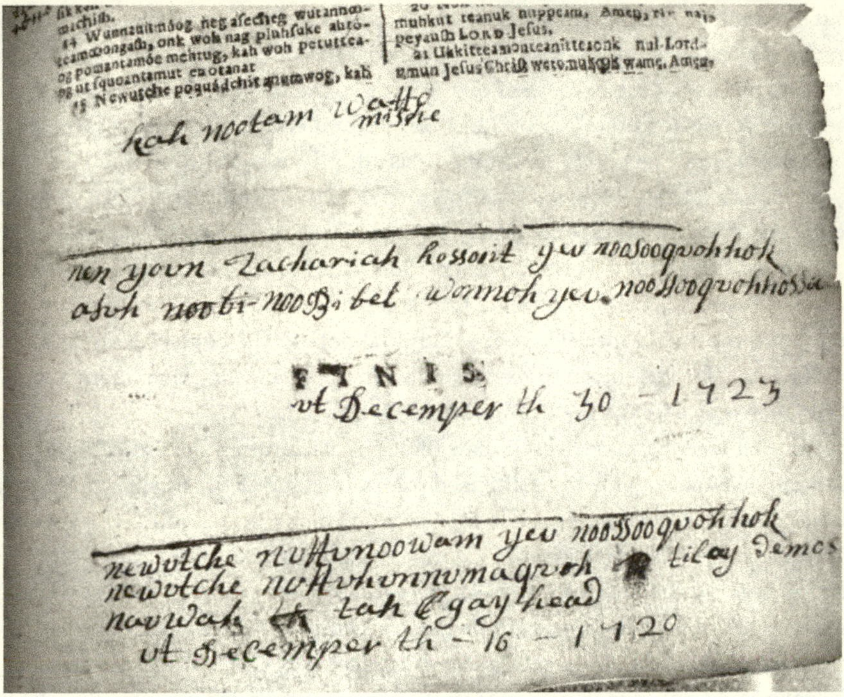

FIGURE 2.3 Indian Bible marginalia, 1685 ed. Photograph by Linford D. Fisher. Collection of the Massachusetts Historical Society, Boston.

The several hundred instances of known and translated Indian-language marginalia in the various copies of the Indian Bible can be classified in different ways. The first is simple marginal notations indicating ownership, or even evidence of borrowing. A Native named Elisha, for example, wrote "I, Elisha, this is my book" not once but in three different places in his Bible. In another Bible someone wrote: "This is Papenau's book. I am looking after it." There is also copious cross-referencing, indications of biblical literacy and the awareness of the interrelatedness of biblical texts. In the margins of Isaiah, for example, a Native wrote "Revelation 1" as a cross-reference. There are statements of readership; in the margins of the book of Nahum, someone wrote: "This chapter I read, the first chapter of Nahum."[31]

Much of the marginalia also simply suggests a personalization in terms of a blank space to write. This is indicated by the examples of handwriting practice—copying out verses, the entire alphabet, or the names of books of the Bible. Some Indian Bibles seem to have served as journals or personal diaries. Writing in their own language, Natives recorded observations about the weather ("five great snows"), reports of illness and recovery ("I am glad that my brother recovered"), plans for a particular day ("I Josiah Attaunitt made this on March 18, 1716. I am going to go to the ocean"); and the recording of the death of friends and family members ("Jacob Seiknout's daughter died May 17, 1727, the one called Sareh"). One marginal note in Jeremiah records the witnessing of an apparent indiscretion: "I Banjmon Kusseniyeutt caught (?) a Negro man and a white woman."[32]

But the bulk of the marginalia reveal a deep and somewhat tortured engagement with the biblical text itself—with the actual content of the Bible. Examples include: "Therefore we are pitiful, because of our sin"; or in the book of Daniel: "You, Thomas, remember: do not fornicate"; or in the book of Numbers: "Pitiful people [are] we. It is not good. Always falsehood is heard among us all."; "I am a pitiful person. I do not like very much to read this book, for I am too pitiful in this world"; and "I am not able to defend myself from the happenings in the world." There are other, more positive notes, too, such as "There is much of this word of God, this bible, and the Lord Jesus Christ, and the one who believes in him shall find eternal life." But the honesty is consistent throughout, captured especially in one marginal note in the book of Numbers, which says: "I do not like very much to read many writings"—a feeling that anyone who has slogged their way through the Pentateuch has surely felt.[33]

But not all Natives valued the Indian Bible for its content. For other Natives, the Bible took on a more symbolic, politicized role, as a stand-in for English religious and political alliance. As just one example of this, in the mid-1660s Charles II sent a copy of the Indian Bible to the Mohegans in Connecticut. It was one of the fancy Bibles that had been specially bound in England as gifts to donors, sponsors, and royal patrons, complete with an English-language title page, a two-page dedication to Charles II, distinctive blue-leather binding, gold gilding, and a brass clasp. The problem was, the Mohegans could not read it, as it was in Wôpanâak (which is linguistically related to but different from the Mohegan-Pequot language). Nonetheless, their sachem, Uncas, apparently received this Indian Bible from King Charles II primarily as a sign of political alliance and English religious authority.[34] This Indian Bible was passed down to successive Mohegan sachems over the following eighty years and was mentioned in correspondence with and/or speeches to royal authorities and colonial magistrates in 1703, 1725, 1737, and 1743 by three different Mohegan sachems.[35]

Most significantly, the first Christianized Mohegan sachem, Ben Uncas II, trotted out the Indian Bible in 1743 during widely attended public hearings on the Mohegan Land Controversy, as both a sign of the Mohegan's Christianization and their long-standing political alliance with the English.[36] This Indian Bible seems to have lost its relative importance in the later eighteenth century, however, for a later sachem of the Mohegans (perhaps Ben Uncas III) regifted it to the nearby Niantic Indians in Connecticut. By the early nineteenth century, the Niantics didn't know what to do with it, either, so in 1812 Joshua Nonesuch, a Niantic man, gave it to Daniel Wauheat to give to John Lyon Gardiner of Gardiner Island, on Long Island, New York. This particular Indian Bible remained in the Gardiner family for over a century, as a curious specimen of an almost forgotten Indian past.[37] In 1923, Lyon Gardiner, not knowing what else to do with it, donated it to the Connecticut Public Library. In 1974, the University of Illinois Library at Urbana-Champaign purchased this Indian Bible, and it remains there today.[38]

This particular Indian Bible is special for several reasons. Its provenance is fascinating—from King Charles II to the Mohegans to the Niantics to John Lyon Gardiner to several public institutions. It also is quite different from some other Native-owned

Indian Bibles, in that there are no Indian-language marginalia in it—reflective, perhaps, of the Mohegans and Niantics not being able to read it and of its political (not devotional) significance. But more important, it is one of the few (if not only) extant Indian Bibles that have a seventeenth-century disappearing fore-edge painting. Fore-edge paintings were usually applied after the printing (and likely the binding) of a book, often by the binder himself or an artist in his employ. It is a special kind of painting that is done on the inside edges of every page so that when the fore-edge of the book is viewed in the normal closed position, only the gold gilding on the ends of the pages is visible. But when the fore-edge of the book is fanned just a bit, the hidden fore-edge painting magically appears. In the case of this particular Indian Bible, traces of the fore-edge painting are visible even when the Bible is closed. But it is really when the fore-edges are fanned a bit that the hidden painting comes into view: mirror images of flowers, cherubs, a crown, a dog, and a deer.[39]

It is worth asking when this fore-edge painting was added and by whom. We know that at least one bindery in England, run by Stephen and Thomas Lewis, was doing fore-edge paintings in the mid-seventeenth century, as early as 1651.[40] The Newberry Library in Chicago has a Bible printed in 1660 that contains some disappearing fore-edge painting by the Lewis brothers. The text on it says "Give attendance to reading." Although it is hard to see, the Lewis brothers also included the date 1660 in this painting. So it is easily possible that at least some of the unbound Indian Bibles that

FIGURE 2.4 Fore-edge painting on the Indian Bible, 1663 ed. Photograph by Linford D. Fisher. Courtesy of The Rare Book and Manuscript Library, University of Illinois Library, Urbana.

were sent to England were bound by binders who were also proficient in the art of dis-appearing fore-edge painting, whether the Lewis brothers or another binder-artist. Since King Charles II also had in his employ an official royal binder by the name of Samuel Mearne, who produced some fore-edge paintings, it is possible that this Bible was originally Charles II's personal copy or that he at least had this fore-edge painting added before it was sent to the Mohegans.[41]

But in addition to serious readership and engagement (as with the marginalia) and more political uses (as with the Mohegans' Bible), there is an underside to the recep-tion of the Indian Bible, namely both the indifference and rejection that a surprisingly large percentage of Native New England exhibited toward it. As a symbol of English colonization and the cultural violence of evangelization, the Indian Bible was most often ignored. That is to say, as many as 80 percent of American Indians in southern New England alone found no reason to pay much attention to the Indian Bible and Christianity more generally in the seventeenth century. But many Natives also explic-itly rejected the Indian Bible—far more than accepted it, one could easily argue. Sometimes this was reflected in more general attitudes toward the English Bible. In May 1656, two colonists testified that they saw an Indian named Tom wad up a page of an English Bible into his gun and shoot it in order to "make the word of God fly."[42] And in the early 1670s, when Eliot offered to preach to Metacom (King Philip) and the Pokanokets, Philip scornfully removed a button from Eliot's coat and said "he cared for his Gospel, just as much as he cared for that Button."[43]

The rejection of the Indian Bible was displayed most vividly during the mass Indian uprising in New England known by later generations as King Philip's War (1675–1676). Once the fighting began, King Philip told the Rhode Island governor, John Easton, that one of his grievances was that he "had a great Fear to have ani of ther Indians should be caled or forced to be Christian Indians"—a process of which the Indian Bible was the foremost symbol.[44] Accordingly, during the war itself, Natives exacted violence against the primary symbols of European presence and colonialism: houses were burnt to the ground; domesticated animals were killed and disembowled; hymn singing was mocked; church buildings were destroyed; and books were torn apart, including Bibles. In one particularly gruesome encounter, an Indian soldier killed a colonist, slit open his gut, and stuffed a Bible inside.[45] In another instance, English soldiers came upon a Bible that had been torn apart, with the pages scattered around.[46] Indian Bibles, too, were targeted, often left behind by fleeing Christian Indians, some of whom were for-cibly removed to Deer Island in Boston Harbor. During King Philip's War, so many Indian Bibles were destroyed that Eliot confessed to some European travelers seeking a copy that he had none to give them, since most of the Bibles had been burned.[47] It is likely the case that both Indians *and* English soldiers and colonists burned, abused, and shredded Indian Bibles.[48] King Philip's War was widely seen as the failure of Eliot's Indian mission from an English perspective, and the Indian Bible was the most famous object representing that process, incurring the wrath of colonists, too.[49]

Nonetheless, despite all of this violence and rejection, some Christian Indians still valued their Bibles and, according to Eliot, a few even carried them into exile on Deer

Island.[50] After the war, Eliot reported that some Christian Indians "still have frag-ments of their old bibles, which they make constant use of."[51] In part due to the mass destruction of Indian Bibles and the requests coming from surviving Christian Indian communities, Eliot started on a second edition of the Bible right after the war, in 1677.[52] In 1685, two thousand complete second editions of the Indian Bible were printed, revised and corrected by Eliot, Cotton Mather, and James Printer.[53] While the first edition was a hybrid product of a contested period in English history and was published partially for English sponsors and partially for Natives (as indicated by spe-cial bindings, dedications, and title pages in English for some of the Bibles), the second edition was almost solely for the consumption of Natives and did not even contain English-language title pages.[54]

By the early eighteenth century, the importance of the Indian Bible was in relative decline, as English missionaries increasingly favored English-language instruction over teaching written Native languages. Despite the two thousand printed copies of the second (1685) edition, Indian Bibles still seemed scarce thirty years later. This is surely in part because not all of the two thousand copies ever reached Indian hands. In 1703, Captain Ephraim Savage rescued twenty-four unbound Indian Bibles from the trash heap at the house of the recently deceased Duncan Cambell. Savage, realizing the value of the Bible pages, had them bound, with a new title page.[55] By the mid-1720s, the New England Company readily purchased any Indian Bibles they could find in the hands of English men and women for the use of Indians.[56] Requests for a third edition in the early eighteenth century were denied by the New England Company, in part be-cause its commissioners believed that the most efficient way to completely Anglicize Natives was to slowly phase out Native languages by teaching the younger generation to read and write in English.[57] Nonetheless, among a few of the older generation who had been taught to read and write in their own language, Indian Bibles remained an important part of spiritual life and practice. Zachary Hossueit, an Indian minister at Gay Head on Martha's Vineyard, as late as 1747 marked his Indian Bible as his own.[58]

In thinking about the long-term legacy of the Indian Bible among Indian com-munities, it is interesting to note that it was essentially of real spiritual value only to a cluster of Native nations who could speak and read Wôpanâak. For most of New England's Natives, it was simply unreadable and largely unusable (although its contents reached a wider population through preaching and oral transmission). Christianity among the Mohegans, Narragansetts, Niantics, Abenakis, and others de-veloped in the eighteenth century mostly without any scripture or other publications in their own languages. The eighteenth century brought a "second wave" of evangeliza-tion in New England, especially among those Indian communities in Rhode Island, in Connecticut, and on Long Island, New York, who had not previously professed Christianity.[59] This second wave of evangelization largely relied on English-language instruction as the foundation for Native Christianity. Even in this English-language context, the value of the English Bible was dismissed by some Indian preachers. The most famous of these was Samuel Niles, the Narragansett minister from the 1740s through the 1770s, who was notably illiterate. Instead of relying on the Bible for instruction and inspiration, he preferred to go straight to the source, as he liked to point out, and relied on visions and dreams from the Holy Spirit and Jesus.[60] Ultimately, however, the emphasis on English-language instruction that remained central to government and missionary interactions with Native communities had a long-term, negative effect on Indian nations. By the mid-nineteenth century, it was widely presumed that there were no living Natives who could read the Indian Bible, and by the early twentieth century, Wôpanâak as a living, spoken language had seemingly died out.[61]

Fortunately, as with most things in Native history, this is not the end of the story. In the present day, the Indian Bible has gained a second life as an important foundation for language revitalization among Native communities in New England, particularly among the various communities of Wampanoags on Cape Cod and Martha's Vineyard. Through the work of Wampanoag linguist Jessie Little Doe Baird, Wôpanâak is once again being spoken, written, and, for the first time in several generations, learned as the first language among Wampanoag children. At the center of this language revitalization is the Indian Bible and the other seventeenth-century Indian language publications. In what can only be described as one of the most supreme ironies of this long history, the very book that was intended to reshape and even eradicate Native religion and culture is now being used to rejuvenate it. Although there are other Indian-language publications that Eliot and his Native translators and printers produced, according to Baird the sheer length of the Indian Bible makes it indispensable for understanding a wider semantic range of words and their uses in a variety of contexts and in different literary genres.

In other ways, the Indian Bible is returning to Native nations. At least one Indian Bible is actually owned by a Native community, the Mashantucket Pequots, in Connecticut, whose profitable casino allowed them to build a highly acclaimed museum, develop a research center, and, ultimately, purchase an Indian Bible (1685 edition) on the rare book market. But like the Mohegans in the colonial period, no one at Mashantucket can actually read it. It is a mute artifact of a distant past but still richly symbolic and important in terms of what it represents and—in terms of sheer cost—a status symbol of sorts.

In sum, a close examination of America's First Bible—the Indian Bible of 1663—is an important window into the role of the Bible in colonial American life, particularly among the Native American population. In the broader span of the history of Christianity, it represents the very first such translation and engagement with the full text of scripture for—and by—any indigenous population in the Americas. And in the history of the United States, it stands as the first of a multitude of translation and evangelistic efforts by American missionaries on behalf of American Indians in North America. In this way, the 1663 Indian Bible cast a long shadow over the subsequent attempted evangelization of Natives and, later, global missionary efforts by American missionaries. After the American Revolution, such efforts were continued by the Society for Propagating the Gospel Among Indians and Others in North America (1787) and the American Board of Commissioners for Foreign Missions (1810), among dozens of other state and denominational missionary societies.[62] These two organizations and other such societies often used Eliot's missionary and translational work as an inspiration for their own efforts, whether in North America or around the world.[63] As such, the Indian Bible represents a chapter in the nation's history that, while too often overlooked, is a critical part of a much larger history of the readership and reception of the Good Book. It also serves as the symbolic fountainhead of colonial and later evangelistic missionary activity, whether at home or abroad.

ACKNOWLEDGMENTS

I am grateful to the staff at the Newberry Library, the Massachusetts Historical Society, the American Antiquarian Society, and the University of Illinois Urbana-Champaign for their archival assistance. Special thanks to Robert Morrissey, Jill Gage, Philip Goff, and Jesse Little Doe Baird for their help and insights.

3

The Debate over Prophetic Evidence for the Authority of the Bible

in Cotton Mather's *Biblia Americana*

Jan Stievermann

ISAIAH 7:14 HAS long been a litmus test for new Bible translations and users of translations. Peter Thuesen has shown how central this verse was in the protracted conflict
over Scripture interpretation that peaked after World War II, when the National
Council of Churches sponsored the Revised Standard Version (RSV, 1946–52; further
revised in 1990 as New Revised Standard Version [NRSV]).[1] Resistance to the RSV
eventually led to the production of the theologically more conservative New
International Version (NIV, 1973–78) and helped to give shape to what is often called
neo-evangelicalism. Among conservative theologians and church leaders, one of the
chief concerns with the RSV/NRSV was how its interpretative choices seemed to
weaken the prophetic links between the Old and New Testaments and the power of
prophetic evidence, thereby generally undermining the authority of the Bible. These
concerns focused on a number of Old Testament passages in which liberal translators
had expunged traditional christological references, but none so prominently as Isaiah
7:14. In translating this famous prophecy, to which Matthew 1:23 explicitly refers when
the angel announces the birth of Jesus, the RSV had replaced the traditional "virgin"
(on which hung so much theological weight) with the philologically more correct
"young woman." When the NIV programmatically restored the traditional "virgin," the
translation of this verse came to symbolize the conservative-liberal divide and assumed central importance in contemporary evangelical-fundamentalist "constructions of biblical 'inerrancy.'"[2]

The intra-Protestant conflicts epitomized by the wrangling over this verse have not
been the exclusive domain of theologians but also inform the attitudes and practices of

lay people. Chapter 1 shows that regular Bible readers today lean toward conservative biblicist doctrines. It reports that among the roughly 50 percent of Americans who engage in personal Bible study outside worship, 45 percent said that they regarded Scripture as inerrant and 46 percent as divinely inspired.[3] This speaks loudly to the vitality of evangelical Protestantism and the general popularity of an exalted view of Scripture. Though of course it is not only evangelicals who say the Bible is the literal and inerrant word of God, a large number of these regular Bible readers likely identify with evangelicalism.[4] Inerrancy and literalism loom very large in evangelical self-under-standing. Through the many debates about who is or isn't an evangelical, this emerges as a crucial characteristic, which both self-identified evangelicals and scholars have emphasized.[5] Evangelicals historically, as Molly Worthen writes, have "shared the conviction that belief in the inerrant truth of the Bible was more than a doctrine. It was the clarifying lens necessary to rightly perceive reality, a biblical 'world and life view.'"[6]

Chapter 1 also shows that the vast majority of regular Bible readers prefer the theologically conservative translations. Among the roughly 50 percent of Americans who engage in personal Bible study outside worship, 19 percent prefer the NIV, and 55 percent the KJV, against a mere 7 percent opting for the NRSV. Obviously, there are many and complex reasons for the widespread rejection of the RSV and NRSV, just as there are for why people prefer the NIV or KJV, including aesthetic concerns. But the choice of a translation is also, culturally, the choice of an affiliation with a translation philosophy, an exegetical method, and a theological stance. Notably, this view of Scripture goes along with a specific commitment to the evidential power of the Bible as a source of factual proof for the truth claims of Christianity. Isaiah 7:14 has consistently served as a kind of shibboleth in this matter. For conservatives, a number of nonnegotiable theological principles came to hinge on the literalist interpretation of this prophecy, including the integrity of the Old and New Testaments as one coherent and errorless revelation of God, a general belief in supernatural prophecy and miracles, and the virgin birth more specifically.[7]

This essay sheds some new light on the very early history of the evangelical engagement with this issue. Long before the rise of German "Higher Criticism" and the modern Bible revision movement,[8] this problem centrally concerned some of the leading theologians of early eighteenth-century British North America, including Cotton Mather (1663–1728) and Jonathan Edwards (1703–1758), the two figures now firmly associated with the origins of evangelicalism.[9] This is no mere historical coincidence. There is a case to be made that the biblicism of American evangelicalism, as it emerges in the exegetical works of Mather and Edwards, was crucially defined by a preoccupation with scriptural evidentialism, and particularly prophetic evidence.[10]

Edwards's biblical exegesis and biblical theology have been receiving more and more attention in recent years,[11] including his engagement with prophetic evidence, to which he gave considerable room in many scriptural annotations as well as sermons, and to which he devoted a large section of his unfinished work "The Harmony of the Old and New Testament."[12] The situation is very different with Mather. This has to do with Mather's poor reputation,[13] but, most important, with the fact that Mather failed to find adequate sponsorship for the publication of his magnum opus of biblical interpretation, the massive "Biblia Americana." Written between 1693 and 1728, the holograph manuscript of the "Biblia" consists of some 4,500 folio pages filled with annotations on all the books of the Bible. It thus stands as the oldest comprehensive scriptural commentary composed in British North America, which, however, has remained almost unstudied in the archives of the Massachusetts Historical Society. Only through the current editorial project to bring this work to light are we beginning to see the riches of what is one of the great untapped resources for American religious and intellectual history. Combining extensive discussions of the most cutting-edge textual and historical scholarship of his day with scientific speculations and advice for practical piety, Mather's scriptural interpretations reflect the growing influence of Enlightenment thought in America as well as the rise of transatlantic revivalism. His commentary also marks the very first beginnings of an involvement among America's theological elite in discussions over revising the translation of the KJV.[14] Here I want to look at Mather's apologetic but critically informed efforts to demonstrate the evidential value of the messianic prophecies of the Old Testament.

As I will argue, the specifically evangelical tradition of evidentialism that we see emerging in Mather took shape in reaction to a key controversy in the early British Enlightenment discussion over the authority of the Bible. One important part of this discussion was the question of whether and how Christian apologetics in the light of new textual and historical scholarship could still legitimately point to the fulfillment of Old Testament prophecies in the New. Especially contested were, of course, the messianic prophecies. While the initial controversy in the English-speaking world peaked in the early decades of the eighteenth century, pitting a group of radical Deists around Anthony Collins (1676–1729) against the clerical establishment, it had considerable reverberations throughout western Christendom into the nineteenth century and even the present period. In many ways the controversy occurred at a decisive juncture in the development of biblical interpretation. The controversy also reflects the changing nature of Christian apologetics more generally, as it shifts its primary emphasis from a polemical engagement with Judaism and Islam to a defense against skeptical voices emerging from within the Christian world. For early evangelical apologists the engagement with Enlightenment thought and the critics of scriptural authority involved a shift toward an empiricist-factualist understanding of the veracity of the Bible. It also entailed a tendency to conceive of the true meaning of biblical texts, especially of the prophecies, as lying in a sharply circumscribed literal sense, determined by authorial intention and historical reference. Only if understood in this literal-historical sense could the prophecies serve as proof for the Christian faith. As it would in the nineteenth and twentieth centuries, Isaiah 7:14 served as a focal point for this debate over prophetic evidence in the early decades of the eighteenth century. This allows me to mostly restrict myself to Mather's annotations on just this prophecy and the neighboring verses.[15]

Prophetic evidence was a key element of apologetics from the very beginning of Christianity's development into a separate religion, and of particular importance in negotiating the complex relationship with Judaism. New Testament authors frequently referenced prophecies from the Old, especially the messianic prophecies, in order to show that they had been fulfilled in Christ or would be fulfilled in the latter days. Thus, 2 Peter 1:16–21 famously affirms the certainty of God's promise in Jesus Christ first through "the eyewitnesses to his majesty" and second through the prophecies fulfilled in him. Demonstrating the fulfillment of Old Testament prophecies subsequently would also become an important argument in the debates over the canon that came to include the Hebrew Bible as part of Christianity's sacred Scriptures. "The struggle to understand Isaiah as Christian Scripture," to cite the title of Brevard Childs's magisterial study of the subject, was key in these debates, with Isaiah 7:14 functioning as a linchpin.[16] Among the various messianic signs spoken of by the ancient Hebrew prophets that Christians claimed to be fulfilled in the birth, life, death, and resurrection of Jesus of Nazareth, the virgin birth—explicitly referred to as a fulfillment of Isaiah 7:14 in Matthew 1:18–25 and mentioned in Luke 1:26–38—assumed a highly prominent and often emblematic role.

After the establishment of Christianity, proof of the fulfillment of ancient prophecies also became part of a larger effort to validate the reasonableness of Christianity, as well as to show the superiority of Christianity over the rising force of Islam. Throughout the Middle Ages and into the early modern period, however, the main function of prophetic evidence was to prop up what had developed into the full-fledged concept of Christian supersessionism: the Jews had not accepted Jesus as the messiah, even though, as the Gospels showed, God had given them more than enough evidence that he was the promised one. As a consequence, God had abrogated his covenant with the Jewish people and made a new one with the followers of Christianity as the "true" or "spiritual" Israel.

Used in these ways, prophetic evidence and typology belonged to what Hans Frei has described as a "precritical" paradigm of biblical realism and mode of scriptural interpretation.[17] While there was a rich tradition of allegorizing many parts of the Scriptures and translating Scripture into dogmatic or edifying propositions, there had always been an understanding that the biblical narratives could and should be read literally. The late Middle Ages and the Reformation period then gave new priority to this understanding. The biblical stories meant what they said because the real world was conceived of as constituted by the sequence of stories contained in the Bible from creation to consummation. In a traditional biblical worldview, the sacred histories of Scripture and "history" were not yet conceptually separated. Indeed, "History" with a capital *H*, understood as one autonomous, developmental continuum, run by immanent laws, was a product of Enlightenment thought. Before that the history of the world tended to be understood as a cumulative story told in the sequence of biblical narratives, which together constituted one larger whole. Prophecies and types were essential means in tying the sequential stories together into this larger, coherent narrative. Just as the hermeneutical lens of typology allowed Christian exegetes to argue not only that persons and events of the Old Testament had parallels in the New but also that the highest meaning of these types was only realized in their antitypes, prophetic evidence made it possible to view the Hebrew Bible as standing in an organic relationship of prefiguration and fulfillment to the Gospels and Epistles. The belief in the Christian fulfillment of Jewish prophecies blended smoothly into a realistic reading of the biblical stories as a sequence of historical occurrences.[18]

Mather's "Biblia Americana" is in many ways a transitional work. While overall it is strongly imbued with the spirit of early historical criticism (about which more below), many of its topical concerns and exegetical methods are still invested in older forms of Christian apologetics and its approach to the Bible. If we look at Mather's commentaries on Isaiah pertaining to prophetic evidence, there is one layer of glosses that is very much "precritical" in nature and primarily geared toward demonstrating the absolute and exclusive truth of the Christian religion over against other religions, especially Judaism. On this level, Mather makes liberal use of apologetic and polemical literature from antiquity, the Middle Ages, and the Reformation period. Examples include the massive *Pugio Fidei adversus Mauros et Judaeos* (1278) by the Spanish Dominican polemicist and scholar of Jewish literature Raimundus Martinus (Ramón Martí; 1220–1285)[19] but also more recent works by early modern Christian Hebraists.[20] These works offered him selections from ancient Jewish commentary literature and classic rabbinic interpretations, which supposedly showed that those parts of the Old Testament prophecies, which had been referenced by the New Testament writers in describing the birth, life, and death of Jesus Christ, had traditionally been read as speaking about the messiah. Like his sources, Mather devotes considerable attention to Isaiah 7:14. To support the Christian interpretation of this prophecy, Mather culls from *Pugio Fidei* a number of "Remarkable Concessions of the Jewes" asserting that the birth from a virgin mother mentioned in the prophecy of Isaiah had traditionally been considered a sign of the messiah in Talmudic and Midrashic literature, even if some modern rabbis denied this to weaken the Christian cause (*BA* 5:605–607).

During this early stage of annotation, Mather also sought to address the thorny questions that surrounded the translation of the Hebrew word עַלְמָה (*almah*) in Isaiah 7:14. These questions had preoccupied Christian theologians since the days of the very early church, as witnessed by Justin Martyr's early second-century anti-Jewish polemic *Dialogue with Trypho* (esp. chs. 43, 66–68, and 84). Following the citation of Isaiah 7:14 in Matthew 1:23, where *almah* had been rendered as παρθένος (*parthenos*)— a word unambiguously denoting sexual inexperience—the Vulgate (which rendered the word as "virgo") and all subsequent vernacular translations of the Old Testament had understood this word to signify a "virgin." The KJV was no exception here. Mather, however, was well aware of the fact that from the beginning of Christianity this interpretation had been challenged by rabbinical exegetes. They argued that *almah* simply meant a "young woman" of a marriageable age,[21] while the word בְּתוּלָה (*bethulah*) more properly signified a virgin, as demonstrated by the usages of these words elsewhere in Scripture.[22]

Behind the lexical problem lurked the issue of whether the New Testament references to the virgin birth corresponded with their Old Testament sources, if read literally and in accordance with their original intent. Was the use of the word *virgin* in the Gospel of Matthew a misinterpretation that originated in the Septuagint version of

Isaiah used by the author of Matthew, where the Hebrew word *almah* was first rendered as *parthenos*? And could the New Testament assertions of Jesus's miraculous
conception by the Holy Spirit really serve as evidence for his messiahship, if the original messianic prophecy in the Hebrew version of Isaiah never associated the coming of
the Immanuel with the idea of a virgin birth?

Mather addressed these issues in the context of an entry on Jeremiah 31:22, "How
long wilt thou go about, O thou backsliding daughter? for the LORD hath created a
new thing in the earth, A woman shall compass a man" (KJV). Following a long tradition, he reads this verse as a kind of parallel prophecy to Isaiah 7:14, which likewise
announces the miraculous birth of the redeemer: "The Meaning is, A Woman shall bee
with Child of a Man. But this were no New Thing, if it refer to no other than the ordinary Way of Generation. It cannot, possibly bee expounded better, than concerning
the Conception of a Virgin; as the Ancient Rabbins did certainly understand it, applying this Prophecy expressly to the Messiah" (*BA* 5:919). Mather draws on the work of
John Turner (b. 1649/50)—an Anglican apologist, hospitaller of St. Thomas Southwark,
and fellow of Christ's College in Cambridge—*A Discourse concerning the Messia* (1685).
With the help of Turner he asserts that, of course, Isaiah 7:14 also spoke of the birth of
the Immanuel to a virgin, and that the "ridiculous Endeavours of the Jewes to wrest
that Scripture from us" were ill-founded. Borrowing from Turner, Mather cites the
authority of Jerome "That the Hebrew Word there is Alma; and the Punic Language, is
almost the same with the Hebrew; but Jerom assures us that Alma, in the Punic, was
the proper & peculiar Name of a Virgin" (*BA* 5:920).[23] In addition to this philological
argument, he cites long Old Testament passages that he sees as containing prophetic
or typological references to the virgin birth of the messiah, demonstrating that Jesus's
immaculate conception, as asserted by the evangelists, was "Typically and Prophetically
Necessary."

Two hundred fifty years later the scholars working on the NIV felt compelled to
reverse the RSV-translation of Isaiah 7:14. On the level of philology, they would
acknowledge that in biblical Hebrew *almah* primarily signified female adolescence and
could but did not necessarily have to imply virginity. Thus the NIV added a footnote
that the word often simply meant "young woman." But theologically, they, like Mather,
were convinced of the absolute necessity of having the major Old Testament prophet
announce the virgin birth that Matthew had enshrined in the Christian tradition.[24]
After all, this announcement is explicitly offered by the preceding verse in Matthew
(v. 22) as an affirmation of the divinity of the Immanuel to be born to Mary, but also of
the authority of Scripture: "Now all this was done, that it might be fulfilled which was
spoken of the Lord by the prophet" (KJV). For today's conservative evangelicals as
much as for Mather, this type of prophetic evidence, along with programmatic statements such as 2 Peter 1:19–21 and 2 Timothy 3:16, were foundational for the doctrine
of biblical authority.

On this level of debate, no deeper questions are raised by Mather about hermeneutical methods, historical contexts, and the nature of prophecy. Yet there are further layers
of annotation and levels of argumentation, where he taps into more recent literature on

prophetic evidence, reflecting the different challenges that Christian apologetics in general was now facing. In addition to Jewish and Muslim "infidels," this more recent literature was directed at a formidable new adversary: skeptical critics from within the Christian world. Since the mid-seventeenth century, in the period often referred to as the early Enlightenment, three closely interlocked intellectual developments had begun to challenge the authority of the Bible among the intellectual elites of Protestant western Europe: empiricism, rationalism, and new historical-contextual methods in biblical criticism. All three forces worked toward a growing intellectual detachment of historical reality from the biblical narratives. Together they gave birth in the long run to a new model of biblical realism that was representational rather than absolute and self-contained.

If empiricism defined the "real" in terms of observable, measurable factuality, this implied the existence of an independent natural and historical reality, whose truth was autonomous and primary. For most interpreters, the biblical narratives still coincided with this reality, but the affirmation of their veracity was increasingly made dependent on a correspondence with a reality situated before or behind the text.[25] At the same time, there was a trend in philosophy to assert the autonomy and authority of human reason as the ultimate arbiter of truth. To be sure, in the early phase of the English Enlightenment most scientists and philosophers tended to assume the harmony of revealed religion and empirical inquiry. But there was even an influential minority of intellectuals already in the second half of the seventeenth century, notably Benedict Spinoza (1632–1677), Thomas Hobbes (1588–1679), and the radical Deist John Toland (1670–1722), who, albeit with very different methods and purposes, began to conceptually divorce the true moral meaning of the Bible from its historical factuality, which they regarded as questionable at best.[26]

The third and arguably most profound challenge to the older form of biblical realism and authority of the Scriptures came from the rise of new historical-contextual approaches in biblical hermeneutics. At least among specialists and the learned classes, these approaches began to slowly displace the traditional "precritical" modes of reading, while raising troubling new questions about authorship, textual integrity, coherence, and more generally the factual reliability of the Scriptures.[27] As early as 1642, the Dutch Arminian theologian Hugo Grotius (Hugo/Huig de Groot, 1583–1645) had shaken the world of Protestant theology with his *Annotationes in Vetus et Novum Testamentum* (1642). Approaching the Scriptures with the same philological rigor and attention to historical and cultural contexts that humanism had applied to the texts of classical antiquity, Grotius in many ways challenged traditional Christian interpretations of the Hebrew Bible, including the use of prophetic evidence.[28] It is important to note that Grotius did not principally call into question the factuality of the Old Testament prophecies or the belief that the prophets, by divine inspiration, had been able to foretell future events. However, he thought that the majority of the prophecies pointed to events no farther into the future than the Babylonian captivity, the return from exile, or, in a few exceptional cases, to the second destruction of Jerusalem by the Romans and the final diaspora of the Jews.

In the preface to his *Annotationes ad Vetus Testamentum*, Grotius wrote about his basic hermeneutic approach:

> In the prophets I put most of my efforts into finding correspondences with specific historical events. In this part I have related quite a few passages, which the exegetes of old related to Christ and the gospel times, to the historical events belonging to the age of the prophets; however, these events nonetheless have wrapped in them the figure of Christ and the gospel times. I proceeded after this manner [in these cases], because I would otherwise see an incoherent succession of words and events in the prophets, which [i.e. the succession] is most beautiful elsewhere. And certainly such passages reveal to us Christians the providence of God, who had the Messiah and the mercy to be shown by him foreshadowed not only in words, but also in deeds.[29]

On the level of their literal-historical sense, which for Grotius was the primary sense, the Old Testament prophets therefore did not refer to "the figure of Christ and the gospel times." Otherwise, for Grotius, the coherence of the prophetic books and the natural succession of the historical events of which they spoke would have been completely confounded. The prophecies would have made no sense as a means to admonish or comfort their immediate addressees. Everything these ancient seers themselves intended in their predictions had their fulfillment within the boundaries of the Old Testament. The vast majority of the Hebrew prophecies stood in no meaningful relation to the New Testament. Not even Isaiah actually foresaw or deliberately referred to the Christ event. Where the "exegetes of old" had established these relations, they had done so as believers, not as scholars. They had often overburdened the text. Only for a precious few of these prophecies could it be argued that the events or figures they predicted had "wrapped in them the figure of Christ and the gospel times" in the manner of an *integument.* Through God's providence these events or figures were of such a nature that they lent themselves to an allegorical interpretation, which retrospectively found in them a mystical foreshadowing of the future Christ.

With a few terse remarks on Isaiah 7:14–16, Grotius's *Annotationes* had, as it were, fired a shot that still echoed through the early years of the eighteenth century. Grotius argued that if one read Isaiah 7:14 literally and contextually, the historical referent of the sign predicted by Isaiah to King Ahaz in Isaiah 7:14 as a token of "God's certain help against the Syrians and Israelites, and in saving the city against Sennacherib" was the future birth of his second son (following the first son, who according to Isaiah 7:3 was symbolically named Shearjashub or "a remnant will return"), here symbolically named Immanuel ("God is with us") but called by yet another symbolic name, Mahershalalhashbaz ("The spoil speeds, they prey hastens") in Isaiah 8–9.[30] This child was the same child spoken of in the two subsequent verses (Isaiah 7:15–16) and would be born to the young woman with whom Isaiah was to be conjoined in his second marriage. While the prediction of the natural birth of this child primarily and immediately was thus a sign for the deliverance of Ahaz and Judah from its enemies before this boy would reach maturity (which is how Grotius understood verse 16, "before the child shall know to refuse the evil, and choose the good"), Grotius thought that, in a mystical way unbeknownst to Isaiah, it also adumbrated the deliverance brought to all mankind by the birth of the messiah to the virgin Mary. The latter fulfillment was, Grotius thought, readily apparent from the perspective of the Christian faith.[31]

Considering the importance traditionally assigned to prophetic evidence and given the period's increasing prioritization of the literal-historical sense, it is not surprising that Grotius's biblical commentary created heated and prolonged controversies on the Continent as well as in the British Empire. Many felt that the way in which Grotius's preterist hermeneutics reduced christological references in the Old Testament to a secondary *sensus sublimior* totally emasculated prophetic evidence for the divinity and messiahship of Jesus and weakened the truth-claims of the Bible more generally. Ultimately it loosened the ties between the Old and New Testaments and threatened to annul any Christian claim to the Hebrew Bible.

As a response to these challenges, the whole nature of Christian apologetics began to change in the late seventeenth century. Seeking to beat their perceived enemies at their own game, Protestant controversialists in particular emphasized the reasonableness of revealed religion, and offered extratextual (historical or scientific) "proof" for the realism and historical accuracy of the biblical narratives. However, this heavy reliance on external evidence indicates that "a logical distinction and a reflective distance between the [biblical] stories and the 'reality' they depict" had also crept into the consciousness of the new apologists.[32] They, too, became increasingly invested in a new kind of biblical literalism that equated the truth of the Scriptures with their historical factuality. In the context of this profound transformation of Christian apologetics, prophetic evidence gained new significance. Now demonstrations of the fulfillment of Old Testament prophecies in the New served not only to prove that Jesus of Nazareth was indeed the promised messiah. Such demonstrations also became a primary means to establish more generally the inerrant veracity of Scripture as well as the coherence of the canon.

The new forms of apologetics proliferated especially in post-Restoration England, where a more conservative Christian Enlightenment was dominant. Countless such works flew from the pens of both Calvinist Dissenters and Anglican scholars,[33] who typically placed a lot of weight on prophetic evidence.[34] For example, John Smith, in his *Christian Religion's Appeal from the groundless Prejudices of the Sceptick, to the Bar of common Reason* (1675), had an extensive chapter with the programmatic title "Instances of Prophecies fulfill'd whose Effects are permanent and obvious to the Atheist Eyes, if he will but open them." If many of these new English apologists attacked Grotius, this bespeaks the fact that half a century after the Dutch scholar had published the *Annotationes*, his preterist approach to the prophecies had considerably gained ground among English biblical scholars.[35]

The "Biblia Americana" must be understood as part of this new apologetically oriented biblical criticism. As Reiner Smolinski has shown, Mather mounts a strong case for the inspiration, inerrancy, and literal truth of the Scriptures by amassing different kinds of proof (prophetical, historical, philological, and empirical) for their factual veracity, even while he makes significant concessions to the emerging historical-contextual scholarship.[36] Mather's commentary on Isaiah specifically mirrors the new debate over prophetic evidence between what might be called "Grotians" and "anti-Grotians."

Sometime in the 1710s, Mather added a layer of annotations, which brings into conversation two contemporary works that were central to this scholarly debate in England. The first is *A Commentary on the Prophet Isaiah, Wherein the Literal Sense of His Prophecy is Briefly Explain'd*, published in 1709 by Samuel White (fl. 1700) of Trinity College, Cambridge. Expanding on Grotius, White sought to demonstrate that many places in Isaiah that had traditionally been read as speaking of the first or second coming of the messiah, the history of the Christian church, and the end times could not be legitimately connected with the New Testament at all. The traditional readings were arbitrary allegorizations of passages that referred to Isaiah's own time. With Grotius, White allowed for a mystical foreshadowing of Christ to be detected by the eyes of faith in some prophecies. But he argued that in their literal and primary sense even these prophecies—with the one exception of the visions of the suffering servant in Isaiah 53—related to events to occur in ancient Jewish history. In reading Isaiah 7:14, he followed Grotius's lead in interpreting the child as "the Son of Isaiah," who to Christian believers retrospectively appeared "as a Type of Christ."[37]

The second work, which Mather read in conversation with that of White, was *A Commentary on the Prophet Isaiah*, put forth in 1714 by William Lowth (1660–1732) of St. John's College, Oxford. Lowth had written his commentary with the explicit aim to rebut White and the other followers of Grotius. Mather much preferred Lowth and cited him approvingly on many occasions. Still, he showed a kind of grudging respect for the scholarship of White, and even more so of Grotius himself. And it seems that he was uneasily aware of the many problems that their historical research had raised about a strictly christocentric interpretation, which saw Isaiah 7:14 as completely transcending the contemporary context and solely referring to the miraculous birth of the messiah. "For my own Part," Mather wrote in an introductory remark to Isaiah,

> I can allow to the wretched Mr. Samuel White, out of whose Commentary on Isaiah, I shall now & then accept an Illustration; (and unto the other Admirers & Followers of Grotius.) That this wondrous Book of Prophecies, had an Eye to the Condition of the People, under their Invasion from Sennacherib, and somewhat before and after it; and then unto the Chaldæan Captivity & their Deliverance from it. But then to deny that the Prophetic Spirit had also in View, the Deep Things of our SAVIOUR, & of the New Testament, & of the Millenium in the Last Day; to which the Terms have a most lively Adaptation. This is an Ignorance by no Means to be countenanced. (*BA* 5:566)

Mather insisted that an exclusively or even predominantly preterist hermeneutics, as that of Grotius and White, was not biblical, nor was such a reduction of the reach of the prophetic Spirit necessitated by the new methods of criticism. As Lowth assured Mather, careful attention to the literal meaning of the original Hebrew and the historical context of the utterance led toward, not away from, a Christian interpretation of the prophecies.

Lowth suggested to Mather a hermeneutic model of multiple fulfillments that expanded on earlier such interpretations of Isaiah in the Reformed tradition.[38] He thought that "many of the Prophecies are not limited to one single event, but may have different Views, and be capable of being fulfilled by several Steps and Degrees." But, in sharp contrast to White's understanding of a "double interpretation," Lowth insisted that the so-called secondary sense, although it was fulfilled later in time, should not be understood as "less principally intended by the Prophets." On the contrary, he thought of the ultimate fulfillment as the principal one.[39] This ultimate fulfillment was the fulfillment of an actual prediction, not just a retrospective application. "This Christian Interpretation of the Prophecies is called the Mystical Sense," Lowth wrote, "because it helps to unfold the Mysteries of the Gospel, not as if it were always opposed to a literal Sense. For in many Cases what we call the Mystical Sense, more exactly answers the natural and genuine Import of the Words, than any other Interpretation that can be given of them."[40]

This is how Mather, on his second level of annotation, dealt with Isaiah 7:14. He allowed for a double application of the prophecy but rejected the devaluation of the secondary sense as an allegorical imposition by Matthew. In the nearest sense, referring to the immediate future, Isaiah promised a sign to King Ahaz for the deliverance of Judah from its enemies Rezin and Pekah. This sign would be that one who is now a virgin will marry and bring forth a son, and when this son comes of age, the two kings of Samara and Damascus will be destroyed. In a secondary sense the prophet promised the birth of the messiah seven hundred years later, who would be conceived without the partnership of man by virtue of the Holy Spirit.[41] Mather held that this secondary sense was not, as Lowth put it, "contrary to a literal reading" but in fact "more exactly answers the natural and genuine Import of the Words, than any Interpretation that can be given of them." On the contrary, "[if] this prophecy can be applied in a lower Sense to Isaiah's Son, or any other Person but Christ; yet it is plain at first sight, that the Historical Sense, which is commonly given of the Words, to denote One that is now a Virgin, but should afterwards marry and bear a Son, comes infinitely short of the true Force and Meaning of them, and contains nothing in it that can deserve to be called a Sign or Wonder."[42]

However, the critics of the traditional use of prophetic evidence would not so easily be silenced. During the last years of Mather's life they in fact became even more vociferous, as the debate over prophetic evidence increasingly evolved into one about the historicity of scriptural revelation as such and its reliability as the foundations of Christian faith. The radicalization of the debate over prophetic evidence is reflected in a final layer of annotations that Mather added to his commentary on Isaiah between the mid-1710s and the time immediately before his death, when he attached a number of smaller pages to the already overcrowded folio pages pertaining to Isaiah 7:14. These smaller pages contain excerpts from the most current apologetic literature written by English divines in defense of the scheme of double application that Mather had also embraced.

The turn of the debate leading toward the scandal surrounding Collins's work had been initiated by William Whiston (1667–1752), Newton's successor at Cambridge and a correspondent of Mather. He had intended to put the use of prophetic evidence on firmer ground, but as things turned out, he helped to undermine it in the long run.[43] In his *Accomplishment of Scripture Prophecies*, Whiston sought to settle once and for all which of the Old Testament prophecies had their full accomplishment within the boundaries of the Old Testament and which were demonstrably predictive of Christ and the gospel times. In keeping with his Lockean understanding of language as well as an increasingly empiricist understanding of evidence,[44] he argued that "we lose all the real advantages as to the proof of our common Christianity" if we allow for secondary applications of the prophecies that were disconnected from the *sensus historicus*. The biblical prophecies could only have one, literal sense, which was accomplished only once in history: "A single and determinate sense of every Prophecy, is the only natural and obvious one, and no more can be admitted without putting a force upon plain words, and no more can be assented to by the minds of inquisitive Men, without a mighty bias upon their rational faculty." If it was not possible to demonstrate that the messianic prophecies in the Old Testament "have been properly and literally fulfilled without any recourse to Typical, Foreign and Mystical Expositions fulfill'd in Jesus," then they could not serve as proper evidence.[45] In making this argument, Whiston contributed to shifting the scholarly discourse on hermeneutics toward a sharp separation of the literal sense, now narrowly understood as historical reference, from any figurative level of meaning. Traditionally, figurative or typical meaning had been viewed as naturally congruent with literal meaning. Now the two were increasingly seen in opposition.

Whiston was ready to give up on a lot of the minor prophecies, including Isaiah 7:15–16, in the sense that he understood them to have been fully accomplished in Old Testament times. He was convinced, however, that it was indeed possible to defend what he considered the most important prophecies concerning the Incarnation and Second Coming of the messiah and the advancement of his kingdom as having only one literal fulfillment in Christ and the gospel, because "the words do most exactly, if not solely agree to him; and that the Coherence of those places is intire without them, if not in some measure inconsistent with them."[46] This, he thought, was certainly true for Isaiah 7:14: "The words are not only impossible to be apply'd to any other than to the Messias; that seed of the Women alone; but the coherence of the other Prophecy [i.e., Isa. 7:15–16] is intire without it."[47]

Whiston unwittingly played into the hand of a group of radical English Deist intellectuals who appropriated his hyperliteralist approach to the issue of prophetic evidence. Principal among these was Anthony Collins, who in his famous *Discourse of the Grounds and Reasons of the Christian Religion* (1724) started out by following Whiston in contending that prophetic evidence was the only solid empirical proof to back up the

Christian claim that Jesus was indeed the Christ and redeemer.[48] In assessing this claim, Collins, like Whiston, would only allow one literal fulfillment of the Hebrew prophecies. And like Whiston he insisted that, as the text stands, the Old Testament passages cited in the New simply could not be applied literally to the situation described in the latter. However, he flatly rejected Whiston's arguments concerning textual corruptions either by accidental scribal errors or by rabbinical manipulations aiming to refute Christianity. Such arguments for Collins amounted to little more than wishful thinking. He was convinced that in their literal and natural sense all the prophecies, which had traditionally been read as referring to the messiah, were really foretelling events of the Old Testament period. While he granted that in some of these prophecies a typological or mystical sense could be found that adumbrated Christ, they could not be said to have actually predicted him. Since the prophets had not intended Christ as the referent of their predictions, the New Testament citations of these prophecies ultimately did not hold any evidential power. With a view to the citation of Isaiah 7:14 in the Gospel of Matthew, Collins wrote that "to understand the Prophet as having the conception of the Virgin Mary and birth of her son Jesus literally and primarily in view, is a very great absurdity." Instead, the words "in their obvious and literal sense, relate to a young woman in the days of AHAZ, King of Judah."[49]

For Collins, then, the tradition of prophetic evidence was for all intents and purposes dead. Its demise showed the indefensibility of regarding the Bible as a coherent supernatural revelation from God. For the Deist Collins, Christianity could and should only be defended to the extent that it corresponded with a universal religion of reason. Unsurprisingly, Collins's attack on prophetic evidence caused a huge uproar on both sides of the Atlantic that reverberated for decades.[50] The stakes were enormously high, as Collins struck at the very heart of Christian apologetics, threatening not only the main proof for Christ's messiahship but also for the unity, harmony, and authority of the Bible as one continuous revelation.

Mather made an effort to incorporate the debate started by Whiston and Collins into his "Biblia" as long as he was able to. In so doing, he gave room to Whiston himself and scholars who followed his lead, but also to defenders of the legitimacy of double applications. It seems that toward the end of his life Mather very much wavered on how the quintessential Isaianic prophecy could and should be understood. Whiston's *Accomplishment of Scripture Prophecies* first makes an appearance in the "Biblia" in an annotation on Isaiah 7:15–16. Here Whiston's opinion is cited that the prophecy of the child—of whom it is said here, "butter and honey shall he eat," and "before the child shall know to refuse the evil, and choose the good, the land that thou abhorrest shall be forsaken of both her kings"—is not literally applicable to the messiah, whose birth was predicted in the prophetic excursion of the previous verse. For Whiston this second prophecy referred solely to Isaiah's own son: pointing to his son Shearjashub, Isaiah foretells to King Ahaz that before this boy will stop eating child's food and come of age the land will be delivered from Rezin or Pekah.[51] When he extracted this annotation from Whiston, Mather seemingly was ready to concede that the primary sense of Isaiah 7:15–16 was pointing to the life and times of the prophet. But almost as a kind of anxious afterthought he added another annotation in which Whiston's exclusively preterist reading of Isaiah 7:15–16 was qualified. This Mather did by reference to the Cambridge scholar and controversialist Nicholas Clagett the Younger, D.D. (1654–1727), who had written an apologetic tract in direct refutation of Whiston's opinion that,[52] as Mather explains, "the Language & Intent of the Prophets, is ever Single: and that their Prophecies are not capable of a Double Sense, & of such Typical Interpretations, as many Christian Expositors putt upon them." While Clagett offered a "Collection of Twenty Five Prophecies, which he allowes to be meant only of the Messiah, & applicable to no other," Clagett maintained, as quoted by Mather, "That there are Prophecies of the Messiah, which carry a Double Sense in them: & that it is fitt there should be so." With good reason, Mather thought, Clagett understood the prophecy of Isaiah 7:15–16 to fall into this category as much as the one in the preceding verse:

> The Sign of Deliverance given to Ahaz, is a Prophecy of the Holy Child, and of Another Child. A Prophecy of a Child, that should be born in Isaiah's, and Ahaz's Time, & of a Child that should not be born till some Hundred Years after. A Prophecy, that within the Time, that a Virgin should marry, & conceive, & bring forth, & the Child should be grown to distinguish between Good and Evil, Ahaz should be delivered from the Two Kings he feared. And a Prophecy that a Virgin, while a Virgin, should conceive, & bring forth, a Son for the Deliverance of Mankind. Here is a Prophecy of a Child, that should be called, Immanuel; as token of the Presence of God, with the House of David. And a Prophecy of a wonderful Child, who should be called, Immanuel, because he should be God Incarnate. (*BA* 5:610–611)[53]

This defense of the possibility of multiple referents in prophecies more generally and of a double fulfillments of Isaiah 7:14 in particular—first to Isaiah's son Mahershalalhashbaz, mentioned in Isaiah 7–9, and then to Jesus Christ—seems to have satisfied Mather for some time.

But then came the controversy surrounding Collins, which, even for the great majority of scholars who rejected the Deist position, made it clear that the legitimacy of double fulfillments was increasingly coming under pressure. While some apologists chose to dig in their heels, others followed Whiston's lead. Significantly the very last work that Mather excerpted for his commentary on Isaiah was the *Letter to the Author of the Discourse of the Grounds and Reasons of the Christian Religion: Shewing, that Christianity is supported by Facts well attested* (1726), by the now forgotten controversialist John Green (d. 1774), curate of Thurnscoe, who leaned toward Whiston's hyperliteralism. Through Green's elaborate historical explanations Mather obviously became convinced that with regard to Isaiah 7:14, one could and should take a stance for one, and only one, literal accomplishment in Christ. Thus Mather writes,

> This Prophecy, cannot in any Sense at all relate unto a young Woman in the Days of Ahaz. But Matthews Interpretation of it, is literal, and obvious, and indeed the

only one that can be given. This makes the Prophecy serve to a considerable End; conspicuously distinguishing the Messiah from all other Persons.... None but JESUS ever was born of a Virgin: And none but He could be called, Immanuel; And of none but Him could it be said, His Name shall be called, The mighty GOD. (BA 5:612–613)

To make this argument hold water, however, one needed to separate the prophecy of Isaiah 7:14 from those of the following verses, whose primary meaning was much more convincingly explained as applying to Isaiah's own time. "Here are evidently Two distinct Prædictions," Mather summarizes Green. "The first, That a Virgin should conceive & bear a Son. The second, That the Land of the Enemies to Judah should be forsaken of its Kings, before Shearjashub should know to Refuse the Evil & Chuse the Good." Although being distinct prophecies, both literally fulfilled in history once, the two were still connected in the sense that the predictions concerning Isaiah's own son in Isaiah 7:15–16 simultaneously constituted a prophesied type of the birth of the messiah foretold in verse 14: "The one of these Prædictions is made a Sign of the other, and was to be fulfilled, in Token, that the other should also come to pass in the Season of it" (BA 5:613).[54]

What made Mather convert to this interpretation in the last year of his life and also adopt it as the final word on the issue in his last unpublished manuscript, "The Triparadisus" (1726/27)?[55] It was not that he came to reject the hermeneutics of double fulfillment altogether. In fact he defended and applied it in the context of many other Old Testament prophecies. And so did his famous successor in the New England tradition, Jonathan Edwards, who in fact read Isaiah 7:14 as a prophesied type.[56] But it seems that for Mather and Edwards, as for many later evangelical exegetes, there was a pull away from the manifold sense of the word when it came to defending key positions from Scripture. This illustrates how much the intellectual debates of the early Enlightenment had affected and would continue to affect views on Scripture. As these debates more and more centered on the historicity and factuality of the biblical text, hermeneutics increasingly shifted toward an equation of "literalism at the level of understanding the biblical text with literalism at the level of knowing historical reality."[57] For conservative apologists, or "critical anticriticism" (to use a term suggested by Mark A. Noll), this made factual inerrancy "the epistemological keystone of Christianity itself."[58]

Within the larger world of today's evangelical theology, some exegetes have come to favor typological readings of Isaiah 7:14 or a sensus sublimior or sensus plenior approach, which are in many ways similar to Grotius's notion of a hidden mystical sense.[59] This had also been the position taken by prominent members of the committee of scholars who had worked on the RSV, when challenged by conservatives on their seemingly irreverent translation of Isaiah 7:14.[60] By contrast, the majority of more literalist-minded evangelical interpreters seem to be conflicted, as Edwards and Mather were, between allowing for a double historical fulfillment of this famous prophecy and insisting on a hyperliteralist reading in which the prediction of the birth of a child called Immanuel to a virgin mother in its primary and exclusive sense refers to Jesus Christ.[61]

4

Navigating the Loss of Interpretive Innocence

READING THE "ENLIGHTENMENT" BIBLE IN EARLY

MODERN AMERICA

Robert E. Brown

SOME OF THE results of chapter 1 seem to indicate a lingering effect of modernity on American Bible reading. Those who think of the Bible as a fable read it the least—but even among those who hold the strongest views of its divine origin, less than half have read it once in the last year. This might suggest that even those who venerate the Bible highly may find it difficult to make it practically relevant, as they find its application increasingly circumscribed from life outside their institutional church communities. For the past century and a half, American Bible readers have been grappling with the loss of "interpretive innocence," as readers of all theological persuasions have become more attuned to the historical processes involved in the creation of the canonical texts of Scripture. The more the human element in the authoring of the biblical texts has been documented, the more difficult it has been to identify the nature of the divine element (inspiration) in them, as well as an authoritative meaning in the texts that compels belief and behavior and, thus, a strong motive for reading.

The transformation of the Bible from mythos to historical artifact—what Jonathan Sheehan has termed the forging of the "cultural Bible"—began in earnest in America well over three centuries ago.[1] Coming to terms with the Bible's own history resulted in increasingly naturalistic accounts of its origins and created a growing awareness of the human element in its formation.[2] This essay will address a central consideration in the concomitant theological reassessment that took place regarding the concept of "inspiration," by examining Cotton Mather's elucidation of the interplay of divine and human elements in the biblical texts, as he came to recognize the historical processes at work in their composition and compilation.

These processes were most cogently articulated in three late seventeenth-century works: Benedict Spinoza's *Theological-Political Treatise* (1670), Richard Simon's *Critical History of the Old Testament* (1678; English 1682), and Jean Le Clerc's *Five Letters concerning the Inspiration of the Holy Scriptures* (1690).[3] The essence of the theory of composition proposed by Spinoza and Simon was this: the political and religious affairs of the early "Hebrew Commonwealth" were written down by "Public Writers" from the time of Moses forward and were maintained by a scribal guild as a kind of repository of national records. However, the historical narratives and prophetic texts now constituting the Old Testament were written considerably later, largely beginning with the priest-scribe Ezra, and continuing down into the second century. Thus the received texts are abridgements drawn from earlier miscellaneous public records, used by scriptural editors for later, religious purposes. The process of transcription and reediting over centuries introduced numberless disjunctions and contradictions, as the texts were reworked with later audiences in mind. This process precluded the possibility of a seamless, infallible narration of Jewish history. Rather, the texts were primarily intended to promote piety; the narrative structure was simply a stylized platform for moral and religious instruction.

Historical criticism of this nature required early modern interpreters to reconcile their discovery that the Bible was subject to the vagaries of historical process, both in its composition and in its compilation, with assumptions that the biblical texts were the product of divine inspiration and thus presumably immune to the limitations of their human authors. The composition theories of Spinoza and Simon undermined traditional theories of biblical authority and meaning, which tied the notion of inspiration to the presumption of a contemporaneous, identifiable autography in the texts. "Inspiration" or divine authorship could only be confidently asserted when the human author who had received divine revelations, or was eyewitness to the miraculous events of Jewish or providential history, committed them to writing in near time. The idea that texts were the product of long historical processes involving anonymous editors far removed from the precipitating events invited skepticism about the accuracy and truthfulness, and thus the divine origin and authority, of the final product.

Furthermore, inspiration was understood to be the product of something like ecstatic possession, in which the subject lost control of his personal will and faculties. This incapacitation was taken to mean that the author was wholly directed by the Spirit, ensuring that the final text was divine and infallible. The Old Testament prophets seemed to be the paradigmatic instance for this theory: their visionary texts postulated the total passivity of the author in receiving and relaying divine revelation. The critical theory of the Old Testament's compilation gave more credit to the authors as deliberative agents who used their rational faculties in writing. This was particularly true for "nonprophetic" genres in the Bible, such as historical narrative, wisdom literature, and epistolary texts. These did not seem to be "inspired" in the traditional, ecstatic sense, making it conceivable that an author's fallible human character shaped the literary substance. The challenge for early modern interpreters was to construct a theory of inspiration that reconciled the divine and the human, the fallible with the infallible, in the Bible's composition.[4]

Spinoza was not particularly troubled by this problem: he understood prophecy or "inspiration" to be the result of human imagination rather than a divine afflatus. As such, human error was inevitable. The real purpose or value of Scripture was only found in its moral and religious piety; so long as the authors did not intend to deceive, their literary productions could be esteemed in some measure.[5] Simon dispensed with this problem by asserting that in their role as public scribes, the authors of the Old Testament *functioned* as prophets. Thus, any writings they produced, no matter how garbled or compromised from a historical standpoint, had the authority that comes from prophetic inspiration. Each author also had the prophetic liberty to arrange the material as he saw fit and to redact the work of his predecessors, as authors sought to fit "them to their own times and design."[6]

Jean Le Clerc on the other hand tackled this issue in a more systematically thorough manner. He argued that while the prophets were inspired, their writings, which depended on their memories (or the memories of their amanuenses), were not necessarily inspired, since memories are by nature faulty. Furthermore, the personality of the prophet shaped the message, such that inspiration pertains not to the words themselves but only the substance of the ideas expressed.[7] For Le Clerc, other literary genres in the Bible fell into a different category. Thus the historical narratives of the Bible were not *in any way* inspired, because historical writing was by nature a rational or deliberative exercise, not one of ecstatic possession. Histories were credible when the authors were known to be honest and well-informed on "principle matters of fact." Historians merely gave "the truth of the history to the best of their knowledge." As such, biblical histories were bound to have the kinds of mistakes in them that were common to all historical writing.[8] The wisdom literature of the Old Testament was similarly uninspired, since it dealt with questions of common morality, answers for which could only attain probability, not complete certainty. Le Clerc concluded, however, that this did not undermine the authority of Scripture; the histories and general doctrines of the biblical texts could be taken to be inspired in their substance, so long as they were found to agree with the general teachings of Jesus, and with reason.

Cotton Mather was no stranger to the critical interpretation of the Old Testament and in fact cautiously embraced its results. Late in life, for example, he came to reject the originality of the Hebrew vowel points, even though he had defended their integrity in his master's thesis at Harvard.[9] Influenced by Simon, he also came to accept the idea that the Old Testament had a long compositional history.[10] In an essay inserted at the end of the *Biblia Americana* (post-1716), "Things done by Ezra, for the Repairing and Preserving of the Sacred Scriptures," Mather acknowledges that the historical vagaries entailed in the compilation of the Old Testament, and the editing that this required, indicated a process that represented a dramatic loss to the notion of a pristine canon largely unchanged since its creation: "Ezra, from as many copies as he could gett, sett forth a correct edition of them; ... [He] ... *added* what appeared necessary to him, for the illustrating, the connecting, and the compleating of them; . . . [changing] the old names of places, which were grown obsolete, into the new names, whereby people now called them."[11] What Mather concluded for the Pentateuch—later editing by public scribes and variations introduced in transcription and editing—he also conceded for most of the Old Testament, as well as much of the New Testament, particularly the four Gospels.[12]

As a result, Mather reshaped his understanding of inspiration.[13] In two additional essays appended to the *Biblia*, he worked out a theory of inspiration that took into account the historical processes and, thus, the human element at work in canonical construction ("Some Remarks, relating to the Inspiration, and the Obsignation, of the Canon"; and "Some Remarks upon the Spirit of Prophecy"). Whereas Le Clerc had tied inspiration to the mechanics of prophecy and to the genre of writing (effectively eliminating it from most of the Old Testament), Mather concluded that inspiration could encompass and transcend historical process and human agency. For example, inspiration does not necessarily mean ecstatic passivity: "Men that are divinely inspired, are not thrown into such a Rage. Tho' their *Inspirations* proceed not from or at their *Wills*, yett they can manage them as they *Will*, for the Circumstances of their producing them."[14] Thus, inspiration did not circumvent the personality of the prophet-author, who retained both his deliberative rational faculties, and his freedom to write as he saw fit: "The inspiration which led the writers of the Scriptures, did not exclude such humane means . . . in matters of discourse and reason, to argue from their own observations. . . . Nor did this inspiration . . . exclude their use of their own words, and of the style that was most natural to them. And as they were permitted the use of these, thus they were permitted . . . sometimes to use the words of others."[15] This meant that no literary genre was excluded by definition from inspiration by the Spirit; Mather's theory theologically reintegrated the whole of the biblical canon.

Following Le Clerc's lead, Mather acknowledged that there were elements in the compilation and composition of biblical text that did not require or involve inspiration; the Bible and the story it told had to be read in a nuanced fashion. For example, matters pertaining to "human prudence" were not the product of inspiration but rather were the result of a more general "conducive power" of the Spirit. Thus, "There is no necessity of saying, that Paul sent for his cloak and parchments, by the inspiration of the Holy Spirit; or that he had an immediate command for every salutation, at the end of his epistles."[16] Similarly, Mather acknowledged that prophetic and apostolic inspiration was neither perpetual nor universal. It came and went, as necessity dictated. Even the apostles had to sort out differences of opinion among themselves; the inspiration of the Spirit was to be found in the process of deliberation: "We might add; that the infallible Spirit, which inspired the sacred writers, was not permanent and habitual; or continually residing in them; nor given for all purposes and occasions. . . . In a matter of great importance to the whole church, the Apostles mett together in council, to decide the controversy, both because according to our Saviour's promise to them, they might expect a more abundant effusion of the Holy Spirit upon them, when they were for that end assembled in His Name." Significantly, Mather allowed for the idea that the apostolic or prophetic understanding of important doctrines showed evidence of change over time *within* the New Testament, suggesting that inspiration itself involved historical process. For example, with regard to the doctrine of the resurrection: "we find the Apostolical Writings, *before* the Second Epistle to the *Thessalonians* cleared that Matter up, speaking as if it were possible to have been the Fate of some living in those Times."[17] Perhaps an even more intriguing example of Mather's belief in progressive revelation can be found in his commentary on Philippians 3.11. In speaking about the order of the resurrection of the dead, Mather understands Paul to be speaking here of mysteries to which he was privileged and that the Spirit had not yet permitted to be revealed. Thus he could only speak of them cryptically, or indirectly:

> What if this thing...should be one of those...which the Apostle was *Forbidden* at present, to publish unto the World as an *Article of Faith*, but he had Liberty to mention as his own Holy Opinion and Persuasion. It being reserved unto *John* more expressly to publish it first as an *Article of Faith*, in the proper Time and Place for it. Our Apostle seems to manage himself in this Point, as he does elsewhere, in things which he proposed only as *a Man*, so far as his Reason might go, and not as *an Apostle*, speaking authoritatively in the Name of God.[18]

In many ways Mather's theory of inspiration closely paralleled Le Clerc's theory in its recognition of the human role in the writing of Scripture. However, Mather's theory was different in one crucial regard. Le Clerc concluded that human reason had free rein in the composition of the Bible, meaning that human foibles would be introduced into its content as a matter of course, suggesting that the authoritative, divine elements must be separated and drawn off from its human dross. Mather was willing to concede that fallible human personality and reason were at work in the writing of Scripture but insisted that the Holy Spirit still superintended the overall outcome toward an infallible end; the divine telos in the composition was still achieved. Though inspiration might be less restrictive of human agency than traditionally thought, it still encompassed the process as a whole and could be identified in the effect. The "Holy Spirit infallibly guided them in the use of those means...[so as to] supply them with suitable apprehensions, and *keep them* in the use of their own rational judgment, *within the bounds of infallible truth, and of expediency for the present occasions.*"[19] For Mather, human authorship did not mask or obviate divine authorship, even if there were what "look[ed] like variations and almost contradictions in our Sacred Scriptures," and even though "the different style[s] of the historiographers from the prophets, of the prophets from the evangelists, of the evangelists from the apostles may make the truths of Scripture seem of different complexions."[20]

Mather's biblical commentary and theology of interpretation represent the beginning of a long history of American attempts to articulate the dynamic between the divine and the human in the creation of Scripture. Like that subsequent history, Mather's reworking of that dynamic is highly rationalistic in nature; unlike much of that history, he seems willing to have held the nature of the divine-human elements of

Scripture together loosely, without trying to specify them too exactly. To describe this, Mather resorted to a common early modern analogy: as with our understanding of the natural world, so too the process of inspiration may entail "methods, which are to us inscrutable."[21] Though the concept does not appear overtly in his discussions of inspiration, his theological reconstruction employs the idea of mystery in the twinning of the divine and the human in scriptural authorship, in much the same manner that the Christian tradition grappled with the inherent tensions to be found in the notion of the Incarnation. It is a concept he readily uses elsewhere in the *Biblia*, and a concept noticeably absent in much of contemporary American Bible reading.

5

Reading the Bible in a Romantic Era

Beth Barton Schweiger

THIS ESSAY ASKS how the enormous popularity of poetry in the early United States may have shaped how people read the Bible in the nineteenth century. The qualification "may have" is important. Reading is one of the most difficult of human actions to interpret. A reader picks up a book, and whether she spends thirty seconds or two hours with it, eventually she closes it, rises from the chair, and walks out of the room, usually without leaving a trace. It is hard enough to describe how the Bible may influence its readers, but these problems are multiplied in trying to understand readers who have been dead for generations. The rare first-hand account—a diary entry or letter—can tell us something about readers, but usually not in detail. Another possibility is to study prescriptive literature such as sermons, biblical commentaries, Sunday school literature, or other didactic texts that tell us how people were *told* to read the Bible. But can we be certain that they followed this advice? A third possibility—the approach taken here—is to explore the assumptions readers took to their Bibles by examining what else they were reading.[1]

People in the early nineteenth century witnessed remarkable changes in how print was produced, what was printed, how it was distributed, and who knew how to read. All of these developments were welcomed by, and in many cases pioneered by, church leaders and laity. American Christians wrote, printed, and published with such abandon that by midcentury the country was awash in pious print. The invention of the steam press and stereotyping, along with innovations in book distribution, allowed the Bible to be mass-produced for the first time in human history. More people owned Bibles and Testaments than ever before, and a growing array of cheap print—newspapers, tracts, pamphlets, magazines, and almanacs—spread Christian texts across the country.

At the same time, the number of skilled readers grew, both those who learned in schools and those who learned informally at home or in Sunday school. This was particularly significant for women, Indians, and African Americans, as historically few of them had learned how to read. Christian colleges and academies trained pastors and laypeople, many from modest backgrounds, to appreciate sophisticated texts. Print fueled the great Anglo-American revivals, feeding the growth of national organizations such as the American Bible Society and other not-for-profit denominational printing concerns that printed Bibles, New Testaments, and other literature. All of this Christian print spread thickly across the country with the help of colporteurs, camp meeting preachers, and Sunday school teachers. The Bible moved to the center of political debates as people struggled without success to find in its pages a final answer on the burning question of slavery. For all of these changes, however, we know little about how ordinary Americans read the Bible in the early nineteenth century. Recent work has begun to change this, but writing a history of Bible readers remains difficult for the simplest of reasons: the Bible was everywhere, and people took it for granted. Bible readers rarely felt inclined to record how they read it.[2]

Popular poetry was one of the primary contexts in which people began to read the Bible in the nineteenth century. People of all stations in life, the educated and uneducated, were mad about poetry. Like the Bible itself, poetry could be found almost everywhere. Books of poetry could be had, of course, but these were relatively expensive. Poems could be found in the pages of magazines, newspapers, or almanacs. Single printed pages, known as broadsides, were printed in every small printing office at the expense of the local poets who penned the verses. People who could not read heard poems recited on the street or in a shop, often as song. Poems were staples of popular hymnody; many sacred songs first appeared as single sheets. At the same time that printed poetry was increasing, scholarship on the literary aesthetics of the Bible found a popular audience. This work argued that poetic language was the purest medium of divine truth. Poetry "arose from those immutable principles of harmony established by Him who originally strung that invisible harp in the nature of man." Not surprisingly, this led to the conviction that the Bible itself was full of poetry and in fact was itself a literary text of the highest quality. This conviction altered how people understood the Bible and, eventually, how they understood God. They became convinced that the creator of the universe valued beauty and good taste in language. Finally, many of the most popular poets of the day evoked the Bible in their writing. Their poems regularly appeared in newspapers, magazines, and even almanacs. But of particular importance was these poems' presence in sacred songbooks and hymnals. Some of the most popular sacred songs were sung to verses penned by popular poets, which were memorized by countless people. This chapter, then, examines in turn poetry's enormous popularity, the conviction that there was poetry in the Bible, and the ubiquity of the Bible in contemporary poetry.[3]

The concern here is not to interpret poetry but simply to describe its presence and to suggest its broad influence among Bible readers. The two poets highlighted here, Felicia Hemans and William Cowper, were among scores of others who wrote about the

Bible and whose work was reprinted in hundreds of hymnbooks. Both Hemans and Cowper were English Anglicans; Hemans was the best-selling female poet of the nine-teenth century, while Cowper was an unhappy eighteenth-century lawyer. Both were appreciated widely in the early United States, underscoring the continuing importance of the Anglo-American context long after the American Revolution. This was particu-larly true of the most modest printed works. Britain was familiar territory for American readers who never set foot on a transatlantic ship, from Jack Horner's corner to the English Reformation to *Oliver Twist* and *Pilgrim's Progress*. As late as 1840, American readers were steeped in reprints and standard works, almost half of which were British in origin.[4]

CHRISTIAN CONFIDENCE IN POETRY

Like the Bible, poetry was on the lips of tradespeople and schoolgirls, copied into com-monplace books, printed in small-town newspapers and on the well-thumbed pages of almanacs. Moreover, aspiring poets were everywhere. Nothing was more common than to write poetry, especially among the young, and many people aspired to be pub-lished. One editor warned would-be poets that there was "postage to pay, paper to waste, and patience to weary" with the piles of submissions he received. Poetry was the inspiration for a new, wildly popular genre known as the gift book, or annual. Lavishly produced, usually with gilded stamped cloth bindings in richly colored cotton or silk, these volumes were filled with fine engravings and the work of some of the best known authors in the Anglo-American tradition. They were attractively priced so they could be offered as a token of tasteful affection to friends and relatives at Christmas, New Year's, and birthdays. In 1838, the *Christian Keepsake and Missionary Annual*, a book full of poetry, claimed that its contents spoke "winningly of Christ and of eternal things," that it had "inscribed upon its gilded pages the words of eternal life," and that it would transform their hearts. In spite of its popularity, some worried about the influence of "new poetry," particularly on young women. Lord Byron was known in some quarters as "the prince of the Satanic school of poetry." Yet he was also read appreciatively by American evangelicals, including missionaries, one of whom invoked Byron's "Childe Harold's Pilgrimage" to describe the Asian landscapes before him.[5]

The popularity of literary sensibilities among nineteenth-century American Chris-tians has been associated with a small coterie of northeastern liberal Protestants. Yet there is abundant evidence that the fascination with poetry flourished far beyond the confines of liberal Boston. Poetry was arguably more important than fiction in lodging sentimental imagery in Christian minds. Nineteenth-century readers read, wrote, and published poetry in magazines and newspapers, Sunday school literature, and school-books. They read hymnbooks and songbooks as poetry and bought volumes of verse by Edward Young and John Milton from circuit riders. Agents hawked volumes of sacred poems by subscription in the countryside. All the most popular poets of the period, including Lydia Sigourney and Felicia Hemans, regularly took up sacred themes. The connections between religious emotion and poetic enthusiasm were believed to be very strong. Reverend John Maffitt, a Methodist editor, noted that while religious sensibility was perhaps of less fervency than poetic ardor, he nevertheless commended poetry as the servant of religion. "It is too late in the age of mental philosophy to make the assertion that poetry has no power to pour its notes of sweet and transporting melody in to the quiet recesses of a deeply humbled heart," Maffitt wrote. The noted Presbyterian cleric James Waddel Alexander, who had two brothers named after eighteenth-century British writers, the essayist Joseph Addison and the poet William Cowper, championed the religious power of poetry. One writer in 1849 "got to ruminating," he said, "upon what the Sabbath had done for poetry and what poetry had done for the Sabbath." Among the many things that came to mind he mentioned silence, church bells, and the noted British poet Felicia Hemans.[6]

What, then, did poetry have to do with Christianity in a period that we associate more with revivals and reform movements than with the reading of blank verse? Interest in poetry was part of a broad expansion of knowledge that was enabled in part by the astonishing growth of common schools, academies, and colleges. Expectations for common learning rose ever higher as the possibility of gaining even a rudimentary liberal education was extended to ambitious laborers. Even the self-taught labored over the pages of their grammars and rhetorics as they sought to master the formal English that they believed would improve their lives. How one spoke and wrote revealed character and position as clearly as dress, manners, family, or piety. In short, the mastery of language and learning of all kinds became increasingly important, even to those in modest circumstances. As their knowledge grew, they cultivated a taste for literature, particularly poetry.[7]

Poetry was certainly at the center of things for an ambitious Methodist editor who labored in an office stacked with books on the corner of Eighth and Main in Cincinnati in 1841. Leonidas Hamline (1797–1865), who would later become a Methodist bishop and leading voice in the Holiness movement, had just begun publishing the *Ladies Repository and Gatherings of the West*. Intended primarily as a pious alternative to *Godey's Lady's Book*, Hamline's magazine featured fine engravings and poetry and essays by popular writers. By the 1850s, musical notation appeared in each number. Methodist readers subscribed in droves, up to forty thousand of them by the end of the journal's first decade alone. The *Repository* remained one of the most enduring and popular periodicals of the period.[8]

Hamline's commitment to publishing poetry was broadly shared by editors of American religious periodicals, most of which were literary publications. The *American Baptist Magazine*, *Christian Spectator*, and *Presbyterian Magazine* (later the *Christian Advocate*) all included critical reviews of poetry and published poetry. Methodist periodicals were among the most successful of the genre, and they were full of poetry. The *Methodist Magazine* featured poetry from its first issue in 1818, and by midcentury the *Methodist Quarterly Review* included page after page of poems and critics. The *Review*'s writers considered eighteenth-century works by Charles and John Wesley, John Newton, Isaac Watts, and Edward Young, but they also celebrated modern verse by Elizabeth

Barrett Browning, Henry Wadsworth Longfellow, and William Cullen Bryant. Editors assumed their audience knew all of these poets well.[9]

What work, then, did poetry accomplish for the legions of pious readers in this generation? Why did they have such confidence in poetry? As it turns out, they believed that special moral powers inhered in poetic language. According to philosophy of mind, the psychology of the nineteenth century, language exercised a tangible power. Reading poetry fostered virtue. "Poetry comes to us clothed in robes of purity, and bearing sentiments of a lofty and truthful character," a writer explained in his conduct manual for young men. The conviction that poetry refined the taste, quickened the imagination, and purified the feelings made it worthy fare for young minds.[10]

The doctrines of Scottish moral philosophy held that the mind was composed of various faculties, including a moral faculty known as taste. Taste was "the power of receiving pleasure from the beauties of nature and art." In essence, taste was a rational reaction to the beautiful. When beauty was apprehended, then the mind would be refined by its presence. But these things could be quite complicated, for not all people could recognize beauty, and some people were more sensitive to it than others. Taste, it turns out, could be improved. Like the human body, it could be strengthened through exercise, such as listening to music, gazing at works of art, and, importantly, by reading poems and other works of genius. Reading, then, wielded powerful physical and moral influence over the mind through language, and this was the chief reason people should read poetry. "Aliment taken into the mind operates like aliment taken into the body, by assimilation. It is converted, as it were, into the very substance of the soul, and imparts to it its own character," an editor explained.[11] The task of poetry, and more broadly of education, was to strengthen the moral faculty and to cultivate a taste for beauty and truth.

POETRY IN THE BIBLE: BISHOP ROBERT LOWTH

Reverence for poetry found its highest expression in claims for the Bible. Just as the Bible belonged to the realm of history in the nineteenth century, it also belonged to literature. American Christians' concern for the truth of biblical history paralleled a growing interest in the aesthetics of Scripture. The Bible's literary qualities, and particularly its aesthetic powers, began to be celebrated by theologians, liberal and evangelical alike.[12]

Their ability to do this rested on the work of the eighteenth-century Anglican Bishop Robert Lowth (1710–1787), who was among the first to argue for the literary merits of the Scriptures. Lowth was himself a poet who had written English and Latin verse. One of his poems later appeared the Episcopal hymnbook of 1871 and was eventually translated into the language of the Dakota people. In 1741 Lowth was elected professor of poetry at Oxford. His *Lectures on the Sacred Poetry of the Hebrews* (1753), delivered over his decade in that post, became the standard on the subject for British and American readers.[13]

Lowth discovered poetry on nearly every page of the Bible, especially in the book of Isaiah, whose author he considered to be the "first of all poets for sublimity and eloquence." His claim for poetry in the Bible rested on two points. First, Hebrew poetry was metrical, and second, it exhibited what he called "parallelism." The repetitive phrasing found in the Old Testament, particularly in the book of Psalms, left Hebrew poetry vulnerable to the claim that it was a poor cousin to classical poetry. Ingeniously, Lowth turned this potential flaw into a virtue. Repetition, he argued, was perfectly suited to express the sublime mystery of man confronting God. The Hebrew poets used a form to express the sublime that was perfectly suited to the human mind.[14]

Lowth's interest in demonstrating the superiority of Hebrew poetry over classical poetry was radical, indeed, in a culture that had revered the classics for centuries. He argued that because the chief purpose of poetry was to express religious truth through beauty, and because the Bible and its poetry was inspired by God, it was the highest and most beautiful of all forms of poetry, surpassing even that composed by the classical poets. The ancient Hebrews not only rivaled the genius of the classical poets, they exceeded them. In an age that revered Greece and Rome, Lowth argued that the Bible was a source of literary excellence on its own terms. It contained the most sublime poetry, the most authentic history, the best devotions, and the most perfect theology. The notion that the chosen people of God would produce a literature that was inferior to that of ancient pagans was absurd, Lowth thought. The British evangelical Anglican Edward Bickersteth (1786–1850), who was widely read by Americans, summarized this confidence in the literary merits of the Bible. "Let no man think that the diligent reading of the Holy Scriptures will leave him with slight and imperfect knowledge . . . he will know the most ancient and authentic history, the most sublime strain of poetry, the most just lessons of deep wisdom to guide his life, the most curious antiquities of nations, the most perfect book of devotions, the only infallible theology. . . . The whole Bible in all its parts is complete and entire; a solution of all the most important questions."[15]

Lowth's work was celebrated by British and European scholars, but it also became a substantial presence for American academics, seminarians, and editors of religious journals. With the help of Moses Stuart, Calvin E. Stowe (husband of Harriet Beecher Stowe) brought out a new edition of Lowth in 1829. "To what strange conclusions should we be led were we to interpret Milton's *Paradise Lost* in the same spirit and by the same rules with which we should read President [Jonathan] Edwards on the *Freedom of the Will*?" Stowe asked, suggesting the rewards of considering the Bible as a literary text with Lowth's help. The standard biblical commentaries of the period all relied on Lowth's insights. Adam Clarke (1762–1832), the Irish Methodist theologian and author of the leading Methodist commentary, echoed Lowth in finding Hebrew authors superior to the finest classical authors and argued that "the whole collection of the Psalms forms a sort of *heroic tragedy*. The redemption of man, and the destruction of Satan, is the plot." Matthew Henry (1662–1714), British Presbyterian author of a popular commentary, followed Lowth's insights. He argued that Hebrew poetry had "a poetic force and flame, without poetic fury and fiction, that could strangely command

and move the affections, without corrupting the imagination. While they gratify the ear, they edify the mind, and profit the more by pleasing."[16] Louisa Payson Hopkins, the wife of a Williams College professor, wrote an essay on the book of Proverbs for John Kitto's *Cyclopaedia of Biblical Literature* (1845) that relied exclusively on Lowth's parallelism argument. Payson had been the principal of a school in New York before her marriage and was proficient in several modern languages in addition to Greek, Hebrew, Latin, metaphysics, and theology. Although she was not credited in the list of contributors and her entry was signed only by her initials, "L.P.H.," it appeared in the first two editions of the two-volume work. Subsequent editions, such as that edited by William Lindsay Alexander in 1871, replaced her essay with another contributor's work.[17]

Lowth's arguments were also cited in popular journals and in children's books. Leonidas Hamline's *Ladies' Repository* argued that "there is no place in which such sublime poetry can be found, as in the Hebrew language of the Old Testament," claiming that biblical poetry put "a perfect impress of the divine Original at once to the mind of the reader." A writer in the *Southern Presbyterian Review* claimed that the great English poets such as Milton, Scott, Cowper, and Byron all learned their craft at the feet of the writers of the book of Psalms. The view that the Bible was full of tasteful poetry began to bear so much weight that some writers even broached the unorthodox view that the authority of Scripture itself rested at least in part on its aesthetic qualities. "The existence of such poetry as is to be found in the Pentateuch, five hundred and fifty years before the age of Homer...Is itself one of the highest proofs of the divinity of the Scriptures," one wrote.[18]

Lowth would have been pleased. He intended his *Lectures on the Sacred Poetry of the Hebrews* for general readers rather than "for what is commonly termed the learned world." Happily for him, his book found a hearing with both audiences. The library at Andover Seminary held three English translations (including Stowe's edition) and one Latin edition of Lowth's *Lectures*. The junior class at Newton Theological Institution read his *Lectures*. Readers across the country read about Stowe's edition of Lowth in the *North American Review*. Methodist (and other) women encountered his authority on poetry in the pages of the *Ladies Repository*, and Lowth was cited in many other denominational organs. Sunday school students were introduced to his expertise in Benjamin Nicholls's popular commentary *The Mine Explored, or Help to the Reading of the Bible*, and Lowth was cited in one of the period's standard texts on moral philosophy.[19]

Ultimately, it seems, Lowth's readers agreed that the beauty and power of biblical poetry was evidence of the divine inspiration of the Scriptures. After all, how could the Creator of the universe inspire bad poetry? The inspired word of God was of course conveyed in the finest human language. In this way, the language of God acquired an aesthetic. More, God himself did so. As these convictions spread in both learned and popular writings, from pulpits and in schoolrooms, divine inspiration and literary inspiration seemed almost indistinguishable.[20] This widespread obsession with poetry thus marked the deepening influence of liberal education on popular understandings of the Bible and of Christian doctrines. As growing numbers of people educated their sons and daughters in the best traditions of Western culture, they celebrated the importance of beauty and taste and the special virtues of poetry. Biblical authors became literary geniuses.

THE BIBLE IN POETRY: FELICIA BROWNE HEMANS AND WILLIAM COWPER

Just as Lowth's *De Sacra Poesi Hebraeorum* convinced readers that the Bible was full of poetry, so, too, was nineteenth-century popular poetry full of the Bible. Of the scores of poets who were well-known to American readers, Felicia Browne Hemans and William Cowper were among the best loved. Neither has received much critical attention, but both were widely read in the nineteenth century. Hemans was only a child when Cowper died in 1800, but together they popularized the Bible as a fitting subject for verse. As their popularity spread, their poems became a standard presence in American hymnbooks.

Born in Liverpool, Felicia Browne Hemans (1793–1835) was the best-selling female poet of the nineteenth century and one of the first women to make a living with her pen. Known as "Mrs. Hemans," she was an ambitious writer who produced nineteen volumes of poems in her lifetime. She was very much a poet of her own day, as her reputation rapidly declined after her death. By the late 1820s, her work was widely celebrated by ordinary readers and critics alike. She had a substantial influence on other poets, especially the popular writer Lydia Sigourney (1791–1865), who became known as the "American Mrs. Hemans."[21]

The first U.S. edition of Hemans, in four volumes, was edited by the Unitarian Andrews Norton, professor of sacred literature at Harvard Divinity School. *Poems of Mrs. Hemans* appeared between 1826 and 1828. Remarkably, Norton hailed her work as superior to Homer and Milton. He praised the "delicate and elevated feelings" of her work in contrast to the darker themes that prevailed among other celebrated poets of the period such as Byron. The ambitious Hemans certainly aspired to the company of Byron and his peers, but they dismissed her as a "bluestocking."[22]

Hemans's chief appeal in the United States, one that underscored her estimation as merely a "female poet" and made her extremely popular with women, was her focus on domestic themes. She turned to explicitly religious poetry only in her final decade. Her domestic history did not accord with the ideals in her poems. Her father left the family for Canada when she was thirteen, and her husband similarly abandoned her to live in Italy, leaving her to raise five young sons on her own. She never remarried, and her furious pace of writing and publishing was driven in the main by financial need. Her final years were spent in Dublin in the household of her brother, the city's chief of police. It was there that she began to publish religious poems. "Female Characters of Scripture: A Series of Sonnets" (1833, 1834) shows the poet explicitly interpreting the women of both Old and New Testaments. Long overlooked, these poems have recently received critical attention. In the estimate of one theologian, Hemans merits being called a key female interpreter of Scripture in her generation for her learned treatment of biblical themes.[23]

Hemans was celebrated by American readers because her verse appeared at the moment when popular interest in education and literature, particularly for women, surged. Her books were found in mercantile libraries along with Byron, Burns, Scott, Coleridge, Swift, Milton, Edward Young, and Hannah More. But much of her warm reception came from students and teachers in the growing ranks of female academies. Hemans was considered appropriate fare for young ladies, along with Hannah More and Maria Edgeworth. She became known as a model female poet for a generation of women readers who were considered to be "peculiarly susceptible to the influence of poetry," as a Tennessee Methodist writer put it. Hemans's work was widely commended in advice literature, much of which was written by schoolteachers and heads of schools. Her work also appeared in schoolbooks and was a popular subject for declamation exercises for both men and women. One influential schoolbook publisher even produced *The Hemans Reader for Female Schools* in 1847.[24]

Hemans's appeal extended beyond schools, however, because she was widely published in periodicals. Two hundred of her poems appeared in Blackwood's *Edinburgh Magazine* over her career. Such magazines were widely read in the United States; more important, much of their content was reprinted in American magazines in an era when such borrowing was commonplace. Editors of the *North American Review* and *Godey's Lady's Book* praised her work.[25] Her poems, along with advertisements for her books, appeared in newspapers across the nation, from East Coast cities to rural Alabama and North Carolina. She was hailed as a genius by virtually every religious periodical in the period. Cherokee readers found her on the pages of the *Cherokee Phoenix* in 1828.[26]

In the end, American Christians probably became most familiar with Hemans's poetry by singing it. Scores of her poems appeared in hymnbooks between the 1820s and 1900, following the trajectory of her literary reputation. Several of her most popular poems appeared in hymnbooks into the mid-twentieth century. Unlike the most popular hymns of the era, Hemans's hymns were not deeply Christological; they did not evoke Jesus at all. Instead, they celebrated the peace of reposing on the bosom of God or the journey of the Pilgrims to New England. Her long-standing presence in the corpus of popular hymnody thus confirmed her as one of the chief sacred poets in the Anglo-American world.

One of the most beloved and frequently printed of hymn writers, William Cowper (pronounced "Cooper") (1731–1800) led an unconventional and tragic life marred by repeated episodes of profound depression, suicide attempts, an unhappy professional life in law, and dependence on genteel women for his livelihood. His long domestic attachment to a widow brought the whiff of scandal. His sudden and joyous conversion to Christianity during a period of depression gave way years later to the conviction that he was irreparably separated from God, a view that he held at his death. Born in 1731 to an Anglican rector and a woman distantly related to John Donne, Cowper lived for many years next door to Reverend John Newton, best known as the author of the popular hymns "Amazing Grace" and "Glorious Things of Thee Are Spoken," in a small village in Buckinghamshire.

Cowper's texts were an important presence in the lives of American Christians. His masterpiece of five thousand lines, *The Task*, was used extensively in schools and was memorized by thousands of students. His poems appeared frequently in hymnbooks, and he was lauded as a model Christian poet, although his reputation, like Hemans's, suffered at the hands of other poets. Byron, for example, denied he was a poet at all. This may have been because of Cowper's unabashed commendation of the Bible as a source of wisdom and eloquence in the face of Romantic skepticism about its reliability. Cowper also spoke boldly about the quality of Hebrew thought over and against the ancient "pagan poets and orators" in the vein of Bishop Robert Lowth. "Is Christ the abler teacher or the schools? If Christ, then why resort at every turn, to Athens or to Rome for wisdom?" His legions of admirers, particularly in the United States, found such boldness refreshing. "Alas! Where are the minds of heavenly mould, who dare to take the Bible as their *standard* in poetry and eloquence, as well as in morality and religion?"[27]

Cowper's influence, like Hemans's, came through his popularity in hymnbooks. Several of his poems rank highly among the hymns most frequently reprinted from the seventeenth to the mid-twentieth century. John Newton's popular *Olney Hymns* (1779), a collection that deeply influenced nineteenth-century hymnbooks, was a full-fledged collaboration between the two men. Cowper's poems featured in hymnbooks through the nineteenth century and beyond.[28]

THE IMPORTANCE OF POETRY IN AN AGE OF REVIVAL AND REFORM

Considering the popularity of poetry for Bible readers who were also devoted to revival and reform opens an important dimension of the story of Christianity in the early United States. Culture offers an alternative context to the narratives of revival and reform, sectionalism, and theological change that have prevailed in our understandings of religion in the period. Literature, poetry, and the aesthetics of language mattered to nineteenth-century American Christians, even the most ordinary of them, in ways we have not yet accounted for. Seeing the importance of poetry for them can help us to understand how religion "worked" in nineteenth-century culture.

It worked, for the most part, through print. The nineteenth century was steeped in print; it was the digital technology of the day. American Christians applauded the technological developments that enabled print to shower the country and, in many cases, pioneered and fostered them. The importance of poetry shows how much of quotidian culture turned on print. The most modest of objects brought the heights of Anglo-American culture, past and present, into the lives of the ordinary Christian people, whether they lived in an eastern city, an Appalachian hamlet, or a midwestern village. William Shakespeare and Percy Bysshe Shelley, Felicia Hemans and John Milton, Edward Young and William Cullen Bryant all arrived on the pages of countless publications—almanacs and newspapers, pamphlets and scuffed hymnbooks—to be memorized, recited, sung, and revered. This happened at the very time that the meanings

of "culture" were shifting, in complicated and dramatic ways, from the older association with agriculture and toward "the best that has been thought and said," in the words
of Matthew Arnold.[29] In the same way, the sons and daughters of farmers left the field
to attend school in ever larger numbers. Some of these, among them many pastors,
continued on to academies, seminaries, and colleges where they learned to appreciate
even more poetry while imbibing the Byzantine rules of formal English grammar and
rhetoric. Many of these students eventually were published themselves in the myriad
small magazines and newspapers that sprouted like mushrooms, only to vanish by
sunset and be replaced by others. The Christian investment in liberal education reaped
an abundant harvest of print.

The embrace of poetry offers one instance of how this growing availability of liberal
knowledge shaped a religious sensibility that differed remarkably from that of earlier
generations. Readers did not divide their thoughts into strict categories of "literature"
and "religion" or of "culture" and "theology." What they read, recited, and learned—in
school or at their mother's knee—formed a single whole with their religious convictions. The writers they encountered in their gift books and annuals, in their school-
books, and in their magazines also appeared in their hymnbooks; Bible stories and
verses appeared in poems they read in the newspaper.

The Bible was the central text in the Anglo-American world in the nineteenth century. It justified empires and underwrote slavery even as it inspired democratic revolutions and strengthened arguments for individual liberty. As Lawrence Levine wisely
noted many years ago, intellectual history can (and should) be written as the history
not of thought but of people thinking.[30] There is little question that in the nineteenth
century, people of all kinds thought about the Bible. They found parallels between its
stories and their own lives, learned to know its characters intimately, and memorized
long passages, sometimes entire chapters, that they rehearsed as they walked the
roads or followed a plow. Increasingly, they questioned the Bible's truth and wrestled
with its meaning. The exalted strains of the Authorized Version described equally their
griefs and their joys. In this way, the language and stories of the Bible connected the
daughters and sons of Yale professors and presidents to those of farmers, tanners, and
slaves. Importantly, this ability to connect the powerful with the powerless did not
rest on whether people knew how to read the Bible; it had always been transmitted as
easily by speech as by the page. Even those who never learned to read knew the book
intimately.

Appreciation of poetry is but one example of how Romanticism and sentimentalism
were insinuated deeply into Christian thought and practice through the expansion of
liberal education. Above all, Romanticism celebrated human agency. The hunger for
change and the belief that people could enact it was a defining characteristic of
Christian practice in the period. The impulse to learn to read, to improve oneself, to go
to school, and to reform society were all deeply Romantic. These desires merged silently
with the soteriological language of individual and social conversion, bridging divisions
between liberal and evangelical, Catholic and Protestant, north and south. Across theological and geographical divides, people hailed education, schooling, reading, and

printing as the salvation of their age, whether it be in a small newspaper in northern Alabama or in the pages of the *North American Review*. This assumption ran deep and broad. Liberal and evangelical, slave and free, Catholic and Protestant alike proclaimed that "knowledge is power." Everyone understood that knowledge offered the leverage to force change in themselves and others. This readers learned from what they brought *to* their reading of the Scriptures from the context of poetry and other literature. It is hard to see the enormity of this silent transformation because we believe this still, two centuries on.

Aaron has a great knowledge of the Bible, but cannot read a word.

—*Light and Truth of Slavery. Aaron's History* (1845)

What happens to the writerly imagination of a black author who is at some level *always* conscious of representing one's own race to, or in spite of, a race of readers that understands itself to be "universal" or race-free?

—MORRISON, *Playing in the Dark: Whiteness and the Literary Imagination* (1992)

6

The Origins of Whiteness and the Black (Biblical) Imagination

THE BIBLE IN THE "SLAVE NARRATIVE" TRADITION

Emerson B. Powery

NINETEENTH-CENTURY AFRICAN Americans were active agents of liberation in their day, despite the social, political, and ideological barriers challenging their involvement. The narratives of the formerly enslaved—or so-called slave narratives—give us one significant window into that period and allow us to hear the words, feelings, and perspectives of those women and men who spoke of freedom over and against their previous reality of bondage. These African-American autobiographical narratives are part of a specific genre, following prescribed themes laid out by the abolitionist community. These individuals began their lives in bondage in the American South and gained their freedom after years of enslavement. These freedom narratives describe the nature of slavery, its effects on the subject, the institutions that governed the lives of the enslaved, and significant events in the subjects' lives that led to their freedom. They were not simply dispassionate rehearsals of these events but were usually (though not exclusively) composed as public, political documents, used to further the abolitionist cause by demonstrating that slavery was an inhumane institution that robbed human beings of not only their liberty but their very lives. As Harriet Jacobs wisely wrote, "there are wrongs which even the grave does not bury."[1] In a country that considered itself to be a "Christian Nation," these Americans—without the rights of full citizenship—wrestled with their Bible and discovered interpretations that allowed for potential liberating possibilities for their cause and their own lives.

In this essay, I want to contextualize William Anderson's 1857 account on 2 Kings—a passage he claimed supported the origins of whiteness—by situating Anderson's discussion in the broader ideological context of the period. After a brief analysis of the "curse of Ham" motif in representative freedom narratives (the "curse of Ham" myth, of course, was one of the more popular ideas to support the peculiar institution), I will turn my attention to Anderson (and a few of his contemporaries). Then I will offer, succinctly, some hermeneutical implications of this African-American approach to the biblical text in light of the topic of this essay on racial origins, or, what we might call "Whiteness and the Biblical Imagination."

DOUGLASS (1845, 1855), JACOBS (1861), AND THE "CURSE OF HAM"

It is widely recognized that the Bible was a primary resource of ideological support for the proponents of the slave institution. The so-called curse of Ham account (see Gen 9) was widely appropriated as a biblical warrant to maintain the prevailing slavocracy. Occasionally, African-American authors would refute its implications for coloration, especially with respect to the ties between "blackness" and "enslavement." They were forced to respond to situations when coloration was presumed in Genesis 9. (For example, Josiah Priest suggested that the *character* of Ham was like the color of Ham's [black] skin.) Rarely, however, was Genesis 9 utilized by the formerly enslaved to discuss the origins of "whiteness."[2] Other biblical passages were more suitable, as I will show.

In the freedom narrative tradition, there was a direct response to the "curse of Ham" argument that was expressed through the contemporary experiences of African Americans. Some recognized that, ethnically speaking, African Americans were *not* part of a pure racial group. Frederick Douglass (both in 1845 and in 1855) and Harriet Jacobs (1861) both express this view. In Jacobs's words: "They [i.e., Slaveholders] seem to satisfy their consciences with the doctrine that God created the Africans to be slaves. What a libel upon the heavenly Father, who 'made of one blood all nations of men!' And then who *are* Africans? Who can measure the amount of Anglo-Saxon blood coursing in the veins of American slaves?"[3] Her biblical allusion confronted the U.S. reality of the crimes that regularly occurred—for example, rape—in addition to enslavement. And Jacobs's story, *Incidents in the Life of a Slave Girl*, would detail examples of the true nature of the blood that flowed through the veins of many so-called Africans. Her critique specifically condemned the leaders of the white church: "If a pastor has offspring by a woman not his wife, the church dismiss him, if she is a white woman; but if she is colored, it does not hinder his continuing to be their good shepherd."[4]

Neither Douglass nor Jacobs argued against the biblical myth of Ham as a source for explaining the origins of *racial* identity. Apparently, they accepted the *blackness* of Ham's (and, Canaan's) skin color despite the lack of evidence in the biblical story. They tacitly agreed with the larger cultural assumption that Genesis 9 was a statement about origins. According to Sylvester A. Johnson, in *The Myth of Ham in Nineteenth-Century American Christianity*, it would have been "exceptional" for any nineteenth-century African American to have questioned this basic assumption.[5] Douglass and Jacobs did not accept, however, that "Ham" was an uncomplicated identification of contemporary African Americans.[6] As Jacobs asserted, using Acts 17, God has "made of one blood all nations." Furthermore, Genesis 9:25–27 might support enslavement but, as Douglass argued,[7] it did *not* support the enslavement of American blacks. For Douglass and Jacobs, Genesis 9 did not promote the enslavement of the types of blacks, racially speaking, who lived in the United States. Their common experience attested otherwise.[8] These authors indicated that a complex color arrangement existed in the Americas that would not allow for the simplistic assertion that enslaved Africans in the Americas were "black" Hamites, instead suggesting that they were an elaborate admixture that necessitated a more nuanced reading of Genesis 9 in relation to slavery.

"A GREAT DEAL HAS BEEN SAID ABOUT COLORS"; THE CULTURAL CONTEXT OF "RACE ORIGINS"

Following congressional fights over the Fugitive Slave Law of 1850, the decade of the 1850s was intense with arguments surrounding slavery. Most religious people in the United States, though not all, believed that the Bible was of primary import for defending the theological rationale for enslavement and ethnic difference.[9] Intimately related to this debate was the underlying racial ideology that surfaced. By 1850, the majority of American scientists, as Donald Swan argued, held to "the principle tenets of the doctrine of polygenism."[10] As diligent as white interpreters were about providing biblical support for the slavocracy of the day, they were much less engaged in biblical interpretation for an analysis of "race." As Mark A. Noll succinctly puts it, "on slavery, exegetes stood for a commonsense reading of the Bible. On race, exegetes forsook the Bible and relied on common sense."[11] This so-called common sense knowledge was supported by institutional structures (i.e., educational, economic, legal) to maintain the superiority of the white race. For many of them, the issue of race was settled by the biblical "Ham" and the ensuing curse on his family.[12] Despite little to no concentrated focus on a "biblical perspective" on race (if you will) by white exegetes, this gap was occasionally filled by black exegetes, who frequently engaged the Bible with "race" at the forefront of their analyses. In 1855, Douglass reacted, "Shall we...fling the Bible away as a pro-slavery book? It would be as reasonable to do so as it would be to fling away the Constitution."[13] In 1857 William Anderson proposed an alternative biblical narrative to account for the origins of race. Rather than attempting to offer an account for (the curse) of blackness, Anderson turned the question on its head: How did whiteness occur?[14]

"WHITENESS" AND THE BIBLICAL IMAGINATION OF WILLIAM ANDERSON

His title reveals his objectives clearly and directly: *Life and Narrative of William J. Anderson, Twenty-four Years a Slave; Sold Eight Times! In Jail Sixty Times!! Whipped Three Hundred Times!!! Or The Dark Deeds of American Slavery Revealed. Containing Scriptural Views of the Origin of the Black and of the White Man. Also, A Simple and Easy Plan to Abolish Slavery in the United States, Together with An Account of the Services of Colored Men in the Revolutionary War—Day and Date, and Interesting Facts.* His lengthy title was attached to a relatively short narrative (only fifty-seven pages). After detailing his story, Anderson tackled the significant trifecta in his appendices: freedom (plan to abolish slavery), race (ethnic origins), and war (contributions of "colored men" to the Revolutionary War).

Like many authors of freedom narratives, the author emphasized that this account was "written by himself." Unlike many others, this narrative provided no prefatory comments from (usually white) dignitaries either to recommend this work, acknowledge the high caliber of the author's character or offer a statement about the relative value of such a project. But this independence allowed him to carry out his objective unhindered, to do what he called "free thinking." Of particular interest is his relatively short analysis of "scriptural views of the origin of the black and of the white man."

Anderson ignored the widely held view that "Ham" was the "father of the black race." Instead, using Genesis 2:7, he believed that, originally, *all* people were black, since "the ground was quite black or dark."[15] In my search through the antebellum narratives, Anderson was the only formerly enslaved writer I found who appropriated Genesis 2:7 in a discussion on racial origins.[16] But he was not the first African American to do so; others (e.g., Robert Lewis) interpreted the book of Genesis in this manner more than a decade before Anderson.[17]

Since Anderson presupposed blackness as the default race of all original humanity, he proposed a theory of racial origins that addressed whiteness as the aberration. To support this idea, he turned his attention to 2 Kings 5, the story of Naaman's healing. In the biblical account, the Syrian captain Naaman has been inflicted with a skin disease. Hearing of the prophet Elisha's healing power, Naaman seeks him out, secures his healing (though reluctant to heed the prophet's advice), and attempts to offer a payment. Elisha refuses payment. The biblical narrator, then, introduces Gehazi, Elisha's servant.[18] Gehazi disagrees (secretly) with Elisha's refusal to benefit financially from this wealthy Syrian (and rival) captain. So he tracks down Naaman without Elisha's permission. He tells Naaman a lie, secures goods, and hides them. But Elisha is not to be fooled. (He is a prophet after all!) Elisha discovers Gehazi's deception and curses him with the same disease Naaman once had. Not only was Gehazi punished, but his descendants would carry this disease forever. And Gehazi, originally black, "went out from (Elisha's) presence," in the King James Version, "a leper as *white as snow*." (my italics).

Anderson classified Naaman's "leprosy" (5:1, 3, 6, 7; KJV) as a "certain bad disease."[19] Though central to the biblical account, Naaman's healing was of much less interest to Anderson than Gehazi's actions and eventual disease.[20] In Anderson's retelling of the story, he ignored a few details.[21] He omitted the words "menservants, and maidservants" from Elisha's list of items that one should not accept from others at that time (5:26; during a war?). Anderson kept his focus on "race" without complicating it with the issue of "status." Many of his white counterparts, in the nineteenth century, recited this story and Gehazi's sin, in particular, to enforce the status quo.

Most early nineteenth-century white, biblical expositors ignored any racialized exegetical possibilities for Gehazi's turning, in the KJV's phraseology, "white as snow."

They concentrated their efforts on other factors in the story to emphasize themes related to (im)piety: (1) Gehazi's sin of *greed*;[22] (2) Gehazi's *lie* to cover up his greed; (3) Gehazi's *sin*, as an outgrowth of Adam's sin; (4) Elisha's "prophetic" foresight (to observe Gehazi's true actions); (5) Elisha's frugality and disinterest in worldly goods (i.e., lack of greed).[23]

Surprisingly, William Anderson did not link Gehazi's "greed" to his new-found "whiteness." Yet such a connection would seem relevant in light of the nineteenth-century arguments surrounding the economic value of the "peculiar institution." White, pious interpreters exposed plenty of "greed" in the passage; Anderson discovered "whiteness" (i.e., the curse of whiteness). Neither combined the two. Most interpreters avoided *race*. More attuned to *status* than race, antebellum white interpreters—in the North and the South—utilized Gehazi's failure and condemnation as an example to teach the "servants" in their midst to "read your Bibles," as in the widely popular "Tracts of the American Tract Society" in the North (in 1825), which included "An Address to Persons in Different Stations of Life, on the Duty of Studying the Bible": "There you will find an account of pious servants; you will see how faithfully Abraham's servant obeyed his master, Gen. 24; how a servant-maid was useful to Naaman, the captain of the king of Assyria's army; you will see the punishment of a lying servant in Gehazi."[24] Or we find examples of the common arguments in the South in support of the institution of enslavement, such as J. B. Thrasher's pamphlet *Slavery: A Divine Institution*:

> Also the prophet Elisha, on whom the mantle of Elijah fell—the man of God who performed so many miracles, and among others, that of raising the dead to life— was a slave holder, and punished his slave Gehazi, by afflicting him with leprosy.... [and just a few paragraphs later] So that we find God ever after entering into the covenant with Noah and his sons, constantly punishing sin and sinful nations, whether Jew or Gentile, with slavery, captivity and death. Hence we believe that the slavery of the negro is of God, which we can trace back to the curse of Caanan [*sic*].[25]

While Thrasher linked, implicitly, the notion of coloration and slavery in 2 Kings, he completely ignored the ending of 2 Kings, with its explicit reference to coloration, and turned his attention to Genesis. Anderson on the other hand (intentionally?) omitted the label of the disease as "leprosy" (in the KJV of 2 Kgs 5:27) in order to concentrate on its coloration. Anderson referred to it simply as a "disease," what we might call the *disease of whiteness*. As the King James Version states and Anderson reiterated, Gehazi departed from Elisha's presence as "white as snow." Commonsense interpretation of the Bible was the prevailing hermeneutical approach of the day; if there was ever a commonsense interpretation in the nineteenth century, this was it.[26]

For Anderson, this was the biblical beginning of "whiteness." Apparently, he had presented this exegesis, as he reported, "a thousand times in the hearing of the learned" and had never been challenged or questioned; even if he exaggerated the numbers of his hearers, what Anderson claimed about the decade was true, as we know from multiple sources, that "a great deal has been said about colors" during the 1850s. The period provided heightened, intense debate over the origins of races, and the Bible was one of the primary sources utilized to help people discern how things came to be. Anderson shared what most people thought before 1860: "we have to do the best we can with the writings that are left for our instruction."[27]

Anderson was right about one thing: a great deal was "said about colors" as arguments surrounding the origins of racial identification increased in the 1850s. The Bible, of course, was not excluded from such racialized interpretive discourse. One need only search the entries on "Ham," "Japheth," and "Shem" in the Bible dictionaries of the day for prevailing sentiments about contemporary racial divisions.[28] On the other hand white interpreters rarely commented on Gehazi's miraculous alteration (to "white as snow") in a racialized manner, though it did occasionally happen in the years prior to the Civil War.

An explicit exploration of coloration appeared in *Illustrations of the Holy Scriptures*, from Reverend George Bush (no relation to the former president), who was at the time (in 1839) professor of Hebrew and Oriental literature at New York City University, in an attempt to read biblical stories in light of contemporary "Eastern" traditions and audiences. In a reflection on the phrase "leper *as white* as snow," the author writes the following about the culture in India: "There are many children born white, though their parents are quite black. These are not lepers, but albinos; and are the same as the white negroes of Africa. To see a man of that kind almost naked, and walking among the natives, has an unpleasant effect on the mind, and leads a person to suspect that all has not been right. . . . The natives do not consider this a disease, but a BIRTH, i.e. produced by the sins of a former birth."[29] Unlike some his contemporaries, Bush thought it logical to locate ancient, biblical "white lepers" in contemporary settings, even if as "albinos" in India or "white negroes" in Africa. This racialized discourse magnifies what Edward Said described as the Western gaze on the "Orient," with its fierce (and usually distorted) description of the "other."[30]

William Anderson had a different interpretive objective in mind. For him, the Gehazi narrative provided a black counter-myth to the prevailing racialized tradition surrounding Noah's sons. Anderson's exegetical conclusion—leprosy equals whiteness—only becomes logical if the interpreter presumes the blackness of humans at the origins of creation; and whiteness—not blackness—as the product of sin. Anderson, of course, upheld such a position based on his reading of Genesis 2:7.[31]

Anderson's independence from others, unlike other formerly enslaved authors, allowed him to stake an interpretive claim on the biblical narrative to explore the racial identities of the peoples who populated his United States.[32] Of course, he didn't go far enough. He offered no ideas about Native Americans or the small (but growing) pockets of Asian and Latino Americans who were part of this diverse landscape in the 1850s. (The "later" Douglass did provide a more global vision.)[33] But what Anderson did offer—a theory of whiteness—was sufficient to challenge the dominant myth of the day that blackness was secondary, inferior, and later in the creative order. Furthermore, he accomplished this feat by using the primary religious source for

Christian readers of his day, simply trying "to do the best we can with the writings that are left for our instruction."

CONCLUSION

No matter how we adjudicate the legitimacy of Anderson's racialized understanding of 2 Kings 5, his interpretation serves as a potent critique of white interpretive tendencies. Why is it that white interpreters failed to see this narrative—that concludes with the offender and his descendants being perpetually cursed to be as "white as snow"—as an etiology of the white race? Clearly 2 Kings has far more content that can be considered "racialized" than does the "Curse of Canaan" account in Genesis 9, which never mentions skin color and curses only the eponymous ancestor "Canaan," with no explicit statement of genealogical perpetuation. Yet the Genesis narrative supported the ideological basis of southern enslavement and the subsequent denigration of African peoples from the 1820s until the 1960s, and the myth still holds sway in some congregations. Anderson's argument is thus helpful, if only to shine a light on the (deliberate?) inconsistencies of the hermeneutical traditions of the proslavery school, who readily chose texts to support their larger economic and political goals but ignored others that could be perceived as detrimental to those in their social location. Had Anderson's reading of 2 Kings 5 prevailed, the understanding of "whiteness" as a curse on Gehazi and his "seed forever," brought about because of greed, might have served as a potent condemnation of a system that dehumanized darker peoples for the financial benefit of lighter peoples and perhaps even fostered conversation about such economic exploitation. Suffice it to say that a significant hermeneutical opportunity offered by Anderson's distinctive interpretive move was missed, as white proslavery advocates were never forced to reconcile their interpretive biases with regard to Genesis with the text in 2 Kings, whose plain meaning should have challenged their assumptions about Scripture's bases, and what they thought of as God's bases, for racial divisions.

These formerly enslaved individuals lifted up the pen to write and raised their voices to speak about an experience of enslavement that included a religious setting in which the Bible was frequently interpreted to enforce and maintain their status and condition. And, for the most part, they sifted through these theological perspectives to reclaim the Bible for themselves and placed it on the side of the oppressed. In light of the conditions of the day, this took an unimaginable ingenuity. They took a text—used against them—and made it their own, often reversing the implications of normative mainline interpretive patterns. These public narratives left behind a legacy of their commitment, a snapshot of their lives, a challenge to the system of bondage, and a critical engagement with the sacred texts of the Christian religious tradition that the dominant race marshaled to read *against* the marginalized and the minoritized. Anderson's interpretive approach called for more than simply the right textual choice, since the Bible was a contested site. It placed at the forefront attention to identity, in light of an ideological presupposition in which he took stock of the margins—that is, a hermeneutical approach that positioned the text and himself, simultaneously, on the side of the minoritized populations. This was Anderson's utilization of what we might call (since Delores Williams) a hermeneutics of survival. This, too, is part of the story of what it means to read the Bible in American life.

7

Biblical Women in the *Woman's Exponent*

NINETEENTH-CENTURY MORMON WOMEN INTERPRET THE BIBLE

Amy Easton-Flake

NINETEENTH-CENTURY MORMONS saw themselves as a new Israel. They appropriated ancient Israelite sentiments, customs, and rhetoric and, most significant, Israel's status as God's covenant people and practice of polygamy. In 1846 they underwent their own exodus as they followed Brigham Young—their own Moses—to the promised land of the Rocky Mountains. Upon settling there, they continued to read their experience through the lens of ancient Israel. As Philip Barlow writes, "the Mormon identification with biblical peoples, events, and prophecies was experientially more all-encompassing than that of any other major group during the nineteenth century."[1] Consequently, when nineteenth-century Mormon women sought to find models for themselves and create their own space within the Mormon community, they often turned to the same place where their male counterparts found a sense of identity: the Bible. In the pages of the *Woman's Exponent* (a bimonthly newspaper that played a significant role in Utah and in the Mormon Church from 1871 to 1914) we find evidence of the rich female heritage these women created, often undergirded by scriptural support, within a self-consciously patriarchal society and theology. Relying on the hundreds of articles in the *Woman's Exponent* that discuss scriptures, I analyze how Mormon women used and interpreted the Bible in the last quarter of the nineteenth century. More particularly, I focus on Mormon women's use of biblical women to promote their ideals of Christian womanhood, their arguments for gender equality and expansion of women's sphere, and their defense of the Mormon practice of polygamy. Through their writings these women joined their female counterparts of other faith traditions in asserting women's authority to interpret scripture and create their own identity.[2]

89

Although Joseph Smith—prophet and founder of the Church of Christ (later to be known as the Church of Jesus Christ of Latter-day Saints and often referred to as the Mormon Church)—introduced a new book of scripture called the Book of Mormon, the King James Bible remained the primary religious text for nineteenth-century Mormons.[3] The majority of church members at this time were first-generation converts from Protestant faiths; consequently, their previous knowledge of and reverence for the Bible likely contributed to its status as the text most frequently cited in Mormons' religious sermons and written documents. A look at the journals of nineteenth-century Mormons also reveals the Bible to be the scripture they turned to for comfort and uplift.[4]

Examining the sermons of nineteenth-century male leaders of the Mormon Church provides valuable insight into how Mormons' understanding and use of the Bible compared to that of their Protestant contemporaries. According to Philip Barlow's extensive study of these sermons, Joseph Smith "shared his era's assumptions about the literality, historicity, and inspiration of the Bible. . . . Like others, he viewed the Old Testament through a New Testament lens, was affected by the perspectives of 'Christian Primitivism' and embraced both a long tradition of typological thought and an emerging train of dispensational thought."[5] Mormonism tended to attract people who interpreted the Bible similarly to Smith; consequently, members of the Mormon faith continued to promote a basic biblical orientation that paralleled the selective literalism and other traits shared by gospel primitivists throughout the nineteenth century. Similar to adherents of other faiths, Barlow found that Mormons used the Bible "to justify opinions held on nonbiblical grounds. They also reflected the national shift in emphasis from the Old Testament to the New Testament . . . and [were] intoxicated with the biblical themes of the millennium."[6] And like most Protestant Americans, they used the Bible as a handbook of faith and practice.[7]

As alike as their approach to the Bible was in many respects, Mormons also used the Bible in distinctive ways that set them apart from their Protestant contemporaries. Barlow argues that Mormons saw the Bible not as "the controlling myth of the national experience," as did many of their religious contemporaries, but rather as "the record of prophecies specifically pointing to the Mormon 'restoration.'"[8] And, as Gordon Irving explains, they often used the Bible to support their own contemporary Mormon practices and theology, particularly the practice of polygamy, their teachings on apostasy and restoration, their understanding of themselves as part of God's covenant relationship with Israel, and their belief in the continuity of the Gospel and the priesthood keys from the time of Adam to the present day.[9] Perhaps most important, Joseph Smith and his followers differed from mainstream Protestant understanding of the Bible in their adoption of an extrabiblical canon and their rejection of *sola scriptura*.[10] Because the Bible had passed through many hands and undergone numerous translations over the centuries, Mormons acknowledged its imperfections along with its sanctity. Stressing the corruption of the biblical text in its current form and dismissing portions, such as the Song of Solomon, as uninspired, Mormons looked to modern-day prophets and their own personal relationships with God in order to interpret unclear portions of biblical text.[11] While Barlow's, Irving's, and others' research illuminates nineteenth-century Mormonism and sets out nicely the religion's points of continuity and departure from other Christians' Bible usage, their narrow focus on male leadership leaves unaddressed many questions about how nineteenth-century Mormon lay members, particularly women, used and interpreted the Bible.

While Mormon women, like their female Protestant contemporaries, saw the domestic sphere as their primary field of action, their religious convictions led them to take an active role in civil affairs.[12] The demands of frontier life and the unconventional domestic structure formed by polygamy further created opportunities for women to become welcome participants in the public sphere. Mormon women, as historians such as Carol Cornwall Madsen, Jill Mulvey Derr, Maureen Ursenbach Beecher, Lavina Fielding Anderson, and Maxine Hanks have amply shown, were a vital force in nineteenth-century Mormon society as they mothered their families, provided social welfare, taught and aided others through the Relief Society (a female-led benevolent organization in the church), actively participated in the educational and electoral processes of their community, and often worked outside the home to support their large families.[13]

What has not been adequately explored, however, is the important role women had in shaping the Mormon community's understanding of the Bible through their teaching of children, their preaching to one another in meetings of the Relief Society, and their writing in the *Woman's Exponent*. One writer for a national magazine claimed that the *Exponent* "wield[ed] more real power in [Utah] state politics than all the newspapers in Utah put together."[14] While such a sweeping statement was certainly an exaggeration, the *Exponent* was clearly a significant force. Never owned or officially sponsored by the Mormon Church—although official church leadership did approve of it—the *Exponent* was entirely carried on by women and, significantly, provided a space for them to freely express their viewpoints and interests.[15] Along with editorials and articles, it regularly published original poems, short stories, and essays, as well as reports from the different women's organizations throughout the church. Topics of particular interest were women's rights and roles in the home, church, and community; suffrage; education for women; church and Relief Society news; and defending polygamy and other aspects of Mormonism.[16] The surprisingly dialogic views expressed in the *Exponent*'s pages provide scholars today with insight into the diverse opinions that existed in the Mormon community, offering a repository of knowledge for analyzing Mormon women in late nineteenth- and early twentieth-century Mountain West.

Of particular interest for this study is the range of Bible usage and interpretation contained in the *Exponent*. Similar to Bible readers of both the nineteenth century and today,[17] Mormon women, as indicated by the *Exponent*, used the text to provide comfort, explain religious doctrine, encourage desired behaviors, and argue for the correctness of certain political or social views.[18] Individuals also devoted a fair amount of time to discussing the benefits of reading scriptures and encouraging all women to know them well and find truth therein.[19] More particular to Mormonism, writers for the *Exponent* also cited passages from the Bible to encourage missionary work and support

Mormon faith claims.[20] Although Mormon women in the nineteenth century were rarely sent on proselytizing missions, letters and editorials in the *Woman's Exponent* indicate that they regularly interacted with and proselytized to individuals of other faith traditions when they traveled or corresponded via mail. The *Exponent* itself was envisioned to be the vehicle by which Mormon women could share their faith and give an accurate presentation of themselves to the world.[21] Though in reality it was read by few outside the Mormon faith, Emmeline B. Wells, editor from 1877 to 1914, frequently sent it to her Protestant associates and credited it with changing the opinions of individuals about the Mormon Church and its female followers.[22] Analyzing these articles reveals these women to be not only well versed in the Bible but also active participants in spreading their beliefs and defending the Mormon faith.

MORMON WOMEN'S USE OF BIBLICAL WOMEN IN THE SCRIPTURES

By narrowing our focus to how Mormon women employed biblical women in the last quarter of the nineteenth century, we may identify trends and methods that allow us to situate Mormon women in the larger context of nineteenth-century female exegetes. This in turn complicates and expands previous understanding of Mormons' interpretation and use of the Bible compared to their Protestant contemporaries. By the mid- to late nineteenth century, biblical exegesis took many forms, as individuals engaged in both "so-called lower criticism—textual criticism that aimed at establishing the original text of scripture free from mistranslations—and higher criticism which sought to discover the historical background of the biblical texts, their authors, sources, and literary characteristics."[23] This historical-critical method encouraged interpreting the Bible with the same methods used to analyze "any other book";[24] both skeptics and adherents of various faith traditions employed this method. However, as Christina de Groot and Marion Taylor have discovered, the majority of nineteenth-century women interpreters writing for both religious and secular publications still predominately practiced noncritical exegesis: "They used modern insights from science, history, and geography to aid their reading but were not willing to dispense with a spiritual and theological understanding of the text. They continued to use traditional methods of discerning God's voice in the book."[25] Summarizing these traditional methods, Taylor and Heather Weir explain that women regularly looked for "connections between their lives and experiences and the biblical characters' lives... sought timeless and universal truths... drew moral inferences from the text... [and] used an associative approach that connected images from various parts of the scripture." In essence, "they appropriated the message of the text, applied it to their own lives, and shared their insights with others."[26] Taylor's, de Groot's, and Weir's findings aptly describe Mormon women's exegesis in the *Exponent* as well. They shared with Protestant women a common Protestant sensibility that scriptures speak directly to contemporary readers and may be interpreted without any mediating guide. And their impetus for writing—which largely came from their self-understanding of their responsibility to inculcate religious and moral values first in their families and then in society as a whole—mirrors that of their female contemporaries who also believed women had a special mandate to teach and minister to the young, the poor, the sick, the uneducated, and the unreligious.[27]

Looking at Mormon women's specific interpretation of biblical women, we find increasing continuity with their Protestant contemporaries as well as significant differences. Like their Protestant contemporaries, Mormon women used biblical women to provide Christian role models who spoke to their own needs, particularly in the contexts of nineteenth-century gender debates, and to authorize the expansion of women's public role.[28] Stark differences surface, however, for Mormon women used biblical women to defend doctrinal positions, most prominently the practice of polygamy. In analyzing their interpretations of biblical women, we learn much about what Mormon women of the late nineteenth century valued, how they perceived their roles in their church and community, and what they expected of themselves. The image that emerges is diametrically opposed to the image of Mormon women as simple-minded, ignorant, oppressed, coerced, and enslaved that often appeared in the American popular press of the day.[29] Instead, Mormon women presented biblical women—and, by extension, themselves—as capable, intelligent, independent agents with crucial roles to play in society and God's kingdom.

PROVIDING CHRISTIAN ROLE MODELS

Mormon women, like other nineteenth-century female interpreters, used the Bible, and in particular biblical women, as a powerful source of self-fashioning. As did other Bible literalists, Mormons believed that examples in the Bible spoke directly to their own time and that the life narratives of individuals in the Bible had the power to shape the subjectivities, expectations, and values of the reader.[30] As one prolific Mormon exegete, Hannah T. King, wrote, women of the scriptures should be used "for models of imitation ... they are admirable specimens of the *genus*. In them is exhibited no vanity, frivolity, no weakness—all is simple dignity, stern duty, and strict obedience to principle."[31] Though not all Mormon writers would depict biblical women in such a romanticized manner, King's statement does encapsulate well the respect Mormon women accorded biblical women in their interpretations. In contrast to many Protestant interpreters (such as Harriet Beecher Stowe, Sophia Goodrich Ashton, and Etty Woosman) who sought to make women of the Bible more relatable by examining their faults and shortcomings,[32] Mormon exegetes almost universally chose to present them in the most favorable light possible in order to use them as ideal role models.

Mormon women's exalted view of biblical women likely had much to do with the place of biblical patriarchs and matriarchs in nineteenth-century Mormon theology. Unlike many nineteenth-century Christians who believed in a progressive theological evolution where God revealed his gospel in incremental phases, Mormons believed that Adam and the patriarchs held the same priesthood keys and possessed the same knowledge of gospel ordinances and principles as the early apostles.[33] Since Mormons

viewed the patriarchs as equals in gospel knowledge yet superiors because of the relationships they had obtained with God, Mormons could not excuse away the patriarchs'
weaknesses as many nineteenth-century interpreters did by portraying them as less
advanced in religious (and often other) terms. Stowe, for instance, often compared
them to children, living in "the world's infancy."[34] Instead, Mormon interpreters in the
nineteenth century most often ignored the questionable aspects of these characters in
order to focus on moments when their examples could be used to inspire nineteenth-
century readers.[35] King's readings are a prime example, as she ignores or mitigates
many of the more interesting and complex parts of biblical women's characters and
stories in order to make the women comply with her image of them. For instance,
Rebekah's plot to obtain the birthright for Jacob by deceiving her husband, Sarah's
ordering Hagar and Ishmael to be banished to the wilderness, and Rachel's and Leah's
competition to bear children are all virtually absent from King's exegesis. When absolutely necessary, King may allude to controversial actions, but she does not mention
them directly.[36] In contrast, her peers in other faith traditions make these moments
central to their exegesis, with some interpreters condemning and others applauding
these women's behavior and choices.[37]

Within the context of nineteenth-century ideals for women, the specific virtues
Mormon interpreters most often promoted in their biblical heroines are largely unsurprising. For instance, Mary was used to encourage women to "choose the better part;
[to] follow not in the way of the Gentiles, but strive to live pure and holy before God."[38]
Ruth was admired for "her integrity, her purity, her constancy," and readers were
encouraged to be as "brave and heroic, or self-sacrificing and unselfish as Ruth."[39]
Sarah, Rebekah, and Rachel were all set forth as examples of "true and faithful" wives
and mothers, and their examples were used to uplift women's status in domestic relationships.[40] Women were shown to be powerful as they remained "pure, chaste, and
good."[41] These expressions of women's exalted piety and purity were standard fare in
nineteenth-century America and Great Britain;[42] thus, many Mormon writers fit nicely
within the ranks of the nineteenth-century interpreters and female activists who used
the Bible to illustrate the power women wielded within traditional gender behaviors
and relationships and how familial roles were not limiting or disempowering but
expansive.[43]

To accomplish this, Mormon writers often had to reimagine male/female relations
within the Bible and what ideal qualities looked like in practice. Adelia B. Cox Sidwell,
for example, asserts Rebekah's superiority over her husband when she refers to the
"obstinacy of Isaac" in not recognizing God's will and explains how "God not only
acknowledged, approved and honored [Rebekah's] will, but relied upon her fine powers
of discretion, and discernment of character" to ensure that Jacob, who was God's son
of choice, received the birthright blessing. Of this episode, Sidwell surmises that
"although [Rebekah] was compelled...to resort to stratagem to obtain it...as women
usually are she was right."[44] Sidwell and more pointedly Emmeline B. Wells also used
the Bible to encourage women to rethink what virtues such as integrity, purity, brav-
ery, and unselfishness actually entail by pointing out discrepancies between the

ancient meaning of the Word of God as depicted by the lives of biblical women and nineteenth-century conceptions of following the Word of God.[45] Wells writes: "We are told by Christian teachers in the world to imitate the examples of the illustrious women of the Scriptures; but let any one do so in reality, the finger of scorn will be pointed at them."[46] Wells calls on women to reject these nineteenth-century constrictions and follow the examples of their biblical foremothers. In making this move, Sidwell and Wells echo Christian interpreters such as Sarah Moore Grimké and Clara Neyman.[47]

ARGUING FOR WOMEN'S EQUALITY AND THE EXPANSION OF WOMEN'S SPHERE

An integral aspect of the *Exponent* was the championing of equal opportunities for women. As Carol Cornwall Madsen reports in her extensive quantitative study of the *Exponent*, "most issues contained at least two editorials advocating the expansion of 'woman's sphere,' with the most common topics being suffrage, polygamy, woman's education, and woman's career opportunities."[48] Similar to women activists in the nineteenth century, Mormon women often rooted their entrance into the civil sphere in traditional domestic roles.[49] Women's spheres would naturally expand as women extended their much-needed motherly concern to all of society.

One particularly notable example of how Mormon women used the Bible to support this position is Thyra's exegesis of Dorcas (also known as Tabitha) from the New Testament. Thyra begins by explaining how men often refer to Dorcas "as a pattern of humility" who "stayed at home and stitched away for the love of Jesus without any ambitious ideas of what she would accomplish" and then use her example to silence women who "desire to vote, to legislate or 'orate.'" Thyra asserts this is a misreading of Dorcas; rather, she was a woman who "had charge of some organization for the poor, the widows and the orphans, that her work was a great one." Thyra justifiably uses the scriptural verses about individuals mourning Dorcas's death to argue that "she was so beloved by the people because she was extensively known for good works . . . and . . . when she died, they felt there was no one to fill her place, and accomplish so much good as she could have done." Thyra's exegesis epitomizes how Mormon women commonly expanded women's spheres and authority by starting within traditional gender boundaries and then redefining understanding of them. For while Thyra applauds and encourages women to fulfill the traditional female role of devoting one's life "to the noble and holy work of elevating, purifying and refining the human family," she redefines what it means "to minister to others, forgetful of self, [to] live for God and His Kingdom," because she does not relegate women to the home or to serving in obscurity.[50] Instead she encourages women to use their "intellect and wisdom" to accomplish as much good as possible. And this, as her reading of Dorcas indicates, most often meant becoming an active participant and leader in benevolent and civil affairs. For Mormon women, as for many of their religious contemporaries, home and public life were compatible. As Grace Aguilar, a nineteenth-century Jewish exegete, wrote, "to a really great mind, domestic and public duties are so perfectly compatible, that the first need never be sacrificed for the last."[51]

Listing the women who had played prominent roles in spiritual and political life in the Bible was a popular rhetorical move of individuals seeking to expand women's opportunities, particularly for women who wanted to offer respected models for their own seemingly unconventional public activity. Deborah, a judge in Israel for forty years, served as the favorite example of society's need for female leadership.[52] As one *Exponent* author wrote, "so beautiful in character, so noble in life, her genius was superior to any recorded in the history of the Hebrews, and she alone has escaped unreproved by prophets and historians."[53] For many within and outside of the Mormon faith, Deborah became a proof text not only of God's approval of female political leadership but also of society's need for motherhood and feminine virtue in the political sphere.[54]

Similarly, nineteenth-century Mormon women referenced the examples of prophetesses Huldah and Miriam to argue that men in the ancient world sought after and highly valued the opinions of women; the use of these biblical examples supported their call for men in nineteenth-century America to behave likewise by giving women the vote.[55] Women in Utah were among the first in the United States to vote—second only to the women of Wyoming—and writers of the *Exponent* were prolific in extolling the virtues of suffrage, particularly once the Edmunds-Tucker Act stripped Utah women of their right to vote in 1887 (an Act put in place because the Mormon's practiced polygamy).[56] In this respect, Mormon women were more progressive than many churchwomen of other faiths who—according to Ann Braude—until the end of the nineteenth century viewed as radical the argument that women needed the vote in order to promote Christian values.[57] Mormon women, in contrast, were with the vanguard of women reformers who commonly cited biblical women such as Deborah, Huldah, and Miriam as examples of how women's abilities were needed in political and civil spheres.[58]

More than showing women's wider sphere of influence and action in the ancient world, however, Mormon women considered it important to show God's approval of that wider sphere and to show women's integral role in helping him achieve his purposes both then and in the present. To underscore this perspective, Mormon women turned to the Bible to provide "abundant testimonies that God acknowledges woman as capable of thinking and acting for herself" and that he trusts them and uses them as significant actors in his work.[59] Like their Protestant contemporaries, Mormon authors were particularly fond of emphasizing these points by referencing Jesus's attitude toward women in the Gospels and women's interactions with him.[60] As multiple authors recount, "it was a woman who oftenest ministered to the wants of the son of God, who believed in and followed him, but it was not a woman who betrayed him."[61] "Woman alone pressed her way to the very foot of the cross....Woman embalmed his precious body. Woman first greeted him when he burst the bonds of death and triumphed over the grave....Twas woman who was first commissioned to go and proclaim the glad tidings of his resurrection, And woman today stands among the foremost in her Master's work—a true disciple and among the purest representatives of His divine life the world affords."[62] Nineteenth-century Mormon women viewed themselves not as second-class citizens but as valued members of God's kingdom who could actively take part in Christian duties and civil affairs as did their foremothers in biblical times.

Perhaps Ella F. Smith summarized most eloquently the dominant vision of women's sphere in the *Exponent*. She writes that only when women are "emancipated, enlightened, and enfranchised" will they be able to "do fully the work God has them given them to do." Then, "commissioned by the Great Father and clothed in the armor of affection, she will go forth to conquer the world with the sword of the spirit. . . . The whole world will surrender to her divine command, and before her triumphant march the powers of darkness flee. Prisons will be transformed into schools, and saloons and brothels will be turned into markets and homes of purity."[63] Like many other nineteenth-century Christians, Mormons believed fervently that Christ's millennial reign was imminent, and in the *Exponent* we see clearly the integral role Mormon women believed they were to play in preparing the earth for Christ's return.

DEFENDING THE PRACTICE OF POLYGAMY

If we focus exclusively on what Mormon women's exegesis of biblical women promotes in regard to women, then Mormons appear to differ little from progressive women of other religious traditions; however, when we shift our focus to the theology promoted in the exegesis, significant differences emerge. The vehement dispute surrounding the practice of plural marriage is the most striking example. Many nineteenth-century exegetes of various faiths routinely denounced the evils of polygamy and mitigated biblical patriarchs' practice of polygamy by simply ignoring it, showing the problems that arose from it, stating that it was never sanctioned of God, or explaining it away as a less advanced religious stage.[64] Notably, this was most often done without any reference to Mormons and simply came as a result of exegetes struggling to comprehend a practice almost universally rejected in Western culture. Mormons, however, brought the patriarchs' polygamous practices to the forefront of their exegesis in order to explain and justify their own practice.

Plural marriage was central to the Mormon faith from its public avowal in 1852 until it was rescinded in 1890. Joseph Smith introduced the practice earlier to close associates, explaining that God had commanded Abraham to practice polygamy and now God had commanded Joseph and chosen others to follow their example.[65] Members of the church saw themselves as modern Israel, living in the "dispensation of the fullness of times" when all ancient principles—such as prophets, priesthood, and temples— would be restored to the earth.[66] Plural marriage was believed to be one of those ancient principles. Consequently, nineteenth-century Mormons lived it and defended it despite intense opposition and condemnation from the American government and its people. Many men, for instance, were imprisoned for marrying multiple wives, and

Utah was denied statehood until the Mormon Church's 1890 Anti-polygamy Manifesto officially ended the practice within the faith.[67]

Although individuals outside the Mormon faith lambasted polygamy and could not comprehend how it could be a part of women's call for greater gender equality, writers for the *Exponent* rigorously defended the practice by claiming its "divine origin, its constitutionality, its biblical precedence, its social value, its emancipating structure, and its elevating influence on society."[68] As Emmeline B. Wells, editor of the *Exponent*, explained, plural marriage gave women "more time for thought, for mental culture, more freedom of action, a broader field of labor, and inculcated liberality and generosity."[69] Many nineteenth-century Mormon women wrote of polygamy not only as a God-given commandment but also as a form of liberation, and nearly 10 percent of the editorials in the *Woman's Exponent* were dedicated to defending the practice from 1871 until 1890, when the practice officially ended.[70]

The defense of choice was biblical precedent; consequently, the *Exponent* and other publications of the Mormon Church contain numerous references to the patriarch's practice of plural marriage. Sarah and Hagar in particular were used to explain the practice to those in the church and to defend the practice to other Christians who attacked the church.[71] Most often these defenses emphasized that in the times of the Old Testament "the Lord sanctioned the practice, and blessed those who lived in that holy order."[72] Indeed, as one editorialist wrote, "God loved the old polygamic tree, for he does not condemn [Abraham], but on the contrary says that in his fruit shall all the nations of the earth be blessed."[73] Writers regularly called fellow Christians into question for "condemn[ing] Mormon women in the present age for accepting the conditions of the Abrahamic covenant, viz., patriarchal marriage" while revering Old Testament men and women involved in the same practice.[74] And writers used the example of God cursing Miriam with leprosy for speaking against Moses's plural marriage to an Ethiopian woman to warn contemporary readers "how dangerous it is to speak against this practice which the Lord approves."[75] Women writers were also particularly fond of interpreting the Lord's answering of Hagar's, Sarah's, and Hannah's prayers as evidence of his divine approval of plural marriage and his personal care for plural wives both in ancient times and in the nineteenth century.[76]

EXEGESIS IN APPLICATION

In presenting biblical women as progressive models of womanhood, Mormon women created a space for moving beyond established nineteenth-century gender norms while also maintaining an air of religious conservatism. As Wells explained in her article about Ruth, Mormon women desired only to follow the examples of the great women of the scriptures; if nineteenth-century society considered these actions to be unwomanly, then society needed to change.[77] The impact of this exegesis and the extensive writings in the *Exponent* that encouraged women's educational, occupational, and political advancement may in part be seen in the lives of the many Mormon

women who pursued advanced degrees, achieved occupational success, and held political offices during the late nineteenth century.[78] Particularly noteworthy are the numerous women who traveled East to receive medical degrees, and women such as
Martha Hughes Cannon, the first female state senator in the United States, and Mary
Chamberlain, the first mayor in an all-female town council in the United States.[79]
While Mormon women in the second half of the twentieth century would largely conform to conservative gender expectations, women at the end of the nineteenth and
beginning of the twentieth century stood at the cutting edge of many women's rights
objectives such as suffrage, social reform, divorce and child custody laws, and educational and occupational opportunities.[80]

Nineteenth-century Mormon women also lived up to the mandate contained in
their exegesis for women to play an integral role in building up the Mormon Church, as
women were central to organizing many of the efforts of the institutional church. For
instance, women of the Relief Society served as Sunday school teachers, officiated in
Mormon temples, and gave blessings of healing to other members.[81] They also raised
their own funds to build meetinghouses and storehouses and were the motivating
force behind the creation of associations that sponsored weekly meetings and activities for young children, youth, and young adults.[82] In terms of helping the larger society and preparing the earth for Christ's millennial coming, Mormon women also advocated for urban reform, antiprostitution activism, community charity, infant health
and nutrition, and disaster relief.

Unfortunately, ascertaining precisely how the *Exponent* and the exegesis it contains
contributed to women's progressive actions is impossible; one can only collect evidence through individuals expressed statements of the *Exponent*'s impact as well as
establish time correlation. However, what one can more precisely explore is the impact
this exegesis may have had on certain Mormon doctrines—a notable example being
that of Eve. As Boyd Jay Petersen explains in his article analyzing how Eve has been
presented in the Mormon Church, nineteenth-century male Mormon leaders uniformly presented Eve in a less favorable light, as one who had been deceived but inadvertently fulfilled God's purpose.[83] In the *Exponent*, however, a theological debate
ensued over "whether Eve was the essentially duplicitous instigator of evil or the noble
initiator of human progress; between the traditional view of Eve that has persisted in
Christianity for millennia and the ennobled portrayal of Eve that many found in
Mormon scripture and theology."[84] Petersen illustrates that "this version of Eve as
hero," which was absent from male Latter-day Saint thought in the nineteenth century
but dominant in the *Exponent*, has now become "the most common in today's [Latter-
day Saint] discourse."[85] Such findings indicate not only that the women who wrote for
the *Exponent* had the ability to shape Mormon theology through their exegesis but also
that scholars today should not lightly dismiss nineteenth-century women's claims
about the vast impact of the *Exponent* on Mormon society.

In the last two decades as scholars have come to recognize how women participated
actively in nineteenth-century theological discourse through the genres of devotional
books, hymns, poetry, periodical articles, and novels, our understanding of these

women and the religions in which they participated has been complicated and enhanced.[86] What my work and the work of Boyd Jay Peterson and Susanna Morrill on the *Exponent* make clear is that Mormon women were involved in similar projects, using similar methods, to those of their female religious contemporaries and that Mormon studies will likewise significantly benefit from the inclusion of female voices found in these genres.[87] In the pages of the *Woman's Exponent*, Mormon women assert their authority to interpret scripture and employ the Bible not only to create an image of their roles as women but also to shape a society and a religion in which the achievement of such an ideal is possible. And when we incorporate their exegesis into the academic conversation, our comprehension of nineteenth-century Mormon theological, cultural, social, and gender issues are all enriched.

8

Scripturalizing Religion and Ethnicity

THE CIRCLE SEVEN KORAN

Sylvester A. Johnson

AMONG THE SALIENT themes of the results from the survey research found in chapter 1 is the overwhelming and enduring importance of the Bible to Americans today. According to the data gathered from this research, about two-thirds of Americans who do not read the Bible still view it as their authoritative, divine source for knowledge and guidance. Since its first appearance in the Americas many centuries ago, the Bible has shaped popular, cultural ideas of narrative, metaphor, tropes, and rationalities. And in a serious way, it continues to function as a symbol of moral authority and religious fidelity in the United States.

In light of this, it is no accident that the early twentieth century saw the emergence of a religious community based on a biblically themed book of scripture that focused on Jesus in order to establish a Moorish, Islamic identity. Since the 1920s, the Moorish Science Temple of America (MSTA) has held its *Holy Koran of the Moorish Science Temple*, also called the *Circle Seven Koran*, as authoritative scripture. In what follows, I explain the scripture of the MSTA, an early community of African-American Muslims that began in 1925. I hope to elucidate two central issues: (1) the process Vincent Wimbush has termed "scripturalizing activity," which should deepen our attention toward the human practices of power and the social context through which scriptures are constituted and deployed, and (2) the relationship between specific scripturalizing tactics and ethnogenesis, the creation of peoplehood as this has emerged in the MSTA.

THEOLOGY AND ETHNOGENESIS

"Noble" Drew Ali, the founding prophet of the MSTA, produced the holy book of the movement as both a practical and symbolic measure for establishing a new religious community. He called it the *Circle Seven Koran*, evidently drawing on the Freemasonry symbol that represented the numeral 7 and the circle as symbols of fullness and completion. As an Islamic book of scripture, the *Circle Seven Koran* was meant to signify in name the Qur'anic scripture traditionally attributed to Muhammad of Arabia, who founded Islam in the seventh century of the Common Era. It was also meant to be distinctive on its own terms, however, emphasizing the specific circumstances of twentieth-century colonialism and race. For this reason, the *Circle Seven Koran*'s preface, penned by Ali, claimed to bear secret knowledge that had been newly revealed after many ages and delivered for the first time into "the hands of the Moslems of America."[1]

Although some scholars and laity alike have typically considered scripturalization to be bizarre, dilettante, trivializing, and categorically heretical, scripturalizing is overwhelmingly common and integral to a range of social formations, frequently becoming part of the context for framing and executing human subjectivities and agencies. The making of scriptures has recurred for thousands of years, and there is no clear reason to expect it will not continue. (By analogy, the same might be said of the rise of prophets, whether self-proclaimed or branded as such by others.) So, although it might be tempting to focus on the novelty or fantastical appearance of new scriptures, it is more fruitful intellectually to engage seriously with social data about tactics and power modes that inhere to scripturalizing practices.[2]

We can examine the *Circle Seven Koran* in precisely this fashion by attending to its historical matrix, its political and narrative architecture, and its deployment by the MSTA. The most important contextual element of its emergence was a turn toward ethnic identity among Blacks throughout the diaspora. At the time, civilization was viewed by elite intellectuals and in popular culture as a Western European property to be disseminated among nonwhite races, commonly demeaned as "savage" or barbaric. The MSTA's ethnic turn, in this context, emphasized that Blacks were a heritage people—they possessed culture and a distinct civilizational genealogy that was fundamentally shaped by their particular religion of Islam.[3]

The ethnic turn was not only about possessing heritage, however. It was also structured as a political formation with the specific aim of opposing colonial forms of political power. Black people in the United States were denied the actual status of citizens and lived under the formal racial architecture of apartheid. This was the racial state. And it created a colonial status for nonwhites. This meant the MSTA's insurgent theology of ethnicity and heritage renewal necessarily sought to resolve the status of Blacks as a political population governed not as members of the political community but as perpetual enemies or aliens of the society in which they lived. This was the political project of anticolonialism, and it featured centrally in the portion of the *Circle Seven Koran* that Ali composed, the final four chapters.[4]

The political texture of the Holy Koran of the MSTA was constituted through its analytical and narrative elements. These obtained chiefly through interpreting Jesus as both a historical and a figural person of Moabite ancestry—as a Canaanite. On this score, it is important to consider Ali's reliance on Levi Dowling's *Aquarian Gospel*, the source for the *Circle Seven Koran*'s narratives about Jesus. (Ali also used selections from *Unto Thee I Grant*.) I raise this not to suggest that Ali lacked creativity or originality but to explain the significance of his selecting this source. The central emphasis of Dowling's text was the Eastern milieu of Jesus and his teaching. At the time, European scholars, particularly those of the German universities, had rendered Jesus as a virtual Western European, an anti-Semite who reviled and contravened racial Jewishness by embodying the spiritual and intellectual capacities of Greek *ratio*, the subjectivity of Western European "Man," thereby transcending fixation on legalism and ethnic particularism. By contrast, the *Aquarian Gospel* attributed Jesus's genius and salvific ministry not to the West but to the East, reveling in the Orientalist manufacture of untamed mystery. This approach romanticized the East and invested in presumptions of irreducible disparity between Eastern and Western sensibilities that ultimately originated with the racial formations of colonialism.[5]

Ali capitalized on this Orientalist theme to substantiate his own effort to extract Jesus from the hegemonic legacy of European Christian interpretation. But Ali was not attempting to claim Christianity for the colonized, "darker" races. Rather, he aimed to demonstrate that Jesus was a Canaanite, an eventual descendant of Ruth the Moabite heroine of biblical narrative. In the racially coded semiotics of biblical interpretation, this meant that Jesus was among the nonwhite races of the world. By Ali's account, Jesus was a victim of the European Roman government, wrongly executed "for seeking to redeem His people from the Roman yoke and law." The *Circle Seven Koran* identified Christianity as the religion of Europeans, represented in biblical narrative by the Roman Empire.[6]

The *Circle Seven Koran* was especially significant as scripture because it was conceived as both an affirmation of ethnic distinction and a strident assertion, by the book's own account, that Christianity was *not* the religion of Black people. It is exceedingly difficult for most observers today to grasp the complicated nature of this claim. So it might be helpful to set it alongside the emergence of the Qur'an in Arabia during the seventh and eight centuries. Early communities of Muslims were surrounded by the empires of Persia and Byzantium (dominated by Zoroastrians and Christians). They were intimately familiar with the many Jewish communities of the region. All of these religious others had scriptures and were called the "people of the book." So it was with considerable reverential pride and honor that early Muslims celebrated the Qur'an, traditionally attributed to the founding prophet Muhammad and written in the Arabic language. This sociohistorical context generated profound and lasting emphasis on the Qur'an as the revelation of an all-powerful deity (the one-god, in the parlance of monotheism) in the Arabic language to a once-scriptureless people. It is in this sense that the MSTA declared the *Circle Seven Koran* to be the scripture of Blacks as a people possessing a Moorish nationality. Because of such, they were no longer without a scriptural incarnation of revelation. They, too (like the Christians who constituted the religious majority in the United States), possessed a book of divine knowledge that asserted a distinct message of redemption in terms unique to their history and circumstance.[7]

The MSTA deployed its book of scripture with conscientious resolve and import. Temple leaders printed and disseminated the Holy Koran to members and clearly identified it as their unique, authoritative scripture prepared by their own "divine prophet." As was the case with other religious groups, the MSTA also prepared study guides based on the *Circle Seven Koran*. This included a catechism that emphasized the substance of the MSTA's salvific message of redemption and national belonging. The MSTA's periodical the *Moorish Voice* expounded on lessons from the *Holy Koran*. It was the sourcebook for the sermons preached in MSTA religious meetings. As a physical object, moreover, the *Circle Seven Koran* depicted the founding prophet, Ali, rescuing a vulnerable person of slight stature, representing the mission to redeem fallen humanity. MSTA literature also employed the Arabic term "Allah" to designate the divine.[8]

One of the most striking forms of the book's deployment was its use to rationalize opposition to the legal structure of racism in the early twentieth century. In Belzoni, Mississippi, for instance, during the spring of 1942, adherents of the MSTA strategically breached racial laws by refusing to follow segregated seating requirements for public transportation. They justified their opposition by asserting that the *Holy Koran* proved they were not Negroes but Moorish and thus not susceptible to apartheid laws.[9]

Throughout its entire history, members of the MSTA have continued to emphasize their Muslim identity by foregrounding the depth and expanse of Islam as a global religion. And the *Holy Koran* that Ali prepared remains at the center of Moorish theology and religious authority.

SCRIPTURALIZING DYNAMICS

Several important themes emerge from considering the scripturalization of the *Circle Seven Koran*. First, it is a distinctly biblical scripture. I mean this in the sense in which the Qur'an has been understood as engaging centrally with major characters, stories, and motifs of biblical texts. The *Circle Seven Koran* is a highly creative *synthesis* of preexisting writings and compositions original to Noble Drew Ali. In this way, like most American scriptures, it reflects the immense influence of the Bible on American culture.

Second, the governing historical condition of the *Circle Seven Koran*'s fashioning as a scripture was the ethnogenetic moment of the early twentieth century. Ethnogenesis was arguably these scriptures' most profound deployment. Theophus Smith has skillfully demonstrated the extent to which the Bible enabled the formation of new iterations of peoplehood in African-American history. It is in a similar sense that the *Circle Seven Koran* merits attention for engendering critical tactics of formation and reformation of peoplehood. Moorish Americans became a people with their own book of scripture. It symbolized and authenticated Moorish Americans as a distinct population rooted in the civilization of Islam. Interestingly enough, this same ethnogenetic formation also elided the historical scope and diversity of African indigenous religions, most of which were varieties of Orisha devotion. The civilizational paradigm that provides the thrust to the theology of Moorish history, moreover, also eviscerates any serious engagement with non-Abrahamic civilizational traditions of Africa.[10]

Third, to the degree that scripture embodies the capacity to function as a cultural force, it has frequently become a weapon—an instrument for participating in conflicted struggle. This function of scripture is as ancient as it is contemporary and proceeds in great measure from the powerful status commanded by literacy and textuality. As Itumeleng Mosala has brilliantly displayed, scriptures are already a product of fundamental struggles for control over material resources and institutional sources of social power. The deployment of scriptures as part of the same forms of struggle constitutes a reciprocal dynamism.[11]

Fourth, the status of scripture is an emergent property. It is a status achieved through specific histories and political processes, so that it cannot be reduced to any of its elements. This historical conditioning is richly demonstrated in Pauline Maier's study of American sacred texts. Maier devoted her career to examining the politics and cultural consequences of the American Revolution. In this study, she turned her attention to the scriptural status of the Declaration of Independence. It is evident from Maier's study of this secular scripture of the state that exceptionalism is by no means a necessary element in the making of scripture. The Declaration did not begin as an exceptional document. It was *made* exceptional several decades after it was written because of events other than the independence of the Anglo-American settler colonies. And this happened largely (though not entirely) through debates over slavery.[12]

Fifth, moral authority features as a major element of scripture. Here again, the Declaration is instructive for its role in authorizing not rebellion or revolution (the document's instantiating *Sitz im Leben*) but rather the pursuit of social and political equality across binaries of race, gender, class, and labor status. In a similar fashion, the *Circle Seven Koran* grounded Black ethnicity and religious particularity as normative in a context that had vilified the racial difference of Blacks. In tandem with this, the MSTA's book of scripture rendered colonialism as a type of original sin that contextualized the criminalization and execution of Jesus. Here was a Canaanite man put to death unfairly to ensure he would not redeem his people—the Jews—from being governed by the paradigmatic Western empire. In Ali's own day, the point was for the MSTA to inspire African Americans and all peoples of the non-white nations to embrace their ethnic identities and organize to combat the epistemology of colonialism and to assert in its place of authority a radically inclusive paradigm for conceptualizing political membership in the United States. This was the centerpiece of the *Circle Seven Koran*'s call for adherence to justice and principles of righteousness.

CONCLUSION

The MSTA poses a drastic demonstration of how American biblical culture has become instrumental in the formation and growth of Islam and the particular way that Muslim identity has been scripturalized in U.S. religious history. This might seem ironic, but it should compel us to appreciate anew the expansive influence that scripture wields as a cultural force and symbolic entity that shapes religious agency.

9

Reading the Bible in War and Crisis to Know the Future

Matthew Avery Sutton

"CAN MAN KNOW the future?" New York educator and fundamentalist Arno Gaebelein provocatively asked during the Great Depression. "We answer without hesitation, Yes. We can know the future through the Bible, the Word of God."[1]

Gaebelein was one of a growing number of Christians who in the late nineteenth and early twentieth century developed new ways for reading and understanding the Bible's prophetic books. Presbyterians, Baptists, Methodists, and pentecostals, male and female, black and white, they made the Bible a malleable tool that allowed them to make sense of the chaos they witnessed around them in order to predict and anticipate what was coming next, at home and around the globe. They believed that they alone understood the past, the present, and the future, which gave them an unwavering sense of confidence and absolute authority. Theirs was a utopian movement that looked longingly to a glorious future. While God had destined the rest of humanity to succumb to the Antichrist, tribulation, and then final judgment, the faithful looked forward to eternal bliss.

But they were not the only ones who read their Bibles to understand the future. The practices and traditions developed by Gaebelein and his network of fundamentalist allies continue to influence a substantial number of modern-day Christians. According to chapter 1, of the 50 percent of Americans who read the Bible at all in the prior year, over one-third claimed that they did so "to learn about the future." Some respondents likely meant that they used the Bible to answer questions about the afterlife, about heaven and hell. But if history is our guide, it is also clear that substantial numbers of these respondents use the Bible to anticipate tomorrow's headlines. In the same way Gaebelein used the sacred text to make sense of the Bolshevik revolution, the Great

Depression, the rise of fascism, and World War II, so, too, do modern-day Christians read the Bible to understand the significance of Obama administration policy initiatives, turmoil in eastern Europe, the growing power of China, tensions and war in the Middle East, and the machinations of leaders like Vladimir Putin. Their reading of the most apocalyptic books of the Bible gives them comfort by allowing them to find ultimate meaning in the most tumultuous issues of their generation.

Critics have long contended that fundamentalists' and evangelicals' apocalyptic hermeneutic fostered indifference and apathy in the faithful. Rather than work to reform this world, detractors said, evangelicals had their heads lost in the clouds. This critique has stuck. But it's wrong. Although evangelicals felt sure that the global apocalypse was imminent, it was never too late for the individual, the nation, or the world to be reborn. Like devout Calvinists who sent missionaries abroad even though they knew that they were powerless to effect anyone's salvation, or orthodox Marxists who challenged the market economy despite believing that capitalism was an inevitable step on the road to the socialist paradise, evangelicals never let their conviction that God had already determined the future lead them to passivity.

The development of the particular apocalyptic hermeneutic popularized by early-twentieth-century fundamentalists marked a new era in American Christianity. The innovative methods they used to understand the future differed from the most prevalent Bible-reading practices of their day. The vast majority of American Christians in the nineteenth century subscribed to a theological view called postmillennialism. Postmillennialists offered Americans an enthusiastic vision of the future, believing that the establishment of a peaceful, utopian kingdom of God on earth was imminent. But theirs was not the only perspective. A group of radical white evangelicals kept a skeptical eye on much of what was occurring around them. Living amid the rise of the modern university system, massive urbanization, political turmoil, and significant Catholic and Jewish immigration, a determined group believed that true Christianity, and perhaps their way of life, was under siege. They feared that churchly conservatives had lost the authentic radicalism of New Testament Christianity and had failed to make faith relevant to the world's changing conditions. They viewed liberal Protestantism and movements like the social gospel as troubling distortions of Christianity that had seemingly transformed religion into little more than a shallow nostrum for curing temporal problems.

As radical evangelicals tried to make sense of the changing times, they began to find in the scriptures verses that they had not noticed before, while vague and obscure passages came into sharper focus. Informed by their historical context, their reading of church history, and the work of a few relatively obscure European apocalypticists, they came to the startling conclusion that they were not preparing the world for a godly millennium. Instead, they were living near the end times—the period of history predicted by biblical writers thousands of years earlier that would immediately precede the battle of Armageddon and the second coming of Jesus. Rather than waiting for the kingdom of God to appear through moral reform or personal regeneration, they saw tribulation and death looming on the horizon. Hence they identified as premillennialists—they believed that the return of Christ would precede the millennium. For them time was short and humankind was careening toward an inevitable apocalypse. They felt the need to warn the nation and the world that Jesus was coming back. And he was coming soon.

Throughout Western history, various Christians have seen in dramatic social changes hints of the coming apocalypse. The Crusades, the Reformation, and the French Revolution inspired short-lived millennial movements that eventually faded into obscurity. In the United States, groups like the Shakers, the Church of Jesus Christ of Latter-day Saints, and other more mainstream Protestants have at times heralded Christ's coming kingdom. Doomsaying has often walked hand in hand with the Christian faith. What made the radical evangelical movement different were the ways massive geopolitical changes in the late nineteenth and twentieth century seemed to confirm adherents' hopes, expectations, and predictions. World events appeared to be lining up with biblical prophecy as never before. The national and global events that seemed to be fulfilling prophecy worked to reinforce the methodology of those Christians who used the Bible as a tool for understanding the future. Over the last 150 years, this particular approach to reading the Bible—seeing it as a roadmap through the coming apocalypse—has become so pervasive among evangelicals that it is now a fundamental way in which many read the Bible.

The modern practice of reading the Bible as a guide to an apocalyptic future was first popularized by William Blackstone. A wealthy Chicago real estate developer and friend of evangelist Dwight L. Moody, Blackstone felt energized by the chaos he saw around him. Certain that time was running out, Blackstone decided to take up a pen and draft *Jesus is Coming* in 1878 to warn as many people as possible about the imminent apocalypse. To illustrate how close the world was to Armageddon, Blackstone cited various signs that touched on almost every aspect of modern life. The precarious states of capitalism and democracy represented one ominous indication that the apocalypse was near. Other signs lined up perfectly with the conditions that inspired Mark Twain's novel *The Gilded Age*. Blackstone viewed "oppressing monopolies, systematic [s]peculation and fraud" as important indicators that the days were numbered. Others had to do with moral issues, such as the rising circulation of "obscene literature," which had provoked the series of so-called Comstock laws that constrained the publication and sale of such works. The future as Blackstone saw it was bleak. "Surely then this wicked world, which is so radically opposed to God, and under the present control of His arch enemy, is not growing better. On the contrary, judgment, fire and perdition are before it. Perilous times are coming."[2]

Despite Blackstone's expectation of such a dire future, his sentiments did not drive him or his fellow believers to apathy or indifference. "We neither despair, nor fold our hands to sleep," the businessman-theologian explained. "On the contrary, we are filled with a lively hope." Explaining that millennial convictions sparked action rather than ennui, he continued, "Surely this positive conviction of coming doom is a mightier incentive to action than can be the quieting fallacy that things are moving on prosperously and that EVEN THE WORLD IS GETTING BETTER." While critics accused men and women like Blackstone of otherworldliness, their convictions seemed to have the opposite effect. Preparing for Jesus's return fostered intense, relentless engagement with the world around them. By the time of Blackstone's death in 1935, over a million copies of his book had been printed in multiple editions in forty-eight languages, making it one of the most influential religious books of the twentieth century.[3]

Blackstone and a growing number of radical evangelicals believed that prophecies supposedly about the last days, outlined in Daniel, Ezekiel, Matthew, and Revelation, would occur in rapid succession just before Christ's return. Such a theology provided adherents with an imminent hope of the second coming without forcing them to identify a specific date. Jesus, they determined, was always coming; they had to be ready at all times.

Radical evangelicals like Blackstone agreed that at the end of the current age a series of extraordinary events would unfold. Most expected the "rapture" to initiate end-times chaos. Blackstone and others taught that after the rapture, those left behind would undergo a seven-year tribulation. A new leader—who would actually be the Antichrist—would take power in this period, assuming control over a ten-kingdom confederacy established within the boundaries of the old Roman Empire. His reign would be characterized by what the prophet Daniel called a combination of "iron" and "clay" (Daniel 2:40–43). Premillennialists interpreted this as a mix of totalitarian rule (iron) supported by popular democracy (clay). Although the Antichrist will have unprecedented political control, his confederation will face enemies to the north, south, and east. Radical evangelicals' preoccupation with anticipating who those enemies would be drove them to become serious students of geopolitical developments.

The Bible, they argued, provided unparalleled insights for those who knew how to read it. Yet because it did not provide the day or the hour of Jesus's second coming, neither did radical evangelicals. They carefully avoided setting specific dates for the coming apocalypse and routinely acknowledged that their speculation was just that. They could keep expectations of an imminent rapture high without being pinned down as false prophets. If the return of Christ was not around the next corner, it was always behind the corner after that. This was and is the genius of evangelicals' use of the Bible for interpreting the future. Like the faithful virgins in Jesus's parable in Matthew 25 who had properly prepared for the return of the bridegroom, they were always ready.

To illustrate the evolving ways American evangelicals have read their Bibles to understand the future, the rest of this essay will focus briefly on three different periods. In each of these eras, Christians thought that contemporary events were lining up exactly with the prophetic books of the Bible. They saw in national and international news signs that the last days had commenced, and believed that the rapture, tribulation, and battle of Armageddon were imminent. Such interpretations imposed a sense of order and meaning onto seemingly dangerous and unpredictable events.

The three main eras I will focus on are (1) the 1930s and fundamentalists' obsession with Mussolini and the restoration of the Roman Empire; (2) the early Cold War and evangelicals' fixation with Stalin and the rise of the USSR; and (3) the 1970s and evangelicals' growing interest in Israel and the Middle East. I will briefly conclude by documenting how American Christians since 9/11 have found creative ways to read the "war on terror" in the context of biblical prophecies.

Premillennial apocalypticism shaped the emerging fundamentalist movement in the early twentieth century. It provided a means of understanding and explaining national and global politics, World War I, the Balfour Declaration creating a Jewish homeland in Palestine, and the League of Nations controversies. But soon fundamentalists felt a new sense of urgency. For generations they had been carefully combing both their Bibles and their daily newspapers for evidence that Jesus's return to earth was nearing. Global events in the 1930s so closely paralleled fundamentalists' long-held predictions that the imminent return of Christ animated everything from their most private conversations to their loudest political expressions. Although the Antichrist had not yet revealed himself, the faithful felt sure that Satan was orchestrating global events in preparation for the coming of a new world leader. William Bell Riley summed up their feelings. The daily newspaper, he explained, was "an index finger pointing down the path of fulfilling prophecy. The age to which we have come is one of which Isaiah and Jeremiah wrote; of which Daniel dreamed; of which the apostles prophesied, and of which Christ Himself uttered alike words of warning and wisdom." Premillennialism consistently provided its adherents with confidence. In a darkening age, they alone understood the significance of cascading world events. While the rest of humanity naively marched toward the coming tribulation, fundamentalists looked forward to the rapture and then millennial bliss.[4]

At the center of fundamentalists' efforts to use the Bible to explain contemporary events and to predict the future was Benito Mussolini. The faithful had long expected the Antichrist to take power through a ten-nation confederacy led by a resurrected Roman Empire. That Il Duce seemed to fit the prophetic bill almost perfectly captivated fundamentalists around the nation. Speculation about Mussolini's significance began shortly after he formed a new government in Italy. Los Angeles Bible teacher Louis Bauman boasted that he had first identified Mussolini in 1922 as the probable Antichrist. A few years later he warned, "If Mussolini does not prove to be Antichrist . . . he is certainly a magnificent fore-shadow of Antichrist!"[5]

As global conditions deteriorated, premillennial speculation snowballed. Evangelist Luke Rader called Il Duce a "curse to the human race" and the possible Antichrist. "Since Mussolini is resurrecting Rome," his brother Paul warned, "the eyes of all students of prophecy are upon him." Texas Tornado J. Frank Norris warned a friend to keep his eyes on Mussolini. "I firmly believe," he explained, "we are coming to the climax of the ages." Southern missionary L. Nelson Bell summarized fundamentalist thought in a letter to his mother. The "way is being paved for the final restoration of the old Roman Empire. . . . What a joy," he wrote, about events that seem less than joyful, "to have the hope of His Coming before us, rather than the mirage of a world getting better and better."[6]

In one of the great ironies in fundamentalist history, Mussolini had no idea how closely he was being watched by fundamentalists. Then he met Ralph and Edith Norton. The Nortons were probably the most influential and well-known fundamentalist missionaries of the interwar era. They ran the Belgium Gospel Mission and corresponded with most of the significant fundamentalist leaders of the era. In the early

1930s, they embarked on a tour of Europe with plans to publish a series of articles based on their impressions in the *Sunday School Times*. A meeting with Mussolini marked the climax of the trip. "Do you intend to reconstitute the Roman Empire?" they asked the prime minister. At first Mussolini had no idea what they were getting at. Then the Nortons walked the Italian fascist through biblical prophecy. As they proceeded, Mussolini apparently "leaned back in his chair and listened fascinated." "Is that really described in the Bible?" he asked the missionaries. "Where is it to be found?" By the time the Nortons were through with him, Mussolini apparently believed—and maybe even hoped—that he was the long-awaited world dictator prophesied in the book of Daniel. True to form, Il Duce had no reservations about taking on the role of the prophesied Antichrist.[7]

In 1935, Italy's invasion of Ethiopia raised fundamentalist interest in Mussolini to new heights. Harold John Ockenga, who would soon emerge as the leading spokesman of evangelicalism in the post–World War II era, second only to Billy Graham, preached an enthusiastic sermon on the relationship between the prophecies of Daniel and the Italian campaign in Africa. He promised that humankind was standing "on the brink of the greatest international upheaval and tribulation of history which will mark the end of the present era." Many fundamentalists agreed that Italy's actions in Africa matched biblical predictions. Prophecy, or at least their interpretation of prophecy, seemed to be coming true. Bauman also saw the invasion as an important step on the road to Armageddon. Inspired by events abroad, John R. Rice preached sermons in his Texas church titled "Is Mussolini the Anti-Christ?" and "Mussolini Restores the Roman Empire." Both were printed in his fledgling newspaper, *Sword of Lord*. The articles produced a flood of positive correspondence and helped Rice eventually make *Sword* one of the most influential Christian papers in the nation.[8]

A few fundamentalists were so sure about Mussolini's role in end-times prophecy that they felt compelled to share God's cosmic plans with national policy-makers. One Atlanta fundamentalist suggested that they open "a Sunday School in Washington to study Prophecy and History and invite the House and Senate and the President and his Cabinet to become students." Others wrote to President Franklin D. Roosevelt directly. A Texan who promised to keep FDR up-to-date on the "signs of the times" named Mussolini as the Antichrist and predicted that out of the Ethiopian crisis "a ten League of nations will come, which shall be governed by Mussolini, which shall stand for seven years" preceding the return of Christ. A Pennsylvania Presbyterian wrote to Roosevelt as well, encouraging him to study prophecy "with its amazing secrets for the Statesman." Roosevelt, he believed, should be making policy on the basis of premillennialism. "In international relationships," he counseled, "it would be of priceless worth to know that the map of Europe will be reshaped according to Biblical Prophecy, of which the strength of Rome to-day is an interesting indication." These letters indicated how seriously the faithful took their analysis. They believed that they could and should help American leaders make wise decisions on the basis of their premillennial interpretations of the Bible.[9]

As they had with Mussolini, fundamentalists were able to line up events in the Soviet Union, England, and Asia with biblical prophecy as well. In an era of unparalleled global crisis, they could not have positioned themselves any better. They promised Americans that only they could explain the causes of global turmoil, only they could anticipate where world events were heading, and most important, only they could guarantee adherents a means of escape from the impending global catastrophe. They and they alone could read beyond the headlines to help humanity navigate its way out of the coming earthly inferno and on to the millennial kingdom. If only the men and women they were trying to reach would listen.

As the war unfolded, fundamentalists proved to have been mistaken. Their greatest error had been placing so much importance on Mussolini. Many had viewed him as the Antichrist's predecessor if not the Antichrist himself. Yet by 1941 most of the world recognized that the Italians had overplayed their hand. The British were driving back the fascists in North Africa, and the Greeks had resiliently fought an Italian invasion. Il Duce was transformed quickly from the potential beast of Revelation into Hitler's weak-kneed lackey. Gaebelein stubbornly refused to acknowledge how he had fostered false hopes; instead he denounced others for doing the same: It had been "through confusion...through date-setting...through calling certain present-day actors in world history the Antichrist, etc.," that prophecy teachers had brought "the Word of God into disrepute." Bauman, who had continued to assert in books, magazines, and sermons that the Roman Empire was ascending, kept faith in Mussolini longer than most. "Just now," he wrote to a friend, "people may be questioning my position with regard to Mussolini." "May it not be," he later suggested, "that the critics are a little premature in their criticism?" Apparently not. A few fundamentalists later joked about the extremes to which prophetic speculation had gone. *Moody Monthly*'s editors, for example, reprinted a story making the rounds in the 1940s. "One prominent Bible teacher, just after the inglorious death of Mussolini, was asked to bring four addresses on prophecy at a Bible conference. He is said to have wired, 'Cannot come; I have only two addresses left.'"[10]

By the end of the war, fundamentalists mostly refused to acknowledge how much they had erred. But by refusing to set dates, they could keep expectations of an imminent rapture high without being labeled false prophets.

The post–World War II generation of fundamentalists, who had begun to call themselves evangelicals, had a clear sense of what "occupying" until Jesus's return meant for their lives, their movement, and especially their nation. The apocalyptic implications of the atomic bomb combined with the increasingly intense Cold War provided an ideal opportunity for them again to relate their faith to the concerns of their communities. Americans knew that an epic battle of good and evil, right and wrong, was in the making. While they longed for a future of peace and prosperity, they understood that an atheistic Soviet Union, nuclear weapons, and global devastation threatened on the horizon. Evangelicals helped Americans make sense of this postwar world by aligning it with their apocalyptic visions of imminent violence, horrific persecution, and world war.

Hiroshima and Nagasaki had convinced radical evangelicals that even if they did not know when the world was going to end, they now knew how it would end: 2 Peter 3:10

said, "But the day of the Lord will come as a thief in the night; in the which the heavens shall pass away with a great noise, and the elements shall melt with fervent heat, the earth also and the works that are therein shall be burned up." Almost as soon as the U.S. army detonated "Little Boy" over Japan, prophetic speculation began anew. Like most Americans, evangelicals did not lament the number of causalities the bomb produced. Instead, they celebrated victory and moved quickly to analyzing how atomic weapons represented another key piece in the prophetic puzzle. Now that humans had the capacity to obliterate the earth, they argued, God had to be planning to intervene soon.[11]

American evangelicals speculated that atomic weapons would soon force God to bring history to an end. But as long as only the United States had the bomb, most saw little risk of humanity destroying itself. The faithful understood, however, that if or when the bomb fell into the hands of the United States' rivals, the train to Armageddon would accelerate. No enemy loomed larger at the time than the Soviet Union. In the late 1940s evangelicals, journalists, and government officials alike worried that Stalin would develop atomic weapons and soon thereafter strike the United States. The Soviets' successful test of an atomic weapon in 1949 confirmed their worst fears. With a nod to old speculation about Ezekiel's prophecy of the end-times rise of the kingdom of Magog, *King's Business*'s editors interpreted the news as "another step in the advance of Russia toward the goal of the Northern Confederacy." Meanwhile, Lowell Blanchard and the Valley Trio translated premillennial ideas into pop culture. They recorded "Jesus Hits Like an Atom Bomb" (1950), fretting that "Everybody's worried 'bout the Atomic Bomb, but nobody's worried 'bout the day my Lord will come when He'll hit— Great God Almighty—like an Atom Bomb when He comes, when He comes."[12]

Although evangelical leaders feared the growing power of the Russians, some relished the fact that the bomb had made apocalyptic expectations part of mainstream American life. Los Angeles pastor Frank Lindgren claimed that the bomb had forced American elites to grapple with what "we 'illiterate fundamentalists'" had been saying for years. Louis Bauman made a similar point in his last series of articles on prophecy before his death in 1950. "Dark indeed are the prognostications of our generation of statesmen, scientists, modernists and men of war," he wrote. "The super-optimists of a few years ago have become the super-pessimists of today." Fuller Seminary professor Wilbur Smith summarized how radically things had changed since he had attended his first prophecy conference in 1914. At that time, fundamentalist doomsayers represented a small minority. In the late 1940s, in contrast, secular authorities, even more than evangelicals, were preaching imminent ruin. "Today," he observed in *Moody Monthly*, "the unbelieving world unites in testifying that we are in an hour of dire crisis—not only an hour of possible, impending calamities, but it would seem on the very verge of the eclipse of civilization and the destruction of humanity." Indeed, the premillennial message of imminent destructions resonated with Americans in new ways.[13]

As Cold War tensions rose, evangelicals returned again and again to the scriptures. While fundamentalists had spent the 1930s fretting over Mussolini and the restoration of the Roman Empire, they spent the 1940s and 1950s obsessed with Stalin and the Soviet Union. Russia had long played an important role in prophetic speculation, and the Cold War simply reaffirmed the USSR's last-days significance. "There is no country in all the world," Bible professor Lewis Talbot observed, "more autocratic than the Union of Soviet Socialist Republics, governed by its man of cold steel, Stalin.... And this is exactly in fulfillment of the prophecy of this Scripture." Wilbur Smith penned a new, up-to-date series of articles on prophecy for the *Sunday School Times*. A widely circulated advertisement for the articles asked readers to identify which world leader—Napoleon, Hitler, Mussolini, or Stalin—was the coming "World Dictator." The only possible answer had to be Uncle Joe—the only one still alive and in power.[14]

During the Cold War, evangelicals taught all Christians to read the Bible to understand the future. Doom and gloom theology even became a prominent theme in the work of some liberal Protestants. Harris Franklin Roll, an influential critic of fundamentalism in the late 1910s, acknowledged in the *Christian Century* that "the First World War brought a marked revival of belief in the imminent second coming of Christ" (which he had vehemently denounced at the time) but World War II produced "a new apocalypticism." Indeed, in the late 1940s postmillennial optimism yielded to a revised expression of liberal Protestantism that was dubbed neoorthodoxy. It grew out of the work of Karl Barth, Reinhold Niebuhr, and Paul Tillich and came to animate central tenets of midcentury political liberalism. As Americans tried to make sense of the wartime carnage and the Cold War arms race, human depravity and original sin became topics of regular conversation not just among evangelicals but also among the nation's leading liberal theologians. Evangelicals accurately sensed that American culture had taken a dark turn. Popular music, movies, literature, and the arts all testified to the fact that in the post-Holocaust, post-Hiroshima world their fellow citizens had embraced apocalypticism in new and profound ways. The whole world now truly understood that the end was near.[15]

While the evolving place of Russia in biblical prophecy has continued to provoke evangelical prophetic speculation, the faithful broadened their focus in new ways in the 1970s. The Middle East—rife with tension, conflict, and turmoil—was rapidly beginning to occupy the center of evangelicals' attention. In the disco decade, no one tapped more into evangelicals' fascination with anticipating the future than the heavily mustachioed Hal Lindsey. In 1970, he published the best-selling *Late Great Planet Earth*, which represented in part a rehashing of the many prophecies that had long mesmerized other premillennialists. The global influence of the USSR and China served as important markers of the times, as did the increasing power of Arab nations and the creation of the European Common Market. More than anything else, however, Israel took center stage in Lindsey's analysis. He believed that as the world moved toward the battle of Armageddon, three events would occur. "First," he wrote, "the Jewish nation would be reborn in the land of Palestine. Second, the Jews would repossess old Jerusalem and the sacred sites. Third, they would rebuild their ancient temple of worship upon its historical site." The first of these steps was accomplished in 1948 with the creation of the state of Israel. The second occurred in 1967 when Israel captured

Jerusalem during the Six-Day War. The final event Lindsey predicted was the reconstruction of the Jewish temple. Many premillennialists believed that the Jewish temple would rise again on the land currently occupied by the Dome of the Rock, a major Muslim holy site.[16]

Over the next few years, eager premillennialists followed Lindsey's lead. They kept readers up-to-date with analyses of the unremitting global turmoil and chaos that defined the period. In 1972, San Diego minister Tim LaHaye laid out an argument for an imminent second coming. "I believe the Bible teaches that we are already living in the beginning of the end," he wrote in his aptly titled book *The Beginning of the End*. "See if you agree." The minister cited wars, rumors of war, global travel, increased knowledge, growing labor-capital conflicts, same-sex relations, Israel's statehood, and the creation of the UN to support his thesis. But he also included some more original signs that reflected the concerns of the seventies, such as the relatively new phenomenon of Satanism and the rise of "scoffers" who denied young Earth creationism. "If you think the above teachings indicate that time is short," he concluded, "you are right."[17]

Two years later, John F. Walvoord published *Armageddon, Oil and the Middle East Crisis*, which marked a new phase in end-times prognostication. Walvoord, a Dallas Theological Seminary president who had long blended analysis of biblical predictions with world events, tackled the swiftly evolving geopolitics of the era. He allocated far more attention to the place of Arab and Persian nations in prophecy than any of his predecessors, demonstrating how the Middle East, like Mussolini in the 1930s and Stalin during the early Cold War, was now driving evangelicals' prophetic speculation. His work illustrated how dramatically evangelicals' expectations were evolving in conjunction with the times. Living amid the rise of OPEC, a severe energy crisis, and long gas station lines, Walvoord thought he knew where global events were headed. He predicted that Arab and European nations would soon establish an Antichrist-led cartel that would regulate the rise and fall of national currencies, control world trade, manage the world's energy reserves, and "eclipse the power of both Russia and the United States."[18]

In making this argument, Walvoord answered a question that had long troubled premillennialists. The faithful knew that in the last days four great confederacies would descend on the Middle East to wage the battle of Armageddon, but they had never understood how or why this would happen. The growing significance of and conflict over Middle East oil finally helped them see how the final conflict could unfold. "The prophetic significance of this rise in power in the Middle East is tremendous," Walvoord concluded, "and from a biblical standpoint it is the most dramatic evidence that the world scene is shaping up for Armageddon."[19]

The success of books by Lindsey, LaHaye, and Walvoord and hundreds of other similar books, tracts, and sermons demonstrated how in the 1970s innovative evangelicals spread the classic apocalyptic message through multiple platforms. Their work resonated with a new generation of young Christians who straddled the divide between the increasingly mainstream and button-downed evangelicalism of their parents and the

youth revolution under way at the time. For these baby boomers, faith in the imminent return of Christ inspired hope in a world that seemed more than ever to be
careening toward Armageddon. This faith also provided adherents with secret knowledge and insight into the past, the present, and the time to come. Despite the chaos
surrounding them, their faith guaranteed them a secure and glorious future. Their
faith also moved them to action. After all, Jesus would soon come back in judgment.

Although premillennial apocalypticism has ebbed and flowed for the last 150 years,
it has succumbed neither to the Antichrist nor to competing theologies. Like a phoenix
from the ashes, premillennialism reappears whenever tragedy strikes. No event illustrates this better than 9/11. As Americans struggled to make sense of the horrific tragedy, some elite evangelical leaders preached caution. *Christianity Today*'s editors, for
example, made few explicit links between the attacks and doomsday beliefs. "I try to
avoid end-times prophecy," Watergate felon and popular Christian leader Chuck
Colson wrote in his post-9/11 regular *Christianity Today* column, "that makes Christians
appear irrelevant to the world."[20]

But his was not the only response to the tragedy. Chuck Smith, leader of the highly
successful Calvary Chapel movement, warned his parishioners that they had better
repent before time ran out. Bishop G. E. Patterson of the Church of God in Christ
admonished his flock that this "could very well be the beginning of the countdown that
will lead to the final world conflict." John Hagee, a Texas minister who in recent years
has authored numerous best-selling apocalyptic screeds, interpreted the terror attacks
as the opening of World War III and the beginning of the end. In the days immediately
following the attack, laypeople turned to books in search of answers, emptying stores
of their stock of evangelical prophecy manuals and apocalyptic novels. A few weeks
later Americans made the new *Left Behind* novel *Desecration: Antichrist Takes the
Throne*, which hit store shelves that October, the best-selling hardcover novel of the
year.[21]

Evangelical apocalypticism once again gave Americans a language with which to
make sense of the tragedy. George W. Bush's rhetoric of an axis of evil, his black and
white, good and bad, you are for-us-or-against-us ultimatums, and his vision for transforming the Middle East reflected the ideals of modern evangelicalism. Bush may have
even invoked Ezekiel's prophecy to French President Jacques Chirac to justify the invasion of Iraq. "Gog and Magog are at work in the Middle East," the American president
apparently explained. "Biblical prophecies are being fulfilled." "This confrontation," he
continued, "is willed by God, who wants to use this conflict to erase his people's enemies before a new age begins." Bush was probably not making decisions on the basis of
premillennial convictions. Nevertheless, he well understood that the neoconservative
ideals that shaped his foreign policy meshed almost perfectly with the ideas of evangelical apocalypticism.[22]

The 9/11 tragedies, the opening of the "war on terror," and the commencement of
military action in Iraq sparked a new series of premillennial books. Hagee rushed into
print *Attack on America: New York, Jerusalem, and the Role of Terrorism in the Last Days*
(2001), which interpreted 9/11 as a sign that Armageddon was just around the corner.

Hal Lindsey responded to 9/11 with a *The Everlasting Hatred: The Roots of Jihad* (2002), a distorted, fear-mongering recap of the history of Islam and Islam's relationship with Jews. John Walvoord's publisher also looked to cash in on the renewed interest in prophecy with an updated edition of the deceased Dallas theologian's classic text, retitled *Armageddon, Oil, and Terror: What the Bible Says about the Future of America, the Middle East, and the End of Western Civilization* (2007). Meanwhile, LaHaye and Jenkins continued to dominate best-seller lists with new *Left Behind* books, while all around the country, various ministers broadcast their own low-budget local and regional prophecy shows. Others still made the most of the internet, including the founders of the popular website raptureready.com, which tracks how close we are to Armageddon (we're really close).[23]

Although historians, sociologists, and journalists continue to debate the future of American evangelicalism just as vigorously as American evangelicals debate what the Bible says about the future, recent surveys have reaffirmed the success and influence of evangelicals' efforts to spread their faith. Millions of Americans now believe that the time is nigh. A 2006 Pew poll revealed that 79 percent of U.S. Christians believed in the second coming; and 20 percent expected it to happen in their lifetime. A 2010 Pew poll revealed that 41 percent of all Americans (well over 100 million people) and 58 percent of white evangelicals believed that Jesus is "definitely" or "probably" going to return by 2050. These polls were further confirmed in chapter 1. While the vast majority of those people polled and surveyed probably have little to no understanding of the complex theology undergirding their opinions, their faith in an apocalyptic second coming reveals how thoroughly evangelical premillennialism has saturated American culture over the last 150 years. Evangelicals' conviction that Jesus is coming has become such a standard part of evangelical rhetoric that few ever question it. The belief that the time is short and that God is going to hold his people accountable for their work has driven generations of believers to reclaim the seemingly secular American culture. The urgency, the absolute morals, the passion to right the world's wrongs, and the refusal to compromise, negotiate, or mediate now defines much of American evangelicalism and a significant part of right-wing politics. We now live in a world shaped by evangelicals' apocalyptic hopes, dreams, and nightmares.[24]

10

Reference Bibles and Interpretive Authority

B. M. Pietsch

PRISONERS IN THE Los Angeles county jail in January 1915 witnessed a unique case of biblical education. Twenty-one-year-old chronic kleptomaniac Harold Lane had been found guilty of stealing a stack of Bibles. The judge overseeing Lane's case offered him a choice: serve seven years in San Quentin, or spend thirty days in the county jail and read the Bible from cover to cover. Seizing on the latter option, Lane told reporters: "I have always wanted to read the Bible...but it has always seemed that I never have had the time." Despite Lane's fortuitous prison sentence that helped facilitate his lifelong desire, the scene in the county jail was described as one of mildly comic anxiety. Lane was scheduled to appear before Judge Wilbur after thirty days to have his biblical knowledge tested, but he struggled with the text. A newspaper account portrayed him reading scrupulously from dawn until lights-out, and said: "Other prisoners heard him murmuring: 'The Kenite and the Kenizzite, and the Kadmonite. And the Hittite, and the Perizzite, and the Rephaim. And the Amorite, and the Canaanite, and the Girgashite, and the Jebusite.'" Still working on the book of Genesis and overwhelmed with the unfamiliar world it described, Lane worried to the reporter: "I only hope that Judge Wilbur will not expect me to remember all of the names I have read in it."[1]

Lane's sentence and his anxiety highlight a key tension animating Americans' uses of the Bible. On one side stood Judge Wilbur's belief in popular perspicuity and the efficacy of personal Bible reading. This view held that an ordinary person—like Lane—could understand and profit from individual reading of the whole Bible. Lane's sentence suggested that a single, private experience of the Bible could be as effective in reforming morals and shaping character as seven years of penitential labor. Belief in popular perspicuity rested on a patchwork of assumptions—from sources as diverse as Reformation rhetoric of "the Bible alone," Common Sense epistemology, republican and revivalist ideas of religious authority, and frontier self-reliance—and dominated public conversations about the Bible.

Yet Lane's actual encounter with the Bible revealed the dissonance between this view and reality. Struggling his way through Genesis, Lane remarked: "I have been told that for nineteen hundred years wise men have been pondering over the Bible's wisdom, so naturally I cannot be expected to understand all I have read."[2] His perplexity mirrored that of his times. Pulpits, lecterns, newspapers, and street corners were filled with strident debates over the Bible's teaching on geology, or women, or entertainments, or modern life. The increasingly divisive uses of the Bible proved alienating to common readers. As responsibility for knowledge production moved increasingly into the hands of experts in the twentieth century, this difficulty was only exacerbated. If "wise men" throughout the ages could not fully agree on the meaning of the Bible, what hope had an average person like Lane?

On the same day that his story appeared in the *Los Angeles Examiner*, Lane sent a letter from prison to California oilman, philanthropist, and fundamentalist patron Lyman Stewart. By 1915, Stewart had built a philanthropic empire, supporting Bible colleges and foreign missions and, most famously, funding the publication of the *Fundamentals*. Lane wrote: "Dear Mr. Stewart: As I have been sentenced to spend 30 days in the County Jail and to read the Bible cover to cover, and as the Bible I now have is of a very fine print and the light rather dim I would like to ask you to loan me a *Scofield Reference Bible* which I will return as soon as my time is up. Altho I am in here for stealing Bibles I assure you most sincerely that I will return yours."[3]

Speculating about Lane's possible motives for the request suggests a number of different ways that reference Bibles were found valuable in the twentieth century. Perhaps it was as simple as Lane claimed: he needed a book with larger type. Perhaps he knew that Lyman Stewart was a dispensationalist and hoped to improve his chances for success by requesting a Bible that had become a symbol of dispensational identity. (Just two years earlier, in 1913, the school Stewart founded—the Bible Institute of Los Angeles, or Biola—had started construction on a new downtown building, and Stewart had a *Scofield Reference Bible* placed in a time capsule in the cornerstone of the building.) Perhaps, as a practiced, if not entirely successful, Bible thief, Lane wanted to get his hands on an expensive edition of the Bible. Or perhaps, frustrated by his attempts to make sense of the Bible on his own (and worried about his fate if he did not), he was seeking help from the system of reference notes found in Scofield's "self-interpreting" Bible.

Annotated Bibles like the *Scofield Reference Bible* had helped guide the hapless in making sense of "the Bible alone" for centuries, offering an ingenious compromise to solve the problems of popular interpretive authority. Lacking durable commitments to historical traditions, often without strong clergy or church structures, and believing the Bible ought to be sufficient on its own, many Protestants were forced to seek other means for gaining assurance that their biblical interpretations were coherent and warranted.

Biblical annotations—helps provided on the pages of the Bible itself—neatly met this challenge. It is unsurprising, then, that the text of Christian scriptures frequently appeared on the page with marginal company. Among the early English translations of the Bible, commentary was the rule rather than the exception, as clergy mistrusted what would happen if the masses tried to interpret the Bible without guidance. For example, the 1560 Geneva Bible included 300,000 words of theological commentary in its margins, making up roughly 30 percent of the printed text.[4]

Alongside this tradition of marginal annotation stood a competing tradition of textual purity. The sixteenth-century translator and Protestant reformer William Tyndale opposed annotation, believing it promoted the power of the church hierarchy by bolstering its interpretive authority. In 1611 the Authorized Version, or King James Version, of the Bible was published without any interpretive commentary. King James felt the heavily annotated Geneva Bible included "some notes very partiall, vntrue, seditious, and sauouring too much of daungerous, and trayterous conceites."[5] His concerns were the mirrored opposite of Tyndale's, and he demanded that no marginal notes be included.

These two trajectories in Bible publishing—for guided interpretation and for the undiluted Word—have remained in tension to the present. Given the status of the Bible in American life, the stakes have been high. By baptizing a single interpretation from amid the "surplus of meaning characteristic of literary works," as philosopher Paul Ricoeur described it, annotation has played a key role in adjudicating theological disputes.[6] Literature professor Evelyn Tribble described the resulting tensions as "the bitter struggle for possession of the Bible, which is framed by competing and contested understandings of authority."[7] Over the centuries, struggles over the right to interpret the Bible pitted professional clergy against lay readers, scholars against uneducated believers, and theologian against theologian. Repeatedly these struggles played out on the very pages of the Bible itself.

These competing impulses—toward annotation or textual purity—immigrated to North America along with the first efforts at Bible publishing and distribution. In 1778, the Scottish minister John Brown published his *Self-Interpreting Bible*, which included marginal notes alongside the text of the Authorized Version, offering "Paraphrases On The Most Obscure Or Important Parts" and "Evangelical Reflections."[8] Dozens of editions of John Brown's Bible were reprinted in North America by the end of the nineteenth century. Focusing on the Bible's resources for interpreting itself and downplaying his annotations, Brown's edition claimed to help lay readers interpret scripture for themselves. This populist appeal played well for nineteenth-century American audiences committed to the premise that every reader was capable of understanding the Bible alone, without clerical guidance.

In mid-nineteenth-century North America, unannotated Bibles, particularly those from the American Bible Society, dominated the religious marketplace. Formed in 1816, the American Bible Society aimed to make the Bible available to every person. Building on populist faith in the efficacy of simple Bible reading, they committed to publishing all Bibles "without note or comment." This decision was partly pragmatic.

The competing denominations that supported the American Bible Society would have been unlikely to agree on any single set of annotations. However, it also encoded assumptions about the clarity and perspicuity of the Bible. Readers were expected to be able to approach the text without guidance from either church tradition or textual commentary and still discover a common set of eternal truths.

Both annotated and unannotated Bibles fought for readers steeped in Common Sense realism. The dominant epistemology for many nineteenth-century Americans, Common Sense philosophy posited that the human mind was designed to understand the natural world accurately through sense perceptions. Many mid-nineteenth-century evangelicals relied on a Common Sense hermeneutic to describe how they found meaning in their Bibles. Believers assumed that the message of the Bible was clear, reasonable, and available to all. Combined with prevailing republican sentiments in the United States, this philosophical position metamorphosed into a stark theological conclusion: that each reader was warranted in drawing theological conclusions and discerning moral truths from individualized readings of the Bible.

By the end of the Civil War, Common Sense realism could not hold back the floodwaters of change. The devastating effects of the war in the United States undermined both popular and elite confidence in Common Sense, as the consequences of Americans' confidence in their interpretations of the Bible—particularly regarding slavery—filled the graveyards of North and South. Questions of authority prevailed: on what basis could readers have confidence in their readings? In both philosophical and everyday ways, Common Sense no longer offered sufficient warrants for confident beliefs.[9]

The failure of Common Sense reasoning to adjudicate theological debates was accompanied by widespread changes in American Protestant life between 1880 and 1920. Despite significant diversity, many mid-nineteenth-century Americans saw themselves as part of a broader "biblical civilization." As the historian Grant Wacker argued, "a broadly evangelical Protestant consensus powerfully gripped mainstream culture... [and] this homogeneity was very much a product of common assumptions about what the Bible is and teaches."[10] It was not to last. Whether real or imagined, by 1920 the sense of belonging to a common biblically based culture was a contentious claim rather than a common assumption. Immigration and urbanization, the rise of consumer culture and secularisms, and the emergence of biblical higher criticism all contributed to the shifting picture. Just as important were the fractures between disparate visions of what it meant to be a "biblical civilization."

Disenchantment took many forms. The Bible contained resources for many visions of the Good, and all of them were prone to crisis and disappointment. Americans struggled to reconcile inherited or innovative biblical interpretations with the flawed world they found themselves in, particularly when the Bible itself seemed the source of the flaws. For some, the stumbling block was slavery and war, for others it was education, or miracles, or the status of women, or the problems of race and poverty, or public morality, or an expanding state, or an increasing sense that all suffering was essentially evil. Many felt the world made by a biblical civilization was decidedly unbiblical. Others believed it was biblical but that the Bible encoded a primitive or oppressive worldview. This diversity of interpretations of the Good proved problematic for everyone. If one group's understanding of the Bible was the source of suffering for their neighbors, how could consensus, or justice, be found?

A brief example will help illustrate. The period from 1880 to 1920 saw fierce battles about the Bible's teachings on women. Some, such as abolitionist and suffragist Sarah Grimké, felt the Bible had played a crushing role in subjugating women and sustaining patriarchy. Disillusioned by the civilization created by Bible-wielding Americans, Grimké argued that "the blasphemies, the monstrosities, the irrationalities of the Bible must be brought face to face with science, reason and common sense."[11] Others, such as suffragist Frances Willard, saw the problem as one of interpretation and believed that although the Bible had been used to oppress women, it could also be a resource for creating a better world. Willard, longtime president of the Women's Christian Temperance Union, wrote: "The whole subjection theory grows out of the one-sided interpretation of the Bible by men." By debunking these outdated interpretations and substituting better ones, advocates for gender equality could use evangelical Protestantism and public reverence for the Bible to forward their campaigns and achieve justice. But in both debunking and reinterpreting, the common reader, guided by Common Sense and tradition, was at a disadvantage. Willard noted: "the plain wayfaring woman cannot help concluding that exegesis, thus conducted, is one of the most time-serving and man-made of all sciences, and one of the most misleading of all arts. It has broken Christendom into sects that confuse and astound." New guidance was needed to break away from unjust or one-sided readings of the Bible. "We need women commentators," Willard wrote, "to bring out the women's side of the book; we need the stereoscopic view of truth in general, which can only be had when woman's eye and man's together shall discern the perspective of the Bible's full-orbed revelation." Willard hoped that women commentators, alongside "the modern impulse toward 'real facts,'" would lead to new, just, and harmonious teachings about the shape that a biblical civilization should take.[12] But this desire was shared just as ardently by proponents of competing and contradictory visions. Consensus did not result. And as the greatest threat to the trustworthiness of the Bible was the presence of so many Christians harming other Christians in the service of their biblical interpretations, the Bible itself seemed endangered.

Changing conceptions about the nature of books only heightened these moral questions. Just what kind of a book was the Bible anyway? A philosophical or ethical treatise? A recipe book for a good life, or an instruction manual for getting into heaven? A fictional moral tale, like a novel? History, either objectively true in every detail or a product of its time and thus prone to errors and mistakes? By the twentieth century, the dramatic increase in book publication complicated the question. More and more Americans felt that knowledge came from reading, yet this was paired with a more sophisticated understanding of how different kinds of knowledge came from different kinds of texts. A novel might offer a stunning evocation of a beautiful garden, but reliable advice about when to plant petunias came from works like *The Art and Practice of Landscape Gardening* or *Gardener's Magazine*. In the atmosphere of the Progressive Era,

Americans became accustomed to discovering useful truths about the world in clear, didactic prose backed by scientific authorities. For example, parents might nod sagely at the biblical proverb "train up a child in the way he should go," but when pressed to make practical decisions they could turn to a plethora of more modern texts that offered more clear and pragmatic advice about every conceivable situation. Worried about rickets, for example, parents found Proverbs less useful than the pamphlets distributed by the U.S. Children's Bureau that prescribed sunlight for babies and instructed: "In the North Temperate Zone it is usually possible for normal babies to begin to have outdoor sun baths by the middle of March or the first of April, provided that the place selected for the sun bath is protected from the wind."[13] The tone, comprehensiveness, and comprehensibility of this newer type of prescriptive literature made the Bible—with its hermeneutic disagreements, its ancient place names and obscure events, and its extraordinary miracles—seem even less intelligible to common readers in their search for the Good.

Given this, why persist in the rhetoric of the Bible alone? Why did Americans such as Judge Wilbur assume that unguided reading produced reliable and useful effects? Again, there was not one reason but many, including the power of tradition, and personal experiences. The denominational structure of American Protestantism provided few alternatives. Rampant anti-Catholicism and nativism used "the Bible alone" as a symbol of Protestant (or American) identity. Minorities who saw the Bible as a potential source of liberation were often invested in preserving its status. Perhaps most important, the rhetoric of "the Bible alone" made possible coalitions of Protestants with differing aims and methods. As historian Adam Laats argued, nearly all Protestants in the early twentieth century supported Bible reading in public schools. Their reasons for doing so differed dramatically. For some, the Bible was a "supernatural tool to save souls."[14] For others, it would indoctrinate children with proper morality and patriotism. Yet others saw the Bible as an instrument for social cohesion, or for inoculating children against the dangers of atheism (or liberalism), or for an understanding of literature and history. If most Protestants thought plain Bible reading for children was efficacious, they did not agree on why, or how, or what causal mechanism was involved.

For those committed to ideas of popular perspicuity, the task was to preserve popular faith in the authority and efficacy of plain Bible reading, while simultaneously giving readers guidance in dealing with the complexities of the text, so as to reduce the diversity of interpretations. One strategy was to preserve the Reformation rhetoric of "the Bible alone" even while religious practices quietly relocated epistemological foundations to higher ground. Annotated Bibles made possible subtle shifts in Bible reading practices. To be sure, the language of popular perspicuity and Common Sense persisted among evangelicals well into the twenty-first century. In a 2013 survey, nearly 80 percent of Americans disagreed with the claim that understanding the Bible correctly required years of theological study, and the 2014 study analyzed in chapter 1 of this book found that less than half of Bible readers claimed to seek any help in interpreting the Bible.[15] Yet changes in the consumption of annotated Bibles and in practices of Bible reading told another story. Hermeneutical authority shifted from the individual empirical mind to the methodological annotations accompanying Bibles and the religious authorities that produced them. In the 1820s, 27 percent of English Bible editions published in the United States included some kind of commentary. By the 1870s, however, that number had jumped to 60 percent, as more and more Americans sought guidance for understanding their Bibles, and by the end of the twentieth century hundreds of different annotated editions and "boutique" Bibles had been published.[16]

The *Scofield Reference Bible* offers a clear example of how this worked. Edited by dispensationalist leader Cyrus Ingerson Scofield and first published in 1909, it sold more than 10 million copies during the next century, ranking it as (probably) the best-selling reference Bible in America. Scholars have most commonly viewed it as a symbol of premillennial theology. Yet advocates more often emphasized its scholarly credentials. With an influential and well-connected editor, a host of credentialed consultants, and Oxford's name on the patent leather spine, the *Scofield Reference Bible* oozed with intellectual authority. Expertise, performed through the professionalized tools of footnotes, citations, and credentials, conveyed authority and confidence.

There were many competing editions of the Bible with comparable credentials. The particular genius of the *Scofield Reference Bible* lay in its ability to navigate the tensions between technical specialization and expertise on the one hand and beliefs about popular perspicuity on the other. Scofield's notes were marketed *not* as theological commentary—which took interpretive power away from readers—but as methodological guidance. The goal was to turn readers into experts. Scofield's initial plans acknowledged this goal of populist hermeneutical empowerment. "The thought," he wrote, "is to prepare an edition of God's Holy Word so clearly and simply divided and arranged that any believer of ordinary intelligence may read the Bible understandingly. People are not interested in the Bible because they do not understand it when they read it."[17] Scofield's ambition was to make true again "the conviction...that the Bible is a self-interpreting Book."[18] Through typological cross-references and taxonomic annotations, this Bible provided readers with interpretive practices that promised the authority of expert interpretations to *any* reader. In doing so, it helped redefine the meaning of "the Bible alone" and played a major role in fortifying popular rhetoric about the Bible's authority and perspicuity in everyday life.

The *Scofield Reference Bible*'s largest appeal came not from its dispensational theology but from its demonstration of how individual readers could employ complex textual methods to derive (mostly) mainstream theology from difficult biblical texts. Sales numbers suggest that for millions of readers it offered a compelling solution to these problems of populist interpretive authority. This is not to say that reference Bibles did not simultaneously develop strong sectarian associations for subsets of the population. Many became intimately associated with particular brands of Protestant piety, or brands in themselves. In 1923, W. P. King, pastor of First Methodist Church, Gainesville, Georgia, wrote an article for the *Atlanta Constitution* highly critical of fundamentalism, lamenting: "The standard text-book of Fundamentalism is: 'The Scofield Bible.' There are many undiscerning Christians who accept the notes and comments as if they were part of the sacred text."[19] Although King evinced a low opinion of the interpretive savvy of Scofield's readers, just as many saw the Scofield Bible's association with fundamentalism as a virtue. Charles Ryrie, a second-generation dispensational leader, recounted how a childhood minister "saw to it that all the pew racks contained *Scofield Bibles*."[20] Offering "old time religion," or "the best of modern scholarship," or some other branded evangelical identity, many reference Bibles became commodities that allowed believers to purchase for themselves a share of the respectability and trustworthiness of specific Christian movements.

For the majority, however, reference Bibles appealed not simply because they offered sectarian credentials, but because they promised to unlock universal, or at least common, meanings from the text. "Serious" laypersons, without access to theological educations and amid the fractured remains of a "biblical civilization," turned to reference Bibles to reconcile belief in both the usefulness of individual Bible readings and the necessity for expert guidance. Like Judge Wilbur, they expressed faith in the popular perspicuity and efficacy of the Bible alone. Like Harold Lane, they chose, in their own versions of the Bible, to avail themselves of the authority, annotations, and aspirations of expert guidance. For these believers, reference Bibles represented the individuation of functions that religious communities used to perform. From interpreting the Bible to claiming religious identities to bestowing authority—a whole array of forms of religious meaning-making became reimagined as part of individual religious experience. Reference Bibles both signaled this shift and accelerated it, as they served as the plain Word and as reliable, modern, scholarly texts.

One last story will help illustrate how reference Bibles helped Americans navigate the tensions between popular Bible reading and specialized interpretive authority. Cameron Townsend founded the Protestant missions organizations Wycliffe Bible Translators and the Summer Institute of Linguistics, and was an untiring translator of the Bible. While on a trip to Central America, someone asked Townsend about his qualifications for Bible translation. "Well," he replied, "I didn't finish college and never went to Bible school. Maybe I'll finish my education sometime. But here [in Guatemala] I seldom see a book on theology or church history. I spend my devotional time studying the Bible and Scofield's notes."[21] For many American Protestants, this answer would prove sufficient. The *Scofield Reference Bible*—with its condensed expert interpretations and taxonomic divisions—offered methodological proficiency and theological confidence to anyone who cared to study "the Bible alone."

ACKNOWLEDGMENTS

Portions of this chapter were previously published in chapter 7 of *Dispensational Modernism* (New York: Oxford University Press, 2015) and have been reproduced by permission of Oxford University Press.

11

The Soul's Train

THE BIBLE AND SOUTHERN FOLK AND POPULAR MUSIC

Paul Harvey

ROBERT JOHNSON WONDERED what happen if he "Had Possession, Over Judgment Day," while Charley Patton, singing under the moniker Elder J. J. Hadley, reproduced familiar lyrics about meeting you on a distant shore in a chilling two-part version of "Prayer of Death"; Sister Rosetta Tharpe practically invented rock-and-roll guitar while updating the Pentecostal favorite "Jesus on the Mainline"; Barry McGuire foresaw an "Eve of Destruction" in the 1960s, while Bob Dylan wove in and wove out of biblical and religious references that kept a generation of interpreters busy; Robbie Robertson and the Band "pulled into Nazareth" only to find no place "where I can lay my head," and reinvented Bob Dylan's "I Shall Be Released" with country gospel harmonies; Sam Cooke came up through a Holiness background in Mississippi and cut memorable sides as a member of a gospel quartet before bursting onto the pop scene and eventually writing the civil-rights-era classic "Change Is Gonna Come"; more recently, artists, styling themselves "No Depression" or "Americana" songsters, have resurrected and reinvented southern-derived traditions of music about darkness, misery, mystery, and transcendence, with bags full of biblical tricks. Johnny Cash's long career, from classics such as "Ring of Fire" to the Folsom County Prison live recordings and to his rediscovery by hipsters in the 1990s and last "American Recordings," suggests how, in so much American music, the southern has become archetypical. And once it had become the archetypical, a stand-in for the authentic, it entered a world rife with imagery and metaphor from a southern biblical worldview.

For much of the twentieth century, if southern churches slumbered in "cultural captivity," southern culture held the nation captive, as people responded to the elemental force of its blues, country, and gospel music, its evocation of the most fundamental emotions of human life, and its literary grapplings with the most profound questions of race and American history. The literature, poetry, music, and other cultural products of those grapplings drew from many sources, of course, but always were deeply imbibed in biblical history and lore. That was true not just of the gospel tradition, but of the bawdier tunes and the blues.

This essay briefly explores how the most violent and inequitable region of the country produced forms of religious music that transformed popular culture internationally. And it will explore how the Bible was translated in American folk and popular music emanating from the American South, from the spirituals to soul and, more recently, "Americana" and the kind of contemporary southern reflections represented in Glory Fires or in modern forms of southern gospel (roughly, the 1830s to the early twenty-first century). Other scholars have studied hymns and diverse kinds of institutionally sanctioned religious music; here I will focus on how biblical themes, modes, motifs, imagery, and philosophy colored popular music, from the spirituals and the blues to country, gospel, and soul, and how those folk and popular forms in turn shaped how Americans changed their understanding of biblical characters over time.

The biblically literalist culture of the American South both inspired and ultimately was overcome by the spectacularly imaginative readings given to biblical passages by southern musicians, from the collectively anonymous authors of spirituals to the carefully rendered character sketches, ribald parodies, or angry manifestoes of contemporary artists ranging from Valerie June to the Glory Fires to the Drive By Truckers. In other words, precisely by taking the Bible as a literal and historical document seriously, southern musicians extrapolated tales that wove their way into deeply American histories of struggle, injustice, triumph, backsliding, and visionary experiences.

More than anyplace else, in music the religious South deeply imprinted and shaped American life. In black spirituals, Americans learned of the deep theology and culture of the nation's most despised and oppressed people. Through black and white variants of gospel music and in the rhythmic intensity that black and white Pentecostals carried forward through the twentieth century, Americans recaptured a deep soulfulness and spiritual dance and listened avidly to thinly veiled secularized versions of those forms in the popular music of the post–World War II era. In the 1960s, as spirituals morphed into freedom songs and religiously based groups such as the Staples Singers envisioned a new hope, biblical imagery empowered movements for social change. Interestingly, in more contemporary forms of Americana, musical artists have returned to the kinds of biblical sketches of the folk musicians of decades ago, usually for the purpose of sketching out stories of mystery, irony, and tragedy. In all these cases, the Bible has proven productive of stories and meanings that stretch far beyond the kinds of renderings given to biblical texts among strict Bible believers in the region. Biblical tales, told and retold and spun into new forms, have inspired creative sound art for those who insisted that they needed nothing but the Bible but clearly needed something more as well.

It's the intense contrast and juxtaposition of a biblically literalist culture and wildly imaginative musical production that is the focus here. I would suggest that it's precisely in that juxtaposition that our answer may be found to how the South produced such a disproportionate share of the culture that we associate as the most deeply American, and has without question been of the most influence in the musical sounds that surround us. It's the tension produced by the text-bound theology and the demands of artistic production; by the stories of justice and the manifest injustice all around; and by the fact that a biblically fundamentalist culture could not contain its own text, for in cultural production that played with the text, the extravagant imagery, metaphor, language, and poetry of the Bible inevitably took center stage.

And there's another set of almost unbearably painful tensions and paradoxes that come into play here as well: the poverty, racism, and violence so endemic in southern history put in contrast to the millennial dreams and aspirations that can be (and in southern history often were) drawn from biblical texts. In the civil rights era, figures such as Martin Luther King were the masters at exploiting that very tension. Scholars have explored this in literature, especially through the figure of Faulkner; here I want to add to that the cultural production of popular music, and explore what it was about southern religious culture's use of the Bible that underlay so much of the creative revolutions in popular sound from the nineteenth century to the present—from the fires of glory in the spirituals to the Glory Fires of contemporary Birmingham.

NINETEENTH-CENTURY BACKGROUND

Southern Protestantism was not exactly a promising place to look for the origins of contemporary American popular music, or for inventive adaptations of biblically inspired lyrics. For much of the nineteenth century, for example, white southerners only grudgingly accepted aesthetic cultivation in worship practice. Qualms on the theology of performance troubled believers who were talented in music but scorned "mere display" as sinful. "Harmony is voluptuous," a nineteenth-century Virginian pondered in his diary. "It requires no pious emotions for a man to love harmony. In fact, by singing base and suffering my mind to be distracted from the words, by the 'lascivious pleasing' of chords, I am often unfitted for the other exercises of the Sanctuary." He felt that "mere accompaniments" should have no place in sacred music.[1]

Over time, Southern evangelicals who had been suspicious of vocal display thus gradually accepted stylistically refined music as spiritually acceptable, even uplifting. By the mid–nineteenth century, congregations were moving away from a capella hymns lined out by individuals to congregational singing accompanied by pianos and organs. Denominationalists initiated training programs in schools, encouraged the use of professional music ministers in wealthier churches, and promoted revivals with professionally skilled song leaders.[2]

In the mid-nineteenth century, educational entrepreneurs established singing schools to provide a rudimentary musical education for plain-folk southerners. Educators generally used a simplified form of notation known as shape notes, a system of representing sounds on the page based on four shapes. Each stood for a note on a scale that retained fixed intervals, obviating the need to learn different key signatures. Musical educators sprang up throughout the region, and the most successful eventually formed publishing companies. Lawrence Vaughan in Tennessee and the Stampps-Baxter company in Texas became dominant forces in religious music publishing and spread the kinds of songs that later generations of popular singers would grow up singing. In the 1930s they were joined by Albert E. Brumley, author of the classics "I'll Fly Away" and "Turn Your Radio On."

Meanwhile, African-American song styles dating from slavery fascinated but also repelled listeners. They fascinated listeners with their "strange," "weird," "primitive" melodic and rhythmic structures, but they dismayed many black church leaders who wanted to lead their congregations to a better day—to sing more "scientifically and correctly," as one denominational leader put it. Part of the politics of respectability dating from the late nineteenth century was to displace African-American styles of church music and assimilate them into a broad Protestant mainstream. But it was precisely those musical forms deemed primitive and beyond the pale of respectability that powered the revolutions of popular music in the twentieth century, in terms of both music and lyrics.

THE RECORDING REVOLUTION OF THE TWENTIETH CENTURY

In the 1920s and 1930s, the birth of the recording music industry brought a new sort of musical education to ordinary southern folk who purchased records put out by Columbia, Okeh, and the Paramount Record Company, which somehow persuaded numerous early black performers to come record at a recording studio hooked into a chair factory near Grafton, Wisconsin. Meanwhile, the Bristol, Virginia, sessions of 1927 and the voluminous early Carter family recordings intermingled the sacred and the secular for white southern audiences. The recording industry grew up alongside, and made possible, revolutions in popular music. These were recordings meant for segregated audiences, but they often and easily found their way to unintended audiences, both through record sales and through the radio.

Among African Americans, preachers and bluesmen offered two seemingly contradictory, but ultimately complementary, versions of black spirituality. Each drew from biblical texts and extended them into artistically compelling renderings, whether it was the powerful rendering of "High Water Everywhere" by Charley Patton or the Mississippi native Reverend C. L. Franklin's recorded sermons on "The Eagle Stirreth Her Nest" or Blind Willie Johnson's stories of John the Revelator. Preachers found in biblical texts stories about overcoming and endurance, while the country blues took from characters both biblical and contemporary a collective wisdom that spoke truth to power but also reinforced social enmities between powerless people.

White southern folk and country music, too, handed down exquisitely painful sagas about the supernatural forces that shaped everyday lives, sometimes inexplicably, and often for the worse. For every "May the Circle Be Unbroken" that expressed evangelical aspirations to heaven, there were songs about the mysterious cuckoo bird warbling, bad luck befalling innocent souls, gambling debts piling up, ghosts and apparitions haunting communities at night, crimes of passion and rage tearing communities apart, and death stalking humans on the brink. And tunes from the shape-note hymnals such as *Southern Harmony*, older folk ballads such as "Poor Wayfaring Stranger" and more recent variations on it such as "Rank Strangers," reinforced that this was a "world of woe," in which "everyone I met / seemed to be a rank stranger." In heaven there would be only family, but on this world of woe there very well could be no one you could actually know, much less trust. The plaintive classic "O Death," which features death as a character coming into the room and the singer pleading to "spare me over another year," all explored how unexplainable happenings affected human life, as do lyric lines such as "Woke up this morning / blues walking like a man / He said come here, give me your right hand."

Perhaps more than anyone else, bluesmen embodied and played out the religious visions of moral ambiguity and outright evil. In this sense, they were as quintessentially religious figures as were the preachers, for in profoundly personal ways they explored the boundaries of the sacred and the profane.

Other performers wavered between their roles as bluesmen and preachers, unable fully to settle into either one but using that tension for memorable metaphorical explorations of the struggle within human souls. The bluesman and preacher Eddie "Son" House serves as a good example of the performer conscious of his own sin as he experienced the torment of desiring to preach the gospel but also enjoy the sinful delights of the world. When he bowed to pray in his room, according to one of his autobiographical compositions, the blues came along and drove his spirit into exile. Son House's struggles duplicated those of a generation of talented men and women who saw the church as an avenue for respectability but could not reconcile themselves to the self-denial required of evangelicals. Son House took his 1930 recording of "Preachin the Blues" (a riff from blueswoman Bessie Smith's 1927 version of the song) and added in his own autobiographical struggles:

> Oh I have religion this very day,
> But the womens and whiskey, well they would not let me pray....
> Oh I'm going to preach these gospel blues and choose my seat and sit down.
> When the spirit comes sisters, I want you to jump straight up and down.[3]

Holiness/Pentecostalism provided fertile ground for musical interchange among white and black southerners, just as the great camp meetings of the early nineteenth century provided a similar forum for cultural interchange. Pentecostalism provided much of the soundtrack and expressive forms that reshaped American cultural styles later in the twentieth century, precisely by so perfectly exploring but also overcoming the kinds of tensions outlined earlier in this essay. Again, coming from the most biblically grounded of cultures, Pentecostals tapped into personal stories that spoke to archetypical themes that gave them near universal appeal. Guitars, tambourines, and other rhythmical instruments, once seen as musical accompaniments for the devil, found their way into black Pentecostal churches in the early twentieth century. C. H. Mason's Church of God in Christ congregations immediately adopted them.

From the earliest songwriters to the pioneering black female guitarist Sister Rosetta Tharpe, gospel performers kept alive the exuberant tradition of black religious music, from the nineteenth century to the black gospel world of the twentieth and eventually into performances on stages, in nightclubs, and on records. Born in Arkansas to a family active in the Sanctified church, Tharpe took the rhythmically expressive music of her upbringing and brought it to the world of street busking, revival tent singing, and later the commercial marketplace of recordings and nightclubs. At the age of four, she stood on some boxes and belted out the song "Jesus Is on the Main Line," kicking off her career as a performer. Like many lyrics from that era, "Jesus on the Mainline" drew a spiritual moral from the use of a modern technology—hearers were urged to call up Jesus on the "main line" (the central line of a telephone system from that era), and "tell him what you want."[4]

Through the interwar years, a number of musicians combined the blues and religious music, importing blue notes, instrumental virtuosity, and the skills of charismatic soloists into what had been highly communal forms of sacred expression. The native of Villa Rica, Georgia, and son of a Baptist minister deserved the title often bestowed on him of the father of black gospel music. But a coterie of people working together, writing hymns and performing them in the unique pastiche that was black gospel, elevated the music to its place in the African–American sacred canon. Dorsey's younger years as a musician took him to juke joints, blues haunts, and Holiness storefront churches as well as some of Chicago's largest and most respectable Baptist congregations. Gradually, he married blues feeling to gospel message. "Blues is as important to a person feeling bad as Nearer My God to Thee," he later said. "I'm not talking about popularity. I'm talking about inside the individual. This moan gets into a person where there is some secret down there that they didn't bring out.... When you cry out, that is something down there that should have come out a long time ago. Whether it's blues or gospel, there is a vehicle that comes along maybe to take it away or push it away." Aside from differences in the words, "you take that blue moan and what they call the lowdown feeling tunes and you shape them up and put them up here and make them serve the other purpose, the religious purpose."[5] The blues moan that serves a religious purpose, of course, became the root of not just gospel, but from there to soul.

Through the twentieth century, the culture developed in Sanctified congregations exemplified the twin poles of black Christian life—protest and praise. Black Pentecostals embraced the cultural creations of gospel music and other forms of black celebration earlier and with more vigor than the mainline black denominations, which still often followed the norms of respectability defined by nineteenth-century church founders and leaders. Moreover, there is a virtually straight line from Pentecostalism to gospel, soul, and R & B and through those into the heart of virtually all popular music that depends on a blue note and a back beat.

The gospel business, according to music historian Bill Malone, evolved from shape-note singing schools and evangelical revivals "but drew much of its dynamism and much of its personnel from the Holiness-Pentecostal movement of the late nineteenth century and early twentieth century. By 1900 a great stream of religious songs, fed by the big-city revivals of the era, flowed into American popular culture." Publishing houses within and outside denominations cranked out paperback hymnals for church meetings and singing schools. Beyond the church walls, white and black secular and religious musicians traded licks, vocal styles, and lyrics.[6]

Opportunity beckoned everywhere for songwriters and performers. As a result, the early musical publishers and impresarios could not retain their most talented employees. One of them, a native of Spiro, Oklahoma, named Alfred E. Brumley, emerged as the premier white gospel songwriter of his era. Brumley worked with a music company in Arkansas, taught in singing schools, played piano, and composed hymns. Brumley left the Stamps–Baxter empire to form his own business with Eugene Bartlett (composer of the gospel standard "Victory in Jesus") in Hartford, Arkansas. In 1931, Brumley penned his classic "I'll Fly Away." Eventually becoming Brumley's signature tune, "I'll Fly Away" perfectly captured the fond hopes for a future life that permeated white gospel music lyrics. During his long and productive career, Brumley composed some seven hundred songs, including "Turn Your Radio On," "He Set me Free," and a bluegrass standard later made famous by Ralph and Carter Stanley (and much later by Bob Dylan), "Rank Strangers to Me":

Everybody I met Seem to be a rank stranger;
No mother or dad, Not a friend could I see.
They knew not my name And I knew not their faces—
I found they were all Rank strangers to me.

The sounds of upcountry singing—lined–out hymnody, *Sacred Harp* tunes, and the widespread gospel tunes—eventually found their way into the repertoire of bluegrass, traditional gospel, and newer country groups, ranging from Roy Acuff and the Smokey Mountain Boys to Flatt and Scruggs and to the Louvin Brothers, the Stanley Brothers, Bill Monroe's bands, the Osborne Brothers, and dozens of others. The familiar themes of focusing on the joys of salvation and eternal life and avoiding worldly entanglements dominated country gospel, heard in such classics of the genre as "Working on a Building":

It's a holy ghost building, it's a holy ghost building,
It's a holy ghost building, for my Lord, for my Lord.

Whether performed by the slicker vocal quartets or by the more country sounding string bands and bluegrass groups, songs in the genre typically portrayed surviving the harsh journeys of life, with a "Bible for my roadmap," to get to "my last stop in heaven some sweet day." Lester Flatt and Earl Scruggs sang of "working on a road, that leads to glory / I want to shake my Saviour's hand." The "gospel highway" would lead to final escape and rest. Aside from "I'll Fly Away," perhaps the best known song of the genre was "I Saw the Light," which Hank Williams adapted freely from the lyrics and music of Albert E. Brumley's "He Set Me Free."[7]

Gospel quartets increasingly followed popular styles, provoking a perplexed southern publisher to ask, "Why should people who love the Lord and clean Christian society have to listen to music of the 'juke box' to find a medium of expression toward God?" Despite such concerns, the music of southern Protestantism and the tunes of the juke box intermingled frequently through the twentieth century—as did the musical worlds of white and black southerners.[8]

BLUES AND BLACK GOSPEL

Black gospel emerged from a tangled history of nineteenth-century spirituals, Moody–Sankey hymns, and a variety of twentieth-century sources, including the blues and bawdy music. Early controversies over the relationship between the blues and sacred song gradually disappeared as the forms increasingly intersected in the commercial world of popular music. In the early twentieth century, however, the tension was very real. The two forms vied for the souls of black American performers and their audiences.

In the mid–twentieth century, those who came from rural traditions, both white and black, purchased instruments from mail–order catalogues, listened to and imitated musicians played on the radio, and gradually created musical forms that merged what had been highly distinct secular and sacred styles. The powerful image of the train, as in the popular tune "Life's Railway to Heaven," written by the white Georgia holiness pioneer Charles Tillman, was a vehicle for physical and spiritual deliverance.

In southern religious song imagery, trains were the path to salvation. In "When the Train Comes Along," Henry Thomas, an itinerant musician and preacher, waited at the depot for Jesus to take him in. Blind Lemon Jefferson, a gifted guitarist and troubadour, added songs about traveling across the Jordan River because "Jesus gonna be my engineer," expressing the popular notion of the train as a vehicle to Canaan land. Through the twentieth century, the train found its way into innumerable song lyrics as well as personal testimonies. One conversion narrative relates how the seeking mourner stood on a platform at a train station, then "knelt to pray. As I knelt Jesus handed me a ticket. It was all signed with my name. I arose to my feet and handed it in at the window and was told to take my place with the three men standing on the platform and wait." The train also symbolized transport in the other direction for sinners who were not right with God. In more than three hundred recordings made in the 1920s, the Reverend J. M. Gates, a popular pastor in Atlanta, recorded classics of chanted sermonizing and singing such as "Death's Black Train Is Coming." His rendition of the well–traveled song sold over 35,000 copies and helped to establish him as one of the best–selling artists for Columbia records.[9]

Ignoring race lines, an ever-growing storehouse of songs, lyrics, tunes, and sermonic lines passed back and forth among musicians and recording preachers and songsters. "O Death," "John the Revelator," "Please See My Grave Is Kept Clean," and numerous gospel tunes from the late nineteenth and early twentieth century coursed through white and black southern sacred song. "John the Revelator," for example, was recorded by a variety of white and black country and gospel singers. The best known version (partly because of the recording's inclusion on Harry Smith's "Anthology of American Folk Music," which introduced a subsequent generation to the music of this era), features the ferociously growling Texas street guitarist and singing evangelist Blind Willie Johnson asking "Who's that writing," his wife, Angeline, answering "John the Revelator," and Blind Willie punching back with frightening intensity, "Hey, book of the Seventh Seal." Charley Patton, perhaps the largest single influence on the first generation of Mississippi Delta blues music, recorded several religious songs, sometimes using pseudonyms (such as "Elder J. J. Hadley") foisted on him by record companies seeking to differentiate their gospel and blues product lines. Even in his sacred recordings, notably the chilling two-part "Prayer of Death," Patton's wicked guitar runs (with a single blue note taking the place of the final word on the obligatory line "I'll meet you on that distant shore") lend an air of devilish power.[10]

White and black performers borrowed freely from just about every musical tradition they could find. Thus, blues runs and African-American syncopation found their way into the styles of white singers, while a hillbilly mandolin graces the 1927 rendition by the black Pentecostal Ford Washington McGee of the "white" gospel hymn "Rock of Ages, Cleft for Me" (in stark contrast to the polyphonic Sanctified revelry of his first recording, "Lion in the Tribe of Judah"). McGee's talented piano player, Arizona Dranes, belted out barrelhouse lines and nascent rhythm-and-blues lines in her records in 1926 and 1928.

Through the interwar years, a number of musicians combined the blues and religious music, importing blue notes, instrumental virtuosity, and the skills of charismatic soloists into what had been highly communal forms of sacred expression. This musical formula came out of Holiness and Pentecostal worship, which emphasized call-and-response singing and intense audience involvement. Gospel legend Mahalia Jackson made Brewster's tune "Move On Up a Little Higher" famous. Surrounded in her hometown of New Orleans by the blues and Pentecostal music, she was happiest in congregations where she could hear foot-tapping and hand-clapping. The Sanctified church next door to her home Baptist church introduced her to drums, cymbals, tambourines, and triangles. "Everybody in there sang and they clapped and stomped their feet and sang with their whole bodies," she remembered. "They had a beat, a powerful beat, a rhythm we held on to from slavery days, and their music was so strong and expressive it used to bring the tears to my eyes.... First you've got to get the rhythm until, through the music, you have the freedom to interpret it." Jackson avoided the temptation of pop music stardom, endearing her to her gospel music fan base.[11] Her very first recording, from 1936, drew deeply from biblical imagery: "Let them do what they will may / Til that great harvest day / God's gonna separate the wheat from the tares," she sang, embarking on a musical career that would be transformative for American culture."

Black gospel quartets, a counterpart to the southern gospel groups popular among whites, elevated innovative styles to a new level of musical sophistication. The jubilee style of quartet singing emerged in the mid-1930s, employing sermonic themes in narrative form. Among black migrants, gospel quartets sang in nearly every community venue—churches, revival celebrations, community outings, and labor union meetings. The foursomes bolstered their popularity by adding special rhythmic touches to their performances. The Soul Stirrers, Blue Jay Singers, Dixie Hummingbirds, Swan Silvertones, and numerous other groups further refined the black gospel quartet sound. By the early 1950s, at the zenith of the quartet era, many groups alternated two lead singers: one for hard gospel and the other for more traditional spiritual styles known as jubilee singing. Packaged shows that traveled throughout the South featured intense competitions between star performers.[12]

In the 1960s, secular popular music drew from an abundance of talented performers who had been honed in the gospel music world among both whites and blacks. Sam Cooke was the perfect exemplar of the gospel singer as pop star. Born in 1931 in Mississippi, he grew up in Chicago as the son of a minister in the Church of Christ Holiness (the creation of the Mississippi black Holiness pioneer Charles Price Jones). As a teenager, he sang in the Highway QCs, a group that served as a farm team for major black gospel groups of the era, including the Soul Stirrers. Later Cooke became a lead singer for the Soul Stirrers, where he developed a style elegantly described as "sophisticated sanctification." In the 1950s he struck out on his own and became the famous crooner of doo-wop and soul classics, ranging from the chart-topper "You Send Me" to social commentary such as "Change Gonna Come." Curtis Mayfield provides another example of the deep influence of the "beat" of the Sanctified church and the politicization of lyrics handed down in folk and commercial traditions, most notably in his classic anthem written to celebrate the 1963 March on Washington, "People Get Ready," with its moving gospel quartet harmonies accentuating the lyrical transformation of the train image as the vehicle to freedom's coming:

> People get ready, there's a train a'comin
> You don't need no baggage, just get on board
> All you need is faith, to hear the diesels hummin'
> Don't need no ticket, just thank the Lord.[13]

Those raised as cultural products of this racial interchange in religious expression entered the public world of broadcasting and performing in the mid-twentieth century. Perhaps more than anyone else, Elvis Presley illustrates this point. The young Elvis borrowed freely from sacred performers in creating his own musical persona. He memorized an entire catalogue of church music from both white and black traditions and could produce it on command. Along with his friends in Memphis, Presley enthusiastically sampled African-American religious culture both in person and on the radio.

Unlike the rowdies who satirized southern religious solemnities, Presley was affected by his encounter with African-American Pentecostalism. He intuitively grasped its kinship to his own Assemblies of God background. He listened avidly to black religious orator W. Herbert Brewster on the radio and frequented local meetings of the Church of God in Christ.

Whites and blacks borrowed theologies, performance styles, and cultural practices freely (if often unwittingly) from one another. Elvis, for example, absorbed the sounds, the rhythms, and the stage manner that shaped his own electric performances. White secular and religious performers learned from—some might suggest they stole—doo-wop (with its own roots in black gospel quartets), religious holy-roller dancing, and the melismatic singing that coursed through African-American church music. In the process, they created entertainments that shaped American popular culture. Sacred passion, expressed most obviously in white and black southern Pentecostalism, was at the heart of R & B and rock–and–roll.[14]

But Jesus was not present or visible enough to forestall descents into self-destruction, or the impulse to enjoy the pleasures of the flesh. Both the more sentimental music of southern evangelicalism and the tunes of southern hard religion come through in the career of Johnny Cash. The persona of the man in black embodied a darkness that symbolized both his own Christ-like identification with the poor and downtrodden in society and his constant struggle with personal demons. His internal battle was between his own desires for piety and his manic pursuits. In the midst of recording classics such as *Johnny Cash at Folsom Prison* and later a similar piece at San Quentin, Cash managed to travel to the Holy Land and film a biographical rendering of Jesus's life, *The Gospel Road: The Story of Jesus*. With salvation by Jesus and the loving hand of June Carter Cash and a Christian community, Cash hoped to have the "kingdom of God building inside you and growing." Less than a decade later, Cash's much less well-publicized struggles with alcohol, and a suicide attempt, showed that he was still chasing a dragon who appeared to him in blackness. Cash's recordings follow a trajectory well known to southerners, and especially to bluesmen, as they struggled within themselves between good and evil impulses and put those struggles in song. Their Jesus came from the hard religion of the southern tradition, one with wide currency in black and white communities.[15]

Cash's recordings toward the end of his life, collected in the five-volume set *American Recordings*, allowed him ample space to explore his lifelong mutually contradictory passions. In his music, Jesus appears as a figure of lightness and grace, but "the beast in me" is more than powerful enough to overcome and simply snuff out His presence on earth. Cash's exploration of characters experiencing a dark night of the soul recurred through his musical career; his periodic reversion to a more triumphalist Christ, as seen for example in his appearance at Explo 72 in Dallas, could not overcome Cash's own attraction to and unforgettable songwriting about the mortal struggle for the soul. Cash was, one writer for *Christianity Today* averred, a "Man in Black" who wore "glorious white," after his death "reunited with his brother and face-to-face with the Lord." But his later music expressed intense struggles with Jesus. In

"Redemption Song," Cash summed up a lifetime of hard living and expressed an older culture of a hard religion, about the blood of Jesus coming from his hands and side, his blood giving life and setting captives free: "Through the fire and the flood Clung to the tree / And were redeemed by the blood." Very late in his life, Cash sang somewhat menacingly of "your own, personal Jesus": "Feeling unknown, And you're all alone / flesh and bone, by the telephone / lift up the receiver, I'll make you a believer. / I will deliver, you know I'm a forgiver." Cash's classic recordings in *Man in Black* and his haunting *American Recordings* captured his conflicted soul and his background in rural Arkansas, where, in the words of Billy Joe Shaver, "Jesus Was Our Savior—Cotton Was Our King."[16]

Cash carried forward a tradition that both white and black artists had sung about, in a variety of musical genres from country to rhythm and blues, through the middle years of the twentieth century. Ultimately, this Jesus was too subversive to be segregated from the realities of everyday life, or to any strictly rendered stories from the Bible.

Johnny Cash's appeal to a diverse cross-section may be compared to that of the late great jazz bassist Charlie Haden, whom I'm just inserting as a footnote here as he is a singular figure. Haden grew up singing gospel music as a young boy with his family's singing group based out of Springfield, Missouri, but an early bout with polio turned him from singing to bass playing. And what a turn that was, as Haden became one of the two or three most influential and revered jazz bassists of the last half century from his epic work with Ornette Coleman, Keith Jarrett, and so many others. In the 1960s Haden became part of the World Liberation Orchestra, and in later years he spoke of how he saw a deep connection between his country and gospel roots and his career as an avant-garde jazz musician. A recent article put it this way: "Haden saw the common link between jazz and country— both are poor people's music related to 'the struggle for independence, identity and to be recognized,' he said in a 2009 AP interview following the release of his first country album, 'Rambling Boy' on which he returned to his roots, playing songs by the Carter Family and other traditional country musicians."[17]

RECENT AND CONTEMPORARY MUSIC

The remembrances of growing up in church, singing in the choir, learning the hymns— they are a nearly universal part of the autobiographies of southern-born popular musical performers, all the way from Dolly Parton, Vince Gill, and Jason Isbell to Aretha, the Staples Singers, and pretty much everyone in the soul and R & B world. For outsiders who want to tap into those traditions, the church and the blues are the place they go.

In more contemporary black gospel, the gospel of hope remains as central as the angry jeremiad is to rap. These two sides emerged also in the respective careers and hit records of the gospel star Kirk Franklin and the rap artist Kanye West. Born in 1970, another scion of a black Baptist family, Franklin led a troubled youth but found his way back to his religious faith in the 1990s. He formed the gospel group The Family, which has dominated the gospel music charts for the last generation. Kirk Franklin's "Why We Sing" led off his 1995 record of that title; it was the first gospel album to sell more than a million copies. Lyrically, his themes reprised the familiar thread of black gospel: Jesus provides hope and can get you through life's troubles. "Someone asked the question / Why do we sing," Franklin begins. His answer: "I sing because I'm happy / I sing because I'm free." God's eye remained on the sparrow, giving the believer hope.

Rappers have explored religious themes, but outside the conventional norms of the black Christian tradition. Lyrics to their more serious or searching raps speak of a profound yearning for, but disconnection from, the historic African-American spiritual themes of redemption from suffering in this world. Kanye West's "Jesus Walks" best exemplifies this feeling and reprises some of the conflicts between bodily desires and spiritual quests, the same internal struggles that ran through the lyrics of many bluesmen earlier in the century:

> God show me the way because the devil trying to break me down (Jesus Walks)
> The only thing that that I pray is that my feet don't fail me now (Jesus Walks)
> And I don't think there's nothing I can do now to right my wrongs (Jesus walks
>   with me)
> I want to talk to God but I'm afraid because we ain't spoke in so long

The literalist biblical culture of the South inspired musical renderings of biblical texts that took their meanings far outside the confines of the readings sanctioned by the southern denominations. That helps explain why a provincial culture, economically crippled by poverty and exploitation and intellectually straitjacketed by a literalist hermeneutic and a suspicion of outside ideas and influences, produced a good deal of the "sound" of twentieth-century American culture and a fair number of its dominant themes, metaphors, and images. It also suggests why the rural southern came to stand in for the authentic. It's what has driven a generation or two now of obsessive record collectors, stealing away 78s in their personal vaults like so many totems of authenticity. It's what sent Bob Dylan off on a search for Woody Guthrie and an early attempt to mold himself in that image; It's where Jerry Garcia and his lyrical partner Robert Hunter went as they composed staples of the Grateful Dead's repertoire such as "St. Stephen":

> Saint Stephen with a rose
> In and out of the garden he goes
> Country garland in the wind and the rain
> Wherever he goes the people all complain....
> Did he doubt or did he try?
> Answers aplenty in the bye and bye
> Talk about your plenty, talk about your ills
> One man gathers what another man spills

It's where Robbie Robertson went, with the deep assistance of his introduction to southern culture at the hands of the Arkansas-born and -bred and multitalented musician and singer Levon Helm, to gather material to write a contemporary classic such as "The Weight." It's where a California-born and Santa Cruz- and Berkelee College of Music–trained performer such as Gillian Welch went before she emerged with her breakthrough sound and first hit "Orphan Girl," with its ending of the orphan girl feasting at the table of God's family after this life was over, and another tune about an aspiring young rock-and-roller who wanted to grab the Savior's hand or reimagine Time itself as "The Revelator"; and more recently, it's what partially drew a privileged New England schoolkid named Ketch Secor to adopt a tobacco-chewing country persona, busk his way across the South and eventually across the country, and put himself in the voice of a southern farmer with no hope:

> Take 'em away, take 'em away, Lord
> Take away these chains from me
> My heart is broken 'cause my spirit's not free
> Lord take away these chains from me

Or to pen his own attempt at prophecy and judgment in "I Hear Them All":

> I hear the crying of the hungry
> In the deserts where they're wandering
> Hear them crying out for Heaven's own
> Benevolence upon them
> Hear destructive power prevailing
> I hear fools falsely hailing
> To the crooked wits of tyrants when they call
> I hear them all, I hear them all, I hear them all.

Biblical references often tossed up offhandedly, as in a recent tune by the Alabama Shakes about a woman desiring her bottle more than the guy who is after her: "Well pass me the whiskey / pass me whatever there's drank left in / Well I don't care if it's seven in the morning / For all I care it could be the second coming." And in their hit "Hold On," the lead singer marvels that "Bless my heart, bless my soul, didn't think I'd make it to 22 year old, There must be someone up above sayin' / 'Come on, Brittany, you got to come on up. You got to hold on." Or from the new and much ballyhooed recording "Deconstructed," from the contemporary southern rock band Glory Fires:

> We were whooped with the Good Book,
> Wound up shamed, sorry and worse.
> But I yearned to burn the wrath out of every chapter,
> And water the love in every verse.
> Water the love in every verse.

Dereconstructed.
Dereconstructed, y'all.

Birmingham-born band leader Lee Bains declares as the aim of his record *Glory Fires:* "Southern cultural identity has been exploited for these regressive, right-wing, draconian, imperialistic movements.... I think that's a contradiction. To me, at its core, Southern culture is opposed to all of those things. To me, what I identify with the Southern identity is this notion of courtesy and Judeo-Christian charity and hospitality and keeping to yourself and respecting people's eccentricities or whatever. These are the things that I equate with Southernness, and I don't see them discussed or highlighted very often. Instead, we're left with the notion of a Southerner as AR-15-waving, angry, judgmental, hateful figure. Those aren't the Southerners that I grew up around."[18] The Drive-By Truckers put it this way, summarizing a version of southern populism which often has emerged from one branch of the religious tradition: Ain't about the races, the crying shame/To the fucking rich man all poor people look the same.[19]

From the nineteenth century to the present, then, southern musicians and those inspired by southern-born forms of music drew from biblical apocalyptic imagery, angry prophecy, gentle reassurances, and archetypical character struggles. It was the potent combination of biblical imagery set within a fundamentalist culture of reading and understanding juxtaposed to a violent and inequitable social and economic system that collectively created the tensions that empowered the most memorably explosive music of American popular culture.

For where two or three are gathered together in my name, there am I in the midst of them.
—MATTHEW 18:20, KJV

…and in many congregations the "Bible class" overshadowed the regular Sabbath worship.
—SYDNEY E. AHLSTROM, *Religious History of the American People* (1972)

12

Where Two or Three Are Gathered

THE ADULT BIBLE CLASS MOVEMENT AND THE SOCIAL

LIFE OF SCRIPTURE

Christopher D. Cantwell

THE PROGRAM CALLED it a banquet, but such a term failed to convey the religious significance many in attendance ascribed to the event. It was more like a love feast, a communion of saints gathered to enrich their relationships with each other and the divine. Held on Friday, October 20, 1905, at the Western Avenue Methodist Episcopal Church in Chicago, the gathering celebrated the twenty-fifth anniversary of the church's Wesleyan Bible Class. Former class members traveled from as far as California to attend not only the dinner, but also the week of prayer meetings, Sunday school rallies, intraclass baseball games, and jaunts into the countryside that preceded it. Yet Friday's meal was, without question, the week's highlight, both the anniversary's climax and an annual tradition begun when the class had a mere fifteen members. The class of now five hundred, made up of members from several Protestant denominations, honored this momentous occasion by hosting a number of dignitaries. Local ministers, municipal court judges, and even the standing bishop of the Methodist Episcopal Church spoke at the meal—although Theodore Roosevelt's personal secretary politely declined the class's ambitious invitation to the sitting president to attend.[1]

In addition to its spread of catered foods, the banquet offered its guests an array of spiritual sustenance. Interspersed between the courses of raw oysters, French peas, and cabbage salad, the class arranged a number of speeches, musical performances, and extended toasts. Right before the main course the class's teacher, doubling as toastmaster, turned over the floor to the audience and invited past and current members to stand and give a one-sentence explanation of why they had joined the class. Nearly half of the reported five hundred guests rose to speak that evening. Yet their answers were surprisingly similar. Each in some way cited friendships as the primary reason they both joined and then remained members of the class. "I liked the friendly atmosphere of the class, and I wanted my friends to be Christian people," relayed one former member named Venia Marie Kellar. Current member George Hutchinson agreed, telling the audience: "After a few visits I found it impossible to stay away. The cords of friendship and sympathy are irresistibly strong and very manifest in the Wesleyan Bible Class." Even when members did express an interest in expanding their knowledge of scripture, this desire to be part of a Christian community coursed through their responses. "A desire to know more of God's word" had brought new member George J. Shand to the class, for example. But he stayed because of "the hospitality shown me, and the pleasant association with members of the class."[2]

While the extent of the Wesleyan Bible Class's anniversary celebration might have been unique, its enthusiasm for the familiarity and conviviality of collaborative Bible study was widely shared. Across the country local ministers and Protestant laypeople had been organizing similar Bible study groups at a rapid clip throughout the turn of the century, each a part of what contemporaries called the "adult Bible class movement." Indeed, the Wesleyan class's anniversary banquet featured an address on the movement delivered by the head of the Cook County Sunday School Association's new Adult Bible Class Committee. Formed two years earlier by several Protestant laymen in order to promote the formation of Bible study groups in the region, the committee inspired a number of similar efforts among other state and local Sunday school associations. By 1922, the International Sunday School Association conservatively estimated that these associations had gathered some 5 million women and men into more than fifty thousand Bible classes nationwide—all with their own anniversary banquets, class socials, and even baseball leagues.[3]

The doctrine of *sola scriptura* notwithstanding, the Bible has long been a social text for Protestants in America. From the "private meetings" of Puritan New England to the cell groups of modern megachurches, Protestants have often read, interpreted, and engaged with scripture in either collaborative or communal settings. According to sociologist Robert Wuthnow, such intimate assemblies constitute the most plentiful social unit in America today, with more than 20 million people participating in some kind of weekly meeting around the study of scripture.[4] Scholars, however, often overlook these ubiquitous institutions when telling the Bible's American history. In the long arc of American religious history, the Bible traditionally appears as the wellspring of America's cultural and political lexicon or the object over which theological conflicts rage. Beginning with the Bible's commodification and subsequent mass marketing in the revivals of the nation's great awakenings, scholars traditionally focus on the Good Book's politicization in the public school battles of the antebellum era, on the challenge evolutionary biology and historical criticism posed to scripture's intellectual authority in the late nineteenth century, and on the fundamentalist-modernist conflicts that resulted from these tensions in the 1920s, often culminating with William

Jennings Bryan's defense of inerrancy on a stage outside a courthouse in Dayton, Tennessee, during the "Scopes Monkey Trial" in 1925.[5]

This history is, of course, true and it accurately traces the Bible's enduring presence in American history. But it is also incomplete. Though at a distance from these more public histories of scripture, Bible study groups are a vital component of the Bible's American history, sites of both cultural reflection and production. In them ordinary women and men locate themselves in the debates of their day, perpetuating the discursive categories of the religious cultures of which they are a part. At the same time, however, these small gatherings are also places where local people creatively adapt the terms of these debates to the material realities of their lives in order to forge communities, shape identities, or make meaning. These adaptations not only anchor specific religious worlds, but can also shape the larger institutions of which they are a part through the religious forms they yield. They may not be as dramatic as the Scopes trial, but the religious histories of lay Bible study are no less important.[6]

Nowhere is this more clearly seen than in the history of the wider movement of which the Wesleyan Bible Class was a part. Though founded in order to enlarge the religious knowledge of young adults, the tens of thousands of classes that became associated with the adult Bible class movement were more often defined by their abiding interest in the formation of meaningful, long-lasting relationships. Bible class teachers extolled the virtues of Christian friendships while classes transformed themselves into sites of Protestant sociability through a variety of recreational activities. For the millions of Americans who joined them, Bible classes provided a needed sense of community in a world they felt lacked any. By the time these classes reached a critical mass in the first decades of the twentieth century, they increasingly became implicated in the nascent theological and ecclesiastical battles of the era as religious leaders took note of their proliferating numbers. Both liberal and conservative theologians attempted to influence these flourishing networks of lay devotion, but it was the loose association of conservative ministers and prominent laymen affiliated with the first wave of Protestant fundamentalism who most successfully mustered Bible class members into their ranks. Connecting the movement's interest in protective devotional communities to their own attempts to purify or separate from existing denominations, these activists turned Bible classes into allies. The resulting coalition would yield a highly politicized conception of community, one that suggested Bible classes were more than just a gathering of friends: there were an embattled minority who needed to move out of their classrooms in order to take back not only their church but also the nation.

Bible classes, of course, have long been a part of the American religious landscape. Founded alongside the establishment of the earliest Sunday schools, they first appeared as early as 1800. Some saw them as a quintessentially American contribution to the British-born Sunday school, a manifestation of the new nation's desire to democratize religious knowledge. By 1830 they had become enough a part of local church life that the American Sunday School Union sponsored special Bible class magazines, ministers published their Bible class lectures, and a number of Sunday school advocates had gathered in Philadelphia to organize an American Bible Class Society.[7]

In addition to their nationalist tendencies, these earliest Bible classes also shared a number of characteristics that would define the organized study of scripture over the next century. First and foremost, as their name suggests, organizers intended Bible classes to deepen people's knowledge of scripture. Published commentaries, denominational curricula, or even the personal reflections of a church elder might guide a class's studies, but classes always claimed the Bible to be their "textbook." This emphasis on religious instruction, however, was almost always accompanied by a more pointed concern over the biblical education of Protestant youth. According to a number of Sunday school workers, local ministers, and anxious Protestant parents, Bible classes provided a needed devotional space for youngsters who considered themselves too old for Sunday school but had yet to become full "accessions to the church."[8] Sufficiently occupied in a Bible class, advocates hoped, young people would not only remain in a local church's fold but also become trained for some future Christian service. Finally, because Bible classes occupied this liminal space between the sanctuary and the Sunday school, they also became sites of devotional innovation as teachers experimented with methods of retention. As the American Bible Class Society discovered, classes could be found not only in churches but also in libraries, in lecture halls, and even on the shop floors of Lowell's factories.[9] Though these devotional departures seemed irreverent to some, Bible class advocates argued they ensured the church's future.

Despite this early interest, however, Bible classes languished throughout much of the nineteenth century. The American Bible Class Society found little denominational support for its endeavors and folded after only three years, while midcentury Sunday school literature paid Bible classes little mind. By the late 1800s some even derided "the old time Bible class" as a relic of the past, the domain of megalomaniacal deacons prone to pontification.[10] But the closing decades of the nineteenth century witnessed nothing short of a Bible class revival. Minister's meetings, Sunday school associations, and denominational gatherings all noted a sudden groundswell of interest in organized Bible study—a development many seem unprepared for. By 1877 the *Sunday School Times* had become so inundated with requests for information on Bible class methods that they had to issue an apology for not publishing pieces on the topic fast enough.[11]

As before, a concern for Protestant youth drove the Bible class's late nineteenth century return. Alongside the rapid urbanization of the American population, where millions of white, native-born Americans from rural areas joined even larger numbers of European immigrants in migrating to the nation's burgeoning cities, Protestant leaders became suddenly and acutely aware of young people's absence from Sunday worship. Widely reported canvases by city minister's meetings estimated that anywhere from 40 to 60 percent of Sunday school enrollment failed to join a church; when they included attendance at the midweek prayer meeting, canvassers found that number dropped to a quarter.[12] Petrified that this Sunday school "leakage" might drain the Protestant church dry, ministers frantically sought organizational remedies. By 1900 the nation's denominations had founded no fewer than fifteen societies aimed at rectifying this perceived "youth problem," from the Young People's Society for Christian Endeavor (1881) to the Luther League (1888) and the Baptist Young People's Union of America (1891). Bible classes were intimately a part of this "young people's movement,"[13] as some called this outburst of Protestant youth groups, but they differed in several crucial respects. First, where most young people's societies entertained juveniles for a time before graduating them to some other church association, Bible classes sought to become the avenue by which Protestant youth as young as fifteen would become, and then remain, mature Christian citizens. The word "adult" increasingly became a mandatory prefix when discussing these classes, a term that not only described an adult Bible class's intended audience but also the maturity teachers expected of their members. They were also far more likely to be organized and led by laypeople, unlike the denominationally supervised young people's societies. While the Methodist Episcopal Church's Epworth League had its own denominational office and appointed staffers, for instance, Bible classes, by virtue of their inclusion under the broader umbrella of the Sunday school, remained organic, congregationally specific affairs. Finally, these local origins in combination with the Bible class's continued identification with lay Bible study would ultimately draw them into doctrinal disputes over their chosen texts.

But before they became implicated in these larger conflicts, Bible classes emerged from far more local concerns. Marshall A. Hudson was like so many other Bible class teachers before he started one in 1890: he hadn't even heard of them before. The owner of several successful crockery stores in Syracuse, New York, and a member of the city's First Baptist Church, Hudson watched with concern as the city slowly filled "with young men who needed Christ, but no extra effort was being made to save them." After attempts to organize a brotherhood or a young people's society proved a failure, Hudson simply began inviting young men to church in order to discuss passages from the Bible. To his surprise, the men agreed. In addition to the Sunday gatherings of this "Baraca Bible Class," Hudson opened his home once a week so the men could fraternize and soon added a weekly checkers club to keep them out of the saloon. By 1893, Hudson had not only grown this class to over two hundred members but also helped found nearly a hundred more across upstate New York, along with a number of Philathea Bible Classes he devised for women.[14]

It was a process repeated countless times across the country. While the story's details always varied, they all followed a similar script. A concerned layperson, church leader, or, occasionally, a minister invited a cohort of young adults to gather regularly to study scripture and shortly thereafter gave the group a name. Like the Baraca and Philathea classes, many classes segregated themselves by sex. But alongside these men's and women's classes were any number of mixed classes, married couple's classes, student classes, businessmen's classes, and other occupationally specific assemblies. The only constant was that every class formed itself around some kind of shared experience or professional status. "The secret to success in adult Bible class work may be summed up in four words," publisher David C. Cook wrote in an early survey of Bible class work: "taking advantage of circumstances." Each seemed to have "grown out of felt needs along some particular line" where the members' similar circumstances quickly bound them together as a group.[15]

The importance of these shared interests is most readily seen in the host of activities classes adopted alongside the study of scripture. The Young Ladies' Bible Class at the Christian Church of Evanston, Illinois, for example, organized child care for its members so mothers could remain involved in church work, while the Howson Fellowship Class at Woodlawn Park Methodist Episcopal Church in Chicago organized mock trials and debate tournaments for law students from the University of Chicago who attended the class.[16] In addition to these accounts of mutual aid, Bible classes also reported innumerable instances of direct assistance to members in need, from helping someone move to funding a member's education through class donations. Some even formalized their welfare work. When International Sunday School Association secretary W. C. Pearce surveyed the landscape of Bible class work in 1908, he found that a number ran employment, lodging, and medical committees that drew on the resources of the church to maintain lists of open positions, respectable boarding houses, or physicians who might waive their fees for Bible class members.[17]

According to Pearce, however, by far the most active Bible class committee was the social committee. Where churches had once left their members "to find their own pleasures without guidance," Bible classes now made sure such needs were "carefully considered and satisfied."[18] At a minimum, Pearce observed, most classes, like the Wesleyan class, adopted some sort of anniversary banquet. "Every successful class that the writer knows makes much of the annual class dinner," he wrote.[19] But in many Bible classes these banquets were but one event on an elaborate social calendar that filled practically every day of the year. The aptly named Pleasant Hour class of the First Presbyterian Church of Olney in Philadelphia, for example, held not only the recommended annual dinner but also lavish quarterly parties, monthly desert socials, a magazine exchange, and weekly coffees at a designated member's home.[20] In many respects, Bible classes came to be defined by their affability. From the weekday lunches of a businessmen's Bible class to the cooperatively owned summer cottages where classes vacationed as a group, most sought the most entertaining way to bring class members into closer association with each other. "Nothing is too good for the adult Bible class," a thoroughly impressed Pearce concluded.[21]

Of course, on one level these activities were a lure, evangelistic bait intended to draw unchurched youth into devotional Bible study. "Social to save" was one Bible class teacher's motto, for a class should never "give a social for itself, but always for others."[22] Yet the extent of Bible class social life suggests that the millions of women and men who joined them primarily desired to deepen and enrich their existing relationships. Chicago's Wesleyan Bible Class, which opens this essay, was actually quite well known in Sunday school circles for its cultivation of class friendships. The teacher, a newspaper editor named Frank L. Wood, claimed he had an "unwritten law" that once someone became a member of the class their spiritual state forever remained the class's concern. "Once a Member, Always a Member," was Wood's phrase, and he enacted this principle through a tightly organized system of correspondence that kept members in contact throughout much of their adult lives. As individuals or families inevitably left Chicago for elsewhere, Wood made sure every departing member was given a proper sendoff and their new locale recorded in the class's records. Wood then regularly met with "expert stenographers" from the class and dictated as many as twenty letters a week to the names recorded in his "absent Wesleyans" address book. He introduced former members to other absent Wesleyans living nearby, alerted them when members would be passing through their area, shared news of the class's ongoing activities, and inquired as to their physical, social, and spiritual well-being. Wood had all of this correspondence composed in green ink in order to distinguish the class's letters from other presumably less important missives and shared the replies he received with the class in the hope that current members might remain in contact with their former classmates through prayer, a personal note, or a special visit.[23]

And remain in contact they did. According to the class's correspondence, Wesleyans who had not known each other in Chicago became friends in their new communities, members planned their travels around visits to former classmates, and the class as a whole became intimately a part of each other's lives. They helped each other find housing, attended each other's weddings, rejoiced over the births of each other's children, and grieved when illness and death inevitably touched them all. For many Wesleyan class members, Wood's plan to keep the class in touch proved so meaningful that when financial considerations forced him to discontinue the use of green ink in 1930—nearly forty years after he sent the first letter—they wrote in to mourn the subtle yet, for them, profound change.[24]

The reason Wesleyan class members valued their Bible class membership stemmed from their location in the industrial economy. Like the majority of Bible class members at the turn of the century, the Wesleyan class was filled with white, middle-class young adults who worked a variety of entry-level jobs. The class's 1905 roster listed bookkeepers, sales agents, teachers, and, of course, stenographers as members, but by far the most common position was the generic category of "clerk." None of the class's members, moreover, were originally from Chicago, all of them having recently arrived in order to take the positions they now had.[25] For these low-level office workers, their entry into the corporate structures of industrial capitalism proved profoundly dislocating. Their Bible class membership provided a necessary sense of security, community, and self-worth in this isolating, bureaucratic world. "Estrangement is one of the saddest experiences of my life," claimed founding member Calla Scott Willard in a letter to the class. "To know some true heart cares for me is one of the strongest incentives to try to be and do."[26]

For members of the Wesleyan Bible Class, as well as countless other Bible class members across the country, the relationships their classes fostered were more than mere supplements to the spiritual discipline of Bible study. Rather, they were a primary source of the class's religious significance. The anniversary banquets and quarterly socials that forged and sustained them were as much religious practices as recreational pursuits, rituals intended to promote a sense of closeness as much as they transmitted traditional forms of religious knowledge. Absent Wesleyan Otto C. Paul, for example, particularly drew religious meaning from his Bible class relations. A native of Sheboygan, Wisconsin, Paul joined the Wesleyan class after moving to Chicago in search of work.

After his search proved a failure, he returned home to Sheboygan, but remained in regular contact with the Wesleyan Bible Class throughout much of his life, replying to Frank Wood's green-printed letters and waiting at Sheboygan's docks for hours at a time in order spend a few minutes with a passing Wesleyan. According to Paul, such moments were vital, no matter how fleeting, because it was in his relationships with fellow Christians that he felt his relationship with Christ became most manifest. "Tell the class I am learning a great lesson," he wrote in one letter to Wood, "That plan of keeping in touch with one another has the Christ spirit in it. Surely even so we retain the friendship of Christ, keeping in touch with him."[27]

This is not to say, of course, that scripture was inconsequential to the growth of adult Bible classes at the turn of the century. Far from it. No matter how many banquets a class held, their most common activity remained the weekly Sunday school meeting. Their ability to generate such feelings of closeness relied on this shared appreciation of the book; a collective reverence that served the foundation on which every Christian friendship supposedly rested—in some instances quite literally.

To promote their upcoming 1906 season, for example, the Cook County Sunday School Association's Bible Class Baseball League circulated a photograph of their 1905 champions. The photograph shows the victorious Haynes' Bible Class team from the Belden Avenue Presbyterian Church proudly posing with their championship banner. The team had good reason to be proud. Not only had they beaten thirteen hundred other athletes from 150 teams in order to claim the league's title, they had done so while adhering to a strict code of piety. In order to participate, the Belden Avenue men had to submit a monthly attendance card signed by a teacher or minister that verified their presence in class. League officials suspended any athlete with more than one unexcused absence a month, as well as any player caught smoking, drinking, chewing tobacco, or using "improper language of any character."[28]

The image's most striking feature, however, is its editing. Some unknown editor decided to crop the team's portrait and superimpose it on top of a sketch of an open Bible. The cropping itself is a revealing move, visually separating the young men from the rest of their world as if to emphasize the importance of these religious relationships over others. But the Bible's presentation as an illegible series of squiggly lines also reveals something of the character of Bible class life. Whether the book was even a Bible at all might be up for debate were it not for such telltale signs as the curled corners of the leather binding, the columned text, and the preinstalled fabric bookmark protruding from the binding. The editor could have chosen to communicate a message through this open text, highlighting a particular book, chapter, or verse. But the editor did not. Rather, what the image does suggest is that the Haynes' Bible Class success— the confidence and pride evident in their faces, and the friendship conveyed in their familiar poses—was based on their shared appreciation for, and study of, the Bible.

The only text the Cook County Sunday School Association chose to feature in this promotional image was the tattered sheet music of "Onward Christian Soldiers" in the background. A nineteenth-century hymn written for an English Sunday school march that became popular in the United States after the Civil War, the tune casts the church

FIGURE 12.1 The Haynes' Bible Class Baseball Team, 1905 champions of the Cook County Sunday School Association's Bible Class Baseball League. Image courtesy of the World-Wide Baraca-Philathea Bible Class Union Archives and the Ockenga Institute, Gordon-Conwell Theological Seminary.

as an army out to vanquish Christ's foes. What battle these Bible class athletes unwittingly engaged in, however, at the time remained unclear.

By 1900, Shailer Mathews was worried. Like many seminarians, he had observed the frenzied organization of Bible classes in churches across the country. But according to this rising modernist divine, such activity was cause for concern. No area of church life, he fretted, was "less subject to rules" than the Bible class. Even the most ordinary layperson could teach one, guided by "no preparation" save his or her own "feeble moralizing and pathetic anecdotes." If they were going to be of service to the church, Mathews demanded, Bible classes should be conducted "in much the same way as a teacher in a college will conduct a college class," with the most recent scholarship in biblical studies.[29] Other, largely liberal theologians agreed. After visiting a number of classes, biblical scholar Iriving F. Wood determined that while most Bible class patrons respected the Good Book's power, most were "unwilling to hear anything about newer views regarding the Bible."[30]

Where Mathews and other modernist theologians saw failure, however, a growing number of evangelists and conservative theologians looked on this groundswell of interest in the Bible and saw an opportunity. In the close-knit devotional communities Bible classes sought to build, these religious activists saw something of their own desire to purify or separate from established denominations. For them the task was less to correct or mold a class general understanding of scripture than to organize it. And throughout the first decade of the twentieth century they did just that, attempting to transform the disparate network of individual Bible classes into a movement.

Much like the formation of Bible classes themselves, this consolidation of individual Bible classes into something like a movement also began from below. After a number of Bible classes in Chicago expressed an interest in forming some kind of Bible class union in 1903, the Cook County Sunday School Association intervened and convinced the group to become a part of their body as an Adult Bible Class Committee. The New York State Sunday School Association followed suit that same year, prompting the International Sunday School Association to take notice. Within two years the International Association formed its own Adult Department and attempted to federate all Bible class work under its aegis. "A new day has dawned," wrote W. C. Pearce, who in addition to overseeing the department also popularized labeling lay Bible study as the "Adult Bible Class Movement." "Through the organized class movement," he wrote in 1908, "the boundless energy of the manhood and womanhood of the world is being utilized."[31]

Emphasis on "utilized." According to the International Sunday School Association, the Adult Department's ostensible purpose was to support the organization of new classes by publicizing the practices of successful classes. But the Department's efforts also suggest they were interested in organizing Bible classes for collective action. The Department, for instance, adopted an "International Emblem" that classes could display to publicize their part in the movement. A red circle wrapped around a blank white space, the emblem represented the blood of Christ that one had to pass through in order attain a pure life. But it was also an attempt to forge a shared identity among Bible classes, "a bond of fellowship because it represents the Bible classes of all the different forms." The Department encouraged classes to place the symbol on all of their published material and sold the emblem as a lapel pin, cufflink, or watch charm so individual members could personally display their affiliation.[32] Alongside these symbolic gestures, the Department also devised a number of activities that stitched together disparate networks of Bible classes into regional alliances. They encouraged classes to collect and share lists of their members with Sunday school associations and sponsored a number of organizing tours and conventions, led by individuals like

Moody Bible Institute faculty member E. O. Sellers, *Fundamentals* editor A. C. Dixon, and a number of lesser conservative divines.[33]

For the ministers and prominent laymen who oversaw these efforts, this consolidation of Bible class activity into local, state, and national associations was vital if they were to contribute to any larger cause. In a revealing 1910 editorial in the *Westminster Adult Bible Class*, the Bible class magazine of the Presbyterian Church, Reverend Edward C. Kunkle disclosed that Bible class federations served to transform individual classes into a coherent "force for righteousness." "The federation develops the sense of mass movement," he argued, "and thereby helps to hold men more steadfastly to their ideals and responsibilities." This sense of "responsibility" was key, Kunkle continued, for Bible classes had so far failed "to live their lives in the sense of the larger whole of which they are a part." The "spirit and sweep" of great reforms like prohibition and world evangelization had "not yet made their impress upon those who constitute the rank and file of our local communities," stalling the progress of both campaigns. Imagine what an association of every Bible class might yield, he implored his readers. "It will bring into expression the note of imperialism in Christianity," Kunkle dreamed, inspiring "the forces of righteousness to claim their rights to the right of way in this world." "Politicians will respect the wishes of the better element of the people when they learn how to assert themselves as the enemies of the good know how to assert their wishes," Kunkle sternly concluded. And in a pointed line almost assuredly aimed at the sociability that defined adult Bible classes, Kunkle asserted that "Isolation, independence, exclusiveness and aloofness, whether as classes or as individuals, make impossible vital fellowships and efficient ministry."[34]

Many Bible classes needed little convincing. In communities across the urban north, a number of local Bible class federations did translate their devotional connections into political action. The Cook County Sunday School Association shared its membership lists with reform organizations they supported, while one New York Bible Class Federation organized a "civic committee" that coordinated letter writing campaigns to alert representatives of their positions on specific issues.[35] Reflecting their foundational interest in shielding young people from temptation, local federations similarly attempted to purge their communities of what they saw as sin. Out of a gathering of the Men's Bible Class Federation in Ashland, Ohio, for example, members formed a Citizen's League in order to support a city ordinance banning the production or sale of alcohol. On the day of the vote in 1904, the League placed Federation members outside every poll and appointed others to remind every Bible class member to vote. The ordinance won by a narrow margin.[36]

Not every Bible class activity translated to electoral success. In fact, most did not. Marshal A. Hudson attempted to run for lieutenant governor of New York on the Prohibition Party ticket in 1908, attempting to utilize the thousand Baraca Bible Classes he had recently federated into the Baraca Bible Class Union as pseudo–field offices, and lost spectacularly.[37] But the increased social and political activity of state and local Bible class associations soon drew these groups into larger, far more recognizable campaigns. In 1910, the World's Sunday School Association organized a "Men's

Bible Class Parade" in support of prohibition in the nation's capital to accompany its triennial convention in the city. A reported ten thousand Bible class teachers and members from across the country marched around the Capitol singing "Onward Christian Soldiers" and carrying banners that read "The Saloon MUST Go." When the procession arrived at a lecture hall to conclude the event, they found waiting on the stage such religious and political luminaries as J. Wilbur Chapman, John Wanamaker, and President William Howard Taft.[38] Such spectacles, however, masked the understated, but no less important, ways Bible classes had become the grassroots base of the first wave of Protestant fundamentalists. City unions became the advance teams for Billy Sunday's rallies, while Bible class newsletters advertised noted Fundamentalist theologian James M. Gray's "inductive method" of Bible study.[39]

Even a figure as renowned as William Jennings Bryan turned to Bible classes in order to resuscitate a damaged career. After his controversial resignation as secretary of state in 1915 left him politically powerless, Bryan attempted to revive his image by organizing an "open-air" Bible class in his new hometown of Miami. Bryan, of course, had long been both a member and an advocate of the Sunday school, but his decision to lead a Bible class had a tactician's touch. Unlike the thousands of Bible classes that preceded him, Bryan's class was built around the teacher, consisting only of a weekly gathering at a public park. But the familiarity of the venue proved a success. The class became a sensation, attracting as many as six thousand attendees during the vacation season. Its renown also soon drew Bryan into several nationwide Bible class speaking tours, which brought him back into the public consciousness in the lead-up to his failed run as moderator of the General Assembly of the Presbyterian Church.[40]

According to Bryan, he had started his Bible class "hoping to reach people who never go to church."[41] The result, of course, was in some ways the opposite. The decades of Bible class work that preceded his own had laid the foundation for his rise in religious circles. While Bryan and others might have thought they were at the beginning of a new campaign, in many ways they were capitalizing on work that had long been under way before them.

Far from insignificant gatherings of ordinary people for the regular study of scripture, Bible classes have been a crucible in which the contours of American Protestantism have taken form. In their emphasis on the singular importance of Christian friendship lay the idiomatic foundations of today's evangelical subculture, a phenomenon that became actualized in the campaigns and institutions of religious leaders who directed this desire for community toward ecclesiastical and political ends.

Nor should we think this dialectical relationship between the devotional lives of ordinary people and religious developments occurring on a larger scale will end. As chapter 1 of this book indicates, nearly a quarter of those who claim to read scripture on a regular basis today continue do so in some kind of group context.[42] What social activities and relationships might form in these intimate gatherings is yet unknown. But as the history of the adult Bible class movement makes clear, even the most private acts of friendship can have dramatic public consequences.

13

"Thy Word Is True"

KING JAMES ONLYISM AND THE QUEST FOR CERTAINTY IN AMERICAN EVANGELICAL LIFE

Jason A. Hentschel

TO DESIRE CERTAINTY is to be human—or so J. I. Packer assured us in 1965 during the aftermath of the controversy surrounding the publication of the Revised Standard Version of the Bible. Packer, one of the engineers of evangelicalism's mid-twentieth-century institutionalization of biblical inerrancy, equates that spiritual starvation decried by the prophet Amos with the "unsure, tentative, and confused" state of the church today. Back then, during the age of Israel's divided kingdom, God spoke a message of instruction and salvation through his prophets; now, his Spirit promises to speak through the scriptures, interpreting and applying them to the church. But, Packer reflects sadly, that is far from reality today. Instead, "preaching is hazy; heads are muddled; hearts fret; doubts drain our strength; uncertainty paralyses our action....We know in our bones," Packer cries, "that we were made for certainty, and we cannot be happy without it."[1]

Postwar Americans and innumerable others throughout the West, such as the aforementioned James Packer, experienced decades of cultural upheaval in the closing half of the twentieth century. Alongside the ubiquitous anxiety of an unknown and unfathomable foreign nuclear threat came an intense unsettling of society at home, the product of escalating battles over race, gender, and sex. Biblical inerrancy took its modern shape within this volatile culture and so inherited an enduring and peculiar apologetic tinge that has colored evangelicals' understanding of God, scripture, and the nature of the Christian life. Evangelicals rigorously reemployed the doctrine of inerrancy as the litmus test used to judge authentic Christian faith and practice, and in doing so lifted up an errorless Bible as the certain answer to the increasing uncertainties of life.

King James Onlyism, an intraevangelical movement likewise come of age in this postwar struggle for certainty, presents a relatively straightforward illustration of how American evangelicals in general view and make use of their Bibles today. Like Packer and the greater evangelicalism he represents, King James Only adherents display a driving desire for certainty in the face of what both commonly refer to as an encroaching and destructive subjectivism. Unlike Packer and greater evangelicalism, however, King James Only adherents claim, often vehemently and usually by reference to the underlying Greek and Hebrew texts, that the Authorized Version is the only wholly and truly Christian translation.[2] Across the board, the King James Bible is understood to be their one rock of certainty. It is that absolutely trustworthy book that grants an assurance that what these individuals know to be true is really true.

This conclusion stems from two separate ethnographic studies I conducted during the spring of 2011 and the summer of 2012, which together involved three King James Only churches in the Dayton, Ohio, metropolitan area. Each of these churches belongs to the "Bible Believers' Church Directory," a loose, 1,000-plus member association of churches from every state and over thirty countries. On admission to the directory, each church must affirm the following doctrinal statement: "*We believe* the King James 'Authorized Version' Bible to be the perfect and infallible word of God. We believe the Bible was inspired in its origination and then divinely preserved throughout its various generations and languages until it reached us in its final form. By this we mean that the Authorized Version preserves the very words of God in the form in which He wished them to be represented in the universal language of these last days: English."[3] The data from these studies suggests that a deep-seated fear of doubt drives these three local Dayton churches and their members to claim that God has providentially preserved the Hebrew, Aramaic, and Greek texts behind—and, by extension, the English text of—the King James Bible, a conclusion supported by many of the movement's major published defenses. For example, when asked about the nature and role of modern textual criticism—a method that many non–King James Only evangelicals feel ensures that the Bible they do have is accurate and trustworthy—one respondent claimed that such criticism is a thinly veiled, rampant exercise in relativistic subjectivism where each text critic serves as his or her own authority. The fear here is that where there is a plurality of authority—where subjectivism and a culture of skepticism reign—objective certainty disappears and Christians are doomed to read their Bibles always in doubt of God's truth and their own salvation.[4]

PROTECTING CERTAINTY

That a fear of doubt and its corollary desire for certainty drive the King James Only position today is evidenced in each of the interviews performed throughout this study, though with varying degrees of emphasis reflective of each respondent's comfort around Christians of other traditions.[5] Whatever the degree of emphasis, however, each respondent felt certain that the King James Bible was the most trustworthy and spiritually meaningful version for American Christians today. Consider the following discussion with George Robertson, pastor of Lowes Baptist Fellowship, a lively and growing congregation averaging 650 on Sunday mornings, which claims on the front page of its Sunday bulletin—next to "independent," "fundamental," and "soulwinning"—that it proudly stands on the old, trustworthy "KJV 1611."

> JASON: Do you personally believe that God has preserved his inerrant word in the King James Bible, and if so, what exactly does that mean to you?
>
> GEORGE: I believe he has preserved it in the King James Bible, and it means to me that when I open up a King James Bible that I have something that's pure and right and I may not understand it all, but if I could understand it, it would all be right. And, I don't have to question it; I don't have to correct it. I use it to correct myself, but it's something that I can't correct. It's perfect, and God has preserved it. For English-speaking people, I believe the King James Bible is the English version or English translation that's been preserved accurately for English-speaking people.[6]

George would go on to confess that while he is familiar with some translations that are close to the King James, there are none that he would hold "with the same respect that I hold the King James." Because no other translation so perfectly preserves God's word, there is a danger that comes with preaching and teaching from any translation other than the King James:

> JASON: What do you believe would be lost or different if God did not preserve his inerrant word in the KJV? This may also be said from a different perspective— or different way around—as, "What may be the danger of these other translations?"
>
> GEORGE: If I was preaching from something that I did not believe was 100 percent true and pure, I don't know that I would have the ability to discern what was the untruth from the truth, and then, therefore...I think I would wonder, "Am I teaching the truth or am I teaching something that's not true?" So, believing that I have a Bible that's 100 percent pure and true then I have the confidence to preach it and know that I'm giving forth the truth. [Whereas] if I didn't believe that [that] Bible was 100 percent pure then I would be putting into the hands of someone something that I would be fearful that they would find the error that's among the truth.[7]

George had a point. A simple walk through the religious section of any bookstore will leave even the well-attuned overwhelmed, if not mystified, by the sheer variety of English translations and editions. Even in 1955, before the flood of new versions and editions took the shelves, James Jasper Ray could gripe that in the face of this "multiplicity of differing Bible versions" we simply are left bewildered and confused. And, he would add, the uncertainty does not stop there.[8] Should we compare just two of these versions, we would find that not only do their translations differ, those differences often reflect deeper conflicts in the very texts being translated. Some versions contain words, phrases, entire paragraphs, or even multiple paragraphs that are missing from other versions. Wilbur Pickering, writing two decades after Ray, sounds the same troubled note: "But if you have used a number of the modern versions you may have noticed some things that perhaps intrigued, bewildered, or even distressed you. I am thinking of the degree to which they differ among themselves, the uncertainty as to the identity of the text reflected in the many footnotes regarding textual variants, and the nature and extent of their common divergence from the King James Version."[9] Note the two reasons Pickering gives for this intrigue, bewilderment, and distress. First, we suffer uncertainty due to the many variants among our Bibles, with some versions offering multiple readings in their own footnotes. Pickering goes on to mourn the "incipient uneasiness" this cacophony of options has on the reader.[10] What was once our one reliable guide in times of trouble and uncertainty is now a source of that trouble and uncertainty.

The second reason concerns the claim that these new versions all diverge from the King James translation, not its underlying Greek and Hebrew texts. A standard calculus of the movement involves comparing the text, language, and meaning of the modern translations up against the KJV. Whatever attention is paid to the textual tradition of the King James, it is done so in defense of the English. Certainty for King James Only advocates is as much a certainty about the English text as it is about what might be present in ancient manuscripts. Understood as such, King James Onlyism exhibits a genuine conservatism.[11]

TRUSTING GOD'S WORD

As if to make this very point, David Brothers of Kiefaber Community Baptist Church, a congregation much smaller than Lowes Baptist, claimed that there is a blessing that comes with simply believing that the King James is God's preserved word. Any believer can legitimately and honestly say that her King James Bible provides peace—a peace rarely spoken of by Christians who use other Bible translations. Such peace is found simply in trusting that the King James is indeed God's pure word. "A lot of the people that have the [New International Version] ... don't argue for its perfection," David explained. "Anybody usually that's arguing about that, or presenting a case for it, is King James. So, to me, I think there is a certain amount of a blessing that comes to an individual when they accept that this is the word of God and allow it to be the authority in their life and the manual for what they're going to do and how they look at it." Notice that David's argument, while structurally the same as other evangelical arguments for biblical authority, has the King James Bible as its specific subject over and against the NIV, today's best-selling evangelical translation.[12]

Consistently, King James Only advocates find to be a useless, if not dangerous, fiction the claim, first formulated in the nineteenth century by theologians at Princeton Seminary, that the Bible is ultimately inerrant only in its original autographs. What use is an inspired Bible, argues Edward Hills in his seminal textual defense of the King James, if we do not have access to it today? In a move that strikes many critics as unbiblical and generally specious,[13] Hills connects the divine inspiration of the scriptures to God's preservation of the King James:

> If the doctrine of the *divine inspiration* of the Old and New Testament Scriptures is a true doctrine, the doctrine of the *providential preservation* of the Scriptures must also be a true doctrine. It must be that down through the centuries God has exercised a special, providential control over the copying of the Scriptures and the preservation and use of the copies, so that trustworthy representatives of the original text have been available to God's people in every age. God must have done this, for if He gave the Scriptures to His Church by inspiration as the perfect and final revelation of His will, then it is obvious that He would not allow this revelation to disappear or undergo any alteration of its fundamental character.[14]

If God truly loves and cares about his people no matter the day and age, then he will not leave them without a trustworthy witness. To deny this is to suggest that he is a faithless, unloving God tragically unconcerned with the salvation of his people.

If any argument can be said to stand at the heart of King James Onlyism, it is this appeal to providential preservation, which here takes the form of a dogmatic presupposition. This is important to remember when trudging through the movement's many and varied arguments for the Hebrew and Greek texts that underlie the King James Bible. Such adventures in textual criticism occupy a central place in the group's apologetic, one that reflects a combination of what James Barr calls the dogmatic and maximal-conservative approaches.[15] When the movement's proponents engage in technical methodological discussions, they do so in order to support a prior dogmatic position—here, that God has preserved his word in the KJV. Hence while any defense of the translation's underlying texts, as a whole commonly referred to as the *Textus Receptus*, may appear to be an objective scientific evaluation of the textual evidence, there is a theological presupposition guiding that evaluation. Moreover, not only does this presupposition serve as a lens through which the evidence is interpreted, but that evidence is in turn interpreted in a way intended to support the original presupposition.

To the chagrin of many of their critics, most King James Only advocates happily admit that they are proceeding under just such a theological presupposition.[16] They locate the error besetting modern textual criticism in the fact that it does not make such a claim and instead argues for taking a neutral position in relation to the text, treating it as any other ancient work. Faithful evangelical Christians who accept the absolute authority of the Bible cannot proceed in such a neutral fashion, however, as they would have to ignore God's promises to preserve his word—promises given in that word itself. Critical neutrality is thus ruled out as an unchristian way of interpreting the textual history of the Bible.[17]

For Paul Brown, founding pastor of Stonemill Baptist Church and one of the lead instructors at Stonemill's King James Only Bible Institute, whether or not one ultimately accepts the King James as the only, truly Christian Bible hinges on whether or not one accepts the Bible as absolutely authoritative. Paul began our conversation with an account of his conversion and then quickly proceeded to stress the importance of maintaining an unwavering faith in what the King James says concerning God's revelation and promises. Instead of reviewing the critical arguments, Paul notably began by insisting upon the importance of faith for the Christian life. His usage of faith in this regard, however, reflects a rather straightforward acceptance of the Bible's testimony about itself and its own preservation. Such faith, Paul explained, referencing Romans 10:17, involves "taking what the Bible says and believing it is true."

The rhetoric shaping Paul's account of when he came to believe in the providential preservation of the King James reflects that of a religious conversion. Sparking his belief in the KJV as God's perfect word was an encounter with Psalm 12:6–7, the movement's banner text:

The words of the Lord are pure words:
As silver tried in a furnace of earth, purified seven times.
Thou shalt keep them, O Lord,
Thou shalt preserve them from this generation for ever.

PAUL: I may not know where it is at the time that I read this, but I say to myself, "Got to be somewhere." If he said that he would preserve them, then they're somewhere. Then all I can say is, "Lord, you show me where they are. I want *the* words." "The" is a definite article that [implies] "one and only." It's got to be "one and only." . . . I know all of the comebacks: "Well, how can he do it in this language, how can he do it in that?" Hey, listen: He messed up the languages all back there in the Book of Genesis. He's got no problem straightening them out anytime he wants! It's just a matter of believing God can do what God wants to do the way God wants to do it, and if you're not looking for the truth, you'll mess your mind up. You got to be careful with God. He'll mess you up just as fast as he'll straighten you out. The Bible says, "Seek and ye shall find." What's the antithesis? What's the opposite?

JASON: Don't seek and you . . .

PAUL: . . . will not find. He'll make absolutely sure you won't. He'll blind you like a bat. You're dealing with a God . . . who knows what you want, and he'll give you what you want. Seek and you will find. The opposite is just as true.[18]

For Paul, to claim to have faith in the internal evidence of scripture means to trust that God can and will do precisely what he says. He will not only inspire the Bible; he will

preserve it for all generations, and that means, most important, for us today. The inherent circularity of this argument was never an issue for Paul. If God says he will do
something, then by definition he will do it. To question God's ability or resolve is to
question God himself—a foolhardy notion indeed and yet one, as Paul never tired of
pointing out, typical of today's evangelicals and liberals alike. The root of the matter is
thus whether or not one thinks God is a liar.

In Stonemill's arguments for the preservation of the "one and only" word in the
King James, this insistence on a presuppositional faith becomes the distinguishing
factor between a "KJV man" and all who deny that the King James is God's divinely
preserved word. Despite the text critical arguments and the remarkably detailed charts
examining the differences between versions, the authority of the King James rests not
in the *Textus Receptus* but, as Samuel Gipp explains, in the "power and promise of God
to preserve His Word."[19]

It is important to note here the shape this argument for the preservation of the
King James takes. Because God is perfect, his revelation must likewise be perfect.
This is a classic argument for biblical inerrancy, one that King James Onlyism applies
directly and solely to a particular English translation. To claim that the King James
is God's perfect word then is to claim it cannot change.[20] To add or subtract from it,
to argue that we need something more or something different than what is found in
it, is to argue against its perfection and thus against God's promise to provide
humanity with salvation. Authority and perfection here represent two sides of the
same coin. At Stonemill, Paul emphasized this particular connection with an appeal
to 1 Peter 1:23 and the incorruptible seed from which true Christians are born again.
Because our first birth came from corruptible seed, we must be born again of the
incorruptible seed, that is, as the apostle says, "by the *word* of God." If the word is
not truly incorruptible, or if we today do not actually have that incorruptible, inerrant word in our hands but only in some lost autographs (and thus not at all), then
we cannot truly be born again incorruptible. Furthermore, our salvation is uncertain
and at risk, being based on an untrustworthy, flawed Bible. Hence, what is at stake
in the doctrine of preservation is the eternal salvation of our souls—that most basic
element of evangelical Christianity. Yet the solid, static perfection of the KJV res-
cues us from this hopeless state by providing the cognitive and emotional assurance
we need.

It might come as a shock, then, to hear Paul not only allow for but emphatically
embrace the possibility of further revelation via future inspirations of the Holy Spirit.
Such an allowance implies that a future translation, even in English, could be—to use
Paul's own words—"a little bit better than it was in the first century."[21] To hold to both
the inerrancy and perfection of the Bible as well as the Spirit's freedom to reveal more
truth in the text itself—and not in the church's or individual's interpretation of the
text—is a paradox threatening Stonemill's entire project. And yet it is this insistence
on the Spirit's freedom to enhance the text in this way that enables Paul and Stonemill
to claim that an English text is *the* perfect word of God over and above the Hebrew and
Greek autographs. The fact that the Spirit may choose to preserve a better—can we

say, more perfect?—revelation in Spanish or French or Cantonese has no effect on the perfection of the English KJV.

That Stonemill fails to see this paradox, needless to say its gravity, testifies to what the King James Only position does for Stonemill as much as it threatens to undermine that same position. It is ironic that an unyielding consistency forces Stonemill Baptist into what appears to be a rather stark inconsistency. But Paul's insistence that the Spirit is free to do what he wants with his word—a pneumatology echoed by the congregation's own celebration of the Spirit's movement in the nitty-gritty of their daily lives—is a necessary consequence of the earlier assertion that God is both able and willing to preserve his word. To deny to the Spirit the ability to enhance the biblical text—to reveal a further, better truth in the biblical words themselves—is to deny once again God's omnipotence and, by extension, what makes the King James Bible alone the final authority.[22]

To be fair, Stonemill's position here stands near the radical fringe of the King James Only movement, and I have found no other pneumatological stance quite like Paul's, though the "double inspiration" of Peter Ruckman, spokesman for that radical fringe, could conceivably allow for it.[23] There is, however, a certain consistency exhibited by Paul and Stonemill here with regard to the freedom and omnipotence of the Spirit that serves quite well to illustrate just how powerful, pervasive, and at times seemingly irrational King James Onlyism's appeal to biblical authority can be.

Edward Hills's retelling of the textual history of the New Testament is a case in point. In a fantastic example of revisionist history, Hills claims that God must have guided Erasmus to include in his edition of the *Textus Receptus* those readings preserved not by the majority of Greek texts at the time but by the Latin Vulgate. The most remarkable of these involved the last few verses of the book of Revelation, which Erasmus, working from a manuscript missing its final leaf, translated backward from Latin into Greek, thus creating a truly unique reading. Here, as with the so-called Johannine comma (1 John 5:7) and other commonly disputed texts, Hills is forced to concoct an elaborate defense of the KJV.[24]

For instance, with regard to the differences found among the multiple editions of the *Textus Receptus*, Hills resorts to a tortured distinction between "providential" and "miraculous." A perfect, difference-free textual tradition of the *Textus Receptus* would have required God to have worked miraculously, apart from any human participation. God, however, chose to preserve his word providentially and through human agents in history, which he did despite the inevitable mishaps that would incur. To be sure, Hills's admittance that such imperfection and uncertainty exist within the history of the biblical text is quickly remedied. Faced with the question of which edition of the *Textus Receptus* to follow as God's preserved word for today, Hills resorts to a sanctifying of the contingencies of history: "Which text do we follow? The answer to this question is easy. We are guided by the common faith. Hence we favor that form of the Textus Receptus upon which more than any other God, working providentially, has placed the stamp of His approval, namely, the King James Version, or, more precisely, the Greek text underlying the King James Version." Here we see clearly the power of taking providential preservation as an all-determining presupposition. The divine inspiration and preservation of scripture demand that the textual evidence be interpreted to fit the promise of God that his people will always have access to his word.[25] The consequence of such a move is that now the text's history must be reverse-engineered from the King James, and so biblically faithful Christians are forced to allow the circumstances of later history to determine how they interpret every preceding historical moment.

Those in the movement believe that it is precisely in such a theologically informed interpretation of the textual history that we can find certainty. If the Bible were to be found only in readings long lost and only recently discovered, as modern critics claim, then our faith "would be always wavering." "We could never be sure," Hills warns us, "that a dealer would not soon appear with something new from somewhere." Fortunately, God has not left us in such a lurch. He did not preserve his text in this "secret way," but publicly in the *Textus Receptus* and the King James. On these texts, King James Onlyism assures us, we can be truly certain.[26]

AGAINST SUBJECTIVISM

Presuppositionalism in American evangelicalism has come under significant critical analysis in recent years. Molly Worthen notes that evangelicals "talk so much of 'the Christian worldview' because they believe in it—but also because it is a powerful rhetorical strategy. It curtails debate, justifies hard-line politics, and discourages sympathetic voters from entertaining thoughts of moderation or compromise."[27] Uninflected, presuppositionalism recognizes no objective facts, and yet evangelicals insist that this does not deny the possibility of absolute truth. Evangelical presuppositionalism is as such a far cry from extreme perspectivalism. In fact, evangelicals reject any notion that might imply that an individual is his or her own authority. They insist instead that the Bible alone, as the objective revelation of the eternal God, should provide the presuppositions that color our lives. This would include in the case of King James Onlyism not only the very methods we use to interpret scripture but also the way we tell the story of the preservation of the text itself.

Cornelius Van Til, the foremost proponent of evangelical presuppositional apologetics in the twentieth century, did not shy away from addressing what he perceived to be *the* false presupposition and, on that account, the challenge to God's authority in his word: "When man became a sinner he made of himself instead of God the ultimate or final reference point. And it is precisely this presupposition, as it controls without exception all forms of non-Christian philosophy, that must be brought into question. If this presupposition is left unquestioned in any field all the facts and arguments presented to the unbeliever will be made over by him according to his pattern."[28] Matthew Tabor of Kiefaber Community Baptist Church put the same point this way: "One of the things I believe: Man's word versus God's word. Do we take God's word at his word and believe it? Or, do we want to start looking at God's word and try to compare it? . . . Does

God's word have to pass the test of man?"[29] For nineteenth- and twentieth-century evangelicals, the terms *humanism*, *subjectivism*, and *modernism* were synonymous with making ourselves this "final reference point," with making God's word subject to human reason. Each of these labels could be used to communicate the same basic belief—that one trusts oneself over the Bible.

For Paul Brown and Stonemill Baptist Church, the problem with modern textual criticism is that it is based on a methodology of skepticism, one that seeks to explain everything through "natural experience" and not the word of God.[30] Zane Hodges, longtime professor at Dallas Theological Seminary and one of the more respected proponents of the Majority Text, of which the *Textus Receptus* is a particular expression, offers a similar analysis: "[Confidence] in modern critical Greek texts depends ultimately on one's confidence in contemporary scholarly judgment. It should be clear, however, that when the whole problem of textual criticism is reduced to a series of arguments about the relative merits of this reading over against that reading, we have reached an area where personal opinion—and even personal bias—can easily determine one's decision....In short, the knowledge possessed by modern textual critics about scribes and manuscripts is so ambiguous that it can, without difficulty, be used to reach almost any conclusion."[31] The result is that modern textual criticism and so our modern Bibles are shot through with "speculation and uncertainty."[32] Hence Edward Hills must spend two chapters recounting the sad rise of "unbelief" and "modernism" before he can enter headlong into any discussion of authentic Christian textual criticism.[33] For King James Onlyism, then, all this talk about discovering the true text only serves to raise the great specter of subjectivism with its ensuing uncertainty.

The path to such uncertainty is usually described by King James Only advocates as being quite subtle, as seeping into one's Bible reading through supposed attempts at academic honesty and transparency. It is on these lines that Paul Brown complains about the brackets often used to set off allegedly inauthentic passages in certain modern translations: "As soon as you put brackets on it, the person looks at it and says, 'I wonder if that can be better?' You have instituted confusion right from the start!" This confusion creates a vacuum of authority. By offering multiple readings of certain verses and casting doubt on entire sections of scripture, modern translations suggest not only that God has failed to preserve his word but that God's truth is subject to our own decision-making—a situation evident in any attempt to purchase a new Bible. "Since there's [a] plurality of all of these Bibles," Paul went on to say, "then you become your own god, and deep down in the heart of every man is that desire. Satan has set up a system so you can just revel in it. You can pick out what you want and what you don't want, and you can call the shots. That's dangerous....That's death in the pot."[34]

For Stonemill Baptist and Lowes Fellowship, uncertainty and subjectivism have become common fare in American Christianity, and yet they see such uncertainty and subjectivism as typical of history and humanity in general.[35] Here is a theme believed to run all the way back to the Garden when Satan deceived Adam and Eve into thinking God to be a liar and humans the true masters of their souls:

JASON: [What] would you say are the impetuses behind the translation debate?

GEORGE: Money. You can only sell so many King James Bibles...I believe it's Bible publishers who are trying to market a Bible and so they put a copyright on it, and they make another Bible and make some changes and advertise it as true and reliable and easier to read, easier to understand...I believe it's satanic. Satan is a deceiver. "Yea hath God said," back in Genesis. The very first thing he wanted to do was cause Eve to doubt what God really said. If you can tear down the Bible, then every man becomes a god unto himself, and that's what humanism is all about. Men proclaiming, "My way. I do my own thing. My way is as right as your way. You have your belief and I have my belief, but we're all going to make it to the same...place..." And, that's the kind of humanism and humanistic thinking [I'm talking about].[36]

Here the battle for the KJV is simply one more expression of that same struggle being fought for millennia between God and the Devil, biblical authority and human pride.

What mainline Protestants originally understood as faithfulness to the true history behind the biblical text King James Only adherents understand as, at best, a sad faithlessness and, at worst, a conspiratorial attempt at deception. As Peter Thuesen notes, evangelicalism's adoption of inerrancy as its rallying cry against the intellectual and social turmoil of the early twentieth century was driven by an attempt to maintain some semblance of a lost religious, moral, and intellectual authority uncorrupted by modernity's love affair with the pseudo-science of liberal historical criticism.[37] From the perspective of today's advocates of King James Onlyism, the use of modern textual criticism not only failed to find that kernel of objective historical truth lying behind the biblical text, it also failed to find any consensus at all—a truly "objective" fact made plain by the plethora of disagreements among modern translators and the plurality of new translations. In other words, the movement's proponents understand modern textual criticism's attempt at historical objectivity to be a thinly veiled, rampant exercise in subjectivism, the result of which can be only confusion and uncertainty.

It is this fear of uncertainty, of perpetual doubt, that undergirds these three King James Only churches' insistence that the Bible is the final authority in all matters of faith and practice, and it is this fear that drives their arguments for the inerrancy of the King James. Yet, if we expand our scope to include the larger evangelical world, we see this same critique of subjectivism and its resultant uncertainty coloring the general evangelical debate over the inerrancy of the Bible. The lone difference is that whereas King James Onlyism directs its attack at modern textual criticism, greater evangelicalism has seen fit only to critique higher criticism and the historical-critical method, leaving "lower" textual criticism relatively free of such charges.

J. I. Packer, for instance, explains subjectivism as the conviction that "the final authority for my faith and life is the verdict of my reason, conscience or religious sentiment." He then links this subjectivism to the higher criticism of nineteenth- and twentieth-century Protestant liberalism. Those who follow such a path "treat the question of the truth and authority of Scripture, which God has closed, as if it were still open; they assume the right and competence of the Christian student to decide for himself how much of the Bible's teaching should be received and authoritative." The only legitimate Christian response to subjectivism, explains Packer, is to take a stance of reverential humility toward scripture: "Christian believers, who acknowledge the authority of Christ as a Teacher in other matters, ought equally to acknowledge it in their approach to the Bible; they should receive Scripture as He did, accepting its claim to be divinely inspired and true and studying it as such."[38] Here Packer safeguards conservative and evangelical conceptions of biblical authority against critical attack by reducing our acceptance or denial of such authority to a strictly moral choice. When we reject the truth of scripture and thus fail to enjoy its certainty, we do so not for any genuine epistemological reason but because we do not have the requisite moral character.

Whether he has full-blown liberals or lapsed evangelicals in mind, Packer's general target is the higher historical criticism that set the agenda for much of nineteenth- and twentieth-century biblical scholarship. Yet, when we compare his critique with that offered by King James Only advocates against modern textual criticism, their arguments, while directed against different targets, are clearly cut from the same cloth. That King James Onlyism, a movement within evangelicalism, shares the same concerns, presuppositional methodology, and often the very same rhetoric as Packer and other leaders of the battle for the Bible should come as no surprise. The substitution of human reason for biblical authority is the clear enemy for both.

If we were to highlight a difference between the two groups, it would lie in how they go about securing certainty in the face of what each one views as the illegitimate encroachment of modern forms of criticism. One final illustration will serve to make this particularly clear. In the commotion following the publication of the RSV in 1952, evangelicals across the board threw up their arms in horror at what the translators of the RSV thought to be a simple case of translational propriety. The issue surrounded the translation of the Hebrew word *almah* in Isaiah 7:14, which the King James for centuries had read as "virgin," with its traditional Christological implications. However, following a precedent stretching as far back as Luther and supported by solid linguistic evidence, the RSV translated *almah* as "young woman," and thereby forced a few evangelicals, like the Reverend Martin Luther Hux, to burn the new version as heterodox.[39]

The issue, most notably, was not textual but translational and theological—the Hebrew of Isaiah 7:14 is certain—yet evangelicals as a whole rejected the change as an attempt to cast doubts on the inspiration and authority of the Bible, particularly Matthew 1:23, which quotes Isaiah 7:14 using the Greek Septuagint's *parthenos*, or "virgin." Some evangelicals went even further, charging the translators of the RSV with deliberately undermining the virgin birth. The latter has become a particularly common cry within King James Only circles, but the point here is that while King James Only adherents and their evangelical cousins agreed that the RSV had seriously mishandled the Bible, the two groups sought to remedy the situation in significantly different ways.

Never questioning the legitimacy of modern textual criticism or the need for modern translations of the Bible, the majority of evangelicals claimed that the RSV translation committee had failed to take into account the unique theological character of the biblical text. In the Gospel of Matthew, the Holy Spirit had seen fit to "translate" Isaiah 7:14 as "virgin"; hence the doctrine of inerrancy demanded that this must be the correct translation of the original Hebrew as well. Otherwise, God and the Bible would both be inconsistent, their infallibility and authority broken. Reeling from the translation committee's insistence that such theological considerations not be allowed to determine the translation of the biblical text, these evangelicals moved to produce a brand new translation—the NIV—which would take such considerations into account and thereby protect Christian orthodoxy.

And yet, these evangelicals' King James Only cousins rejected altogether any attempt at making a new translation, choosing instead to defend the orthodox Bible they already had. What united the two groups was a shared concern to protect those traditional doctrines thought threatened by the RSV, a concern—it must be stressed—said to be seated not in linguistic evidence or even in the interpretation of individual texts but in one's general acceptance of the Bible's authority.

In his anthropological study of Creekside Baptist Church, Brian Malley argues that evangelicals have inherited certain defined patterns of belief, including specific doctrines that they then attribute to the Bible. The direction of this attribution is important: "The tradition presents the text as an object for hermeneutic activity, but the goal of that hermeneutic activity is not so much to establish the meaning of the text as to establish transitivity between the text and beliefs."[40] According to Malley, then, evangelicals actually attribute meaning to the text instead of deriving meaning from it, despite their claims to the contrary. In evangelical lingo, their exegesis is actually eisegesis.[41]

The evangelical reaction to the RSV controversy supports Malley's argument. The RSV was said to be heterodox in those places—such as Isaiah 7:14—where the new version prompted a different interpretation from that traditionally assigned to the passage in question, even if the general doctrine or belief was affirmed elsewhere in the same Bible (e.g., the RSV maintained the "virgin" reading in Matthew 1:23). In other words, evangelicals together criticized the RSV because its apparent meaning did not match up with their preconceptions about what it should mean—that is, the RSV stood in conflict with their inherited interpretive traditions. For a community defined by its insistence on biblical authority and letting God speak, it is surprising how much effort has gone into defining what the Bible is supposed to mean and what God is supposed to say.

THE STRUGGLE WITH HISTORICAL CONSCIOUSNESS

It would seem that King James Only advocates and their evangelical cousins are struggling with the same issue, what Grant Wacker described three decades ago as our increasing historical consciousness.[42] Evangelicals of whatever stripe have for two centuries now attempted to minimize, if they have not simply ignored, the implications of historical consciousness on scripture. The appeal to a providentially preserved Bible, one that we can personally touch with our hands and know to be eternally true, is just such an attempt to escape history. Greater evangelicalism's appeal to the inerrant autographs, though possibly less consistent, is another. It would seem that the reason why these two positions remain strong among their respective constituencies in the face of liberalism's wholehearted embrace of historical consciousness lies in the fact that evangelicals and liberals tend to play by a different set of rules, what we may call "core values." In his *Four Cultures of the West*, John O'Malley argues that the history of Western Christianity betrays a number of discursive traditions driven by substantially different values that in turn grant to each culture distinctive rules for discussion and expression. The first of these cultures, what O'Malley labels the "prophetic," is characterized by an indomitable insistence on commitment and purity. It is a decidedly uncompromising culture built on black-and-white dichotomies and inviolable first principles—a culture that would rather maintain an apparent absurdity than hand over the farm.[43] This is the culture of King James Onlyism and of much of today's evangelicalism, both of which value as much as anything a certainty that what they know to be true is indeed true.

Often opposed to the prophetic is the "academic" or "professional" culture. Here the unending search for that elusive truth is all defining. The academic culture values pure rationality and the "close examination of particulars that lead to precise distinctions formulated in sharply defined concepts," which then lead to further and further questions—the end goal being a coherent system, yet one always under revision.[44] Modern textual criticism most closely resembles this culture.

It is important to note that no pure expression of either of these cultures exists. Every actual manifestation of one is at least partially colored by another. For instance, both classic fundamentalism and today's evangelicalism have utilized rational argumentation. However, and this is the crucial point, such argumentation serves not as a core value but as a means of support for those values. The relentless, questioning rationality of the academic culture is foreign to its prophetic cousin, which will gladly "tweak" or even discard such rationality when it ceases to support the latter's core values. (Recall Hills's distinction between miracle and preservation or evangelicalism's insistence that theology hold sway over principles of translation.) What past opponents of the King James Only position failed to realize was that their heavily reasoned arguments hardly addressed the movement's core concerns. The same could be said for much of the criticism directed at greater evangelicalism's appeal to biblical inerrancy. Of course, it is questionable whether any attack on these core concerns would have succeeded, given the prophetic culture's proclivity to defend its beliefs at any cost.

It might be tempting then to throw up our hands at the apparent futility of such debates, but that, it seems to me, would be rash and unnecessary. If anything, this look into King James Onlyism reminds us that behind these often bizarre claims and questionable arguments stand normal folk who are affected like the rest of us on any number of levels. The fear of doubt is as much psychological and emotional as it is intellectual, and so while appealing to the King James may provide a temporary salve for the pains caused by a growing historical consciousness, doubt will continue to color the faith of those in the movement, even as the debate itself continues to do so.

Historian David O'Brien has noted that it is in the very nature of modern society to doubt: "We learn from the Enlightenment that, in the modern context, belief is always accompanied by doubt, by questions about its truth that are there from the start." Indeed, O'Brien warns us, it is not doubt but dogmatism that makes faith and belief impossible.[45] This is a far cry from greater evangelicalism's insistence that certainty is both desirable and possible. It would appear that the faith professed by many evangelicals and their King James Only cousins is an odd type of faith, one far removed from the traditional understanding of faith as trust in the face of a lack of rational certainty.[46] It would then seem to be in paying attention to this desire for certainty that we have the best opportunity to reengage not only King James Only adherents like those in Dayton but evangelicals in general with a renewed discussion of how best to understand the nature and function of the Bible in American life.

ACKNOWLEDGMENTS

Two notes of thanks should be mentioned. First, this work has been supported in part by the University of Dayton Office for Graduate Academic Affairs through the Graduate Student Summer Fellowship Program. Second, heartfelt thanks go out to the three congregations and their pastors who graciously welcomed me into their communities and generously shared their thoughts and experiences.

14

Selling Trust

THE *LIVING BIBLE* AND THE BUSINESS OF BIBLICISM

Daniel Vaca

"KIDS!," A WOMAN groans, turning to the television camera while taking a break from picking up toys in a child's bedroom. "You bring 'em into the world…watch 'em grow…then spend a lifetime worrying about how they'll turn out." The woman begins walking down a flight of stairs, as two children rush by her, heading upstairs. Reaching a living room, she picks up a book, gazes upon it, and holds it up for viewers to see. "Here's something I found that helps a lot. *The Living Bible.*" She explains: "It's not a children's Bible but it's written in today's language so everyone—even children—can understand it. I like to think this *Living Bible* has made a big difference in our family."

Part of an advertising campaign known as "Mother Jr." that aired on televisions in fifty markets in 1974, this advertisement sought to do more than merely raise awareness about a new version of the Bible. Above all, the advertisement set out to convince viewers that responsible parents—and responsible mothers, in particular—not simply could but should purchase *The Living Bible*, published by Tyndale House Publishers of Carol Stream, Illinois. As one of Tyndale House's marketing strategists explained, the advertising campaign attempted "to demonstrate that the *Living Bible* could help every mother in her responsibility to impart values to her children…in a language that both she and her children could understand." Attempting to capitalize on notions of Christian womanhood that assigned responsibility to mothers for the moral and soteriological well-being of both their children and their husbands, Tyndale's advertising agency aired the ad on television programs popular with women, such as the medical drama *Medical Center* and the detective show *Banacek*.[1]

As its advertising campaign suggests, *The Living Bible* was an object designed, produced, and otherwise designated for commercial consumption; it was, in short, a commodity. Most Bibles are commodities. Of course, not every reader of the Bible in the present or past has acquired it through a commercial transaction. Bibles regularly have circulated as gifts, heirlooms, and articles of charitable distribution. Since the early nineteenth century, however, as commercial publishing companies not only began producing a great variety of Bibles but also elaborated the consumer channels through which they distributed their products, even Bibles that ultimately have passed freely from one person to another often have circulated temporarily as articles of purchase.[2] Especially as the evangelical book industry expanded in the second half of the twentieth century, Bible sales increasingly served the commercial interests of for-profit publishers, distributors, and booksellers.

To be sure, the Bible's commodity status is not necessarily remarkable. Insofar as contemporary American society is a consumer society, most articles of everyday life are commodities. And as Colleen McDannell notes, advertisers have encouraged their publics to perceive virtually every commodity as no less "numinous and inspiring" than the Bible.[3] Yet the Bible's commodity status does not demand attention because commodities are peculiar; that status merits notice because it is essential to the story of the Bible in American life. Commodity status has configured how Americans have acquired and engaged their Bibles, for example, and has helped determine why Americans have engaged particular Bibles.

Although evangelical book businesses generally have presented their activity as a form of Christian service to their consumers, their commercial activities have not simply attempted to meet existing consumer demand. In addition to designing Bibles that consumers want, the book and Bible industry also has sought to teach consumers what they should want. Tyndale House's "Mother Jr." advertisement provides just one example of that labor, illustrating how companies have both cultivated and catered to their consumers' desires, anxieties, aspirations, purchasing preferences, and gender roles.[4] As this chapter accordingly argues, commodity status not only shapes the form that particular Bibles take and the audiences they attempt to reach but also orients how Bibles conjure authority and justify their existence. By analyzing the commodity status of *The Living Bible*, this chapter asks how consumer capitalism determines the rationales that lie behind Bible production, distribution, and consumption.

COMMERCIAL CONCERNS

In a sense, the Bible's commercial history is an old story, which several historians of American religion and culture have examined. Focusing on the nineteenth century, for example, a number of historians have chronicled the rise of industrial Bible production and consumer-oriented design, exploring how changing conceptions of status, taste, and family have shaped Bible consumption and use.[5] While studies of the nineteenth-century Bible industry have tended to focus more on the material design of American Bibles than on their translations and texts, Peter Thuesen explores how American Protestants increasingly fought during the late nineteenth and twentieth centuries over Bible translation, production, and interpretation. Arguing that Biblical debates between "liberal" and "conservative" Protestants fundamentally have manifested a shared obsession with "textual and historical veracity," Thuesen points out that publishing companies have supported one side of a hermeneutical debate over another for reasons that have "reflected pecuniary as well as theological motives."[6]

Yet if the Bible's commodity status seems historiographically evident, conversations about how Christians engage and understand the Bible often privilege other concerns. As chapter 1 observes, for instance, scholars should devote further analysis to the "enduring popularity" of the King James Bible, especially among people with relatively low incomes. Proposing potential lines of research, the chapter further suggests that explanations for the King James Version's popularity might include readers' aesthetic preferences, denominational policies, or theological beliefs. While each of these explanations holds its own explanatory potential, however, other explanations might acknowledge how practical circumstances shape the preferences, policies, and beliefs that people understand and articulate. Consider, for example, that the copyrights to many translations of the Bible belong to particular corporations, which typically demand licensing fees to use their translations. Meanwhile, the text of the King James Version resides in the public domain (outside the United Kingdom), which allows American publishers to reproduce its text without paying licensing fees. As a result, editions of the King James Version are abundant and inexpensive. As chapter 1 notes, readers who insist on the King James Version seem to claim more regularly that "the Bible is the literal word of God." But commercial accessibility allows more people to put that perception into practice; and if, as Susan Harding suggests, "speaking is believing," then greater access enables more people to adopt that perception.[7]

Attention to the Bible's commodity status might help explain additional findings from chapter 1. The majority of survey respondents claimed, for example, that they do not seek help in understanding or interpreting the Bible. This finding reflects respondents' reply to a question about their engagement with the following categories of assistance: clergy; published commentaries; Bible study groups; radio/television; and internet.[8] But one category of potential assistance proved conspicuous for its absence: the Bible itself. For well over a century, even "Bible only" Protestants often have not read the Bible only, in a literal sense; instead, they have read the Bible's text in formats that have offered varied cross-references, footnotes, and other interpretive aids.[9] By providing readers with sufficient interpretive assistance within a Bible's covers, such formats have allowed their readers to avoid or deny seeking assistance from outside the Bible. Meanwhile, by continually creating Bibles with new annotations and study aids, publishing companies have been able to continue selling new editions of the Bible to customers who already own at least one. To recognize the Bible as a commodity is to recognize that the act of buying a particular kind of Bible from a particular kind of outlet is itself an act of receiving external interpretive assistance. By considering how commercial impulses orient understandings of the Bible and its use, scholars need not ignore traditional emphases, such as aesthetic preferences or theological beliefs; to the contrary, such an approach helps scholars understand how people develop beliefs, live them out, and transmit them across space and time.

THE LOGIC OF AUTHORITY

Created by Kenneth N. Taylor (1917–2005), portions of *The Living Bible*'s Living Translation began appearing as early as 1962, while the complete Bible appeared in 1971. *The Living Bible* would become the best-selling book in the United States in 1972 and 1973, and it has remained relatively popular. According to chapter 1, 5 percent of survey respondents reported that they read a Bible containing the Living Translation most frequently. That translation's continued popularity stems in part from its continued appearance in new formats—including *The Book* (1985), a version designed to look like an attractive novel, which Tyndale House marketed through a $10 million advertising campaign.[10] Yet Bibles containing the Living Translation have touted more than an innovative appearance. Above all, the Living Translation has emphasized its use of "today's language." Because that emphasis has conflicted with prevailing paradigms of Biblical authority, the success of *The Living Bible* demands explanation.

Strictly, the Living Translation is not a translation; it is a paraphrase of an English-language translation, the American Standard Version. Published in 1901, the American Standard Version was an American-audience variation of the Revised Version, published in 1881 (New Testament) and 1885 (Old Testament). So called because it revised the King James Version, the Revised Version reflected translators' desire to produce what Peter Thuesen describes as a "pure, uncorrupted biblical text." Viewing their endeavor as a kind of objective science, translators hoped that a modern Bible would serve as a foundation for Protestant ecumenism and secure confidence in the Bible's authority by correcting the textual errors the King James translators had made centuries earlier.[11] To claim authority for their revision, both these translators and most subsequent translators have highlighted their translations' proximity to the Bible's original languages and the most ancient manuscripts. Manifesting this principle, the Revised Version and American Standard Version both proved "slavishly literal."[12] In a sense, this literalism made the American Standard Version an ideal candidate for a paraphrase. Yet insofar as a paraphrase fundamentally distances itself from the textual proximity that literalism endorses, the same logic that lends the American Standard Version its authority simultaneously undermines the authority of paraphrases and more colloquial translations. The latter Bibles accordingly have claimed authority by other means.

Rather than generating authority by appealing to "formal equivalence" with the Bible's untranslated words, paraphrases and colloquial translations claim "dynamic" or "functional equivalence." The justification for functional equivalence rests principally on the notion that rigid adherence to the formal structure of the Bible's original languages invariably obscures its functional meaning for contemporary readers, who neither speak with ancient syntax nor understand many ancient concepts. As one biblical scholar says of dynamic equivalence, "the criterion for translation is the response of the reader, and the ideal seems to be an immediate response." Readers of Bibles that rely on this appr2oach not only presume that they "should be able to understand it on their own terms" but also trust that their Bible's creator will define those terms responsibly.[13]

Premised on adapting the Bible to the reader's textual preferences and devotional sensibilities, functional equivalence has proven consonant with publishers' inclination to cater to potential consumers' desires; in a way, consumer capitalism has justified the legitimacy of functional equivalence. At the same time, however, attempts to create Bibles that cater to consumer preference through functional equivalence must reckon with the precariousness of their authority. Although all Bibles generate authority by convincing readers to trust their creators' judgment, some versions demand more trust than others. By relying almost entirely on functional equivalence, paraphrases transform their creators' judgment not just into an operating logic and a marketing strategy but also into a potential object of attack. Although Kenneth Taylor was not the first person to render the Bible in accessible language, his singular success relied largely on his ability to forestall attack and cultivate trust through the market.

In addition to championing their own ability to judge the Bible's functional meaning, earlier paraphrases and colloquial translations also invited potential and actual criticism. With the first of its six volumes published in England in 1739, for example, Philip Doddridge's *Family Expositor* became the first paraphrase that North American booksellers imported. A Massachusetts printer eventually reprinted it in 1807.[14] Recognizing that his English-reading Protestant consumers generally expected their Bibles to contain the King James text, Doddridge anticipated and addressed potential criticism in his Bible's preface. Acknowledging that his paraphrase often deviated so significantly from the King James text that "I should not be able to guess from the *paraphrase* itself, what the *scripture* was which it pretended to explain," Doddridge admitted that such interpretive liberty "must undoubtedly give the greatest advantage for disguise and misrepresentation." To defend his version against accusations of misrepresentation and to evidence his sound interpretive judgment, Doddridge not only presented his paraphrase alongside the relevant King James texts but also flagged words in the paraphrase that he offered as his own "improvement." While words paraphrased directly from the Bible appeared in italics, Doddridge's improvements appeared in standard font. He instructed readers to study the King James text first, the italicized portions of the paraphrase second, and his own improvements last.[15] With the risk of misrepresentation accordingly minimized, Doddridge insisted that the potential advantages of a paraphrase outweighed the dangers. In addition to helping "to promote *family religion*," a paraphrase offered what Doddridge described as the "most agreeable and useful manner of explaining it to common readers," who might lack yet desire "the benefit of a learned education." Especially as Doddridge's *Family Expositor* traveled beyond the religious communities that knew and trusted him, the design and rationale of his text helped to protect it from criticism.[16]

Throughout the nineteenth and twentieth centuries, paraphrases and colloquial translations continued to claim authority by appealing to original languages, to their laudable objectives, or to the trustworthiness of their creators.[17] In the 1920s, for example, the University of Chicago biblical scholar Edgar Goodspeed defended his colloquial translation, *The New Testament: An American Translation* (1923), by appealing to his belief that the Bible should appear in "the simple, straightforward English of everyday expression." Noting that the New Testament was written not in classical or literary Greek but rather in "the common language of everyday life," Goodspeed argued that a colloquial translation might capture the "unpretending vigor" of the original.[18] As Bryan Bademan explains, Goodspeed hoped such vigor might allow the Bible to "have a key role to play in integrating, preserving, and extending American Protestant culture."[19] Yet even though Goodspeed based his translation on the original biblical languages, he ultimately drew criticism from varied Protestant perspectives. While many mainline Protestants insisted that only the King James Version "contained the raw materials for sustaining liberal democracies," some conservative Protestants saw Goodspeed's avowed theological modernism as evidence that colloquial language would invite the same sort of misrepresentation Doddridge had cautioned against.[20] In contrast with Goodspeed's case, both mainline and conservative Protestants proved less critical of a colloquial translation of the Bible known as Today's English Version, which appeared as a New Testament entitled *Good News for Modern Man* in 1966 and as the complete *Good News Bible* in 1976. But that version escaped the criticism that befell Goodspeed's Bible because its creator and that creator's stated objective received widespread support. The American Bible Society, the translator and producer of Today's English Version, explicitly presented it as an evangelistic aid, restricting its vocabulary and syntax so that people who spoke English as a second language might understand its meaning.[21]

In comparison with these predecessors, *The Living Bible* initially lacked a firm claim to the criteria that generally have conferred authority on paraphrases and colloquial translations. As a paraphrase of an English translation, it held an indirect connection to the original languages; some critics derided it as a "translation once removed."[22] Created by an individual, it initially laid no claim to an institution's sound reputation. Written in language geared less toward readers in missionary contexts than toward American readers who shared Kenneth Taylor's own middle-class, conservative aesthetic, *The Living Bible* did not seem to possess objectives that set it apart from colloquial translations that had relied on the original languages.[23] As a result, several conservative Protestant publishers turned down opportunities to publish it.[24] One of the leading evangelical publishers of the day, Zondervan Publishing House, reportedly claimed "misgivings about the concept."[25] Taylor later recalled that "theologically liberal scholars" initially praised it, while "evangelical scholars could not tolerate a paraphrase translation, insisting that any translation must be on a word-for-word basis, rather than expressing the *meaning* of the Greek text."[26] Eventually, however, *The Living Bible* would achieve bestseller status and solicit substantial evangelical acceptance by using commercial strategies to elevate its creator's reputation, to cultivate support for his objectives, and to recalibrate how consumers assessed a Bible's utility and authority.

THE PURPOSE OF PARAPHRASING

Kenneth Taylor generally touted two principal reasons for creating *The Living Bible*. The first and more conventional objective centered on the urgent need for people to read the Bible. The second objective involved children. Insofar as other colloquial translations already had claimed that their accessible language would incite Bible reading, Taylor and Tyndale House distinguished *The Living Bible* by emphasizing the second objective. Market research and market success testified to that strategy's success.

"It is my hope," Taylor explained to a reporter from the *Saturday Evening Post* in 1975, "that this will open a window to fresh changes in millions of lives. The Bible, as the Word of God, can transform lives unbelievably if only people will give it a chance."[27] An objective with a long lineage, the desire to saturate American society with the Bible's transformative power had animated organizations like the American Bible Society since the early nineteenth century. That objective also had served as a guiding principle for the religious cultures in which Taylor grew up. The son of a conservative Presbyterian minister, Taylor was raised in Oregon but attended college at Wheaton College, near Chicago. After graduating in 1938, he began graduate study at Dallas Theological Seminary before ultimately graduating in 1944 from Northern Baptist Theological Seminary, in Illinois. Considered centers of fundamentalist Protestantism, all of Taylor's educational institutions trained their students to advocate for Bible reading and study as a primary means of opposing theological modernism.[28]

While Taylor's educational experiences nurtured his fundamentalist devotion to the social and soteriological importance of conservative biblicism and morality, subsequent experiences cultivated an emphasis on diffusing that devotion as widely as possible. This emphasis lay behind Taylor's claim that a paraphrase would serve as an ideal conduit for the Bible's power. "A *readable* Bible," he insisted, "can revitalize our time."[29] Taylor developed this emphasis on accessibility as a participant in the burgeoning neo-evangelical movement—which, like Taylor, had matured in moderate fundamentalist institutions. Before and during his time in seminary, for example, he and his wife worked for InterVarsity Christian Fellowship, an evangelical group devoted to college students, which hired Taylor to edit its magazine, *HIS*, in 1943.[30] Together with his interest in Christian writing and journalism, Taylor's evangelical orientation provided him with opportunities to develop new institutions and initiatives dedicated to disseminating conservative biblical and moral perspectives.

The logic of evangelicalism justified Taylor's paraphrase. As it developed in the late 1930s and 1940s, the evangelical movement of Taylor's time committed itself above all to diffusing conservative Protestant sensibilities throughout American culture. That aspiration even lay behind evangelical leaders' rehabilitation of the term "evangelical," which they hoped would appeal more widely than labels that connoted denominational particularity or doctrinal rigidity, such as variations on the term "fundamental."[31] More important, this evangelical movement perpetuated a broader shift away from what Timothy Gloege describes as "churchly" Protestantism and toward an orientation that located authentic faith not in church membership or creedal affirmations but rather in an individual's relationship with God. To be sure, an emphasis on individual understanding can be seen as part of a centuries-long tradition of Protestant concern for lay interpretive authority. But individual understanding became a hallmark of the evangelical mode especially in the late nineteenth century. Embracing consumer-oriented sensibilities while also challenging new theories of human development focused on random mutations and inherited traits, many evangelicals renewed their focus on the social necessity of individual choice.[32] This individual authority received enhanced support in the twentieth century, as expanding consumer markets encouraged consumer choice and drew upon evangelical ideas to make mass consumption socially acceptable.[33] Insofar as it privileged individual readers' understanding of the Bible and cultivated that priority through consumer pathways, *The Living Bible* manifested evangelicalism's social logic. It affirmed its readers' authority, over and against biblicism's conventions.

Deviating from the models of biblical authority that other institutions and translators had adopted, *The Living Bible* claimed that its approach conveyed the Bible's meaning even better than competing colloquial translations. As a 1966 profile illustrates, for example, Taylor sometimes appealed to the original biblical languages. "Before publication," the profile notes, "the manuscript was checked by a number of Greek scholars."[34] Over time, Taylor intensified and revised that appeal; in 1979, for instance, a writer from *Christianity Today* challenged Taylor by asking him to respond to the criticism that "it is based on English versions and not on Hebrew and Greek originals." Insisting that his Bible did in fact rely on the originals, Taylor disparaged translations that relied principally on the original languages. Because translations typically begin with "rough translation" from original languages and receive stylistic revision secondarily, Taylor complained, they usually "produce a somewhat stilted 'feel.'" By comparison, he argued, his approach "begins with the flowing thought of a paraphrase and then turns it over to . . . scholars to check and recheck." More than merely equating the authority of the two methods, Taylor argued that "the paraphrase method is the ultimate method of understandability with accuracy."[35]

In addition to claiming a unique ability to deliver an individual understanding of the Bible, Taylor and Tyndale House also distinguished *The Living Bible* by arguing that its intelligibility served a singular objective: a flourishing family. Taylor claimed authority for his paraphrase above all by highlighting its ability to edify children—including his own children. Beginning in the mid-1960s, when Taylor began publishing portions of the Living Translation, articles about his paraphrase and interviews with him invariably featured this objective. "It was because of his children that Taylor undertook paraphrasing," a 1966 profile explained. In 1974, with sales of the complete *Living Bible* exceeding 14 million copies, the *Wall Street Journal* began its profile of Taylor and his paraphrase by explaining that he "was concerned that the nine children he had at the time weren't getting the most out of the family's devotional reading of the venerable but archaic King James Version of the Bible."[36]

Before writing *The Living Bible*, Taylor had devoted much of his professional attention to children and younger adults. In 1948, for example, he published *Is Christianity Credible?*, a small booklet that attempted to provide college students with "a better understanding of the reasonableness of Christianity and why their pagan professors didn't believe in Christianity."[37] Several years later, he began writing books for younger children, including *Stories for the Children's Hour* (1953). Taylor later explained that he focused on writing for younger children due in part to his own experience as a father. With his first child born in 1942 and his final child born in 1956, Taylor and his wife, Margaret, had ten children. In Taylor's telling, he grew frustrated when he "could not find a book that covered the entire Bible for very young children." As a result, he wrote *The Bible in Pictures for Little Eyes* (1956).[38]

Recalling *The Living Bible*'s creation in his autobiography, Taylor would explain that it emerged out of continued difficulty engaging his children with the Bible. As his oldest children reached adolescence and his own storybooks no longer proved suitable, he began reading to them from "the Bible itself." But he found that it became "hard to hold the children's attention even though I stopped the reading every few verses to explain and ask a question or two." Admitting that he, too, had struggled to understand the Bible as both a young person and adult, Taylor decided in 1955 to try paraphrasing passages from the King James Version. When he shared the results with his children, Taylor "was elated to note that ... they had understood." Taylor also admitted that he "enjoyed reading my paraphrase too, and got much more out of it than from other Bible reading." While his preference for his own words may not have surprised anyone but him, he was encouraged by receiving positive responses from his children whenever he paraphrased new passages. Eventually, he decided to paraphrase the epistles of the New Testament. As the basis for his work, he selected the American Standard Version because "it was, and still is, in my opinion, the most accurate of the word-for-word English translations." Writing with "vocabulary and construction that would be acceptable for the average reader at *Reader's Digest* level," he completed his paraphrase of the epistles in December 1960 and titled it *Living Letters*.[39]

Why did Taylor highlight the superiority of his "thought-for-thought" method and its supposedly incomparable ability to nourish children and their families? While personal experience undoubtedly informed Taylor's concern for children, market research also suggested that an emphasis on children would resonate with consumers. In order to identify the best way to market *The Living Bible* among varied potential consumer groups, Tyndale House commissioned a number of market research studies in the early 1970s. Focusing especially on the "middle to upper class professional population," for example, one 1972 study identified housewives and mothers as "the decision maker in the area of Bible purchasing." In 88 percent of the 300 families surveyed, "the mother was directly involved in need recognition and actual purchase." Insisting that "the *Living Bible* must be shown as the answer to the most important needs which Bible readers have," Tyndale House's marketing strategists pointed out that many house-

wives cited lack of time, lack of habit, preference for other religious literature, or difficulty understanding the Bible as their reasons for not reading it. Meanwhile, the same
respondents "agreed overwhelmingly with the statement 'My family is the most
important thing in my life.'" In-depth interviews also revealed that Taylor's account of
writing "the paraphrase primarily so his children could understand the Bible seemed
very effective in reminding respondents of similar problems with the Bible." As a
result, the final research report recommended that marketing material should capitalize on the tendency for "the typical housewife" to be "very concerned about raising her
younger children and giving them social, moral, and religious guidelines on which they
could base their lives."[40]

Based on this recommendation, Taylor's publishing firm developed the "Mother Jr."
ad and created related advertisements for periodicals. "Their future lies in your hands,"
one print ad trumpeted in bold letters above an image of children playfully dressing
themselves in costumes. "Paraphrased thought for thought rather than translated
word for word," the ad explained in smaller print, "The Living Bible is written the way
people talk today, not hundreds of years ago.... Your children are depending on you
and you can depend on the Living Bible."[41] Picking up this advertising campaign's
strong emphasis on the interests of children, subsequent articles about Taylor's paraphrase focused recurrently on that theme. Having minimized the prevailing view that
a Bible translation should emerge directly from the original biblical languages, Taylor
cultivated authority for his paraphrase by highlighting objectives that market research
had endorsed.

To be sure, both Taylor and many of his readers valued an emphasis on children due
in part to a longer tradition of evangelical preoccupation with children. While middle-
class Victorian-era evangelicals had attempted to discipline working-class children outside the home and emphasized moral discipline within the home, for example, Taylor's
contemporaries transformed the welfare of children into a salient strategic tool through
campaigns against issues like desegregation and gay rights.[42] Midcentury evangelical
initiatives like Youth for Christ expressed a version of this same concern for children
and families.[43] Through his own work for InterVarsity and his emphasis on *The Living
Bible*'s benefit to children and families, Taylor both participated in this tradition and
engaged it strategically. Illustrating how such priorities achieved prominence through
consumer contexts, Taylor's commercial success helps explain why corporations like
Wal-Mart later would achieve success by cultivating what Bethany Moreton describes as
the notion that "mass buying could mean procuring humble products 'for the family.'"
To the extent that Wal-Mart would sanctify itself by selling books like Taylor's, it did so
by capitalizing on the authority those books already had cultivated.[44]

MARKETING A BIBLE AND AN AUTHOR

In addition to cultivating trust by claiming laudable objectives, Bibles also have touted
the reputation of their creator. Hewing to this paradigm, *The Living Bible* ultimately

would leverage Taylor's reputation. Although Taylor's education and work experience had enlarged his standing among evangelicals, the evangelical book industry would enhance it further. Taylor would receive support from that industry partly because he had helped spearhead its creation. That experience would enable him to take greatest advantage of the commercial opportunities that the industry afforded.

Taylor became familiar with the evangelical book industry not just through his work for InterVarsity's publications but especially through his subsequent work for Moody Press, which he joined in 1947. He became its director the following year. In that position, he learned which books sold best. Early in his time at Moody, for example, he discovered that the publisher of Charles B. Williams's *New Testament in the Language of the People* (1937) had allowed it to go out of print. A Southern Baptist professor who taught Greek and New Testament interpretation, Williams had based his translation on original biblical languages yet had written it in colloquial language, with extensive annotations. After securing Williams's permission to republish his version of the New Testament, Moody Press cultivated readers' trust by adding an introduction that contained testimonials to the translation's accuracy. At the same time, Moody removed many of Williams's annotations.[45] Williams's Bible would become one of Moody's bestsellers, and Taylor would cite it as inspiration for his subsequent paraphrase experiments.[46]

In addition to familiarizing him with consumer demand for particular book genres, Taylor's time at Moody also attuned him to issues that constrained or enhanced sales volume. As director of Moody Press, he recognized that the evangelical book industry operated regionally, with limited large-scale, national distribution. Taylor saw this as a problem because it held back the scale of literature that his company and others could produce and sell. To remedy this problem, Taylor and his assistant director, Bill Moore, set out to expand the industry's distribution capacity by creating an evangelical counterpart to the American Booksellers Association.[47] In the fall of 1950, Moore and Taylor organized the Christian Booksellers Association (CBA). Among its many contributions to the shape of the postwar evangelical book industry, the CBA's legacy lay especially in the growth and professionalization of evangelical bookstores. The organization would devote substantial resources not only to connecting publishers to distribution outlets but also to helping people start, operate, and maximize profits from their bookselling businesses.[48] By the mid-1960s, articles in evangelical magazines regularly remarked on the attractive lighting, racks, displays, and general store experience the CBA had helped create.[49] During the 1960s, the growth of Christian bookstores helped Christian book sales to rise dramatically, notably faster than the book industry in general.[50]

Taylor's success testified to the value of the CBA. After finishing *Living Letters*, Taylor bound several copies and brought them to the annual CBA convention in 1962, where he set about drumming up interest from book distributors and bookstores. Having decided to publish the book himself, he named his new publishing business Tyndale House Publishers, after the sixteenth-century English Bible translator William Tyndale. Under that commercial banner, Taylor secured distribution through CBA bookstores and wholesalers. He also piqued the interest of Billy Graham, who offered to give away copies to viewers of his *Hour of Decision* television program in the fall of 1963. That same fall, Taylor decided to leave Moody Press to focus on paraphrasing the entire Bible and soliciting more books for his publishing business. By the 1970s, such authors as David Wilkerson, Tim LaHaye, and James Dobson all would publish books with Tyndale House. Taylor launched the full *Living Bible* at the July 1971 CBA convention. Familiar with the intricacies of book distribution due to his CBA experience, he arranged a corporate partnership with the firm Doubleday, which allowed him to distribute *The Living Bible* not just through Christian bookstores but also through secular bookstores, drugstores, grocery stores, and such department stores as J. C. Penney.[51]

But the CBA ultimately did more for Taylor than provide him with distribution knowledge and outlets; it also helped elevate his reputation and cultivate authority on his paraphrase's behalf. In 1975, for instance, the official trade magazine of the CBA, *Bookstore Journal*, published an article titled "Can You Really Trust a Paraphrase?" Written by Paul Mouw, the article set out to train booksellers in how to understand and respond to customer anxiety about paraphrases. Acknowledging that some evangelical customers were convinced that *The Living Bible* was not a legitimate Bible, Mouw dismissed such criticism. "No translation can possibly be exactly accurate and trustworthy—not even the King James," he insisted. Based on this claim, he argued that all translations must deviate from the literal text, so that "today's American, who thinks and lives differently than the writers of the Scriptures, can understand *exactly* what God meant." Insofar as a paraphrase allows an author to emphasize the "usual understandings of the passage by evangelicals," Mouw explained, an "honest, careful paraphrase . . . is as valid and safe as a word-for-word type. On balance, perhaps safer."

But Mouw also cautioned that the safety of a paraphrase ultimately depends on its creator. Rather than asking whether the paraphrase method is valid, Mouw suggested that consumers should recognize that every "translator brings his own theological and educational understandings and limitations to the manuscript." Pointing out that most translation initiatives attempt to mitigate individual theological priorities by using teams of translators, Mouw described team translation as a problem. Because "various team members will hold different positions," he explained, "the resulting compromise doesn't fully satisfy either side." Instead of privileging the ideal of team translation, Mouw advised booksellers to consider the possibility that "one unique man" might create a translation that "is as accurate as possible in transferring God's meaning." Identifying "Dr. Kenneth Taylor" as such a man, Mouw insisted that "the theology of a translator is important." Having made that case, he concluded by quoting a variety of Bible and theology professors who could attest to the "extreme value" of Taylor's work.[52]

Just one example of CBA articles and Tyndale House advertisements dedicated to elevating Taylor's reputation and marketing his Bible, Paul Mouw's article illustrates how *The Living Bible* received authority not from a denomination, ecclesiastical organization, or any single individual but rather from a trade group devoted to boosting the sales volume of its affiliates. Recognizing evangelical anxieties about the authority of a paraphrased Bible, Mouw and *Bookstore Journal* attempted to assuage them. The article not only addressed evangelical bookstore owners' potential theological reservations about *The Living Bible* but also exhorted those salespeople to shift their consumer's perceived needs. In this way, the market for evangelical books both generated and circulated understandings of biblical authority and authenticity.

CONCLUSION

By 1979, when the journalist Harold Myra interviewed Kenneth Taylor about *The Living Bible* in the flagship evangelical magazine *Christianity Today*, sales of Taylor's Bible reportedly accounted for almost half of Bible sales in the United States. As an ad in the magazine claimed, over 24 million copies had sold. "Some versions gain popularity—then fade away," the ad explained, "while *The Living Bible* remains the people's choice." On another page, the words "The People's Choice" occupied an entire page, virtually unadorned. How had Taylor's Bible achieved such success?

Harold Myra asked Taylor a version of that question. "Sometimes I've been asked," Taylor responded, "whether I expected such a vast circulation to occur, and I really don't know how to answer that because God did give me some intimations that it was going to have a wide usefulness."[53] Although Taylor did not elaborate on the intimations he reportedly received, they perhaps included some of the business experiences explored in this chapter. Whether or not Taylor held particular moments from his career in mind, however, his general experiences in both publishing and business undeniably shaped the strategies he and his company used to generate authority for his paraphrase and to cultivate consumer interest in it.

Yet this does not make *The Living Bible* an exception to the proverbial rule by which contemporary Americans have encountered, experienced, and engaged the Bible. To the contrary, by using commercial strategies to conjure support for his Bible's objectives, to solicit respect for his authorial status, and to generally confer authority on his product, Taylor simultaneously embraced and entrenched at least two principles that conjoin the stories of modern consumer capitalism and the Bible in American life. Since the early 1800s, one principle has demanded that publishers acknowledge that consumers have attained a kind of sovereignty. As technologically reliable printing and cheaper methods of production and distribution have enabled publishers to multiply their aesthetic presentations and sites of commercial activity, consumer preference has oriented Bible production and consumption.[54]

In addition to catering to consumers' aesthetic preferences, a second principle has seen publishers in the twentieth century focus especially on cultivating particular preferences and priorities. In addition to biblical ideals, those preferences and priorities include social and soteriological anxieties. When the "Mother Jr." ad aired in 1974, for example, a middle-class, Christian housewife might not have considered that the key to her children's future morality and salvation might be found in the pages of an unusual "thought-for-thought" Bible. But Tyndale House, its advertisements, and its sales outlets would make that case, attempting to revise her understanding of her family, her Bible, and the relationship between the two.

As the market became a primary venue for evaluating material and metaphysical concerns, even classic ministerial endorsements came to serve this commercial strategy. "In this book I have read the age-abiding truths of the Scriptures," the revivalist Billy Graham explained in another Tyndale House ad, "as though coming to me direct from God." Read alongside other ads in the same issue of *Christianity Today*, the message of Graham's endorsement was clear: *The Living Bible* was "the People's Choice" because it was God's choice. Reading this ad, a mother possessed no strict obligation to choose *The Living Bible* herself. As ever, the choice to purchase a Bible ultimately remained with the consumer. In that choice, however, lay her family's potential future, and her own.[55]

15

The Bible and the Legacy of First Wave Feminism

Claudia Setzer

THE NINETEENTH CENTURY witnessed strong currents of social change that brought into relief the question of women's participation in public life. First, the Industrial Revolution shifted society away from agricultural models to an urban, production orientation. This affected the family structure by separating the worlds of work and home, contributing to the sense of the home as a refuge from the bruising world and the woman in the family as the one presiding over the moral and spiritual training of the children. The family farm, by contrast, had been an enterprise that engaged the whole family, at the same site. Second, the Second Great Awakening, a religious revival movement at midcentury, encouraged an egalitarian ideal of individual reception of the Spirit happening outside traditional church structures. Women and men alike took on preaching and teaching roles as the revival fanned out across the country. Third, reform movements like temperance and abolitionism featured women and men in public roles, speaking to public groups, writing, and engaging in political actions. The temperance movement, in its leadership and its rank and file, was dominated by women. The movement for women's suffrage, whose official starting date is often identified as 1848, when the first women's rights convention met in Seneca Falls, also participated in these changes.

The lines of influence crossed back and forth. Antisuffrage writers (who were mostly women) may have underscored the spiritual role of women in the domestic sphere, but so too could Elizabeth Cady Stanton hold forth on the moral weight of motherhood. Suffragists advocated participation of women in political processes and public life, but some antisuffrage writers also assumed a public role for women in social reform, arguing that they would be more effective without the vote. The temperance movement in particular confounds categorization, as it revolved around public meetings, sit-ins at saloons, and destruction of stores of alcohol, while presenting itself as "the home going forth into the world." Religion, and the Bible in particular, were part of the mix of events, and could be found on both sides of controversies.

The Bible evoked mixed responses from women's rights advocates in the nineteenth century. Some, like Sarah Grimké, Lucretia Mott, and Frances Willard, regarded it as an ally in the struggle, teaching above all the essential dignity and equality of men and women. Only corruption, mistranslation, and deliberate misuse of the text could make it teach women's subordination. For others, like Matilda Joslyn Gage and Elizabeth Cady Stanton, the Bible was a major tool in the centuries-long oppression of women. Ernestine Rose represents a third response: the Bible, like religion on the whole, was irrelevant to the struggle for women's equality. *The Woman's Bible* (1895–1898), the commentary produced by Cady Stanton and her committee of women interpreters, exhibits all three of these approaches. For all of these commentators, from Grimké to Gage, the authority of the Bible is never absolute, as they also argue from natural law, experience, Nature, and human rights.

Grimké first defended the cause of women's equality using the Bible in her *Letters on the Equality of the Sexes* (1837), written to Mary Parker, the president of the Boston Female Anti-Slavery Society, and published in abolitionist newspapers. A convert to the Society of Friends, from childhood Grimké rejected both slavery and the limitations on women, both features of life on her family's plantation in Charleston, South Carolina. Sarah, her sister Angelina, and brother-in-law Theodore Dwight Weld became prominent campaigners for abolitionism. Grimké believed that the Bible itself was free from patriarchy, citing Genesis 1:26–27 as the *locus classicus* of women's equality, establishing that God created male and female in his image, and Galatians 3:28, where Paul seems to reject all forms of difference between those baptized into Christ. Even the story of woman's creation from Adam's rib indicates equality:

> Surely no one who contemplates, with the eye of a philosopher, the design of God in the creation of woman, can believe that she is now fulfilling that design. The literal translation of the word "help-meet" is a helper like unto himself; it is so rendered in the Septuagint, and manifestly signifies a companion. Now I believe it will be impossible for woman to fill the station assigned to her by God until her brethren mingle with her as an equal, as a moral being; and lose, in the dignity of her immortal nature, and in fact of her bearing like himself the image and super-scription of her God, the idea of her being female. The apostle beautifully re-marks, "as many of you as have been baptized into Christ, have put on Christ. There is neither Jew nor Greek, there is neither bond nor free, there is neither *male* nor *female* [italics hers]; for ye are all one in Christ Jesus."

Woman's equal status was God's design, and to say otherwise is unscriptural and blasphemous.[1] Similarly, Grimké maintains that the Sermon on the Mount preaches ethical commands to women and men alike. Like later feminists, she understands Jesus as teaching an egalitarian message, despite the absence of any explicit teachings on women. Examples of individual biblical heroines, like Miriam and Deborah in the Hebrew Bible and Phoebe and Priscilla in Paul's letters, shore up her argument.

To undermine biblical statements that seem to teach women's subordination, Grimké engages in an early form of cultural criticism. The original text is inspired, she insists. Yet translators have infected the texts with values gleaned from their own culture, one that sees women as slaves or empty-headed dolls, and have read those values back into the narrative. The King James Version is particularly suspect, for example, turning a rueful prediction of women's suffering into a divine curse against Eve in Genesis 3:16: "Your desire will be for your husband, and he shall rule over you." "Shall," indicating command, should be rendered as "will," indicating mere prediction.[2]

A decade later, Lucretia Mott (1793–1880), one of the organizers of the Seneca Falls convention and a fellow Quaker, asks "has there not been an unworthy resort to this volume to prove the usefulness of slavery and of crushing woman's powers, the assumption of authority over her, and indeed of all the evils under which the earth, humanity has groaned from age to age?"[3] Like Grimké she thought that the first creation story, Sinai's laws, and Jesus's precepts taught women's equality but "the pulpit has been prostituted, the Bible has been ill-used. . . . The practice has been, to turn over its pages to find example and authority for the wrong, for the existing abuses of society."[4] Both Grimké and Mott belonged to the Society of Friends, a group that does not see the Bible as the sole source of truth but always subject to "the inner light" that each person possesses.

Fifty years after Grimké, Frances Willard produced an astute and lively defense of women's rights using the Bible. In her *Woman in the Pulpit* (1888) she argued for women's ordination in the Methodist church, using methods that suggest some knowledge of emerging biblical criticism. The influential president of the Women's Christian Temperance Union, Willard backed a broad set of social reforms, including abolition of slavery, child labor laws, and free kindergarten.

True to her Methodist upbringing, Willard loved the Bible from childhood, but rejected literalism as a straitjacket she could not wear. Tweaking those men who justify women's subordination by citing the curse against Eve, she suggests that those men had better take care to fulfill the curse aimed at Adam "to eat his bread in the sweat of his face."[5] Literalism cuts both ways.

To counter statements by Paul recommending women's silence, Willard lines up verses from Judges, Joel, and Luke that show women praying and prophesying in public. By demonstrating multiple voices and views in her charts, she is congenial to the scholarly method of source criticism that was coming from Europe at the time. Whether she consciously borrowed their approaches or was simply a sensitive reader of text, we cannot say. We do know she was acquainted with one of the primary practitioners of the new methods, Charles Augustus Briggs. Like Grimké, she decries the effects of a patriarchal culture on interpretation and even on translation. She notes one case where a missionary to China leaves out Paul's references in Philippians 4:3 to fellow preachers and leaders who are women, fearing it will alienate the Chinese.[6]

African-American women saw the Bible as a fundamentally liberationist text devoted to human dignity. Sojourner Truth drew liberally from the Bible in her famous address in Akron, in 1851,[7] suggesting that if Eve's sin upset the world, she should have a chance to set it right again. Jesus, she reminds us, came into the world through God and a woman, minus any help from a man. Virginia Broughton (1858–1934), a traveling Baptist preacher, gathered biblical verses that supported women's right to preach, disseminating it to her Bible Bands, groups of women who studied the Bible daily. Anna Julia Cooper (1858–1964), educator and college president, learned biblical languages at Oberlin College and went on to earn a doctorate at the University of Paris (Sorbonne). Citing biblical and Christian ideals, this daughter of a slave mother argued for increased education and rights for black women in *A Voice from the South* (1892). African-American women had been strong advocates for universal suffrage but suffered from racism within the suffrage movement in the nineteenth and early twentieth century. Rosalyn Terborg-Penn recounts how some white women tried to suppress Truth's remarks and how divisions arose in the American Equal Rights Association over whether the fight to enfranchise African Americans by the Fifteenth Amendment should include black women or accept the "gradualist" approach to extend rights to men first.[8] The "southern strategy" adopted by the National American Woman Suffrage Association, the suffrage organization formed from two earlier groups, led Susan B. Anthony to ask Frederick Douglass to skip their 1895 convention. In 1903 the association's executive board proposed that southern states be allowed to determine their own approaches, thus guaranteeing exclusion of black women from their definitions of suffrage in those states.[9]

African-American women formed their own women's clubs and continued to press for inclusion in political and religious arenas. In churches like the African Methodist Episcopal church, women such as Jarena Lee and Sophie Murray preached, evangelized, and held prayer meetings, even as their requests for licenses to preach and formal recognition were refused.[10] While rightly critical of institutions in their own communities and in American society, these women did not critique the Bible but seemed to understand it as a thing apart, an unfailing ally in their fight for justice.

Impatient with attempts to harmonize the Bible and women's rights, Matilda Joslyn Gage (1826–1898) and Elizabeth Cady Stanton saw it as a weapon wielded by those in power to keep women in submission. Gage, one of the commentators in *The Woman's Bible*, indicts the Bible as the chief cause of patriarchy in Western society, "the tendency of the Bible has been to crush out aspiration, to deaden human faculties, and to humiliate mankind. From Adam's plaint, 'the woman gave me and I did eat,' down to Christ's 'Woman, what have I to do with thee?' the tendency of the Bible has been the degradation of the divinest half of humanity—woman.... But our present quest is not what the mystic or spiritual character of the Bible may be; we are investigating its influence upon woman under Judaism and Christianity, and pronounce it evil."[11] Even so, she admits that it is misread and highlights powerful women like the queen of Sheba and Bathsheba, who helped her son become king. For her, God is a "spirit or vivifying intelligence," who possesses male and female attributes.[12]

Like Gage, Cady Stanton identifies God with nature, and uncouples "pure religion" from institutions like scripture and churches. Raised a Presbyterian, she was acquainted with virtually every major figure in the abolitionist and suffragist movements. The commentary of her *Woman's Bible*, composed chiefly by American Protestant women, contains disparate attitudes. Cady Stanton rejects anthropomorphism, dubbing the historically contingent narratives of the Hebrew Bible as primitive bids for power over women: "Does anyone seriously believe that the great spirit of all good talked with these Jews, and really said the extraordinary things they report? It was, however, a very cunning way for the Patriarchs to enforce their own authority, to do whatever they desired, and say the Lord commanded them."[13] Similar arguments about the stories around Noah, Isaac and Rebecca, Sarah and Hagar contribute to general condemnation of the Hebrew Bible and "the Jews" as benighted but unduly influential in the long history of subordination of women.

Some contributors to the commentary are less judgmental, retaining the possibility that some revelations are genuine. Like Grimké and Willard, Clara Bewick Colby suggests that the early translators and interpreters shaped the text to conform to their own prejudices. Yet Colby also avoids the trap of assigning all negative views of women to the "Jewish" past of the Old Testament. She suggests that Rebecca, for example, enjoyed personal freedom and that Jewish women fared better than women of other ancient peoples. Nor does Cady Stanton view the New Testament as any improvement on the Old, as she grants that "while there are grand types of women presented under both religions [Judaism and Christianity], there is no difference in the general estimate of the sex. In fact, her inferior position is more clearly and emphatically set forth by the Apostles than by the Prophets and the Patriarchs."[14]

The New Testament receives far less space in the *Woman's Bible* than the Old, but Elizabeth, Anna, and Jesus's mother come in for praise; Mary becomes the subject of Cady Stanton's expansive remarks on motherhood. Jesus is regarded as innocent of patriarchy, while Paul takes the blame for women's subordination in Christianity. Like Grimké, some commentators blame it on Paul's Jewish background. The question of anti-Judaism in feminist interpretation has been discussed for second wave feminism, but it was also a temptation for some of these first wave feminists.

For some, the Bible was neither ally nor enemy in the struggle for equality but something of a bystander. Lucy Stone (1818–1893), for example, considered the Bible significant only in that it bolstered the position of the church and clergy. She does not focus on verses and only generally invokes the notion of women's power given by God, saying "I have confidence in the Father to believe that when he gives us the capacity to do anything He does not make a blunder."[15]

Ernestine Rose, a declared atheist who began life as the daughter of a rabbi in Poland, thought that wrangling over the Bible was a grand irrelevancy. Women's rights rested on values more profound and earlier than biblical ones. When Reverend Antoinette Brown introduced a resolution at a women's rights convention in Syracuse in 1852 that included extended biblical exegesis to show that the Bible supported the rights of women, Rose successfully blocked it. She argued that neither the Book nor

Brown's interpretation should be in the convention's statement. "Here we claim human rights and freedom based upon the laws of humanity and we require no written authority from Moses or Paul, because those laws and our claim are prior even to these two great men....It has done mischief enough. A book that is so ambiguous as not to convey any definite idea, can furnish no authority to this convention."[16] Rose's proposal to table Brown's resolution passed unanimously. Even Lucretia Mott, then president of the association, said that the discussion of the Bible was a distraction and that the association should avoid the pitfall of early abolitionism, when there was too much preoccupation with the Bible. Women's rights were self-evident from reason and universal human rights.

I characterize these three positions of first wave feminists as seeing the Bible as ally, the Bible as enemy, or the Bible as bystander. The categories may overlap, and as with Lucretia Mott, positions may change with circumstances. Cady Stanton, who hardly revered the text, nevertheless recorded her horror when a visitor wanted to use their family Bible as a booster seat for a child at table, saying "It seemed such a desecration. I was tempted to protest against its use for such a purpose, and this, too, long after my reason had repudiated its divine authority."[17] She also admires certain biblical women like Jesus's mother and Mary Magdalene, while failing to note others like Hagar.

These theorists both borrowed the authority of the Bible and pushed against it. Grimké, and Willard, especially, were certain that the pure message of the Old and New Testaments was women's equality. Yet even critics like Cady Stanton thought its teachings might be separated from historically contingent stories, the trappings of culture, and institutional uses by church and clergy. Gage allowed that strong women models appeared, even if suppressed by later interpreters. All of these women rejected literalism.

The women's rights movement was intertwined with the two great social movements of the nineteenth century, abolitionism and temperance. Grimké and Mott publicly campaigned against slavery. Willard grew up in an abolitionist family and included it in her reforms. Cady Stanton first heard the tales of an escaped slave at the home of her cousin, Gerritt Smith, whose house was a stop on the Underground Railroad. In her teens at the time, she said "we needed no further education to make us earnest abolitionists."[18] She credits Boston abolitionist Theodore Parker for many of her ideas. Smith and Parker were members of the Secret Six, wealthy northerners who funded John Brown's uprising.

Abolitionists had to confront the narratives that showed patriarchs owning slaves, Jesus's silence on slavery, and Paul's apparent indifference to it ("Were you a slave when called? Never mind." 1 Cor. 7:21). They developed a critical exegesis that employed philology, extrapolation of certain verses, and emphasis on broader themes to render the Bible the opponent of slavery. For example, some argued that "slave" really meant "servant" in Greek and Hebrew, so the patriarchs were not slave owners. Jesus's teaching, though silent on slavery, was a "seed growing secretly" that would one day bear fruit in the demolishing of injustice. The temperance movement was less biblically oriented, but it could not afford literalist exegesis either, as—Willard noted—it would make Jesus "a glutton and a wine-bibber."[19] Temperance, however, did make women's organizing and public agitating respectable.

Habits of thought learned in abolitionism, including uses of the Bible, naturally, though not automatically, carried over into the women's rights movement. As Cady Stanton says in her autobiography, "all through the Anti- Slavery struggle every word of denunciation of the wrongs of the Southern slave was, I felt, equally applicable to the wrongs of my own sex."[20] The movements shared not only rejection of literalism and use of philological solutions (Grimké's claim that Eve's curse meant it "will" happen, not it "shall," i.e., it was not commanded by God) but also suspicion of tampering with translations (Willard) and recognition of the effect of culture on translation and interpretation.

Two other rather different developments aided feminist exegesis—the Second Great Awakening and the development of historical criticism of the Bible. The Second Great Awakening amplified the Protestant idea of individualism in receiving the spirit. It also gave rise to women preachers, leaders, and circuit-riders. Phoebe Palmer, for example, led the Holiness movement coming out of Methodism. At the same time, historical-critical methods in studying the Bible were coming from Europe, undermining literalism and contextualizing narratives while retaining an allegiance to the text. Discussions of "Higher criticism" appeared in the popular press, in magazines like *Harper's* and *the Independent*, the latter containing a column titled "Biblical Research" that reported the latest finds in archaeology and biblical studies. Roughly fifty articles on historical criticism, pro and con, appeared in the paper between 1880 and 1888. Willard read and contributed to both publications. Both Willard and Cady Stanton refer to the discipline of Higher Criticism as something readers will recognize.

The Bible was a frequent player in the debates about women's rights, but its authority was never absolute. The failure of Brown's "Bible resolution" at the women's rights convention as early as 1852 and Mott's remarks about the limited value of exegetical debates suggest that some leaders saw the Bible as a distraction. When the National American Woman Suffrage Association met in 1896, it passed a resolution saying that it had no connection to "the so-called *Woman's Bible*, or any other theological publication." This was no doubt because the commentary was too much of a political hot potato but may also reflect a growing sense that women's rights would not be won on biblical grounds.

Nor did antisuffrage arguments of the early twentieth century invoke the Bible as much as one might expect. A series of antisuffrage essays by Massachusetts women published in 1916 generally recommended that women emulate Christ by self-sacrifice and bearing the cross and crown of motherhood as he bore his cross;[21] but these essays did not pull out the expected verses from the creation story or Paul's letters. Their arguments more often emphasized the value of women in the home, the notion that no one could juggle home and public life well, and the distinctive role women already played in charitable and reform work. Minister Horace Bushnell argued from women's nature;[22] James Cardinal Gibbons claimed to preserve woman's honor and her privileged position in the home.[23] Gibbons also claimed that wives and mothers already voted by proxy by way of their influence on their sons and husbands.

The three approaches of seeing the Bible, and by extension religion, as ally, enemy, or bystander appeared in second wave feminism, although the Bible was less a presence and had lost considerable authority in the culture compared to Victorian society. Thinking of the "common feminism" of the sixties, seventies, and early eighties in America, I have looked at three canonical works of early second wave feminists noteworthy for their public visibility: Betty Friedan's book *The Feminine Mystique* (1963), Kate Millett's *Sexual Politics* (1970), and issues of *Ms.* from 1972 to 1989. The first two mention the Bible and religion almost not at all. Millett looks at the development of the ideology of patriarchy as it is embedded in literature, especially in works by Norman Mailer, Henry Miller, and D. H. Lawrence. She also argues that Freud's views on penis envy and women as incomplete men have been translated into the culture with insidious and overwhelming effect. She mentions religion only rarely, citing the Fall as one of the leading myths of Western culture.[24] Friedan also ignores religion for the most part, seeing it as a mere servant to larger societal trends. Freud comes for an extended critique;[25] and she does not resist the urge to attribute some of his patriarchal ideas to his Jewishness. *Ms.*, as the work of multiple authors of different religious and humanist upbringings, is quite mixed on religion. A long article in the December 1972 issue recounts the Lilith myth in Judaism, a midrash on the Eve story. In July 1974 three women debate "Is It Kosher to Be Feminist?" A poem of protest against biblical patriarchalism appears in the same issue ("The Tree of Begats"). In January 1980, the article "Eighty Women to Watch in the 80's" includes only three religious activists or theologians; the November issue includes an article on feminist exiles from Russia, one of whom cites an "opposition" Orthodox church as a haven for women. "The Minister's Wife," in the December issue, recounts the challenges of a woman minister in a New England town and echoes early feminists who see religion as ally: "Religion is not traditional. That's the mistake people make. From the first, Christianity has been a dynamic force. Christ said 'go forward, Break with tradition, take the risk, don't be afraid of change.' "

Academics have paved the way for nonscholars to grapple with the Bible. The *Journal of Feminist Studies in Religion*, founded in 1985, is accountable to both the academy and the feminist movement. Elisabeth Schüssler Fiorenza's book *In Memory of Her* (1983) inaugurated feminist New Testament scholarship, introducing a "hermeneutic of suspicion" by which to approach biblical material about women.[26] Her *Searching the Scriptures* (1993–1997) provided feminist commentary on every canonical book.[27] Judith Plaskow's work of theology *Standing Again at Sinai* (1991) sought to reclaim the Torah to include women's experiences.[28] Rosemary Radford Ruether called for a reexamination of primary Christian symbols in *Sexism and God-Talk* (1993).[29] *The Women's Bible Commentary*, an anthology of women's interpretation of biblical texts, was first published in 1992 and its third edition in 2012.[30] All of these works attempt to reach beyond the boundaries of the academy.

Third wave feminism is sufficiently diffuse and diverse that it may not clearly be called a "wave." The same deep suspicion of religion as an obstacle to women's progress appears in remarks like Gloria Steinem's at the MAKERS conference in February 2014 in Palos Verdes, California, a conference devoted to women's empowerment in the workplace. In response to an audience member's question as to the biggest problem in feminism today, Steinem cited antifeminism and economic issues but also said "What we don't talk about enough is religion. I think that spirituality is one thing. But religion is just politics in the sky. I think we really have to talk about it. Because it gains power from silence."[31] At the same time, *Ms.* includes in its online blogs articles like "The Bible, Biology, and Bigotry," by Michael Kimmel (June 18, 2012), which says only a misreading of the Bible valorizes inequality, and "Elizabeth Cady Stanton: More Than a Suffragist," by Christina Maria Paschyn (March 16, 2015), which celebrates *The Woman's Bible*. Blogs on faith and feminism promote women who insist that their religious texts and traditions teach fundamental equality and inclusiveness. The flourishing of organizations like the Jewish Orthodox Feminist Alliance and the Evangelical and Ecumenical Women's Caucus and the increasing number of women leaders of all faiths suggest that the Bible will continue to be a well from which some feminists will draw.

16

Let Us Be Attentive

THE ORTHODOX STUDY BIBLE, CONVERTS, AND THE DEBATE ON ORTHODOX LAY USES OF SCRIPTURE

Garrett Spivey

IN A 1995 *Church History* article, Stephen Stein described the current state of Bible publications as a "proliferation of designer bibles" flooding the American market. He further defined "designer bibles" as "study bibles for specific denominational clusters."[1] As examples, he listed Oxford University Press's *Catholic Study Bible* as well as several offerings from the world's largest Bible publisher, Thomas Nelson. These included the *New Geneva Study Bible*, a Bible aimed at Pentecostals titled the *Spirit-Filled Life Bible*, and *The Orthodox Study Bible* (OSB). These study Bibles offered familiar translations alongside denomination-specific commentary crafted to appeal to niche demographics. While such a significant shift taking place over the past thirty years should certainly draw attention as a generalized movement in the Bible market, there is also benefit in examining the development of a singular example of these niche market Bibles. A brief exploration of the history of one of these projects, the OSB, demonstrates a wide range of motives driving those responsible for its publication. One must consider the personal beliefs of not only the translators and the writers of the study material but also of the senior executives and editors at Thomas Nelson. The history of the OSB reveals a surprising story of how important players in the world of Christian publishing developed a Bible that was significant for their own deeply held religious convictions.

Products designed for public consumption are never utilized only in ways their creators specifically intend. More than other Bibles, these niche study Bibles are designed for very specific uses. Publishers intend for study Bibles to be read in specific locations, for personal and devotional reading, or for group study rather than for liturgical dictation. While the OSB's publishers designed the OSB with specific audiences in mind, hopefully using it in prescribed ways and defined locations, readers found other uses that helped shape and define the its legacy for a generation of modern Orthodox Christians.

The editors state in their introduction to the OSB that it was intended for two audiences: "1. English-speaking Orthodox Christians the world over and...2. Non-Orthodox readers interested in learning more about the faith of the historic Orthodox Church."[2] Lead editor Father Jack Sparks described what he envisioned the uses of the OSB to be, such as "personal use—including recalling the doctrines of the Orthodox Church and their biblical foundation—Church School lessons, Bible studies, answering the issues raised by Protestants as well as heretical sects, and teaching your child."[3] Ultimately, the OSB had two intended goals or uses: to become English-speaking Orthodox Christians' primary Bible for personal reading and study and to be a tool for proselytizing non-Orthodox, especially evangelical Protestants. While the OSB garnered a mixed reception from its intended audiences, Orthodox Christians found a third use for it, namely, as the focal point for a debate over the future trajectory of American Orthodoxy.

The OSB project began in 1988 as a New Testament and Psalms. Thomas Nelson published it in 1993 and after four years began working on a complete Bible with an Old Testament, including the apocryphal or deuterocanonical books found in the Eastern Orthodox canon. Thomas Nelson published this completed project in 2008. It is important to note that while much of what this essay argues may also be said of the earlier New Testament and Psalms, this essay primarily concerns issues surrounding the later Old Testament project.

The OSB was first conceived by a group of former evangelical Protestants who converted to Eastern Orthodoxy in 1987. Their spiritual journey to the Orthodox Church began in the late 1960s, when seven regional directors of Campus Crusade for Christ resigned their positions in order to pastor house churches across the country. They wanted to replicate the churches of the New Testament period to the best of their ability, but after studying the history of Christianity together, they became increasingly drawn away from their evangelical background and toward liturgical worship. This led to the formation of an independent denomination named the Evangelical Orthodox Church and later attempts to formally join Eastern Orthodoxy in North America.

Most of these former Campus Crusaders became bishops in the Evangelical Orthodox Church, responsible for dioceses across the United States and Canada while continuing to shepherd specific churches that they had personally planted in the early 1970s. Jack Sparks, however, became increasingly drawn to intellectual pursuits and the desire to educate new priests in their movement. As a result, he developed an independent research institution in 1976, the St. Athanasius Academy of Orthodox Theology, in order to develop a correspondence course for the training of new clergy and to pursue other research projects. This institution would become the driving force behind the later development of the OSB.

While members of the former Evangelical Orthodox Church certainly altered many of their past beliefs and practices in order to enter canonical Orthodoxy, they held on to some aspects of their evangelical Protestant background, including a devotion to personal scripture reading and a fervor for evangelism. It is not surprising, then, that immediately following the mass conversion of nearly three thousand Evangelical Orthodox Church members to Orthodoxy, one of the first projects the group undertook was the publication of a Bible meant for evangelizing other Protestants and reforming the personal scripture-reading habits of North American Orthodox Christians.

In addition to their role as leaders of the Evangelical Orthodox Church, several of the men responsible for this first wave of conversions also had surprising connections to the world of Christian publication. All of the seven former Campus Crusade directors were authors, mostly through Thomas Nelson or Zondervan. Peter Gillquist, the presiding bishop of the Evangelical Orthodox Church, was also an employee of Thomas Nelson, serving at different points in his tenure as a senior editor and editor-in-chief. Sam Moore, the CEO of Thomas Nelson during much of the OSB's development, was a Lebanese immigrant to the United States. Though he was not a practicing Orthodox Christian, he had a soft spot for Orthodox Christianity. His mother was a devout Lebanese Orthodox Christian, and he had been baptized into the Greek Orthodox Church as an infant in Lebanon. When Peter Gillquist and other former leaders presented the idea for the OSB to Moore, he agreed to pursue the project despite believing that it would not be profitable. He simply did it as a favor for his longtime employee and friend. There were two stipulations, however. Moore agreed to help fund the project as long as they at least made up the cost of production, and he agreed only if they used the New King James Version, which was owned by Thomas Nelson, as the basis for their study Bible. While this was not a significant issue in publishing the New Testament, it proved to be of some consequence years later when developing the Old Testament OSB.

Despite initial estimates that the OSB would not be profitable, the planned publication in 1993 quickly sold out in preorders, and the company rushed to print new copies. After four years of moderate success, the OSB developers believed it was time to tackle the Old Testament in order to produce a complete OSB. Though Sam Moore was still the CEO of Thomas Nelson when the Old Testament project began, he later retired, and the new CEO, Michael Hyatt, oversaw the remainder of the project. Hyatt was an influential member of the former Evangelical Orthodox Church and a deacon in the Eastern Orthodox Church. While the success of the initial OSB proved that such a project could indeed be profitable, Thomas Nelson, the world's largest publisher of bibles, produced the OSB because of the personal beliefs of some of its most senior employees and leaders. But why did Gillquist, Hyatt, Sparks, and others believe that a study bible for Orthodox Christians was necessary? To understand that, one must consider the importance that the Eastern Orthodox Church places on the Greek Septuagint.

Unlike the New Testament project, the Old Testament had a particularly unique set of challenges. All Old Testament translations in Eastern Orthodox Christianity are based on the Septuagint, a Greek translation of the Old Testament books dating to the third century BCE. Almost all Old Testament translations in modern English bibles are based on the Hebrew Masoretic text, including Thomas Nelson's own NKJV, which was used in the OSB New Testament and Psalms. The OSB team decided that if they were going to complete an Old Testament, it must be an English translation of the Septuagint, something that at that point had not been done since 1851. It quickly became apparent, however, that the OSB project did not have the resources to produce a completely new translation. The editors settled on a compromise, for a variety of reasons. They would use the NKJV as the basis for their Old Testament, only altering the text where the Greek and the Hebrew varied significantly. The New Testament would be exactly the same as the older OSB, meaning that it was just the NKJV with the additional study notes. The editors and translators argued that this would keep a continuity of language between the two testaments and greatly reduce the time needed to produce the Old Testament translation.

In addition to a somewhat new translation of the Old Testament, the complete OSB contained a great many aspects that set it apart from other study Bibles on the market. First, it contained all of the books of the Septuagint, including the deuterocanonical books that the Eastern Orthodox Church considers fit for reading, such as the Wisdom of Sirach, Tobit, and 1–3 Maccabees. Second, the margin notes contained commentary from both patristic sources and modern authors. As one translator noted, "among modern Christians the voice of the Fathers regarding scripture is unknown, so it is nice to see what John Chrysostom says versus C. I. Scofield."[4] Third, along with the commentary, the OSB contained several insets that focused on aspects of Orthodox belief and practice. Often these short articles covered parts of Orthodoxy that other Christian denominations find fault with or misunderstand. Examples include articles on the uses of icons in Orthodox worship and the importance of Mary in the Orthodox faith. Other inclusions attempted to meet the needs of both Orthodox and non-Orthodox readers, such as a lectionary for helping Orthodox faithful follow the liturgical calendar for their Bible reading and a more general schedule to guide a reader through reading the Bible in a year.

While the initial OSB met with some success, the leaders of the project believed the general public would need some education as to why such an Old Testament was necessary if the complete OSB was to also be profitable. They felt many of the American Orthodox faithful, especially recent converts, were completely unfamiliar with issues surrounding translation or the history of the deuterocanonical books. They therefore undertook an education campaign through every media outlet available to them, including publishing articles in Orthodox magazines and websites, giving interviews, and producing their own radio programs and podcasts. The standard line of argument began by demonstrating why the Septuagint rather than the Masoretic Text was the foundation of the Orthodox Old Testament, usually by using passages familiar to the audience. One prime example used Isaiah 7:14, the verse that had been at the center of the controversy between conservative and liberal Christians over the Revised Standard Version in the 1950s.[5] The OSB's proponents argued that it was not the fault of supposedly liberal translators that they had changed the verse from what the KJV rendered "Behold, a virgin shall conceive," to "Behold, a young woman shall conceive." The RSV translators were properly translating from the Masoretic Text. It was only once one compared the Septuagint to the Masoretic, they argued, that one saw how the Masoretic Text rendered passages in ways intended to shroud the clear Old Testament allusions to Christ in ambiguous language. While in the eyes of Orthodox believers the Septuagint was divinely inspired, proponents of the OSB argued that the transcribers of the Masoretic Text had ulterior motives; "particularly, they did not want to use in their services texts that the Christians could use to demonstrate that Jesus Christ is the Messiah promised by the Prophets of the Old Testament."[6] The OSB campaigners also pointed to the historical fact that the Septuagint was the translation in use during the life and work of Jesus and his apostles. Any time the New Testament quotes the Old Testament, one is most likely reading the Septuagint. The OSB creators expected those skeptical of the necessity of such a project to ultimately be persuaded by the argument that if it was good enough for Jesus, then it should be good enough for them.

Because the OSB was published first as a New Testament and Psalms collection in the early 1990s and later with a full Old Testament in the 2000s, most of its history has taken place during the internet age. As a result, the development of the project and the contentious debate after its publication have all been available in a very public way. Interested parties could sign up for a newsletter received through either the mail or email, and the webmaster updated the website monthly with news of the project's progress. Once the OSB was published, one could find every review of it online. Even if the review originated in print, transcriptions regularly made their way to Orthodox blogs and online forums. Those who participated in the translation of the OSB also regularly participated in the public conversations surrounding it.

Many Orthodox Christians in North America lauded the complete OSB, finding that it succeeded in meeting its goals for its different audiences. Praise for the OSB usually came in one of two forms. First, reviewers provided anecdotal evidence of how the content of the OSB was exposing Orthodoxy to others and bringing converts into the church, and second, they talked of how the OSB had strengthened their faith, primarily by revealing so-called gems in the scriptures that had been obscured by bad translations or an ignorance of deuterocanonical books. For example, Father Chad Hatfield, a professor at St. Vladimir's Orthodox Seminary, said:

> What impressed me the most about the OSB were the footnotes. It was the footnotes in the first OSB that attracted many non-Orthodox readers to explore Orthodoxy further. Many people are impressed by the footnotes and commentary because the notes appear to be written by Christian believers. This may sound strange, but it is not always the case with the notes in other study Bibles. This Bible has the potential to be a great tool for evangelism. One Episcopalian parish in Indiana ordered twelve copies of the OSB from the St. Vladimir's bookstore for use in their parish Bible study.[7]

Other reviewers recalled several dozen inquirers at their parish who were given the OSB to study and subsequently converted to Orthodox Christianity. Still others gave their approval of the study material, not just for inquiring non-Orthodox, but for all seeking an Orthodox view of the Old Testament: "We are pleased with the commentary. Finally, someone has written a Bible commentary that has as its reason to exist the revelation of Christ in the Old Testament. I am a Christian and I am interested in knowing how the Old Testament relates to Christ. I am not interested in the historical or literary aspect of the Old Testament. It's the mystical Christological aspect of the Old Testament that gives me nourishment."[8] The most common positive use of the OSB, however, was to uncover passages and stories that took on a new meaning for reviewers after reading them in an English Septuagint translation. Reviewers frequently used terms such as *gems*, *pearls*, or *hidden treasures* when discussing passages that had drastically different translations in the OSB compared to their past Bibles of choice or when discussing the deuterocanonical books and chapters of books completely left out of their other modern translations. For one priest, it was the discovery of the story of Sussana, the first chapter of Daniel in the Septuagint and the thirteenth chapter in Latin-based texts, that impressed on him the significance of the OSB.[9] In general, positive reviewers accepted the argument put forth by the OSB education campaign, finding allusions to Christ in the Old Testament that they believed modern translations based on the Masoretic text had shrouded behind deceitful language.

Immediately after its publication, however, a vocal group of Orthodox Christians in North America began publicly criticizing the OSB. Ultimately, these critics used their vitriol as a tactic to voice their discomfort with the current trajectory of American Orthodoxy, namely the attention paid to the waves of converts coming into the church. The issues these critics found with the OSB, such as sloppy editing, imprecise language, and a lack of focus on the traditions of the Orthodox Church, were as much labels for the converts themselves as for the OSB. These critics decided that the OSB did not meet the goals of both of its audiences. As one critic put it, "what we have here is a Bible produced to attract Protestants to the Orthodox Church...but what about the rest of us?"[10]

The New Testament and Psalms version of the OSB had already developed an infamous reputation in some circles of English-speaking Orthodoxy. A highly critical 1993 review by Archimandrite Ephrem Lash may be summarized by this often-repeated line: "It feels far too much like a piece of evangelical propaganda decked out in the trappings of Orthodoxy, like an eighteenth century New England chapel or meeting house with a golden onion dome stuck over the pediment of the porch."[11] After fifteen years of development, reviewers of the complete OSB often reiterated this review, quoting this biting line, because they felt that the editors and translators of the OSB had made no attempt to address the issues raised years before but rather had added to them.

In addition to inheriting the reputation of its ancestor, the complete OSB had many new issues that reviewers considered to be deficiencies. Among online critics, the OSB quickly gained a very unfortunate nickname, the Slop Bible, because of a bizarre error in Luke 10:2 that read "Then He said to slop," rather than the correct, "Then He said to them." Several errors led to the inclusion of an errata sheet with the OSB's later editions. While poor editing was a sign for many of the OSB's lackluster execution, others debated the wisdom of the publisher's selected print materials.

The two camps paid equal attention to the physical nature of the OSB, with negative critics frequently commenting on the less than appealing binding, gilding, and even scent of the newly published work. "The cover of this one feels more like cardboard, of much lesser quality than even the first OSB, which wasn't of great quality at all. And the binding is glued, not stitched, which is truly unfortunate (and cheap)."[12] Kevin Edgecomb battered the OSB's publishers for choosing cheap materials, stating, "the OSB stinks, quite literally. It smells very bad, almost like gasoline fumes."[13] More positive reviewers, unsurprisingly, found the OSB visually stunning, tactilely pleasing, and aromatically appealing. "First things first, it smelled nice.... I'm also in favor of leather bindings, as they tend to wear better, and I side with the woman with the alabaster flask (Mar. 14:3) when it comes to Holy things."[14] Some reviewers celebrated the fact that the OSB's publication represented the first time that an English translation of the Septuagint existed in a single bound volume. This was particularly important for those who wanted to encourage more personal, devotional reading among Orthodox believers, including the practice of bringing one's Bible to services and Bible studies. In response to such views, one critic believed this concern with ease of transport to demonstrate a lack of understanding of the Orthodox perspective on lay devotional practices: "It is certainly a convenience of the highest order to have the entirety of Scripture in a single volume, but asking who would read a three-volume Bible...also seems a little odd. Reading the Scriptures...is an ascetic endeavor—as opposed to a quiet time devotion, or any other such nonsense—and hardly caters to our sense of comfort. As such, then, one would think that the three-volume printing...would be the least of an Orthodox reader's worries in that ascetic struggle!"[15] While debates did sometimes delve into the significance of sloppy editing or smelly pages, negative reviewers reserved most of their ire for the issues they believed demonstrated that this Bible was not for Orthodox Christians but rather a tool for proselytizing Protestants.

The most common criticisms dealt with issues concerning the translation of the Old Testament. While the advertising program for the OSB had been forthcoming in letting its potential readers know that the NKJV would be the boilerplate for the Septuagint translation, many were dubious about this strategy for producing a fresh translation of the Septuagint. When reviewers finally received their copies of the OSB, several found that the effect was even worse than they had expected. Not only was the OSB not a faithful translation of the Septuagint, in their opinion, but it also failed to alter the NKJV in places where the Masoretic and Septuagint texts clearly disagreed. Detractors took the same strategy to demonstrate their points, highlighting familiar excerpts from scripture such as the twenty-third Psalm. They effectively showed that the translator of Psalm 23 had not actually translated anything. It was almost exactly the same as the psalm in the NKJV. This critic capped his findings by stating: "The intention seems to be 'not to rock the boat' by providing a translation that is too different from what people are accustomed to, even when the (supposedly!) underlying text of the Septuagint is quite different than the Hebrew. As some monarch somewhere has sometime undoubtedly said, 'We are not pleased.'"[16] Other reviewers began openly criticizing the editors and Thomas Nelson executives for derailing what they believed had begun as a promising project but became corrupted by business concerns and convert naiveté. One reviewer laid the blame squarely on Michael Hyatt and Thomas Nelson, citing "overriding pressure by Thomas Nelson...to market the NKJV by making this an 'Orthodox NKJV' or some such beast," therefore creating a "dubious, embarrassing 'translation.'" The same reviewer stated that the OSB was clearly a product of the "hubris of the Americanist brand of convertitis [sic]."[17]

Other criticisms centered on the fact that while the OSB was filled with commentary and insets that attempted to educate readers on the differences between Protestantism, Catholicism, and Orthodoxy, the writers and editors still shied away from using language that was truly Orthodox and could potentially offend Protestants. As one reviewer put it: "Take, for example, the article 'Types of Mary in the Old Testament.' Firstly [sic], why just 'Mary' and not a properly Orthodox reference to the Champion of the Faithful like 'The Virgin Mary Theotokos'? How about even 'Mary, Mother of God'? Oh, that's right, I forgot that this OSB is actually directed at Protestants, not Orthodox, so we couldn't possibly call her what we actually call her in what is supposed to be our own Bible!"[18] Critical reviews of the OSB often devolved into diatribes against the behavior of new converts in Eastern Orthodox churches. Anecdotal evidence sufficed to demonstrate their supposed lack of commitment to the church and her traditions. One reviewer recalled a conversation with a priest who said, "The average shelf-life of a convert in one of their parishes was 4 or 5 years, but that at least they always got new ones in the door to replace the ones who leave." Another anecdotal example was a family of converts who, after discovering that they must fast on Sunday mornings before church, even from their morning coffee, in order to take communion, left the church and never returned. Negative reviewers frequently used the terms *immature*, *uneducated*, or *naïve* to describe new converts to Orthodoxy.[19]

The problem for the detractors was not just simply with converts as a whole. Many of the highly critical reviewers were themselves converts to Eastern Orthodox Christianity from other Christian sects or denominations. What drew their scorn was their belief that through the OSB, a specific group of converts, namely former evangelical Protestants, were introducing to American Orthodoxy new and, in their opinion, heterodox or borderline heretical approaches to scripture. For some, the OSB represented an American transformation of their church into a more Protestant version of Eastern Orthodox Christianity that they could not tolerate: "The backdoor (or, nowadays, frontdoor) importation of Protestant models, trends, aesthetics, apologetics, etc. into American Orthodoxy will have long-term, detrimental consequences for the Church. There seems to be a lack of awareness that importing 'Americanism' (in its religious sense) is little distinct from importing 'Protestantism' (in its Evangelical sense) and, from there, little distinct from embracing secularism (in its totalizing sense). Exacerbating this problem is the fact that many of its 'movers and shakers' also appear to be clouded by no small amount of jingoism and that their socio-politico *Weltanschauung* is only a generation removed from the John Birch Society."[20] While one could laud margin notes that introduced a Christological interpretation of the Old Testament to readers, why not simply use more commentary from early Church Fathers? Critics argued that reading patristic commentary was the more Orthodox method of studying scripture. In their opinion, the OSB traded the wisdom of the saints for the inane, jejune commentary of amateurs.

There were others who argued that while the OSB's approach to the scriptures might not be completely in tune with Eastern Orthodox practice, it was needed in the mostly Protestant domain of North America. A reviewer named Sarah stated:

> Study Bibles are bad, but in an America which is quickly becoming biblically illit-erate, I see the need for a Bible which includes explanatory notes.... The prob-lem with modern America is nearly every English-language Bible on the market has overlayed the biblical text with a Protestant veneer which makes it difficult to make the jump from the biblical text to liturgical worship. Because of this, I think the OSB is useful in introducing the biblical text to lay people. The prob-lems I have with it are not nearly as numerous as the problems I have with the translations I see many Orthodox lay people using for their personal reading, if they even have a Bible at all.... I must admit that the OSB is no worse, and per-haps a bit better, than a Protestant-produced study Bible, and as such I think I would encourage lay people to get it and use it. Orthodox need to read the Bible more, and this is perhaps the least-dangerous way to encourage that.[21]

Others echoed this sense of using the OSB to bolster the biblical literacy of Orthodox faithful in a largely Protestant culture: "In America this is a Protestant world. Orthodox need to dialogue with Protestants and not just wall them off—our liturgical language and general approach to the faith is completely different from them. In the facts-based rational world of the Protestants, many unstudied Orthodox simply lack the informa-tion—or tools if you will—to properly engage them. This Study Bible is important for that reason alone."[22] While one can see that the OSB met with mixed results for its intended audience and uses, its unintended use as the spark for a contentious debate over the trajectory of American Orthodoxy remains its current legacy. Would the sev-eral American Orthodox archdioceses continue to focus on converts through other publications and methods of outreach like the OSB? On the other hand, as one re-viewer put it, "what about the rest of us, whose use of Scripture doesn't hinge on strengthening our personal commitment to Christ through Bible reading and prayer, who are not embarrassed to speak the language of the Church, and who prefer to re-place personal devotion with the communal experience of the worshiping Church?"[23] Did the OSB represent an Orthodox Church that was going too far, in the opinion of its adherents, toward making indefensible concessions to their American Protestant milieu? Or was the OSB a necessity, something that filled a gap in the spiritual lives of English-speaking Orthodox Christians? At the very least, the OSB forced English-speaking Orthodox laity to face issues that the shifting demographics of the American Orthodox church had created.

PART THREE

Present

17

The Continuing Distinctive Role of the Bible in American Lives

A COMPARATIVE ANALYSIS

Corwin E. Smidt

THE BIBLE CONSTITUTES one of the most influential books, if not the most influential book, in Western civilization, and it likely serves as the text that has most fully shaped American culture. Certainly, in earlier periods of American history, the Bible not only provided a "common frame of discourse" but, "more often than not," also served as "the ultimate court of appeal."[1] The cultural relevance of the Bible in America, however, is not limited to its historical significance. To the extent that American culture does cohere, one component "helping to sustain that cohesion remains a common set of symbols, imagery, values, assumptions, and expectations rooted in the Bible."[2] Moreover, the Bible continues to be a central text in American society today. A variety of statistics point to this fact: each year the Bible is continually the best-selling book in America, with millions of copies of the Bible being sold annually;[3] almost all (nearly nine in ten) households report that they possess a Bible,[4] with the average number of Bibles found in a household being more than three per household.[5] And when American adults are asked to identify their favorite book, without clarifying the type of book or providing any multiple choice selection, national surveys reveal that the Bible continues to be the most commonly identified book.[6]

Given these statistics, it is probably not surprising that scholars have long contended that the Bible has played a more central role in the liturgical and devotional life of American Christians than for Christians of other Western nations.[7] This distinctive feature of American religious life is likely due to several factors: (1) the relatively strong presence of the evangelical Protestant tradition in American religious life, a tradition with a strong emphasis on the authority of the Bible and its use in devotional life,[8] and (2) the American victory in the Revolutionary War—an outcome that prompted a "democratic revolution" in American life that, in turn, diminished the authority of educated clergy and fostered the emergence of a populist hermeneutic in regard to biblical interpretation.[9] Furthermore, this movement toward hearing the voice of the people in religion clearly facilitated another distinctive feature of American religious life—the propensity of Americans to adopt a more literal interpretation of scripture, as without theological training, competency in Old and New Testament languages of Hebrew and Greek, or appreciation for church tradition, readers were left with few tools with which to interpret scripture.[10]

Nevertheless, though this portrait of American religious life is generally accepted by scholars in terms of its historical accuracy, there are various factors that raise questions about (1) the extent to which the Bible continues to play a distinctive role in American religious life, and (2) the particular level of cultural distinctiveness that the Bible exhibits in American religious life. First of all, a number of changes occurring in American religious life raise questions related to the current place of the Bible in it. For example, over the past several decades, technological innovations have changed the reading habits of the American people, as visual learning continues to supplant textual learning, with "subjective experience...continuing to eclipse textual authority as the mark of true religion."[11] In addition, the relatively recent phenomenon of some Americans claiming to be "spiritual, but not religious" suggests that patterns of Bible reading may occur less frequently, if at all, among those who label themselves spiritual as opposed to religious. Furthermore, given more recent immigration patterns, there has been a growth in the percentage of Americans whose religious faith fall outside the Christian tradition, reflected in part in the growing diversity of different houses of worship in American society.[12] And, finally, the percentage of Americans who claim they never go to church or have no religious affiliation has also grown over the past several decades,[13] particularly among the younger members of society—suggesting that Bible reading among Americans may have well have declined over the past several decades as well.

Second, despite the various claims related to the cultural distinctiveness of the role of the Bible in American religious life, there has never been any real empirical analysis of the extent to which this actually holds true. Certainly, given its greater religious vitality,[14] there are likely to be higher levels of Bible reading in American society than in other Western countries with a Christian heritage. But this in itself does not demonstrate that the Bible plays a more central role in American religious life than in other countries, as higher levels of Bible reading may simply be a function of the higher level of religiosity evident in American society or the particular pattern of religious affiliation found in the United States.[15] If the Bible does play a distinctive role in American religious life, then there should be differences related to the Bible between Americans and people of other countries who share similar religious characteristics. For example, if this cultural argument holds true, then weekly church–attending Catholics in the United States should attribute higher levels of authority to the Bible and exhibit a higher level of Bible reading than weekly church–attending Catholics in other countries. Likewise, views of biblical authority or levels of Bible reading among those with no religious affiliation should be much different in American society than in other societies.

This chapter therefore seeks to engage in a comparative analysis of the role of the Bible in daily life. Three different comparisons will drive the analysis: comparisons across time, across cultural settings, and across religious traditions. Three different topics will be addressed: (1) the extent to which there is any evidence of a decline in attributions related to the authority of the Bible or in terms of the level of Bible reading found among the American people over the past several decades, (2) the extent to which Canadians and Americans who exhibit similar religious characteristics differ in terms of their views of biblical authority and in terms of their practice of Bible reading, and (3) the extent to which Americans of different religious traditions use the Bible for different purposes. Thus, though the analysis is empirically driven, it seeks to provide a broader context in which the other chapters of this book might be placed.

SURVEY RESEARCH RELATED TO THE BIBLE IN AMERICA

When questions related to the Bible are asked in omnibus social surveys, they typically involve one of two different questions: (1) the respondent's view of the authoritative nature of the biblical text,[16] and (2) the respondent's relative frequency of Bible reading outside the context of public worship. The nature of biblical authority is a matter of some dispute even among those Christians who subscribe to a "high" view of the scriptures. Briefly stated, some Christians may adhere to an infallible point of view, other Christians to an inerrant point of view, and still others to a literal point of view; these positions can be arrayed in an ascending order of authority, from infallibility to literalism.[17] Scholars have typically taken responses to questions related to biblical authority at "face value"—namely, such responses are viewed as reflecting doctrinal views (i.e., religious beliefs) rather than some form of group identity (religious belonging).[18]

Much of the existing literature that examines solitary Bible reading as a measure, whether as part of a scale or as a separate measure, tends to treat it simply as a measure of religiosity that may affect other attitudes and/or behavior, rather than focusing on Bible reading in terms of a behavior itself.[19] As a result, little attention has been given to aggregate changes in levels of Bible reading reported by Americans over time.

Not surprisingly, those who hold higher views of biblical authority are far more likely than those holding lower views to engage in reading the Bible outside the context of public worship, as "those who with higher views of the Bible read it more often."[20] However, regular Bible reading is not confined to those who hold literal views of biblical authority, as nearly half of those who read the Bible on nearly a weekly basis or more are not biblical literalists.[21] Hence, it is helpful, when possible, to examine views of biblical authority and patterns of Bible reading as separate objects of investigation.

When viewed comparatively in terms of a cross-national perspective, Americans are far more likely than members of other Western nations to attribute relatively high levels of authority to the Bible. This is evident in table 17.1, which assesses views of biblical authority across thirteen different European countries, Canada, and the United States. These data were gathered through an international cooperative survey endeavor in 1998,[22] in which respondents were asked whether they believed the Bible to be "the actual word of God," "the inspired word of God," or an "ancient book of man." The first two responses obviously attribute religious significance to the biblical texts, whereas the third option does not. And of the two responses attributing religious significance to the Bible, the response indicating that the Bible is "the actual word of God" is a "higher view" of biblical authority than the response that it "the inspired word of God."

Of the thirteen different countries examined in table 17.1, the United States outranks all other countries, except Poland, in terms of the percentage who indicate that they hold the Bible to be "the actual word of God," as 30 percent of Americans and 32 percent of Poles responded accordingly. This stands in stark contrast to the other countries examined, as most other countries have 10 percent or less of their population attributing such authority to the Bible. On the other hand the United States ranked only behind Italy in terms of having the lowest percentage of respondents who reported that they viewed the Bible to be nothing more than "an ancient book of man" (17 percent v. 13 percent, respectively). In contrast, 68 percent of the respondents in Sweden reported that the Bible was simply "an ancient book of man," as did half or more of the Norwegians (with 30 percent of more of respondents giving such an answer in nine of the thirteen countries examined). Overall, therefore, Americans are far more likely than those of most all other Western nations to view the Bible as either the actual or inspired word of God.

TABLE 17.1

The Distinctive Nature of American Views of Biblical Authority: A Cross-national Comparison

What comes closest to your beliefs about the Bible?	Actual word of God	Inspired word of God	Ancient book of man	Other	Total	(N)
Austria	13%	45	33	10	101%	(904)
France	5%	36	47	12	100%	(1018)
Germany (West)	9%	40	39	11	99%	(900)
Great Britain	5%	38	49	9	101%	(732)
Italy	26%	54	13	8	101%	(909)
Netherlands	9%	40	31	20	100%	(1923)
Norway	11%	35	50	5	101%	(1357)
Poland	32%	43	21	4	100%	(962)
Spain	13%	52	27	7	99%	(2252)
Sweden	5%	17	68	11	101%	(1102)
Switzerland	10%	45	34	11	100%	(1101)
Canada	10%	42	42	7	101%	(907)
United States	30%	49	17	3	99%	(1190)

Source: International Social Survey Program 1998.

Unfortunately, questions tapping views of biblical authority in national surveys have been quite varied in terms of question wording and response options (see appendix A). And, given the fact that question wording affects response patterns, one cannot therefore directly compare survey results from different survey organizations using different question formats.[23] Rather, one must confine one's analysis to an examination of changing responses given to the same question. Fortunately, various Gallup Polls and the General Social Surveys have periodically asked Americans about their views of biblical authority using the same question format, with the Gallup Polls doing so earlier, primarily in the 1970s and 1980s, and the General Social Survey beginning in 1984.

Based on these data, table 17.2 presents that changing percentages of Americans who, since 1976, have reported that the Bible is "the actual word of God," "the inspired word of God," or "an ancient book of man." When American views of biblical authority are examined comparatively across time, several distinct patterns emerge from the data presented. First, most Americans (80 percent or more) have viewed, and continue to view, the Bible to be the word of God, whether as the actual word or the inspired word of God. Even in 2014, the most recent date for which data are available, far more Americans viewed the Bible to be the actual word of God (32 percent) than viewed it simply as a book written by human beings (23 percent).

Second, over the past four decades, there has been a marginal shift in how Americans view the authority of the Bible. Between 1976 and 1987, the percentage of Americans who viewed the Bible as the actual word of God ranged between 37 and 39 percent (with 41 percent in 1987 being the exception). However, beginning in 1988 until the present, the percentage of Americans who subscribe to such views has ranged between 31 and 35 percent (with 29 percent in 2002 being the exception).

Third, the percentage of Americans who view the Bible to be simply an old book written by human beings—devoid of any divine nature—has marginally increased over the past four decades. Prior to the late 1980s, only about 15 percent of Americans or less reported that they viewed the Bible to be simply an ancient book of man, but between 1988 and 2008 that percentage fluctuated between 15 and 18 percent (with 14 percent in 2002 being the exception). However, in the four General Social Survey surveys of 2008, 2010, 2012, and 2014 that percentage has now risen to slightly above 20 percent.

Thus, over the past four decades there has been some increase in the percentage of Americans who hold rather low views of biblical authority. However, this marginal increase must be kept in perspective. First, far more Americans attribute the highest level of authority to the Bible (i.e., it is the actual word of God) than contend that it is simply a human creation. Second, despite the marginal increase in the percentage of Americans who view the Bible simply as a human creation, Americans exhibit views of biblical authority that are distinctively different from patterns exhibited by Canadians and members of many Western European societies (see table 17.1).

It is one thing to view the Bible to be the word of God, but it is quite another to read it. Despite the fact that approximately four-fifths of all Americans view the Bible to be either the inspired or actual word of God, far fewer Americans report that they read the Bible on any consistent basis. Various national surveys have, since the early 1940s,

TABLE 17.2

AMERICAN VIEWS OF BIBLICAL AUTHORITY OVER TIME

What comes closest to your beliefs about the Bible?	Actual word of God	Inspired word of God	Ancient book of man	Other[+*]	Total	(N)
GALLUP SURVEYS						
1976	38%[a]	45	13	4[+]	100%	nr
1980	39%[b]	nr	nr	nr	nr	nr
1981	37%[b]	nr	nr	nr	nr	nr
1983	39%[b]	nr	nr	nr	nr	nr
1984	37%[b]	nr	nr	nr	nr	nr
1991	32%[c]	49	16	3[+]	100%	nr
1993	35%[d]	48	14	3[+]	100%	nr
GENERAL SOCIAL SURVEY						
1984	38%	47	14	1	100%	(963)
1985	37%	50	13	*	100%	(733)
1987	41%	43	15	1	100%	(1166)
1988	35%	48	17	1	101%	(1450)
1989	32%	51	17	*	100%	(970)
1990	33%	51	16	*	100%	(901)
1991	35%	49	15	1	100%	(1002)
1993	34%	50	15	1	100%	(1052)
1994	32%	52	15	1	100%	(1928)
1996	31%	51	18	1	101%	(1908)
1998	32%	51	17	1	101%	(2296)
2000	35%	48	16	1	100%	(2251)
2002	29%	54	14	3	100%	(1345)
2004	34%	48	17	2	101%	(1319)
2006	34%	46	17	3	100%	(2943)
2008	32%	47	20	2	101%	(1987)
2010	33%	45	20	2	100%	(4827)
2012	31%	46	21	1	100%	(4741)
2014	32%	45	23	1	101%	(3784)

Sources: Gallup Polls and General Social Surveys

Note: nr: not reported

[a] Gallup Poll, August 27–30, 1976

[b] Gallup Report No. 236, May 1985, p. 47

[c] Gallup Poll, November 21–24, 1991

[d] Gallup Poll, June 18–21, 1993

[+] Includes no answer

[*] Less than 1 percent

examined the frequency with which Americans report that they read the Bible outside the context of public worship. Unfortunately, the manner in which respondents are asked these questions varies greatly. Sometimes, respondents are simply asked whether they have read any part of the Bible in the past year. Other times, they are asked whether they read the Bible daily, weekly, monthly, or some combination of options that entail responses less often than monthly.

The top portion of table 17.3 examines the frequency over time with which Americans report having read a least some portion of the Bible over the past year, with response options simply being either yes or no. In 1942, in the midst of World War II, approximately three-fifths of all Americans (59 percent) reported that they had read the Bible at home within the past year. Though later surveys tended to reveal somewhat higher percentages of Americans reading the Bible at least on a yearly basis, it is interesting to note that, in 1998, more than fifty years after Gallup's 1942 survey, basically the same percentage of American reported that they had read the Bible in the past year (58 percent) as had done so in 1942 (59 percent). However, the most recent iteration of the General Social Survey containing a question related to Bible reading (the one conducted in 2012), revealed that only one-half (50 percent) of all Americans reported that they had read the Bible in the last year. Whether this result represents a true decline in Bible reading among Americans or simply some form of statistical "outlier" is unclear. Certainly, some decline in reported levels of Bible reading might well be expected given the marginal decline over time among Americans reporting "high views" of biblical authority. But the rather substantial drop in the percentage doing so over a relatively short period of time suggests that the percentage found in 2012, though perhaps within the margin of error associated with surveys, may be somewhat lower than the "true" percentage found within American society.

TABLE 17.3

REPORTED FREQUENCY OF BIBLE READING AMONG AMERICANS OVER TIME: LIMITED RESPONSE OPTIONS

	1942	1952	1974	1978	1986	1988	1990	1998	2000	2005	2012
Have you read (any part of) the Bible at home within the last year?	59%	68%	63%	x	x	62%	x	58% (1)	x	x	50%
Read Bible daily	11%	x	x	12%	11%	x	17%	14% (2)	16%	20%	x
Rarely/never	x	x	x	x	x	x	x	x	41%	x	x
Never	x	x	x	24%	22%	x	20%	26%	x	17%	x

Note: Data sources: 1942: Gallup Poll, November, N=1500; 1952: Gallup Poll, December, N=1500; 1974: Gallup Poll, December, N=1517; 1978: Christianity Today Survey, N=1533; 1986: Gallup Poll, October, N=1559; 1988: General Social Survey, February, N=1481; 1990: Gallup Poll, November, N=1021; 1998(1): General Social Survey, February, N=1416; 1998(2): Gallup Poll, November, N=1070; 2000: Gallup Poll, October, N=1052; 2005: Newsweek Poll, N=1004; 2012: General Social Survey, N=1485.

This interpretation receives some support when the bottom portion of table 17.3 is examined. When respondents are asked the relative frequency with which they read the Bible rather than whether they have read it in the past year, a somewhat different picture emerges. Gallup's 1942 survey employed two different forms, with each form asking the frequency of Bible reading in a different format. The second form asked respondents the relative frequency with which they read the Bible, with 11 percent of Americans in 1942 reporting that they read it on a daily basis. More than 40 years later, a Gallup survey in 1986 revealed that 11 percent of Americans continued to report that they read the Bible on a daily basis. Moreover, a variety of subsequent surveys suggest that the percentage of Americans who read the Bible on a daily basis has actually increased since 1986, as somewhere between 14 and 20 percent of Americans reported doing so between 1990 and 2005. And, when one examines the percentages who report that they never read the Bible, one does not find any real increase in the percentage of Americans responding in such a manner.[24]

These same observations can be discerned in table 17.4, which presents the frequency distribution of reported Bible-reading patterns based on the relative frequency

TABLE 17.4

REPORTED FREQUENCY OF BIBLE READING AMONG AMERICANS OVER TIME: EXPANDED RESPONSE OPTIONS: PERCENTAGES

How often do you read the Bible?	1942	1978	1981	1986	1996	1998	2008	2012
Once a day or more	11	12	15	11	19	14	19	24
Once a week or more	15	18	18	22	20	24	20	20
Once a month or more	11	11	12	14	8	14	16	8
Less than monthly	22	28	25	26	x	20	x	x
Occasionally	x	x	x	x	26	x	x	19
Once or twice a year	x	x	x	x	x	x	21	x
Not in last year	41	x	x	x	x	x	x	x
Do not read the Bible	x	24	24	22	x	26	x	x
Can't say/recall	x	7	6	5	x	1	2	x
Never	x	x	x	x	27	x	21	29
Total	100	100	100	100	100	99	99	100

Sources: 1942: Gallup Poll, N = 1500; 1978: Christianity Today Poll, N = 1533; 1981: Gallup Poll, N = 1483; 1986: Gallup Poll, N = 1559; 1996: Second National Survey of Religion and Politics, N = 4037; 1998: Gallup Poll, N = 1070; 2008: Religion & Ethics NewsWeekly Survey, N = 1400; 2012: Sixth National Survey of Religion and Politics, N = 2002.

of daily, weekly, monthly, and less than monthly options. Once again, the data do not reveal any real decline in American habits of reading the Bible. In fact, if anything, the data suggest that there has been an increase in daily and weekly Bible-reading practices,[25] with the percentage of Americans who report that they either do not read the Bible or that they never read it (two different response options associated with different surveys) remaining below 30 percent between 1978 and 2012.

Thus, Americans continue to report that they read the Bible with some regularity. There has not been any substantial decline in reported levels of Bible reading and, if anything, Americans are more likely today than seventy years ago to report that they read the Bible on a daily basis. All this prevails despite the fact that any social pressures to report possible "socially desired" responses that one reads the Bible on some relatively frequent basis were likely far greater several decades ago than today (see also table 17.5 for a cross-national comparison).[26]

Of course, some might contend that regardless of any lessening of social pressures to provide "religious" responses, Americans often overreport their religious practices. And the extent to which Americans may over report certain religious practices has been a matter of some scholarly discussion.[27] Nevertheless, regardless of the extent to which, if at all, Americans overreport engaging in religious practices, it is less likely that individuals "overreport" their religious beliefs—and the percentage of Americans who report that the Bible is the actual word of God has only declined marginally since

TABLE 17.5

PERCENTAGE OF REPORTED WEEKLY CHURCH ATTENDANCE OVER TIME: A CROSS-NATIONAL COMPARISON

	1981	1990	2001	2008
France	11	10	8	6
Germany (West)	19	18	16	14[a]
Great Britain	14	14	14	12
Italy	32	38	40	32[a]
Netherlands	26	20	14	13
Norway	5	5	5	4
Spain	40	29	26	16
Sweden	6	4	7	5
Canada	31	27	27	25[a]
United States	43	44	46	44[b]

Sources: 1981–2001 World Values Survey, adapted from Pippa Norris and Ronald Inglehart, *Sacred and Secular: Religion and Politics Worldwide* (New York: Cambridge University Press, 2004), table 3.6, and European Social Survey 2008 (includes values for both the old West and East Germany).

[a] Not included in the European Social Survey 2008; values are taken from the World Values Survey of 2005.
[b] Not included in the European Social Survey 2008; value taken from the Fifth National Survey of Religion and Politics.

1976 (see table 17.2). Thus, the major conclusions that can be drawn from the first four tables presented are the following: (1) the overwhelming majority of Americans continue to hold very "high views" of biblical authority, (2) these views of biblical authority have not changed substantially over the past forty years, (3) Americans continue to hold far higher views of biblical authority than Canadians and members of most other European societies, and (4) Americans continue to read the Bible as often as, if not more often than, they did seventy years ago.

THE CULTURAL SIGNIFICANCE OF THE BIBLE IN AMERICAN LIVES

As noted earlier, there has been very little empirical analysis of the extent to which the Bible plays a culturally distinctive role in American religious life. Though there may be higher levels of Bible reading in American society than in other Western countries with a Christian heritage, this does not by itself demonstrate that the Bible plays a more central role win American religious life than in other countries. If the cultural argument holds true, then Americans with identical religious characteristics to those in other countries should, for example, attribute higher levels of authority to the Bible and exhibit a higher level of Bible reading than similar religionists in other countries.

In order to test these expectations, I will limit my analysis to a comparison of Americans and Canadians. This more narrow examination of cultural differences is due to the limited availability of data to test these differences. As a result, the primary source of data to test these expectations of cultural differences is the God and Society in North America Survey of 1996, in which approximately 3,000 Americans and 3,000 Canadians were asked the same survey questions related to religion and public life. Though conducted nearly two decades ago, this survey nevertheless constitutes the most recent comparative study that permits an examination of both views of biblical authority and relative frequency of Bible reading. I will supplement these data, however, with three earlier Canadian (along with other U.S.) surveys conducted at roughly similar cross-sections in time.

Table 17.6 examines the percentages of Canadians and Americans over time who (1) report that they never read the Bible, and (2) report that they read the Bible on a daily basis. Though the data for the two countries are drawn from different surveys, they are taken from surveys conducted in each country at approximately the same cross-section in time. The analysis is limited to frequency of Bible reading because the three Canadian surveys of 1975, 1980, and 1995 did not ask respondents their views of the authority of the Bible.

As can be seen from the table 17.6, Americans were far more likely than Canadians at each roughly equivalent cross-section of time to report that they read the Bible on a regular basis. In the late 1970s, Americans were six times more likely than Canadians to report that they read the Bible on a daily basis and half as likely to indicate that they rarely or never read the Bible. This pattern continued into the 1980s and 1990s, though

TABLE 17.6

Differences in Reported Frequency of Bible Reading
among Canadians and Americans

Reported frequency of Bible reading	Canada	United States
1975/1978		
Daily	2%	12%
Never/rarely	55%	24%
1980/1981		
Daily	3%	15%
Never	55%	24%
1995		
Daily	6%	x
Never/hardly ever	72%	x
1996*		
Daily	9%	20%
Never	37%	14%

Sources: 1975: Project Canada, N = 1917; 1978: Christianity Today
Poll, N = 1533; 1980: Project Canada, N = 1482; 1981: Gallup Poll,
N = 1483; 1995: Project Canada, N = 1764; 1996: God and Society in
North America, Canada: N = 3000; United States: N = 3023.

* Phrasing: "read Bible or other religious material"

differences in the ratio between Canada and the United States diminished over time as reports of daily Bible reading increased in both countries over time.

Of course, such differences in reported levels of Bible reading between the two countries may be simply a function of other religious differences evident in the two countries. As a result, table 17.7 examines the same data presented in table 17.6—but this time controlling for frequency of church attendance. If the Bible does play a culturally distinctive role in the United States, then Americans should be more likely than their Canadian counterparts exhibiting similar levels of church attendance to indicate that they read the Bible with greater regularity. And this expectation holds true. Among those who reported that they never attended church, for example, Americans were far more likely than Canadians to report that they read the Bible on a daily basis. And the same is true among weekly church attenders: weekly church-attending Americans were far more likely than weekly church-attending Canadians to respond that they read the Bible on a daily basis.

However, it is also true that the differences exhibited in table 17.7 may be a function of different distributions of Christian faith traditions found in the two countries. Not only is there a larger percentage of evangelical Protestants in the United States than in Canada,[28] but there is also a larger percentage of Catholics in Canada than in the

TABLE 17.7

Cross-national Differences in Reported Frequency of
Bible Reading, Controlling for Level of Church
Attendance

	Attend church	
	Never	Weekly
Canada		
1975		
Read Bible never/rarely	80%	32%
Read Bible daily	0%	10%
1980		
Read Bible never	87%	23%
Read Bible daily	0%	13%
1995		
Read Bible never/hardly ever	82%	10%
Read Bible daily	1%	29%
1996		
Read Bible never	63%	8%
Read Bible daily	2%	30%
United States		
1978		
Read Bible never	76%	14%
Read Bible daily	3%	33%
1981		
Read Bible never	*	*
Read Bible daily	*	*
1996		
Read Bible never	44%	21%
Read Bible daily	6%	38%

Sources: Canada: 1975: Project Canada; 1980: Project Canada;
1995: Project Canada; 1996: God and Society in North America.
United States: 1978: Christianity Today Poll; 1996: God and
Society in North America.

* No percentages reported for (1981 Gallup Poll (see table 17.6)
because the survey does not permit this form of analysis.

United States.[29] Moreover, at least in the United States, evangelicals typically report
that they read the Bible more frequently than either mainline Protestants or Roman
Catholics, and Catholics are less likely to respond that they read the Bible on a daily
basis than either evangelical Protestants or mainline Protestants.[30] Finally, as religious
traditions, those affiliated with evangelical Protestant denominations tend to ascribe

higher levels of authority to the biblical texts than do those affiliated with either mainline Protestant denominations or the Catholic Church.[31]

Given these patterns, table 17.8 controls for both religious tradition and church attendance using data drawn from the God and Society in North America survey, the only international survey that permits direct cross-national comparisons of respondents in terms of both views of biblical authority and patterns of Bible reading. And, even when controlling for both religious tradition and frequency of church

TABLE 17.8

DIFFERENCES IN ATTRIBUTIONS OF BIBLICAL AUTHORITY AND REPORTED FREQUENCY OF BIBLE READING AMONG CANADIANS AND AMERICANS, CONTROLLING FOR BOTH RELIGIOUS TRADITION AND CHURCH ATTENDANCE

	Canada		United States	
	Attend church		Attend church	
	Never	Weekly	Never	Weekly
Bible is inspired word of God				
Evangelical Protestants				
Strongly disagree	12%	x	2%	x
Strongly agree	x	96%	x	95%
Mainline Protestants				
Strongly disagree	15%	x	11%	x
Strongly agree	x	72%	x	78%
Roman Catholics				
Strongly disagree	20%	x	9%	x
Strongly agree	x	63%	x	73%
Unaffiliated				
Strongly disagree	40%	x	34%	x
Strongly agree	x	67% (N=12)	x	55% (N=33)
Frequency of Bible reading				
Evangelical Protestants				
Never	27%	x	24%	x
Daily	x	59%	x	53%
Mainline Protestants				
Never	50%	x	25%	x
Daily	x	21%	x	37%
Roman Catholics				
Never	70%	x	43%	x
Daily	x	16%	x	15%
Unaffiliated				
Never	66%	x	52%	x
Daily	x	17%	x	31%

Source: God and Society in North America, 1996

attendance, Americans typically attribute greater authority to the Bible than their Canadian counterparts. For example, nearly three-quarters (73 percent) of weekly church-attending Catholics in the United States strongly agreed that the Bible is the inspired word of God, whereas only about three-fifths (63 percent) of weekly church-attending Catholics in Canada did so. So, too, weekly attending mainline Protestants in the United States were more likely than their Canadian counterparts to strongly agree that the Bible is the inspired word of God. On the other hand nearly all weekly church-attending evangelicals, regardless of country, strongly agreed that the Bible is the inspired word of God (96 percent and 95 percent in Canada and the U.S., respectively)—a finding consistent with Reimer's ethnographic study (1996) that revealed relatively similar central religious beliefs across the two countries. Nevertheless, among those evangelicals who never attended church, six times as many Canadians as Americans expressed strong disagreement with the statement that the Bible is the word of God (12 v. 2 percent, respectively). The same pattern was true among the religiously unaffiliated who never attended church: Canadians were more likely than Americans to express strong disagreement with the statement that the Bible is the inspired word of God.

The only exception to the expectation that Americans attribute greater authority to the Bible than their Canadian counterparts occurs among those religiously unaffiliated who nevertheless claim to attend church weekly. However, given the small number of people who exhibit these characteristics (only twelve respondents in Canada and thirty-three in the United States), these percentages are highly unstable. But even if these results were to stand, the overall pattern found in table 17.8 reveals that even when controlling for religious differences across the two countries, Americans generally attribute higher levels of authority to the Bible than Canadians with religious characteristics similar to those of their American counterparts.

Likewise, when one controls for both religious affiliation and frequency of church attendance, Americans generally continue to report more frequent levels of personal Bible reading than Canadians. For example, among mainline Protestants who never attend church, Canadians are twice as likely as Americans to report that they never read the Bible (50 v. 25 percent, respectively), and among weekly church–attending mainline Protestants, Americans are nearly twice as likely as Canadians to indicate that they read the Bible on a daily basis (37 v. 21 percent, respectively). The same pattern is true among the religiously unaffiliated, regardless of their relative level of church attendance: Americans report higher levels of Bible reading than Canadians. Among weekly church-attending Catholics, the percentage of Canadians and Americans who report daily Bible reading is approximately the same (16 v. 15 percent, respectively), but among non-church-attending Catholics, Canadians are nearly twice as likely as Americans to report that they never read the Bible (70 v. 43 percent, respectively). The only exception to this pattern involves evangelical Protestants: among evangelicals who never attend church, roughly one-quarter report that they never read the Bible, regardless of the country analyzed, whereas Canadian evangelicals are somewhat more likely than American evangelicals to respond that they read the Bible on the daily basis (59 v. 53 percent, respectively).

Thus, though the patterns are not fully uniform, the overall evidence suggests that the Bible does tend to hold a different cultural position in the United States than in Canada. Even when one controls for level of church attendance and patterns of religious affiliation, Americans are far more likely than their Canadian counterparts to ascribe higher levels of authority to the Bible and to report more frequent patterns of reading.

The idea that religion is enmeshed in American culture in ways that are distinctive from other cultures has had a long history in American scholarship.[32] In testing these contentions, Reimer had earlier shown that (1) levels of "orthodox belief and practice" was indeed higher among those who did not attend church in America than among nonattenders in Canada, and (2) there were greater differences in levels of "orthodox belief and practice" between nonattenders and attenders in Canada than in the United States.[33] Reimer, however, never controlled for differences in patterns of religious affiliation across the two countries, and the analysis presented here reveals that even when one controls for the differences in distributions of evangelical Protestants and Roman Catholics across the two settings, the cultural differences in relationship to both the attributions given to biblical authority and the practice of solitary Bible reading still tend to prevail.

THE USES OF BIBLE READING OUTSIDE PUBLIC WORSHIP

Neither the authority attributed to the Bible nor the frequency with which it is read provides any indication of the purposes for which people use the Bible. The idea that people use media (whether print, audio, or visual) for different reasons and purposes has a long history in media and communication studies. Known as the "uses and gratifications approach," this perspective focuses on how people use media and whether they use different media (or even different forms of the same media) to meet different desires and needs. In other words, according to this framework of understanding, some may use the newspaper to gather national political information, others to learn about community events, and still others to be entertained through reading the comics; some may use television to gather political news, others to be entertained.[34] In the same fashion, not everyone may read the Bible for the same reason(s); different people may read the Bible for different ends and purposes.

Various ethnographic studies have examined how different people may use the Bible, particularly in terms of the practice of small-group Bible study.[35] More recently, Ronald's (2012) qualitative study analyzed the practice of solitary Bible reading and the diversity of ways people used Bible reading in their lives.[36] Though this study provides evidence that different individuals read the Bible for different purposes, it cannot

TABLE 17.9

THE EXTENT TO WHICH AMERICANS READ SCRIPTURE FOR DIFFERENT
PURPOSES

Purpose for reading scripture	Extent to which one reads scripture			Total	(N)	Mean Score*
	Not at all	Small/ moderate	Considerable/ Great			
For personal devotions	10%	47	44	101%	(742)	3.29
To learn about your religion	16%	50	35	100%	(738)	2.99
To make decisions about personal relationships	35%	40	25	100%	(739)	2.44
To prepare to teach or lead	49%	32	20	101%	(742)	2.17
To learn about the future	44%	39	17	100%	(740)	2.16
To learn about attaining health or healing	44%	41	15	100%	(739)	2.15
To learn about issues like poverty and war	60%	29	12	101%	(741)	1.79
To learn about issues like abortion or homosexuality	62%	27	12	101%	(740)	1.75
To learn about attaining wealth or prosperity	62%	28	10	100%	(740)	1.74

Source: General Social Survey 2012.

* Based on five responses with these scores assigned for each response: Not at all, 1; Small, 2; Moderate, 3;
Considerable, 4; Great, 5

assess the extent to which Americans as a whole generally do so for these different
purposes.

In 2012, however, the General Social Survey asked respondents to report whether
they read the Bible for any of nine particular purposes. Five different response options
were provided for each of these nine purposes—ranging from "not at all" to "a great
extent." The responses obtained are presented in table 17.9, though with the categories

of "small extent" and "moderate extent" combined, as well as the options of "considerable extent" and "great extent" combined. In addition, the right-hand column of the table presents the resultant mean score obtained when the full fivefold response options are analyzed.

The two most common reasons why people read the Bible are for the practice of personal devotions and for learning more about their religious faith, with the former being the most widely cited purpose. More than two-fifths of Americans (44 percent) report that they read scripture to a great or considerable extent for devotional purposes, while slightly more than one-third of Americans indicate that they read scripture to a great or considerable extent to learn more about their religious faith. At the opposite end of the spectrum, only one in ten Americans (10 percent) report that they do not read scripture for devotional purposes, and slightly more than one in six Americans (16 percent) indicate that they do not read the Bible in order to learn more about their religion.

On the other hand most Americans rarely, if ever, read the Bible to learn more about what the Bible has to say about "attaining wealth or prosperity." However, neither do Americans as a whole necessarily search the scriptures to learn about what the Bible may have to say about current political issues—regardless of whether such issues are more salient to socially conservative Christians (e.g., "issues like abortion or homosexuality") or more social gospel–oriented Christians (e.g., "issues like poverty and war"). On these matters, more than three-fifths of all Americans report that they never read the Bible for such purposes, while only about one-tenth do so to a "considerable or great extent" for such purposes.

But Americans read the Bible for a variety of other purposes as well. Many note that they read scripture for the purpose of making "decisions about personal relationships" (with only 35 percent of Americans noting that they never read scripture for such a purpose). Others note that they search the Bible, at least to some extent, to "learn about the future" or to learn more about "attaining health or healing," though slightly more than two-fifths of all Americans (44 percent) report that they never read the Bible for either reason. Finally, some read the Bible in preparation to "teach or lead," presumably in terms of some adolescent or adult Christian education class—with nearly one-half of those surveyed (49 percent) indicating that they never read the Bible for this particular end.

Of course, it may be that different religious communities choose to read scripture for different purposes. After all, Ronald has emphasized the important role played by interpretive communities, even when one engages in reading the Bible alone.[37] Hence, table 17.10 presents the mean scores for each purpose of reading the Bible, broken down by those affiliated with different religious traditions: evangelical Protestants, mainline Protestants, Black Protestants, Roman Catholics, and the religiously unaffiliated.

The major conclusions that can be drawn from table 17.10 are several. First, the relative extent to which people use the Bible for different purposes varies across religious traditions—as the mean scores are far from identical as one moves across the rows of

TABLE 17.10

THE EXTENT TO WHICH AMERICANS READ SCRIPTURE FOR DIFFERENT
PURPOSES, CONTROLLING FOR RELIGIOUS TRADITION

Purpose for reading scripture	Mean score for each religious tradition*				
	Evangelical Protestant	Mainline Protestant	Black Protestant	Roman Catholic	Unaffiliated
For personal devotions	3.62	2.98	3.71	2.84	2.43
To learn about your religion	3.22	2.73	3.62	2.39	2.27
To make decisions about personal relationships	2.79	1.89	3.07	1.94	1.80
To prepare to teach or lead	2.34	2.10	2.49	1.80	1.61
To learn about the future	2.37	1.76	2.77	1.66	1.71
To learn about attaining health or healing	2.25	1.65	3.07	1.83	1.77
To learn about issues like poverty and war	1.96	1.45	2.13	1.51	1.51
To learn about issues like abortion or homosexuality	1.96	1.46	2.01	1.36	1.63
To learn about attaining wealth or prosperity	1.79	1.36	2.53	1.48	1.50

Source: General Social Survey 2012.

* Based on five responses with these scores assigned for each response: not at all, 1; small extent, 2; moderate extent, 3; considerable extent, 4; great extent, 5

data presented. For example, Black Protestants exhibit a mean score of 3.71 in relationship to reading scripture for the purpose of personal devotions, whereas the mean
score for the religiously unaffiliated is 2.43.

Second, regardless of religious tradition, the major end for which people read scripture is for personal devotions (first) and for learning about their religious faith
(second)—as the rank order from the smallest or the largest scores for each religious
tradition reveals that the scores for these two purposes are the two largest. This is true
even for the religiously unaffiliated.

Third, Black Protestants report that they read the Bible for a great many different purposes. For example, when using 2.0 as an arbitrary cutoff point, one finds that only three of the expressed reasons for reading the Bible fall below that score among evangelical Protestants, whereas seven of the scores do so for mainline Protestants, Catholics, and the religiously unaffiliated. In contrast, none of the scores for Black Protestants do so.

Fourth, for some purposes examined, even the religiously unaffiliated report that they read the Bible to a greater extent than do Catholics.[38] The mean scores exhibited among the religiously unaffiliated "to learn about the future" and "to learn about issues like abortion or homosexuality" exceed those exhibited by Catholics and mirror Catholics in terms of learning "about issues likely poverty and war" and "about attaining wealth and prosperity."

CONCLUSIONS

Several important conclusions can be drawn from this broad overview of the ways Americans view and use the Bible. First, the evidence suggests that the Bible continues to play an important role in American lives. The overwhelming majority of Americans (relatively four-fifths) today continue to view the Bible as a sacred text—constituting either the actual or inspired word of God. Likewise, many Americans continue to read the Bible with some regularity. Moreover, it appears that despite many social and cultural changes that have transpired over the past several decades, Americans continue to ascribe relatively similar levels of authority to the biblical text and read the Bible with levels of frequency similar to those of Americans several decades ago.

Second, the (limited and somewhat dated) existing evidence suggests that American views of biblical authority and their relative levels of Bible reading are culturally distinctive in nature. Not only do church-attending Americans hold higher views of biblical authority and read the Bible at higher frequency levels than church-attending Canadians, but so do non-attending Americans in comparison to non-attending Canadians. Furthermore, such differences continue to largely hold when controlling for both patterns of church attendance and religious affiliation simultaneously: Americans continue to be more likely to attribute higher levels of authority to biblical texts and to report greater frequency of Bible reading than Canadians exhibiting similar religious characteristics.

Finally, Americans read the Bible for a variety of reasons. However, the primary reasons for which they do so are to engage in personal devotions and to learn more about their religious faith. Americans are far less likely to report that they turn to the Bible to learn about contemporary issues of politics—regardless of whether such issues are related to the political agenda associated with either the "ideological right" or the "ideological left." Nor do Americans turn to the Bible to acquire information related to what is known as the "health and wealth" gospel. Though some do, most do not. Overall, how Americans choose to use the Bible varies little across religious traditions—even when one includes those who do not report any particular religious affiliation. Thus, regardless of the particular religious tradition with which one may be affiliated, the extent to which such Americans report using the Bible for specific purposes is relatively similar in nature.

A SAMPLING OF QUESTION WORDING AND RESPONSE ITEMS

FOR BIBLICAL AUTHORITY QUESTIONS

Gallup Polls 1
Which one of these statements comes closest to describing your feelings about the Bible?

1. The Bible is a collection of writing representing some of the religious philosophies of ancient man.
2. The Bible is the Word of God but is sometimes mistaken in its statements and teachings.
3. The Bible is the Word of God and is NOT mistaken in its statements and teachings.

Gallup Polls 2
Which one of these statements comes closest to describing your feelings about the Bible?

1. The Bible is the actual Word of God, and is to be taken literally, word for word.
2. The Bible is the inspired Word of God but not everything in it should be taken literally.
3. The Bible is an ancient book of fables, legends, history, and moral precepts recorded by man.

General Social Surveys
Which one of these statements comes closest to describing your feelings about the Bible?

1. The Bible is the actual Word of God, and is to be taken literally, word for word.
2. The Bible is the inspired Word of God, but not everything in it should be taken literally.
3. The Bible is an ancient book of fables, legends, history, and moral precepts recorded by man.

National Election Studies

Which of these statements comes closest to describing your feelings about the Bible?

1. The Bible is the actual word of God and is to be taken literally, word for word.
2. The Bible is the word of God, but not everything in it should be take literally, word for word.
3. The Bible is a book written by men and is not the word of God.

National Surveys of Religion and Politics (potentially a two-part question).

A. Which of the following comes CLOSEST to your view of the Bible? It is

1. The inspired word of God
2. A great book of wisdom and history
3. A book of myths and legends

B. (If answered "The inspired word of God" then) "Is the Bible...

1. True, to be taken word for word
2. True, but not to be taken word for word
3. True for religion, but with some human errors

18

Emerging Trends in American Children's Bibles, 1990–2015

Russell W. Dalton

CHILDREN'S BIBLES REPRESENT a significant but understudied aspect of the use of the Bible in American culture. In the process of adapting and repackaging the Bible and its stories, children's Bibles often carry with them a host of religious, ethical, and cultural assumptions and agendas that go well beyond the content of the canonical text of the Bible itself. A study of the diverse and changing ways that children's Bibles have adapted the Bible can help index America's diverse and changing approaches to theology, the Bible, and how the Bible should be used with children.[1]

Since the beginning of the republic, when American publishers republished British children's Bibles, and especially since the explosion of American Christian book buying in the late nineteenth century, Americans have been purchasing and reading a large number and wide variety of children's Bibles. In recent decades, however, children's Bible sales have reached unprecedented heights. The 1990s saw a significant increase in publication and sales of children's literature in general,[2] and the publication of children's Bibles has increased at an even greater rate. *Publisher's Weekly* reported that in the year 1990 Americans spent over $40 million on children's Bibles.[3] According to a book buyer for Family Christian Stores, a popular chain of Christian bookstores, in 1999 children's Bibles accounted for 10–12 percent of their total company sales and 28 percent of their children's book sales.[4] The popularity of children's Bibles has continued to grow since the turn of the new century. As LaVonne Neff reported in her 2001 article "Bible Stories: Facing a Floodtide," "today the flood of Bible-related products continues unabated, and many Bible story books are bankrolling their companies."[5] What is more, these children's Bibles often have a profound impact on their readers, providing many Americans with their first impressions of what the Bible is and how it should be read.

In the years from 1990 to 2015, the year in which this essay is written, several trends have emerged in American Protestant Christian children's Bibles in particular that are instructive in understanding the current landscape of America's religious culture at a grassroots level. This essay will examine the following six emerging trends: presenting Bible stories as fun stories for very young audiences, adding anthropomorphic animal friends to the stories, presenting dinosaurs living alongside humans, presenting the entire Bible as one unified story about redemption in Jesus Christ, writing and illustrating children's Bibles from African-American perspectives, and packaging children's Bibles specifically for either male or female readers. I will place these trends within the longer context of children's Bibles throughout American history and note these trends' significance for understanding contemporary trends in American culture and American Protestant Christian culture in particular.

YOUNGER READERS AND A FRIENDLY GOD

Through the years many have debated whether or not the Bible, with its tales of sex and violence and its complex subject matter, should be used with children at all.[6] Throughout American history, however, children's Bibles have been published for increasingly younger readers. While some nineteenth- and early twentieth-century children's Bibles were aimed at younger readers,[7] the late twentieth and early twenty-first centuries saw a dramatic increase in the number of children's Bibles written and illustrated for preschoolers, toddlers, and even babies. These children's Bibles present their young audience with fun and happy stories that feature a kind and friendly God.

Those who are only familiar with these more recent children's Bibles may be shocked to read some of the children's Bibles of the eighteenth and early nineteenth centuries. During those years of high infant and child mortality rates and residual Puritan beliefs, and before the era of modern childhood development studies, many Christian educators saw it as their primary task to convince children of their own sinfulness, warn them of the righteous judgment of God, and remind them that death might come at any time and to be prepared for it. As Steven Mintz writes in his book *Huck's Raft: A History of American Childhood*, "children's early consciousness of their mortality and the severity of divine judgment was considered a particularly useful tool for shaping behavior."[8] Children's Bibles of this time often used the stories of the Bible to teach children to fear an all-powerful God. In the early to mid-nineteenth century, for example, if a children's Bible in the United States included only ten stories, chances were that one of them would be the story of the children of Bethel taunting Elisha and God sending two she-bears out of the woods to maul and kill them. This story was often used to teach children the lesson that God could kill them at any time if they did not stay obedient to God's laws. In 1863's *Scripture History for the Young*, for example, John Howard retold the story and concluded: "Let the young therefore fear to speak wicked words, for the Lord who hears all they say, and beholds all their actions, will assuredly visit their transgressions."[9] As late as 1877, the children's Bible *Dear Old Stories Told*

Once More concluded the story: "Oh, how little we think what a dreadful thing it is to disobey and hate the blessed God."[10] Meanwhile, early American children's Bible versions of the story of Noah's ark often included horrific illustrations of the floodwaters overcoming despairing children and their families. The text of these stories often closed with a direct warning to children. For example, Samuel G. Goodrich, author of *Peter Parley's Book of Bible Stories* from 1834, closes his account of the flood by warning children: "Oh! How dreadful it is to disobey such a powerful God, who can destroy us in a moment, if he please!"[11] God, again, is presented to children as someone who is to be feared and who may destroy them.

Children's Bibles of more recent decades set a decidedly different tone. Children's Bibles are increasingly designed for very young children of preschool age and even younger, leading to popular titles such as *The Toddler's Bible* (1992), *The Preschooler's Bible* (1994), *The Baby Bible Storybook* (1994), *The Beginners Bible for Toddlers* (1995), *Baby's First Bible* (1996), *Baby's Bible* (2003), *Baby Blessings Baby's Bible* (2004), *The Sweetest Story Bible for Toddlers* (2010), *Baby's First Bible* (2012), and *The Big Picture Interactive Bible Stories for Toddlers from the Old Testament* (2014).[12] This younger target audience, combined with theological shifts and wider awareness and influence of childhood development studies, has led to a friendlier image of God and faith in these books as well. The story of Elisha and the children of Bethel, for example, has long since disappeared from almost all but the most comprehensive children's Bibles and is included in none of these children's Bibles for younger children. While the story of Noah's ark continues to be a perennial favorite, illustrations of people being overcome by waves have largely been replaced by the ubiquitous image of a smiling Noah and his happy animal friends in an overstuffed ark smiling at the reader. In these children's Bibles there is often no mention that anyone drowns in the flood, only the phrase found in dozens and dozens of children's Bibles that "God keeps us safe."[13] God is not a judge to be feared but a loving parent or a friend to be loved.[14]

Parents appear to want their children to relate warm, friendly feelings with the Bible and with God, and some publishers have responded to this desire by introducing a tactile element to their Bible stories. In 2001, the board book *Jesus and the Miracle of the Loaves and Fishes* was packaged with a plush Jesus doll complete with hair and beard of yarn under the product title "Jesus Hugs Me."[15] More recently, several books published by Zondervan's children's division, ZonderKids, have built this theme directly into the children's Bibles themselves. Sally Lloyd-Jones's *Tiny Bear's Bible* (2007) was published with a huggable plush cover designed to look like a cute smiling teddy bear with blue overalls that doubles as a stuffed animal that children can cuddle.[16] The *Baby's Hug-a-Bible* (2010), also written by Lloyd-Jones, is designed with a soft, faux lamb's wool cover. The official product description reads as follows: "A Bible you can hug! In this soft and cuddly book, little ones will find a collection of ten favorite Bible stories in rhyme, filled with comforting truths and promises. Keep God's word close to baby's heart in this perfect introduction for the very young to the stories of the Bible and to God's great love for them."[17] In the same way, P. J. Lyons's *Little Lion's Bible* (2011) has a cover made of soft artificial fur in the shape of a small lion. The packaging invites children to "Cuddle Up with Little Lion and Know God's Love."[18] Zondervan also published Lyon's book in alternate packaging, presumably for the Easter season, as *Little Bunny's Bible* (2011), a plush-covered book that looks like a bunny head complete with floppy ears that has a packaging that says: "A bunny to hug, a Bible to love";[19] *Little Chick's Bible* (2011) was a plush-covered book made to look like a cute yellow chick complete with beak and packaging that read: "A chick to hug, a Bible to love."[20] The stories included in these books are full of smiling people and animals and are happy and friendly in tone. More significant than the details of the text of the stories themselves, however, is the fact that the Bible itself, and by extension the God who is described within it, has literally become a warm and fuzzy feeling for children.

By the end of the twentieth century the image of God presented in most children's Bibles was not that of a God who is demanding and judgmental but rather that of a loving heavenly friend who keeps them safe in times of trouble. In this way, the theology presented in these children's Bibles parallels the findings of the National Study of Youth and Religion conducted from July 2002 to March 2003. According to that study, the prevailing view of God held by American teenagers (ages 13–17) across religions and denominational boundaries is one of a God who makes few demands on humankind. Furthermore, the study suggests that most teenagers believe in a God who wants people to be nice, to be happy, and to feel good about themselves but is not particularly involved in their lives. Still, God is there for them if they need help to protect them or to rescue them if they are in a bind. Researchers Christian Smith and Melinda Lundquist Denton refer to this prevailing view as "Moralistic Therapeutic Deism."[21] Given this religious climate, the cultural factors at work, a concern for what is age-appropriate for children, and a growing emphasis on God's love in American theology, it is not surprising to find that the image of God presented in children's Bibles is not a God who is frightening, demanding, or judgmental but rather a loving heavenly friend who keeps children safe in times of trouble.

ANTHROPOMORPHIC ANIMAL FRIENDS

On the basis of the sorts of children's books found on twenty-first-century bookstore shelves, it would be easy to assume that children's literature in the United States has always consisted of wildly imaginative stories of fantasy, fairy tales, and smiling, fun-loving animals. Throughout much of the eighteenth and nineteenth century, however, American adults, and religious American adults in particular, were very uneasy about the prospect of their children reading fictional stories or any stories that contained fantastical elements or were intended primarily for their readers' amusement. As Gillian Avery notes in her review of American children's literature, most Americans, throughout much of the nineteenth century, viewed fairy tales and other works of the imagination as "irrational, and irrelevant to modern needs."[22] One of the reasons children's Bibles were so relatively popular in the nineteenth century may have been that they were considered "true" stories, as evidenced by children's Bible titles such as

Mother's True Stories and *Tell Me a True Story*,[23] and their somber, serious content held little in common with frivolous fairy tales that included fantastical elements such as talking animals. These attitudes persisted in some form even into the twentieth century.

These concerns regarding fiction and fantasy appear to have diminished, however, over the course of the twentieth century. By the end of the twentieth century, nonreligious children's literature was filled with fun, fantasy, and talking animals, and many children's Bible authors and illustrators began to follow suit. These children's Bibles include textual descriptions and illustrations of cartoon-style, anthropomorphic animals that do things that real animals could not do, especially when they illustrate and retell the story of Noah's ark. In *The Big Big Big Boat, and Other Bible Stories about Obedience* (1993) a male monkey wears a top hat and bow tie and a female monkey wears a pearl necklace as they carry suitcases onto the ark.[24] In *God Loves Me Bible* (1993) giraffes, birds, and elephants are seen doing the laundry and hanging it up on Noah's ark.[25] In Mack Thomas's *The First Step Bible* (1994) a smiling brown bear, alongside many other upright smiling animals, gives Adam a big, friendly hug,[26] and Noah is shown playing marbles on the ark with a cute group of smiling animals, including a rabbit, turtle, bird, and raccoon.[27] In *The Preschooler's Bible* (1994) a tiny bear and monkey kneel, close their eyes, and fold their hands in prayer along with Noah and his wife;[28] and in *My Very First Book of Bible Heroes* (1998) a bear, rabbit, and lion smile big smiles and dance for joy on two feet as they leave the ark while a little mouse looks on with his hands folded in prayer.[29] In *The Beginner's Bible: All Aboard with Noah!* (2009) a smiling elephant helpfully carries a log to Noah while he is building the ark.[30] The story of a fun boat ride with anthropomorphic animal friends is certainly age appropriate, but it bears only scant resemblance to the story as it appears in the book of Genesis. It also effectively presents the story of Noah's ark not as a realistic historical event but rather as a fantasy story that has more in common with the stories in fairy tales than those in history books.

One might suspect that more conservative publishers, those with a primary readership that tends to hold to the historical inerrancy and infallibility of Scripture, would take care to present their stories as somber, historical events with texts that stay close to the canonical text and to include illustrations that were quite realistic. Furthermore, one might expect that they would carefully avoid trivializing the stories as though they were cartoons, with animals acting in ways that only humans could act. On the other hand one might suspect that children's Bibles created for secular publishers and Christian publishers of moderate or liberal denominations would be more inclined to take greater liberties with the Bible stories, allowing their authors and artists to use more creative expression than their more conservative counterparts, not being bound by the desire to depict the stories as realistic historical events or by the need to be consistent with the biblical text. In many cases, however, the opposite is true. The children's Bibles that include illustrations of anthropomorphic animals tend to come from more theologically conservative publishers such as Zondervan, Cook Communications, Thomas Nelson, and Gold 'n Honey Books. Meanwhile, many secular publishers and those with a wider or more mainline readership treat the stories as realistic ancient stories with realistic illustrations, such as 1994's *Children's Illustrated Bible* from Dorling Kindersley, or retell the stories in ways that stay close to the events of the text, offer impressionistic illustrations that convey a sense of awe and wonder, and resist adding morals to the end of the stories, such as the *Reader's Digest Bible for Children*.[31]

This phenomenon perhaps may be explained by conservative Christian parents' strong desire to make the Bible (and, by extension, their faith) fun and engaging. Just as children's Bibles of past centuries resembled the secular children's literature of their day, many of these late twentieth- and early twenty-first-century children's Bibles resemble the children's literature of their day as well. These children's Bibles are fun and engaging and compete with the many entertainment options children have been given.[32] These fun children's Bibles fit the model of popular contemporary children's storybooks, even if they no longer bear much similarity to the stories as they are told in the Bible. The books offered by theologically conservative authors and publishers, then, may not reflect a longing for children to learn accurate accounts of Bible stories. Instead, they meet a consumer demand for books that present the Bible, and by extension the Christian faith, to the next generation as something that is fun and engaging.

DINOSAURS IN THE BIBLE

An extensive survey of children's Bibles from throughout American history suggests that for over two hundred years none contained a description or illustration of a dinosaur living alongside human beings.[33] Beginning in 1996, however, in response to a growing movement of young Earth creationists, several publishers began to offer versions of Bible stories that presented children with text descriptions and illustrations of dinosaurs, humans, and other animals living side by side.

Mary Hollingsworth's *Bumper the Dinosaur Bible Stories*, published in 1996 by Chariot Family Publishing, a division of Cook Communications, tells two stories of a cartoonish green dinosaur named Bumper. "Bumper and Adam" shows a young, toddler-aged Adam naming the animals, including Bumper, and even riding piggyback on Bumper's back.[34] In the story "Bumper and Noah," Bumper is seen marching into the ark beside a pink dinosaur and behind pairs of elephants, giraffes, rabbits, bears, and parrots.[35] While some children may take the stories to be pure fantasy, the book still effectively establishes the image of dinosaurs being present in the Bible's stories.

According to their website, the publisher Master Books "is the world's largest publisher of creation-based material for all ages including apologetics, homeschool resources, reference titles, and quality children's literature."[36] Master Books has published several children's Bible story collections featuring dinosaurs. Gloria Clanin's collection *In the Days of Noah* (1996), for example, presents a greatly expanded version of the story of Noah that describes dinosaurs such as apatosauruses, velociraptors, triceratops, and pterodactyls among the deer, giraffes, lions, rabbits, wolves, frogs, and turtles as they enter, live on, and leave the ark.[37] Earl and Bonita Snellenberger's accompanying illustrations include labels with the names of these dinosaurs so that readers cannot miss their presence.

Ken Ham, president/CEO and founder of Answers in Genesis-U.S. and the Creation Museum, wrote *The Dinosaurs of Eden* for Master Books in 2001. The illustrations, again by Earl and Bonita Snellenberger, place dinosaurs in the Garden of Eden with Adam and Eve, on a hillside as Cain murders Abel, on the ark with Noah, and with Noah and his family as they make a thanksgiving offering to God and even show people riding saddled dinosaurs during the building of the tower of Babel.[38] Ham inserts into these stories arguments for his belief that dinosaurs lived alongside humans.

Later, in 2012, Ham wrote *The True Account of Adam and Eve*, which features Bill Looney's beautiful illustrations, including one of Adam naming a group of animals that include a wolf, pink flamingos, hippopotamuses, giraffes, and raptors,[39] and another of a lion, monkey, goat, mastodon, and another two-legged dinosaur living peacefully together.[40] In one illustration, a cheerful chimpanzee observes while Adam and Eve feed a piece of fruit by hand to a gentle but sharp-toothed dinosaur that appears to be a velociraptor.

Ham's book on Adam and Eve serves as a companion piece of sorts to Tom Dooley's earlier book *The True Story of Noah's Ark*, published by Master Books in 2003. Bill Looney provides the illustrations, including one in which one of Noah's sons motions to a beautiful woolly mammoth who is lifting lumber in his tusks to help build the ark.[41] Later, Looney presents a two-page panoramic view of Noah standing with his staff as he watches a majestic procession of animals marching two by two that includes ostriches, mammoths, giraffes, chimpanzees, buffalo, bears, and, in the rear, two apatosauruses.[42] Looney does not draw attention to the apatosauruses by placing them in the forefront but just presents them as a natural part of the menagerie of animals entering the ark.

These children's Bible stories are primarily marketed to homeschooling parents and churches that hold to the young Earth view of the history of the world but are also available in many Christian bookstores along with other children's Bibles. Though the children's Bibles that include dinosaurs represent only a small percentage of children's Bibles available, the fact that they have been published in recent decades speaks to the importance of the issue for some Christians in the twenty-first century. As belief in young Earth creationism increasingly becomes a litmus test in some circles for one's standing as a conservative Christian in the early twenty-first century,[43] these books, through their text and illustrations, seek to pass on their authors' and publishers' views of creation to members of the next generation.

THE BIBLE AS THE STORY OF JESUS AND REDEMPTION HISTORY

American Christians have long had a faith that has been particularly focused on the person of Jesus Christ,[44] and throughout much of American history children's Bibles have adapted Bible stories in ways that point to salvation in Jesus Christ. During the early 1800s, for example, some children's Bibles pointed out "types of Christ" in the Hebrew Bible,[45] and later in the century many children's Bibles followed the lead of revivalist preachers and used stories such as Noah's ark to urge children to accept salvation in Christ.[46] In the twentieth century, fewer children's Bibles drew connections between Hebrew Bible stories and Jesus Christ, though it was still done by some authors.[47] In the twenty-first century, however, a trend in children's Bibles emerged that took a different approach to the connection between Jesus and the stories of the Hebrew Bible. Not only could a handful of Hebrew Bible characters and objects be seen as "types" of Christ, and not only could an analogy be drawn between salvation for Hebrew Bible characters and salvation for people in the present day, but an increasing number of children's Bibles began to suggest to their readers that the entire Bible is actually a unified story about salvation in Jesus Christ.

Sally Lloyd-Jones's *The Jesus Storybook Bible: Every Story Whispers His Name* (2007) is a case in point. The book's back cover describes the book: *"The Jesus Storybook Bible: Every Story Whispers His Name* tells the story beneath all the stories in the Bible. At the center of the story is a baby, the child upon whom everything will depend. Every story whispers his name. From Noah to Moses to the great King David—every story points to him. He is like the missing piece in a puzzle—the piece that makes all the other pieces fit together."[48] After recounting the story of the Tower of Babel, for example, Lloyd-Jones adds: "You see, God knew, however high they reached, however hard they tried, people could never get back to heaven by themselves. People didn't need a staircase; they needed a Rescuer. Because the way back to heaven wasn't a staircase; it was a Person."[49] The story, then, is framed as one that is ultimately about the coming Savior, Jesus Christ.

Mary Machowski's *The Gospel Story Bible: Discovering Jesus in the Old and New Testaments* (2011) takes a similar approach. According to the publisher's description, "it is easy to forget Jesus in the midst of frantic schedules, family squabbles, and conflicting priorities. But the truth is that he is the hero of every story, including these ordinary ones. This is why Marty Machowski puts God's plan of salvation in Christ on continuous display in *The Gospel Story Bible*. The easy-to-read storybook introduces your family to many captivating people, places, and events from the Bible's Old and New Testaments, showing how each one ultimately points to Jesus."[50]

Every single Hebrew Bible story, then, concludes with a connection to a message of salvation through Jesus Christ. For the story of God's promise to Abram, for example, the message is "Through Abram we have all been blessed, just as God promised, because it is by the death and resurrection of his great-far-off grandson Jesus that all those who believe inherit the promise of Abraham forever!" Regarding God's covenant with Abram: "Like Abram, we are saved when we trust in what Jesus did for us." For baby Moses: "Jesus, like Moses, grew up to rescue God's people from slavery. But it was a different kind of slavery—a slavery to sin." Regarding the Ten Commandments: "None of us can obey God perfectly. None of us except Jesus! When we put our faith in him, Jesus takes away our sin and gives us his perfect record of obedience."[51] Machowski, then, links every Bible story to Jesus and the message of salvation.

Likewise, Rondi DeBoer and Christine Tangvald's 2011 *My Favorite Bible* frames the entire Bible around the motif of Jesus as "the Promised One." According to the book's introduction, "this promise of God is the focus of the whole Bible. Every story reflects the Promised One. Every event prepares the way for His coming. Every page proclaims the truth that **Jesus** is our one and only Savior."[52] In the same way, Sarah Young writes in the preface to her *Jesus Calling Bible Storybook* (2012): "This book tells the wonderful story of God's great love for His people. It shows that the center, the beginning, and the end of this story all focus on Jesus." She begins her story of creation telling children: "In the beginning there was nothing but God the Father, His Son—Jesus—and the Holy Spirit." Young ends each of her stories with a "Jesus Calling" reflection. After telling the story up to the creation of animals, the "Jesus Calling" segment is "I am the Alpha and Omega. That means the Beginning and the End. Most people call me Jesus. I am God's Son. I made the heavens and the earth. Even then—before you were even born—I thought of you and loved you."[53] Each story that follows also alludes to Jesus and ends with a "Jesus Calling" segment.

These, and several other twenty-first-century children's Bibles,[54] clearly promote to potential buyers the fact that they are explicitly connecting each story of the Bible, those from the Hebrew Bible as well as those from the New Testament, to salvation and Jesus Christ. Many Christians in the twenty-first century, out of respect for the Jewish faith and a sense of ecumenicity, have begun to avoid using the name Old Testament and have instead spoken of the Hebrew Bible or First Testament. These children's Bibles, however, are evidence that many Christians at the beginning of the twenty-first century approach their Old Testament as a thoroughly Christian and Christ-centered book. In the process, they reflect many American evangelical Christians' concern that their children understand their view of God's plan of salvation through Jesus Christ as a central theme of the entire Bible.

BIBLE STORIES FROM AN AFRICAN-AMERICAN PERSPECTIVE

African-American religious educators have a long tradition of *telling* Bible stories to children, but arguably only since 1995 have any children's Bibles been published that have been written and illustrated specifically from an African-American perspective.

For most of American history, there has been very little in the way of children's literature of any kind tailored for African-American children.[55] This has been true of children's Bibles as well. Several somewhat related books, however, have been published. In the early twentieth century, for example, African-American pastor and scholar R. A. Morrisey wrote *Bible History of the Negro* (1915) and *Colored People in Bible History* (1925).[56] While Morrisey wrote these stories for adults, he noted that they could be used to instruct children as well. Some related attempts are ones that African-Americans and others would rather forget, such as the misguided attempt by white author Betty Smith Foley to retell Bible stories in the "slavery dialect" of a slave era "Mammy" in *Bible Chillun* (1939).[57] Published in the same year as the release of the film *Gone with the*

Wind (1939), the book reflects a troubling nostalgia for the stereotypical portrayal of slaves. On a more positive note, in 1946, African-American missionary and author Lorenz Bell Graham first published a series of Bible stories written in the idiom of the West African native storytellers he had met there in his book *How God Fix Jonah* (1946).[58] Still, as Ruth Bottigheimer noted as she wrote about children's Bibles in the early 1990s, at the time of her writing no children's Bibles had been written or illustrated specifically for African-American children in the United States.[59] Instead, almost all American children's Bibles were written from a white, Western European perspective, and the illustrations in the majority of children's Bibles and children's Sunday School curriculum materials from throughout American history have depicted Bible characters as white people of European descent.

One benefit of recent developments in the book publishing industry and marketplace, however, has been the recognition of particular marketplaces. According to Leonard S. Marcus, in his book *Minders of Make-Believe*, the emergence of more children's books published by and for diverse groups of people, such as books for African-American children, emerged especially in the 1990s.[60] Since the mid-1990s, a number of children's Bibles have been published from an African-American perspective and created especially for children of color.

Patricia and Fredrick McKissack's *Let My People Go* (1998) offers one of the more creative examples of a children's Bible for African-American children. The wife-and-husband writing team put stories from the Bible into the narrative voice of Price Jefferies, a fictional free black abolitionist, who tells the stories in response to questions asked by his daughter Charlotte in Charleston, South Carolina, in the years 1806–1816. The authors integrate the story of a freed slave with stories of the Bible and in the process draw connections between God's liberating work in the Bible, in the days of slavery, and in more recent times as well. The illustrations in the book, however, may be as significant as the way the stories are told. In his introductory "illustrator's note," James E. Ransome explains that he was determined that while previous Bible illustrations would influence his work, his illustrations would have one key difference: "The people would resemble those from the region of North Egypt and what we now know as Israel, Lebanon, Syria, Iraq, Jordan, Ethiopia, and north of Saudi Arabia— where most of the Old Testament stories took place. I would draw people with brown and olive complexions, Semites. I felt compelled to dispel the myth created by the European representations of Bible characters, so fixed in the minds of most of us." Ransome further explains: "I felt it was time to start educating our children about the true images of the people who gave the world the concept of one God and three religions: Judaism, Christianity, and Islam."[61]

The *Children of Color Storybook Bible with Stories from the International Children's Bible* (2001), published by Thomas Nelson Publishers, does not veer much from the text of the International Children's Bible. Here again, however, the illustrations are key. Victor Hogan illustrates the characters with a variety of facial features and variety of skin tones that are appropriate to the African and Middle Eastern settings of the stories. The book's introduction makes the case that it will help connect children of color to their Biblical heritage and, in the process, help build their confidence and self-esteem.[62]

Likewise, *My Holy Bible for African-American Children*, a study Bible for children published by Zondervan in both King James Version and New International Version editions in 2009, does not retell Bible stories from an African-American perspective but does include supplemental materials such as popular Negro spirituals, inspirational quotes from African Americans, and illustrations by African-American artists.[63]

None of the artists of these children's Bibles follows the pattern of so many white artists before them in depicting Bible characters just as members of his or her own race. Instead, they have chosen to depict the people of the Bible as people of color, with a variety of types of facial features and variety of skin tones, and to show the diversity of races and ethnicities represented by the people of the Bible.

The majority of American children's Bibles throughout American history have and still do depict Bible characters with the coloration and facial features of white people of Western European descent.[64] The last decades of the twentieth century and first decades of the twenty-first century, however, have seen a growing number of children's Bibles, including those not specifically targeted toward children of color, that illustrate the people of the Bible as people of color with a variety of skin tones.[65]

GENDER-SPECIFIC CHILDREN'S BIBLES

In the late twentieth and early twenty-first centuries, evangelical Christian leaders have voiced grave concerns over what they see as the loss of traditional gender identity in the United States. James Dobson, the founder of the conservative Christian organization Focus on the Family, for example, urges parents to encourage and support "the soft, feminine nature of girls";[66] and the "powerful, masculine characteristics" of boys.[67] Earlier in American history, on occasion, children's Bibles were published that offered separate volumes of Bible stories *about* boys or girls, such as Harvey Albert Snyder's *Boys of the Bible* and *Girls of the Bible*.[68] It is only in the twenty-first century, however, that many Christian publishers have focused their efforts on offering separate children's Bibles for male and female readers.

Some children's Bibles designed for either boys or girls retell Bible stories for young children in storybook form. In some cases, the difference between the two volumes is primarily cosmetic. For example, David C. Cook's *The Baby Bible Storybook for Boys* and *Baby Bible Storybook for Girls*, both published in 2008, have identical texts retelling Bible stories on the inside. On the outside, however, they include different titles, and the storybook for boys has a blue cover while the storybook for girls has a pink cover.[69] Other children's Bible authors rewrite the Bible and do so quite differently, depending on the gender of their intended readers and the gender-related virtues they have in mind. In Carolyn Larsen's Baker Book House offering, *The Little Girls Bible Storybook for Mothers and Daughters* (1998), for example, each story ends by passing on a characteristic of a "Woman of God."[70] The story of "Mrs. Noah," for example, is titled "Whatever You Say Dear." In the story, Mrs. Noah goes along with whatever Noah says, and the story concludes with the lesson "A Woman of God is Obedient." Larsen tells readers that as they lived on the ark, "Mrs. Noah kept busy cleaning up after the animals and keeping her family fed and the clothes cleaned."[71] By way of contrast, in Larsen's *Little Boys Bible Storybook for Fathers and Sons* (2001), each story ends with a lesson titled "Becoming a Man of God," followed by a feature, titled "Dad's Time," that provides hints for how a father should talk to his son about the story.[72] In this book's story of Noah, Noah's young sons help build the ark and in the process learn that they should not be afraid of hard work.[73] Girls and boys, then, are presented with different lessons to glean from the story of Noah's ark.

Other children's Bibles designed specifically for either girls or boys in the twenty-first century are devotional Bibles or study Bibles that include full translations of the Bible. These publications do not retell Bible stories in ways that teach and reinforce certain gender roles, but the way they are packaged and the notes they include pass on a host of cultural norms and values related to gender.

A couple of noteworthy examples of gender-specific devotional Bible are the Thomas Nelson's "Biblezines" titled *Revolve* and *Refuel*. *Revolve* 1 first came out in 2003 and was intentionally designed to be a hybrid between a teenage girl's fashion magazine, such as *Seventeen* or *Teen People*, and a devotional Bible. *Revolve* used portions of the New Century Version translation alongside photographs of attractive teenagers and boxed blurbs featuring lifestyle advice. A few years after publishing *Revolve* as a stand-alone magazine, Thomas Nelson published *Revolve 2008: The Complete New Testament*, a trade paperback that included the New Century Version of the entire New Testament interspersed with similar photographs and spiritual and lifestyle tips somewhat randomly placed on the pages next to the text of the Bible. The cover blurbs promised girls features like "True Beauty: How Do You Get It?" and "He Said What? Guys Tell It Like It Is."[74] *Refuel* was a Biblezine targeted at boys. The cover of *Refuel: The Complete New Testament* features a photograph of an electric guitar being played, along with inserts of photographs of skateboarders, a snowboarder, and soccer players. The cover blurbs promise features such as "Extras: Girls, Cash, and Cars," "Girls Spill It All!," "100 Practical Ways to Live Out Your Faith," and "Today's Hottest Songs!"[75] These Biblezines' cover images, cover blurbs, and features reflect and reinforce certain assumptions about female and male adolescents and reveal what their producers believe might entice them to purchase or read the Bible.

In the twenty-first century, Bible publishers have offered consumers a plethora of more traditional devotional and study Bibles designed specifically for either boys or girls. Thomas Nelson's children's division, Tommy Nelson, published an International Children's Bible titled *Shiny Sequin Bible Holy Bible* (2011); it sports a pink cover filled with pasted-on sparkly flowers and glittering hearts.[76] Thomas Nelson's description of the Bible explains that when other girls ask "What kind of book is that?" a girl can "show her sparkly shiny Bible, thus sharing the 'light' of Jesus."[77] For boys, Thomas Nelson published *The Compact Kids Bible: Green Camo* (2007),[78] an ICB version Bible that has a military-style camouflage cover. According to Thomas Nelson, "this Bible is perfect for adventurous boys."[79]

Tyndale House Publishers offered a pair of gender-specific children's Bibles for pre-teens and teens as well. *The Girls Life Application Bible* (2006) sports a pink cover with a butterfly that says: "Finally, a Life Application Bible just for Girls!"[80] Tyndale's *The Guys Life Application Study Bible* (2007) features a black cover with a blue and forest green design.[81]

In similar fashion, Zondervan's *NIV FaiThGirLz! Bible* (2011), available with a pink cover illustrated with flowers, promises to help girls aged nine to twelve learn the "Beauty of Believing" through features such as "Dream Girl," which tries to help girls imagine what it might be like to be in the stories of the Bible.[82] Meanwhile, Zondervan's comparable Bible for boys aged nine to twelve, *The NIV Boys Bible* (2011), does not get as creative a name and features a pretty basic brown cover. Boys also do not get as much in the way of inspirational messages related to the stories of the Bible. One of the recurring features, for example, is "Grossology: Notes on the Grossest and Most Disgusting Stuff in the Bible."[83]

Thomas Nelson's descriptions for two devotional Bibles written by Sheila Walsh, published in 2012, make their assumptions regarding the differences between the genders explicit. Walsh's *God's Mighty Warrior Devotional Bible* sports a blue cover illustrated with a shield and crossed swords.[84] According to Thomas Nelson's official description, "Even though they are often filled with energy and imagination, boys may not always feel very mighty. With this devotional Bible in storybook format, boys can learn how to be strong, honorable, courageous, and true. Selections of Bible text from the International Children's Bible® are combined with delightful articles to help a budding warrior earn his armor and grow strong in the Lord."[85] The corresponding devotional Bible for girls is titled *God's Little Princess Devotional Bible* and sports a predictably pink cover illustrated with a jewel-encrusted tiara.[86] According to the book's description, "A good dose of God's truth combined with lots of sparkle, *God's Little Princess Devotional Bible* will help your little girl blossom into the faithful princess she was created to be! Actual *International Children's Bible®* text is joined with devotionals and activities that focus on such virtues as compassion, generosity, and kindness in fun and engaging ways. Girls are sure to love the updated, extra-shimmery cover, and the content speaks to every family's felt needs as they work to raise daughters of the King."[87] According to these children's Bibles, then, boys should become strong, brave warriors while girls are to become kind and compassionate princesses.

Consumer demand for children's Bibles that tell little girls that they are God's little princesses has appeared to be particularly high in the years 2010–2015. A survey of Christian bookstore shelves reveals over a dozen of these, in the form of both study Bibles that include the entire text of the Bible and Bible storybooks that retell selected tales, with titles such as *The Princess in Me Storybook Bible* (2008), *My Princess Bible* (2010), *The Precious Princess Bible: The Holy Bible for Every Princess* (2010), that Zondervan claims "will delight little girls with Bible verses that assure her she is God's precious princess," *The Princess Bible*: New King James Version, *My Beautiful Princess Bible* (NLT) (2012), *Princess Bible Tiara Edition* (2012), which is embellished with a tiara of glitter and sparkly jewels, *Sweet Dreams Princess: God's Little Princess Bedtime Bible Stories, Devotions, and Prayers* (2008), *God's Little Princess Holy Bible* (NKJV) (2014), *My Princess Bible Purse* (2012) (a pink die-cut board book shaped like a purse), *Bible Stories for His Beautiful Princess* (2014), *The Princess in Me Storybook Bible* (2008) which comes with a shiny mirror built into the pink cover of the book, *Promises for God's Precious Princess* (2013), and *Bible Stories for His Beautiful Princess* (2014).[88] An equal or even greater number of pink-covered "God's princess" themed devotionals for girls also fill Christian bookstore shelves.

Carolyn Larsen's *Princess Stories: Real Bible Stories of God's Princesses* (2011) is an interesting example of this type of children's Bible. Larsen begins each story of a woman in the Bible with a variation of the traditional poem from Snow White that begins "Mirror, Mirror on the Wall" and a page-height illustration of the Bible "princess" drawn in a manner similar to a glamorous Disney princess. The story of Eve, for example, begins "Mirror, mirror on the wall, / Who was the very first princess of all? / A long time ago, before your birth, / Eve was the very first woman on earth." In the illustration on the page, Eve is depicted as a beautiful blond white woman with a flower in her long flowing hair wearing a gorgeous off-the-shoulder purple gown.[89]

While the growing popularity of "Princess culture" for little girls raises concerns for many cultural observers,[90] these examples attest to the fact that many twenty-first-century Christian parents embrace it and seek to have girls link their love of being a princess with the Bible and their faith.

As these examples illustrate, in the last decade of the twentieth century and early decades of the twenty-first century, evangelical Christian concerns over issues of traditional gender roles have been addressed by a number of children's Bibles. Whether due to marketing concerns or ideological concerns, the stories of the Bible are being framed to children and teenagers in ways that reflect and reinforce certain images of gender identity, thereby linking the Bible and faith to those gender roles. The Bible, then, becomes integrally connected to the cultural norms for gender roles, at least as they are understood in a certain portion of American Christianity.

CONCLUSION

The children's Bibles examined in this essay do not provide a comprehensive survey of children's Bibles published in the United States from 1990 to 2015. One of the most popular trends in children's Bibles of the past century that continues to the present day, for example, has been the practice of using Bible stories to teach children status-quo-reinforcing values such as obedience, the value of working hard without complaining, and submission to those who are in authority.[91] The children's Bibles examined here, however, represent six new trends since 1990 that may provide insights into contemporary American culture and American Christianity in particular.

Many adults purchase children's Bibles assuming that they are merely contributing to the biblical literacy of their children. Parents often choose them based on how fun or interesting the cover illustration is, and they are seldom reviewed by clergy or committees before being distributed by faith communities. As the examples in this essay attest, however, children's Bibles reflect assumptions about what the Bible actually is and how it should be used with children. They also reflect a wide variety of cultural values and theological beliefs held by those who have produced and purchased them. In the process, they help reflect and reinforce to the next generation a host of extrabiblical values and beliefs and lend insight to America's diverse and changing cultural and religious landscape.

19

The Curious Case of the Christian Bible and the U.S. Constitution

CHALLENGES FOR EDUCATORS TEACHING THE BIBLE

IN A MULTIRELIGIOUS CONTEXT

John F. Kutsko

THE BIBLE

Chapter 1 highlighted a paradox: "According to the General Social Survey, nearly eight in ten Americans regard the Bible as either the literal word of God or as inspired by God. At the same time, other surveys have revealed—and recent books have analyzed—surprising gaps in Americans' biblical literacy."[1] Section 1 of chapter 1 also notes that 50 percent of all Americans read some form of Scripture in the past year—overwhelmingly the Bible. However, "less than half of those who read the Bible in the past year sought help in understanding it." Furthermore, we learn that a four-hundred-year-old translation—the King James Version—outstrips any other modern translation for regular reading (55 percent).

We may not be surprised that nearly everyone who reads the Bible (91 percent) considers it either inerrant or inspired (though I imagine that the public surveyed does not fully understand the distinction between inerrant and inspired). But at first it is a bit surprising that 65 percent of those who did not read the Bible in the past year also think the Bible is inerrant or inspired. In other words, over 77 percent of all Americans believe the Bible is either inerrant or divinely inspired, whether or not they read it. In our highly simplified political theater and pandering for votes, candidates will exploit these facts.

Finally, chapter 1 says Americans read the Bible especially for prayer, personal direction, and comfort.[2] And while "those with less education read the Bible at twice the rate of someone with a college degree for the purposes of learning about culture war issues," it stands to reason that when most Americans turn to social issues, to understand the world around them, or to understand other religious traditions, they are likely to read the Bible the same way they do for personal comfort—that is, as a largely literal, easily understood text without the need for note, comment, or assistance from specialists. Even so, "frequent readers consulted the Bible three times more often about abortion, homosexuality, poverty, and war."

The survey numbers cited in chapter 1 track closely the numbers found in the Barna Group's research conducted last year for the American Bible Society: "The State of the Bible, 2013."[3] It is worth reviewing these studies together, though I will not do that here. When we do, none of these new findings especially surprises us. The 2006 Pew Forum on Religion and Public Life found that 78 percent (eight in ten) of *all* Americans say the Bible is the "word of God," and of this group, half believe "it is to be taken literally, word for word."[4] A 2000 Gallup poll also tracked closely the reading habits and beliefs reported in chapter 1.[5] A 2001 Barna survey reported: "60% of all adults agree that 'the Bible is totally accurate in all of its teachings' (44% agree strongly, 16% agree somewhat)."[6]

Martin Marty observed that the Bible is America's iconic book par excellence.[7] In a speech delivered on the occasion of the Society of Biblical Literature's centennial annual meeting, Marty begins his well-known 1980 remarks by citing the 1896 words of a scholar at the Theological Seminary of America: "We are all critics, I trust, and higher critics too." This was about as premature a declaration of victory as President George W. Bush's "Mission Accomplished" on the deck of the aircraft carrier USS *Abraham Lincoln*. Marty deadpans it: "The public...did not share those conclusions." He also cites an 1892 article in the Savannah, Georgia, *News* reporting on the 1892 trial of Union Theological Seminary professor Charles Briggs for heresy: "The great majority of Christians regard the Bible as the inspired word of God, and therefore, [believe it] cannot contain errors....To the average mind the whole Bible is true, or it is not the inspired word of God."[8] Marty also cites a Gallup poll and several other surveys going back to 1963 on the dismal level of biblical literacy, even as people consider the Bible a supreme authority yet resist secondary study or the help of so-called biblical critics. Marty in 1980 reads like today: "An idea that the American churches and in some ways the society have adopted and put into practice is the uncritical acceptance of the Bible's worth."[9] Not a new diagnosis then or now. It has been a chronic disease; members of the Society of Biblical Literature continue to lament the paltry impact of their scholarship.[10]

Witness the contradictions in the longstanding attitude regarding the Bible in America. Americans believe that the Bible is the Word of God, inerrant and infallible. Yet surveys demonstrate the embarrassing degree of biblical illiteracy. Furthermore, few readers seek help in understanding or interpreting the Bible from scholars and academic resources. Given that the Bible plays such a central role in American culture, these contradictions are like individual meteorological cells that meet to form a perfectly dangerous storm.

Offhandedly, it seems, Marty notes: "America...has more than the Declaration of Independence and the United States Constitution enshrined in a vault in its archival heart. The Bible also is there."[11] I want to explore this comment and its implications.

THE CONSTITUTION

The close relationship of the Bible to the Constitution deserves itself an extended treatment, but here I have to be suggestive, in outline. In short, we have an uncanny parallel between how Americans regard, read, use, and interpret the Constitution and the Bible, reflecting the same paradoxes for the Constitution in American life that we find in chapter 1.

We can start with a surprising fact. The U.S. Constitution holds a unique place in the world. The 2009 study *The Endurance of National Constitutions* and its Comparative Constitutions Project collected data from nearly every constitution ever written (almost eight hundred).[12] No country has a constitution close in age to the United States. The average life span of a nation's constitution is nineteen years, exactly the time Thomas Jefferson famously said was naturally optimal.[13] Notwithstanding amendments, the U.S. Constitution has not been rewritten, and that is not the norm.

In his 1986 book *A Machine That Would Go of Itself*, Michael Kammen, a Pulitzer Prize–winning professor of American cultural history, explores the Constitution's iconic place in our public consciousness and its role as a symbol in American life, from ratification to the late twentieth century.[14] Kammen's thesis sounds like what we see in chapter 1: "This most crucial document, so essential to the lives of all Americans, is paradoxically cherished but misunderstood. So many citizens assertively invoke the Constitution...yet so few actually know what the text contains, never mind actually *comprehending* its contents."[15]

Consider several other themes in Kammen's study that are relevant to the Bible in American life. First, the Constitution very early achieved a sacred status, often expressed using language of divine inspiration. Kammen traces this "cult of the Constitution" back, noting that "it appeared that Constitution worship had begun immediately in 1789." Critics described it as "fetish worship."[16] This is an ironic outcome, because Jefferson mocked (fittingly with biblical allusion) those who "look at constitutions with sanctimonious reverence, and deem them like the arc of the covenant, too sacred to be touched."[17] In 1811, Georgia senator William H. Crawford complained that people considered the Constitution to be perfect.[18]

A second theme in American's constitutional history is the repeated concern about constitutional illiteracy.[19] Generations of polls and studies back to the nineteenth century bear this out. Kammen then traces the consistently failed attempts to close the gap on constitutional worship or fetishism, blind allegiance to the literal text, and ignorance of the text itself. For example, in 1847 the Senate even bought copies of a manual to the Constitution, out of concern for this illiteracy, and distributed thousands of volumes.[20] None of these efforts was successful, in spite of state legislation that mandated constitutional instruction in public schools and even as some universities required at least one course on the Constitution in order to graduate.

With characteristic detail and comprehensiveness, Kammen traces these themes of populist constitutionalism in American history. And these themes track closely with populist biblicism in America. His work is a rich resource that begs further reflection and comparison to American attitudes toward the Bible. This summary is only an outline of these parallel histories.

Another observation further expands the comparison of the Bible and the Constitution. Peculiar to American interpretation is constitutional originalism, an active topic in constitutional law scholarship in the last decade;[21] including an article in 2014 by Yale Law School scholar Jack Balkin.[22] Originalist interpretations, he notes, "have in common the idea that the U.S. Constitution should be interpreted according to the meanings, purposes, intentions, or understandings of those who framed or adopted the Constitution."[23] Balkin's insights into the origins and peculiarity of constitutional originalism in America are particularly interesting, as they help to explain a relationship between the Bible and the Constitution.

There is much research on the origins of originalism and how far it goes back as a formal, self-conscious interpretative principle appealed to by jurists and legislators. We are most familiar with its recent popularity since the onset of Reagan conservatism.[24] Balkin, however, has shown that the self-conscious use of the device was not just a conservative strategy.[25] And others have shown that originalism was used as justification for legal and legislative positions in the early nineteenth century.[26] Ilya Somin notes: "Modern theories of originalism developed by academics and judges are elaborating longstanding ideas more than inventing completely new ones."[27]

Here an academic-public divide bears acknowledging. Scholarly approaches to historical context might include understanding the framers' limitations even while avoiding a blind allegiance to all the framers' wishes. Indeed, this is similar to historical-critical biblical scholarship as well as formal hermeneutical approaches in many, if not most, faith traditions, in which reason, tradition, and experience are applied.[28] But Balkin notes: "Among the general public . . . the idea of originalism is captured by the deceptively simple notion that judges should interpret the Constitution according to 'what the framers wanted.' "[29] In the popular mind, it is a form of literalism—*sola scriptura, sensusliteralis*, the plain sense of the text—and this is important: it is peculiar to America.

Let me repeat that: it is peculiar to America. Originalism is more common in the United States than in any other nation, and it lends itself to a very simplified view of constitutional interpretation and application. Says Balkin: "What makes originalism controversial in the United States—and largely unheard of outside it—is . . . the claim that judges must interpret and apply the Constitution in the same way that people living at the time of adoption would have. . . . If judges do not . . . they act illegitimately and lawlessly."[30] He says this is problematic, since (as in the case of the Bible) "most Americans know comparatively little about what the framers and adopters actually wanted or sought to achieve in creating the Constitution. . . . Nevertheless, the idea of fidelity to the founders and a desire to follow their example...is a powerful trope in American constitutional argument, although not in most other constitutional democracies."[31]

Why is constitutional originalism so prominent in American culture? Balkin gives six reasons that are a mix of historical and cultural. Two reasons are particularly noteworthy here: "The long dominance of a protestant religious tradition with its emphasis on close reading of scriptural texts and redemptive calls for a return to origins...and a long tradition of reverence for the Constitution and the Declaration of Independence as foundational scriptures in the American civic religion."[32] Balkin sees this as a way Americans work out their ambivalence toward change.[33] They celebrate both pioneerism and constancy. In many ways the reformation spirit of Americans has given them license to break with past traditions while also being deeply traditional, tethered to a religious and political scripture.[34]

Popular biblical and constitutional hermeneutics are a match made in heaven.[35] Balkin says, "The Constitution belongs to We the People—it is written in a comparatively brief text that anyone can read and that each citizen has the right to understand and interpret for themselves. This protestant tradition is populist and anti-elitist."[36] The "We the People" tradition legitimates the interpretive authority of anyone reading the text. Like *sola scriptura*, wherein the Bible must be "delivered from interpretations to speak for itself,"[37] popular constitutional originalism, then, moves beyond establishing original intent. It combines literalism and authority with a naïve assumption that the text requires neither mediation nor displacement in order to meet the needs and challenges of modernity.[38]

Saul Cornell said of the popular ideology of originalism: "citizens need not have much, if any, formal training in law to understand the meaning of constitutional and legal texts, which ought to be interpreted according to their plain meaning."[39] Consider how closely that sentiment aligns with American attitudes toward the Bible and its interpretation. Those attitudes, furthermore, are deeply rooted and deeply prized in religion and politics. Our politicians are quick to seize the plain sense as a sign of solidarity. President Grover Cleveland's statement in the late nineteenth century is, alas, not surprising: "The Bible is good enough for me, just the old book under which I was brought up. I do not want notes or criticisms or explanation about authorship or origin or even cross-references. I do not need them or understand them, and they confuse me."[40]

THE CHALLENGE

It is this combination of sacredness, sufficiency, literalism, and inerrancy, not just in the twentieth century but throughout American history, in religion and politics, with the Bible and the Constitution, that I want to highlight as a challenge to educators teaching the Bible and religion. Why is this a challenge?

First, educators seek to foster respect in our multicultural and multireligious communities and universities. To do so requires creating the environment for tolerance and understanding. The first challenge is our multireligious context itself.

Educators are aware of the rapidly changing contexts in which we live, as Diana Eck showed in her 2001 study *A New Religious America*.[41] The State Department notes that Islam is one of the fastest growing religions in the United States. By 2030, the Muslim population is expected to double,[42] a faster rate of growth than in any other region of the world.[43] Nashville, one of the buckles of the Bible belt and called "the Protestant Vatican," has an estimated one thousand churches and the headquarters of several Protestant denominations and their presses, as well as other Christian publishers and organizations. It also has the largest Kurdish population in America and has the nickname "Little Kurdistan."[44] A recent *Washington Times* story lists the runners-up for this population as Birmingham, Indianapolis, Louisville, and Charlotte, which have all doubled their foreign-born populations between 2000 and 2011.[45] The *Times* story notes: "These states are Republican friendly, and don't fit the profile of a liberal immigrant haven."

The most recent Pew Study should prove the urgency of this conversation.[46] Islam will continue its pace as the fastest growing faith, making up nearly one-third of the world's total projected population. More significant, and contrary to assumptions that religion would decline in the modern world, the size of nearly every major faith is expected to increase. Religions will become increasingly diverse and increasingly important and will increasingly rub shoulders in every urban, suburban, and rural community. Assumptions about Christian identity in America and about the simplicity of reading *any* text, sacred or secular, will be critical factors in how Americans adapt to change.

Second, literalist religion breeds a certainty that is combustible in this context. Every day the news has examples involving the Bible. Consider, for instance, the so-called white supremacist Bible and the use of scripture by hate groups.[47] Timothy Beal examines one such piece of propaganda based on a story in the book of Numbers, chapter 25. This piece makes the case for the so-called Phineas Priesthood,"[48] is replete with biblical proof texting, and is typeset in such a way that the scriptural references "appear to have authority to speak for themselves. They need no interpretation."[49] He says, "Although seldom recognized as such, radical white supremacist culture in the US is in many respects a textual culture. More precisely, it is a biblical culture. Its primary text is the Christian Bible."[50]

Even setting aside such extreme cases, the personal and therapeutic use of the Bible, the use of it in cultural wars, and the use of it to justify intolerance are not unrelated. Chapter 1 suggests that the Bible is used to feel good or feel justified in the context of a simple, unstudied understanding. In all these cases, it is applied to oneself, to the world around oneself, or to one's neighbor without modern hermenueutics—resulting in interpretation that brooks no ambiguity, inconsistency, or uncertainty. The iconic, inerrant, infallible, stand-alone Bible, with its black-and-white certainty, is fuel for the fires of intolerance and hostility.[51] We have a dangerous textual stew with three ingredients: illiteracy, inspiration, and simplicity.

Of course, we know this is a global issue and not limited to the Bible or the United States, and that is why the 2015 Pew Study is so important. A year ago, during Nigeria's so-called whisper campaign, authorities were using churches and mosques to round up gay men. The BBC's reporter, Will Ross, said, "Everybody quoted the Bible or quoted the Koran" to justify this help.[52] Eboo Patel, the founding president of the Interfaith Youth Core, raises the concern that "all too often, people are killing each other to the soundtrack of prayer."[53] Again, this makes this matter more urgent to us as educators in our increasingly diverse communities at home and abroad.

Third, the Bible is a bona fide factor in American culture and public opinion, as chapters throughout this book attest. A 2006 national survey by the Pew Forum on Religion and Public Life found that most Americans (59 percent) continue to say that religion's influence on the country is declining, and most of those who express this view believe that this is a bad thing.[54] In Barna's 2013 State of the Bible survey, 58 percent report that the Bible's influence on their voting is "a great deal or somewhat"; 56 percent said the Bible has "too little influence" in the United States today.[55]

Fourth—and this is my main point—we are facing a deeply rooted and reinforced trait in American culture.[56] A 2009 survey published in the *Columbia Law Review* found that 76 percent of supporters of constitutional originalism also believed the literal truth of the Bible.[57] What is more, the two together, the Bible and the Constitution, bear moral claims and judgments. In the originalist and literalist worldview, to be "unconstitutional" is inherently un-American, just as to be unbiblical is immoral and un-Christian.[58] In law and the Bible, legal scholars Peter Smith and Robert Tuttle note, "literalism and originalism share a core commitment to the idea that their relevant texts have a timeless, fixed meaning that is readily discernable," and "both maintain that all other approaches to their relevant texts are fundamentally illegitimate."[59] The Bible and the Constitution support and reinforce each other in public opinion; and from public opinion to public policy. A Muslim scholar of the Qur'an reminded me that this sounds like America's Sharia law.

We are all familiar with the many arguments for biblical literacy as an important component of cultural literacy.[60] But that's not the problem, is it? Interpretive naïveté is.[61] Nor is it enough to teach the facts of other religious traditions, as if that naturally, necessarily inculcates understanding and tolerance. As Diane Jacobson emphasized in her conference paper, literacy is not fluency. A 1923 editorial on teaching the Constitution in elementary schools noted, "Perhaps the task of memorizing the entire Constitution need not be laid upon the children. Perhaps the accomplishment of such a feat would be of no service to them whatever unless it were accompanied by competent explanations of the origin, history, meaning, value, and philosophy of the Constitution."[62] It sounds funny and obvious when we hear this for educating civics. Yet we face this same situation with the Bible—not Bible memorization (and the findings in chapter 1 are interesting on this, too) but educating for meaning, context, and understanding.

Findings from chapter 1 track so well with American attitudes toward the Constitution to warn us that we are dealing with a veritable national trait. We face a far more complex educational challenge, namely, the assumed homogeneity and certainty, biblical or constitutional, so embedded in our culture.[63] Americans feel fully armed with the Bible, a newspaper, and the Constitution.[64]

The study's general findings, even when nuanced by demographic factors (age, gender, race, education, income, and region) suggest broad concerns for us as educators in a nation that is increasingly religiously diverse. If the results of chapter 1 were a report card, it would suggest that our students—namely, Americans—have failed, and their teachers, us, have to take stock and reconnoiter. The good news is the bad news: we are not alone in our failure. Our challenge is deeply established and complex, and we should look to our allies facing similar challenges across the humanities and social sciences. The task ahead, for mutual understanding, for civil discourse, for the common good, is urgent.

Biblical scholars perform regular, corporal mortification over the "yawning abyss"[65] between academic and public understanding of the Bible. I am not trying to mount a defense for the poor job performance of my guild or to acquit biblical scholars of our responsibility. I am, however, claiming the problem is not unique to biblical scholarship, and the challenge is not ours alone to solve. One of the goals of this book is "to understand...how scripture is used by Christians in the United States in their daily lives apart from worship, especially as that practice is related to other aspects of American life." I think Americans' use of the Bible is related to this other aspect of American life: namely, the Constitution in the public square.

In an emergency, you may hear someone shout, "Is there a doctor in the house?" I can think of no such emergency that compels someone to shout with the same urgency, "Is there a humanities Ph.D. in the house?" But perhaps there is. When it comes to teaching religious understanding and tolerance in our increasingly multireligious communities, we should be the ones opening our medicine bags. Religious tolerance is an urgent matter, for which our colleagues in the STEM fields are not equipped to respond with preventative medicine that brings more civility and understanding to the public square. Stanley Fish observed, "In every sector of American life, religion is transgressing the boundary between private and public and demanding to be heard in precincts that only a short while ago would have politely shown it the door."[66] He recognized "a growing awareness of the difficulty, if not impossibility, of keeping the old boundaries in place and of quarantining the religious impulse in the safe houses of the church, the synagogue, and the mosque."

The humanities and the humanistic social sciences recognize the importance of addressing grand challenges. Religious diversity in a civil society is a grand challenge, because religion in America is deeply imbedded in its culture, and the practices of religion are reinforced each year by the interwoven nature of America's sacred texts. A civil society and its ability to achieve the common good depend on the skills of educators—in history, literature, sociology, anthropology, political science, and religious studies, among others—to take shared responsibility for addressing the challenges we face in an unprecedented time of shifting religious demographics in America. Indeed, the humanities and social sciences are particularly well-tooled to foster deep reflection on diversity and the common good. They teach us how to understand the past, to recognize how texts are interpreted contextually, and to engage in techniques for mutual understanding within and between social and cultural traditions. A special contribution of the humanities is to help complicate dominant traditions, to question assumptions, and to provide the social skills to nurture cultural competence. The humanities can directly address the challenges associated with converging cultural experiences, polarizing political commitments, and religious diversity. The humanistic fields specialize—in ways the STEM fields do not—in the great questions: law and order, interpretation and tradition, tradition and change, individuality and community, conflict and resolution, authority and resistance, war and peace. Technology and science will not solve these challenges of the twenty-first century. And individual disciplines in isolated institutions, institutes, and institutional projects cannot do it either.

Perhaps Stanley Fish's finale in his *Chronicle of Higher Education* article is an opportunity for the academy: "When Jacques Derrida died I was called by a reporter who wanted know what would succeed . . . race, gender, and class as the center of intellectual energy in the academy. I answered like a shot: religion."

I hope we might envision an interdisciplinary forum that deals with this problem—a problem that is reinforced in American history and culture over hundreds of years. It is a problem that the biblical scholar, religion scholar, political scientist, legal scholar, sociologist, and historian all share.

Education systems (elementary through postsecondary) have struggled with results. To achieve the results educators seek, such as the Berkeley Center's Religious Freedom Project at Georgetown University, Harvard University's Religious Literacy Project, or its Pluralism Project, enhancing religious literacy, biblical literacy, and even cultural sensitivity is not enough.[67] Educators must first overcome fundamental challenges in American culture—challenges rooted in our social soil—challenges manifest in how Americans read their two scriptures.

20

Transforming Practice

AMERICAN BIBLE READING IN DIGITAL CULTURE

John B. Weaver

BIBLE MEDIA IN RECENT NATIONAL SURVEYS

Two recent surveys that inquire about practices of reading the Bible in digital form are especially noteworthy. Chapter 1 reports that among those who have read the Bible in the past year, 31 percent read it on the Internet, while 22 percent employed "e-devices." It further delineates the identity of these digital readers by age, income, and education, concluding "that younger people, those with higher salaries, and most dramatically, those with more education among the respondents read the Bible on the Internet or an e-device at higher rates." Chapter 1 offers a tantalizing suggestion of the growing importance of digital forms of Scripture among readers of the Bible, especially given the progression of generational differences that will likely continue to increase the percentage of digital readers of the Bible in society. We notice, for example, that the usage of Internet Bibles averages around 39 percent for individuals under fifty-nine years old. However, the chapter does not make clear how exclusively readers of the Bible use the Internet or e-devices, or whether these two categories overlap or are exclusive of each other. Presumably they overlap, but to the extent that they don't, then the total number of readers of digital texts might be a significantly higher percentage of the total number of those who have read the Bible in the past year.

Another recent survey is the Barna Group's study "The State of the Bible, 2014," conducted for the American Bible Society.[1] This survey has been conducted since 2011 with longitudinal comparison provided in each successive year of the survey. Two questions are especially germane. First, "What format of the Bible did you read in the past year?" While the percentage of print Bible readers has remained consistently high since 2011, around 89 percent, the percentage of Bible readers utilizing digital Bibles on the Internet, smartphones, and e-readers has consistently increased.

Internet: 37% in 2011, 44% in 2014

Smartphone: 18% in 2011, 35% in 2014

E-reader: 12% in 2011, 24% in 2014 (The first iPad was released in April 2010)

Two observations are most relevant: first, the 2014 levels of digital readership of the Bible are significantly higher that those reported in chapter 1 (44 percent v. 31 percent of overall readership on the Internet, and 35 percent smartphone and 24 percent e-reader v. 22 percent e-devices). The higher percentages of digital readers in the "State of the Bible" survey are more in line with the results for the respondents who are fifty-nine years old and younger in chapter 1.

Second, the rise in number of digital readers has not been at the expense of print readers. In other words, the media ecology of Bible reading is increasingly mixed or hybrid, with the Bible increasingly read in digital formats, while use of printed Bibles remains relatively unchanged at high levels. The importance of this hybrid situation cannot be overstated. Rather than digital media eclipsing print, the two are coexisting in increasingly equal measures. It remains to be seen whether or not this trend continues, but it raises a number of questions about why and how this media hybridity is increasing, and why or how it might be sustained or begin to change.

One reason for the continuing high use of print Bibles is indicated by a second question from the "State of the Bible 2014" survey. The question is worded in this way: "All things considered, in what format do you prefer to use the Bible—print, digital, or audio?" This is a question of *preferred* format, not *used* format. The results show a high preference for printed Bibles (84 percent) versus digital (10 percent) in 2014, with consistency in this ratio of preferred media since the question was first asked in 2012 (83 percent print v. 7 percent digital). As one would expect, a preference for digital goes up among younger generations, for example, "millennials," but preference for print remains high (80 percent print v. 15 percent digital). These results suggest that though the use of digital media is rapidly rising, and in some cases doubling, as in the case of e-readers, there is a significant preference of print over digital that remains steady among Bible readers.

How might we explain the persistence of this high use of, and preference for, print Bibles in an increasingly digital culture, wherein the use of digital formats is rapidly expanding? I know of no survey that addresses this question about Bible reading specifically.

TYPES OF BIBLE READING

Some answers to this question are suggested by surveys about digital reading habits that are not focused on Bibles per se but are more broadly concerned with reading of all types. In his 2005 survey and report "Reading Behavior in the Digital Environment," the information scientist Ziming Liu investigates "how people's reading behavior has changed over the past decade by self-reported measures of their overall reading experiences (including work-related and leisure reading)."[2]

By asking about the percentage of time that respondents spent over the past decade on different reading behaviors (e.g., reading all types of documents, reading electronic documents, browsing and scanning, keyword scanning, etc.), Liu identifies reading behaviors that correlate to reading of electronic documents. First, 67.3 percent of the participants reported that they spent more time on reading of all types. Zero percent reported a decline in reading. As Liu notes, this is attributable to both information explosion and digital technology. The latter is indicated by the 83.2 percent of survey respondents who report an increase in time devoted to reading electronically. In this context, the other general changes in behavior are correlated to this increase in digital reading.[3]

The clear distinction in behaviors is among the first five and the last three types of reading, which are correlated to the rise in reading of electronic documents. In this context, Liu introduces the concepts of "extensive" and "intensive" reading. Extensive reading is directed to reading widely, across a large number of books or documents. Intensive reading is reading deeply, with concentrated, more focused attention. The written comments by survey participants quoted by Liu indicate that the extensive "skimming," "jumping," and "multitasking" of online reading and information overload inhibits intensive reading, which is better enabled by reading of print documents. In addition, Liu surveys the differences in readers' propensity to annotate and highlight printed materials compared to screen-based documents. The results are predictably in favor of the ease of marking the printed page versus the digital screen.[4]

What this study highlights is the different behavioral types of reading and the ways digital and print formats differ in their service to these different types of reading. For my purposes, this begins to explain why digital Bibles are increasingly used, due to their utility in extensive types of reading (namely, scanning, spotting, searching) but also are not preferred by a preponderance of readers because of their inability to service well other intensive types of reading (namely, sustained, in-depth, concentrated

TABLE 20.1

PERCENTAGE OF TIME PARTICIPANTS SPENT IN VARIOUS READING ACTIVITIES OVER TIME

Percentage of time spent	Increasing	Decreasing	No change	Don't know
Browsing and scanning	80.5	11.5	8.0	0
Keyword spotting	72.6	2.7	16.0	8.8
One-time reading	56.6	8.0	29.2	6.2
Reading selectively	77.9	2.7	16.8	2.7
Nonlinear reading	82.3	0	15.9	1.8
Sustained attention	15.9	49.6	29.2	5.3
In-depth reading	26.6	45.1	23.0	5.3
Concentrated reading	21.2	44.2	26.5	8.0

reading). Correspondingly, it also helps to explain how use of printed Bibles appears to remain unchanged in recent years. One of Liu's survey questions asks what "document media" the participants prefer to read. Out of all the participants, 89.4 percent preferred print; 2.7 percent preferred electronic, and 8 percent said either one was fine. Recall that this level of preferring printed media is similar to the 84 percent of participants in the "State of the Bible 2014" survey who preferred printed Bibles.

Liu's survey on reading behaviors in the digital environment provides data to support the anecdotal evidence from the many commentators on the relative merits of print and digital Bibles. Both scholarly and popular media are replete with praise for the accessibility and browsability of digital books and other electronic texts (e.g., Christian missionaries often highlight the importance of digital bibles to spreading the Christian message around the world); conversely, commentators bemoan the loss of "sequentiality" and "integrity" in the digital text.[5] There is now something of a cottage industry in publishing books on the profit and pleasure of reading printed books in a digital age of distraction.

BIBLE READING AND THE HYBRID MEDIA ECOLOGY: IMPLICATIONS FOR RELIGIOUS PRACTICE

These past studies of digital media and reading practices raise a number of questions for future research. For example, is there evidence that Bible readers are consistently turning to digital media for "extensive" reading of Scripture (e.g., searching and scanning) while turning to print media for "intensive" reading of Scripture (e.g., sustained and concentrated reading)? If this evidence exists, to what extent are these differences changeable over time and social space? Are they variable according to age, income, gender, and education? Of course, as chapter 1 shows, variable access to digital technology across different socioeconomic groups is an important factor in levels of digital readership. More specifically, will new digital technology and increasing familiarity with digital technology diminish the attraction of the printed book for intensive reading? Another question is what are the theological implications of increased reading of digital Bibles, especially for doctrines of Scripture, such as inspiration, canonicity, and clarity? Further, what are the implications for teaching biblical reading and interpretation in the church and academy?

In the remainder of this essay, I will probe two questions. First, do readers who primarily read digital Bibles maintain a practice of reading printed Bibles, and why? And second, to what extent do these readers value religious practices that are often associated with printed Bibles in recent centuries, namely the practice of memorizing biblical passages and the practice of buying and transferring a Bible as a gift?

To address these questions in a preliminary way, I posted a survey on the public discussion boards of two of the most popular Bible software companies in North America: BibleWorks and Accordance Bible. This twenty-question online survey was completed by 112 participants. My purpose in choosing this participant pool was to attempt to obtain a broad sample of individuals from different religious backgrounds, many of whom were likely to have utilized digital tools for reading and studying the Bible on some occasions.

Of all the respondents, 13 percent were millennials (age 15–34), 36 percent were generation Xers (age 35–49), 47 percent were baby boomers (50–68), and 5 percent were members of the so-called silent generation (69–89); 93.6 percent of respondents were Christian; 2.4 percent were Jewish, 0.8 percent were "none," and 3.2 percent were "other."

Of all the respondents, 86 percent affirmed that they "read portions of sacred Scripture (e.g., the Bible) regularly in a digital format"; 16 percent did not. Unlike the surveys reviewed earlier, which asked about reading of digital texts one time per year, or over the course of ten years, this question addressed the practice of reading Scripture in a regular, recurrent, or patterned way. As might be expected from a population seemingly interested in Bible study software, a large percentage reported frequent use of digital formats of Scripture.

The most common digital formats of Scripture used were "an app or other software on my phone or tablet" (73.32 percent) and "a software program on my desktop or laptop" (53.57). These were followed in frequency of use by "an online website on my desktop or laptop" (25 percent), "a website on my phone or tablet" (14.29 percent), "a dedicated e-reader" (8.93 percent), and "other" (1.79 percent). Finally, 7.89 reported this was not applicable. The predominance of mobile applications and downloadable software is again to be expected from a population interested in Bible software available both for desktops/laptops and also mobile devices.

Of all the respondents, 57.52 percent reported that they "read Scripture in digital text more often than printed text"; 23.01 percent reported that they read Scripture in digital text "less often" than printed text; 14.16 percent reported that they read Scripture in digital text "about the same" as printed text; 5.31 percent reported this was not applicable. Here, nearly three-fifths of respondents indicated a preference for digital format, and nearly three-fourths (72 percent) indicated at least a parity in their use of print and digital texts.

The survey asked this question: "Does the digital format of Scripture help you to read Scripture more often than if you only had a printed version?" Of all the respondents, 51.33 percent responded yes, 20.87 reported no, and 20.87 reported "no difference"; 6.19 percent responded "not applicable." By a slight majority, the practice of reading Scripture in digital form was thought to enhance the frequency of reading, perhaps a more extensive reading, though a significant percentage reported no difference.

Of special importance is the fact that 69 percent of respondents affirmed that they "regularly use printed Scripture for specific times or types of reading, when not primarily using the digital text"; 38.39 percent responded that they did not do this.

Among those who responded yes, there was a text-box option to explain why this was the case. The fifty-six open responses to this question were consistent. Forty-five responded that the print Bible was used habitually for individual or group "devotional" reading. Nine responded that the print Bible was used consistently for public preaching and teaching. The two outliers were one who did not understand the question and one who avoided a digital device on the Sabbath, which is itself a form of devotional practice. Of special note are the respondents who emphasized the regular use of printed Scripture for devotional use. Key words in these responses are "daily," "morning, midday, and evening," "undistracted," "quiet time," "in depth," "serious," "at length," "long form," and "memorable." These are indicators of the "intensive" reading that, in Ziming Liu's survey, were diminished by increased engagement in "screen-based" behaviors of reading. These intensive practices are indicative of the sustained, in-depth, concentrated reading associated with print-based reading. We might reasonably conclude that a significant number of participants in this survey were purposefully reading printed Scripture because they experienced it as having a relative and distinctive capacity for devotional reading that was deep and focused in nature.

Future study of this phenomenon might further explore the extent to which devotional or careful reading is unique to the printed Bible and should be supported as such by religious and academic communities alike. Future study might also explore the extent to which these intensive reading practices are transferable to digital forms of reading. For example, present-day websites and mobile apps are configuring digital technologies to support habitual and contemplative reading of Scripture, whether through mobile apps for practicing *lectio divina*, web applications that block digital communications for a digital Sabbath, or mobile apps that guide the spiritual discipline of *examen*, the prayerful reading and reflection on Scripture. I hypothesize that we will discover an intensifying hybridization of media in Bible-reading practices whereby digital reading technologies support the devotional reading of printed Scripture as a valued Christian practice. This type of transformation of digital media in support of traditional religious values and practices is a current focus of a number of recent cultural studies of digital religion, such as Heidi Campbell's recent *Digital Religion: Understanding Religious Practice in New Media Worlds*.[6]

Another survey question asked, "How important to religious life is the memorization of Scripture in an era with digital Scripture?" Of all the respondents, 11.01 percent responded "not important"; 32.11 percent said "somewhat important", 47.71 percent replied "very important," and 9.17 percent responded "most important."

Another question was "Is the memorization of Scripture more or less difficult in an era with digital Scripture?" Of all the respondents, 31.53 responded "more difficult," 10.81 percent said "less difficult," and 57.66 percent stated "no difference."

Another question was "How important to religious life is the giving and receiving of printed copies of Scripture in an era with digital Scripture?" Of all the respondents, 11.93 percent stated "not important," 29.36 percent indicated "somewhat important," 33.03 percent said "important," and 25.69 percent reported "very important."

CONCLUSIONS

The media of Bible reading in North America are characterized by increasing hybridity of print and digital formats and practices. Digital reading is increasing, but print reading is holding steady and is heavily preferred.

Digital texts are often more accessible and searchable, promoting an extensive practice of reading, while print texts are more sequential and contextual, supporting extensive reading that is more sustained and concentrated.

This difference in Bible media is transforming religious practices so that two types of Bible reading are developing in parallel: a digital reading more conducive to convenience and higher quantities of brief or broader reading and a print reading that is often intentionally maintained as a form of devotional or deeper reading.

These types of reading and their respective media are interrelated and overlap, and the demonstrable interest in devotional reading of the Bible has potential for ongoing transformation of digital technology in support of traditional religious values and practices related to close, reflective reading of Scripture.

21

Readers and Their E-Bibles

THE SHAPE AND AUTHORITY OF THE HYPERTEXT CANON

Bryan Bibb

BIBLICAL SCHOLARS HAVE traditionally been concerned more with the *content* of biblical books than with the conditions of textual production, dissemination, and use. This is changing in recent years as major works have appeared on the subject of Israel's scribal practices, translation in ancient contexts, and literacy and book-collecting in the Greek world. In addition, a major shift in recent scholarship has been the new focus on the Bible's "reception" across space and time. Texts have meaning when they are read, and we must learn more about who reads the Bible, when, how, and for what purposes.

One important aspect of reception history addresses the material realities of translation practices; that is, how translators are constrained by the contexts for which they are translating, and how translations influence the shape of theological and political controversies in churches. In examining this topic, it has become clear that one decisive trend moving forward will be the significance of electronic tools and texts in the ways people encounter the biblical text.

Academic analysis of biblical translation has generally focused on major print-based projects such as the King James Bible and the Revised Standard Version. However, it is likely that electronic forms of biblical text and paratext will constitute the fastest changing and most decisive aspects of Bible "translation" in years to come. This essay will consider how electronic media have already impacted the ways nonexperts experience and interpret the biblical text and how they might do so in the future. The current shift from *codex* to *screen* will be every bit as decisive as the historic shift from *scroll* to *codex* in the Greco-Roman world, or the shift from hand-lettered to printed manuscripts in the late Middle Ages. It is not certain, however, that these changes will lead to more interpretive sophistication or biblical literacy among nonexpert readers. Without significant changes in the public's understanding of translation as a complex interpretative act, electronic platforms may actually reinforce and empower existing assumptions about the biblical text and canon.

FROM SCROLL TO SCREEN

Electronic biblical texts and tools have been available for decades. Accordance was a commercial product for the Mac in 1994, and its founder's first project, called ThePerfectWord, dated back to 1988. In those early days, the computer was still a niche device, and even after every office and desk in the country had a computer, ebooks remained a tiny market. The development that brought ebooks into the mainstream, of course, was the emergence of mobile devices. The earliest enthusiasts of ebooks used the Palm Pilot, but the shift of ebooks into the mainstream was not possible until the introduction of the Amazon Kindle and the Apple iPhone in 2007. The first Kindle was huge, clunky, and cost $400. It wasn't until the Kindle 3 in 2010 that it became a truly mass market device, both well-designed and affordable at $140. Kindles now sell for less than $100, but they have been dwarfed in the ebook market by tablets. In the year Amazon hit the sweet spot with the Kindle 3, it was marginalized by Apple's new iPad and the hoards of Android tablets that followed it. In the years since the introduction of these popular tablet models, ultra-high screen resolutions have made screen reading even more comparable to the paper-and-ink experience. Today, readers are able to access the Bible on their phones, in their pockets, and everywhere else. The majority of Bible readers still prefer printed Bibles, but the market has passed the tipping point by which electronic biblical texts will inevitably overshadow the use of paper Bibles in churches.

There are similarities between this new screen reading and the oldest biblical technology, that is, scrolls and codices. Simple e-texts recreate the "scrolling" experience of seeing paginated chunks of text that flow past the reader, with the mouse or touchscreen replacing wooden rollers. Like the codex, screen reading makes texts easily reproducible and collectible. One important aspect of electronic texts is that the costs of copying, storage, and distribution are minimal. Consider for example the Theological Commons, a digital library of 78,924 books and periodicals on theology and religion, including 29,322 volumes from the Princeton Theological Seminary Library.[1] These volumes all date before 1923 due to overly restrictive copyright laws, but electronic platforms like this have made books accessible to the masses in an unprecedented level. To be sure, technology is unevenly distributed in this world of uneven material distribution. However, many places in the developing world have more or less skipped the computer age and jumped directly into the mobile age. The prevalence of smartphones across the world is a perfect environment for more electronic reading of the Bible.

Chapter 1 provides valuable data about the emerging use of electronic Bibles. A growing number of readers use online and electronic texts, and it seems that e-readers and tablet devices may eventually replace printed Bibles in private and corporate reading of the Bible. The percentage of Bible readers who use the internet is fairly stable between the ages of eighteen and fifty-nine, with 36–41 percent reporting that they have done so, compared to only 19 percent of 60- to 74-year-olds. The use of electronic devices showed a more significant spread, however. Only 10 percent of 60- to 74-year-olds and 19 percent of 45- to 59-year-olds report that they use an electronic device for reading the Bible. The percentage increase among the younger population is striking: 33 percent of 30- to 44-year-olds and 38 percent of 18- to 29-year-olds use these devices, a rate double that of their parents' generation. It seems unlikely that these 18- to 44-year-olds will stop using their phones and tablets when they hit fifty. Rather, it is probable that we will see increases among every age group until electronic devices, supplemented by computer browsers, are the primary means of Bible reading in America.

What effect will this trend have on the *other* areas covered by the survey? There is need for more research (quantitative, qualitative, and hermeneutical) into the transformative influence that digital interfaces may have on the way people understand, interpret, and use the Bible privately and in community. Two developments in biblical reading that may result in particular from the use of electronic Bibles are (1) unparalleled access to competing translations, and (2) shifting functional definitions of the biblical "canon." The definition and nature of "the Bible" will shift as people increasingly encounter the text outside the physical boundaries of the printed volume. Electronic platforms have the potential to destabilize traditional notions of what the Bible is and how it functions.

THE BIBLE IN PARALLEL

First, there is the potential for readers to develop more awareness of alternative translations and to make wider use of "parallel" versions. Chapter 1 confirms that the KJV is still the most commonly read translation by far, although the NIV is dominant among evangelicals. What impact will the free availability of online Bibles have on readers' knowledge of and opinions about different translations? Since the appearance of the controversial RSV in 1952 and the large number of evangelical projects started in reaction, churches in America have tended to evidence a certain kind of translation tribalism. In particular denominations, or even individual congregations, it is common to find one translation accepted as *the* Bible, perhaps with a small range of options for the most progressive members. In this restrictive environment, "parallel Bibles" have long been a gentle way to explore translations beyond a traditional version such as the KJV, and, in theory, a tool for examining translations more critically. Although the ability to read and analyze different translations has never been greater, will this be enough to overcome translation factionalism in churches?

Eager lay readers have long had "parallel" Bibles available to them, the most common being parallel KJV and NIV, or Zondervan's four-part KJV, NASB, NIV, and NLT Bible, called "Today's Parallel Bible." The use of these resources indicates that readers understand something of the vagaries of translation, even while they hold to traditional forms of textual authority. In most cases the King James Bible is the base text. However, in supplementing what they believe to be their authoritative version with "modern language" Bibles, readers display a recognition that language changes over time and that new Bible translations might be more "readable" or "natural" to modern readers. However, the parallel volume also provides the "real" Bible so that one can be sure to have the more "accurate" reading as well. In this sense, one version functions as the "ur-text" against which readers may compare newer, possibly suspect, translations. Even so, a parallel Bible may represent the first step in a reader's move from a traditional to a modern Bible version.

Will the multitext capabilities of electronic and online texts function in the same way as traditional parallel Bibles, or perhaps even enhance the legitimacy of translation plurality? The "parallel panes" feature at sites such as Youversion.com and BibleGateway.com has the potential to play a more radical role in the destabilizing of translation factionalism. These online platforms give readers the ability to place any translation alongside any other and make dozens of different translations available with no one "base" version. This capability is well-suited for readers who have *already* moved beyond allegiance to a particular version and works best for those with an active curiosity about how different translators handle particular verses. These online tools could possibly lead to more openness. However, preliminary data from these sites suggests that very few readers even open parallel panes, much less actively explore different versions, and that they always use the same version when they return to a site. At the moment, it appears that online platforms have largely untapped potential in opening up space for competing translations. Although they might function this way for a subset of adventurous readers, the majority of users replicate their print Bible habits even when online.

In addition to parallel panes, the availability of Greek and Hebrew tools makes possible a level of textual analysis that was previously inaccessible to nonexpert readers. Users of Accordance and other packages are able to search for particular Hebrew and Greek words and thereby compare translations in terms of how they render the same key terms and phrases. For example, readers can not only look up how translations describe the "virgin"/"young woman" in Isaiah 7:14 but also see how those translations render the same underlying term in other verses. This simple searching of the Hebrew and Greek text is available even to readers without knowledge of the ancient languages. Will this analytical searching lead to greater interpretive sophistication or mostly to bad exegesis based on the root fallacy, now that the errors of the first-year seminarian are available to everyone?

Early anecdotal evidence suggests that we are a long way from this sophisticated search being mainstream or useful. Recently, I taught an upper-level religion course for undergraduate students titled "The Digital Bible," which was at its heart an introduction to exegesis using the electronic Bible platform Accordance. These were bright students who were skilled in using computers and mobile devices, but they struggled to make effective use of complex searches even in Accordance, which has a very easy interface. Even when students were able to perform "key number" searches in a Strong's Concordance tagged text, many never quite grasped why they might want to do that, or when it would be most helpful in their textual analysis. These were bright students with direct classroom instruction in using these techniques. It is unclear how many among the laity will have the curiosity, facility, and access to electronic tools required to make this sort of electronic study a common practice in the church.

It is also true that the best searching tools are available only in expensive software packages that only scholars and scholarly-minded pastors will buy. Free Bible websites and apps excel in presenting the English text to readers, while most sophisticated applications are cost-prohibitive and marketed mostly to pastors and scholars. The search windows of online texts are useful, but it is generally difficult to explore underlying Greek and Hebrew terminology. For example, a search for "virgin" in the NIV on biblegateway.com yields fifty-five verses in a list, with links to explore the immediate context of each verse, as well as other translations. This is valuable information, though it requires a lot of clicking. Most important, there is no indication that the English word "virgin" may reflect more than one Hebrew term or that the Hebrew term might be translated differently in other passages. A few sites provide access to key term and original language searches, but they are of uneven quality. Promising options include studylight.org, biblestudytools.com, and blueletterbible.org. Although the Blue Letter Bible has a Strong's Concordance feature, the site incorporates fundamentalist material without marking its perspective or source. For example, in Job 40:15, the site provides a lexical entry for the Strong's term number H930, "behemoth," but then adds tendentious information that is not found in Strong's, indicating that *behemoth* is "perhaps an extinct dinosaur . . . a Diplodocus or Brachiosaurus, exact meaning unknown," and that the translation "elephant" or "hippopotamus" is "patently absurd."[2] This extra information comes from young-earth creationist Larry Pierce but is shown in the information pane in a way that misrepresents this creationist interpretation as a simple lexical fact. The *behemoth* may or may not be a hippopotamus, though scholars argue that this is the origin of the mythological image in Job. Regardless, the *behemoth* certainly is not a brachiosaurus.

TRANSFORMING THE CANON

If the innovative potential of parallel versions and complex searches in electronic Bible platforms remains unfulfilled, another trend may work in another direction. Electronic Bible platforms have the effect of reshaping the canon itself because they enable readers to take current reading strategies to extreme new levels. For present purposes, this essay will define "canon" as "the authoritative text established and used by a community." "Canon" here does not refer primarily to the formal list of particular biblical books but to the *effective* canon, the form and content of the scriptures as they are experienced in a particular community or by an individual.

The fact that Bible applications and websites are *interactive* leads to a revolution in the text's interface, the environment in which the text is experienced. In addition to searching and parallel translation features, Bible apps provide a platform through which readers experience the text of the Bible in radically new ways. This section will describe two transformations of the canon that go in opposite directions. One degrades the notion of the canon by providing more text, and one degrades the notion of the canon by providing less.

First, consider the interface of the Accordance Bible software. The system is built around the concept of "amplifying" a particular word or text with another resource, making it possible to have any number of resources scrolling in sync with the biblical text.[3] For instance, a reader can have a single verse or passage shown in one box, along with a lexicon, a commentary, another translation, a dictionary entry, and a map all in windows around the text. The question is not only what range of resources might be placed alongside the Bible, but why readers would choose particular texts and commentaries. These paratext resources provide useful information for understanding the words of the text. More important, many readers will use this feature to situate authoritative interpretations *alongside* the biblical text. Readers in the Reformed tradition, for instance, can have constant access to the interpretative commentaries of John Calvin or John Piper.[4] These readers are not simply studying the Bible for themselves; they are also participating in an interpretive community for whom particular texts have precise, theologically significant meanings. Traditional "study Bibles" have long provided this sort of catechetical instruction, but the possibilities in the electronic realm are exponentially greater.

The first study Bible in Protestant history was the 1560 Geneva Bible. Preceding the KJV by a generation, the Geneva Bible was the first edition to include commentary and apparatus alongside the text. It provided readers with textual cross-references, book introductions, maps, and other visual appendices. The Calvinist theological perspective of the Geneva Bible had a tremendous influence on English Protestantism. Other important study Bibles in the last century were the dispensationalist Scofield Reference Bible of 1909 and the Ryrie Study Bible, published in 1978. The commentaries in these Bibles provide authoritative answers about what the Bible means, point readers toward the most important passages, and provide a comprehensive framework for dealing with difficult questions. Communities that develop around these study Bibles are fiercely loyal to them and their interpretations. In practical terms, a study Bible defines for the committed reader what the Bible is and thereby reshapes the canon in its own image.

There are at least two dozen study Bible modules available in Accordance, but Accordance takes this expansion of the canon even further by providing a greater range of resources and by enabling the reader to consult more interpretations and information at one time. A reader looking for the classic study Bible experience can purchase that study Bible text and consult it along with his or her favorite translation. Where Accordance is most powerful, however, is when readers personalize and modify their study environment depending on the task at hand and thereby create an endless variety of custom study Bibles. So, while the canon gets restructured in tightly knit communities devoted to particular translations and study Bibles, Accordance is an individualistic deconstruction of that paradigm: your Bible just the way you want it. Do you want a different canon? It's at your fingertips.

Second, these electronic interfaces enable readers to jump quickly to particular texts and even to isolate them from their literary contexts. In the ancient world, as printing technology shifted from scroll to codex, a much greater number of people were able to read the Bible in printed form rather than experiencing it only as an orally mediated text. The chief benefits of the codex seem to have been in portability, durability, and collectability. The development of the New Testament was integrally tied with the library-building practices of the first four centuries, which were made possible by the codex. Most significant for the modern context, the codex made a new reading technique possible: the *flip*. Readers of a bound codex can turn quickly to a particular section, read what they find there, and then quickly turn to a different section. Individual passages can be bookmarked, highlighted, or annotated. This new technique, the flip, is the essential ingredient in many bad student papers I have read, papers that should perhaps be subtitled "a romp through the scriptures." This flipping technique is empowered as well by the addition of biblical verse numbers in the late medieval period. The existence of verse numbers gives modern readers the illusion that the Bible is a list of verses. In fact, there is no such thing as a "verse" of the Bible, but only biblical passages making up interconnected sentences and paragraphs.

In other words, the technique I have called the "flip" enables another reading technique called "ignoring the context," which might be the single most dominant reading strategy among students and church laity. It is interesting to compare modern readers who quote verses out of context with ancient readers who used midrash and *pesher* to apply particular verses to their own times or with Reformation preachers who peppered their arguments with extensive verse citations. Whether citing individual verses is a new phenomenon or based on a larger historical precedent, the ascendancy of "the verse" over "the text" in the modern world is complete, made possible by the physical form of the codex.

The reading strategy of flipping to isolated verses grows more powerful as the codex gives way to the screen. Readers have long memorized or highlighted particular verses that they find useful, but electronic Bibles allow readers actually to excise unwanted texts from the reading window, leaving only the most "relatable" passages. In a process of targeted reduction, hyperlinked and searchable Bibles break all formal boundaries, creating a canon of aphorisms, self-help, and rhetorical ammunition. Thus, the searching of electronic texts has perfected the flip, enabling expert levels of ignoring the context.

The purest expression of this destruction of the canon by reducing it to a list of verses is the remarkable website topverses.com. Here is the description that was originally at the top of the Top Verses homepage, though it is no longer present:

Why Top Verses Bible?

You will like TopVerses because we sorted every Bible verse by popularity. Now search the Bible and find verses in a useful order. We counted how many times each Bible verse (all 31,105 of them) is referenced anywhere on the internet and then ranked them all! Join us on social media to share your faith one verse at a time.

There must have been negative reaction to this language, because the site now invites readers merely to "rediscover your favorite scriptures or try our Bible search with verses sorted by popularity." Gone is the reference to the Bible in a "useful order," though the site's tagline remains "The Bible. Sorted." This approach to reading the Bible in "sorted" fashion raises profound questions about the nature of the canon. Although readers of the print Bible are able to flip through the text, they still encounter biblical passages in "canonical order," depending on which form of the canon they are using. The "sorted order" of Top Verses is based on the notion of "popularity," using Google metrics to list verses in the order of their common quotation and usage in online conversation. This model destabilizes the Christian canon and radically restructures the visibility and importance of different kinds of biblical texts.

For instance, what status does the Hebrew Bible/Old Testament have in the Top Verses sorted canon? In their list of the top twenty verses, there are two from the Hebrew Bible: Genesis 1:1 and Genesis 1:26. The top fifty include those two passages plus Genesis 1:27, Isaiah 9:6, and two verses regularly quoted out of context in Christian theologies of self-help and prosperity gospel: Proverbs 3:5 and Jeremiah 29:11. That Jeremiah passage is part of a "salvation oracle" in which God promises to restore the people of Israel from their Babylonian captivity. In this atomized, individualized interpretation, however, God's reassurance that "I know the plans I have for you" sounds like promises of blessing for individuals. Reading that verse by itself, as one does at TopVerses.com, provides no window into the text's literary and historical context and reinforces the individual interpretation powerfully.

Less "popular" books of the Bible are bypassed almost completely. No passage from the top one hundred comes from the book of Leviticus, although number 101 is Leviticus 18:22, a key passage in the Christian rejection of homosexual relationships. Leviticus 20:13, also about homosexuality, is number 333, but "love your neighbor as yourself" from Leviticus 19:18 does not show up until number 460. From Top Verses, one would never encounter themes of Israelite ritual and holiness, since the list marginalizes any text that doesn't "predict" Jesus or provide argumentative evidence to support conservative Christian social agendas.

One suspects that the Top Verses algorithm presents a fairly clear picture of what average readers think the Bible is and is about. In this view, the Bible is a collection of verses to give people hope and encouragement, to tell people about the coming of Jesus the Messiah, and to make sure we know that Jesus is the only way to salvation.[5] The central purpose of the Bible in this usage is evangelism and self-help, with passages related to history, social justice, or Judaism relegated to the back pages. Since few readers find their way to those "obscure" passages, they have effectively ceased to function within the canon. The "popularity" data in chapter 1 resonates with this list in showing how readers value passages that have a comforting or encouraging message. Electronic Bibles now allow readers to remove these verses from their context completely.

CONCLUSIONS

Scholars may shudder at the Gospel According to Google and push back as printed books make way for mobile devices and Christian social media. However, these trends are powerful indicators of where the Bible and biblical interpretation are headed in the not so distant future. Critical biblical scholars and progressive Christian leaders have long worked to dispel myths about the origins and nature of the biblical text and about the complicated, human processes of textual production, editing, translation, and publishing. With the availability of electronic resources, there is more potential than ever that lay readers can learn something about the Bible's textual complexity and so open themselves at least somewhat to different perspectives. The Bible is being used for self-help and for sociopolitical arguments, and so it is more important than ever to help people understand what the Bible is and how it might best be used, or not used.

A powerful strategy for teaching readers about basic biblical hermeneutics is to help them perceive textual fluidity, and the most effective tool for this task is the use of parallel and multiple translations. Lay readers have long assumed that one Bible version is the "real" Bible and that other translations are more or less inadequate. What is needed now is the recognition that all translations are interpretations and all Bible versions reflect decision-making at several stages in the process. These decisions determine what manuscripts are used, what translation philosophy is followed, and what theological assumptions guide the translators in their handling of contested passages, and so on. Even without knowledge of the ancient languages, students and lay readers can glimpse the complexity of this process by using parallel translations, carefully selected paratext resources, and sophisticated searches. However, this potential will remain untapped as long as teachers and leaders assume that electronic Bibles are a niche market or that they function in the same way as print Bibles. By researching carefully the hermeneutical and practical impact of electronic Bible reading, scholars can open pathways for higher levels of biblical literacy, more careful engagement with the biblical text, and in general a more open-minded approach to differences of interpretation.

In addition to the research and teaching of scholars, one strategy that would help would be to adapt the interface of online Bibles and mobile apps in order to present the Bible in a more dynamic and effective format. First, since readers rarely open a second column for comparing texts at sites such as BibleGateway.com, these sites should show two or more different translations *by default*. These could be chosen to maximize the amount of textual fluidity in view, perhaps with a traditional version such as the NIV alongside something more innovative such as The Voice, or with something that challenges Christian assumptions about the meaning of words, such as the Tanakh.

Second, these sites should show better judgment about what paratext materials are made easily available and how they are presented. The great majority of the commentaries and dictionaries available in free sites and apps are old, out-of-print volumes of limited usefulness. Lay readers do not automatically understand the difference between a nineteenth-century textual commentary and one produced by modern critical scholars. These old and outdated resources appear fresh and authoritative when delivered alongside the electronic biblical text, which works against the need for more critical comprehension. Biblical scholars should produce more free and open-licensed introductory materials that could be used in these platforms and perhaps displace common but problematic titles such as the *Treasury of Scripture Knowledge* (originally published in

1830). By increasing their reliance on current scholarly resources and by carefully labeling and marking the source of all information found on the site, these Bible platforms can help readers become more informed and critical consumers of biblical "helps."

Finally, educational programs in churches, colleges, and seminaries should embrace the potential of these electronic platforms. My "Digital Bible" course that used Accordance rather than a traditional print text or Bible translation is a good illustration of the challenges and possibilities of this approach. Students initially struggled to understand the concepts and importance of what we were doing in class, but by the end they were uniformly enthusiastic about using an electronic Bible for their personal and academic studies. Several of them have reported that they continued to use Accordance regularly after the semester was over. Without instruction, readers will map their traditional reading practices onto the electronic format, which is a waste of potential. Or they may also be drawn to problematic sites that present the Bible in highly flawed or skewed ways, such as TopVerses.com. These electronic tools might lead to an increased biblical literacy in churches, but readers must first develop basic facility with the tools before they can benefit from them.

This essay has argued that the emergence of electronic Bibles has the potential to broaden the availability of biblical translations and to help readers develop more sophisticated reading practices. However, this shift in the form of the Bible may end up reinforcing traditional reading practices while at the same time changing the nature of the Bible-as-read and deconstructing the canon. We need more research to understand the nature of these trends, as well as the hermeneutical and social implications for lay readers of the Bible. When the biblical canon no longer resides within the boundaries of a printed book, what will it become? That, it seems, is still an open question.

22

How American Women and Men Read the Bible

Amanda Friesen

SOCIOLOGISTS HAVE LONG debated the relationship between gender and religion; "the fact that women display higher patterns of religiosity than men is one of the most consistent findings in the sociology of religion".[1] Much of the debate has centered around the origins of these differences, whether it be physiological, psychological or sociological, as well as the examination of various forms of religiosity, such as church attendance, religious salience, closeness to God, frequency of prayer, strength of affiliation, and sometimes biblical orthodoxy.[2] Very little attention has been given to the nature of possible gender differences surrounding reading scriptures. Do women read the Bible more than men? Are there motivational differences between the sexes regarding personal reading?

Bible reading is a key practice in many Christian denominations and could be a behavior that helps explain a woman's approach to religion. Though perspectives on the Bible and individual Bible reading are used as variables to predict various outcomes (e.g., attitudes on abortion or gay marriage), very little is known about why this is the case. Investigating the motivations behind a common religious activity like Bible reading has the potential to empirically unlock some of these connections. Using the Bible in American Life module (see appendix of chapter 1) of the General Social Survey, I test a series of hypotheses related to the above questions to gain a better understanding of whether and how men and women read the Bible differently, which may contribute to the many differences in religiosity between the genders that may have consequences outside church walls.

GENDER AND THE BIBLE

When examining religious practice in the United States, there is little debate that women tend to exhibit higher levels of religious belief and behavior when compared to men.[3] As mentioned earlier, there are few studies that examine the difference in scripture reading, but a brief description of the debate about gender differences in other religious activities may help illuminate expectations for findings in the chapter 1 dataset. Sociologists and psychologists mainly debate whether gender differences have biological or social explanations, and the competing theories involve risk aversion, power control, and affective versus active and extrinsic versus intrinsic approaches to religion.

Some scholars posit that women are naturally risk averse (for biological and evolutionary adaptive reasons), on average, compared to men in most parts of life.[4] Thus, religion is the ultimate insurance against the risk of eternal damnation or other consequences of nonbelief. Other scholars suggest a power control theory that patriarchal households socialize women into this risk aversion as well as religious belief and behavior.[5] In that vein, John P. Hoffman and John P. Bartkowski offer one of the few studies that incorporate scripture variables into the origins of sex differences in religiosity. They find that women are significantly more likely than men to adhere to literal views on the Bible when they belong to "patriarchal" denominations compared to mainline congregations.[6] Hoffman and Bartkowski explain that because women are denied leadership and other organizational positions in conservative Protestant churches, they compensate by accepting a stricter conception of biblical authority that demonstrates dedication and personal piety to a "key schema of their faith." While the current study is more concerned with Bible reading and motivation than literalism, Hoffman and Bartkowski's theory is a helpful step in establishing expectations of gender differences on my religious variables.[7] Conservative denominations are not the only place women have not achieved parity with men in formal roles, and thus Bible reading may be a mechanism that cultivates female religiosity by keeping women engaged and tied to the faith, even if they feel excluded in areas of congregational organization.

To wit, religiosity for women may be driven more by internal motivations such that reading the Bible and seeking to know more about God is an end in itself; whereas men may approach religion for external purposes such as leadership skill–building and networking. Though the current study does not employ this battery, there is a long line of research related to the study of intrinsic and extrinsic religious motivation.[8] These scholars suggest that "the extrinsically motivated person uses his religion, whereas the intrinsically motivated person lives his religion,"[9] indicating that individuals may be approaching religious belief and behavior using different psychological processes. Those who view religion in terms of what it can do for them are extrinsically motivated and answer affirmatively to statements like "What religion offers me most is comfort in times of trouble and sorrow," while intrinsically motivated individuals are more likely to say, "My whole approach to life is based upon my religion."[10] Men and women can be either intrinsically or extrinsically motivated, but there is some evidence that men take a more instrumental approach to their religious activity. Indeed, when examining the gender differences in religiosity across cultures, men tend to be more involved in active, public displays of religiosity in religions like Judaism and Islam that are generally sex-segregated, whereas women, across many cultures and religions, are more "affectively" religious than men when it comes to measures of personal piety.[11]

Currently, there is little scholarship on gender and its relation to one of the most common devotional behaviors of our nation's most influential and pervasive religion. The current study's findings have the potential to further the debate about the nature of gendered differences in religiosity, including whether Bible reading might be the mechanism that contributes to women exhibiting higher levels of religious salience, private devotion, and greater sense of denominational belonging, providing further evidence that a woman's religious experience may be more internally motivated and may explain why women may be more involved in religious activity then men, while men are more likely to ascribe to leadership positions both inside the congregation and in the community.

EMPIRICS AND DISCUSSION

Leveraging the unique questions contained in the Bible in American Life module of the General Social Survey (n = 1,551),[12] I am able to test a series of hypotheses related to how men and women read and experience the Bible. To begin, participants were asked if they read scripture outside a worship service in the past year (yes: 50.4 percent; men saying yes: 43.1 percent; women saying yes: 56.4 percent). A bivariate logistic regression reveals that the odds of reading scripture in the past year are greater for women than men (odds ratio = 1.65, p = 0.00). This relationship holds even when controlling for age, income, education, marital status, and religious tradition (which will be detailed more below). Women also read the Bible more days than men, on average, in the past thirty days (11.267 v. 8.812), and this difference is significant in an analysis of variance (F = 7.57, p = 0.006) and holds when controlling for age, income, education, martial status, and religious tradition. It is possible that women may read more books generally than men;[13] but I am unable to test this assumption, as there are no measures of general book reading in the 2010 General Social Survey.

Why might women read the Bible more than men? As noted, scholars have posited several theories to explain why women tend to be more religious than men, but little work has been completed on how this phenomenon specifically might relate to a behavior like scripture readings. For participants who indicated they had read scripture in the past year, the Bible in American Life module asked a series of unique questions to uncover the motivations behind this textual study. Because the overwhelming majority of the sample indicated the Bible was the predominant scripture they had read (95 percent), the following analyses will focus on this text, and excluding those who read another book drops the sample to 1,508.

Participants were given the following scenario/question battery: "The Bible is used in many ways. In the past year, to what extent have you used the Bible in the following ways? Please use a scale of 1–5 with (1) being 'not at all,' (2) being 'to a small extent,' (3) being 'to a moderate extent,' (4) being 'to a considerable extent,' and (5) being 'to a great extent.'" The follow-up statements are listed in the appendix. Specifically, in keeping with gender differences in the extant literature on affective religiosity, I expected women to be more likely to indicate they read the Bible for private reasons like personal devotion and help with relationships,[14] as well as concerns for health or healing.[15] Figure 22.1 displays the one-way analyses of variance testing the mean difference between men and women on each of the Bible-reading motivation items. The first observation to note is that men and women read the Bible for personal devotional reasons over any other, followed by learning about religion and making decisions about personal relationships. That is, the primary motivators to study scripture outside worship services were due to personal reasons and a desire to learn.

There are some important, significant differences between the genders, though. As expected, women were higher on personal devotion ($p < 0.000$), making decisions about relationships ($p = 0.07$), and learning about attaining health or healing ($p < 0.05$). Women were also more likely to read the Bible to learn about attaining wealth and prosperity, though this effect did not reach traditional levels of statistical significance ($p = 0.10$). There was no relationship between gender and reading the Bible to learn about what the future holds ($p = 0.67$) or to learn about religion ($p = 0.16$), though women did score higher than men in the latter.

Several of the questions conflate two concepts that may have gender differences separately but when put in the same question will muddle gender effects. For example, men are probably more likely to "prepare" to teach a study group, but women are more likely than men to "participate" in a study group;[16] so I would not expect to see a gender difference in that measure—indeed, there is no gender effect ($p = 0.79$). Similarly, women may be more likely to seek answers regarding poverty, as they tend to be more interested than men in social welfare issues;[17] but this would not necessarily be the case in considerations of war. Similarly, the conflation of learning about

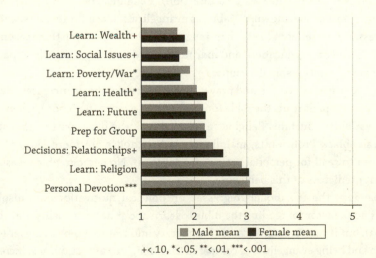

FIGURE 22.1 Mean difference of Bible reading motivation, by gender

"issues like abortion and homosexuality" could wash away any gender effect—though there doesn't seem to be a gender difference in actual public opinion on these matters.[18] Contrary to my predictions, men are more likely than women to read the Bible to learn about poverty and war (p < 0.05) and abortion and homosexuality (p = 0.08). It is important to keep in mind that all participants reported reading the Bible less for these political reasons than for private devotional purposes, but there is a gender difference nonetheless. Women are more likely than men to read the Bible to further their spirituality or to seek counsel on items that affect them personally. Men read for these reasons as well but edge out women when reading for topics with political undertones.

Several factors could influence Bible reading and manifest in bivariate results because gender is perhaps serving as a proxy for something like socioeconomic status.[19] Thus, I included a series of demographic variables to further test my hypotheses regarding reading the Bible for relationship help, private devotionalism, and learning about homosexuality and abortion, as well as poverty and war. I narrowed my analyses to these four dependent variables because they best represent the theoretical justifications of gender differences in religiosity due to public/private sphere[20] and active versus affective approaches.[21] Tables 22.1 and 22.2 display the results. Gendered differences still appear when accounting for age, income, education, marital status (with single, never married as the missing category), and religious tradition (using the RELTRAD [religious tradition] coding used by Brian Steensland and colleagues, with religious "nones" being the missing category).[22] Nones and non-Christians are included because some of these individuals read the Bible in the past year, and it is interesting to note for which reading motivations specific Christian traditions are similar or dissimilar to the unaffiliated.

Women and men were equally likely to indicate the extent they read the Bible to assist in making personal relationship decisions (p = 0.146), though women did score higher on this measure (the expected direction). Religious tradition seems to be the driving force on this dependent variable, as evangelicals, black Protestants, and mainline Protestants were more likely than religious nones to read for this reason. Being Catholic, age, income, education, and marital status do not significantly impact reading for personal relationship decisions.

Turning to private devotion and prayer, however, being female increases the extent to which a participant reads the Bible for this reason by 0.377 (p= 0.000), when holding all other variables constant. Religious affiliation tells the other part of this story, as evangelicals, black Protestants, mainliners, and Catholics are more likely than religious nones to read for personal prayer and devotion. No demographic measures are significant predictors of this behavior.

In table 22.3, the full models regressed on political motivations are displayed.[23] Gender is not a factor for reading the Bible to learn about homosexuality and abortion (p = 0.203), but it matters significantly for poverty and war (p = 0.025). Lower levels of education and being evangelical, as compared to no religious affiliation, also increase the extent to which individuals read about poverty and war. Increased age and lower levels

TABLE 22.1

ORDINARY LEAST SQUARES REGRESSION OF REASONS AMERICANS READ
THE BIBLE

	Decisions about personal relationships		Personal prayer and devotion	
	Coeff. (S.E.)	p	Coeff. (S.E.)	p
Female	0.153	0.146	0.377	0.000
	(0.105)		(0.095)	
Age	-0.004	0.230	0.001	0.811
	(0.004)		(0.003)	
Education	-0.062	0.165	-0.021	0.613
	(0.045)		(0.041)	
Income	-0.018	0.476	-0.003	0.912
	(0.026)		(0.041)	
Married	-0.124	0.380	-0.171	0.183
	(0.141)		(0.128)	
Divorced/wid- owed/separated	0.262	0.116	0.106	0.485
	(0.167)		(0.151)	
Evangelical	1.119	0.000	1.305	0.000
	(0.197)		(0.178)	
Black Protestant	1.111	0.000	1.094	0.000
	(0.278)		(0.252)	
Mainline Protestant	0.583	0.007	0.882	0.000
	(0.216)		(0.195)	
Catholic	0.218	0.323	0.452	0.024
	(0.221)		(0.200)	
Non-Christian	0.472	0.501	0.957	0.134
	(0.702)		(0.637)	
Constant	2.146	0.000	2.219	0.000
	(0.355)		(0.322)	
N	669		670	
R^2	0.122		0.146	

of education are the only significant predictors of reading to learn about homosexuality
and abortion. The only significant relationships between religious tradition and these
sociopolitical motivations is being evangelical on reading about poverty and war,
which is somewhat surprising because of all of the religious traditions, followers of
evangelicalism tend to be less concerned with social welfare and foreign policy issues.[24]

TABLE 22.2

ORDINARY LEAST SQUARES REGRESSION OF REASONS AMERICANS
READ THE BIBLE

	Learn about abortion and homosexuality		Learn about poverty and war	
	Coeff. (S.E.)	p	Coeff. (S.E.)	p
Female	-0.117 (0.092)	0.203	-0.207 (0.092)	0.025
Age	0.006 (0.003)	0.056	-0.001 (0.003)	0.733
Education	-0.111 (0.039)	0.005	-0.085 (0.039)	0.030
Income	-0.023 (0.023)	0.311	-0.028 (0.023)	0.212
Married	0.053 (0.124)	0.671	-0.048 (0.124)	0.700
Divorced/wid-owed/separated	0.041 (0.146)	0.778	0.188 (0.146)	0.199
Evangelical	0.086 (0.172)	0.615	0.466 (0.172)	0.007
Black Protestant	-0.097 (0.243)	0.691	0.373 (0.244)	0.126
Mainline Protestant	-0.143 (0.188)	0.447	0.264 (0.189)	0.162
Catholic	-0.533 (0.193)	0.006	-0.029 (0.193)	0.881
Non-Christian	-0.047 (0.616)	0.939	0.376 (0.616)	0.542
Constant	2.043 (0.315)	0.000	2.132 (0.311)	0.000
N	669		670	
R^2	0.062		0.057	

It is important to note the low explanatory power of these models ($R^2 = 0.057$–0.146), indicating that there are other variables that better explain the variance in these measures. For example, it is likely that politically interested individuals and/or those who are strong ideologues with intense policy preferences read the Bible to learn about these issues, which is beyond the scope of the current analysis.

Moving beyond reading motivation, there are a few other gender findings of note in this unique dataset on Bible reading. The survey asked a series of questions related to whether individuals sought help in "interpreting and understanding what you read" in scripture in the past thirty days. Women and men were equally likely to have sought help in interpretation, and there are no differences in whether they solicited help from clergy, study group leaders, or members, published commentary, an Internet site, or a television or radio program.[25] There was also no difference in the likelihood between genders of individuals choosing to memorize scripture.

Though men and women were just as likely to indicate they had a favorite book of the Bible, there were some interesting contrasts in the preferred book. Of the people who indicated a favorite book (n = 469), women overwhelmingly mentioned Psalms (female n = 103; male n = 22), whereas the modal book for men was Revelation (male n = 18; female n = 12). This, too, fits with the theory that women read the Bible more for personal, comforting, possibly psychological reasons than do men.

CONCLUSION

Results from the Bible in American Life module confirm extant findings about the differences in male and female religiosity in the United States. Women edge out men on Bible reading, demonstrating that personal piety (affective) is a driving force behind their religious participation and their motives are more likely personal devotion rather than political reasons. Future research should explore the institutional structures that encourage individual Bible reading within congregations and whether personality or socialized differences between men and women interact with these structures to result in differential Bible behaviors. Women may see dedicated Bible reading as a controllable outlet for their faith expression:[26] as increasing their religious participation and depth of faith without translating into leadership or civic skill development within congregational structures or the community.[27] Men may not see the benefit in personal piety behaviors like scripture reading because their time and efforts are recruited for and dedicated to organizational participation.

Appendix

"The Bible is used in many ways. In the past year, to what extent have you used the Bible in the following ways? Please use a scale of 1–5 with (1) being 'not at all,' (2) being 'to a small extent,' (3) being 'to a moderate extent,' (4) being 'to a considerable extent,' and (5) being 'to a great extent.'"

To learn about your religion
As a matter of personal prayer and devotion
To prepare to teach or participate in a study group
To make decisions about your relationship with your spouse, parents, children or friends
To learn about attaining wealth or prosperity
To learn about attaining health or healing
To learn about what the future holds
To learn about issues like abortion or homosexuality
To learn about issues like poverty or war

23

Feels Right Exegesis

QUALITATIVE RESEARCH ON HOW MILLENNIALS READ THE BIBLE

J. Derrick Lemons

FOR OVER A decade, scholars have called for more research about the spiritual lives of American millennials, the age cohort born between the 1980s and early 2000s.[1] While much progress has been made, DeHaan, Yonker, and Affholter conclude that religion and spirituality in emerging adults remains understudied.[2] Scholars are especially interested in the religious-to-spiritual shift of American millennials, which is characterized by highly individualistic millennials leaving traditional forms of religious practice while maintaining a deeply spiritual identity.[3] This study seeks to understand the use of the Bible by millennial college students in the southeastern region of the United States. In particular, this essay uses Ralph Turner's theory of self-conception to understand how millennials exegete the Bible and how they apply their exegetical model to the social issue of same-sex marriage.

Born between 1980 and 2000, millennials are currently fourteen to thirty-four years old; 88 million Americans are millennials.[4] During their college years, millennials concern themselves with discovering what they believe about religion and politics.[5] Arnett and Jensen conclude that "whatever they choose for themselves" is the most accurate description of young-adult millennial religion.[6] In regard to their social orientation, today's millennials seem to be more liberal than their older counterparts on all issues, except for abortion.[7] Compared to older adults, millennials are more accepting of evolution, more likely to think Bible reading should be banned in public schools, and more likely to say homosexuality should be accepted by society.[8] According to the National Survey of Youth and Religion, overall 50 percent of millennial college students never read the Bible, and only 6 percent of millennial college students read the Bible on a daily basis. Among conservative Protestants, 31 percent never read the Bible, and 10 percent read the Bible on a daily basis.[9] Millennials are the least likely age cohort to view the entire Bible as the "literal word of God," with only 28 percent taking it literally word for word.[10]

Ralph Turner's theoretical framework of self-conception is a useful model for interpreting data about the religious views of millennials. Turner describes how individuals vacillate between an institutional pole and an impulse pole in a quest to find their real selves.[11] The institutional pole offers external rules with formalized standards to discover an authentic self; an individual's impulse pole allows for more freedom devoid of external rules that limit the real self from emerging. Turner developed his theoretical framework of self-conception in 1976, before millennials were even born. At that point, he noted an important shift that was occurring in American culture: a shift toward individuals finding their real selves in the impulse pole rather than the institutional pole. Phillip Vannini and Alexis Franzese (2008) further explain these two poles by saying, "Individuals on the institutional pole are future oriented and see the true self as related to standards and as something to be constructed. These individuals must be in control to reveal the true self, relying heavily on roles and adherence to role guidelines. Individuals who identify with the impulse pole are grounded in the present, link the true self to spontaneity, believe that the self is discovered when inhibitions are released, and believe that exposure of emotions is admirable."[12] The data from this project will be connected to Turner's theory of self-conception in order to explain how millennial college-aged students interpret the Bible.

METHODS OF THE STUDY

This qualitative study utilized ethnographic interviews of southern millennial college students from the American southeast to provide a deeper understanding of their use of the Bible. A total of 67 participants were interviewed with 15 participants' interviews being excluded because 1 participant was not from the south and 14 participants self-identified as non-Christian. All remaining 52 participants were from the south and self-identified as Christian. The specific demographic profile can be seen in table 23.1.

To collect interviews, sixty-seven students from two sections of an introductory religion course at the University of Georgia were recruited and trained to complete an ethnographic interview with one of their peers. This collaborative ethnographic project used semistructured interviews to collect data on the theological and social orientations of college-aged millennials.[13] In a semistructured interview, interviewers followed a uniform interview format with predetermined questions but adapted the delivery of the questions to maintain a natural flow of conversation with the interviewee.[14] Each interviewer was trained to ask relevant follow-up questions based on the responses from the predetermined questions. The questions examined the theological and social orientation of millennials.

Each interview was audiotaped, and verbatim transcripts were developed from each audio recording. All interviews were uploaded to MaxQDA (VERBI GmbH), a software package for qualitative data analysis. Inductive content analysis was used to code for trends and similar phrases by the author and a research assistant.[15] Only codes that

TABLE 23.1

PROFILE OF CHRISTIAN PARTICIPANTS (N = 52)

Demographic	n	%
Race/ethnicity		
White	43	83
Latino/a	1	2
Black	4	8
Asian	4	8
Gender		
Female	33	63
Male	19	37
Average age 21		
Home community type		
Urban	7	13
Suburban	32	62
Rural	13	25
Religious affiliation		
Catholic	8	15
Evangelical Protestants	10	19
Mainline Protestants	11	21
Other Christian	23	44
Importance of religion		
Most important	32	62
One among many important things	14	27
Not as important as other things	5	10
Not important	1	2
Regularity of worship attendance		
Most weeks	33	63
Every other week	3	6
Monthly	10	19
A Couple of times a year	4	8
Never	2	4

were agreed on by both the author and a research assistant were used in this study to ensure the reliability of codes.[16]

RESULTS

Participants described an intimate relationship with God that relied heavily on prayer or conversations with God. Because of their strong, personal relationships with God, the participants did not view traditional forms of religiosity, like church attendance and regular Bible reading, as necessary to connect with the divine (see table 23.2). As reflected in Smith and Snell's research, my participants also placed the final exegetical authority with the individual reader.[17] That said, the participants in this study did often hold up the Bible as an authoritative moral guide; they just felt it necessary for readers to decide what the text meant to them and make life application of the text to fit this exegesis.

THE BIBLE MEANS WHAT I THINK IT MEANS

To investigate how millennials exegete the Bible, participants were asked, "Do you think the Bible should be viewed literally or non-literally? Explain." In response to this question,

TABLE 23.2
RELATIONSHIP WITH GOD (N = 52)

How personally involved do you think God is with you?	Invoked meaning through interview (%)	Example
God is intimately involved with me and the details of my life	75	I would say that God plays a role in everything I do. From the moment that I wake up until the moment I go to sleep, I think about God and how I am going to follow Jesus Christ. I just pray every day that I can live up to all of the expectations and be a good person.
God ultimately judges but individuals can limit God's involvement in their lives	25	I don't think I am that close to him because I am not living up to my full potential according to the principles of the Bible. My spirituality has been shaken for a long time now, but I am slowly trying to rebuild my faith in God.

the majority of participants (62 percent) said that they interpreted the biblical text both literally and nonliterally, depending on the biblical and present-day context (see table 23.3). However, none of the participants utilized any historical-critical methods in deciding the meaning of a text, nor did any cite any biblical scholars or religious leaders. They shared a belief that generally the Old Testament should be taken nonliterally and the New Testament should be taken literally. Within the New Testament, the authoritative words of Jesus were of special importance. Biblical meaning was ultimately decided based on a gut feeling of what feels right, which they often described as God inspired. For example, one participant plainly stated, "If God thinks that you need to take the Bible literally, then that's how you'll view it. But if God thinks that you need to view the Bible non-literally, then that's how you'll view it." In many ways, the participants shared a belief in an instantaneous form of *lectio divina* (divine reading), minus the need for prayer and contemplation. The emphasis was on God creating meaning of a biblical passage for the individual student. With this emphasis on an individualized divine meaning, the participants valued present-day interpretation over how people in the past interpreted the biblical text. On this continuum of time, millennials

TABLE 23.3

CHRISTIAN PARTICIPANTS' VIEWS OF THE BIBLE AND TRADITION (N = 52)

TEXT AND TRADITION: DO YOU THINK YOUR SACRED TEXT SHOULD BE VIEWED LITERALLY OR NONLITERALLY? AND WHY?		
Subcategory	Invoked meaning through interview (%)	Example
Literally	15	I believe that the Bible should be taken as literally as a history book. God created the world. Moses led the Israelites. God parted the Red Sea. And Jesus died on the cross.
Both literally and nonliterally	62	For the most part, many of the lessons one can learn can be viewed literally. It's basically to each their own. You view it as you want. Your background changes your views and your perspective on how things are.
Nonliterally	23	I don't think it should be viewed literally. Those texts were written a long time ago, most of them are just metaphors. They should be taken with a grain of salt.

attributed the most authority to God speaking to them now, the second greatest authority to Jesus speaking in the Gospels, and the least authority to anyone speaking in the Old Testament.

APPLICATION OF BIBLICAL EXEGESIS

The participants in the study further revealed their use of the Bible when discussing their thoughts about same-sex marriage. The participants were asked, "What is your opinion about the importance of religious groups advocating for or against same-sex marriage?" This open-ended question was chosen so that respondents did not have to support or protest same-sex marriage, nor did they have to use the Bible to justify their answers. However, participants often referenced the Bible when articulating their answers.

Overwhelmingly, 87 percent of the participants said that the church should stay out of the same-sex marriage debate and that they personally supported same-sex civil marriages (see table 23.4). Perhaps the most interesting finding is that only 13 percent of the participants felt that same-sex marriage should be accepted within churches. Participants often generally referenced the creation account in the Bible and said, "God intended marriage to be between man and woman." As another example, participants would say things such as "Legally, I think people should be able to marry whomever they want to marry. By getting married in a church, you assume the beliefs of that church. And churches for the most part do not support same-sex marriages." Another participant did qualify her statement by stating that while the biblical standard might be appropriate within the church, "we live in a world where not everyone is a Christian and should not be bound by Christian interpretations of the Bible." Another person believed that regardless of marriage preference, those wanting to participate in same-sex civil marriages should "have the same rights as any other human being." To summarize these results in a sentence: participants felt the Bible says that same-sex marriage is not what God intended but same-sex couples should have recourse to civil laws that protect their sovereign individual right to marry.

While supporting the autonomy of churches to abstain from performing same-sex marriages, the participants were adamant that churches should not follow the example of Westboro Baptist Church of Topeka, Kansas, known for its militant, abusive style of protest. One participant said, "Gay sex is a sin but so is gluttony," and another said, "It says in the Bible that you're not supposed to marry someone of the same sex, but I'm not going to judge." As exemplified by this quote, participants were very concerned that they not hurt the feelings of same-sex couples, be viewed as hypocritical, or be thought of as judgmental.

Interestingly, very few students argued for same-sex marriage based on the Bible. Most of the participants appealed to the concept of civil rights to argue for same-sex marriage. When the reading of the Bible was depersonalized and based on the collective lens of the organized Christian religion, the participants felt churches must maintain the view that Christian marriage is between a man and a woman.

TABLE 23.4

CHRISTIAN PÁRTICIPANTS' VIEWS OF CHURCH INVOLVEMENT WITH SAME-SEX MARRIAGE (N = 52)

Religious institution involvement with same sex marriage	Invoked meaning through interview (%)	Example
Against same-sex marriage in the church but supports same-sex marriage as a civil right	87	Legally, I think people should be able to marry whomever they want to marry. By getting married in a church, you assume the beliefs of that church. And churches for the most part do not support same-sex marriages.
Churches should adapt and accept same-sex marriage	13	Gay marriage is going to happen; it will soon become a human right. All religions care about kindness and compassion and caring for one another.

DISCUSSION AND CONCLUSION

College-aged millennials in Georgia judged the meaning of the biblical text based on what felt right. This finding directly coincides with the findings of Smith and Snell that millennial college students follow a "what seems right to me" authority.[18] However, college-aged millennials' discussion of same-sex marriage reveals that a more complex exegesis was going on in their minds. At face value, participants supported an individual's right to personalize interpretation of the Bible but expected a more traditional interpretation of the Bible from a church community.

Turner's theoretical framework of self-conception helps explain millennial exegesis.[19] The participants in this study appealed to both the impulse and the institutional poles when utilizing their exegetical models. They highly valued individualized impulses in the exegesis of the Bible. As they see it, God speaks directly and through the Bible to the individual. As this happens, people find their authentic selves. In addition, participants believed that God will make self-evident the meaning of the Bible according to the needs of the individual. In contrast, the participants referenced the need of the church to uphold the rules in the Bible, showing that they value the institutional pole.

Based on work by Turner and Schutte, the status of being married and belief in religion leads people to connect with the institutional pole.[20] Based on my research, millennials connect with the institutional pole when discussing the issue of same-sex marriage. First, participants say that the institution of the government should provide rules to allow for same-sex marriage. Second, participants say that the institution of the church should not be forced to validate same-sex marriage because same-sex marriage contradicts most churches' beliefs, which are based on the Bible. The view of the participants seems to be that the role of government is to protect individual rights, like the right to marry whomever one chooses.

Interestingly, the participants in this study also appealed to the impulse pole. They suggested that the church should stay out of same-sex marriage. Participants perceived that if churches keep quiet, they are protecting the impulse pole of individuals who participate in same-sex marriage. Of course, this perception more likely protects the impulse of the participants in the study and not the impulses of those who value same-sex marriage.

The participants displayed an interesting exegetical decision-making process. They supported an interpretation of the Bible based on what feels right, and they believed that what feels right is created by God. However, when confronted with the polarizing issue of same-sex marriage, they viewed the Bible, and by extension the church, as against same-sex marriage. The participants seem to be saying that an individual's feels-right interpretation of the Bible can, after all, be wrong if it differs from the church's traditional interpretation of the Bible. On the issue of same-sex marriage, the southeastern Christian millennials in this study were caught between the poles of institution and impulse. When the impulsive pole directly conflicts with the institutional pole, the rules of the institution are upheld. One participant said, "If a church believes that same-sex marriage is contrary to the Bible, it's wrong for an individual to come inside and say, 'Hey, you need to support my same-sex marriage.'" Of course, a question begs to be answered—If the Bible is to be interpreted based on what an individual feels is right, how can an individual's interpretation of the Bible be wrong?

The findings reported here suggest that Christians in this study find their true selves intimately linked with the institutional pole and are simultaneously influenced by the desire to find one's self through impulsive means.[21] To reconcile the contradictions between these poles, participants argued for civil, but not religious, validation of same-sex marriage.

In conclusion, Turner's theory of self-conception helps to explain the tension between the impulse and institutional poles that southern Christian millennials feel during exegesis of the Bible. They want to support the impulsive religious pole but usually side with the institutional religious pole because it aligns most closely with their personal impulses. To further explore this topic, it would be interesting to find out if millennials are protecting their personal impulsive interpretation of the Bible by appealing to the institutional pole of the traditional church.

24

Crowning the King

THE USE OF PRODUCTION AND RECEPTION STUDIES TO DETERMINE THE MOST POPULAR ENGLISH-LANGUAGE BIBLE TRANSLATION IN CONTEMPORARY AMERICA

Paul C. Gutjahr

THIS ESSAY EXPLORES finding the answer to a seemingly simple question: What is the most popular English-language translation of the Bible today in the United States? It is a far easier question to ask than to answer.

In attempting to answer it, scholars have primarily used two approaches. In the broadest terms, these two approaches focus either on the number of Bibles of a certain English translation (also frequently denominated as a "version") produced or the number of Bibles of a certain English translation actually being used. To put it another way, those who study the Bible in America have sought to determine a Bible version's popularity by using the differing lenses of American Bible production and reception. While scholars of the Bible in America—including myself—have strongly favored the production approach in answering the question of a given Bible version's popularity, chapter 1 offers an unprecedented glimpse into the actual Bible-reading habits of contemporary Americans.

Chapter 1 reveals the marked limitations of production-centered determinations of a given English Bible version's popularity. In turn, the data recorded in chapter 1 makes it clear that only through the complementary use of production and reception approaches can one hope to arrive at a more nuanced—and thus more accurate—answer as to which Bible version enjoys the greatest popularity in the United States today.

Chapter 1 also makes it clear that while the production lens of Bible scholarship may lead one to believe that various editions have posed significant challenges to the reign of the four-hundred-year old King James Version (KJV) as the most popular Bible version among Americans, the actual survey data leaves little doubt that the KJV still holds the preeminent place among Bible versions in the hearts and minds of contemporary Americans.

PRODUCTION STUDIES

Production studies of the popularity of various English Bible versions have mainly centered on examinations of Bible translators, publishers, and distributors in an attempt to determine what translation is most used among Americans. Production approaches have been favored for the simple reason that production-focused data is more readily available than broadly sampled, systematically collected reception data. Examples of production-oriented evidence include figures on how many new English-language translations have appeared in the United States over a given period of time, as well as the occasionally released figures from publishers concerning print runs of various Bible editions. Considered with appropriate amounts of scholarly skepticism about the truthfulness of publishers and the accuracy of publishing statistics, such numbers can lead to some idea of a given Bible version's popularity.

The production approach also encompasses a great deal of scholarship on English-language biblical translation work. When publishers undertake a new English translation of the Bible, they do so with the desire to reach the widest possible American audience. Both nonprofit and trade publishers attempt in their new translations to remain true to the meaning of the ancient text while also trying to reach the widest possible modern Bible-reading audience. Thus, such translation work is a constant balancing act between textual accuracy and accessibility.

In considering the grand sweep of American history, beginning with the arrival on the eastern seaboard of Puritans from England and the Pilgrims from the Netherlands, no English-language translation has enjoyed greater popularity in the United States than the King James Version, commissioned by its namesake British king in 1604. James I empaneled a forty-seven-person translation team (composed entirely of male scholars of the Church of England) to produce a new Bible that would "be understood even by the very vulgar."[1] It was a translation bent on reaching the most common readers and listeners, and in this spirit the translators simplified its language to favor one-syllable words whenever possible and paid attention to cadences that would allow it to be easily read aloud.[2]

James's Bible enjoyed immense popularity in the years after its first appearance. In the American colonies, by 1700 it replaced the Geneva Bible as the preferred version used by New England Puritans, and it has remained in wide use ever since. In fact, so popular has the KJV been in America that the popularity of every subsequent English-language translation of the Bible has been measured against it.

The towering popularity of the KJV in the United States, however, did not stop Americans from embarking on other English-language Bible translation projects.

Americans began producing new English translations of the Bible as early as the first decade of the nineteenth century, but it is not until the 1820s and 1830s that one notices a marked increase in the number of translators attempting to bring Americans the Bible in a more contemporary idiom.[3] Most often, these translators were driven by the twin desires to incorporate new scholarship on the biblical texts and to clarify the archaic language of the KJV, which many increasingly argued obscured more than it illuminated. Even when the KJV was first released in the early seventeenth century, it was using grammar and vocabulary that was a bit dated and formal for its time. Problems associated with word forms ending in "eth" and vocabulary full of "thees" and "thous" were only exacerbated over the next two centuries as the English language continued to evolve and Americans with increasing frequency took the language in new national and regional directions.

While over twenty Americans (most often working alone, but sometimes in groups) tried their hands at producing new English-language translations of the Bible in the early nineteenth century, it was not until the Revised Version of 1881 that a large-scale, scholarly effort was mobilized to revise the KJV for a new era.[4] Appropriately enough, this new revision of the KJV was simply called the "Revised Version."

The RV was the product of a decade-long translation enterprise that included many of America's and England's greatest biblical scholars. Over seventy men, working in teams on both sides of the Atlantic, made use of the most current biblical textual scholarship available to revise and correct the KJV's core text. At the same time, these scholars also worked to update the KJV's language into a more contemporary idiom. All told, it was the largest and most scholarly English-language Bible translation project since the appearance of the KJV almost three centuries earlier.

The translators released the RV's New Testament in 1881 and its Old Testament in 1885. Its publisher, Oxford University Press, sold some 3 million copies of the New Testament in the first year of release (365,000 of them in the United States).[5] Interest in the RV was so intense when it first appeared that American newspapers such as the *Chicago Times* and the *Chicago Tribune* used their Sunday sections to reprint the entire New Testament over a series of weeks.[6] Demand for the RV quickly cooled, however, as most Americans saw no compelling reason to move away from their familiar and much beloved copies of the KJV. By the 1890s, it is estimated that the RV composed somewhere between 5 and 10 percent of Bible sales in the United States.[7] The KJV clearly remained king.

While the British translators involved in the RV project disbanded in the 1880s, their counterparts in the United States continued to fine-tune this revision for American Bible readers. Their interest lay not only in continuing to refine the text in terms of current biblical scholarship but also in adopting the language of the text to a more American idiom. The American translators also wished to make the text more accessible through the use of revised page headings, altered paragraphing and punctuation, the use of italics, and revised marginal readings with a new cross-referencing system. The American translation team pursued all these changes in the hope of creating a text both more accurate in its rendering of the original sources and more intellectually accessible to contemporary readers. Out of these efforts came the American Standard Version (ASV) in 1901. While the ASV became more popular than the RV in America because of its careful textual recovery work and more Americanized vocabulary, it did not come close to displacing the KJV as the Bible of choice.[8]

Other English-language translations in the United States followed the RV and ASV in the twentieth century, including another momentous team translation effort in the 1940s that gave birth to a revision of the ASV christened the Revised Standard Version (RSV). The RSV New Testament appeared in 1946. Its Old Testament appeared six years later in 1952. The RSV promised to be a significant threat to the long-established primacy of the KJV in America as an "unprecedented first printing of nearly a million copies" was readied for distribution.[9] Added to this considerable commitment by the publishers of the RSV, the newly formed National Council of Churches (NCC) decided to offer its official endorsement to this version. Founded in 1950, the NCC "represented twenty-nine Protestant and Eastern Orthodox denominations with a combined membership of thirty-three million," and it put is substantial institutional weight behind advertising and distributing copies of the RSV.[10] The institutional imprimatur of the NCC allowed the translators of the RSV to proclaim it as a "new *authorized* version," and for a period it seemed as though the KJV had finally met its match, as the RSV's broad institutional support among Mainline and Greek Orthodox churches, coupled with its use of a more common, less King Jamesean English, offered American Bible readers an academically robust, linguistically accessible new version of the Holy Scriptures.[11] In the end, however, while gaining some Bible market share in the United States, the RSV did not come close to displacing the KJV as the favorite Bible version in America.

The drive toward textual accessibility reached new heights in the 1960s with the advent of a new translation strategy that marked a major shift in American Bible publishing. In 1966, the American Bible Society produced a small paperback version of the New Testament, its new Today's English Version (TEV), under the title *Good News for Modern Man*, which became the more popular name for it. The TEV represented a revolutionary change in American Bible translation as it created its text using the translation theories of Eugene Nida, the executive secretary of the American Bible Society's Translation Department. Nida introduced a theory of dynamic or functional equivalence in biblical translation, rather than the formal equivalence methods heretofore used in every major revision of the English Bible since the KJV. Functional equivalence focused far more on reader experience than on formal accuracy in translating the words of a text. Functional equivalence promised a thought-for-thought rather than a word-for-word translation of the biblical text. The basic idea of a passage was Nida's primary concern, not translating each word from the original language in a way that would map onto its most appropriate contemporary equivalent. Nida concentrated on a wholistic rendering of the original text's meaning. He further underscored his desire for biblical accessibility by coupling his emphasis on thought-for-thought translation with a pronounced stress on using the simplest possible English vocabulary in composing the text.

The American Bible Society turned to Robert G. Bratcher, a Baptist minister and one-time missionary to Brazil, to use Nida's theories to create what would become the TEV's New Testament. (The entire TEV Bible appeared in 1976.)[12] Bratcher carefully worked through the New Testament, attempting to represent the primary meaning of passages without using complex vocabulary, obscure references to ancient rituals and behaviors no longer familiar to contemporary readers, or overly theological terminology. For example, the ancient rite of anointing a head with oil was translated as being welcomed as an honored guest (Psalm 23:5).[13] Bratcher—and the TEV translators who followed him—had the main goal of engaging the contemporary American Bible reader with the core meaning of the biblical text. Although the TEV was reviled by biblical scholars as simplistic and overly interpretative, a huge number of Americans embraced it. Within a year of its release, the American Bible Society had distributed over 5 million copies of the TEV. Over the next two decades, that number grew to 75 million.[14]

As popular as the TEV proved to be, the best-selling new twentieth-century English translation of the Bible in the United States appeared in 1978: the New International Version (NIV). The NIV was a revision of the RSV that sought to appeal to more theologically conservative American evangelical and fundamentalist circles. For example, the RSV had received significant criticism in these more conservative circles for a number of its translation decisions. Perhaps the most famous point of contention was its failure to underline the virgin birth of Christ by choosing to translate Isaiah 7:14 using the words "young woman" rather than "virgin."[15] This choice—and others like it—led many conservative members of the American clergy to turn their backs on the RSV, including one North Carolina pastor who publically burned a copy of it using a blowtorch, calling the translation "a heretical, communist-inspired Bible."[16]

Although a close analysis of the NIV shows just how little its translation actually differs from the RSV, the editorial board of the NIV made a number of strategic changes to placate more theologically conservative American Bible readers, including a return to the KJV's translation of the Isaiah 7:14 passage using the word "virgin" rather than "young woman," underscoring the close connection between Isaiah's messianic prophecies and the mother of Jesus found in the Gospel accounts. Zondervan, one of the country's largest Christian publishing houses, invested $8 million in the development and translation work that resulted in the NIV. At every stage Zondervan trumpeted the NIV's editorial board's theologically conservative views of scripture.[17]

Zondervan did more than make sure that its translators were conservative enough to appeal to American evangelical and fundamentalist Bible readers. It made sure that its new translation appeared in a highly reader-friendly format. Zondervan published the NIV in a single-column style and had the text composed using an easy-to-read type font. It also provided new section titles to help the reader transition through various Bible chapters and books. Its emphasis on the reader and its more conservative, formal equivalence approach made the NIV an instant hit among conservative American Protestants. The initial press run of 1.2 million copies sold out before it was printed, and within weeks of its release sales "topped two million copies."[18] So successful did the version prove to be that it came to be considered the first Bible version to outsell the KJV in the American marketplace, laying claim to overtaking KJV in annual sales in 1986.[19]

Here is where scholars of American Bible translation, including myself, have stumbled. Because the NIV began supposedly outselling the KJV in 1986 and its strong sales continue, scholars have used this production-oriented data to point to the NIV as the most popular English-language Bible version circulating in America today. After all, decades of translation work focused so heavily on reader engagement coupled with sales statistics as strong as the NIV's can easily lead one to believe that the NIV was the final culmination of decades of various versions chipping away at the KJV's American popularity. While the production approach might logically lead to such a conclusion, reception data concerning the Bible in America tells a different story.

RECEPTION STUDIES

Bible reception studies are focused on examining the actual reading practices and preferences of American Bible readers, largely through the use of surveys and other means of data collection. Because of their more direct focus on actual reading practices, one might think that reception studies would be the most prevalent method used to determine a translation's popularity. Such is not the case, for two reasons. First, survey data is usually not available for determining readership preferences from the past. Prior to the twentieth century, no organization was surveying American Bible readers in any systematic, broad-based way to determine their preferences when it came to which version of the Bible they used. Second, when such surveys began to be used in the twentieth and twenty-first centuries, the data generated from such surveys was usually a closely guarded secret by those (most often publishers) who had paid for the data to be collected. Publishers commissioned such surveys to help them plan their own Bible development and sales strategies. Simply put, Bible publishing is big business, and as in any business, there are trade secrets that publishers guard in order to retain their competitive edge. Surveys cost a great deal of money, and when organizations invest their resources, they wish to exercise tight control over the data they have gathered.

Thus, the available survey data outside Bible publishing itself has always been scant. This condition changed, however, in 2011, when the Lilly Endowment gave over a half million dollars ($507,140 to be exact) to the Center for the Study of Religion and American Culture at Indiana University-Purdue University Indianapolis to study the Bible in everyday American life. The grant, aptly named "The Bible in American Life," consisted of several elements, but what concerns us here is the approximately $120,000 Lilly provided for the execution of two surveys centered on Americans' everyday Bible usage.

To determine actual American Bible usage patterns, the project bought questions on two large surveys focused on Americans' Bible-reading preferences and everyday practices . For roughly $100,000, they commissioned questions on the General Social Survey. This survey, conducted every other year by the National Opinion Research Center at the University of Chicago is largely funded by the National Science Foundation, has been used since 1972 to track various American demographics, attitudes, and behaviors. Questions were purchased for the 2012 survey, and responses were gathered from a sample size of 1,551 Americans. An additional $20,000 was spent to place questions on the National Congregations Study III (NCS III). The NCS has been used since 1998 to gather information about religious congregational life in America, and the Bible in American Life project focused its attention and questions on Christian congregations.

The Lilly Endowment's grant to the Bible in American Life project provided the resources to execute unprecedented research on American Bible usage habits that was not controlled by a single publishing entity. The results of the surveys are striking and add a much needed reception-oriented dimension to the study of the Bible in America. When it comes to the question of which English-language translation is still most favored by American Bible readers, the survey data is particularly telling. While the production data and the long-established trend toward more functionally equivalent Bible translations seems to point to the NIV as the most popular version used by Americans today, the reception data tells a different story.

The Bible in American Life part of the General Social Survey sought to answer this question: Which English translation from the original Hebrew and Greek do most Americans use in their everyday lives? Responses to the GSS survey confirmed that the NIV and KJV Bibles were indeed the two most popular versions used today by American Bible readers, but in an order different from the one pointed to in the production data. More specifically, 55 percent of Americans who read the Bible used the KJV, while the NIV enjoyed a much lower 19 percent rate of use. The KJV clearly remained the king of English-language Bible translations used by contemporary Americans.

With this reception data in mind, one inevitably needs to seek to understand why the production data might lead one to certain conclusions that do not concur with the reception data. Arguments through production data have centered on proving the NIV to be the most popular English translation of the Bible in America.[20] The reception data on the other hand clearly points to the enduring popularity of the KJV. Four explanations foreground themselves in attempting to reconcile the conclusions of the production and reception approaches. These explanations also provide the framework for understanding why the KJV is still almost three times as popular as its nearest competitor among American Bible readers.

First, it is helpful to keep in mind the underlying principle that religious artifacts and rituals are among the cultural materials and practices that are slowest to change in any society. The anthropologist James Deetz, in his studies of early American burial rituals and of several early American archaeological sites, makes a convincing case for this reluctance to change religious rituals and totems. Examining American colonial gravestones, Deetz argues that the gravestones most closely tied to religious belief are the slowest to evolve in terms of their style and content when compared to more secular gravestones. In the same manner, Deetz argues that religious objects and practices remain in use decades longer than other more secular cultural objects and practices.[21] The Bible, it would seem, is no exception to Deetz's insight, as one sees a pronounced reluctance to change both the binding and the content of American Bibles when studying

American Bible publishing practices. For example, Bibles have been one of the slowest books to move away from the tradition of being bound in leather, and the Bible is one of the few categories of books today that can still be found in leather bindings in large numbers.[22] In a similar way, American Bible readers have been slow to relinquish their attachment to the KJV.

Second, while scholars might point to 1986 as the pivotal year when the NIV finally outsold the KJV, sales statistics are often incomplete. Bibles are among the trickiest books in this regard, simply because there are entire organizations such as Gideons International and the American Bible Society—not to mention denominations and individual churches—who give Bibles away for free. Such free Bibles often do not show up in traditional sales data but nevertheless have a huge influence on what Bible versions are in circulation in a given culture in a specific historical moment. For example, Gideons International has distributed 1.9 billion copies of the Bible around the world in the last century; many of those copies have been given away in the United States free of charge.[23] In English, the Gideons have long favored giving away the KJV. There is also a host of other for-profit and nonprofit Bible publishers who produce the KJV. Collecting sales data from one, or even a handful, of such publishers does not promise to give an entire picture of how many KJV's were sold or distributed in a single year. The 1986 date pointing to the ascension of the NIV to the place of America's most popular English-language Bible translation was based on incomplete Bible production and distribution data, an easy mistake to make since Bible publishing is such a vast and diffused endeavor in the United States.

Third, sales statistics are often only an indicator of a single type of popularity. Just because a certain Bible version is selling does not mean that it is actually being used. Sales figures might be able to offer an idea of how many copies of a book are in circulation, but such figures tell us little about how that book is actually being used once it has been sold. When it comes to sales statistics and religious texts in the United States, it is instructive to consider the case of L. Ron Hubbard's book *Dianetics*. An absolutely pivotal sacred text for Hubbard's Church of Scientology, *Dianetics* was for years listed on a number of prominent best-seller lists because it was enjoying astounding sales in national bookstore chains. *Publishers Weekly*, the publishing industry's most popular publicity and news organ, awarded L. Ron Hubbard (after his death) a plaque commemorating the appearance of *Dianetics* on its best-seller list for one hundred consecutive weeks.[24] It was learned only later that the Church of Scientology was buying up massive quantities of this book to inflate the book's sales profile to attract the notice of best-seller lists such as the one sponsored by *Publishers Weekly*. Unopened boxes filled with unread copies of *Dianetics* were bought by the Church of Scientology and then distributed right back to bookstores so that they would be offered for sale again.[25] Obviously, sales data can be manipulated to mislead.

Fourth, the simple fact is that there have been literally centuries of the production and distribution of KJV Bibles in the United States. There is an aggregate effect to such saturation. There are literally millions of KJV Bibles sitting in American homes and churches. Recently sold, newer English translations of the Bible have a long way to go to match the KJV's high degree of cultural saturation. Following Deetz's insight above, it is easy to believe that Americans often pass on old Bibles to friends and families to use. A certain copy of the Bible can be in use for years, if not decades and even generations. New sales statistics of a given Bible version, as a result, do not necessarily mean that the new version is being used or even retained by its owner.

CONCLUSION

Americans have long loved the King James Bible—its cadences, its phrasing, its seemingly changeless and reliable nature. That love may be facing some erosion with the growing popularity of new English-language translations like the NIV, but the transition to a new dominate English-language Bible version is still under way. The extensive survey work of the Bible in American Life project reveals that newer English translations of the Bible have yet to unseat the massive popularity and extensive use of the KJV among Americans. In the end, while production-oriented book history methods give us insight into various trends in American Bible publishing, they do not give us an accurate idea of what actual Bible versions are being used by Americans, a gap in knowledge that reception-oriented survey data allows us to help fill. Taken together, Americans surveyed concerning their Bible reading preferences overwhelmingly still bear witness that the King James Version remains the king.

25

Literalism as Creativity

MAKING A CREATIONIST THEME PARK, REASSESSING

A SCRIPTURAL IDEOLOGY

James S. Bielo

FROM BIBLE READING TO EXPERIENCING "THE BIBLE"

How do everyday Americans engage the Bible outside formal worship services? The quantitative findings of chapter 1 productively contribute to this question. The analysis provides a detailed portrait of such dynamics as disjunctures between Bible belief and practice, translation preferences, motivations for Bible reading, and how sociological variables such as race, age, gender, and class correlate with reading practices. The focus in chapter 1 on Bible reading is particularly resonant for me because it highlights core questions that animated my first book project, *Words upon the Word: An Ethnography of Evangelical Group Bible Study*.[1]

In *Words upon the Word* I used linguistic anthropology methods to analyze talk and interaction among congregational small groups. A significant focus was on the reading and interpretive practices groups collaboratively created and re-created for scriptural and nonscriptural texts. This discourse-centered approach complemented a rich, but still relatively small, literature on the social life of the Bible among white, conservative Protestants in the United States. For example, there were studies of how the Bible worked as an organizing cultural symbol for congregations, schools, and movements.[2] There were studies of how biblical texts were engaged as a narrative resource in producing public rhetoric and verbal art.[3] And there were studies that illustrated how tightly formed ideologies about the Bible became complicated amid actual uses of the Bible.[4] Chapter 1 provides much-needed quantitative data to help frame the thick descriptions and nuanced analyses of Bible reading in this body of ethnographic work.

One of the most intriguing findings in chapter 1 is that Americans do more than just "read" the Bible. For example, Bible memorization remains a thriving practice. Forty-eight percent of Americans have memorized a verse within the past year, and 64 percent of congregations organize Bible memorization events for children.[5] This observation echoes other scholarship that has documented a variety of Bible uses that go beyond the textual and literacy act of reading. For example: Colleen McDannell has examined how popular biblical commodities are displayed in homes and public spaces, and Tim Beal has explored the phenomenon of Bible-based attractions, which materialize biblical texts in consumer sites of lived religion.[6]

Bible-based attractions are particularly fascinating because they expand our sense of how the cultural category of "Bible" is performed and expressed. The Bible exceeds its identity as a book when it is materialized through genres of place such as museum, theme park, theatre, replica, and garden. When people visit Bible-based attractions they engage more as experiencers of the Bible than readers. In this chapter, I capitalize on this theme of experiencing the Bible through an ethnography of a creationist theme park in the making. Through an analysis of the cultural producers and process of production behind this Bible-based attraction, I revisit the widely stated scriptural ideology of biblical literalism and argue that scholars must recalibrate their conceptions of what literalism is and what it allows for. I begin with a brief overview of the case study: Ark Encounter.

ARK ENCOUNTER

In December 2010, the governor of Kentucky held a press conference to announce a new addition to the state's tourism industry: Ark Encounter. The park is a joint venture between the young Earth creationist ministry Answers in Genesis and the for-profit Ark Encounter LLC. Founded in 1994, Answers in Genesis is the same ministry that opened the $30 million Creation Museum in northern Kentucky in 2007. Set on eight hundred acres of Kentucky rolling hills—forty miles south of Cincinnati, Ohio—the park's centerpiece will be an all-wooden re-creation of Noah's ark, built to creationist specifications from the text of Genesis 6–9.

The governor was joined by local politicians and Ark personnel. The press conference was intended to clarify why a biblical theme park was applying for the sales tax reimbursement program under the Kentucky Tourism Development Act. The brief question-and-answer session with journalists was predictably dominated by the oil-and-water register of church-state conflict. However, a few journalists were more creative; one asked if the re-created ark would have *live* dinosaurs on board.

Ark Encounter is a more than $150 million creationist theme park. The completed ark was built from nearly 4 million board feet of timber, stands 85 feet wide, 51 feet tall, and 510 feet long, and contains more than 100,000 square feet of themed exhibit space. From October 2011 through June 2014, I conducted ethnographic fieldwork with the creative team in charge of conceptualizing and designing Ark Encounter.[7]

Visitors to the park progress through three decks on the ark filled with a mix of sculpted animals, animatronic figures, interactive displays, multimedia exhibits, food vendors, and children's play areas. Each deck is organized as a particular affective experience. Deck One centers on the emotional drama of Noah and his family following the closing of the ark door. They are relieved to have escaped a terrifying storm, they have just witnessed mass death, and they are anxious about the weeks ahead. The creative team always talked about Deck One as the "darkest" of the decks, indexed sensorially by low levels of lighting. The storm would be audible, and visitors would hear sounds of wind, rain, thunder, and debris banging against the ark's sides. Noah and his family would be comforting the animals and each other amid these difficult conditions.

Deck Two focuses on the tasks and challenges of living on the ark. Noah and his family are settled, going about their liminal existence while onboard: the daily grind of tending the onboard garden, caring for the animals, and managing daily routines. The creative team envisioned Deck Two as the primary "how-to" deck, addressing numerous "practical" issues about the Noah story. How did they feed all the animals? What did they do with all the animal waste? How were air, water, and sunlight distributed? What did Noah's workshop and library look like? By addressing these questions, Deck Two emphasizes the creationist claim that "ancient" people were capable of incredibly sophisticated technology because of their long lifespans (Noah living to the ripe old age of 950).

Deck Three continues themes from the first two decks and introduces several new experiences. More exhibits teach about the creationist category of animal kinds. More exhibits address how-to matters, such as what the passengers' living quarters were like and what technology Noah used to build the ark. Deck Three also captures the salvific realization that God's wrath has been expended, the storm is over, the waters have receded, the eight passengers have been spared, and the whole world is now theirs. This affect transitions into further creationist teaching points about post-Flood life, such as the Tower of Babel dispersal of languages and people groups. Deck Three is the place where the creationist typological theology, which links the story of Noah to the story of Jesus, is taught most explicitly.

As visitors move through these three decks, 132 exhibit bays (44 per deck) combine to present a creationist narrative about the steadfast faithfulness of Noah and his family, their salvation, and ultimately the evangelical Gospel of salvation. The iconicity of moving from darkness to light, from judgment to salvation, was very self-conscious for the creative team; they wanted visitors to experience this progression. Through this story of Noah and his family, Ark Encounter teaches creationist history, theology, and the creationist critique of evolutionary science.

Ark Encounter is, among other things, a $150 million testimony. It is missionization, massively materialized, performed in the key of biblical literalism. But the creative team understood their task as much more complicated than a mere presentation of the creationist message. First, they had to demonstrate the historical plausibility of the Genesis story. If the ark could be built from wood now, then Noah could have done it then. This Bible miracle would be no less miraculous, just very doable. If it could have happened, then maybe it did happen, and if it did happen, then the story is true, ratifying the whole of scripture. However, plausibility alone was not enough. Noah's story could not merely be told; it had to be felt. What was it like to see the door close? To hear the fierce storm outside? The cacophony of animals? To live on the ark day after day? And what was it like when the dove did not return? To see the rainbow and be the center of God's saving grace? An immersive experience promises to bridge the gap between plausibility and believability, and the logic of immersive entertainment was the primary engine of the team's creative labor.[8]

LITERALISM

Ark Encounter emerges from the cultural lifeworld of American Protestant fundamentalism. Literalism is the scriptural ideology most associated with creationism and fundamentalism, as both an etic category of classification and an emic term of self-identification. According to chapter 1, biblical literalism continues to be significant among the American public. Eighty-three percent of respondents on the National Congregations Study answered yes to the question "Does your congregation consider the Bible to be the literal and inerrant word of God?" And on the General Social Survey, 29 percent of respondents (c. 96 million Americans) claimed the Bible to be "the literal, inerrant word of God."[9] (Just think: if only 5 percent of these respondents attend Ark Encounter in its opening year, at $40 per person, the admission revenue will be nearly $200 million.)

A series of ethnographic studies have advanced a solid social scientific understanding of how literalism works among conservative Protestants. For example, Brian Malley has demonstrated how literalism circulates and functions as a language ideology, a scriptural ideology, and a cultural symbol more than any actual, systematically executed system of interpretive procedures.[10]

A detailed exploration of literalism is Vincent Crapanzano's *Serving the Word: Literalism in America from the Pulpit to the Bench*. Crapanzano compares the textual ideologies and practices among fundamentalist Protestants and conservative jurists to argue that literalism is an increasingly dominant interpretive mode in American society. Crapanzano outlines a family resemblance of ten features that define literalism: elevating language's referential/semantic dimension over its performative function; unambiguously correlating word and thing; focusing on single, essential lexical meanings; viewing textual meaning as ultimately decidable; reducing figurative meanings to being distorting or relevant only within specialized genres; stressing authorial intention; valuing certain texts as fundamental; pervasively recontextualizing fundamental texts; giving written texts priority over oral texts; and requiring that texts be interpreted on their own terms before they can be applied.[11]

Taken together, the existing scholarship informs us that literalism exerts a widespread influence among American Protestants (even if they are not fundamentalist and, as chapter 1 suggests, even if individuals are not regular Bible readers). However, much of this scholarship also has a normatively critical orientation. Crapanzano exemplifies this. For example, he writes that literalism "engenders intolerance because it can admit no deviance from a single, unambiguous meaning."[12] Explicitly or implicitly, literalism is typically construed by social scientists in negative terms: confining, simplistic, restrictive, narrow, rigid, dogmatic. More often than not, biblical literalists are positioned as a particular kind of textual user: defined by an either/or logic; having little tolerance for ambiguity, polysemy, or uncertainty; hemmed in by a strict originalist fidelity; and confined to the genre of written text. Any possibility that literalism can be anything else, anything more than a closed interpretive universe, is foreclosed. The one feature in Crapanzano's list that might invite this direction—pervasive recontextualization—he construes more as a redundant crutch than a productive resource.

My ethnographic work with Ark Encounter's creative team demanded a reassessment of literalism. As the team worked to materialize the Bible, to transform the Genesis story of Noah into a multisensory, immersive, pedagogic, entertaining experience, literalism became a space for artistic imagination and design creativity. This required an analytical recalibration away from plotting literalism as only ever a restrictive ideology. In turn, the central question I pursue in this chapter is this: in what ways did the creative team engage with literalism as a generative mode? I argue that as the team pursued their literalist imperative, as they performed their creative labor, interpretive opportunities, gaps, and dilemmas emerged to which the team had to respond as religious actors and professional artists. Ultimately, the team used their artistic agency to navigate the promises and constraints of literalism.

CREATIVE CREATIONISTS

Ark Encounter is the second major project of the ministry Answers in Genesis, which began in 1994 when three staff members at the Institute for Creation Research in southern California left to start a new organization for promoting creationism. The founders had two primary goals. First, they wanted to create a "populist ministry" that would complement the Institute's more technical creation science reputation. This presentation of self is revealing. A populist ministry would aim to be as widely accessible as possible. It would not be exclusionary, the kind of institution that only few could appreciate or benefit from. Populism also has a missionary quality. Reaching the masses means casting the evangelistic net as widely as possible. From its origins, Answers in Genesis has been oriented toward the broadest possible audience, not elite academic echelons or specialized public niches. The second goal was the first major project of Answers in Genesis: the Creation Museum. After nearly thirty years of planning and six years of construction, that museum, approximately 70,000 square feet in area, opened in northern Kentucky in 2007 to creationist fanfare and secular skepticism, protest, and ridicule.

The anthropologist Ella Butler has provided an excellent analysis of the Creation Museum. Butler's main argument is that it combines a secular-derived science studies critique (à la Bruno Latour) with elements of conspiracy theory. For the former, "scientific practice is always influenced by the starting assumptions of its practitioners," which prompts the widely accessible conclusion that creationism and mainstream science merely begin with diverging ideological commitments ("human reason" v. "God's Word"). For the latter, "like the conspiracy theorist, the creationist is here positioned as a kind of knowing subject who is enabled to see the truth behind the [evolutionist] façade." Alongside equipping the already converted with teaching and witnessing tools, the Creation Museum seeks to "destabilize scientific claims to objectivity" and, by extension, the cultural capital and authority of mainstream science. All this is performed through the populist registers of cinematic film, multisensory displays, interactive media, replicas, animatronics, and a narrative presentation of materialized biblical figures and scenes. The same creative team who designed the Creation Museum led the production of Ark Encounter. The core team was small, just four members: Patrick, Jon, Kristen, and Travis.

Patrick was the creative director. Now in his sixties, he had joined Answers in Genesis in 2001 to lead the production of the Creation Museum after working for several years as a theme park designer in Tokyo. Before Japan, Patrick's impressive resume included working on the 1984 Summer Olympics, the 1986 Statue of Liberty refurbishing, and Universal Studio's Jaws and King Kong attractions. As the creative director, Patrick had the primary task of managing the vision for the project as a whole, ensuring that every small piece (e.g., exhibits, landscaping, music, lighting) proceeded according to plan and fit as it should into the whole. In the early phases of the project, Patrick was also the primary "script writer," which means he wrote content for publicity and fundraising materials. In my experience Patrick was usually more serious than playful, a consummate taskmaster who maintained a mostly all-business attitude.

Jon had been one of the first artists Patrick hired for the production of the Creation Museum. He was the team's lead illustrator, producing "concept art" at various stages that bridged the team's initial brainstorming, prototypes, and finalized versions. He grew up in Brazil, the child of missionaries, returning to the United States at age eighteen to attend a Christian college. Before working for Answers in Genesis, Jon had served as illustrator for a Christian educational book company and a non-Christian studio firm that contracted with major entertainment corporations like Milton Bradley and Fisher Price. After the Creation Museum was completed, Jon took a two-year hiatus from Answers in Genesis to teach art at a Christian college in Florida. His experience teaching art created a very useful ethnographic effect: Jon was practiced at explaining his work as he created it and adept at articulating his artistic vision in more abstract terms. Throughout my fieldwork Jon was an ideal consultant: always answering questions thoughtfully, often preemptively showing me his latest work before I could ask.

Kristen had been hired in 2005 to help complete the production of the Creation Museum. She had returned to Ohio after earning a master's degree in theatre design from the California Institute of the Arts, the private university founded by Walt Disney in 1961. Patrick hired her specifically for her expertise in spatial, building, and set design. My ethnographic relationship with Kristen remained uncertain throughout the fieldwork. On the one hand she was always kind and often made time, like Jon, to explain her work in detail, even amid hectic schedules and looming deadlines. However, her interactions with me always suggested a sense of caution. It was Kristen who pressed me most about why I was interested in their work and what kind of book I wanted to write. Kristen seemed to put little effort into hiding this caution, which was consistent with my primary impression of her: she was intensely honest. Of all the biographical interviews I did with the artists, Kristen was the most emotionally transparent. She shared intimate details about her life, including her only son's serious health problems as a newborn and infant.

Patrick had hired Travis in 2005, two years before the Creation Museum opened. Travis was eighteen at the time and had just completed his homeschool education in Michigan. In lieu of pursuing a college art degree, he decided to remain with Answers in Genesis. At the opening of Ark Encounter in 2016 Travis was thirty years old, his resume boasting the title of "lead production designer" on two major projects without any formal art training. Travis's expertise was in sculpture and costume design. He was also the team historian, deeply interested in collecting reference details in order to accurately depict "ancient cultures." Measured by minutes and hours, I spent the most time with Travis. This was not by design; it just so happened that Travis traveled least and spent less time in meetings than the others. He was the artist who was most often at his desk working during my days spent at the studio. I always found him to be good-natured, and more talkative than Kristen or Patrick, though much less adept at explaining his art than Jon.

The ethnographic backbone of this project was the team's daily creative labor: spending mornings and afternoons at the design studio while they drew freehand, illustrated concept art, worked with raw materials, sketched exhibit schematics, edited and critiqued each other's work-in-progress. I talked with them at their cubicles, took notes during planned and impromptu team meetings, listened to lunchtime work talk, and photographed the ubiquitous art sitting on tables, hanging on walls, and torn up in trash cans. I arranged semistructured interviews with team members, but the majority of audio recordings and field notes addressed the work of a small team working from small desks: often doing tedious work, frequently working under deadline, ever conscious of budgetary constraints, and constantly seeking the next imaginative breakthrough.

From this project's inception, I approached it as an ethnography of cultural production. This entailed an important theoretical conceit. By following a process of production—"the making of"—distinctive insight is gained about cultural content, aspiration, and identity, compared to analyses that are limited to completed products and/or acts of consumption.[13] Studies in cultural production afford unique access to crucial acts of decision-making and logics for actualizing deeply held assumptions. For the creative team, this included documenting their creative collaborations and differences and mapping the changes between discarded drafts and finalized creations.

The two examples I will present both come from an early stage of the team's work. Early fundraising for Ark Encounter included the creation of a promotional book that was distributed to potential donors and investors. From December 2011 through May

2012 the team worked to produce a nearly sixty-page, glossy promo book that presented the basic rationale for Ark Encounter, explained the purpose of the three decks, and presented concept art for exhibits and attractions. The primary audience for the promo book was the already converted (really, the financially flush already converted), but the organizing elements of the team's cultural production were fully present: immersive entertainment, historical plausibility, materialization of a biblical experience, and scriptural literalism.

INTERTEXTUAL GAPS

The team's creative labor was defined by a dilemma that was productive in nature. As a biblical literalist, how do you materialize a biblical experience when the biblical text provides a relatively sparse amount of detail? In an early interview, Jon reflected on this basic dilemma:

> "It leaves us creatives in a world where we can kind of dream up a world that is believable because it did exist. These people lived many, many, many times, many years more than we do…Imagine what the technologies could have been like if you had hundreds of millions of people that we're living really, really long lifespans and the technology, we have no clue. But, for us as creatives it leads into a world that we can explore, we can create, we never want to, we're never gonna go against what the plain written word is. But, there is that artistic liberty to envision a world that we can immerse somebody in. Of violence, of evil, a world that's kind of similar to maybe what we are dealing with today…Only eight people are doing right and everybody else is out there, absolute hedonism doing whatever they want to do. Imagine a world like that. I can't even imagine it. And, how do you pull that off in a theme park environment where you're not going to offend anybody?"

The ark itself exemplifies this literalist dilemma. The textual specifications from God to Noah in Genesis are minimal: "So make yourself an ark of cypress wood; make rooms in it and coat it with pitch inside and out. This is how you are to build it: the ark is to be three hundred cubits long, fifty cubits wide and thirty cubits high. Make a roof for it, leaving below the roof an opening one cubit high all around. Put a door in the side of the ark and make lower, middle, and upper decks."[14]

Historically, this paucity of detail has been no deterrent to efforts—artistic, pragmatic, sincere and pious, mocking and irreverent—to materially render versions of the ark. Historian Janet Brown observes a "long artistic tradition, in paintings and sculpture" of the ark in the West, and that "science, religion, literalism, and allegory have always been closely intertwined in understanding this narrative."[15]

Material renderings of Noah's ark survive from as early as the fourth century—on the walls of St. Peter's tomb.[16] In the seventeenth century, Athanasius Kircher produced one of the earliest realist-oriented portraits. Anticipating Ark Encounter's commitment to plausibility, Kircher estimated the number of stalls, beasts, snakes, and birds, and "the logistics of stabling, feeding, and cleaning the animals were worked out in exhaustive detail."[17] Many contemporary ark portraits resemble a 1985 artistic representation that resulted from a 1970s evangelical archaeological expedition on Mount Ararat to search for physical remains of the ark.[18] More cartoonish versions abound as well (think: long giraffe necks sticking out of a small boat). The countless iterations of "the bathtub ark" are a definitive object of critique for contemporary creationists. They consider these nonrealist renderings to be complicit in secular-derived schemes to undermine scriptural authority by dismissing the ark's historicity.

On one hand, then, Ark Encounter participates in a long tradition of re-presenting the ark. However, the creative team's task was different because their re-creation was not just visual but was an embodied, multisensory immersive experience. Throughout my fieldwork, the team were uncomfortable with terms like "replica" and "reconstruction" to describe the park's centerpiece. They were keenly aware that any attempt to re-create the ark was densely mediated. In fact, I was never able to identify what term they most preferred. They typically referred to the ark nominally ("the ark") or, on occasion, would call it a "symbol" (of salvation). While the team were supremely concerned with demonstrating the "plausibility" of the Noah story, they maintained a cautionary attitude around "authenticity" in terms of re-creating the ark precisely as Noah built it. For example, the team were always quick to add that Noah never had to deal with design details like fire codes, restrooms, and American Disability Act accessibility requirements.

This tension of historical authenticity extended to all of their creative labor to re-create the pre-Flood world. Because that world was destroyed by the Flood, no direct physical evidence remains. This dilemma is integral to distinguishing between the historian's problem and the artist's opportunity. As artists, as theme park designers, these differences (plausibility v. authenticity, scriptural detail v. material remains) helped delimit for the team the spaces where artistic agency could flourish.

From the earliest days of my fieldwork, a crucial element of the team's labor was obvious: a constant reliance on nonbiblical intertextual references. Linguistic anthropologists have fruitfully developed the concept of "intertextuality," or "the relational orientation of a text with other texts."[19] This concept has primarily been used to analyze the narrative performance of oral poetics, but the fundamental dynamic translates well to the material performance of designing a creationist theme park. The Ark Encounter team would describe their intertextual references using the expressions "something for inspiration," "something to get me thinking," "a foundation to work from," and other such codings.

Jon kept on his desktop a large cache of jpeg files of artwork and images he "liked" for various reasons. When needing an inventive spark, he would scan through this cache until he found an inspiring something. A diverse collection of illustration books was constantly on the move throughout the studio, from bookshelves to cubicle desks to drawing boards. There were film art books from *Star Wars, Jurassic Park, Lord of the*

Rings, Chronicles of Narnia, Star Trek, Avatar, The Last Airbender, and *King Kong.* "Comics" and "Fantasy Cartooning" books sat near professional how-to magazines (e.g., *Make-Up Artist*). The fantasy series *Dinotopia* resided next to a storybook for Disney's *Haunted Mansion*, which resided next to history books about ancient Rome, Greece, and the Middle East, which resided next to numerous Answers in Genesis publications (e.g., *Answers Magazine*).

All of these intertextual references were fodder for the artistic hopper. Some were purely inspirational; others were more informational. The team would also view films together. I arrived one morning in December 2011 to find them watching *Pulse: A Stomp Odyssey* to "get ideas going" for Ark Encounter's "pagan areas." These included the pre-show film that visitors view before entering the ark and the one-quarter-mile pathway that connects the ark entrance and the beginning of Deck One. They viewed Mel Gibson's *Apocalypto* for the same reason. The team regularly went on trips together to museums (one of their favorites was the Abraham Lincoln Presidential Library and Museum in Springfield, Illinois) and themed amusement parks (e.g., Dollywood) to collect design and concept ideas for different exhibit spaces. Their most elaborate trip was a multicity tour of Morocco, which Patrick insisted was necessary for everyone to grasp the sensory and aesthetic dimensions for one of the park's future attractions. Taken together, this ever-expanding matrix of reference, inspiration, and information formed the intertextual universe the team used to fill in and elaborate the paucity of detail in Genesis 6–9.

Bauman and Briggs observe how intertextual relations always produce interpretive gaps that result from a necessarily imperfect fit between a text that has been decontextualized from its original context and recontextualized in a new context. As a cultural and semiotic process, social actors strategically work to minimize or maximize these gaps. Maximizing an intertextual gap is one way to "[build] authority through claims of individual creativity and innovation."[20] This approach is especially useful for thinking about biblical literalism as a generative mode because intertextual gaps constitute spaces of artistic agency. The question I ask of the following examples is this: how did the team negotiate the intertextual gaps that emerged between the limited detail in the text of Genesis 6–9 and their effort to materialize a biblical experience?

Fantasy

In January 2012 I sat with Jon while he worked on a map for the promo book. His eyes darted back and forth between dual monitors. One screen featured an early version of the map in Photo Shop, and he busily clicked keyboard keys, redrawing rivers, erasing mountains. The second screen displayed an online version of the New King James Bible open to Genesis 4. The exact future use of the map was unknown, but it featured prominently in subsequent fundraising materials and eventually became part of Ark Encounter's attempt to immerse visitors in the pre-Flood days of Noah. It was a regional map of the pre-Flood world focused on the Garden of Eden. Jon's task, he clarified to me as he worked, was to represent history in a biblically faithful way, while using his artistic imagination to fill in details that were not provided.

From the vantage point of fantasy-world-making, the use of a map is not a surprising strategy. In his analysis of world-building, Mark J. P. Wolf observes that "the oldest and perhaps most common tool used to introduce a world and orient an audience is the map."[21] Similarly, in his literary history of the fantasy genre, Michael Saler writes: "maps in particular were important for establishing the imaginary world as a virtual space consistent in all its details."[22] This strategy of mapping worlds is evident in works ranging from Thomas More's *Utopia* (1516) to A. A. Milne's *Winnie the Pooh* (1926), J. R. R. Tolkien's Middle Earth trilogy (1937), George R. R. Martin's *A Song of Ice and Fire* (1996), and a great many others.

The Bible says very little about the Garden of Eden or its location. It says the garden was east of Eden and names a few places, rivers, and minerals. Jon did the rest. He described parallels between this work and creations like *Avatar* and Middle Earth, except for the key difference that he was representing an actual world. More accurately, he added, his work was closer in kind to Mel Gibson's Mayan world in *Apocalypto*.

As an earnest biblical literalist, how do you construct a map when the coordinates are so few? In fact, the literalism of this map is not in its physical coordinates, it is in the history it presumes to capture: a past place that did exist, because scripture says so, but no longer does, because God said to Noah, "I am going to put an end to all people, for the earth is filled with violence because of them. I am surely going to destroy both them and the earth."[23] If literalism animates the signified, fantasy is the chosen signifier. Unlike other creationist renderings of Eden, which are constructed using realist registers of modern geography (e.g., longitude and latitude), Jon's map used the register of fantasy world-building.[24] Many who see Jon's map are immediately reminded of Middle Earth. This is not incidental, as Jon kept a matted version of Tolkien's map in his cubicle for reference and inspiration throughout the process of creating his map of Eden.

Jon's double-voiced map suggests an elective affinity between biblical literalism and fantasy world-building. Both are geared toward immersing adherents/consumers in an experience not empirically available. We can never know what the pre-Flood world looked like. But with the help of Jon's map, we can imagine. Imagine the beauty of an Eden with dew still on it. Imagine eight-hundred-year human lifespans, the accumulated intelligence and skill born from eight hundred years of learning from your own mistakes. Imagine a world so wicked that it incited God's wrath. And imagine the end of the rain and the power of God's grace. By banking on park visitors giving themselves over to these imaginings, the creative team sought to ignite our capacity as *homo ludens* to engage in playful reverence for biblical miracle, history, and truth.

Surprise

Jon also showed me four images previewing the brief (c. four-minute) live action pre-show film that visitors view before entering the ark. The film depicts scenes from Noah's final pre-Flood days: meeting with Methuselah before his death, Methuselah passing scrolls to Noah, Noah being tempted by "prostitutes," Noah preaching his final sermon, and the start of the rain. The content of this film's script exists almost entirely in an intertextual gap. All of these events are possible and perhaps even reasonable, given the text of Genesis 5, but none are explicitly named in that text. Methuselah was Noah's grandfather, and one translation of the biblical Hebrew name Methuselah can be glossed as "his death will bring judgment." The scrolls function indexically to mark the historicity of direct scriptural transmission (their content is not revealed, but presumably they are an early manuscript version of the first chapters of Genesis). The prostitutes function symbolically to mark Noah's righteousness (resisting sexual advances represents moral purity). The rain would had to have started at some point, but to portray Noah catching the first drop in his palm (which Jon did in an early pencil sketch on a small, square notepad) is more about creating a dramatic, multisensory effect than stating a pivotal theological claim.

In early May 2012 I ate lunch with Jon in the kitchen of the design studio. We talked candidly about the preshow script. He thought the current approach was "good," but he was feeling discontent and certain that a "better, more creative" idea could still be discovered. I asked what he meant. Depicting Noah's final pre-Flood days would "work just fine," but he thought it was "too event-driven." The "so-what" was being lost. Without any further prompting, Jon recalled a film he had recently seen that he thought could work as a model: *Remember Me,* a romance drama set in New York City. He walked me through the film without much attention to plot details. When I read the summary later that day it was clear his retelling was quite partial. But this is no matter; it was the film's ending that Jon cared about.

While the viewer of *Remember Me* knows that it is set in contemporary times, no exact date is provided. In the final part of the film, the main character is shown staring out the window of one of the World Trade Center towers. The camera zooms out to set the towers against a clear blue sky. It is the morning of September 11, 2001: the scenes that follow show the first reactions to the events at street level. Ash is floating. Another central character, a policeman, is barely managing chaotic traffic. The other central characters are shown staring upward. The object of their stare is not revealed. It would be unnecessary, gratuitous, to do so. Jon "loved" how this dramatic ending "totally changed" his viewing of the entire film. He wanted to show it to the team, and use this logic of audience surprise to revise the preshow script away from "giving everything away up front."

I don't know if Jon ever showed the film to the team, but the preshow script was not revised in this direction. Still, Jon's critique and intertextual imagining help us understand how the team's creative process involved a disposition of continually revisiting the task of materializing the Bible with a literalist imperative.

CONCLUSION

In this chapter I have argued that for Ark Encounter's creative team, biblical literalism was more a generative mode than a restrictive ideology. For them, materializing the biblical text of Genesis 6–9 was tethered to the entertainment imperative of immersing an audience. To accomplish this, their artistry relied on an ever-expanding intertextual universe of potential reference, inspiration, and information. The team worked to maximize a variety of intertextual gaps by "creat[ing] indexical connections that extend[ed] far beyond the present setting of production or reception, thereby linking a particular act to other names, places, and persons."[25] In each of the two examples, art did not emerge from an unmediated biblical literalism but from a literalist commitment imbued with a dense intertextuality.

The example of Ark Encounter urges us to recalibrate our understanding of biblical literalism and to not foreclose possibilities that might exceed the conception of literalism as a narrow, dogmatic ideology. This recalibration results from a methodological expansion. The existing scholarship about literalism comes from studies of preachers preaching, everyday readers reading, and proof-texters proof-texting. This chapter explores what happens when we look elsewhere; say, behind the scenes at a creationist design studio. From this ethnographic vantage, the paucity of scriptural detail is not a straitjacket of confining limits; it is a bonanza of artistic opportunity.

An ethnography of a creationist theme park in the making capitalizes on the productive contribution of the analysis found in chapter 1. In particular, my work in this chapter encourages us to understand Bible reading as one possibility in a diverse field of Bible uses. Ark Encounter joins other Bible-based attractions in an effort to materialize biblical texts so that people can experience the Bible, not just read it. A pivotal question for scholars moving forward will be how these various uses of the Bible fit together in the lives of individuals and communities. What are the contours of the feedback loops that connect reading and experiencing? For example: how might the experience of Ark Encounter's re-creation of Noah and the ark impact subsequent acts of reading this biblical story?

ACKNOWLEDGMENTS

This manuscript originated and developed as part of the 2014 The Bible in American Life Conference graciously hosted by the Center for the Study of Religion and American Culture. I would like to recognize the volume editors for their editorial guidance, as well as friends and colleagues who have enriched my thinking about biblical literalism over the years: Timothy Beal, Jon Bialecki, Simon Coleman, Omri Elisha, Matthew Engelke, Jeff Guhin, Susan Harding, Brian Malley, Steve Watkins, and Vincent Wimbush. Finally, select portions of this chapter, revised here, appeared in the edited volume *Scripturalizing the Human: The Written as the Political* (Routledge, 2015).

26

The Bible in the Evangelical Imagination

Daniel Silliman

DETECTIVE ROLAND MARCH sees a Bible. In some ways this is a strange scene, because the protagonist of J. Mark Bertrand's acclaimed evangelical crime novel *Back on Murder* stands in the well-established tradition of hard-boiled detectives, who guide readers through the "mean streets" of modern American confusions. Here, though, the jaded detective finds himself, of all places, in a modern megachurch. "As we pass through one of a dozen glass double doors into the sub-zero entry, a vaulted shopping mall-style atrium hung with vibrantly colored banners," the detective narrates, "I'm slightly in awe."[1]

In the Houston megachurch, the detective meets with a woman, the mother of a missing girl. He takes in the scene with a detective's eye. He sees a Bible: "On the coffee table between us, next to her tea, a fat Bible lies open, its crinkled pages bright from highlighting. A block of pink. A section of yellow. Tiny handwritten notes creeping into the margins. The book, it gives physical forms to the woman's hopes."[2]

There are three critical elements to how the Bible is represented in this fictional portrayal. The Bible is seen first of all as an object. It is a thing, weighted with physicality. Second, it is presented as having an ideal reader. There is a woman who embodies right reading. She loves the book. This is closely related to the third element: the Bible is portrayed as lending itself to particular reading practices. These are all essential to how the Bible is imagined in contemporary evangelical fiction. Detective March, however surprised he may be at contemporary American forms of Christian faith, has a good eye.

This essay surveys thirty-three evangelical novels with contemporary settings, in genres from crime to romance and war to supernatural awakening, written by evangelicals and published by large and small evangelical presses between 2004 and 2014.[3]

The survey shows the importance of these three things in how the Bible is imagined by evangelical fiction: it is a physical object, it has an ideal reader, and it lends itself to certain reading practices.

These are, of course fictional representations. They are not reliable pictures of how the Bible actually is in the world. Nevertheless, they represent ways in which the Bible is imagined. These novels reveal evangelical conceptions of the Bible and expectations of the Bible, the background understanding that shapes and informs engagement with the scripture.

EVANGELICALS' "PARTICULAR REGARD" FOR THE BIBLE

American evangelicals cannot be rightly understood without an account of their relationship to the Bible. This is part of the core identity of this broad religious movement, which currently includes about a quarter of Americans and, as Steven P. Miller recently argued, "resides at the very center of recent American history."[4] Though there are many different evangelical denominations and institutions and quite a variety of beliefs and practices, biblicism is basic to what it means to be evangelical. In his classic definition of evangelicalism, historian David Bebbington described biblicism as "a particular regard for the Bible."[5]

A lot of the study of that particular regard has focused on internal and external struggles over doctrinal understandings, especially doctrinal understanding of interpretive methods.[6] This makes sense and is important because battles over inerrancy and literalism have given shape to modern evangelicalism. Evangelicalism today cannot be understood apart from these struggles, apart from—as one popular evangelical book in the 1970s put it—the *Battle for the Bible*.[7] It is also the case that many evangelical themselves consider these doctrines to be fundamental. To take one recent example, Gregory Alan Thornbury, president of The King's College in New York City, writes that biblical inerrancy is the "bedrock principle of classic evangelicalism" and that "in the veracity of scripture, everything is at stake."[8] This is typical of evangelical leaders.

It must be noted, however, that evangelicals' relationship to the Bible is not only a matter of beliefs. As anthropologist Tanya Luhrman found in her study of Vineyard churches, evangelicals are actually often less occupied with beliefs about the Bible than with particular reading practices.[9] An increasing number of scholars have turned their attention how the Bible is read—including Corwin E. Smidt, John B. Weaver, Bryan Bibb, Amanda Friesen, and J. Derrick Lemons in this book. These studies show evangelicals' particular regard for the Bible cannot be reduced to doctrinal affirmations, as important as such statements may be. Bible reading, as anthropologist James S. Bielo shows, serves evangelicals as "a site where individuals are able to critically and reflexively articulate the categories of meaning and action that are central to their spiritual and social life."[10] The lived religion of evangelicals' relationship to the Bible needs to be accounted for in the study of this core aspect of evangelical identity, in addition to historical accounts of the doctrinal disputes.

An additional approach can usefully supplement these studies. The Bible is not only an object of evangelical beliefs and practices. It is also an object of imagination. Beliefs about the Bible and practices of engaging with the Bible are wrapped up in what might be called an evangelical imaginary. The imaginary is part of the "background understanding" of beliefs and practices, to take an idea from the philosopher Charles Taylor. The imaginary, for Taylor, is "the largely unstructured and unarticulated understanding . . . within which particular features of the world show up for us in the sense they have."[11] The imagination is important because it is the field of the assumptions that inform beliefs and orient practices. It is in the imagination that descriptive accounts are infused with normative claims, establishing the unspoken standard for what it means for something to "feel right" or "work." It is through the imaginary, as Taylor writes, that "we have a sense of how things usually go, but this is interwoven with an idea of how they ought to go."[12]

A number of scholars, including historian Molly Worthen, have called in recent years for increased attention to the evangelical imagination. As yet, however, only a few studies have looked at this aspect of evangelicalism in this way.[13] This chapter proposes to take up the task of looking at how the Bible in particular is imagined in American evangelicalism, given how central it is to evangelicalism. The suggestion is not that such a study could or should replace accounts of beliefs and practices but rather that it can deepen and broaden accounts of evangelicals and evangelicalism.

Novels can be a good source for the study of an imaginary. This study is based on a survey of thirty-three evangelical novels with contemporary settings. They each have their own respective genres and genre conventions, but the survey was restricted to exclude genres that would require separate analysis.[14] Each of these novels was written by an evangelical and published by evangelicals between 2004 and 2014. They are largely read by evangelicals as well. As works of fiction, they combine realistic, recuperative representations of contemporary American life with idealized and aspirational depictions. They are sometimes didactic, or have didactic qualities, but are not best understood as arguments. They are works of imagination. They stage evangelical imaginaries in ways that enable readers to play with and try on faith, to suspend disbelief in what can be thought of as games of "not-quite belief."[15] The representations, even at their most realist, are fictive. This means, as literary theorist Wolfgang Iser puts it, that through the conventions of fictionality, the novels' representations are framed as "as-if constructions," where "the represented world is not a world, but the reader imagines *as if* it were one." This works in such a way that the "'as if' triggers acts of ideation in the recipient."[16] Fictive representations of the Bible work to move the reader to an act of imagination about the Bible. This corpus of evangelical fiction, then, cannot rightly be taken as evidence for the way the world is. Yet it can reveal how and where facts of are interwoven with expectations and imperatives that inform and shape real-world engagements with the Bible.

Fiction is not unique in engaging the imagination, but fiction has had a large role in giving shape to evangelicals' imagination. Three of the authors surveyed in this corpus have sold books in the millions and ranked on national best-seller lists.[17] One industry expert recently estimated evangelical fiction sales gross between $75 and $85 million, annually. And there's not just a lot of it: this fiction has also often served as an important site of evangelical identity construction. As Amy Frykholm noted in her landmark study of evangelical readers of the *Left Behind* novels, "readers use the books as an authority over and against clerical authority; they use it to defend their faith in a hostile environment and also to make their environments more commodious, to claim a greater expanse of the social realm of 'home.'"[18]

Though few have studied these novels to understand contemporary evangelicalism, they are widely available and can be quite revealing. Surveying these thirty-three novels, looking specifically at portrayals of the Bible, shows important aspects of the "particular regard" that defines evangelicals' relationship to their sacred text. It shows how the Bible is imagined, as the fictional Detective March observed, to give a physical form to faith.

THE BIBLE AS AN OBJECT

The Bible is imagined first as an object. Before the Word of God is words, in evangelical fiction, it is a thing. The Bible is often quoted and referenced, both directly and indirectly, but the most notable way the Bible appears in this corpus is in descriptions of a material object. In the novels surveyed, there are more than sixty distinct physical Bibles portrayed. There are fifty references to Bibles as objects that do not involve reading.

In a small number of these, the unread book is a negative judgment on someone's spiritual state. A woman sees "the Bible lying next to the clock," as in Candace Calvert's novel *Trauma Plan*, and it is "closed, in need of a dusting...in need of reading." The object affects the character. "Familiar regret," Calvert writes, "laced with guilt, washed over her."[19] In these cases, the object itself is important apart from and prior to the text and prior to reading. It moves and convicts as an object. It is the material representation of an individual's relationship with God. This is not only true in the negative cases, however, where the dusty Bible evidences neglect.

In most cases, in these thirty-three novels, the Bible-object is depicted as the manifestation of robust faith, a personal, loving relationship with God. This can be seen with the adjectives most used for Bibles—"worn," "well-worn"—and the synonyms most used, such as "frayed." These words account for more than 26 percent of the descriptions of Bibles in this corpus. These books are imagined not as maltreated but as well loved. In each instance, the rough condition of the Bible is presented as witness to the faith of the object's owner. This is true in Randy Singer's novel *The Last Plea Bargain*, where a born-again felon "opened a Bible that was literally falling apart at the binding," and in Chris Farby's *Every Waking Moment*, where an elderly woman's Bible is seen under a lavender lampshade, "so worn and falling apart that it might have been printed by Gutenberg himself."[20]

The condition is the product of reading, of course, but is also more than that. The Bible-object is portrayed as powerful, apart from and before being read. Bibles are not just to be read. They are to be hugged close. In Meg Moseley's novel *A Stillness of Chimes* a group of young women are described as walking in a rising storm. "They clutched their Bibles," Moseley writes, "like anchors to hold them to earth in the strong wind."[21] Other depictions of this act give the same sense of the book's importance. The protagonist in Tracie Peterson and James Scott Bell's novel *City of Angels* is an orphan who clutches her father's well-worn Bible, holding it as a connection to him and as a key part of the identity she refuses to surrender to the orphanage system. She is described as clutching the book five times in the first twenty pages. She doesn't read it, however, for another one hundred pages and doesn't find peace and a faith of her own in the Bible's words for another two hundred.[22]

In some cases, in this corpus, religious experiences are even connected more directly to clutching than reading. The protagonist in Janice Thompson's romance *Fools Rush In*, for example, experiences God when she stops reading. "Clutching the Bible," the character says, "I closed my eyes for some alone time with God."[23] The Bible is conceived of as an object; its physicality is important. The Bible is imagined in these novels as something to hold close.

While the Bible-object is significant in and of itself, as an object, certain features receive more attention than others. The translation, or the brand, of the Bible is only rarely mentioned. Some commonly quoted translations in these fictions are the New International Version, the New American Standard Bible, and the New Living Translation, but that information often only appears on the copyright pages. The NASB and the NLT are never mentioned in the narratives. The NIV is mentioned only once in the surveyed corpus, in the form of a smartphone Bible app.[24] Two Bible brands, the King James Version and Gideons', are mentioned occasionally, normally in a way that is significant to the plot. In Francine Rivers's romance *Bridge to Haven*, for example, a woman who has left home reads a Gideon Bible, which she gets at a motel. It is a sign of her distance from home. Later, she accepts a replacement, a well-worn Bible that is given her by the man who loves her. The older object signifies her return to where she belongs.[25] In more than 90 percent of the cases, however, the Bible is just "the Bible," with no visible evidence of the human hands at work in its production. Bibles are unbranded in the evangelical imagination.

Other aspects of the books relevant to their status as commodities also are only occasionally mentioned. About 5 percent of the Bibles are described as having gilt-edged pages. Almost 10 percent are described as having leather binding. Seventeen percent are described having a color: maroon, burgundy, brown, or black.

Despite the object's obvious status as a commodity, the Bible is also not imagined as part of the system of economic exchange, for the most part. Of the more than sixty physical Bibles imagined in these thirty-three novels, including a smartphone app and an audio Bible, only one is described as being purchased.[26] The others are given as gifts, appear out of nowhere, are inherited, or date to time immemorial. Though the object-ness of the books is critical, it's not conceived of as an object like other objects but instead is set apart. This is the first aspect of how the Bible is imagined in evangelical fiction.

THE IDEAL READER

After Bible ownership, the surveyed novels emphasize readership. This is an important part of how the Bible is imagined: The Bible has an ideal reader. The ideal reader is not normally the protagonist of these thirty-three novels, but rather someone who performs reading for the protagonist, presenting a kind of engagement with the Bible that the main character longs to and often learns to emulate. It is an aspirational presentation of what good Bible reading is like.

Most often, the ideal reader is an older woman. This image is repeated throughout these books: an older woman in an easy chair reads the Bible. In Richard L. Mabry's thriller *Code Blue*, for example, the protagonist finds the elderly "Dora Kennedy, her hair in curlers, her flannel robe pulled around her neck...in an easy chair in the front room, reading a Bible."[27] In Lynette Eason's crime novel *Too Close to Home*, a character is presented with this same scene. "He spied his mother asleep in the recliner," Eason writes, "the television still on, the Bible open in her lap."[28] The scene evokes a longing in the protagonists, love for the Bible reader mingling with the desire to have the comfort of faith that she has. In Alice J. Wisler's romance *Rain Song*, the protagonist recognizes her own lost heritage of faith in the same scene. First she finds her aunt asleep. The familiar picture: "On a small TV tray, her bifocals rest on top of her maroon Bible. A cloudy orange bottle of heart medication leans against the remote control."[29] Later in the novel, the protagonist is reminded of a similar image of her grandmother, establishing this as a family legacy. "I imagine my grandmother," the narrator says, going "back home to her ginger tea brewing in her bone china teapot...to her maroon-covered Bible and her chair where she can fall asleep with ease during episodes of *Columbo*."[30]

As can be seen in these examples, this ideal image is present in a variety of genres. It's not just female authors. It's not just in novels targeted at middle-aged women. This picture of reading has a real purchase on the evangelical imagination.

Notably, the ideal reader in this corpus of fiction is not a formal religious authority. There are actually very few members of the clergy in these novels. When they do appear, they're often presented as antagonists. There are thirteen references to religious authorities reading the Bible in this corpus. Five are negative. They are negative because they attempt to delegitimize individual and everyday readings of the Bible. They insert themselves as mediators between the protagonist and the Bible, claiming professional status that bars amateurs from direct access to the text. There is an associate pastor in William Paul Young's novel *Cross Roads*, for example, who is described as "the guy with the big Bible."[31] He uses that big Bible to tell a woman that she is under his authority. Challenged on this point, he claims the Bible can only be rightly read by someone who has been formally trained and has an official position as a legitimate interpreter of the text. "Did you go to a Bible school or seminar that I don't know about?" he demands when challenged. "Have you suddenly gotten ordained so that you understand all the mysteries?"[32] Authority mystifies reading in order to preserve authority.

In a number of cases, this mystification takes the form of denying the doctrine of inerrancy, which has been so important to the development of evangelicalism. A liberal minister in Tracie Peterson and James Scott Bell's novel *City of Angels* explicitly preaches higher criticism. He claims "the Germans had shown that the Bible was a collection of merely human writings, full of errors and contradictions, and was to be viewed with a skeptical eye."[33] It's quickly apparent, however, that the battle over inerrancy is a battle over authority and access, a battle of who has the right to read the Bible. "I have a doctorate from one of the finest seminaries in the country. I think I know whereof I speak," the minister says. The hero retorts, "My seminary is the Word of God and in it God speaks."[34] The novel imagines the access an amateur has to the Bible is at stake in the doctrine of inerrancy. Professionals, in the evangelical imagination, are sometimes the enemies of the Bible. In this corpus, that's true about 38 percent of the time that clergy are mentioned. These clergy are imagined to be obstacles to faith. In the other cases, the clergy still are not modeling right-reading, however. They are not imagined to enable Bible reading or faith but rather serve an affirmative function in the narratives. When they read a text aloud, often from the pulpit, it confirms what the protagonist already knows. In a number of cases, the clergy are shown at the climax or denouement, reading a verse that summarizes the theme of the novel. These men (all of them are men) are not presented as ideal readers but are imagined as having the authority to represent God's "amen" to those who have read the Bible for themselves.

The ideal reader in these novels is the reader who models Bible reading. She—most of them are women, though there are exceptions—performs reading in a way that others can emulate and eventually appropriate. She reads in such a way that her image itself is a witness. She reads so others can learn to rightly read by how she has been reading, even without any didactic instructions.

In some cases, in these fictions, that act of imitation is presented as quite literal. In Creston Mapes's novel *Nobody*, for example, the main character is moved by the memory of his mother's Bible reading. He recalls that she read so religiously that she was in the act even as she died.[35] He has inherited her worn Bible but at the beginning of the novel doesn't remember where it is. At the end of the novel, struggling to recover his faith, he picks it up and tries to do what she did. "I turned the pages," he narrates, "looking for anything that would jump out at me, that would chase away the helplessness and give me hope. I landed in Proverbs where several lines of text had been circled in blue."[36] The mother's reading becomes the son's as he follows her lead. This happens multiple times in the thirty-three novels surveyed here: the image of the modeled reading compels the protagonist to pick up the book, and the inherited Bible flops open, as if of its own accord, to verses that were important to the model reader and now speak directly to the protagonist's own crisis.[37]

The ideal reader's influence is not always so direct, though. What's more common is for the protagonist to simply assume the reading posture and practice that has been modeled. The main character in Chris Farby's *Every Waking Moment*, for example, sees an old woman at a nursing home who reads the Bible every morning. The protagonist responds, initially, by saying, "I wish I had your faith.... I believe. I just don't know if it makes any difference. God seems awfully disinterested in my life. But your faith is real and vibrant."[38] Nearly two hundred pages later, the protagonist has changed and has taken up the ritual of morning Bible reading. "Miriam was finishing her cup of coffee," Farby writes. "She had her Bible open, reading in the book of John, marveling at the simple truths she encountered."[39]

Regardless of whether the influence is direct or indirect, the new reader, with newfound faith, is seen to imitate the ideal reader, repeating the often-repeated aspirational image of devotional reading. This is a core element to how the evangelical "particular regard" for the Bible is imagined in these novels.

PREFERRED READING PRACTICES

In the analysis of the ideal reader, it becomes apparent that particular reading practices are also portrayed in these evangelical novels as especially powerful. The Bible is imagined to lend itself to certain sorts of reading. The most powerful reading practice portrayed in this corpus might be called simple reading. This can be associated with biblical literalism, a common hermeneutic among evangelicals, but the hallmarks of literalism, such as the insistence on historical rather than allegorical interpretations of certain passages, are almost entirely absent. Simple reading, distinct from literal reading, is the idea that one should just read. There are no special requirements beyond opening the Bible. In fact, after "worn" and "well worn," the most common description of a Bible in this corpus is "open." About 25 percent of the descriptions of Bibles emphasize it being open.

Again and again, what might be taken for a very complicated act, requiring certain specialized training or education, is shown, instead, to be a simple matter. In addition to the cases where the book seems to open itself, this instruction is given explicitly. "All you have to do," one character says in Katie Ganshert's romance *A Broken Kind of Beautiful*, "is pick it up and listen."[40] The act of opening the Bible is portrayed in these novels as itself sufficient. In a pivotal scene in Francine Rivers's *Bridge to Haven*, for example, the Bible "lay open on the bed," with the result that the "words broke through the walls" the character had "built around herself and brought them tumbling down."[41] The novels portray the Bible readers as being met, in a sense, halfway. They open the book; the book responds.

In some cases this event has a quasi-mystical character. In others, though, the characters find the Bible lends itself to simple reading in more mundane ways. The main character in Alison Pittman's romance *All for a Song* does not magically open the Bible to a verse that exactly speaks to her situation. She finds, nevertheless, that the Bible itself helps her know what to read. "She took the Bible from the drawer and opened to the front pages," Pittman writes, "seeking the list of Scripture references intended to guide the reader to passages that would provide comfort and instruction in times of need . . . she ran her finger down the page, registering the verses meant to give 'Courage in Time of

Fear.'"[42] The reader doesn't need a hermeneutic. The reader need not know what a hermeneutic is. No special skills are required. In evangelical fiction, the most important practice of reading is simply reading, and the Bible is imagined to lend itself to this.

Implicit in the practice of simple reading is an idea about the purpose of reading, which is intertwined with a portrayal of a particular kind of devotional reading. The Bible is portrayed as lending itself especially to therapeutic life-applications. People read and find comfort and affirmation that applies to their lives and their situations.

In a small number of cases in these thirty-three novels, the Bible is read for moral instruction. In Bradilyn Collins's novel *Deceit*, for example, a character uses the Bible to argue against even white lies.[43] And in a small number of cases, it is used to explain points of doctrine, such as Jake Smith's baseball novel *Wish*, where a character references "the 'many mansions' verse in the Bible" to talk about heaven.[44] These cases are in a distinct minority, though. About 7 percent of the portrayals of Bible reading are theological explanations; another 7 percent involve moral instruction.

Mostly, the Bible is read for comfort. It is imagined in these novels as being read for the purpose of finding something personally and emotionally relevant. The Bible is depicted as applying to the contemporary American characters' lives, and in a therapeutic way. An example of this can be found in Lisa Harris's crime novel *Dangerous Passages*. The heroine takes a break from catching a serial killer to sit "curled up in her father's leather chair beside the office window, reading the Bible."[45] She is reassured by her reading. She doesn't find specific answers in the Bible, she says, "as much as the familiar reminder that even though life is tough—sometimes even dark and horrible— that doesn't change who God is. He's still in control."[46] In this fiction, this is the main motive people are imagined to have for reading the Bible.

This therapeutic reading is shown to be sustained by reading practices that evangelicals sometimes call "devotions." About 58 percent of the Bible readings in this corpus could be classified as devotions. Devotional reading has this therapeutic orientation, visible not only in the purpose of reading but in the practice. Devotions typically involve quiet mornings, a nice place to sit, coffee, and a calm state of mind. In the opening lines of Karen Kingsbury's *Fifteen Minutes*, for example, a main character practices this sort of reading, with the expected result. He feels close to God. This is the scene that opens the novel: "Zach Dylan," Kingsbury writes, "held a steaming mug of black coffee in one hand and his Bible in the other. He stood on the wraparound porch of his parents' farmhouse and watched a pair of Arabian horses run through the Kentucky bluegrass.... He loved Jesus more than his next breath. He could feel Him as close as his skin."[47]

Other details of devotional reading practices are also portrayed, including practices of note taking, Bible-praying, and journaling.[48] All those worn Bibles literally bear the markings of devotional reading, in which the reader reads the text and responds to the text with text.

In other instances, characters are seen struggling to engage in these devotional rites, but the portrayal nonetheless reinforces the therapeutic value of this approach to reading. The main character in Janice Thompson's *Fools Rush In* struggles to find the peace of mind to read in this best way but is rewarded for persisting. "I took the time to reach for my Bible," the character narrates, "determined not to let yesterday's events determine today's attitude. So what if everything had crumbled around me last night? . . . I stumbled from Scripture to Scripture, finally landing on just the right one."[49] In Lynette Eason's *Too Close to Home*, a woman makes the mistake of not finding a comfortable place to sit, but her reading is portrayed as being so rewarding that it doesn't matter. "Her kitchen table wasn't exactly the most comfortable spot in the house," Eason writes, "but she'd started reading 1 Peter as she waited for her coffee to brew and hadn't been able to stop. . . . How comforting to know God was on her side and she held power against that evil."[50]

This is the main reason to read the Bible as imagined in evangelical fiction. It is also how to read the Bible. Practices and promises, enactments and expectations are woven together in a biblicist imaginary. The Bible, which is portrayed as an object, first, and also as having an ideal reader, is also imagined as being accessible, available, and very emotionally rewarding to read.

To an extent these presentations of Bible reading are didactic, of course. They can be seen simply as attempts to teach readers how to read the Bible. It is also the case, though, that the reading of the Bible is staged as fiction. The novels don't make arguments for particular practices as much as they prompt readers to an ideation of Bible reading, inviting them to suspend disbelief, identify with the characters, and imagine the Bible. These novels actually don't stray too far into the didactic. Even when they do, however, it is in the context of fiction. Bible-reading instruction is presented within the frame of an invitation to imagination, the novels portraying how those who have this particular regard for the Bible expect Bible reading to work. What can be seen in these representations of Bible reading is the development of an evangelical sense of how things go and how things should go, a "background understanding" that informs and shapes the way many people approach the Bible.

CONCLUSION

In a number of interesting ways, the findings of the Bible in American Life survey align with the evangelical imaginary that is visible in evangelical fiction. The survey found that devotional reading predominates in America. In fact, chapter 1 reports that "Bible readers consult scripture for personal prayer and devotion three times more than they do to learn about abortion, homosexuality, poverty, or war." Amy Plantinga Pauw connects this therapeutic reading to an evangelical attitude, where "Scripture is a companion in the journey of faith" and the question that guides reading is "What does this verse mean to me?" In evangelical novels, one finds an invitation to an ideation of a Bible that works like this, to expect Bible reading to provide comfort and reassurance. The novels reveal this imaginary, the background expectation of how the Bible is effective comfort.

The study also found that most Americans who read the Bible do not seek interpretive assistance, they simply read. A majority—56 percent—said they don't ask for assistance in their Bible reading. Whether or not they practice a particular method of reading, it could be the case that they don't ask for help because of expectations of what Bible reading should be like. The Bible, if it works the way it is imagined in evangelical fiction, will open itself to the reader.

Among Americans who read the Bible in the last year, the study found only 21 percent of Bible readers and 11 percent of the population as a whole consulted clergy for help in understanding the Bible. One could think about this fact in the context of expectations of clergy. In evangelical fiction, clergy are not portrayed as helpful in understanding the Bible. They can affirm Bible reading, but also they often, in defense of their specialized authority, make it harder to read the Bible. It can be argued that at least some of the people who are reading religiously and who don't ask the clergy for help act that way because authoritative reading clashes with their unarticulated normative descriptions of the Bible. If one imagines the Bible as a quasi-sacred object that offers itself to simple reading, asking for a specialist's help is tantamount to denying the Bible's power.

The study also found that Americans have a somewhat conflicted attitude toward Bible translations. Rates of Bible ownership are known to be quite high, in America, and yet people buy more Bibles every year.[51] Christian bookstores report that sales of Bibles have continued to grow in recent years, and the number of available editions of the Bible continues to proliferate.[52] The New International Version, under copyright by Zondervan, has long surpassed the King James Version as the best seller. Nevertheless, the Bible in American Life survey found that the older version, which is not copyrighted, persists as the most popular among those who read the Bible. Fifty-five percent of Bible readers said they used the KJV (if at a less frequent rate than NIV readers).[53]

Historian Mark Noll notes that these decisions about buying Bibles and which Bibles to buy, reading Bibles and which Bibles to read, are made in the context of bookstores "now crowded with alternative versions" of the text. The argument of this essay is that that context is very important. It is important to consider those bookstores and to take into account the many other books besides the Bible that crowd the shelves at evangelical retail outlets and that also do brisk business at secular chains, big-box retailers, and online booksellers.[54] Careful consideration of the evangelical novels that sell alongside Bibles can usefully supplement studies of beliefs and practices by revealing an evangelical biblicist imaginary that shapes the expectations of a sizable group of people in American culture today. These fictions, to borrow a line from a fictional detective, give imaginary form to faith in the Bible.

It is not down on any map; true places never are.

—HERMAN MELVILLE, *MOBY-DICK*

27

Feeling the Word

SENSING SCRIPTURE AT SALVATION MOUNTAIN

Sara M. Patterson

IN 1971 LEONARD Knight walked into the Raven Balloon Industry building in South Dakota with a plan. Knight wanted to purchase a hot air balloon for the $700 he had in his pocket. He recalled that "it was like trying to buy a brand new Cadillac for seven hundred dollars, and they weren't interested. And as I was walking out I saw some big bags of balloon material and they said they sold them for five dollars a bag because it was material that'd been cut wrong."[1] Knight quickly had a new plan to use those bits of material to create his own balloon. The balloon Knight constructed took over a decade to sew. In the early 1980s, Knight went out into the desert of southern California to fly the handmade hot air balloon that he had built to celebrate his born-again Christian experience.

That hot air balloon that proclaimed God's love never flew because some of the material had begun to rot. Knight also never consulted an industrial pattern but rather followed his instincts about size and shape. In the end, there was only one problem, and it was an insurmountable one. Knight "made it too big; it was two hundred foot high and one hundred foot wide, four times as big as the ones they ride in."[2] Though in that moment he felt like a failure, he claimed that it was "not because of God. I felt like a failure because Leonard didn't listen properly. Leonard was too far ahead of God. Leonard wanted to do it his way."[3] And so despite his failure, Knight still felt a call to thank God in some big, beautiful, and public way for the gifts he had been given. He stayed in the desert and decided that instead of a balloon he was called to build a mountain to honor his God and to share his faith with others.

The site where Knight chose to build his mountain is on the outskirts of what is today known as Slab City, California (a free recreational vehicle camp). The "slabs" of

Slab City were left behind when the U.S. government deemed the area an unnecessary military base in 1961. Slab City, in California's Imperial Valley between the Salton Sea and the Chocolate Mountains, is a community full of retired "snowbirds" (who live across the continent but head to the desert of Southern California during the cold months of the year) and social dropouts who travel around doing odd jobs and eschewing the middle-class lifestyle of economic achievement celebrated by most Americans. Slab City is a unique spot that has been described as "not so sinister as it is a strange, forlorn quarter of America. It is a town that is not really a town."[4] The town is not really a town because of its shifting cast of characters, lack of a structured governmental system, and lack of utilities. Perhaps the ethos of Slab City is best encapsulated in a song about it from the film *Into the Wild*: "We ain't got much money, but we got lots of class. If you don't like my style—kiss my ass."[5]

Knight fit right in with his Imperial Valley neighbors who valued the freedoms that distance from society offered. No one ever questioned the fact that Knight set up shop on lands owned by the state of California. No one ever wondered if it would be all right or appropriate for Knight to build a public expression of his private religious experience on land owned by the state. No one bothered Knight, and he never bothered anyone. He just wanted the freedom to honor his God. And so Knight's first mountain was built out of cement, scraps he had found in nearby junkyards, and paint. Knight spent around five years working on his "God is Love" mountain until, in 1989, a small rainstorm caused a crack.[6] That crack led to the collapse of the entire mountain: "Everybody thought I'd be discouraged, and people said—God must not want you to put that mountain up. But my thought was—Thank you, God, for taking the mountain down. Nobody got hurt. . . . And I just looked up and I said—'God, I'm gonna have to do it again. But I'm gonna have to do it with more smarts.'"[7]

Undeterred, and still finding fault in his own choices rather than concluding he had maybe misunderstood his divine call, Knight rebuilt the mountain with more smarts; he used materials and techniques he learned in the desert. Knight took straw bales often donated by local farmers and turned them into adobe bricks by mixing clay and water and adding it to the bales. He then shellacked over those bricks with thousands of gallons of paint. With additional "junk" that he collected in the desert—discarded tires, parts of cars, windows—Knight created the mountain that stands to this day.

Knight's life follows the patterns of early Christian desert ascetics who escaped a society and church they found too materialistic, too complicated, and too corrupt and fled to the desert to focus on their relationship with God. These desert hermits rejected the social categories and expectations of their time and fled to the wilderness to experience the freedoms of that place. In the desert they were sought out by fellow believers who could not or chose not to leave their communities but believed the desert hermits had found a special type of wisdom alone in the desert—a type of wisdom they and everyone else needed. It was precisely because the desert teachers had renounced the values their society held dear that they were perceived as having a special and necessary type of wisdom.[8] Pilgrims travel to Salvation Mountain today for precisely the same reasons.[9]

FIGURE 27.1 Salvation Mountain

It was *away* from the culture he found too materialistic and too attached to a false notion of success that Knight was able to set up an alternative world with a distinct system of exchange. Knight's alternative system had at its base the notion of gift giving. His God gave him the gifts that enabled him to build a mountain; that mountain was then his gift to the world. Pilgrims gave gifts in exchange for the wisdom Knight offered them—the wisdom he found in the sacred spaces of the California deserts—*away* from society. It was in this space set apart that Knight fashioned his mountain to serve as an invitation to all peoples to participate in a peaceful and loving millennium.

In the middle-of-nowhere desert Knight created a world of gift giving as a direct critique of the capitalist market in the United States. His world, his sacred space, is a challenge to the larger economy in the United States, where money and status mark an individual's identity and where the "little guy" never seems to matter to anyone. Knight set up his mountaintop as a prophetic platform from which he critiqued the capitalist market economy, Christian denominationalism, and Christian exclusivism toward the world's other religious traditions.

In this essay I will explore two facets of the biblical interpretation that takes place at Salvation Mountain. The first portion of the essay is an analysis of the juxtaposition of biblical texts in the artwork on the mountain. Salvation Mountain offers a visual worldview that stands out precisely because the colors and shapes are so different from the landscapes of the desert. Salvation Mountain invites people to it, asking them to step closer and experience the small and distinct world it offers. I will then move to investigating visitors' experiences of the biblical text as object at Salvation Mountain. I will examine the way touch plays a prominent role in their accounts. Touching "the Word" inspires a sensory, aesthetic response, an embodied experience of and acceptance of the religious worldview offered at the mountain. Over and over visitors suggest that they have *felt the Word* in deep and profound ways at Salvation Mountain.

Visitors to the site describe this "feeling" of the Word as a much more profound and *real* experience of the biblical text. Such experiences trouble the privileging of sight and sound in the study of religion. Scholars have accepted the Protestant claim that "the Word" is significant as a way to encounter the divine through biblical texts that people read and sermons that people hear. In order to fully understand the ways believers encounter the biblical text, we must expand our study of the various sensory ways that "the Word" is engaged and rethink our assumptions about how believers engage the text.

Let's begin by exploring how "the Word" is portrayed on the mountain and developed into a distinct worldview through the juxtaposition of various biblical passages. The largest letters on the mountain proclaim "God is Love"; this sentiment is affirmed and expanded on the right side of the mountain with large letters announcing: "Love is Universal." For Knight, God's love is universal while also being eminently personal, recognizing the particularity and individuality of each person. The second largest message on the face of the mountain is one that encourages pilgrims to say Knight's version of the Sinner's Prayer, the same prayer he said the day he became a born-again Christian: "Jesus I'm a Sinner Please Come Upon My Body, and Into My Heart." Knight's image of Jesus is one of a man knocking at the door of the heart of every human, waiting to be let in. He claimed that the sacrifice Jesus made was for everyone and each individual could receive the promise of salvation and heavenly reward if willing to accept the offer and let Jesus in.

Although Knight's message is universal, it has a subtext with a particular flavor in the Christian tradition. Like many Pentecostals, Knight's favorite biblical passages to quote were often from the book of Acts. Acts 2:38, specifically ("Then Peter said unto them, Repent, and be baptized every one of you in the name of Jesus Christ for the remission of sins, and ye shall receive the gift of the Holy Ghost") and Acts 2:2–4 ("2: And suddenly there came a sound from heaven as of a rushing mighty wind, and it filled all the house where they were sitting. 3: And there appeared unto them cloven tongues like as of fire, and it sat upon each of them. 4: And they were all filled with the Holy Ghost, and began to speak with other tongues, as the Spirit gave them utterance").

What aligned Knight with trends in the Pentecostal and Holiness traditions was not just his literalist interpretation of the Bible but also his focus on a second baptism by fire. For Knight this was a second embodied experience of his faith: "This happened to me the second day I got saved. Shi-ya-comma-mulk-you-lu....And I said, 'What's that?' I didn't know what it was, but it's in the Bible. Speaking in tongues is in the Bible. So God blessed me with his tongue."[10] Knight understood tongues to be a gift given to true believers since the time of the disciples. For him, the gift of tongues confirmed the

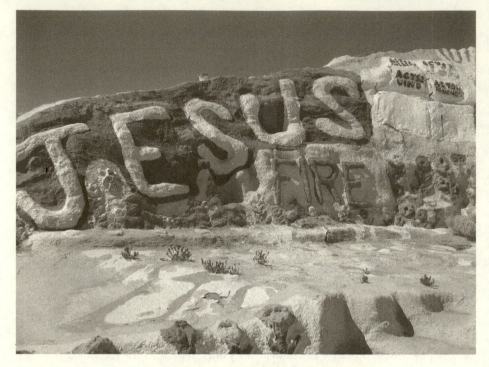

FIGURE 27.2 Jesus Fire portion of Salvation Mountain

truthfulness of the individual's born-again experience. Throughout his life Knight kept up a private, frequent dialogue with God and so understood speaking in tongues as a special prayer language that only God could understand.

Knight embraced a profoundly *embodied* theology. Perhaps the two most significant aspects of that embodied theology come in his version of the Sinner's Prayer and his concept of baptism by fire. Knight's version of the Sinner's Prayer on the front of the mountain is rather distinct: "Jesus I'm a sinner. *Please come upon my body* and into my heart."[11]

When asked about the "enter into my body," Knight said: "I got that in there. In Revelation . . . Jesus stands at the door and he knocks to come in." In the narrative of his own born-again experience it was only when he said the Sinner's Prayer that Knight claimed he felt his body change: "I started to repent . . . I could feel it. . . . It felt so beautiful, like the sensation of God. [The] sensation of a scripture that no other man had hardly seen and [I've] seen it." Here it is clear that "the Word" became real for Knight when he experienced it in a fully embodied way, an experience he believed to be profoundly unique, aesthetically beautiful, and accessible to anyone open to the message.

Knight also discussed the Holy Spirit in an embodied way. At times he saw the spirit like a comforter (and for him "comforter" indicated a bed comforter). Citing John 14:26, John 15:26, and John 16:7, Knight explained that "a comforter is a quilt. You can feel a comforter. . . . And sometimes I feel comforted, because I ask for it."[12] When Knight explained this perspective to me, he grabbed a bed comforter off the floor of

FIGURE 27.3 Leonard Knight

one of the cave-like structures attached to the mountain and wrapped it tightly around himself, showing in a visible way just how close he believed the Holy Spirit could be and just how comforted he could feel by it.

Just as nineteenth-century Baptists and Methodists and twentieth-century Pentecostal and Holiness believers did, Knight placed emphasis on *experience* over education as the site of religious authority. This is most evident in the way he described himself; he often referred to himself as stupid and silly, thus simultaneously reinforcing God's power and his own experiential authority. He claimed that "God scraped the bottom of the barrel to have me work on that mountain. Maybe he just wanted to prove that he could pick somebody that really couldn't do it and then make him do it."[13] In telling this part of his story, Knight repeated to visitors a core Pentecostal message: that God and the Holy Spirit choose who they choose. The message is ultimately a democratic one. The Holy Spirit may enter into and fill the body of anyone, and humans are not to judge that choice. In embracing this belief, Knight had the theological underpinnings for his social outlook. If humans are not to judge, then he had no right to judge anyone or discriminate based on the racial, economic, and gender categories that society, not God, had created. Knight felt a religious call and command to love everyone.

Within American Christianity, Knight's theology and exegetical method are closely allied with the Pentecostal and Holiness traditions, yet these traditions are not often linked with inclusive claims about other religious traditions. Yet Knight claimed that his God-Is-Love message transcended the boundaries of all the world's religions.

He accepted the validity of other religious traditions and did not believe that people of other traditions, Muslims, Hindus, Jews, and Buddhists, were going to hell. In fact, Knight's theology of hell was relatively nonexistent, particularly in the last decade of his life. Knight was not concerned about people receiving some ultimate judgment in the next life but was concerned with developing and encouraging love in this one. Knight claimed Jesus as *his way* of finding God's love and transforming his life. In the end, though, his concern was that others were experiencing God's love and living that love in the world; how they got there, their faith tradition, was less important.

Knight disagreed with Christian exclusivists and also with premillennialists who believe that the world will get much worse before it gets any better, stating that "the rapture is not in the bible... [it's] a man-made thing." Instead, "God is going to come down with a love. Everybody is going to love better.... And it's coming." While the mountain serves as the promise of things yet to come, it is also evidence of movement toward that promise. For Knight and many of his visitors, the mountain is the message and evidence of the truth of the message all in one.

I'd like to turn now to exploring how the mountain serves as evidence—tactile evidence—of the truth of the message for visitors. To do so, though, we must first begin with what people see. The vision of Salvation Mountain is, at first, just that. It is image. It is an assault on the colors and textures of the desert. One visitor explained that he was "not sure what to expect. When I got across the railroad tracks and began to turn the corner I saw the Mountain. It was truly breathtaking. 'God is Love,' can be seen from far away."[14] Another pilgrim remembers quite clearly her approach to Salvation Mountain, an approach that began with a sense of feeling lost, transitioned into disappointment, and then became awe as she came closer to the mountain and *saw* it. "'What mountain? It is a desert out here!' but I kept on driving. As I got closer, my nerves and fear started to set in, mind you; I was alone in a very odd location. I had passed several hitchhikers, dreadlocked hippies, campsites of leftover 'Flower Children' from the 60s, desert people, campers and seekers of the strange, like myself. . . . There it was, Salvation Mountain! I pulled over to the side of the road to park, and yes, somewhat in disbelief. My initial thought was 'You have got to be kidding; I drove out here for this?' I cannot express to you enough this is where first impressions can be so WRONG!...As I walked closer, I found myself in complete and utter 'Awe.'"[15] This pilgrim traveled with expectations, expectations that were first disappointed and then met in spades. And they were met only as she came closer to the mountain and it engaged all of her senses.

William T. Vollman, a historian of the Imperial Valley, described his experience of Salvation Mountain in a similar way: "Up close, it became the world; a few steps away it began to resolve into the puny production of a single human being."[16] What was it that made these two visitors feel both unimpressed *and* full of wonder? Perhaps it was the scattered paint cans, the junk littering the area, or the mountain itself. The scale seems to inspire two types of responses in people, at times even in the same person. There is at one and the same time a "*This* is it?!" response and a "How could one person do all *this*?!" response. In part, it is hard for anyone to imagine what a thirty-year project will look like. Yet this strange juxtaposition captures something deeper that is occurring. From a distance the sight of Salvation Mountain invites one to it because of its colorful landscape juxtaposed against miles of dusty brown and sagebrush green landscape. It does not seem large or mountain-like, though. It does not jut up from the earth in a particularly impressive way. Yet when one draws nearer and accepts the invitation to focus on all of its intricate details, and when one stands at its base and looks up, the mountain does, indeed, "become the world," filling the field of vision and dramatically altering the horizon. It is in the midst of these contradictory sensory experiences that pilgrims often experience a sense of awe.

To complicate matters further, people do not always articulate religious experiences in terms of word and belief. Those experiences often remain in a category beyond full expression precisely because they are the most profound. Religious studies scholar David Morgan argues throughout his work that religious belief, even though we think of belief as an intellectual activity, is actually an embodied activity. "Making, exchanging, displaying, and using artifacts are principal aspects of human doing," he reminds us. Most religious peoples "live their religion in the grit and strain of a felt life that embodies their relation to the divine as well as to one another. The transcendent does not come to them as pure light or sublime sensations in most cases, but in the odor of musty shrines or moldering robes or the pantry where they pray."[17] Religion resides in the self and the stuff, and dualisms imposed by scholars are often not significant distinctions to the person experiencing it all.

Morgan has also challenged the way scholars of art and image tend to understand religious believers' interactions with sacred objects. First, he disputes the ideas that sight is the primary sense and that sight is primarily an intellectual sensory activity. He asserts that sight is often thought of as a "pristine and distant form of contemplation" and that we imagine it as disembodied and immaterial. He argues instead that we must think about sight in relation to other senses and that we must remember that seeing is an embodied activity. Morgan emphasizes the way senses work together in order to create experience. In particular he asserts that sight anticipates touch—by seeing "mass relative size, distance, movement, and texture." If seeing functions to anticipate what something will feel like, then, "religious seeing would mean encountering the sacred in material terms."[18] As I will show, in the instance of Salvation Mountain, Knight has constructed a world emphasizing *felt* religion. And so at Salvation Mountain the senses often work together toward a tactile experience of religious ideas, claims, and experiences.

It was not until I had collected well over one hundred visitors' accounts and started to read through them all at the same time that I realized something. Over and over again, visitors begin by talking about what they saw but quickly turn to what they touched and what they felt when they touched the mountain. And it made me realize that touch was really what the mountain was all about. Our experiences of sight seem to maintain a distinction between self and other, between the viewer and the viewed— there is me and there is the thing or person that I am looking at. In this way, sight can reinforce a dualistic perspective. Touch, however, troubles such dualisms. When I touch something, my hand conforms to the shape of it. My body is affected by its interaction with whatever I touch. Similarly my touch can transform the object that I am touching. Thus the relationship between self and other, between me and the thing I am touching, becomes more complicated. Self and other, subject and object, are two dualisms that Salvation Mountain collapses. For this reason, touch can often surface as the most profound aspect of a religious experience. The power of touch to transform and burst through dualisms—and the fact that Knight invites people to touch and to feel in a culture that suggests that such activities are often inappropriate, especially around artwork—helps explain why so many pilgrims have such profound experiences at Salvation Mountain and why they believe that they experience the divine there.

Touch is an interesting sensory experience to explore. It troubles the easy dualisms that some of our senses appear to reinforce. It also is a sense that is highly regulated in our culture. We are told from our youth, perhaps especially in our youth, not to touch certain things. The things that we aren't supposed to touch are especially important, special, we are told. A common phrase repeated to children is "You see with your eyes, not with your hands." What does this saying imply? That to truly behold something, our impulse is often to actually hold it. Touching makes sight more powerful; it confirms what we see. One of the many sets of things we are told we should not dare to touch is art. We are to behold it but not to hold it. We are to be moved by it, but through our eyes. Knight's mountain crashes through those cultural regulations. He has built a piece of art that invites viewers to come closer, to climb, to experience it. In so doing, he is asking visitors to transgress the boundaries that their culture upholds. They transgress boundaries as they climb a mountain of transgressed boundaries. He asks them to behold it and to hold it.

The mountain serves as evidence that precedes words and expressed emotions. It is the experience and the emotion itself. That the mountain exists in the middle of nowhere contributes, for those who believe, to the claims it makes. In this regard the narrative is the same: only a crazy man would spend thirty years in the desert, *unless* that crazy man was sent there by divine command. The fact that Leonard Knight placed the mountain outside the capitalist marketplace, never offering to sell it, always offering small mementos as gifts to visitors, has also led to visitors sensing it as a place set apart, an alternative world, a sacred space.

Pilgrims respond to the space. They receive Knight's message as embodied beings and react in ways that become standardized as visitors begin to share their experiential stories with one another, both in person and in the online world.[19] Pilgrims begin with what they saw: they admire the artwork and realize the size and complexity of it. They then begin to talk about what they hear at the mountain, the stories of Knight's own embodied experience of his faith, his welcoming, inclusive theology, and his message that God loves everyone. Then pilgrims to the mountain often note that being able to climb the mountain serves as a deeper level of *feeling* the mountain's message. They use such words and phrases as "unique," "mind boggling," and "welcoming" in their efforts to articulate what it means to them to be able to climb Knight's witness to God's love. One woman visiting from Germany claimed that "climbing the mountain [was] like being a part of it. It's like the heart in the desert."[20]

In visitors' accounts it becomes clear that touch is a central component of the religious experience of Salvation Mountain, both physical touching and being "touched" in the sense of being "moved by." These two types of being "touched" are related in intriguing ways. There is the touch of a physical body against another body or object, as when visitors to Salvation Mountain place their hands on the mountain, climb the mountain, and feel the material reality of it. Then there is the sense that they have *felt* the truthfulness of the mountain's claims about God. Both types of touching—the sensory and the internal—occur frequently in pilgrim narratives. This is not surprising. Knight's most intense experience of the divine came through a warming of his heart, feeling touched by the spirit, and then seeing and hearing the ways the intense experiences of *feeling* manifested in his life.[21] That he would then create an artwork that invites pilgrims to engage all of their senses but to ultimately focus on *feeling* makes sense. His mountain is a witness that can be seen, smelled, felt, and touched, asking its visitors to serve as witnesses and to feel in their own right. It asks them to *feel the Word*.

Climbing the mountain is a distinct way of touching and feeling that surfaces again and again in pilgrim accounts, and in these accounts the act of touching and climbing changes one's perspective, how one sees and understands. One pilgrim recounted:

> He encouraged me to climb . . . [e]specially with that camera. So I half climbed and half crawled up the sunshine-yellow stairs and foot path that wind across the face of the mountain. My backpack shifted alarmingly and I put my hand down for support. I noticed in places that the paint had chipped off in great thick chunks and I wondered how many years of dedication and how many layers of acrylic it takes to produce something like that. As I climbed I tried not to think about safety measures and building codes and I was quite relieved upon finally reaching the top. Slab City lay quietly to the east, a field of tiny white boxes. To the west, the sparkling Salton Sea. A giant cross made of what appeared to be telephone poles cast a shadow hundreds of feet long across the dirt. Below me, the creator of the crumbling beast squinted through the sunlight. He was smiling at me, delighted. Looking down at him, I couldn't decide if the man was crazy or brilliant. Then I realized that I was the one who had just spent the afternoon climbing to the top of a giant art installation in the middle of the desert.[22]

Perspective changes as one climbs, as this narrative so clearly recounts. The bodily experience of being disoriented and righting herself, of shifting her vision from the immediacy of the mountain's paint, to the horizon of the Salton Sea, to the shadow of the cross, all affect the way she *sees* things. No longer is Knight the crazy one, or if he is, she is too. If he is brilliant, then she is too. A shift in her perspective changes the way she sees the world, affirming Knight's mission of building the mountain. Her experience of climbing then affirmed to her the artistry of the mountain *and* its inclusive message.

A common theme in pilgrims' stories is that of feeling a divine spirit in the place. This theme is expressed in Cindy Holleman's account:

It all started when I was a child approximately 8 years old. Although we live in a desert, my mom and dad liked to go camping in the desert....Each time we would go camping to the east it would include a trip to the mountain. I don't really remember Leonard at that time but I remember my dad would take paint and explain Leonard's mission to me. I saw it literally grow over the years. I remember as a small child the mountain only being a little more than the size of a big-rig. Then each year or every other year or so it grew. During my early 20s I went to college in San Diego and I didn't get to the mountain or camping much but I never forgot the message. When I had a child we started going to the mountain infrequently but I wanted her to see what Leonard had created over the years. It still continued to grow the times we took her there. About 4 years ago, my church group was looking for a field trip and we went to the mountain. This is when I met the man I had only heard about for my entire life! It was like an Oprah moment or something. Truly, God filled the space we were in when Leonard was talking about all the years he'd been there, how the mountain (and now the surrounding creations) were built and mostly to remember 'Keep it Simple, God is Great and he loves us.' My now 17-year-old daughter felt a real kinship with Leonard....Like I said—it's kind of a short but sweet story but it's my story.[23]

Holleman's narrative stands out for a number of reasons while also tapping into themes that run throughout pilgrim stories. Unlike single-visit pilgrims, Holleman has seen the mountain evolve over decades and witnessed how Knight's dedication has played out over the course of several years. Before she knew what it was, she knew that it was a work-in-progress, and she was able to see the material reality of the mountain develop over time. She saw the evidence of Knight's message, an aspect that is so important to so many pilgrims, evolve. Salvation Mountain became a familial place, Knight a point of reference in her family's constellation of narratives. They understood who they were as religious people and as family members in terms of how they connected to the ongoing evolution of Salvation Mountain. Part of their family narrative merged with the narratives of Salvation Mountain and their connection with the holy there. Because of this intersection of stories in her life, Cindy felt the spirit in the place. For her, God was present and surrounding them at each moment, making her describe it as an "Oprah moment" full of intense emotional experience. She hoped that that kind of presence would continue on in the life of her daughter. Her constellation became her daughter's, and Knight showed the spirit to another generation of her family.

For yet another visitor to Salvation Mountain, the most important touch was a feeling in her heart: "As a spiritual person, a believer, but very private about my religion, my beliefs, and not one to ever preach to anyone . . . as one who has visited and prayed in some of the most historical and ancient churches still standing, I must say this modern day monument touched my heart without a doubt."[24] Touching becomes a way of making the mountain and the experience it attempts to articulate *really real*. Touching is a means toward an embodied experience of beliefs. At the mountain it

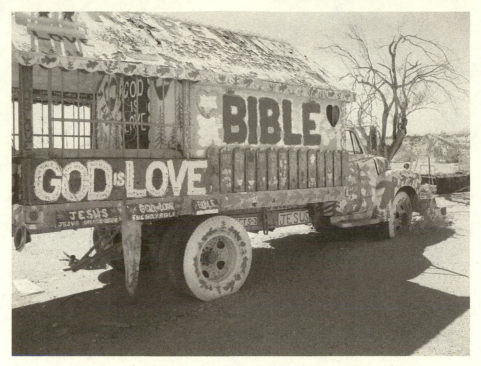

FIGURE 27.4 Art truck at base of Salvation Mountain

affirms these beliefs, that God is present, that God is love, and that these are things we can *know* in our bodies.

In account after account, there is the sense that the pilgrim has *felt* the truthfulness of the mountain's claims about God being love and about that love being the salvation for the world. Religious believers have at times called this feeling a sixth sense, an internal movement or conviction that they might describe as being touched by the Holy Spirit. That internal sense is often caused by the physical act of touching something one believes to be sacred. As one pilgrim described it, "God is love" is today's mantra … and I *felt* it."

ACKNOWKEOGMENTS

This essay is based on materials from my book *Middle of Nowhere: Religion, Art, and Pop Culture at Salvation Mountain* (Albuquerque: University of New Mexico Press, forthcoming). I thank the Society for the Arts in Religious and Theological Studies and the Faculty Development Committee at Hanover College for financial support of my research.

PART FOUR

Retrospective

28

The Bible

THEN AND NOW

Mark A. Noll

THE BIBLE REMAINS nearly ubiquitous in American public life. Wherever you care to look, examples abound—on the internet, in the movies, on television, in bookstores, in public rhetoric, in the names of people and places, and (not least) in political conflict keyed to the nation's culture wars.

The *New York Times* recently reported on the amazing success of a free Bible app, YouVersion, marketed by LifeChurch.tv, which is headquartered in Edmond, Oklahoma. This app with its over 600 Bible translations in over 400 languages has been downloaded over 100 million times since its launch in 2008.[1] Shortly after the *Times* article appeared, *Christianity Today*, as if to ratchet up the e-universe wow-factor, reported on "The Bible in the Original Geek," with coverage of an array of fast-expanding digital firms, platforms, and initiatives, including BibleWorker, AdaptiveBible, Accordance, Logos, the Franken-Bible, BibleGateway, and BibleTech.[2]

On July 30, 2014, Amazon.com's ranking of movie and television programs liked the History Channel's *The Bible: The Epic Miniseries* at a respectable 1,315, with over 2,700 customer reviews. But the same source listed the Blu-ray/DVD/Digital HD version of *Noah*, starring Russell Crowe, at number 1 in its ranking of Blu-ray Drama and number 2 in Blu-ray Action and Adventure. The circulation of Darren Aronofsky's *Noah* once again confirms that controversy sells, since at least some of the film's notoriety came from the well-publicized objections of a few critics who charged that it distorted what the biblical story from Genesis, chapters 6 to 9, actually communicated.[3]

Less publicized but still remarkable testimony to the staying power of Scripture can be found on the Social Security Administration's webpage that tabulates the names that American parents bestow on their children. Doomsayers of Biblical Decline, a number that includes not a few historians, must deal with the fact that in the first decade of the twenty-first century, the five names most often given to American male children came from Scripture (Jacob, Michael, Joshua, Matthew, Daniel), as did three of the ten most frequent for girls (Hannah, Abigail, Elizabeth).[4]

The Bible as a publishing phenomenon continues as an underreported but nonetheless significant feature of commercial life. At least two or three firms each gross over $100 million annually from Bible sales. One careful judgment from 2006 estimated that at least 25 million Bibles had been sold the year before, with the total take from all publishers probably well over a half billion dollars.[5] The American Bible Society distributes millions of complete Bibles or New Testaments each year, including its own Good News Bible and the Contemporary English Version, along with many more tracts and booklets featuring smaller scriptural portions. In 2005 the Museum of Biblical Art opened its doors at the Bible Society's New York headquarters to highlight the historical importance of Scripture in literature and art. The Gideons International, with worldwide Scripture distribution nearing two billion copies, and Wycliffe Bible Translators, with projects sponsored in scores of countries, head the list of American-originated mission organizations devoted to disseminating the Scriptures. Numerous commentary series, special publications like the hand-lettered illuminated Saint John's Bible, and an array of cleverly marketed t-shirts, writing implements, and refrigerator magnets keep the Bible as image, along with words from Scripture, squarely in the view of most Americans.

To be sure, quotation or allusion to the Bible in everyday public rhetoric has increasingly been crowded out by burgeoning references to sport, popular music, on-demand videos, international military crises, simple self-indulgence, and other marks of modernity. It is nonetheless intriguing to note how regularly the referencing of Scripture continues. For example, we find this paragraph in a Supreme Court ruling of April 29, 2014, where Justice Ruth Bader Ginsburg spoke for the Court to mandate that the Environmental Protection Agency enforce regulations respecting pollution blown from the Midwest to states along the East Coast: "Further complicating the problem, pollutants do not emerge from the smokestacks of an upwind State and uniformly migrate downwind. Some pollutants stay within upwind States' borders, the wind carries others to downwind States, and some subset of that group drifts to States without air quality problems. 'The wind bloweth where it listeth, and thou hearest the sound thereof, but canst not tell whence it cometh, and whither it goeth.' The Holy Bible, John 3:8 (King James Version)."[6] The political sphere is the domain where the Bible remains most contentiously visible. Nothing seems to excite the blood sport of contemporary American politics more than efforts to claim the biblical high ground. So it was on February 2, 2012, when President Barack Obama delivered a substantial address in Washington, D.C. at the United States' sixtieth annual National Prayer Breakfast. In the speech, which began with the president "giving all praise and honor to God for bringing us together here today" and included a quotation from C. S. Lewis about the impossibility of deriving a specific political platform from the Christian faith, Obama quoted or paraphrased at least ten passages from the Bible. His scriptural repertoire included a full quotation, from the New International Version, of 1 John 3:17–18 (with its emphasis on love through action instead of just words) along with allusions—echoing the wording of the King James Version and several modern translations—to passages from Genesis, Leviticus, Proverbs, and Isaiah in the Old Testament and Matthew, Luke, and Romans in the New.[7]

President Obama's speech was noteworthy not only because it featured skillful biblical quotations that the nation's first African-American president used to articulate his vision for the country. Also noteworthy was the immediate opposition the speech generated from other Bible believers who chastised the president for abusing the Scriptures. On the day after the prayer breakfast self-identified Christians associated with the Republican Party called the president's remarks "theologically threadbare" and the product of "laughable theology."[8]

Another example of the same kind of controversy arose in December 2013 when Arkansas Democratic senator Mark Pryor released an early reelection video in which, rather than commenting on public policy, he shared his personal faith. Dressed in shirtsleeves with Bible in hand and with a gentle piano melody playing in the background, Pryor spoke directly into the camera: "I'm not ashamed to say that I believe in God and I believe in his Word. The Bible teaches us no one has all the answers, only God does, and neither political party is always right. This is my compass, my North Star. It gives me comfort and guidance to do what's best for Arkansas." The inevitable response blew back immediately, but with a twist, since Pryor's opponents could refer to what he himself had been quoted as saying only a few months before, that the Bible "is really not a rule book for political issues" since "everybody can see it differently."[9]

A different kind of biblical political intervention took place in late July 2014 when a coalition of five religious organizations filed a lengthy amicus brief in the U.S. Seventh Circuit Court of Appeals. It asked that the court overturn the ruling of a District Court in Indiana that had invalidated that state's ban on same-sex marriage. The brief's first substantive argument began with these words: "We Defend Traditional Marriage out of Fidelity to Religious Beliefs that Include but Transcend Teachings about Human Sexuality, Not out of Animus." A biblical argument followed immediately: "Let us first dispel the myth that hostility lies at the root of religious support for husbandwife marriage. Jesus expressed no disapproval or hostility when he taught, 'Have you not read that he who made them from the beginning made them male and female, and said, "For this reason a man shall leave his father and mother and be joined to his wife, and the two shall become one flesh?"' Matthew 19:45 (RSV). Nor were the ancient Jewish scriptural texts that Jesus referenced based on animosity toward anyone. See Genesis 1:27, 2:23 (RSV)."[10] And so we could go on with such examples for a very long time. But...but...but. All even semiserious observers want to know what the near ubiquity of Scripture in modern America actually means. *How many* people actually ever read the Bible, and *what proportion* of Americans does that number constitute? Do biblical references reflect a deeply engrained spirituality or are they merely left-over survivals of earlier, more genuinely religious times? An even more consequential question concerns the integrity of scriptural usage: does the public presence of the Bible indicate something solid, well rooted, and praiseworthy? Or, to paraphrase Marx, are references to Scripture only a kind of holy water that exploiters sprinkle on their guilty consciences? Or perhaps they exist only as white noise deployed cynically to sanctify the manipulative designs of gun-toting libertarians, self-serving political scoundrels, and brain-destroying mass media moguls. For many historians there is a further set of important questions: whatever we might conclude about the Bible in America today, how does the present compare with the past for the distribution of Scripture, for the relative weight of Scripture in public discourse, or for whether the Bible is being read, marked, learned, and inwardly digested for good?

Any number of approaches offer hints for answering such questions. National comparisons offer such a pathway. As one instance, Canada, where as late as the early 1960s religious adherence and Bible usage were both more widespread than in the United States, now registers much lower measures for both church attendance and Bible reading.[11] Probing the contexts underlying the diverging national histories offers the prospect of real insight.

Consider also the use of names. The fact that parents today draw regularly on a biblical repertoire for naming their children establishes continuity with an American past where the same repertoire was exploited to name the landscape. Travelers who get off I-65, I-69, I-70, and I-74 and meander through the collar counties surrounding Indianapolis, for example, will find themselves journeying through cities and towns called Bethany, Carmel, Eden, Mt. Zion Corner, New Palestine, Ninevah, North Salem, Providence, and Samaria. Farther afield in Indiana, many places reflect a similar biblical source: four varieties on Salem, two each on St. Mary's, Mt. Zion, Jordan, and Antioch, with a host of others (Canaan, Gospel Grove, Bethlehem, Titus, Palestine, St. Joseph, Jericho, Goshen, Hebron, and more).[12] As with the naming of children, so also the naming of places requires interpretation. But at least on the surface, both personal names and place names testify to a continuing biblical fixation widespread at some level in the past as well as the present.

However much such random forays might accomplish to illuminate the historical place of Scripture, they lack scholarly depth and systematic breadth. It is precisely in pursuit of such depth and breath that the Center for the Study of Religion and Culture at Indiana University-Purdue University Indianapolis (IUPUI) has sponsored the research appearing in this book. It is also entirely fitting that an Indiana agency is making this effort. While serious scholarship on Scripture as a force in American history has existed for well over a century, only in the recent past have historians carried out wide-ranging research with full attention to the many contexts in which the Bible has functioned in American history. Among the leaders of such study have been a trio of Indiana-based historians: David Paul Nord of the University of Indiana-Bloomington, with path-breaking studies on the voluntary societies that did so much to distribute the Bible in the first decades after American independence; Paul C. Gutjahr, also of the University of Indiana-Bloomington and author of a deeply researched book on the production and physical form of Bibles in the nation's first century; and Peter Thuesen of IUPUI, whose study *In Discordance with the Scriptures* documented the cultural earthquake when alternative translations began to compete with the King James Version.[13]

Similarly, although significant survey research with attention to the Bible has been carried out for at least seventy years, we now enjoy a new level of sophistication with the study (see chapter 1 here) from IUPUI's Center for the Study of Religion and Culture. This study, constructed and interpreted by chief investigators Philip Goff, Arthur Farnsley, and Peter Thuesen, has moved decisively beyond sensationalistic, polemical, eccentric, and anecdotal treatments. In their own words, the IUPUI investigators set out to "learn how ordinary Americans use scripture, . . . [whether] they read the Bible outside formal services, and if so, how and why." Through the use of two extensive national surveys, they also wanted to "learn more about the use of scripture in American congregations . . . how contemporary Bible use fits into American historical patterns at the individual and congregational level, . . . [whether we] are . . . seeing big changes, or . . . there is a recognizable continuum on which we can understand contemporary use in its appropriate context."

Although no single effort can deal comprehensively with all important questions, this carefully constructed investigation has yielded many important findings as well as posing unusually thoughtful questions for further study. It is revealing in many ways. For example, it should come as no surprise that the most regular readers of Scripture are older Americans and that Bible reading prevails more widely in the South than in other regions. It is also not surprising that more women than men are regular readers, and probably not a surprise that Bible reading rates decline as education levels rise. Again, while hardly a revelation, it is nonetheless welcome to have firm data documenting the fact that of Americans who read any sacred writings, the Bible is the choice for 95 percent. More surprising in an age of cascading electronic stimuli is the finding that half of American Bible readers also take time to memorize the Scriptures, a practice also encouraged by two-thirds of the nation's congregations. I was at least mildly surprised to learn that Americans who claim no religious adherence read the Bible at higher rates, at least for certain purposes, than some who claim membership in one of the Christian traditions. It may also be surprising that less than half of the Bible readers surveyed ever seek help for interpreting what they have read, and of those who do seek such help, most turn to the clergy of their churches while very few turn to the internet. Yet the impact of the newer media is certainly evident from the survey, for it reveals that about one-third of Bible readers now access the sacred text via the internet, while more than a fifth do so through e-devices.

The IUPUI project abounds in such useful information. But in this chapter I would like to draw special attention to four of the findings that seem especially significant—from the standpoint of both the past and the present, both the then and the now. They are also among the most pertinent results that begin to address the question of how much has changed over time with respect to Scripture in the infrastructures of American culture. These four, treated in what strikes me as an ascending scale of importance, are (1) Bible reading by Roman Catholics, (2) the continued use of the King James Version, (3) Bible reading by African Americans, and (4) the general accounting of who reads the Bible and why they read it.

First, the IUPUI survey shows what might be considered a surprise when it documents the Bible-reading habits of Roman Catholics. In the words of the investigators, "while the difference between Catholic and Protestant traditions is still noticeable, those who think Catholics only read scripture in services are missing an important point: over one-third of Catholics consult scripture outside formal services, and among those readers, about half do so for their personal devotions and to learn more about their faith."

The use of Scripture among Catholics outside formal worship is an intriguing subject by itself. The long-standing Protestant charge that the Catholic Church prohibited lay Bible reading was never technically true. In 1876, James Gibbons, then a bishop but soon to become cardinal archbishop of Baltimore and the leading spokesman for the American church, published one of the best-selling books of any kind in American history. Titled *The Faith of Our Fathers*, Gibbons's temperate apology for Catholicism responded at great length to Protestant charges about Catholic scriptural practices: "If you open an English Catholic Bible," he wrote, "you will find in the preface a letter of Pope Pius VI, in which he strongly recommends the pious reading of the Holy Scriptures." Then after citing several more official statements, Gibbons concluded: "These facts ought . . . to convince every candid mind that the Church, far from being opposed to the reading of the Scriptures, does all she can to encourage their perusal." At the same time, Gibbons expended much greater effort to explain why, though the Church approved Bible reading, it wanted that reading to take place under strict ecclesiastical guidance: "God never intended the Bible to be the Christian's rule of faith, independently of the living authority of the Church."[14]

Gibbons's approach, affirming the acceptability of lay Bible reading but hedging that permission with careful instruction about the Church's authoritative role as Bible interpreter, long had the practical effect of making the Bible an unread book for lay Catholics outside the mass. Yet since the 1943 papal encyclical, *Divino Afflante Spiritu*, and even more since the Second Vatican Council, that situation has changed significantly. While not yet in Protestant quantities, Catholic publishers now supply a great deal of material for scriptural study aimed at both scholars and the laity; a few institutions now exist, like the St. Paul Center for Biblical Theology associated with Steubenville University, that energetically promote Catholic engagement with the Bible;[15] and although again not with Protestant frequency, it is even possible to find Catholics arguing among themselves about the acceptability of different Bible translations.

The importance of this shift for the internal life of Catholicism is matched by its importance for Catholics' involvement in the wider society. To take only one example, the amicus brief I quoted earlier concerning same-sex marriage represented the kind of ecumenical effort unimaginable fifty years ago. Its five sponsors were the U.S. Conference of Catholic Bishops, the National Association of Evangelicals, the Church of Jesus Christ of Latter-day Saints, the Ethics and Religious Liberty Commission of the Southern Baptist Convention, and the Lutheran Church-Missouri Synod. While this amicus brief contained references to the Catholic Catechism and pronouncements by the Mormon First Presidency, the uniting point for its religious argument rested on Scripture. Along with many other factors, a deeper Catholic engagement with the Bible has been building bridges with Protestants, but also Mormons, that extend from religious arenas into the public sphere. One of the important results of the IUPUI survey, therefore, is to document the changing place of Scripture in the broader reaches of American Catholic history.

If that finding points to a significant difference between then and now, a second finding of the IUPUI survey documents what many observers have to regard as a surprising note of continuity between the past and the present. This finding concerns Bible versions. The surprise is that despite a century or more of very well-publicized and very skillfully marketed alternative translations, the 1611 King James Version remains the text of choice for a majority of American Bible readers and a near-majority of Christian congregations. Specifically, 55 percent of Americans who read the Bible do so from the KJV, while 40 percent of congregations polled used the same text for public worship. Other surveys of actual Bible usage, as contrasted to Bible sales, deliver similar findings.[16]

The surprise, of course, is the durability of the KJV, which has been much praised by literary scholars and much studied for its cultural, religious, and even political impact everywhere in the English-speaking world, but which also has been overshadowed by the extraordinary array of alternative versions produced in the United States since the mid-nineteenth century. Even in the heyday of the KJV, with Protestants firmly fixed as the nation's cultural arbiters, Bible publishing *not* connected to the KJV was a major enterprise. American Roman Catholics have long been supplied with the Douay-Challoner-Reims version and, since 1970, the New American Bible. Beginning in the early twentieth century, American Jews have produced a number of significant translations of the Hebrew Scriptures. And among church communities using languages other than English, Scripture publication has also been a big business. For the period 1860–1925, when distribution of the KJV was at its height, American publishers brought out at least 136 non-KJV English-language editions of forty-two separate English translations of the Scriptures. During the same period, *American* publishers also produced at least 316 editions of complete Bibles (or complete Hebrew Scriptures) in forty languages other than English, including one hundred editions of complete German-language Bibles.[17] Contemporary best-seller lists reflect the continuing popularity of non-English versions *in the United States*, especially a 1960 revision of the sixteenth-century Reina-Valera Spanish translation.

As almost everyone knows, the publication of non-KJV English translations emerged as very big business over the course of the twentieth century. When the New Testament of the Revised Standard Version was published in 1946, it became the first Bible beside the KJV to gain a broad national readership. Since then, a number of translations based on the KJV, but with substantial alterations, have sold very well, some into the hundreds of millions. They include the full RSV, completed in 1952, then the New Revised Standard Version of 1989, but also the New American Standard Bible (1973), the New King James Version (1982), and most recently the English Standard Version (2001).

Not until 1956 and the first publication of what became known as The Living Bible did a version deviating substantially from the KJV gain a wide American readership.

But when that happened, such Bibles proliferated. In fact, for a few years in the mid-1970s, The Living Bible, which Kenneth Taylor had paraphrased loosely from a King James Version so that his children would understand what was read at family devotions, accounted for nearly half of all Scriptures sold in the country.

In this environment a number of new translations won the kind of broad following that was impossible so long as the KJV dominated the English-speaking market. They included notable imports from Britain, like the New English Bible (New Testament, 1961; complete, 1970), J. B. Phillips's New Testament in Modern English (1962); and the Catholic-sponsored Jerusalem Bible (1966). Since 1970, Americans have themselves produced at least twenty-five new translations or paraphrases of their own. Most have appeared under Christian auspices, although the Jewish Publication Society also sponsored a notable translation in 1985 of the Hebrew Scriptures, Tanakh.

The most important of these post-KJV efforts grew out of dissatisfaction among some conservative Protestants with the 1952 RSV. It was sponsored by the New York International Bible Society and led in 1978 to the publication of the New International Version. The support this version garnered from a wide range of moderate and conservative Protestants, during another period of evangelical resurgence, has led to the distribution of well over 400 million copies. For at least a quarter century the NIV has topped the regularly published list of best-selling Bibles put out by the Association for Christian Retailers.

When, however, a revision committee brought out a revised Today's New International Version in 2002, which replaced some male-specific pronouns with gender-neutral renderings, the history that led to the NIV was repeated. Conservatives who objected to this translation strategy expressed their criticism as vociferously as earlier foes of the RSV had done. They also moved to sponsor new texts like the English Standard Version and the Holman Christian Standard Bible (from the publishers for the Southern Baptist Convention).

Another phenomenon that makes the strength of the KJV surprising is that it has weathered the vigorous promotion of these alternatives. When American commercialism entered a new phase in the 1950s, so too did the translation and marketing of the Bible. Not so much theology or ecclesiastical decisions but a society experiencing unprecedented wealth, mobility, college education, and merchandising through the new medium of television created a new era for Bible publishers.

With Thomas Nelson, Zondervan Corporation (publisher of the NIV), and Harper-SanFrancisco (the main publisher of the RSV and the New RSV) leading the way, the new versions have been marketed with a vengeance. Niche publishing, which characterizes American book distribution as a whole, dominates Bible sales as well. In 2004, six of the ten best-selling editions were different marketing vehicles for the same translation: the NIV Study Bible, the Life Application Bible (NIV), the Student Bible (NIV), the Teen Study Bible (NIV), NIV Thinline Bible, the Adventure Bible (NIV). Large advertising budgets now support the sale of editions like Seek Find: The Bible for All People, The Bible in 90 Days, The 100-Minute Bible, Grace for the Moment Devotional Bible, and Bibelzine Redefine in snappy magazine format.[18]

Before the IUPUI survey was published, I had thought that the most important conclusion about Bible translations in the recent past concerned the new situation created
by the nearly inexhaustible variety of English-language Bibles read by believers and
available to the public at large. From this perspective I saw both positive and negative
results. Positively, Scripture can now be read in a more contemporaneous and more
understandable book than when it appeared in the language of the early seventeenth
century. But negatively, the proliferation of texts would seem to disqualify any one of
them from speaking with natural familiarity to those who use other versions; the
once-common practice of scriptural memorization becomes much more complicated;
and debates over which new translation best captures the original Hebrew and Greek
can sometimes turn nasty, with the particular venom generated by what Freud called
"the narcissism of small difference."

Yet now, according to the IUPUI survey—and even after an extended period where
new translations have proliferated in wild diversity—55 percent of Americans report
that they still use the King James for personal reading (the competition includes 19
percent for the NIV, 7 percent for the NRSV, 6 percent for the New American Bible,
5 percent for the Living Bible, and 8 percent for all other translations). The same goes
for Scripture read in churches. The survey reports that after the 40 percent of congregations that use the KJV, 21 percent of congregations promote the NIV, and 10 percent
use the NRSV, with no other translation showing up as often.

"Clearly," as the project investigators have written, "the King James Bible is far from
dead." But just as clearly, as they also say, "the full reasons for the KJV's enduring popularity remain to be investigated.... Is the version's appeal mostly aesthetic...? Or do
particular denominational cultures account for much of the KJV's popularity—its venerable status in black churches, for example?" Sylvester A. Johnson has noted that the
language of this one translation continues to function as "a type of lingua sacra or sacred
dialect" for surprisingly large segments of the American Bible-reading population. Yet
despite a wealth of informative studies, including numerous publications to mark the
version's quadricentennial in 2011, no fully satisfactory explanation exists for the continuing popularity of the King James Version. That situation certainly attests the iconic
status of this one translation. But what does it say about American Bible readers?

A third significant finding of the IUPUI research concerns the use of the Bible by
African Americans. This finding speaks to a very strong continuity in American history, but a continuity that, until recently, has not received the attention it deserves.
The IUPUI analysis in chapter 1 is unequivocal: "the strongest correlation with Bible
reading is race. Specifically, black people read the Bible at a higher rate than people of
other races, and by a considerable margin.... 70% of all blacks said they read the Bible
outside of worship at least once in the past year, compared to 44% for whites [and]
46% for Hispanics." Furthermore, "nowhere else in our data is there such a clear linkage between one descriptive variable—self-identification by race—and such a high
level of interaction with the Bible."

In the fairly recent past, a remarkable cornucopia of scholarship has provided the
necessary historical perspective for understanding these results. Beginning with David

Brion Davis, Eugene Genovese, and Albert Raboteau, a host of expert historians have documented a very great deal about black history, including the deep connections between African Americans and the Bible.[19] When the efforts of these scholars are synthesized, they describe a history with at least three major phases that help interpret the survey's results.

First, kidnapped slaves initially encountered Scripture as an integral component of European Christendom, a Christendom that was fully complicit in their captivity. So long as the Christianity Africans knew was simply the religion of that Christendom, few conversions took place. In the middle decades of the eighteenth century, however, the situation began to change when advocates of the transatlantic evangelical revivals proclaimed a biblical message strongly focused on the New Birth. Although many of the foremost preachers of the awakenings either owned slaves or made no protest against slavery, their version of Christianity so strongly stressed a biblical message of personal renewal that it could operate more or less on its own, liberated from the entanglements of Christendom. The intensity of that biblical presentation resulted in black conversions. As a result, black converts became People of the Book much more than adherents to any particular Christian tradition.

The very first English-language publications by black authors illustrated this mode of scriptural Christianity. The first, or perhaps second, of those efforts was an eighty-eight-line poem composed on Christmas Day, 1760, by Jupiter Hammon, an enslaved person on Long Island. His effort began with the word "salvation," a word he then repeated twenty more times in the poem, and with a direct evocation of Scripture specifying the origin, nature, and availability of that salvation:

> Salvation comes by Jesus Christ alone,
> The only Son of God;
> Redemption now to every one,
> That love his holy Word.[20]

The poem that followed overflowed with scriptural phrases: "Lord unto whom now shall we go" (paraphrasing John 6:68); "Ho! every one that hunger hath" (echoing Isaiah 55:1); "Salvation be thy leading Staff" (alluding to Psalm 23:4); "Our hearts and Souls do meet again, / To magnify thy Name" (echoing Psalm 34:3); and "Now Glory be to God on High" (derived from Luke 2:14).[21] Significantly, Hammon's poem focused tightly on the Bible's salvific message rather than on anything imperial, military, cultural, political, or ecclesiastical.

That Bible-centered, Christendom-averse approach rapidly became paradigmatic for almost all of the publications of the eighteenth-century Black Atlantic. Phillis Wheatley's justly celebrated poetry was a partial exception, since she added both contemporary politics and classical motifs to her verse. For the rest, all drew pervasive inspiration directly and narrowly from the Bible, including *A Narrative of the Most Remarkable Particulars in the Life of James Albert Ukawsaw Gronniosaw, An African Prince, as Related by Himself* (1772); *A Narrative of the Lord's Wonderful Dealings with*

John Marrant a Black, (Now going to Preach the Gospel in Nova-Scotia) (1785); the memoir of David George published in Britain but describing his early life as an American slave and his stay in Canada before taking part in the settlement of Sierra Leone (1793); Quobna Ottobah Cugoano's *Thoughts and Sentiments on the Evil and Wicked Traffic of the Slavery and Commerce of the Human Species* (London, 1787); and above all *The Interesting Narrative of the Life of Olaudah Equiano, or Gustavus Vassa, the African, Written by Himself* (1789 and several subsequent editions). The biblical religion that was so thick in these works might be viewed as only a variant on what others experienced in the eighteenth-century evangelical revivals. But that view would be deceptive. The difference lay in the nearly total emphasis on a scripturally derived message of liberation for the individual, apart from the structures of Christendom.

The next phase in this story concerns the anchor that Scripture provided for enslaved persons and free blacks in the parlous decades between American independence and the constitutional prohibition of slavery. That anchor can be illustrated from 1792, when one thousand black colonists, most of them former American slaves, sang a hymn by William Hammon as they marched ashore to start a new life on the West Coast of Africa in Sierra Leone: "Awake! And sing the song, of Moses and the Lamb. . . . The Day of Jubilee is come / Return ye ransomed sinners home."[22] In Albert Raboteau's authoritative summary, "it would be hard to exaggerate the intensity of [African American] identification with the people of Israel."[23] That identification, especially with Exodus and divine deliverance, eventually proved strong enough to overcome an intense effort by well-positioned white leaders, in the North as well as the South, to argue that the Bible legitimated the American slave system.

So it was that David Walker in his 1829 *Appeal . . . to the Colored Citizens of the World, but in Particular and Very Expressly to Those of the United States of America* could insist that not the actual unfolding of American history but an understanding of liminal divine reality was required to read the Scriptures correctly. Of the many aspects of American slavery that Walker contended the Scriptures condemned, he found especially galling the treatment of slave children, which he felt constantly violated Jesus's command of Matthew 18:6: "Whoso shall offend one of these little ones which believe in me, it were better for him that a millstone were hanged about his neck, and that he were drowned in the depth of the sea." Walker had only scorn for those who disregarded such passages: "Now the avaricious Americans think that the Lord Jesus Christ will let them off, because his words are no more than the words of a man!!!" Such rhetoric struck fear into some white hearts, in part because of its vehemence, but also because of how effectively Walker evoked the Scriptures: "Will not those who were burnt up in Sodom and Gomorrah rise up in judgment against Christian Americans with the Bible in their hands and condemn them?"[24] Walker's favored Bible translation—favored as well by Richard Allen, Daniel Coker, Frederick Douglass, Lemuel Haynes, Jarena Lee, Daniel Alexander Payne, James Pennington, Sojourner Truth, and all other African Americans who addressed the public in those crucible years—was of course the King James Version.

The third phase of this story brings us to the present and the remarkable prevalence of Scripture among African Americans, primarily in the form of the KJV. Many

Americans know something intuitively about the public dimensions of that deep bibli-cal commitment, since it featured prominently in one of the signal moments of post-war American history. On August 28, 1963, during the March for Jobs and Freedom in Washington, D.C., Martin Luther King, Jr., pointed provocatively to the uncashed promissory note of American democracy and spoke movingly about abstract ideals of justice. But when near the end of his address King set aside his manuscript and reprised phrases he had used in earlier speeches, he invoked an even higher authority than the Declaration of Independence: "I have a dream that one day every valley shall be exalted, every hill and mountain shall be made low, the rough places shall be made plain, the crooked places shall be made straight and the glory of the Lord will be revealed and all flesh shall see it together."[25] King's quotation from Isaiah 40:4–5—and in the words of the KJV—demonstrated the thorough confluence of African American experience, American public life, and the Bible.

Now the IUPUI survey has spotlighted the prominence of Scripture, usually as the KJV, that continues to this day as a powerful force in African-American life *outside* the political arena. The survey reveals what common sense should have made clear: that the powerful words of a Martin Luther King, Jr., could stir the American public only because those same biblical words had long before given life and hope to the private lives of black Americans.

The most comprehensive finding of the IUPUI survey is almost certainly its most important one. It compounds several individual aspects of the survey. Those aspects and the comprehensive conclusion to which they point are laid out clearly in the inves-tigators' executive summary: "48 percent of Americans read the bible at some point in the past year. Most of those people read at least monthly, and a substantial number...read the Bible daily....Among Bible readers, about half had a favorite book, verse, or story. Psalm 23, which begins, 'The Lord is my shepherd...' was cited most often, followed by John 3:16. Bible readers consult scripture for personal prayer and devotion three times more than to learn about culture war issues such as abortion, homosexuality, war, or poverty." In other words, the major conclusion arising from this ambitious project is that a lot of Americans continue to read the Bible, and they do so primarily for religious instruction and support.

Again, this finding should not be a surprise. Why argue about President Obama's public quotation from the Bible unless private engagement with Scripture is impor-tant? Why invest the technical learning, the thousands of working hours, and the mil-lions of dollars to produce an endless array of new Bible translations unless such expertise, such efforts, and such expenditures meet a demand for personal strength-ening from the books produced? And then, to ask a question that draws on many sur-veys going back to the beginning of public polling on the Bible: why is the percentage of the population who consider the Bible divinely inspired or even inerrant always higher than the percentage who can answer even the most rudimentary questions of Bible knowledge? The answer must be that the Scriptures matter for American life in the aggregate because so many individual Americans accept the notion that God speaks to human beings in human words.

Details from the IUPUI survey flesh out this actually existing situation. To repeat, it showed that almost half of the population reported reading the Bible at least once at year, almost two-fifths at least monthly, over one-fourth at least weekly, and about 10 percent daily. So there are more readers of the Bible each and every day than the record-breaking number of Americans who watched the recent World Cup final. And why do Americans read the Bible? Overwhelmingly the chief reasons are "for prayer and personal devotion," "to learn about religion," and "personal relationship decisions." Then, quite a bit less frequently, "to learn about health and healing" and "to learn about the future"; and then much less frequently "to learn about poverty or war," "to learn about obtaining wealth," and "to learn about abortion or homosexuality." To be sure, the survey does reveal interesting differences keyed to age, region, sex, education, wealth, and religious tradition with respect to the purposes for which individuals turn to Scripture.

Yet the big picture is more important than the admittedly interesting variations. The big picture, to quote the survey again, is that "individuals are actually far more likely to read the bible for personal edification and growth than to shape their views of culture war issues. Indeed, Bible readers consult scripture for personal prayer and devotion three times more than they do to learn about abortion, homosexuality, poverty, or war."

It is important to be clear about the meaning of these findings. They do not resolve any of the very difficult questions about how sincere people are in their Bible reading, how or in what ways personal Bible reading shapes character, whether or not what is read in Scripture is true, or if true is true in what sense, and many other questions of fundamental importance. The findings do, however, indicate decisively that the most important story about the Bible in American life is not politics. It is not culture wars. It is not well-publicized defenses or attacks on Scripture. Instead, the major story about the Bible in American life unfolds in the private spaces, religious societies, and voluntary organizations where spiritual purposes dominate. As Alexis de Tocqueville and many others have suggested, the *upshot* of what happens in these private spaces can mean a very great deal for politics, culture wars, arguments over truth claims, and much else. But spinoff consequences are not the same as what underlies the consequences. The IUPUI survey has gone a long way to illuminate the base structure to which politics stands as only superstructure.

Religion has been a major subject of popular American journalism since the civil rights movement, and even more since the rise of the Religious Right. Such journalism has often reported accurately on how the Bible has been brought into public life. What it has often missed, however, is that political uses of the Bible have never been its most important uses. These IUPUI surveys should bring sanity back into journalists' reporting on religion, at least to the extent that they show how important nonpolitical use of Scripture continues to be in modern American life.

The chairman of the translation committee of the NRSV was Bruce M. Metzger, who by the time he worked on that project had been active as a New Testament scholar at Princeton Theological Seminary for over half a century. His words of introduction to this translation state formally what the IUPUI survey documents implicitly:

In traditional Judaism and Christianity, the Bible has been more than a historical document to be preserved or a classic of literature to be cherished and admired; it is recognized as the unique record of God's dealing with people over the ages.... The Bible carries its full message, not to those who regard it simply as a noble literary heritage of the past or who wish to use it to enhance political purposes and advance otherwise desirable goals, but to all persons and communities who read it so that they may discern and understand what God is saying to them.[26]

Exactly what has changed and what has remained the same for the Bible in American life certainly requires further careful investigation. Yet to explore such questions without starting where Metzger begins, and where the main conclusions of the IUPUI survey point, will be to misunderstand that history completely.

INTRODUCTION

1. Nathan O. Hatch and Mark A. Noll edited *The Bible in America: Essays in Cultural History* (Oxford: Oxford University Press, 1982).

2. David L. Barr and Nicholas Piediscalzi, eds., *The Bible in American Education: From Source Book to Textbook* (1982); Ernest Robert Sandeen, *The Bible and Social Reform* (1982); Giles B. Gunn, ed., *The Bible and American Arts and Letters* (1983); Allen Phy-Olsen, ed., *The Bible and Popular Culture in America* (1985); James Turner Johnson, ed., *The Bible in American Law, Politics, and Political Rhetoric* (1985); and Ernest F. Frerichs, ed., *The Bible and Bibles in America* (1988).

3. Mark A. Chancey, Carol Meyers, and Eric M. Meyers, eds., *The Bible in the Public Square: Its Enduring Influence in American Life* (2014).

4. Paul C. Gutjahr, *An American Bible: A History of the Good Book in the United States, 1777–1880* (Stanford, Calif.: Stanford University Press, 1999); and Peter J. Thuesen, *In Discordance with the Scriptures: American Protestant Battles over Translating the Bible* (New York: Oxford University Press, 1999).

5. Hannibal Hamlin and Norman W. Jones, eds., *The King James Bible after 400 Years: Literary, Linguistic, and Cultural Influences* (Cambridge: Cambridge University Press, 2010); Vincent L. Wimbush, ed., *African Americans and the Bible: Sacred Texts and Social Textures* (New York: Continuum, 2000); Claudia Setzer and David A. Shefferman, eds., *The Bible in American Culture: A Sourcebook* (London: Routledge, 2011).

6. Bible in American Life conference, Indianapolis, August 6–9, 2014.

CHAPTER 1

1. Hereafter, all quoted comments from the project advisors are from email correspondence with the editors between December 2013 and February 2014.

2. For an explanation of the liberal and conservative ideologies behind the RSV and NIV, respectively, see Peter J. Thuesen, *In Discordance with the Scriptures: American Protestant Battles over Translating the Bible* (New York: Oxford University Press, 1999), 67–144.

3. Paul C. Gutjahr, "From Monarchy to Democracy: The Dethroning of the King James Bible in the United States," in Hannibal Hamlin and Norman W. Jones, eds., *The King James Bible after 400 Years: Literary, Linguistic, and Cultural Influences* (Cambridge: Cambridge University Press, 2010), 164; see also chapter 24 here.

4. On "King James Onlyism," see chapter 13 here.

5. Mark Twain, *The Adventures of Tom Sawyer: Authoritative Text, Backgrounds and Contexts, Criticisms*, ed. Beverly Lyon Clark (New York: Norton, 2007), 29.

6. "Poll Finds Teens Don't Know Bible," *Chicago Tribune*, April 29, 2005.

7. On biblical inerrancy as a kind of shibboleth or "common sense," see Molly Worthen, *Apostles of Reason: The Crisis of Authority in American Evangelicalism* (New York: Oxford University Press, 2014), 24. For the classic statement on fundamentalist use of Baconian logic in interpreting scripture, see George M. Marsden, *Fundamentalism and American Culture: The Shaping of Twentieth-Century Evangelicalism, 1870–1925* (New York: Oxford University Press, 1980), 55–62. Marsden argues that "inerrancy" became a code word for the movement, assuming a "scientific quality" of truth as directly apprehended.

8. Among many studies on African American religion in the United States, see Michael Emerson and Christian Smith, *Divided by Faith: Evangelical Religion and the Problem of Race in America* (New York: Oxford University Press, 2001) and C. Eric Lincoln and Lawrence Mamiya, *The Black Church in the African American Experience* (Durham, N.C.: Duke University Press, 1990).

9. For another view on reasons for Bible reading, see the 2015 Barna Group report, "The State of the Bible," conducted for the American Bible Society, http://www.americanbible.org/features/state-of-the-bible-2015.

10. Amy O'Leary, "In the Beginning Was the Word; Now the Word Is on an App," *New York Times*, July 26, 2013.

11. For more on digital Bible reading see R. G. Howard, *Digital Jesus: The Making of a New Christian Fundamentalist Community on the Internet* (New York: New York University Press, 2012) and Heidi Campbell, "Who's Got the Power? Religious Authority and the Internet," *Journal of Computer-Mediated Communication* 12 (2013): 1043–1062.

12. *Exploring the Digital Nation—America's Emerging Online Experience*, United States Department of Commerce, June 2013, www.ntia.doc.gov/files/ntia/publications/exploring_the_digital_nation_-_americas_emerging_online_experience.pdf.

13. For more on education and religion, see Philip Schwadel, "The Effects of Education on Americans' Religious Practices, Beliefs, and Affiliations," *Review of Religious Research* 53 (2011): 161–182.

14. "Religion and the Unaffiliated," Pew Research Center, October 9, 2012, www.pewforum.org/2012/10/9/nones-on-the-rise-religion/. Pew puts the "seeker" rate of Nones at about 10 percent.

CHAPTER 2

1. Spanish authorities prohibited the printing of Bibles in Spanish as early as the mid-sixteenth century. Two early printed Spanish Bibles were printed outside Spain, in 1569 (Basel) and 1602 (Amsterdam). Benjamin Wills Newton, *Valera's Spanish Bible of 1602. Appeal to*

Protestant Christians Respecting the Reprinting of This Version. (London: Houlston and Stoneman, 1856), 3–7. Jesuits in Peru translated catechisms and other smaller portions of the Bible into Aymaran in the sixteenth century, but never the entire Bible. They also did not have access to a printing press in Peru. Sabine MacCormack, "Grammar and Virtue: The Formulations of a Cultural and Missionary Program by the Jesuits in Colonial Peru," in *The Jesuits II: Cultures, Sciences, and the Arts, 1540–1773*, ed. John W. O'Malley (Toronto: University of Toronto Press, 2006). The first full English Bible was not printed in North America until the eighteenth century.

2. Although the language of the Indian Bible has often been called the "Massachusett" language, it is actually Wôpanâak, according to Wampanoag linguist Jessie Little Doe Baird. Wôpanâak is part of the Eastern Algonquian family of languages indigenous to North America and is spoken by the Wampanoag people of southeastern New England. See also "Wampanoag," Summer Institute of Linguistics' Ethnologue website, https://www.ethnologue.com/country/US/languages, accessed September 8, 2015.

3. Eames Wilberforce, *Bibliographic Notes on Eliot's Indian Bible: And on His Other Translations and Works in the Indian Language of Massachusetts* (Washington, DC: U.S. Government Printing Office, 1890), 14–15. Robert Boyle, the president of the New England Company, reported presenting a copy to Charles II in person, who "looked a pretty while upon it, & shewd some things in it to those that had the honour to be about him in his bed-chamber, into which he carryd it." Robert Boyle to John Eliot, April 21, 1664, quoted in Wilberforce, *Bibliographic Notes*, 15.

4. James Axtell, *The Invasion Within: The Contest of Cultures in Colonial North America*, The Cultural Origins of North America 1 (New York: Oxford University Press, 1985).

5. See the Treaty of Hartford, 1638, http://hdl.handle.net/10079/digcoll/2389, accessed August 21, 2015.

6. Although these sachems are more usually referred to as "Massachusett" sachems, they were part of the larger Wampanoag population of Natives in southeastern Massachusetts. I am grateful to Jessie Little Doe Baird for this insight.

7. This missionary society was formed in 1649, dissolved with the Restoration in 1660, and rechartered in 1662.

8. As Eliot worked on the Bible, several times the commissioners for the New England Company and the United Colonies requested in the 1650s that his translation of the Bible into the Indian language be done in such a way it would be understood by as many New England Native nations as possible, which was an unrealistic request. For example, see Commissioners of the United Colonies to John Eliot, August 29, 1655, quoted in Wilberforce, *Bibliographic Notes*, 5. For more on universal language theories in this time period and how the Indian Bible fit into them, see Sarah Rivett, *The Science of the Soul in Colonial New England* (Chapel Hill: University of North Carolina Press, 2011), 162–165.

9. George Parker Winship, *The First American Bible* (Boston: Merrymount Press, 1929), 14.

10. For the Massachusetts and Connecticut missions, see Richard W. Cogley, *John Eliot's Mission to the Indians before King Philip's War* (Cambridge, MA: Harvard University Press, 1999). For Martha's Vineyard and the work of the Mayhews, see David J. Silverman, *Faith and Boundaries: Colonists, Christianity, and Community among the Wampanoag Indians of Martha's Vineyard, 1600–1871* (New York: Cambridge University Press, 2005).

11. Winship, *Cambridge Press*, 221.

12. Ongoing archaeology of Harvard Yard and of the location of the old Indian College building that housed the Cambridge Press has revealed a significant quantity of two items in particular: first, dozens of very small type pieces from the press, and second, fragments

of many rum bottles. See https://www.peabody.harvard.edu/exhibits/current?q=node/282, accessed August 7, 2015.

13. Winship, *Cambridge Press*, 210. Given that, in the end, the New Testament was printed before the Old Testament, this simultaneous printing plan might have been abandoned or modified.

14. Justin Winsor and Clarence F. Jewett, *The Memorial History of Boston, Including Suffolk County, Massachusetts, 1630–1880*, vol. 1 (Boston: Ticknor, 1880), 470.

15. John Wright, *Early Bibles of America* (T. Whittaker, 1894), 1. Even in 1975, one author insisted: "Throughout his work Eliot had no assistance." Edward H. Davidson, "The Eliot Indian Bible," *Non Solus*, no. 2 (1975): 2. Scholars have only recently begun to fully recognize the robust roles Natives had in the translation, typesetting, and printing of the Indian Bible. The work of the linguist Jessie Little Doe Baird (most of which is unpublished to date) will be the most important argument about Indian contributions to the translations of the Indian Bible. See also Hilary E. Wyss, *Writing Indians: Literacy, Christianity, and Native Community in Early America*, Native Americans of the Northeast (Amherst: University of Massachusetts Press, 2000), 42.

16. John Eliot to Edward Winslow, July 8, 1649, quoted in Wilberforce, *Bibliographic Notes*, 1.

17. Daniel Gookin, "An Historical Account of the Doings and Sufferings of the Christian Indians in New England," in *Archaeologia Americana: Transactions and Collections of the American Antiquarian Society*, vol. 2 (Cambridge, MA: Folsom, Wells, and Thurston, 1836), 444. Wilberforce, *Bibliographic Notes*, 1. Increase Mather, Cotton Mather, and Samuel Gardner Drake, *The History of King Philip's War* (Boston: Printed for the editor, 1862), 48–49.

18. Letter of John Eliot, April 28, 1651; letter of John Eliot, 1654, quoted in Wilberforce, *Bibliographic Notes*, 1, 5.

19. John Eliot to Thomas Thorowgood, June 18, 1653, quoted in Winship, *Cambridge Press*, 167. See also Wilberforce, *Bibliographic Notes*, 5.

20. Mather et al., *History of King Philip's War*, 172n1.

21. Mather et al., *History of King Philip's War*. There are other supposed mistakes by Eliot and the Indian translators that past generations of historians have noted, particularly with regard to Judges 5:28 ("lattice" translated as "eelpot lattice") and Matthew 25:1–12 (where "virgins" is supposedly rendered in the masculine). Recent linguistic analysis by Jessie Little Doe Baird has revealed these former, older analyses of the translation to be wrong.

22. I am grateful to Jessie Little Doe Baird for this insight. Taken from personal conversations and a presentation she gave, "John Eliot's Wôpanâak Bible: The King James Bible and Its Place in Wampanoag Language Reclamation," at the Mashantucket Pequot Museum and Research Center, Ledyard, Connecticut, March 1, 2014. See Psalm 9:17, for example, which reads (in the King James Version) "The wicked shall be turned into hell, and all the nations that forget God." In the Indian Bible, "hell" in this verse is rendered *chepiohkomukqut*. Scholars have noted the presence of "unorthodox" translations in other Native contexts as well. Trace Leavelle, for example, has noted the misrendering of key concepts in the Miami-Illinois language, for example in the Apostles' Creed, instead of "born of the Virgin Mary," the Miami-Illinois rendering is "the virgin Mary unintentionally gave birth." Tracy Neal Leavelle, *The Catholic Calumet: Colonial Conversions in French and Indian North America* (Philadelphia: University of Pennsylvania Press, 2011), 103.

23. United Colony Commissioners to the New England Company, September 10, 1660, quoted in Wilberforce, *Bibliographic Notes*, 9. One unanticipated result of the Indian Bible was that it aided in somewhat standardizing spoken Wôpanâak between the mainland and the islands (Martha's Vineyard and Nantucket). Colonists reported slightly different linguistic differences on Martha's Vineyard and Nantucket. But as a result of the Indian Bible, these two vocabularies came into greater conformity over time. In 1722, Experience Mayhew, a longtime missionary on Martha's Vineyard, observed: "Indeed the difference was something greater

than now it is, before our Indians had the use of ye Bible and other Books translated by Mr. Eliot, but since that the most of ye Litle differences that were betwixt ym, have been happily Lost, and our Indians Speak, but especially write much as those of Natick do." "Experience Mayhew to Paul Dudley," Chilmark, Martha's Vineyard, March 20, 1721/22, *New England Historical & Genealogical Register* 39 (1885), 12.

24. Jill Lepore, *The Name of War: King Philip's War and the Origins of American Identity* (New York: Knopf, 1998), 36–37.

25. As early as 1653 the United Colony commissioners wrote to the New England Company expressing their doubts about Eliot's linguistic ability and stating their desire that Thomas Stanton be involved in the translation process, describing Stanton as "the most able Interpreter wee have in the countrey for that Langwige." Nonetheless, the evidence does not suggest that Stanton's skills were ever utilized. Quote from Winship, *Cambridge Press*, 158. See also William Kellaway, *The New England Company, 1649–1776: Missionary Society to the American Indians* ([London]: Longmans, 1961), 124–125.

26. Roger Williams, *The Bloody Tenent yet More Bloody*, in *The Complete Writings of Roger Williams* (New York: Russell and Russell, 1963), 4:373. For a brief discussion of this critique of Eliot, see Michael Clark, *The Eliot Tracts: With Letters from John Eliot to Thomas Thorowgood and Richard Baxter* (Westport, CT: Praeger, 2003), 34n2. Williams's critique of Eliot lasted late into his life. See Linford D. Fisher and Lucas Mason-Brown, "'By Treachery and Seduction': Indian Baptism and Conversion in the Roger Williams Code," *William and Mary Quarterly*, 3rd ser., 71, no. 2 (April 2014): 175–202; Linford D. Fisher, J. Stanley Lemons, and Lucas Mason-Brown, *Decoding Roger Williams: The Lost Essay of Rhode Island's Founding Father* (Waco, TX: Baylor University Press, 2014).

27. As bibliographers have pointed out, there were also fewer substantial errors, whether through translation or typesetting, throughout the entire Bible. *A List of Editions of the Holy Scriptures and Parts Thereof Printed in America Previous to 1860: With Introduction and Bibliographical Notes* (Albany: Munsell & Rowland, 1861), 2–3, 7–8.

28. As reported by Cotton Mather, in a memorial to the New England Company, 1710, quoted in Wilberforce, *Bibliographic Notes*, 30–31.

29. Ives Goddard and Kathleen Joan Bragdon, *Native Writings in Massachusett*, Memoirs of the American Philosophical Society 185 (Philadelphia: American Philosophical Society, 1988), 423.

30. The note is in Malachi: "In Boston the 17th of the 5th month (July), 1670." Goddard and Bragdon, *Native Writings*, 383.

31. Goddard and Bragdon, *Native Writings*, 411, 417, 377, 379.

32. Goddard and Bragdon, *Native Writings*, 447, 449, 453, 459, 451.

33. Goddard and Bragdon, *Native Writings*, 377, 409, 423, 431, 443, 423.

34. From the beginning, individuals involved in missionary and language work realized that the several languages in New England differed enough in to warrant separate translations. In the 1650s, Abraham Pierson began a translation of the Indian catechism into Quinnipiac (south/central Connecticut). The New England Company commissioners planned in 1656 to have Eliot's Indian catechism translated into "the Narragansett or Pequott Language," which was different from the Wôpanâak Eliot was working with. Modern linguists have identified Wôpanâak as an "N" dialect; Mohegan-Pequot is a "Y" dialect, which is distinct enough that English missionaries who were fluent in the one required a translator when speaking to Natives who spoke the other. Eliot himself made similar distinctions in the seventeenth century: "We *Massachusetts* pronounce the *n*. The *Nipmuk Indians* pronounce *l*. And the *Northern Indians* pronounce *r*." The example Eliot gave is Anum, Alum, and Arum, meaning "dog." John Eliot, *The Indian Grammar Begun* (Cambridge, MA: Marmaduke Johnson, 1666), 4.

See also Winship, *Cambridge Press*, 160. Ives Goddard, "Eastern Algonquian Languages," in *Handbook of North American Indians: Northeast*, ed. Bruce G. Trigger, vol. 15 (Washington, DC: Smithsonian Institution, 1978), 70–77.

35. Owaneco mentioned the Bible from Charles II in his petition regarding land loss to Queen Anne in 1703, saying it had been given along with a sword. Ben Uncas II referenced the Bible in a speech to John Mason, a missionary on Mohegan lands in 1725. Mahomet II, in his petition to King George II in 1736, invoked the Mohegan's long-standing treaties with England, which King Charles II renewed in the 1660s "by sending them a Sword & a Bible." "Petition of Mahomet, or Mamohet, to the King," Joseph Talcott, *The Talcott Papers* (Hartford: Connecticut Historical Society, 1895), 1:369; John Mason, "The Speeches of the Moheegs," New England Company Records, London Metropolitan Archives, London, MS 7957, doc. 14; "Memorial of Mahomet [II] to King George II, 1736," quoted in Learned Hebard Papers Regarding Mohegan Indians, Connecticut State Library, Hartford. See also Linford D. Fisher, *The Indian Great Awakening: Religion and the Shaping of Indian Cultures in Early America* (New York: Oxford University Press, 2012), 102–103.

36. "The humble address and declaration of Ben Uncas, chief Sachem of the Mohegan Indians, to his majesty's court of commissioners holden at Norwich...," July 20, 1743, in Connecticut, Uncas, and John Mason, *Governor and Company of Connecticut, and Moheagan Indians* (London: W. and J. Richardson, 1769), 109. For more on Ben Uncas II, see Linford D. Fisher, "An Indian Bible and a Brass Hawk: Land, Sachemship Disputes, and Power in the Conversion of Ben Uncas II," *Journal of Social History* 47, no. 2 (December 1, 2013): 319–343. Regarding the Mohegan Land Controversy, see David W. Conroy, "The Defense of Indian Land Rights: William Bollan and the Mohegan Case in 1743," *Proceedings of the American Antiquarian Society* 103 (1993): 395–424.

37. Wilberforce, *Bibliographic Notes*, 18.

38. Davidson, "Eliot Indian Bible," 3.

39. John Eliot, *Mamusse Wunneetupanatamwe Up-Biblum God Naneeswe Nukkone Testament Kah Wonk Wusku Testament* (Cambridge [Mass.], 1663), Rare Book and Manuscript Library, University of Illinois Urbana-Champaign, Urbana. I am grateful to the Rare Book and Manuscript Library's staff for the opportunity to view and photograph this book. I am also thankful to Robert Morrissey for alerting me to its presence.

40. Jeanne Bennett and Sam Ellenport, *Hidden Treasures: The History and Technique of Fore-Edge Painting*, 1st ed. (New York: Calliope Press, 2012), 23.

41. Regarding Samuel Mearne, see Bennett and Ellenport, *Hidden Treasures*, 20–22.

42. Testimony of Samuel Dudley and Edward Hilton, May 7, 1656, vol. 31, Indian, 1705–1750, Massachusetts Archives, Boston, p. 645.

43. Cotton Mather, *Magnalia Christi Americana: Or the Ecclesiastical History of New England from 1620–1698* (London, 1702), 199.

44. John Easton, "A Relation of the Indian War," in *A Narrative of the Causes Which Led to Philip's Indian War, of 1675 and 1676*, ed. Franklin B. Hough (Albany: J. Munsell, 1858), 10.

45. Lepore, *Name of War*, 105.

46. William Hubbard, *A Narrative of the Indian Wars in New-England, from the First Planting....* (William Fessenden, 1814), 77.

47. Wilberforce, *Bibliographic Notes*, 28.

48. Many Indian Bibles were also likely inadvertently lost when Indian and English towns were burned to the ground. Some colonists reported losing their entire libraries, and many

Indians lost everything during the war, including any books—like the Indian Bible—they might have had.

49. Lepore, *Name of War*, 43, 43n90.

50. Wilberforce, *Bibliographic Notes*, 28.

51. John Eliot to Robert Boyle, November 27, 1683, *Collections of the Massachusetts Historical Society* (Boston: The Society, n.d.), vol. 3, ser. 1, p. 182.

52. Wright, *Early Bibles of America*, 17.

53. Wilberforce, *Bibliographic Notes*, 30.

54. Wright, *Early Bibles of America*, 19. A very few were printed with English language dedications and sent to England. The one curious and unique feature of the 1685 edition is that it contains brief chapter summaries throughout, and in English.

55. Minutes of the NEC Boston Commissioners, April 26, 1703, Manuscript Records of the New England Company, London Metropolitan Archives, 7953, item 9.

56. In 1726, the New England Company commissioners ordered "that a Good English Bible be procured & exchanged with the Revd R. White of Attleborough for an Indian Bible." Minutes of the NEC Boston Commissioners, August 19, 1726. In 1731, Samuel Gerrish was authorized to purchase half a dozen used Indian Bibles, "no new ones being had." February 8, 1731. Manuscript Records of the New England Company, London Metropolitan Archives, 7953, item 9.

57. In response to requests for a third edition of the Indian Bible, Cotton Mather, a New England Company commissioner in Boston, listing reasons why the New England Company should decline. Some of the reasons were financial; printing such a large book was costly, as they knew from experience. But more important were cultural, linguistic, and theological factors. Cotton stated this clearly: "The best thing we can do for our Indians is to Anglicise them in all agreeable Instances; and in that of Language, as well as others. They can scarce retain their Language, without a Tincture of other Salvage [sic] Inclinations, which do but ill suit, either with the Honor, or with the design of Christianity." Furthermore, Mather worried that important concepts were being lost in translation: "the great things of our Holy Religion brought unto them in it, unavoidably arrive in Terms that are scarcely more intelligible to them than if they were entirely in English." *Collections of the Massachusetts Historical Society*, ser. 6, vol. 1, p. 8.

58. Goddard and Bragdon, *Native Writings in Massachusett*, 1:415.

59. Fisher, *Indian Great Awakening*, chap. 2.

60. Joseph Fish to Andrew Oliver, November 15, 1762, Miscellaneous Bound Manuscripts, Massachusetts Historical Society, Boston.

61. Miscellaneous Readings, Eliot's Indian Bible, *Farmers' Cabinet*, April 1, 1869, vol. 67, issue 37, p. 1.

62. For more on the founding of the Society for Propagating the Gospel Among Indians and Others in North America and its relation to both the colonial period and nineteenth-century global missions, see Linford D. Fisher, "'Not in Our Neighborhood': The SPGNA, American Indians, and the Turn to Foreign Missions in the Early Republic," *Common-Place* 15, no. 3 (spring 2015), http://www.common-place.org/vol-15/no-03/fisher/#.VW9AzmRVikr.

63. For a helpful analysis of how missionaries from the American Board of Commissioners for Foreign Missions found inspiration in Eliot and the colonial period, see Ussama Samir Makdisi, *Artillery of Heaven: American Missionaries and the Failed Conversion of the Middle East* (Ithaca: Cornell University Press, 2008), chap. 1.

CHAPTER 3

1. Peter J. Thuesen, *In Discordance with the Scriptures: American Protestant Battles over Translating the Bible* (New York: Oxford University Press, 1999), esp. 121–155.

2. Thuesen, *In Discordance*, 11.

3. See chapter 1.

4. According to the 2008 study of religious beliefs and practices by the PEW Forum on Religion and Public Life, 63 percent of all Americans consider the Bible the word of God; of these, 33 percent consider it the literal word of God. Among American Protestants, 77 percent consider the Bible the word of God; of these, 46 percent consider it the literal word of God. Within this larger group, self-identified evangelicals clearly tend toward a literalist view (59 percent literalists v. 25 percent nonliteralists; with 7 percent regarding the Scriptures as "written by men, not by God"), while self-identified members of Protestant mainline churches tend toward a nonliteralist understanding of Scripture (22 percent literalists v. 35 percent; and 28 percent regarding the Scriptures as "written by men, not by God"). It is noteworthy that members of the historically black churches are strongest in their commitment to literalism: 84 percent consider the Bible the word of God; of these, 62 percent consider it the literal word of God, against 18 percent nonliteralists and 9 percent who regard Scriptures as "written by men, not by God." See *Religious Landscape Survey: Religious Beliefs and Practices*, May 2008, 30; http://religions.pewforum.org/pdf/report2-religious-landscape-study-full.pdf.

5. Even the introductory literature on American evangelicalism is vast, and literalism and inerrancy figure in virtually all introductions and historical surveys. The locus classicus is of course David W. Bebbington, *Evangelicalism in Modern Britain: A History from the 1730s to the 1980s* (London: Unwin Hyman, 1989), where a particular regard for Scripture is part of the famous quadrilateral definition (2–19), and the tendency of evangelical biblicism toward insisting on "inerrancy, verbal inspiration, and the need for literal interpretation" (14) is highlighted. The other classic is George M. Marsden, *Understanding Fundamentalism and Evangelicalism* (Grand Rapids: Eerdmans, 1991), esp. 37–39, 75–76. From the spate of recent introductory literature, compare the following on literalism/inerrancy: Mark A. Noll, *American Evangelical Christianity: An Introduction* (Oxford: Blackwell, 2001), esp. 59–60; Randall H. Balmer, ed., *Encyclopedia of Evangelicalism*, rev. ed. (Waco: Baylor University Press, 2004) 351, 410; Douglas A. Sweeney, *The American Evangelical Story* (Grand Rapids: Baker, 2005), esp. 157–161; Barry Hankins, *American Evangelicals: A Contemporary History of a Mainstream Religious Movement* (Lanham, MD: Rowman and Littlefield, 2008), 23–26, 182–183; Daniel J. Treier, "Scripture and Hermeneutics," in *The Cambridge Companion to Evangelical Theology*, ed. Timothy Larsen and Daniel J. Treier (Cambridge: Cambridge University Press, 2007), 35–50.

On the development of modern views on inerrancy and literalism in American Protestantism, see Jack B. Rogers and Donald K. McKim, *The Authority and Interpretation of the Bible* (San Francisco: Harper and Row, 1979); Mark A. Noll, *Between Faith and Criticism: Evangelicals, Scholarship, and the Bible in America*, rev. ed. (Grand Rapids: Baker Book House, 1991), and "Evangelicals and the Study of the Bible," in *Evangelicalism and Modern America*, ed. George M. Marsden (Grand Rapids: Eerdmans, 1984), 103–121; Thomas H. Olbricht, "Biblical Primitivism in American Biblical Scholarship, 1630–1870," in *The American Quest for the Primitive Church*, ed. Richard T. Hughes (Urbana: University of Illinois Press, 1988), 81–98; George M. Marsden, "Everyone One's Own Interpreter? The Bible, Science, and Authority in Mid-nineteenth-century America," in *The Bible in America: Essays in Cultural History*, ed. Nathan O. Hatch and Mark A. Noll (New York: Oxford University Press, 1982), 79–100.

6. Molly Worthen, *Apostles of Reason: The Crisis of Authority in American Evangelicalism* (New York: Oxford University Press, 2014), 17. Worthen generally belongs to those revisionist scholars who argue against tight, essentialist definitions of American evangelicalism and who emphasize that under its broad tent, evangelicalism "includes a definition-defying array of doctrines, practices, and political persuasions" (3). Still, she considers literalism to be one of the few indisputable hallmarks of the many diverse churches, groups, and movements associated with the term. For the irreducible plurality of evangelicalism, see Donald W. Dayton and Robert K. Johnston, eds., *The Variety of American Evangelicalism* (Knoxville: Tennessee University Press/InterVarsity, 1991).

7. This connection can be seen in many classical statements of faith in the history of conservative biblicism in American Protestantism. See, for instance, Archibald Alexander Hodge and Benjamin Breckenridge Warfield, "Inspiration," *Presbyterian Review* 2 (April 1881): 225–260; and Benjamin Breckenridge Warfield, "The Supernatural Birth of Jesus," *American Journal of Theology* 10 (1906): 21–30. Compare the famous statement of faith by the Presbyterian General Assembly of 1910 that declared both "the inerrancy and full authority of the Bible" and "the virgin birth of Christ" to be fundamentals (qtd. from Hankins, *American Evangelicals*, 29). *The Fundamentals* (1910–15), of course, contained numerous essays on inerrancy, inspiration, and the fallacies of "Higher Criticism." The very first essay in the original 12-volume edition was a piece by James Orr, "The Virgin Birth of Christ." W. B. Riley's well-known essay "The Faith of the Fundamentalists," *Current History* 24 (1927): 434–440, makes the virgin birth an essential among "the greater Christian doctrines" together with inerrancy. The connection is also highlighted by John Gresham Machen, *The Virgin Birth* (New York: Harper, 1930), esp. 288–291; and Harold Lindsell, *The Battle for the Bible* (Grand Rapids: Zondervan, 1976), esp. 39–40. For more recent examples, see: Norman L. Geisler, ed., *Baker Encyclopedia of Christian Apologetics* (Grand Rapids: Baker Book House, 1998), 132, 135, 759–764; the entries "Bible, Inerrancy and Infallibility of" and "Virgin Birth of Jesus" in *Evangelical Dictionary of Theology*, ed. Walter E. Alwell (Grand Rapids: Baker Academic, 2011) 156–159; 1247–1250. Here, J. M. Frame makes the connection explicit by stating: "The virgin birth is doctrinally important because: (1) The doctrine of Scripture. If Scripture errs here, then why should we trust its claims about other supernatural events, such as the resurrection?" (1249).

8. On the history of "Higher Criticism" in America, see Jerry Wayne Brown, *The Rise of Biblical Criticism in America, 1800–1870* (Middletown: Wesleyan University Press, 1969); John H. Giltner, *Moses Stuart: The Father of Biblical Science in America* (Atlanta: Scholars Press, 1988); Glenn T. Miller, *Piety and Profession: American Protestant Theological Education, 1870–1970* (Grand Rapids: Eerdmans, 2007), esp. 88–132; Mark S. Massa, *Charles August Briggs and the Crisis of Historical Criticism* (Minneapolis: Fortress Press, 1990); J. G. Williams, *The Times and Life of Edward Robinson: Connecticut Yankee in King Solomon's Court* (Atlanta: Society of Biblical Literature, 1999); Paul C. Gutjahr, *Charles Hodge: Guardian of American Orthodoxy* (New York: Oxford University Press, 2011).

9. Edwards's status as a founding father of American evangelicalism is long-standing and virtually indisputable. For recent works that foreground his centrality in the rise of evangelicalism, see, for instance, George M. Marsden, *Jonathan Edwards: A Life* (New Haven: Yale University Press, 2003); Mark A. Noll, *The Rise of Evangelicalism: The Age of Edwards, Whitefield and the Wesleys* (Downers Grove: Intervarsity Press, 2003); Douglas A. Sweeney, "Evangelical Tradition in America," in *The Cambridge Companion to Jonathan Edwards*, ed. Stephen J. Stein (New York: Cambridge University Press, 2007), 217–239; Philip F. Gura, *Jonathan Edwards: America's Evangelical* (New York: Simon and Schuster, 2006); Thomas

S. Kidd, *The Great Awakening: The Roots of Evangelical Christianity in Colonial America* (New Haven: Yale University Press, 2007). Mather's association with early evangelicalism is less established but increasingly recognized. Works that emphasize the connection include Robert Middlekauff, *The Mathers: Three Generations of Puritan Intellectuals, 1596–1728* (1971; reprint, Berkeley: University of California Press, 1999), 191–367; Richard L. Lovelace, *The American Pietism of Cotton Mather: Origins of American Evangelicalism* (Grand Rapids: Christian University Press, 1979); Michael J. Crawford, *Seasons of Grace: Colonial New England's Revival Tradition in Its British Context* (New York: Oxford University Press, 1991); and Rick Kennedy, *The First American Evangelical: A Short Life of Cotton Mather* (Grand Rapids: Eerdmans, 2015).

10. For the Baconian tradition of evidentialism in American Protestant theology, see Theodore Dwight Bozeman, *Protestants in an Age of Science: The Baconian Ideal and Antebellum American Religious Thought* (Chapel Hill: University of North Carolina Press, 1977); Mark A. Noll, *America's God: From Jonathan Edwards to Abraham Lincoln* (Oxford: Oxford University Press, 2002), esp. 227–253; and Noll, *American Evangelicalism*, esp. 156–158; E. Brooks Holifield, *Theology in America: Christian Thought from the Age of the Puritans to the Civil War* (New Haven: Yale University Press, 2003), esp. 159–394. Holifield explicitly acknowledges that Cotton Mather and his father Increase stand at the beginning of "what would become an American evidentialist tradition" (70). Michael J. Lee has recently argued that this tradition of evidentialism in American Protestant apologetics inadvertently contributed as much to the long-term erosion of biblical authority as openly skeptical critics, since this tradition, too, increasingly argued over the factual veracity of Scripture in naturalistic-historical terms that would ultimately prove indefensible. See his *The Erosion of Biblical Certainty: Battles over Authority and Interpretation in America* (London: Palgrave MacMillan, 2013), esp. 25–51 on Mather, and 53–85 on Edwards.

11. For a comprehensive study of Edwards's biblical interpretations that also includes an up-to-date survey of the burgeoning literature on Edwards and the Bible, see Douglas S. Sweeney, *Edwards the Exegete: Biblical Interpretation and Anglo-Protestant Culture on the Edge of the Enlightenment* (New York: Oxford University Press, 2015). Important recent works on Edwards's biblical criticism and his immersion in contemporary biblical scholarship include Stephen R. C. Nichols, *Jonathan Edwards's Bible: The Relationship of the Old and New Testament* (Eugene: Wipf and Stock, 2013); Stephen J. Stein, "Edwards as Biblical Exegete," in *The Cambridge Companion to Jonathan Edwards*, ed. Stephen J. Stein (New York: Cambridge University Press, 2007), 181–195; Robert E. Brown, *Jonathan Edwards and the Bible* (Bloomington: Indiana University Press, 2002); Stephen J. Stein, "The Spirit and the Word: Jonathan Edwards and Scriptural Exegesis," in *Jonathan Edwards and the American Experience*, ed. Nathan O. Hatch and Harry S. Stout (New York: Oxford University Press, 1988), 118–130; as well as Stein, editor's introduction to Edwards's *Apocalyptic Writings*, *Notes on Scripture*, and *Blank Bible*, *Works of Jonathan Edwards Online* (hereafter *WJEO*), 5:1–93, 15:4–12, 22–24, and 24:59–75; and Peter J. Thuesen, editor's introduction to Edwards's *Catalogues of Books*, *WJEO* 26:1–107.

12. This massive apologetic work was to have three parts: the first would have addressed prophecies of the messiah and their fulfillments; the second would have detailed Old Testament types and their New Testament antitypes; the third would have outlined the coherency of Old and New Testaments in terms of doctrine and precept. The extensive notes that survive on section 1 are contained in the Miscellanies Nos. 891, 922, and 1067 ("Prophecies of the Messiah") as well as 1068 ("Fulfillment of the Prophecies of Messiah"), which are not contained in the letterpress edition. Large parts are accessible online through *WJEO* 30. On this work see

Kenneth P. Minkema, "The Other Unfinished 'Great Work': Jonathan Edwards, Messianic Prophecy, and 'The Harmony of the Old and New Testament,'" in *Jonathan Edwards's Writings: Text, Context, Interpretation*, ed. Stephen J. Stein (Bloomington: Indiana University Press, 1996), 52–65.

13. For a historical explanation of Mather's image in American culture, see Jan Stievermann, "General Introduction," and Brooks E. Holifield, "The Abridging of Cotton Mather," in *Cotton Mather and Biblia Americana—America's First Bible Commentary*, ed. Reiner Smolinski and Jan Stievermann (Tübingen: Mohr Siebeck, 2010), 1–58; 83–109.

14. So far, the first four of the ten volumes (which together will amount to about 10,000 pages in print) have been published: *Biblia Americana: America's First Bible Commentary, A Synoptic Commentary on the Old and New Testaments*, vol. 1, *Genesis*, ed. Reiner Smolinski (Tübingen: Mohr Siebeck, 2010); vol. 3, *Joshua—2 Chronicles*, ed. Kenneth P. Minkema (Tübingen: Mohr Siebeck, 2013); vol. 4, *Ezra-Psalms*, ed. Harry Clark Maddux (Tübingen: Mohr Siebeck, 2014); and vol. 5, *Proverbs-Jeremiah*, ed. Jan Stievermann (Tübingen: Mohr Siebeck, 2015). For an assessment of the edited materials, see my *Prophecy, Piety, and the Problem of Historicity: Interpreting the Hebrew Scriptures in Cotton Mather's Biblia Americana* (Tübingen: Mohr Siebeck, 2016).

15. The manuscript commentary on Isaiah consists of 90 pages of different sizes, ranging from folio pages to little pieces of scrap paper sealed to the margins. In the following, parenthetical references will be made to the edited version of this commentary contained in vol. 5 (*BA* 5:565–860).

16. Brevard S. Childs, *The Struggle to Understand Isaiah as Christian Scripture* (Grand Rapids: Eerdmans, 2004). On precritical debates over Isaiah, see chs. 1–14. See also John F. A. Sawyer, *The Fifth Gospel: Isaiah in the History of Christianity* (Cambridge: Cambridge University Press, 1996), chs. 1–8.

17. Hans W. Frei, *The Eclipse of Biblical Narrative: A Study of Eighteenth and Nineteenth Century Hermeneutics* (New Haven: Yale University Press, 1974). For a recent study of this crucial transition, see Michael Legaspi, *The Death of Scripture and the Rise of Biblical Studies* (New York: Oxford University Press, 2011).

18. Even typological readings, as Frei points out, were not perceived as "being in conflict with the literal sense of biblical stories, [but] figuration or typology was a natural extension of literal interpretation. It was literalism at the level of the whole biblical story and thus of the depiction of the whole of historical reality." Frei, *Eclipse*, 1–2.

19. Mather used the first print edition with annotations by the Hebraist Joseph de Voisin of the Sorbonne (d. 1685), which was issued under the title *Pugio Fidei Raymundi Martini Ordinis Prædicatorum Adversus Mauros et Judæos* (Paris, 1651). On the *Pugio Fidei* in the larger context of medieval anti-Jewish polemics, see Ora Limor, "Polemical Varieties: Religious Disputations in 13th Century Spain," *Iberia Judaica* 2 (2010): 55–79; Jeremy Cohen, *The Friars and the Jews: The Evolution of Medieval Anti Judaism* (Ithaca: Cornell University Press, 1982), esp. 126–169; and Robert Chazan, *Daggers of Faith: Thirteenth-Century Christian Missionizing and Jewish Response* (Berkeley: University of California Press, 1989), 115–136. On the peculiarities of anti-Jewish polemics and philosemitism in Puritan thinking generally and Mather's work specifically, see Michael Hoberman, *New Israel/New England: Jews and Puritans in Early America* (Amherst: University of Massachusetts Press, 2011).

20. On early modern Christian Hebraism, see Stephen G. Burnett, *Christian Hebraism in the Reformation Era (1500–1660): Authors, Books, and the Transmission of Jewish Learning* (Leiden: Brill, 2012); and Allison P. Coudert and Jeffrey S. Shoulson, eds., *Hebraica Veritas? Christian*

Hebraists and the Study of Judaism in Early Modern Europe (Philadelphia: University of Pennsylvania Press, 2004).

21. For other uses, compare, for instance, Gen. 24:43; Ex. 2:8; Ps. 68:26; Song 1:3, Song 6:8; and Prov. 30:19.

22. For other uses, compare, for instance, Gen. 24:16; Lev. 21:3, 13, 14; Deut. 22:14, 19, 20; Judg. 19:24; 2 Sam. 13:2, 18.

23. Mather's explanation is based on Turner, *A Discourse concerning the Messia* (1685), 24. Through Turner, Mather refers to Jerome's annotation on Isa. 7:14 in *Commentarii in Isaiam Prophetam libri XVIII*, bk. 3, ch. 7 (PL 24.108): "Lingua quoque Punica, quae de Hebraeorum fontibus manare dicitur (Al. ducitur), proprie virgo alma appellatur." "Also in the Punic language, which is said to derive (or: 'which is drawn') from the sources of the Hebrews, the virgin in fact is called 'alma.'" For a modern assessment of Jerome's philological argument, see Childs, *Struggle*, 95.

24. Thuesen, *In Discordance*, 124–127.

25. On this, see Peter Harrison, *The Bible, Protestantism, and the Rise of Natural Science* (Cambridge: Cambridge University Press, 1998); and Jitse M. van der Meer and Richard J. Oosterhoff, "God, Scripture, and the Rise of Modern Science (1200–1700): Notes in the Margin of Harrison's Hypothesis," in *Nature and Scripture in the Abrahamic Religions: Up to 1700*, vol. 2, ed. Jitse M. van der Meer and Scott Mandelbrote, Brill's Series in Church History (Leiden: Brill, 2008), 363–396.

26. On the religious debates during the early Enlightenment in England, see J. C. D. Clark, *English Society 1688–1832: Ideology, Social Structure, and Political Practice during the Ancièn Regime* (1985), 2nd ed. (Cambridge: Cambridge University Press, 2000); B. W. Young, *Religion and Enlightenment in Eighteenth-Century England: Theological Debate from Locke to Burke* (Oxford: Clarendon Press, 1998); and Joel C. Weinsheimer, *Eighteenth-Century Hermeneutics: Philosophy of Interpretation in England from Locke to Burke* (New Haven: Yale University Press, 1993).

27. On the rise of historical criticism see Jonathan S. Sheehan, *The Enlightenment Bible: Translation, Scholarship, Culture* (Princeton: Princeton University Press, 2005); Henning Graf Reventlow, *Epochen der Bibelauslegung, vol. 4, Von der Aufklärung bis zum 20. Jahrhundert* (Munich: Beck, 2001); and the two classic studies by Hans-Joachim Kraus, *Geschichte der historisch-kritischen Erforschung des Alten Testaments*, 2nd ed. (Neukirchen-Vluyn: Neukirchner Verlag, 1969) and Klaus Scholder, *The Birth of Modern Critical Theology*, trans. John Bowden (London: SCM Press, 1990). A host of important early modern Old Testament scholars are treated in Magne Sæbø, ed., *Hebrew Bible/Old Testament: From the Renaissance to the Enlightenment* (Gottingen: Vandenhoeck & Ruprecht, 2008). On Spinoza's biblical criticism more specifically, see J. Samuel Preuss, *Spinoza and the Irrelevance of Biblical Authority* (Cambridge: Cambridge University Press, 2001); and Travis Frampton, *Spinoza and the Rise of Historical Criticism of the Bible* (New York: Clark, 2006).

28. In Nellen's apt description: "As a rule, Grotius searched for explanations by clarifying the historical context. From this starting point he arrived at an exegesis that loosened the ties between the two Testaments. As a humanist he was focused on the literal meaning of the text. He rejected the idea that the Old Testament prophecies were fulfilled in a way that would have been meaningless to a contemporary audience. In his opinion there was a 'splendid coherence' between biblical prophecies and events described in the books of the prophets. Anyone who neglected this coherence read the Bible wrongly." J. J. M. Nellen, "Growing Tensions between Church Doctrines and Critical Exegesis of the Old Testament," in Sæbø, *Hebrew Bible/Old Testament*, 802–826, esp. 813. See also Kraus, *Geschichte*, 50–53; Childs, *Struggle*, 230–235.

29. The original reads: "In Prophetiis plurimum posui operæ, ut singulas ad respondentes ipsis historias referrem.... In hac parte locos nonnullos, quos veteres ad Christum et Evangelii tempora retulere, retuli ad historias aevo Prophetarum propriores, sed quae tamen involutam habent Christi et Evangelicorum temporum figuram. Feci autem hoc, quod ni id fieret, viderem male cohaerere verborum rerumque apud Prophetas seriem, quae caeteroqui pulcherrima est. Et talia quidem loca nobis Christianis Dei consilium patefaciunt, qui non per verba tantum, sed et per res nobis Messiam et beneficia per ipsum exhibenda adumbraverit." My translation. In the *Opera* edition, the one-page preface is located right before the beginning of the Genesis annotations. See *Opera omnia theologica, in tres tomos divisa*...(London, 1679) (1:1).

30. "Significat nomen Emmanuel certum Dei auxilium contra Syros & Israelitas, & in urbe conservanda contra Sennacheribum." *Opera* (1:279). Compare also Grotius's commentary on Mt. 1:22–23 in *Opera* (2:12–13).

31. "Atque his quidem nobis videtur simplex primoque obvius esse sensus verborum Esaiae, in quibus tamen inesse...*Arcanum* de Christo Christum agnoscentibus liquido apparer" ("And to them just as much as to us the meaning of the words of Isaiah seem obvious and foremost; that in these is inherent the mystery of Christ which will appear transparent for understanding to the Christian"; my translation). *Opera* (2:13).

32. Frei, *Eclipse*, 5.

33. W. M. Spellman, *The Latitudinarians and the Church of England, 1660–1700* (Athens: University of Georgia Press, 1993); Justin A. I. Champion, *The Pillars of Priestcraft Shaken: The Church of England and Its Enemies, 1660–1730* (Cambridge: Cambridge University Press, 1992); Gerard Reedy, *The Bible and Reason: Anglicans and Scripture in Late Seventeenth-Century England* (Philadelphia: University of Pennsylvania Press, 1985); and Robert M. Burns, *The Great Debate on Miracles from Joseph Glanvill to David Hume* (Lewisburg: Bucknell University Press, 1981).

34. Among such works that Mather used are: John Smith, *Christian Religion's Appeal from the groundless Prejudices of the Sceptick, to the Bar of common Reason* (London, 1675); Richard Kidder, *Demonstration of the Messias. In which the Truth of the Christian Religion is proved, against all the Enemies thereof; but especially against the Jews* (London, 1684); John Edwards, *A Discourse concerning the Authority, Stile, and Perfection of the Books of the Old and New Testament*, 3 vols. (London, 1693–95); and Robert Jenkins, *The Reasonableness and Certainty of the Christian Religion* (London, 1696–97).

35. The most prominent English follower of Grotius had been Henry Hammond (1605–1660); see esp. his *A Second Defence of the Learned Hugo Grotius* (London, 1655).

36. See his "Authority and Interpretation: Cotton Mather's Response to the European Spinozists," in *Shaping the Stuart World, 1603–1714: The Atlantic Connection*, ed. Alan I. Macinnes and Arthur Williamson (Leiden: Brill, 2006), 175–203, and "How to Go to Heaven, or How Heaven Goes? Natural Science and Interpretation in Cotton Mather's 'Biblia Americana' (1693–1728)," *New England Quarterly* 81.2 (2008): 278–329; Smolinski also broaches the debate on prophetic evidence in his introduction to the edition of Mather's work *The Threefold Paradise of Cotton Mather: An Edition of "Triparadisus"* (Athens: University of Georgia Press, 1995), 3–78, esp. 11–19.

37. Samuel White, *A Commentary on the Prophet Isaiah, wherein the literal Sense of his Prophecy's is briefly explain'd* (London: J. B., 1709), 52–53.

38. In his commentary on Isaiah, Calvin had already operated on the assumption that the fulfillment of prophecies must not be limited to one person or happening. Rather, in the formulation of Brevard Childs, he often "employed a dynamic understanding of historical events that unfolded in a process that anticipated in stages the full realization of the initial

promise." If Isaiah, for instance, predicted the freeing of Israel from its Babylonian captivity, Calvin simultaneously viewed this as "a forestaste [*sic*] of the divine deliverance in the reign of Christ." Childs, *Struggle,* 223. On this, see also Richard A. Muller, "The Hermeneutics of Promise and Fulfillment in Calvin's Exegesis of the Old Testament Prophecies of the Kingdom," in *The Bible in the Sixteenth Century,* ed. David C. Steinmetz (Durham, NC: Duke University Press, 1990). However, in his reading of Isa. 7:14, Calvin insisted on a single fulfillment in Christ. See John Calvin, *A Harmony of the Gospels Matthew, Mark and Luke,* ed. David W. Torrance and Thomas F. Torrance, trans. A. W. Morrison, 3 vols. (Grand Rapids: Eerdmans, 1972), 1:65–69.

39. William Lowth, *A Commentary upon the Prophet Isaiah* (London: W. Taylor, 1714), pref., x–xi.

40. Lowth, *Commentary,* pref., x.

41. Lowth, *Commentary,* x–xi. Ironically, to support this view, Mather also cites (*BA* 5:603) the apologetic work of the French Catholic scholar Pierre Daniel Huet (Huetius; 1630–1721), *Demonstratio Evangelica ad serenissimum Delphinum* ([1679] 1722), proposition 9, ch. 12, p. 359. However, Huet, as White notes (*Commentary,* 52), understood the secondary, messianic sense of Isaiah 7:14 in a typological rather than a strictly predictive manner.

42. Lowth, *Commentary,* x–xi; see also 56–57.

43. For an in-depth treatment of this debate, see Henning Graf Reventlow, *The Authority of the Bible and the Rise of the Modern World,* trans. John Bowden (Philadelphia: Fortress Press, 1985), 354–369; James E. Force, *William Whiston: Honest Newtonian* (Cambridge: Cambridge University Press, 1985), chs. 3–4. See also Stephen Snobelen, "The Argument over Prophecy: An Eighteenth Century Debate between William Whiston and Anthony Collins," *Lumen: Selected Proceedings From the Canadian Society for Eighteenth-Century Studies* 15 (1996): 195–213.

44. As Nichols explains, a Lockean understanding of language made the prophecies into "deliberate predictions by the human author. He had subordinated the meaning of a text to its historical referent on the ground of the interpreter's assessment of the human authorial intention. A prophecy could only have one meaning, that which the interpreter deemed to have been intended by the human author." Nichols, *Jonathan Edwards's Bible,* 37.

45. William Whiston, *The Accomplishment of Scripture Prophecies. Being eight Sermons preach'd at the Cathedral Church of St. Paul, in the Year MDCCVII* (1708), 16, 13, 16.

46. Whiston, *Accomplishment,* 51. This insistence, of course, put Whiston in the awkward position of dealing with the fact that the citations of these quintessential messianic prophecies in the New Testament were often incomplete and their wording did not fully accord with the received Masoretic text of the Old Testament. Whiston's solution, put forth in his *Essay towards Restoring the true Text of the Old Testament* (1724) was that the respective key passages in the Septuagint, from which the Apostles had invariably and accurately quoted the Hebrew Bible, had been subsequently corrupted together with the Masoretic text by conniving rabbis who sought to weaken the cause of Christianity by strategically undermining its central proof-texts. Whiston took it upon himself to restore what he believed to be the original text of the Old Testament in order to demonstrate that its key messianic prophecies had been correctly cited in the New and either had their one literal fulfillment in Christ and the gospel times, or could be expected to be fulfilled in the latter days.

47. Whiston, *Accomplishment,* 51.

48. See James O'Higgins, *Anthony Collins: The Man and His Works* (The Hague: Martinus Nijhoff, 1970), esp. 155–199.

49. Anthony Collins, *A Discourse of the Grounds and Reasons of the Christian Religion....*(London, 1724), 41–42.

50. For the enormous English print output of this debate in England, see Thomas R. Preston, "Biblical Criticism, Literature, and the Eighteenth-Century Reader," in *Books and Their Readers in Eighteenth-Century England*, ed. Isabel Rivers (Leicester: Leicester University Press, 1982), 97–127, esp. 116–118. For a fascinating study of the role of Jewish learning and Hebraism in this debate, see David B. Ruderman, *Connecting the Covenants: Judaism and the Search for Christian Identity in Eighteenth-Century England* (Philadelphia: University of Pennsylvania Press, 2007), 61–76.

51. See Whiston, *Accomplishment*, 57, 87–94.

52. *Truth defended, and Boldness in Error rebuk'd: or, a Vindication of those Christian Commentators, who have expounded some Prophecies of the Messias.... Being a Confutation of part of Mr. Whiston's Book, entituled, The Accomplishment of Scripture-Prophecies* (London, 1710).

53. Mather here summarizes pp. 78–87 of Claggett's work.

54. A summary of Green, *Letter to the Author*, 80–81.

55. Compare the *Triparadisus*, 165–166, where Mather reused the *Biblia* annotation on Isa. 7:14 derived from Green, while ignoring the alternative interpretations he had previously entertained.

56. On Jonathan Edwards's engagement with the major prophets and Isaiah especially, see David P. Barshinger, "'The Only Rule of our Faith and Practice': Jonathan Edwards's Interpretation of the Book of Isaiah as a Case Study of His Exegetical Boundaries," *Journal of the Evangelical Theological Society* 52 (December 2009): 811–829; and Jeongmo Yoo, "Jonathan Edwards's Interpretation of the Major Prophets: The Book of Isaiah, Jeremiah, and Ezekiel," *Puritan Reformed Journal* 3 (July 2011): 160–192. In the extensive notes for his *Harmony*, Edwards, like Mather, frequently defends the possibility that Old Testament prophecies could have double referents. At times, as Nichols explains, Edwards argues "that a prophecy may be dissected in such a way that it is seen to respect two events; one immediate, the other more distant." In other cases, he "endorses the notion of prophesied types," according to which a more immediate historical event predicted by the prophet simultaneously serves as a type foreshadowing an antitype relating to the messiah or the gospel period. Nichols, *Jonathan Edwards's Bible*, 33.

In Misc. no. 1067, sec. 19 (unedited), there is a passage on Isa. 7:14 in which Edwards embraces a reading of this verse as having had a primary historical accomplishment in the birth of Isaiah's son, while also being a prophesied type subsequently fulfilled in Christ. Edwards notes that sometimes in the Old Testament prophecies a sign (i.e., the birth of the child as the sign promised to Ahaz) occurs after the thing immediately signified (the deliverance of Judah). Edwards then also emphasizes that the complete fulfillment of this prophecy was only accomplished in Christ: "The utmost that is aimed at in this prophecy, is not the birth of Mahershalalhashbaz [i.e., Isaiah's own son]..., the birth of Mahershalalhashbaz was upon no account a great wonder, who seems to be born only to be some faint type of this person here foretold. Sometimes those things that are mentioned in Scripture as signs of things predicted, do not come to pass till after the thing signified has been accomplished." Qtd. from Nichols, *Jonathan Edwards's Bible*, 55. In the *Blank Bible* entry on Isa. 7:14, a similar interpretation is offered that argues that the birth of Isaiah's son "denotes and is typical of the purity of Christ's conception." Edwards, *WJEO* 24:636.

57. Thuesen, *In Discordance*, 11.

58. Noll, *Between Faith and Criticism*, 156.

59. A good entry point into the contemporary evangelical debate on this matter is Kenneth Berding, ed., *Three Views of the New Testament Use of the Old Testament* (Grand Rapids: Zondervan, 2009). David L. Turner offers a good survey of the current positions among evangelical scholars on the Isa. 7:14–Mt. 1:23 nexus, helpfully distinguishing between adherents of a strictly predictive view (Jesus Christ as single referent and fulfillment of Isa. 7:14), adherents of a multiple fulfillment approach, which posits a "partial fulfillment in the days of Ahaz but also a climactic fulfillment in New Testament times," and adherents embracing a typological understanding, which Turner himself prefers. According to such a typological understanding of Old Testament prophecies, "the biblical historical events contain theological motifs that anticipate the Christ event when seen with Christian hindsight." "Thus Isa. 7:14 is viewed as a sign to Ahaz that was fulfilled during his days, and Matthew sees in this passage a historical pattern that comes to climactic fulfillment with Jesus." David L. Turner, *Matthew, Baker Exegetical Commentary on the New Testament* (Grand Rapids: Baker Academic, 2008), 69–73.

60. They all insisted, as Thuesen explains, that "young woman" was the most correct translation and that the primary and literal meaning of Isa. 7:14 had to be understood as referring to the prophet's immediate historical context. Yet they also argued that such an interpretation did not exclude the possibility of a secondary, typological significance, for which the original authorial intention (and hence the lexical problem) was largely irrelevant. Luther Weigle, for example, pointed out "that if the prophet had really been referring to the virgin birth of Christ— an event seven hundred years in the future—then he was 'trifling' with King Ahaz by falsely promising him an imminent sign." Weigle consistently defended the New Testament doctrine of the virgin birth and seemed to hold out the possibility that Isa. 7:14 had a second, typological fulfillment in Christ. Yet his argument that Isa. 7:14 was fulfilled in Ahaz's time implied a view of the Old Testament prophecy as essentially self-contained, with meanings and referents existing prior to those identified by the New Testament authors. See Thuesen, *In Discordance*, 128.

61. For evangelical representatives of the single-fulfillment view, compare, for instance, Machen, *Virgin Birth*, 288–291; Edward J. Young, *The Book of Isaiah* (Grand Rapids: Eerdmans, 1965), 1:277–295, and "The Immanuel Prophecy: Isaiah 7:14–16," *Westminster Theological Journal*, 15.2 (May 1953): 97–124. For more recent representatives of this view, see Louis A. Barbieri, "Matthew," in *The Bible Knowledge Commentary*, ed. John F. Walvoord and Roy B. Zuck (Wheaton: Victor, 1983), 20; Harold Fowler, *The Gospel of Matthew*, 4 vols., Bible Study Textbook Series (Joplin, MO: College Press, 1968), 1:38–42; William Hendriksen, *The Gospel of Matthew* (Grand Rapids: Baker Academic, 1973), 134–141; and Geisler, *Baker Encyclopedia of Christian Apologetics*, 759–762. For modified versions of this view, see J. A. Motyer, "Context and Content in the Interpretation of Isa. 7:14," *Tyndale Bulletin* 21 (1970): 118–125, and *The Prophecy of Isaiah: An Introduction and Commentary* (Downers Grove: InterVarsity Press, 1993), 84–88; and Donald A. Carson, *Matthew*, in *The Expositor's Bible Commentary*, ed. F. E. Gaebelein, vol. 8 (Grand Rapids: Zondervan, 1984), 78–79. For evangelical representatives of the double fulfillment approach, see, for instance, Craig L. Blomberg, *Matthew, New American Commentary* (Nashville: Broadman, 1992), 60, "Matthew," in *Commentary on the New Testament Use of the Old Testament*, ed. G. K. Beale and D. A. Carson (Grand Rapids: Baker Academic, 2007), 3–5; Robert H. Gundry, *Matthew: A Commentary on His Literary and Theological Art*, 2nd ed. (Grand Rapids: Eerdmans, 1994), 24–25; Donald A. Hagner, *Matthew 1–13*, Words Biblical Commentary 33a (Dallas: Word, 1993), 20; Herman N. Ridderbos, *Matthew*, in *Bible Student's Commentary* (Grand Rapids: Zondervan, 1987), 29–30; Stanley D. Touissant, *Behold the King: A Study of Matthew* (Grand Rapids: Kregel, 1980), 44–46; Walter C. Kaiser, "The Promise of Isaiah 7:14 and the Single-Meaning Hermeneutic," *Evangelical Journal* 6 (1988), 55–70; Paul D. Wegner,

"How Many Virgin Births Are in the Bible? (Isaiah 7:14): A Prophetic Pattern Approach," *Journal of the Evangelical Theological Society* 54.3 (September 2011), 467–484; and Amber Warhurst, Seth B. Tarrer, and Christopher M. Hays, "Problems with Prophecy," in *Evangelical Faith and the Challenge of Historical Criticism*, ed. Christopher M. Hays and Christopher B. Ansberry (Grand Rapids: Baker Academic, 2013), 99. Interestingly, Grant R. Osborne even speaks of a "growing consensus" among evangelical exegetes that prefers a double fulfillment. See his *Matthew, Zondervan Exegetical Commentary on the New Testament*, vol. 1, gen. ed. Clinton E. Arnold (Grand Rapids: Zondervan, 2010), 78–79. This is also the position embraced by the popular *Zondervan Illustrated Bible Backgrounds Commentary*, vol. 1, *Matthew, Mark, Luke*, gen. ed. Clinton E. Arnold (Grand Rapids: Zondervan, 2002), 13.

CHAPTER 4

1. See Jonathan Sheehan, *The Enlightenment Bible: Translation, Scholarship, Culture* (Princeton, 2005), ix. This process in American intellectual history has also been documented of late; see Reiner Smolinski, "Authority and Interpretation: Cotton Mather's Response to the European Spinozists," in *Shaping the Stuart World 1603–1714*, ed. Allan I. Macinnes and Arthur H. Williamson (Leiden, 2006), 175–203; and Robert E. Brown, *Jonathan Edwards and the Bible* (Bloomington, 2002).

2. For a recent history of these developments, see Michael J. Lee, *The Erosion of Biblical Certainty: Battles over Authority and Interpretation in America* (New York, 2013).

3. Published in 1685 as *Sentimens de quelques theologiens de Hollande sur l'histoire critique du Vieux Testament composée par le P. Richard Simon.*

4. For a fuller discussion of the early modern debate over inspiration, see Reiner Smolinski's introduction to Cotton Mather, *Biblia Americana*, vol. 1 (Tubingen, 2010), 149–157.

5. Benedict de Spinoza, *Theologico-Political Treatise* (New York, 1951), 14, 153–154.

6. Richard Simon, *Critical History of the Old Testament* (London, 1682), bk. 1, ch. 3, p. 27.

7. Jean Le Clerc, *Five Letters concerning the Inspiration of the Holy Scriptures* (London, 1690), 26.

8. Le Clerc, *Five Letters*, 27, 93. The epistles of the New Testament are susceptible to this analysis as well. It is clear from the book of Acts, for example, that the early apostles disagreed with each other on occasion about fundamental issues of teaching and practice. Thus whatever inspiration they may have had was episodic rather than perpetual. The process of letter-writing is a mundane, rational exercise that does not require inspiration, and so inspiration is not an applicable category for the New Testament epistles. The imperfect process of canonization further complicates the matter: some epistles may even be forgeries, such as 2 Peter, a "fiction of some ancient Christian." Le Clerc, *Five Letters*, 43, 112, 114. Le Clerc's theory of inspiration is deeply indebted to Hugo Grotius as well as Spinoza; see Samuel A. Golden, *Jean Le Clerc* (New York: Twayne Publishers, 1972), 134–137.

9. This cautious but open-minded approach put Mather at odds with a significant portion of the orthodox Protestant theological community. On the vowel points, for example, many Reformed divines had resisted the idea that the received text differed in any way from the original. The great divine François Turretin helped to engineer the *Helvetic Consensus* (1675), a confession that not only insisted on the originality of the vowel points but also on the inviolability of the received text from errors of transmission. (Turretin's son, Jean Alphonse, who eventually succeeded him as a professor of theology in Geneva, was instrumental in having the *Consensus* abolished in 1706.) See Mather, *Biblia Americana*, 121.

10. See Smolinski, "Authority and Interpretation," 189–191.

11. Cotton Mather, "Things done by Ezra, for the Repairing and Preserving of the Sacred Scriptures" (this essay, which appears at the end of the *Biblia*, will be published in vol. 10 of the critical edition by Mohr-Siebeck). Mather also acknowledged that the form of the Old Testament, particularly the Pentateuch and the Prophets, was conditioned by liturgical use (each had fifty-four divisions, or partitions, to conform to annual reading practices). He also conceded that several works (e.g. Chronicles, Ezra, Nehemiah, Esther, and Malachi) were very late, either third or second century BCE. It is in this essay that he discusses his change of mind about the lateness of the vowel points, conceding that this potentially makes the readings unclear or problematic, should the points be mistaken: "It follows form hence, that the Text of the Sacred Scriptures, will be left unto an arbitrary and uncertain reading" (though Mather is confident such problems can be readily cleared by context).

12. See Mather, *Biblia Americana*, vol. 1, 117–144.

13. On his general theory of inspiration, see Mather, *Biblia Americana*, vol. 1, 149–161. It is also the case however that Mather embraces a suprarationalistic understanding of inspiration, in which a biblical author can write about a circumstance at hand, but also write proleptically about the future, beyond his cognition; see his essay at the end of the *Biblia*, entitled "Some Remarks upon the Spirit of Prophecy" (ms. pp. 1–10).

14. See his commentary on 1 Cor. 14.32 in the *Biblia*. Curiously, Mather's understanding of the actual *experience* of inspiration minimized the rational component of the process in favor of the ecstatic. In his terminal *Biblia* essay "Some Remarks upon the Spirit of Prophecy," he argues that the process of inspiration is largely nonrational, something that overwhelms the recipient, and may involve angels, mysterious voices, dreams, trances, visions, and signs. Thus Balaam may be thought of as a prototype of this experience of prophetic passivity, in that he could not prophesy as he desired but could only speak as God directed.

15. See Mather's essay at the end of the *Biblia*, entitled "Some Remarks, relating to the Inspiration, and the Obsignation, of the Canon" (ms. p. 1). Mather's source here is Robert Jenkin, probably his *Reasonbleness and Certainty of the Christian Religion* (1698). Jenkin (1656–1727) was a dissenting minister but late in life was made Lady Margaret's Professor of Divinity at Cambridge. On the element of personality in the authorship of the New Testament texts, see Mather's full comment on 2 Corinthians 5.1, which begins: "there are *Eight* Writers of the *New Testament*, they every one of them, in their Holy Writings, have Expressions, that carry some Character of their own former Circumstances, and show that they were not forgetful of what once they were."

16. Mather, "Some Remarks, relating to the Inspiration," ms. p. 1.

17. See Mather's commentary on 2 Cor. 5.3, which refers to the belief that the resurrection would occur during the apostolic era. This is a somewhat puzzling comment, since Mather dates 2 Thessalonians to 53 AD, the second earliest epistle in the New Testament. It may be that he is referring to the confusion about the resurrection that the apostles evidenced in the Gospels and the book of Acts, or simply to the misunderstanding mentioned in passing in 2 Cor. 5.3.

18. See Mather, *Biblia Americana*, Phil. 3.11.

19. Thus the Spirit preserved "that Book from error, which was to be the standard of truth for all ages." "Some Remarks, relating to the Inspiration," ms. p. 1. An author like Paul might have full use of his rational judgment in writing, but his "doctrine was inspired by the Holy Spirit; and the Holy Spirit, who might suffer him to putt it into his own words, yet never suffered him to express it otherwise, that in such a manner, as was agreeable to His intention."

20. "Some Remarks, relating to the Inspiration," ms. p. 2. Mather's source here is John Arrowsmith (1602–1659), possibly from his *Armilla catechetica* (1659), a posthumous collection of sermon excerpts. Arrowsmith was a member of the Westminster Assembly, and later Regius Professor of Divinity and Master of Trinity College at Cambridge. His *Theanthropos, or God-man* (1660) appears in the Mather libraries; see Mather, *Biblia Americana*, vol. 1, 329.

21. Mather, "Some Remarks upon the Spirit of Prophecy" (ms. pp. 1–10).

CHAPTER 5

1. Robert Darnton, "First Steps toward a History of Reading," in *The Kiss of Lamourette: Reflections in Cultural History* (New York: Norton, 1990), 154–187.

2. Mark A. Noll, "Review Essay: The Bible in America," *Journal of Biblical Literature* 106 (September 1987): 493–509; David Paul Nord, *Faith in Reading: Religious Publishing and the Birth of the Mass Media in America* (New York: Oxford University Press, 2004); Candy Gunther Brown, *The Word in the World: Evangelical Writing, Publishing, and Reading in America, 1789–1880* (Chapel Hill: University of North Carolina Press, 2004); Paul C. Gutjahr, *An American Bible: A History of the Good Book in the United States, 1777–1880* (Stanford, Calif.: Stanford University Press, 1999); and Nathan O. Hatch, *The Democratization of American Christianity* (New Haven, Conn.: Yale University Press, 1989), esp. 179–183. The five-volume, 3,200-page *History of the Book in America*, completed in 2010, does not include a stand-alone essay about how the Bible was printed and read, although references to the Bible appear throughout. The five volumes are as follows: Hugh Amory and David D. Hall, eds., *The Colonial Book in the Atlantic World*, (New York: Cambridge University Press, 2000); Robert A. Gross and Mary Kelley, eds., *An Extensive Republic: Print, Culture, and Society in the New Nation, 1790–1840* (Chapel Hill: University of North Carolina Press, 2010); Scott Casper et al., eds., *The Industrial Book, 1840–1880* (Chapel Hill: University of North Carolina Press, 2007); Carl F. Kaestle and Janice A. Radway, eds., *Print in Motion: The Expansion of Publishing and Reading in the United States, 1880–1940* (Chapel Hill: University of North Carolina Press, 2009); David Paul Nord et al., *The Enduring Book: Print Culture in Postwar America* (Chapel Hill: University of North Carolina Press, 2009).

3. William Cowper Scott, "Poetry—the Dignity of Its Nature," *Southern Literary Messenger*, (April 1846): 193–198; Ingrid Satelmajer, "Print Poetry as Oral 'Event' in Nineteenth-Century American Periodicals," in Sandra M. Gustafson and Caroline Sloat, eds., *Cultural Narratives: Textuality and Performance in American Culture before 1900* (Notre Dame, Ind.: University of Notre Dame Press, 2010).

4. James N. Green, "The Rise of Book Publishing," in Gross and Kelley, *Extensive Republic*, 75–127.

5. Michael O'Brien, *Conjectures of Order: Intellectual Life and the American South, 1810–1860* (Chapel Hill: University of North Carolina Press, 2004), 706; Beth Abney, "The Orion as a Literary Publication," *Georgia Historical Quarterly* 48 (December 1964): 411–424, quote on 415; Frederick W. Faxon, *Literary Annuals and Gift Books, A Bibliography, 1823–1903* (1912; reprint, Middlesex, UK: Private Libraries Association, 1973); Ralph Thompson, *American Literary Annuals and Gift Books, 1825–1865* (New York: H. W. Wilson, 1936); Alonzo Potter, D.D., "Influence of Literature on the Moral Sentiments," in John A. Clark, ed., *The Christian Keepsake and Missionary Annual* (Philadelphia, 1838), 281–291, quoted in Thompson, *American Literary Annuals*, 27; "Extracts from Mr. Mason's Journal," *Baptist Missionary Magazine* (Boston, 1836), 165.

6. John Newland Maffitt, "Religion and Poetry," in *The Cabinet of Religion, Education, Literature, Science, and Intelligence* (New York, 1830), 57–59, quotes on 57, 59; Waddel Alexander, *Thoughts on Preaching Being Contributed to Homiletics* (New York, 1863), 435, 503; "The Sabbath in Its Poetical Aspects," *Southern Literary Messenger*, April 15, 1849, 223. Historians have paid little mind to evangelicals' obsession with poetry. An exception is Bridget Ford, "American Heartland: The Sentimentalization of Religion and Race Relations in Cincinnati and Louisville, 1820–1860" (Ph.D. diss., University of California, Davis, 2002), chap. 9, "Belief in Poetry." See also Brown, *Word in the World*, 204–205.

7. Beth Barton Schweiger, "A Social History of English Grammar in the Early United States," *Journal of the Early Republic* 30 (Winter 2010): 533–555.

8. James E. Kirby, Russell E. Richey, and Kenneth E. Rowe, *The Methodists* (Westport, Conn.: Greenwood Press, 1996), 303–304; Frank Luther Mott, *A History of American Magazines, 1850–1865* (Cambridge, Mass.: Harvard University Press, 1938), 301–305.

9. For example, see P., "Miss Barrett's Poems, *Methodist Quarterly Review* (January 1846): 54–68; "Henry Wadsworth Longfellow," *Methodist Quarterly Review* (October 1859): 568–585; "Bryant's Poems," *Methodist Quarterly Review* (January 1859): 41–46.

10. Rufus W. Clark, *Lectures on the Formation of Character, Temptations and Mission of Young Men* (Boston, 1853), 99.

11. Alonzo Potter, "Influence of Literature on the Moral Sentiments," in John A. Clark, ed., *The Christian Keepsake and Missionary Annual* (Philadelphia, 1838), 281–292, quote on 282; Hugh Blair, "Lecture II—Taste," in James L. Golden and Edward P. J. Corbett, eds., *The Rhetoric of Blair, Campbell, and Whately* (Carbondale: Southern Illinois University Press, 1990), 37–40.

12. Jerry Wayne Brown, *The Rise of Biblical Criticism in America, 1800–1870* (Middletown, Conn.: Wesleyan University Press, 1969), 22.

13. James Turner, *Philology: The Forgotten Origins of the Modern Humanities* (Princeton: Princeton University Press, 2014), 78–80.

14. David S. Katz, *God's Last Words: Reading the English Bible from the Reformation to Fundamentalism* (New Haven, Conn.: Yale University Press, 2004), 153–157, quote on 154.

15. Bickersteth, *Works of the Rev. E. Bickersteth* (New York, 1832), 550–551.

16. Robert Lowth, *Lectures on the Sacred Poetry of the Hebrews*, ed. Calvin E. Stowe (Andover, Mass., 1829), xv; Adam Clarke, "Introduction to the Book of Psalms," in *The Holy Bible . . . . With a Commentary and Critical Notes*, vol. 3 (London, 1854), 1919, 1924; Matthew Henry, "Preface to the Poetical Books," in William Jenks, ed., *Matthew Henry's Comprehensive Commentary of the Holy Bible with Scott's Marginal References* (Brattleboro, Vt., 1836), 593.

17. John Kitto, *A Cyclopaedia of Biblical Literature*, vol. 2 (New York: Ivison & Phinney, 1854), 571–574; Margaret Sumner, *Collegiate Republic: Cultivating an Ideal Society in Early America* (Charlottesville: University of Virginia Press, 2014), 148–150; Elizabeth Stuart Phelps et al., *Our Famous Women: An Authorized Record of Their Lives and Deeds* (Hartford, Conn.: A. D. Worthington & Company, 1884), 541; Sarah Josepha Hale, *Woman's Record: or, Sketches of All Distinguished Women* (New York: Harper & Brothers, 1853), 830.

18. D., "Hebrew Minstrelsy," *Ladies' Repository, and Gatherings of the West* 4 (December 1844): 362; review of Halsey's *Literary Attractions of the Bible*, *Southern Presbyterian Review* 11 (1859): 442; Thomas Smith Grimké, *Reflections on the Character and Objects of All Science and Literature* (New Haven, Conn., 1831), 132.

19. Lowth, *Lectures on the Sacred Poetry of the Hebrews* (1787; Hildesheim, Germany: Georg Olms Verlag, 1969), vi–vii; Oliver A. Taylor, ed., *Catalogue of the Library of the Theological*

Seminary at Andover, Mass. (Andover, Mass., 1838), 283–284; "Annual Report of the Faculty to the Trustees of the New Theological Institution," *Baptist Missionary Magazine* 15 (1835): 415; "Review," *North American Review* 31 (October 1830): 337–379; "Hebrew Minstrelsy," *Ladies Repository* 4 (December 1844): 362–363; Benjamin Nicholls, *The Mine Explored, or Help to Reading the Bible* (Philadelphia: American Sunday School Union, 1853); Jasper Adams, *Elements of Moral Philosophy* (Philadelphia, 1837), 75.

20. David Norton, *A History of the English Bible as Literature* (New York: Cambridge University Press, 2000), 272–298.

21. S. Gilman, D.D., *Poetical Remains of the Late Mary Elizabeth Lee* (Charleston: Walker & Richards, 1851), n.p. Lydia Sigourney wrote a memoir of Hemans. Hemans's reputation after her death moved from "polite discouragement, to emerging appreciation, to celebrity, to condescension, to obscurity, to critical and scholarly recovery, to renewed classroom interest." Susan J. Wolfson, ed., *Felicia Hemans: Selected Poems, Letters, Reception Materials* (Princeton: Princeton University Press, 2000), xiv.

22. Ann Douglas, *The Feminization of American Culture* (1977; reprint, New York: Anchor Press, 1988), 113; Andrews Norton to Felicia Hemans, spring 1831, quoted in Wolfson, *Felicia Hemans*, 569; Gary Kelly, ed., *Felicia Hemans: Selected Poems, Prose, and Letters* (Peterborough, Ontario: Broadview Press, 2002), 59–65.

23. Julie Melnyk, "Hemans's Later Poetry: Religion and the Vatic Poet," in Nanora Sweet and Julie Melnyk, eds., *Felicia Hemans: Reimagining Poetry in the Nineteenth Century* (New York: Palgrave, 2001); "Felicia Hemans," in Marion Ann Taylor, ed., *Handbook of Women Biblical Interpreters: A Historical and Biographical Guide* (Grand Rapids, Mich.: Baker Academic, 2012), 249–254.

24. Richmond Mercantile Library Association, *Catalogue of Books* (Richmond: Shepherd & Colin, 1839); Almira H. Lincoln Phelps, *Lectures to Young Ladies, comprising Outlines and Applications of the Different Branches of Female Education* (Boston: Carter, Hendee and Co and Allen and Ticknor, 1833), 40; "Extracts from the Prospectus of The Columbia Female Institute," *Guardian, A Family Magazine* (Columbia, Tenn.), January 1, 1841; "Felicia Hemans," *Home Circle, A Monthly Periodical Devoted to Religion & Literature* (Nashville), October 1855, 437–442; William Bentley Fowle, *The New Speaker* (1829), in Sister Marie Leonore Fell, ed., *The Foundations of Nativism in American Textbooks, 1783–1860* (Washington, D.C.: Catholic University of America Press, 1941), 60; T(imothy) S(hay) Pinneo, *The Hemans Reader for Female Schools* (New York: Clark, Austin & Smith, 1847).

25. Wolfson, *Felicia Hemans*, 612. Andrews Norton wrote extensively about Hemans for the *North American Review*.

26. Hemans appeared in the "Poetry Corner" of an Alabama newspaper in the 1820s, for example. Rhoda Coleman Ellison, *Early Alabama Publications: A Study in Literary Interests* (Tuscaloosa: University of Alabama Press, 1947), 45. See also advertisement for works of Mrs. Hemans along with Sigourney's memoir of her in seven volumes, *Raleigh Register and North Carolina Gazette*, May 14, 1841, 2; Mrs. [Felicia] Hemans, "The Wounded Eagle," *Cherokee Phoenix*, May 6, 1828, 4.

27. Henry Theodore Tuckerman, "Cowper," *Southern Literary Messenger* (December 1840), 838–842; "Biblical Eloquence and Poetry," *Princeton Review* 3 (October 1831): 447–454, quotes on 452, 450.

28. Stephen A. Marini, "American Protestant Hymns Project: A Ranked List of Most Frequently Printed Hymns, 1737–1960," appendix 1 in Richard J. Mouw et al., eds., *Wonderful Words of Life: Hymns in American Protestant History and Theology* (Grand Rapids, Mich.: Eerdmans, 2004), 251–264.

29. Raymond Williams, *Keywords: A Vocabulary of Culture and Society* (New York: Oxford University Press, 1976), 76–82.

30. Lawrence W. Levine, *Black Culture and Black Consciousness: Afro-American Folk Thought from Slavery to Freedom* (New York: Oxford University Press, 1977), ix.

CHAPTER 6

1. *Incidents in the Life of a Slave Girl* (Boston: Published for the Author, 1861), 294. http://docsouth.unc.edu/neh/texts.html.

2. Some white interpreters certainly utilized this text for their explorations of racial origins. See Thomas Virgil Peterson, *Ham and Japheth: The Mythic World of Whites in the Antebellum South* (Metuchen, NJ: American Theological Library Association, 1978).

3. *Incidents in the Life of a Slave Girl*, 69. Jacobs cites Acts 17:26 from the King James Version: "And hath made of one blood all nations of men for to dwell on all the face of the earth, and hath determined the times before appointed, and the bounds of their habitation." The NRSV offers the following translation for 17:26–27: "*From one ancestor he made all nations* to inhabit the whole earth, and he allotted the times of their existence and the boundaries of the places where they would live, so that they would search for God and perhaps grope for him and find him—though indeed he is not far from each one of us." The Greek has "out of one" without any noun to be modified by "one" (whether "blood" or "ancestor").

4. "There is a great difference between Christianity and religion at the south. If a man goes to the communion table, and pays money into the treasury of the church, no matter if it be the price of blood, he is called religious" (*Incidents in the Life of a Slave Girl*, 115).

5. Sylvester A. Johnson, *The Myth of Ham in Nineteenth-Century American Christianity: Race, Heathens, and the People of God* (New York: Palgrave McMillan, 2004), 10. There is evidence that a few did move in a different direction (e.g., William Anderson, James Curry, James Pennington).

6. A decade later, in a speech titled "The Composite Nation," Douglass broadened out his argument to include observations about the influx of Asians on to the American soil: "The Chinese are likely to be even more difficult to deal with than the negro. The latter took his pay in religion and the lash. The Chinaman is a different article, and will want the cash. He has notions of justice that are not to be confused or bewildered by any of our 'Cursed be Canaan' religion"; cited in Frederic May Holland, *Frederick Douglass, the Colored Orator* (New York: Funk and Wagnalls Company, 1895), 321.

7. "It will do away the force of the argument, that God cursed Ham, and therefore American slavery is right," in *The Narrative of the Life of Frederick Douglass* (Boston: Anti-Slavery Office, 1845), 5.

8. The biblical account is an etiological story about Canaan's downfall and provides justification for the "eventual" (following the biblical timeline) destruction of the land of Canaan. One major difference between nineteenth-century enslavement and its counterpart in antiquity was that, in antiquity, anyone could be enslaved; in its contemporary version, only dark-skinned peoples could be enslaved. See Paul Finklemann, *Defending Slavery: Proslavery Thought in the Old South* (Boston: St. Martin's, 2003), 8; Finklemann ignores the fact that Native Americans were enslaved for a period of U.S. history.

9. See Mark A. Noll, *The Civil War as a Theological Crisis* (Chapel Hill: University of North Carolina Press, 2006).

10. Swan, "The American School of Ethnology," *Mankind Quarterly* (October 1971): 90.

11. Mark A. Noll, *America's God: From Jonathan Edwards to Abraham Lincoln* (Oxford: Oxford University Press, 2002), 418.

12. Peterson claims that there was only *one* southern clergyman in the antebellum South who "unequivocally rejected Ham as the progenitor of the black race" (*Ham and Japheth*, 102); this Lutheran pastor in Charleston, John Bachman, asserted that "environmental factors" were the cause for the color variety in America (102).

13. Speech in Boston, Massachusetts, February 8, 1855, cited in J. Albert Harrill, "The Use of the New Testament in the American Slave Controversy: A Case History in the Hermeneutical Tension between Biblical Criticism and Christian Moral Debate," *Religion and American Culture* 10 (2000): 160.

14. As in Toni Morrison's words in the epigraph; *Playing in the Dark: Whiteness and the Literary Imagination* (New York: Vintage Books, 1992), xii.

15. *Life and Narrative of William J. Anderson, Twenty-Four Years a Slave* (Chicago: Daily Tribune Book and Job Printing Office, 1857), 61. "And the Lord God formed man of the dust of the ground, and breathed into his nostrils the breath of life; and man became a living soul" (Gen 2:7; KJV).

16. Others—e.g., Henry Box Brown, in Charles Stearns, *Narrative of Henry Box Brown* (Boston: Brown and Stearns, 1849), and David West, in Benjamin Drew, *A North-Side View of Slavery* (Boston: J. P. Jewett and Company, 1856)—provided oral statements (to white narrators) reflecting on this biblical passage, but it was utilized to discuss *status* rather than *race*. Without reference to Genesis, Leonard Black wrote about a common knowledge regarding the blackness of King Solomon; *Life and Sufferings of Leonard Black* (New Bedford: Benjamin Lindsey, 1847), 52–53.

17. See Robert Benjamin Lewis, *Light and Truth: From Ancient and Sacred History* (Augusta, ME: Severance & Dorr, 1843; reprint, Ithaca, NY: Cornell University Library Digital Collections, 2012). Equally important, for Lewis, was the etymology of the Hebrew word *'adam*, which meant, according to Lewis, "earthy."

18. Gehazi was introduced, earlier in the biblical narrative, in the story of the Shunamite woman (2 Kings 4).

19. Anderson, *Life and Narrative of William J. Anderson*, 61.

20. Naaman received 2.5 lines; Gehazi received 14.5 lines. In the (KJV) text, Naaman is described as a "Syrian," who—as captain of the army—had captured an Israelite girl to serve his wife (5:1–2, 20).

21. Anderson ignored the following: (1) Gehazi's request is for "two prophets"; in Anderson's retelling, the clothes were apparently for Elisha himself; (2) it was Naaman's "two servants" who carried the goods back; instead, it seems as if Gehazi carried the items away himself.

22. In nineteenth-century secondary sources on the Bible, Gehazi was frequently associated with *Achan* (in OT) and *Judas* (in NT) as preeminent biblical thieves.

23. Extremely rare was a focus on the leprosy as God's "theocratic punishment."

24. In *Tracts of the American Tract Society: General Series*, vol. 6 (New York: American Tract Society, 1825). No author is listed. Digital Presentation in the Theological Commons (DPTC), http://commons.ptsem.edu/.

25. *Slavery: A Divine Institution* (Port Gibson, MI: Southern Reveille Book & Job Office, 1861), DPTC.

26. See Mark A. Noll on the dominance of commonsense hermeneutics in the nineteenth century. Anderson added to the biblical account only Gehzai's feelings when he departed from Elisha: he was "scared" (Anderson, *Life and Narrative of William J. Anderson*, 62).

27. Anderson, *Life and Narrative of William J. Anderson*, 62.

28. With respect to Japheth, "Their posterity peopled the north half of Asia, almost all the mediterranean isles, all Europe, and I suppose, most of America." John Brown, *A Dictionary of the Holy Bible*; vol. 2 (Pittsburg, PA: The Ecclesiastical and Literary Press of Zadok Cramer, 1807).

29. George Bush, ed., *Illustrations of the Holy Scriptures, Derived Principally from the Manners, Customs, Rites, Traditions and Works of Art and Literature, of the Eastern Nations . . . with Descriptions of the Present State of Countries and Places Mentioned in the Sacred Writings* (Brattleboro, VT: Brattleboro Typographic Company, 1839). The statement was republished in the 1856 edition. DPTC. Most of this comment, if not all, Bush derived from Joseph Roberts's *Oriental Illustrations* (London, 1829).

30. Edward Said, *Orientalism* (New York: Vintage Books, 1978).

31. See Robert Benjamin Lewis, *Light and Truth*. It does not seem that Lewis or James Pennington, in *A Textbook of the Origin and History of the Colored People* (Hartford: L. Skinner, 1841), account for "whiteness," though Lewis was also interested in reporting on the origins of Native Americans. Following Genesis 2:7, Lewis concluded that Adam must have been "black" since "the soil of Eden was very rich, and black" (*Light and Truth*, 1). A few pages later Lewis also suggested that Adam was "reddish in color" (7). James Pennington turned to the Genesis passage to make his case for the human intellect of African Americans, without privileging any racial identification (*Textbook*, 57). Lewis's goal was to explore the greatness of ancient Ethiopia to counter contemporary claims to the contrary. For Josiah Priest, the origins of whiteness, like blackness, began at Genesis 9, since Noah and his wife were originally red, as were the first created humans.

32. Anderson's digression into theories of racial origins was partly due to the lack of sponsorship on his project. Apparently, Anderson had no need for such financial (and editorial) support. He owned three farms and ran other successful businesses and simply had the means to carry out this literary project unencumbered by the political necessities of his formerly enslaved colleagues. In many ways, his appendix gives us a rare glimpse into the biblical imagination of the black mind to account for the color of whiteness in the contemporary world. If a lot was "said about color" in his day, it was from a white perspective, what whites postulated about the origins of blackness, as a way of organizing their social institutions in antebellum America. What was less well known—because the political, economic, and media outlets would not allow for it—was what African Americans thought, said, and wrote about the origins of whiteness.

33. See Robert Lewis, who briefly attempted to account for "red" people groups (i.e., Native Americans).

CHAPTER 7

1. Philip Barlow, *Mormons and the Bible: The Place of the Latter-day Saints in American Religion*, rev ed. (New York: Oxford University Press, 2013), 109.

2. Gerda Lerner explains how the "act of critique and reinterpretation [of the Bible] would be a prime example of their subversion and transformation of patriarchal doctrine, in itself a feminist act. Such an act implies that the person engaging in reinterpretation considers herself fully authorized and capable of challenging expert theological authority." Gerda Lerner, *The Creation of Feminist Consciousness: From the Middle Ages to Eighteen-Seventy* (New York: Oxford University Press, 1993), 138. Rebecca Styler has also written

about how "through the genre of collective Bible biography, series of short life accounts of scriptural women, nineteenth-century women took interpretive control out of the hands of experts and analyzed these characters in more empowering ways." Rebecca Styler, *Literary Theology by Women Writers of the Nineteenth Century* (Farnham, Surrey: Ashgate, 2010), 69.

3. Grant Underwood writes, "As we step back to take a larger look at Book of Mormon usage in early years, we can make a number of general observations. First, compared to the Bible, the Book of Mormon was hardly cited at all.... To a people who have come to prize the Book of Mormon as 'the keystone' of their religion, it may come as a surprise to learn that in the early literature the Bible was cited nearly twenty times more frequently than the Book of Mormon." Grant Underwood, "Book of Mormon Usage in Early LDS Thought," *Dialogue* 17 (autumn 1984): 52.

4. For a cross-section of journals see "Diaries, Journals, and Autobiographies of Contemporaries of Joseph Smith Jr.," Book of Abraham Project, http://www.boap.org.

5. "Christian Primitivism" refers to Christian groups that are restorationist in their outlook, believing that a purer form of Christianity should be restored using the early church as a model. Barlow, *Mormons and the Bible*, 10.

6. Barlow, *Mormons and the Bible*, 106.

7. Mark A. Noll has noted that the Bible for most Protestant Americans has been first a "compendium of instructions for faith and practice." Mark A. Noll, "The Image of the United States as a Biblical Nation, 1776–1865," in *The Bible in America: Essays in Cultural History*, 39–58, ed. Nathan O. Hatch and Mark A. Noll (New York: Oxford University Press, 1982), 43.

8. Barlow, *Mormons and the Bible*, 106.

9. Gordon Irving, "The Mormons and the Bible in the 1830s," *BYU Studies* 13 (summer 1973): 473–488, 474–476.

10. "By Scripture alone." It is the doctrine that the Bible contains all knowledge necessary for salvation and holiness. For Mormons, the canon was still open, and they would add other texts revealed to Joseph Smith, such as the Book of Mormon, the Doctrine and Covenants, and the Pearl of Great Price, to their canon of scripture.

11. For more information, see Barlow, *Mormons and the Bible*, 94–111.

12. Two of the best works of scholarship documenting this phenomena in Protestant America are Lori Ginzberg, *Women and the Work of Benevolence: Morality, Politics, and Class in the Nineteenth-Century United States* (New Haven: Yale University Press, 1990), and Nancy A Hewitt, *Women's Activism and Social Change, Rochester, New York, 1822–1872* (Ithaca: Cornell University Press, 1984).

13. For a good overview of nineteenth-century Mormon women's lived reality, see Maureen Ursebach Beecher and Lavina Fielding Anderson, eds., *Sisters in Spirit: Mormon Women in Historical and Cultural Perspective* (Chicago: University of Illinois Press, 1987); Carol Cornwall Madsen, ed., *Battle for the Ballot: Essays on Woman Suffrage in Utah* (Logan: Utah State University Press, 1997); Jill Mulvay Derr, Janath Russell Cannon, and Maureen Ursenbach Beecher, eds., *Women of Covenant: The Story of Relief Society* (Salt Lake City: Deseret Book, 1992); Maxine Hanks, ed., *Women and Authority: Re-emerging Mormon Feminism* (Salt Lake City: Signature Books, 1992). For examples of individual women, see Richard E. Turley Jr. and Brittany A. Chapman, eds., *Women of Faith in the Latter Days*, vols. 1–3 (Salt Lake City: Deseret Book, 2011–14).

14. "Emmeline B. Wells," *Tullidge's Quarterly Magazine* 1 (January 1881): 252, cited in Sherilyn Cox Bennion, "The Woman's Exponent: Forty-Two Years of Speaking for Women," *Utah Historical Quarterly* 44, no. 3 (summer 1976): 222–239.

15. For historical background on the *Woman's Exponent*, see Bennion, "Woman's Exponent," 226–239; Carol Cornwall Madsen, *An Advocate for Women: The Public Life of Emmeline B. Wells, 1870–1920* (Provo, UT: BYU Studies, 2006): 34–66.

16. See Carol Cornwall Madsen, "Voices in Print: The Woman's Exponent, 1872–1914," in *Women Steadfast in Christ*, ed. Dawn Hall Anderson and Marie Cornwall (Salt Lake City: Deseret Book, 1992), 69–80, 71–72. "A categorical breakdown of the editorial content reflects the *Exponent*'s emphasis. More than 20 percent of the editorials addressed the subject of woman's rights, another 20 percent discussed Church and Relief Society news, 10 percent defended polygamy, and 7 percent supported woman suffrage" (72).

17. See chapter 1.

18. See for example Eliza R. Snow, "A Synopsis," *Woman's Exponent* 3, no. 23 (1875): 178–179; Anonymous, "Sisters Be in Earnest," *Woman's Exponent* 5, no. 10 (1876): 76; Emile, "Woman's Voice," *Woman's Exponent* 5, no. 13 (1876): 101; Anonymous, "F R Society Reports," *Woman's Exponent* 1, no. 3 (1872): 2.

19. See for example Excellette, "Woman's Voice," *Woman's Exponent* 2, no. 20 (1874): 147; Mary Ann M. Pratt, "For What Are We Called in Question?," *Woman's Exponent* 12, no. 23 (1884): 178; Mary Ann M. Pratt, "Questions Answered," *Woman's Exponent* 10, no. 21 (1882): 162; Anonymous, "Wise Women of Scripture," *Woman's Exponent* 8, no. 10 (1879): 76; Hope, "Divinity of the Bible," *Woman's Exponent* 11, no. 17 (1883): 129–130; M. E. Kimball, "The Bible," *Woman's Exponent* 4, no. 16 (1887): 27.

20. See for example E.M., "Home Missionaries," *Woman's Exponent* 1, no. 17 (1873): 135; Mary Ann M. Pratt, "Bible Doctrine," *Woman's Exponent* 10, no. 24 (1882): 189; Hannah T. King, "Mrs. Emily Scott," *Woman's Exponent* 10, no. 24 (1882): 189; Mary Ann M. Pratt, "Question," *Woman's Exponent* 22, no. 16 (1894): 124–125; Anonymous, "Letter from Mrs. M. I. Horne," *Woman's Exponent* 4, no. 21 (1876): 4–5; M. E. Kimball, "Why Offended," *Woman's Exponent* 18, no. 5 (1889): 36–37; M. E. Kimball, "Not So Fast," *Woman's Exponent* 18, no. 13 (1889): 97; Julia Cruse Howe, "An Address," *Woman's Exponent* 18, no. 13 (1889): 101–102.

21. As proclaimed in the inaugural edition, the stated impetus of the *Woman's Exponent* was to help one another progress through the "diffusion of knowledge and information" and to correct the "gross misrepresent[ations]" of Latter-day Saint women found within the popular press by providing them with a means of representing themselves. Louisa Lula Greene, "A Utah Ladies' Journal," *Woman's Exponent* 1, no. 1 (1872): 8.

22. Bennion, "Woman's Exponent," 225–226.

23. Carolyn De Swarte Gifford, "American Women and the Bible: The Nature of Woman as a Hermeneutical Issue," in *Feminist Perspectives on Biblical Scholarship*, ed. Adela Yarbro Collins (Chico, CA: Society of Biblical Literature, 1985), 22.

24. Benjamin Jowett, "On the Interpretation of Scripture," in *Essays and Reviews* (London: Parker & Sons, 1860), 377.

25. Christiana de Groot and Marion Ann Taylor, "Recovering Nineteenth-Century Women Interpreters of the Bible," in *Recovering Nineteenth-Century Women Interpreters of the Bible* (Atlanta: Society of Biblical Literature, 2007), 9. See also Gerald Bray, *Biblical Interpretation: Past and Present* (Downers Grove, IL: InterVarsity Press, 1996), 306.

26. Marion Ann Taylor and Heather E. Weir, *Let Her Speak for Herself: Nineteenth-Century Women Writing on Women in Genesis* (Waco, TX: Baylor University Press, 2006), 15–17.

27. Taylor and Weir, *Let Her Speak*, 6. See also de Groot and Taylor, *Recovering Nineteenth-Century*, 5. With the feminization of religion in the nineteenth century, mothers became the parents who read and instructed children in the Bible and became increasingly responsible for nurturing proper morals in young people and society. For more information see Barbara Welter, "The Feminization of American Religion: 1800–1860," in *Clio's Consciousness Raised: New Perspectives on the History of Women*, ed. Mary S. Hartman and Lois Banner (New York: Harper and Row, 1974), 137–157.

28. For findings of this in Protestant female exegesis, see Styler, *Literary Theology*, 78; Julie Melnyk, "Women's Theology and the British Periodical Press," in *Reinventing Christianity: Nineteenth-Century Contexts* (Aldershot, England: Ashgate, 2001), 191.

29. Terryl L. Givens, *The Viper on the Hearth: Mormons, Myths, and the Construction of Heresy*, rev. ed. (New York: Oxford University Press, 2013), 157–163.

30. For information on this in a Protestant context, see Styler, *Literary Theology*, 71–78.

31. Hannah Tapfield King, *The Women of the Scriptures* (Salt Lake City: privately published, 1878), 1; originally published serially in the *Woman's Exponent*.

32. For examples of this, look at each of these women's exegesis of Sarah, reprinted in Taylor and Weir, *Let Her Speak*, 149–172. Taylor and Weir also surmise from their vast research that "most [nineteenth-century interpreters] seemed to delight in discussing Sarah's imperfections" (187).

33. Joseph Smith, *Teachings of the Prophet Joseph Smith* (Salt Lake City: Deseret Book, 2006), 181, 59–61. See also Barlow, *Mormons and the Bible*, 57, 119; Irving, "Mormons and the Bible," 474.

34. "Men and women, in that age of the world, seem to have practiced deceit and spoken lies, as children do, from immaturity and want of deep reflection" (12). According to Stowe, the patriarchs and matriarchs lived during "the world's infancy," and "the Father God…looks down on [them]…as a mother on the quarrels of little children in the nursery." Harriet Beecher Stowe, *Woman in Sacred History* (1873; reprint, New York: Portland House, 1990), 37.

35. Interestingly, this reverence for the Old Testament prophets continues in the Mormon Church today. One may readily see this by looking at an Old Testament Sunday school manual and noting what it emphasizes and ignores.

36. King, *Women of the Scriptures*, 5–6.

37. For good primary examples of this see Grace Aguilar, Sarah Hale, and Elizabeth Julia Hasell's exegeses of Rebekah, reprinted in Taylor and Weir, *Let Her Speak*, 268–280, 283–286, 302–307.

38. M.H., "Paul," *Woman's Exponent* 3, no. 17 (1875): 131.

39. Aunt Em, "The Integrity of Ruth," *Woman's Exponent* 7, no. 12 (1878): 89.

40. King, *Women of the Scriptures*, 2–6.

41. King, *Women of the Scriptures*, 14.

42. For an overview of nineteenth-century gender norms and the use of the image "angel in the house," see Anne Hogan and Andrew Bradstock, *Women of Faith in Victorian Culture: Reassessing the Angel in the House* (Charlottesville: University of Virginia Press, 1966), 1–5. See also Barbara Welter, "The Cult of True Womanhood: 1820–1860," *American Quarterly* 18 (1966): 151–174.

43. Catherine A. Brekus, *Strangers and Pilgrims: Female Preaching in America 1740–1845* (Chapel Hill: University of North Carolina Press, 1998), 149–153. For primary examples from nineteenth-century female exegetes, see Taylor and Weir, *Let Her Speak*, 84–90, 269–280, 377–382.

44. Adelia B. Cox Sidwell, "Women of the Bible," *Woman's Exponent* 18, no. 17 (1890): 136.

45. Sidwell, "Women of the Bible," 136–137; Aunt Em [pseudonym for Wells], "The Integrity of Ruth," 89.

46. Aunt Em, "Integrity of Ruth," 89.

47. See Joy A. Schroeder, *Deborah's Daughters: Gender Politics and Biblical Interpretation* (New York: Oxford University Press, 2014), 148, 169, for more details on Grimké and Neyman.

48. Tarla Rai Peterson, "The *Woman's Exponent*, 1872–1914: Champion for 'The Rights of the Women of Zion, and the Rights of the Women of All Nations,'" in *A Voice of Their Own*, ed. Martha M. Solomon (Tuscaloosa: University of Alabama Press, 1991), 168. Peterson is drawing from Madsen's MA thesis.

49. Brekus, *Strangers and Pilgrims*, 149–151; Aileen S. Kraditor, *The Ideas of the Woman Suffrage Movement 1890–1920* (New York: Norton, 1981), 96–122.

50. Thyra, "Our Modern Dorcas," *Woman's Exponent* 5, no. 13 (1876): 97.

51. Cited in Schroeder, *Deborah's Daughters*, 163.

52. For examples, see Anonymous, "Be Wise and Hearken to Counsel," *Woman's Exponent* 5, no. 11 (1876): 84; Lillie Devereux Blake, "Women in History," *Woman's Exponent* 16, no. 9 (1887): 65–66; Sidwell, "Women of the Bible," *Woman's Exponent* 18, no. 17 (1890): 136–137; Anonymous, "Wise Women," 76; Anonymous, "The Days of the Judges," *Woman's Exponent* 18, no. 19 (1890): 149.

53. Ella F. Smith, "Woman's Mind Equal to Man's," *Woman's Exponent* 18, no. 22 (1890): 177.

54. For a discussion of this outside the Mormon faith see Schroeder, *Deborah's Daughters*, 155, 161, 180–184.

55. Emily H. Woodmansee, "Lawn Fete," *Woman's Exponent* 19, no. 4 (1890): 29; Anonymous, "Wise Women," 76; Anonymous, "Days of the Judges," 149; Blake, "Women in History," 65–66; Aunt Em, "Integrity of Ruth," 89.

56. See Peterson, "*Woman's Exponent*," 171–178.

57. Speaking of the Women's Temperance Union, Ann Braude writes: "However it was phrased, the idea that women needed the vote in order to promote Christian values was a radical notion to the relatively conservative churchwomen who made up the rank and file of the WCTU." Ann Braude, *Sisters and Saints: Women and American Religion* (New York: Oxford University Press, 2007), 79.

58. For information on women of other faiths, see Gifford, "American Women," 11, 17; Brekus, *Strangers and Pilgrims*, 217; Schroeder, *Deborah's Daughters*, 140–141, 155; Nancy Hardesty, *Women Called to Witness: Evangelical Feminism in the Nineteenth Century*, 2nd ed. (Knoxville: University of Tennessee Press, 1999), 62–63.

59. Anonymous, "Wise Women," 76.

60. For Protestant examples see Hardesty, *Women Called to Witness*, 63, and Beth Bidlack, "Olympia Brown: Reading the Bible as a Universalist Minister and Pragmatic Suffragist," in *Breaking Boundaries: Female Biblical Interpreters Who Challenged the Status Quo*, ed. Nancy Calvert-Koyzis and Heather Weir (New York: Bloomsbury, 2010), 140.

61. Phebe C. Young, "Woman and Her Sphere," *Woman's Exponent* 17, no. 18 (1889): 139.

62. Smith, "Woman's Mind Equal," 177–178.

63. Smith, "Woman's Mind Equal," 177–178.

64. Taylor and Weir, *Let Her Speak*, 396; For specific examples from different nineteenth-century female interpreters see Taylor and Weir, *Let Her Speak*, 115, 140, 178, 284, 327–328, 368, 389–390, 393, 396.

65. See Doctrine and Covenants 132:34–38, 61–66.

66. See Doctrine and Covenants 112:30, 124:41, 128:18.

67. For more information, see "Plural Marriage in Kirtland and Nauvoo" and "Plural Marriage and Families in Early Utah," lds.org. https://www.lds.org/topics/.

68. Peterson, "*Woman's Exponent*," 173.

69. Emmeline B. Wells, "Women Talkers and Women Writers," *Woman's Exponent* 5, no. 6 (1876): 44. Originally cited in Peterson, "*Woman's Exponent*," 173, and Madsen, "Voices in Print," 75.

70. Madsen, "Voices in Print," 72.

71. For a list of some of these see note 72 (p. 112) in Andrew C. Smith, "Hagar in LDS Scripture and Thought," *Interpreter: A Journal of Mormon Scripture* 8 (2014): 87–137. Examples in the *Woman's Exponent* include Anonymous, "A Few Reflections," *Woman's Exponent* 6, no. 1 (1877): 3; Anonymous, "A Few Reflections," *Woman's Exponent* 6, no. 2 (1877): 9; Mrs. Jennie Tanner, "The Ladies' Mass Meeting," *Woman's Exponent* 14, no. 20 (1886): 159; Sarah A. Fullmer, "Our Franchise," *Woman's Exponent* 11, no. 24 (1883): 185.

72. Fullmer, "Our Franchise," 185.

73. Anonymous, "Few Reflections," *Woman's Exponent* 6, no. 1, 3.

74. Anonymous, "Mormonism Will Live," *Woman's Exponent* 9, no. 20 (1881): 156.

75. Anonymous, "Few Reflections," *Woman's Exponent* 6, no. 2, 9. See also A Plural Wife, "My Views on Celestial, Plural Marriage," *Woman's Exponent* 15, no. 15 (1887): 115; Mary J. Morrison, "Celestial Marriage," *Woman's Exponent* 10, no. 17 (1882): 135.

76. As many recounted, "The Lord sent His angel to Hagar" "and blessed her, and promised that she should become the mother of a 'great nation.'" "God also blessed Sarai and said she should be called Sarah and should bear a son, and become a mother of nations, and kings of nations should be of her posterity." Likewise, "the Lord heard and answered the prayers of Hannah, the [plural] wife of Elkanah, and gave her a son, even the Prophet Samuel." A Plural Wife, "My Views," 115; Fullmer, "Our Franchise," 185; Anonymous, " Few Reflections," *Woman's Exponent* 6, no 2, 9.

77. Aunt Em, "Integrity of Ruth," 89.

78. For good brief overviews of some of these women's lives and their accomplishments, see Turley and Chapman, *Women of Faith in the Latter Days*.

79. For information on Martha Hughes Cannon see Mari Grana, *Pioneer, Polygamist, Politician: The Life of Dr. Martha Hughes Cannon* (Guilford, CT: TwoDot, 2009). For information on Mary Chamberlain see Kylie Nielson Turley, "The Politics of Politics: Remembering Mary Woolley Chamberlain, Mayor of Kanab," in *New Scholarship on Latter-day Saint Women in the Twentieth Century*, ed. Carol Cornwall Madsen and Cherry B. Silver (Provo, UT: Joseph Fielding Smith Institute for Latter-day Saint History, 2005), 40.

80. "Mormonism and Women," in *Mormonism: A Historical Encyclopedia*, ed. W. Paul Reeve and Ardis E. Parshall (Santa Barbara: ABC-CLIO, 2010), 354. For more information, see note 15.

81. For more information, see Todd Compton, "Kingdom of Priests': Priesthood, Temple and Women in the Old Testament and in the Restoration," *Dialogue* 36, no. 3 (fall 2003): 41–59. Linda King Newell, "A Gift Given: A Gift Taken: Washing, Anointing, and Blessing the Sick among Mormon Women," *Sunstone* 22, nos. 3–4 (June 1999): 30–43.

82. Matthew Bowman, *The Mormon People: The Making of an American Faith* (New York: Random House, 2012), 136–139.

83. Boyd Jay Petersen, "'Redeemed from the Curse Placed upon Her': Dialogic Discourse on Eve in the *Woman's Exponent*," *Journal of Mormon History* 40, no. 1 (2014): 142.

84. Petersen, "'Redeemed from the Curse," 149.

85. Petersen, "'Redeemed from the Curse,'"157.

86. For a good overview of this, see Julie Melnyk, "Women, Writing and the Creation of Theological Cultures," in *Women, Gender and Religious Cultures in Britain, 1800–1940*, ed. Sue Morgan and Jacqueline deVries (New York: Routledge 2010), 32–53.

87. Susanna Morrill, *White Roses on the Floor of Heaven: Mormon Women's Popular Theology, 1880–1920* (New York: Routledge 2006).

CHAPTER 8

1. *Circle Seven Koran*, 1. This and all subsequent references to the *Circle Seven Koran* are based on the "Moorish Science Temple of America" files of the Federal Bureau of Investigation, FBI file no. 62-25889 (hereafter MSTA-FBI file), available at https://vault.fbi.gov, accessed July 17, 2015.

2. Vincent L. Wimbush, ed., *Theorizing Scriptures: New Critical Orientations to a Cultural Phenomenon*, Signifying (on) Scriptures (New Brunswick, N.J.: Rutgers University Press, 2008).

3. S. A. Johnson, "The Rise of Black Ethnics: The Ethnic Turn in African American Religions, 1916–1945," *Religion and American Culture: A Journal of Interpretation* 20 (summer 2010): 125–163; Michael Gomez, *Black Crescent: The Experience and Legacy of African Muslims in the Americas* (Cambridge: Cambridge University Press, 2005), 230–235.

4. Johnson, "Rise of Black Ethnics."

5. Richard Brent Turner, *Islam in the African-American Experience*, 2nd ed. (Bloomington: Indiana University Press, 2003), 94; Herbert Berg, *Elijah Muhammad and Islam* (New York: New York University Press, 2009), 14–15.

6. *Circle Seven Koran*, 60.

7. Sidney H. Griffith, *The Bible in Arabic: The Scriptures of the "People of the Book" in the Language of Islam* (Princeton, N.J.: Princeton University Press, 2013).

8. FBI field office report, Jackson, Mississippi, "Moorish Science Temple of America," April 7, 1942, p. 3, MSTA-FBI file, file no. 100-793, in FBI file no. 62-25889, pt. 1 of 31.

9. "Moorish Science Temple of America," pt. 2 of 31.

10. Theophus H. Smith, *Conjuring Culture: Biblical Formations of Black America: Biblical Formations of Black America* (Oxford: Oxford University Press, 1994).

11. Itumeleng J. Mosala, *Biblical Hermeneutics and Black Theology in South Africa* (Grand Rapids, Mich.: Eerdmans, 1989).

12. Pauline Maier, *American Scripture: Making the Declaration of Independence*, 1st Vintage Books ed. (New York: Vintage, 1998).

CHAPTER 9

1. Arno Gaebelein, *World Prospects: How Is It All Going to End?* (New York: Our Hope, 1934), 18.

2. William E. Blackstone, *Jesus Is Coming*, 2nd ed. (London: Partridge and Co., n.d.), 94, 99, 100.

3. Blackstone, *Jesus Is Coming*, 94, 95.

4. William Bell Riley, "Prophecy and Present Problems," in T. Richard Dunham, ed., *Unveiling the Future: Twelve Prophetic Messages* (Findlay, OH: Fundamental Truth, 1934), 42.

5. Louis Bauman, "The Reappearance of the Empire on the Fateful Hills of Rome," *King's Business* (July 1936), 257; Louis Bauman, "Is the Antichrist at Hand? What of Mussolini?," *King's Business* (January 1926), 15.

6. "Pastor Attacks Parental Laxity; Mussolini Flayed," *Boston Globe*, June 14, 1926; Paul Rader, *The Coming World Dictator* (Chicago: World Wide Gospel Couriers, 1934), 40; J. Frank Norris to I.

E. Gates, March 30, 1928, folder 743, box 16, collection 124, J. Frank Norris Papers, Southern Baptist Historical Library and Archives, Nashville; L. Nelson Bell to mother (Ruth Lee McCue Bell), May 21, 1930, folder 3, box 1, collection 318, Lemuel Nelson Bell Papers, Billy Graham Center Archives, Wheaton, Illinois. See also J. Frank Norris, "The Candidacy of Al Smith," in *Is America at the Crossroads? Or Roman Catholicism vs. Protestant Christianity* (Fort Worth: J. L. Rhodes, 1928), 15; and G. A. Griswood, "The Coming World Dictator," *Our Hope* (January 1931), 417.

7. Ralph C. and Edith F. Norton, "A Personal Interview with Mussolini," *Sunday School Times* (August 13, 1932), 423.

8. Harold J. Ockenga, "The Ethiopian Situation—or—The Meaning of the Present World Crisis," n.d., 2, sermon manuscripts, Harold John Ockenga Papers, Gordon Conwell Theological Seminary, South Hamilton, Massachusetts; Louis Bauman, "Socialism, Communism, and Fascism," *King's Business* (August 1935), 292; John R. Rice, "Is Mussolini the Anti-Christ?," *Sword of the Lord* (August 30, 1935), 1; John R. Rice, "Mussolini Restores the Roman Empire," *Sword of the Lord* (May 22, 1936), 1.

9. "Armageddon Just Ahead," *Baptist & Commoner* (June 16, 1926), 5; Chester Jackson to FDR, October 14, 1935, Texas file, and Howard E. Oakwood to FDR, October 3, 1935, Pennsylvania file, both in Collection 21-A, President's Personal File, Franklin D. Roosevelt Presidential Library, Hyde Park, New York.

10. Arno Gaebelein, "Confusion in Prophetic Interpretations," *Our Hope* (February 1941), 521; Louis Bauman to A. Stirling Mackay, November 29, 1940, Louis S. Bauman Papers, Bob Jones University Library, Greenville, South Carolina (microfilm); Louis S. Bauman, "Have Mussolini and His 'Resurrected Roman Empire' Both Collapsed?," *King's Business* (April 1941), 164; "Prelude to Prophecy," *Moody Monthly* (February 1948), 397.

11. See for example "Prophetic Aspects of the Atomic Bomb," *Sunday School Times* (September 1, 1945), 666; Robert B. Fischer, "The Message of the Atomic Bomb to the Church," *Moody Monthly* (March 1946), 426, 450; Wilbur M. Smith, *The Atomic Bomb and the Word of God* (Chicago: Moody, 1945), 17.

12. "Russia Has It—Now What?," *King's Business* (November 1949), 6; Lowell Blanchard with the Valley Trio, "Jesus Hits Like an Atom Bomb," on *Atomic Platters: Cold War Music from the Golden Age of Homeland Security* (Bear Family, 2005).

13. Frank E. Lindgren, "The Atomic Bomb," *King's Business* (January 1946), 9; Louis S. Bauman, *The Approaching End of This Age* (Grand Rapids: Zondervan, 1952), 6; Wilbur M. Smith, "World Crises and the Prophetic Scriptures," *Moody Monthly* (June 1950), 679. See also Herbert Lockyer, *It Is Later Than We Think* (Grand Rapids: Zondervan, 1951), 8.

14. Louis T. Talbot, "Palestine, Russia and Ezekiel 38," *King's Business* (January 1948), 11; "Prophecy's Light on Our Times," advertisement, *Moody Monthly* (November 1948), 201.

15. Harris Franklin Roll, "The War and the Second Coming," *Christian Century* (August 18, 1943), 941.

16. Hal Lindsey with C. C. Carlson, *The Late Great Planet Earth* (Grand Rapids: Zondervan, 1970), 50–51.

17. Tim LaHaye, *The Beginning of the End* (Wheaton: Tyndale House, 1972), 8, 169.

18. John F. Walvoord, *Armageddon, Oil and the Middle East Crisis* (Grand Rapids: Zondervan, 1974), 20, 21.

19. Walvoord, *Armageddon, Oil and the Middle East Crisis*, 55.

20. Charles Colson, "Wake-up Call," *Christianity Today* (November 12, 2001), 112.

21. William Lobdell, "Religion; in Aftermath of Attacks, Talk of 'End Days' Soars," *Los Angeles Times,* September 22, 2001; Jim Remsen, "Apocalypse Now? Some Wonder They Find

Parallels between the Sept. 11 Attacks and Prophecies in Scripture and Elsewhere," *Philadelphia Inquirer,* September 30, 2001; J. M. Parker, "Hagee Sees Approach of Apocalypse," *San Antonio Express-News,* September 17, 2001; Kevin Sack, "Apocalyptic Theology Revitalized by Attacks," *New York Times,* November 23, 2001.

22. Bush quoted in Kurt Eichenwald, *500 Days: Secrets and Lies in the Terror Wars* (New York: Simon and Schuster, 2012), 459. See also Stephen Spector, "Gog and Magog in the White House: Did Biblical Prophecy Inspire the Invasion of Iraq?," *Journal of Church and State,* Advanced Access, published online March 28, 2013.

23. John Hagee, *Attack on America: New York, Jerusalem, and the Role of Terrorism in the Last Days* (Nashville: Thomas Nelson, 2001); John F. Walvoord and Mark Hitchcock, *Armageddon, Oil, and Terror: What the Bible Says About the Future of America, the Middle East, and the End of Western Civilization* (Carol Stream, IL: Tyndale House, 2007). The title alone of Hagee's more recent 2010 *Can America Survive? 10 Prophetic Signs That We Are the Terminal Generation* (Brentwood, TN: Howard Books, 2010), makes his convictions explicit.

24. "Many Americans Uneasy with Mix of Religion and Politics," Pew Research Center (August 24, 2006), http://www.pewforum.org/Politics-and-Elections/Many-Americans-Uneasy-with-Mix-of-Religion-and-Politics.aspx; "Jesus Christ's Return to Earth," Pew Research Center (July 14, 2010), http://www.pewresearch.org/daily-number/jesus-christs-return-to-earth/.

CHAPTER 10

1. "Must Read Bible 30 Days: Sentence Follows Theft," *Los Angeles Examiner,* January 14, 1915, II.1.

2. "Must Read Bible 30 Days," II.1.

3. Harold A. Lane to Lyman Stewart, January 14, 1915, Lyman Stewart Papers, Biola University Archives, LaMirada, California.

4. Harry S. Stout, "Word and Order in Colonial New England," in *The Bible in America: Essays in Cultural History,* ed. Nathan O. Hatch and Mark A. Noll (New York: Oxford University Press, 1982), 21. See also: Karen H. Jobes, "Bible Translation as Bilingual Quotation," paper presented at the annual meeting of the Evangelical Theological Society, 2007.

5. Quoted in Evelyn B. Tribble, *Margins and Marginality: The Printed Page in Early Modern England* (Charlottesville: University Press of Virginia, 1993), 52.

6. Paul Ricoeur, *Interpretation Theory: Discourse and the Surplus of Meaning* (Fort Worth, TX: Texas Christian University Press, 1976), 45. As legal scholar Laurent Mayali argued: "the relationship of annotation to the text is less a relation of meaning than it is a relation of power." Laurent Mayali, "For a Political Economy of Annotation," in *Annotation and Its Texts,* ed. Stephen A. Barney (New York: Oxford University Press, 1991), 185.

7. Tribble, *Margins and Marginality,* 17.

8. David Daniell, *The Bible in English* (New Haven: Yale University Press, 2003), 601.

9. See, for example: Mark A. Noll, *America's God: From Jonathan Edwards to Abraham Lincoln* (New York: Oxford University Press, 2002).

10. Grant Wacker, "The Demise of Biblical Civilization," in Hatch and Noll, *Bible in America,* 122.

11. Quoted in David Hempton, *Evangelical Disenchantment: Nine Portraits of Faith and Doubt* (New Haven: Yale University Press, 2008), 99.

12. Frances E. Willard, *Woman in the Pulpit* (Boston: D. Lothrop Company, 1888), 37, 23, 21, 26.

13. Proverbs 22:6; "Sunlight for Babies" (pamphlet), U.S. Department of Labor, Children's Bureau, 1926.

14. Adam Laats, *Fundamentalism and Education in the Scopes Era* (New York: Palgrave Macmillan, 2010), 140.

15. American Bible Society, *The State of the Bible 2013* (New York: American Bible Society, 2013).

16. Paul C. Gutjahr, *An American Bible: A History of the Good Book in the United States, 1777–1880* (Stanford: Stanford University Press, 1999), 37.

17. Arno C. Gaebelein, *The History of the Scofield Reference Bible* (New York: Our Hope Publications, 1943), 52.

18. Gaebelein, *History of the Scofield Reference Bible*, 52.

19. W. P. King, "Things New and Old about the Bible: The Continued Conflict in Theological Thought," *Atlanta Constitution*, October 7, 1923, D22.

20. Charles Caldwell Ryrie, *Dispensationalism* (Chicago: Moody Press, 1995), 9.

21. James C. Hefley and Marti Hefley, *Uncle Cam: The Story of William Cameron Townsend, Founder of the Wycliffe Bible Translators and the Summer Institute of Linguistics* (Waco, TX: Word Books, 1974), 59.

CHAPTER 11

1. *South Carolina Baptist*, May 8, 1868; John Bailey Adger to F. W. McMaster, July 14, 1871, Adger Papers, Presbyterian Historical Society, Montreat, North Carolina; Aquila Peyton, entry of March 12, 1860, Diary of Aquila Peyton, Virginia Historical Society, Richmond.

2. For an example of this ridicule, see *South Carolina Baptist*, August 22, 1867, which referred to the typical singing of rural congregations as an "inharmonious jingling of nasal sounds."

3. Son House, *Preachin the Blues* (CD, Catfish Records, 2000).

4. Jerma Jackson, *Singing in My Soul: Black Gospel Music in a Secular Age* (Chapel Hill: University of North Carolina Press, 1993).

5. Last two paragraphs from Boyer, *How Sweet the Sound: The Golden Age of Gospel* (Washington, D.C.: Elliott and Clark, 1995), 21; Michael Harris, *The Rise of Gospel Blues: The Music of Thomas Andrew Dorsey in the Urban Church* (New York: Oxford, 1992), 99–100. See also Robert Palmer, *Deep Blues: A Musical and Cultural History of the Mississippi Delta* (New York: Penguin, 1982), and Jon Spencer, *Blues and Evil* (Knoxville: University Press of Tennessee, 1993), which provide some of the most recent compelling discussion of the relationship between the blues and African-American spirituality.

6. Bill Malone, *Southern Music, American Music* (Lexington: University Press of Kentucky, 2003), 67–68, 76–78; Don Cusic, *The Sound of Light: A History of Gospel Music* (New York: Popular Press, 1990); Bill Malone, *Singing Cowboys and Musical Mountaineers: Southern Culture and the Roots of Country Music* (Macon: Mercer University Press, 2003), 32.

7. James Goff, *Close Harmony: A History of Southern Gospel* (Chapel Hill: University of North Carolina Press, 2002), 94–96.

8. Quoted in Goff, *Close Harmony*, 215.

9. Clifton Johnson, ed., *God Struck Me Dead: Voices of Ex-Slaves* (Pilgrim Press, 1969), 147; John Giggie, "God's Long Journey: African Americans, Religion, and History in the Mississippi Delta" (Ph.D. diss., Princeton University, 1997), 120–140; *Complete Recorded Works of the Reverend J. M. Gates* (Document Records, 1996); Gates's version of "Death's Black Train Is Coming" may also be heard individually on *Roots 'n Blues: The Retrospective, 1925–1950* (Columbia Records, 1992), disc 1.

10. Preceding two paragraphs from *F. W. McGee: Complete Recorded Works*, vol. 1; Document Records, 1996; Ken Romanowski, liner notes to *Arizona Dranes: Complete Recorded Works in Chronological Order*; Document Records, 1994. Giggie, "'When Jesus Handed Me a Ticket,'" 249–266; Patton recording from *American Primitive: Raw Pre–war Gospel*; Revenant Records, 1997.

11. Mahalia Jackson, *Movin On Up* (New York: Avon Books, 1969), 56–59.

12. Clifton Taulbert, *Once upon a Time When We Were Colored* (n.p.: Council Oak Books, 1991), 95–100.

13. Kip Lornell, *Happy in the Service of the Lord: African American Sacred Vocal Harmony* (Knoxville: University Press of Tennessee, 1995), 15–16, 22–24, 28–29, 37–38, 46, 66; Cusic, *Sound of Light*, 124.

14. For a fuller analysis of Elvis's religious upbringing, see Peter Guralnick, *Last Train to Memphis: The Rise of Elvis Presley* (New York: Little, Brown, 1994).

15. George Vecsey, "Cash's 'Gospel Road' Film Is Renaissance for Him" (1973), reprinted in *Ring of Fire: The Johnny Cash Reader*, ed. Michael Streissguth (Cambridge, Mass.: Da Capo Press, 2002), 126.

16. "The Beast in Me," from *American Recordings* (CD, Lost Highway Records, 1994); Billy Jo Shaver, "Jesus Was Our Savior, Cotton Was Our King" (Sony Music Entertainment, 1974); "Personal Jesus" and "Redemption Song" from Johnny Cash, *American IV: The Man Comes Around* (CD, Lost Highway, 2002); Ted Olsen, "Johnny Cash's Song of Redemption," *Christianity Today* 47 (November 2003), reprinted in Streissguth, *Ring of Fire*, 60–62.

17. Charles Gans, "Jazz Bassist Innovator Charles Haden Dies at 76," SF Gate, July 12, 2014, https://www.yahoo.com/music/jazz-bass-innovator-charlie-haden-dies-76-142851380.html.

18. Chuck Reece, "Glory: Lee Bains III & the Glory Fires," http://bittersoutherner.com/lee-bains-iii-dereconstructed#.V6EtYBUrKM9.

19. "The Southern Thing," *Southern Rock Opera*; Lost Highway Records, 2002.

CHAPTER 12

1. The above summary of the Wesleyan Bible Class's anniversary is drawn from *Quarter Century Anniversary Souvenir & Program of the Wesleyan Bible Class: The Twenty-Fifth Year since its Foundation* (n.p.), unpaginated, oversize folder 1, Wesleyan Bible Class Records, Special Collections and Preservation Division, Harold Washington Library Center, Chicago Public Library (hereafter WBC Records). The quotation in the epigraph is from Sydney E. Ahlstrom, *A Religious History of the American People* (New Haven, CT: Yale University Press, 1972), 741.

2. "Why I Joined the Class," in *Quarter Century Anniversary Souvenir & Program*.

3. Raymond A. Smith, "The Adult Bible Class Movement" (B.D. thesis, University of Chicago, 1922), 27. Smith frustratingly does not cite the source for this estimate. His research, however, suggests it may have come directly from the International Sunday School Convention, whose headquarters were in Chicago.

4. Robert Wuthnow, *Sharing the Journey: Support Groups and America's New Quest for Community* (New York: Free Press, 1994), 76. On "private meetings" among the Puritans see David D. Hall, *Worlds of Wonder, Days of Judgment: Popular Religious Belief in Early New England* (Cambridge, MA: Harvard University Press, 1990), 163; and for contemporary cell groups see Kevin D. Doughtery and Andrew Whitehead, "A Place to Belong: Small Group Involvement in Religious Congregations," *Sociology of Religion* 72 (2011): 91–111.

5. The literature here is, of course, immense, but see for example Nathan O. Hatch and Mark A. Noll, eds., *The Bible in America: Essays in Cultural History* (New York: Oxford University Press, 1982); Paul C. Gutjahr, *An American Bible: A History of the Good Book in the United States, 1777–1880* (Stanford, CA: Stanford University Press, 1999); David Paul Nord, *Faith in Reading: Religious Publishing and the Birth of Mass Media in America* (New York: Oxford University Press, 2004); Mark A. Noll, *Between Faith and Criticism: Evangelicals, Scholarship, and the Bible in America* (San Francisco: Harper and Row, 1986); George Marsden, *Fundamentalism and American Culture* (New York: Oxford University Press, 2006).

6. My thinking on the cultural functions and theoretical workings of Bible study groups has been shaped by James S. Bielo, *Words upon the Word: An Ethnography of Evangelical Group Bible Study* (New York: New York University, 2009); Simon Coleman, "The Social Life of the Bible," in *The Social Life of Scriptures: Cross Cultural Perspectives on Biblicism*, ed. James S. Bielo (New Brunswick, NJ: Rutgers University Press, 2009), 194–211; and Robert A. Orsi, "Everyday Miracles: The Study of Lived Religion," in *Lived Religion: Toward a History of Practice*, ed. David D. Hall (Princeton, NJ: Princeton University Press, 1997), 3–21.

7. See *Second Annual Report of the American Bible Class Society, Presented in Philadelphia, May 26, 1829: Together with the President's Address and an Appendix* (Williamstown, PA: Ridley Bannister, 1830), 6. For more on the early history of Bible classes see Edwin Wilbur Rice, *The Sunday-School Movement and the American Sunday-School Union* (Philadelphia: Union Press, 1917), 27–30, 101–103; and Anne M. Boylan, *Sunday School: The Formation of an American Institution, 1790–1880* (New Haven, CT: Yale University Press, 1988), 109–114.

8. *First Report of the American Bible Class Society, Made at Philadelphia, May 22, 1828: With an Appendix* (Philadelphia: W. F. Geddes, 1828), 4. See also B.C., "Sunday School Bible Classes," *American Sunday School Magazine* 3 (March 1829): 75–76.

9. *First Report of the American Bible Class Society*, 4–5.

10. On the Society's frustrations see *Second Annual Report of the American Bible Class Society*, 6. On late-century perceptions of Bible classes see Cyrus Northup, "A Glimpse at an Old Time Bible Class," *Sunday School Times* 25 (February 24, 1883): 126. And on the lack of interest in Bible classes at midcentury, one need only look at the annual reports of the American Sunday School Union throughout the 1850s.

11. "The Bible Class and Its Methods," *Sunday School Times* 19 (January 27, 1877): 53. On the emerging interest in Bible classes see R. G. Pardee, *The Sabbath-School Index: Pointing Out The History and Progress of Sunday-Schools, With Approved Modes of Instruction, Examples in Illustrative, Pictorial, and Object-Teaching; Also the Use of the Blackboard, Management of Infant-Classes, Teachers' Meetings, Conventions, Institutes, Etc., Etc., Etc.* (Philadelphia: J. C. Garrigues & Co., 1868), chap. 16; *The First International (Sixth National) Sunday School Convention, Held at Baltimore, MD., May 11, 12, 13, 1875* (Newark, NJ: Executive Committee of the International Sunday School Association, 1875), 30–32; and *The Fifty-Sixth Annual Report of the American Sunday-School Union, 1880* (Philadelphia: American Sunday School Union, 1880), 37; "Saving our Young People," *Christian Advocate* (March 25, 1880), 200.

12. For examples of these canvases, see "The Church and the Young," *Congregationalist* 33 (April 27, 1881): 2; and James J. Hill, "Sunday School Leakage," *Sunday School Times*, July 25, 1896, 423–474. On the broader concern over the exodus of youth from the Protestant church see Christopher Lee Coble, "Where Have All the Young People Gone? The Christian Endeavor Movement and the Training of Protestant Youth, 1881–1918" (Ph.D. diss., Harvard University, 2001), 253–254.

13. On the Young People's Movement see Frank Otis Erb, *The Development of the Young People's Movement* (Chicago: University of Chicago Press, 1917); Joseph F. Kett, *Rites of Passage: Adolescence in America 1790 to the Present* (New York: Basic Books, 1977), 192, 217–221; and Christopher Coble, "The Role of Young People's Societies in the Training of Christian Womanhood (and Manhood), 1880–1910," in *Women and Twentieth-Century Protestantism*, ed. Margaret Lamberts Bendroth and Virginia Lieson Brereton (Champaign: University of Illinois Press, 2002), 74–92.

14. According to Hudson, the names of his Baraca and Philathea classes come from the Greek words for "blessed" and "truth," respectively. Marshall A. Hudson, "Autobiography of the Man Who Got His Million," 28–32, box 11, World Wide Baraca Philathea Bible Class Union Archives, Gordon-Conwell Theological Seminary, Wenham, MA (hereafter WWBPU Archives); Ann Elizabeth Olson, *A Million for Christ: The Story of Baraca Philathea* (n.p.: World Wide Baraca Philathea Union and Gordon-Conwell Theological Seminary, 2003), 16–19.

15. David C. Cook, *Successful Adult Bible Classes and What They Are Doing: Also Reports from Sunday School Superintendents pm Adult Bible Class Work and Needs and Conditions of the Work as Seen by Adult Class Teachers of the Ordinary Sort* (Elgin, IL: David C. Cook, 1905), 3–4.

16. "Class Act as 'Little Mothers,'" *Young Ladies' Class Weekly* 6 (January 16, 1916): 4; Carleton J. Corliss, *History of the Howson Fellowship Bible Class, 1911–1952* (Chicago, 1952), 23.

17. W. C. Pearce, *The Adult Bible Class: Its Organization and Work* (Philadelphia: Westminster, 1908), 16–17, 40–42. See also "The Social Life of a Boy's Class," *Sunday School Times* 37 (May 23, 1896): 325; "Class at Work," *Westminster Adult Bible Class* 2 (January 1919): 9.

18. Pearce, *Adult Bible Class*, 57.

19. Pearce, *Adult Bible Class*, 59.

20. See articles in the *Pleasant Hour* 1 (Nov. 1906): 4–5; 1 (May 1907): 6; 1 (October 1907): 4; 2 (November 1907): 4; 4 (December 1909): 3.

21. Pearce, *Adult Bible Class*, 66. For other class activities see *Wesleyan Advocate* (May 1908): 5–6 and (August 1910): 6; Rev. J. S. Armentrout, "A Year's Social Program," *Westminster Adult Bible Class* 10 (October 1918): 370; Cook, *Successful Adult Classes*, 12, 23–25, 46–47, 58–59.

22. J. H. Bryan, *The Organized Adult Bible Class* (St. Louis: Christian Publishing Company, 1909), 82.

23. Frank L. Wood, "How I Keep in Touch with My Class," *Report from the Forty-Sixth Annual Convention, Cook County Sunday School Association*, reprinted in *Quarter Century Anniversary Souvenir*, oversize folder 1, WBC Records; "Wesleyan Bible Class, Chicago Celebrates 'Absent Members' Year," *New Adult Bible Class Monthly* 5 (February 1910): 4–5; Pearce, *Adult Bible Class*, 56–57. State and local Sunday school associations regularly requested Wood to speak to their assemblies about his method of correspondence.

24. "Midyear Letter," March 1, 1930, oversize folder 2, WBC Records. Evidence for the Wesleyan Bible Class's collective intimacy is drawn from Christopher D. Cantwell, "The Bible Class Teacher: Piety and Politics in the Age of Fundamentalism" (Ph.D. diss., Cornell University, 2012).

25. "Our Members," in *Quarter Century Anniversary Souvenir*, oversize folder 1, WBC Records.

26. "What Our Absent Members Think of It," in *Quarter Century Anniversary Souvenir*.

27. "What Our Absent Members Think of It."

28. "Cook County Bible Class Athletic Association," *World-Wide Baraca* 7 (May 1906): 1. For more on the Bible Class Athletic Association see *Forty-Ninth Annual Convention and Statistical Directory, 1908* (Chicago: Cook County Sunday School Association, 1908), 44–46.

29. Shailer Mathews, "The Conduct of the Adult Bible Class," *Biblical World* 14 (November 1899): 363–366.

30. Irving F. Wood, "What Shall the Adult Bible Class Do with Modern Biblical Scholarship?" *Biblical World* 21 (May 1903): 375–378. See also Smith, "Adult Bible Class Movement," 45–66.

31. *Organized Sunday-School Work in America, 1905–1908: Triennial Survey of Sunday-School Work Including the Official Report of the Twelfth International Sunday School Convention Louisville, Kentucky, June 18–23, 1908* (Chicago: Executive Committee of the International Sunday-School Association, 1908), 298. See also W. C. Pearce, "The Adult Bible Class Movement," in *The Development of the Sunday School, 1780–1905: The Official Report of the Eleventh International Sunday School Convention, Toronto, Canada, June 23–27, 1905* (Boston: International Sunday School Association, 1905), 642–645.

32. *The Adult Department: It's History, Departmental Organization for Associations, Plans for Extending the Work*, Adult Department Leaflet no. 1, in Bryan, *Organized Adult Bible Class*, 143–146.

33. *Organized Sunday-School Work in America, 1905–1908*, 285–299, 353–356; *Organized Sunday School Work in America, 1908–1911: Triennial Survey of Sunday School Work Including the Official Report of the Thirteenth International Sunday School Convention, San Francisco, California, June 20–27, 1911* (Chicago: Executive Committee of the International Sunday School Association, 1911), 302–305.

34. Rev. Edward C. Kunkle, "The Advantages of Federation," *Westminster Adult Bible Class* 2 (March 1910): 93.

35. *Forty-Ninth Annual Convention and Statistical Directory, 1908*, 50; "The Work of One Civic Committee," *Westminster Adult Bible Class* 2 (July 1910): 252.

36. Mary Whiting Adams, *A Working Bible Class* (Anti-Saloon League, n.d.), cited in Smith, "Adult Bible Class Movement," 25; Pearce, *Adult Bible Class*, 44–47.

37. "Prohibitionists to Notify Mr. Hudson, Candidate for Lieutenant-Governor," *Syracuse Herald*, October 1, 1908; "Candidates on Hand," *Syracuse Herald*, August 28, 1908; George M. Hammell, *The Passing of the Saloon: An Authentic and Official Presentation of the Anti-liquor Crusade in America* (Cincinnati: Tower Press, 1908), 264.

38. William N. Hartshorn, ed., *World-Wide Sunday-School Work: The Official Report of the World's Sixth Sunday-School Convention, Held in the City of Washington, U.S.A. May 19–24, 1910* (Chicago: Executive Committee of the World's Sunday School Association, 1910), 37, 545–547; "S.S. Men Parade," *Washington Post*, May 21, 1910.

39. See Roger A. Burns, *Preacher: Billy Sunday and Big-Time American Evangelism* (New York: Norton, 1992), 103, 183, 211; Cantwell, "Bible Class Teacher."

40. William Jennings Bryan and Mary Baird Bryan, *The Memoirs of William Jennings Bryan* (Philadelphia: John C. Winston, 1925), 453; Michael Kazin, *A Godly Hero: The Life of William Jennings Bryan* (New York: Knopf, 2006), 243–258; Lawrence W. Levine, *Defender of the Faith: William Jennings Bryan, The Last Decade, 1915–1925* (New York: Oxford University Press, 1965), 289.

41. Bryan and Bryan, *Memoirs of William Jennings Bryan*, 453.

42. My rough estimate of a quarter of all Bible readers comes from the finding that of the 44 percent of Bible readers who reported seeking counsel in their study, 49 percent cited Bible study groups as a resource they used.

CHAPTER 13

1. J. I. Packer, *God Has Spoken: Revelation and the Bible*, 3rd ed. (Grand Rapids: Baker, 1994), 24. The first edition of this work (Hodder and Stoughton, 1965) was published in a series called

Christian Foundations and did not include the introduction found in the second and third editions. Packer's reflection on Amos here, tellingly placed in a section entitled "The Infection of Uncertainty," functioned then in the first edition to lead off Packer's overall argument.

2. A small, more radical contingent of King James Onlyism further proclaims the KJV to be the product of a second inspiration, which can on that account correct the original autographic texts. This position, referred to as "double inspiration," is often linked to the thought of popular spokesman Peter Ruckman. See the chapter "Correcting the Greek with the English," in *The Christian's Handbook of Manuscript Evidence* (Pensacola: Bible Baptist Bookstore, 1970), esp. 138–139, where Ruckman stresses that *"Mistakes in the AV 1611 are advanced revelation!"* For a generally helpful taxonomy of King James Onlyism, see James R. White, *The King James Only Controversy: Can You Trust Modern Translations?*, 2nd ed. (Minneapolis: Bethany House, 2009), 23–29.

3. "Statement of Faith," *Bible Believers' Church Directory*, accessed March 21, 2014, http://www.biblebelievers.com/churches. Emphasis in original.

4. Interview with Paul Brown, Stonemill Baptist Church, February 23, 2011. All names, both of the churches and respondents, are pseudonyms.

5. For example, both respondents from the relatively moderate Kiefaber Community Baptist Church were open to the use at home of Bibles other than the King James. They described this openness as stemming from either cultural upbringing or a significant past event. Whereas Matthew Tabor, a third-generation Christian from India, emphasized how his familiarity with non-English Bibles and non-Western cultures granted him a rather unique perspective on the preeminence of the KJV, David Brothers, the lead pastor at Kiefaber, pointed to his experience as a hospital chaplain and the necessity there of appreciating a wide spectrum of different people and beliefs. "I don't go in to convince them they're wrong or to show them that," David explained. "I journey with them where they're at to be a spiritual support, and I can do that. And, I think that kind of helps me also in my Christianity. I don't believe everybody has to dress the same way I dress and do everything exactly the way I do, and that's the reason why a lot of the—what you would call a King James Only church— they're almost cultish in some ways. That's probably another reason why we don't advertise [that we're King James Only]." Interview with David Brothers, Kiefaber Community Baptist Church, July 16, 2012.

6. Interview with George Robertson, Lowes Baptist Fellowship, August 2, 2012. Edward Hills makes the same point more directly. See his *The King James Version Defended*, 4th ed. (Des Moines: Christian Research Press, 1984), 106.

7. Interview with George Robertson, Lowes Baptist Fellowship, August 2, 2012.

8. James Jasper Ray, *God Wrote Only One Bible* (Eugene: Eye Opener, 1983), 1. For an account of this flood of translations and editions hitting the market, see Paul C. Gutjahr, "From Monarchy to Democracy: The Dethroning of the King James Bible in the United States," in *The King James Bible after 400 Years: Literary, Linguistic, and Cultural Influences*, ed. Hannibal Hamlin and Norman W. Jones (New York: Cambridge University Press, 2010), 164–178.

9. Wilbur N. Pickering, *The Identity of the New Testament Text*, rev. ed. (Nashville: Thomas Nelson, 1980), 17.

10. Pickering, *Identity of the New Testament Text*, 18.

11. This particular brand of conservatism is ironically at odds with that exhibited by the movement's evangelical critics. See Daniel Wallace, "Inspiration, Preservation, and New Testament Textual Criticism," in *New Testament Essays in Honor of Homer A. Kent, Jr.*, ed. Gary T. Meadors (Winona Lake: BMH, 1991), 80.

12. Interview with David Brothers, Kiefaber Community Baptist Church, July 16, 2012. For the story of how the New International Version became the "authorized" modern translation for American evangelicals, see Peter Thuesen, *In Discordance with the Scriptures: American Protestant Battles over Translating the Bible* (New York: Oxford, 1999), esp. 121–155.

13. For example, see D. A. Carson, *The King James Version Debate: A Plea for Realism* (Grand Rapids: Baker, 1979), 68–74; Wallace, "Inspiration, Preservation, and New Testament Textual Criticism"; W. Edward Glenny, "The Preservation of Scripture and the Version Debate," in *One Bible Only? Examining Exclusive Claims for the King James Bible*, ed. Roy Beacham and Kevin Bauder (Grand Rapids: Kregel, 2001), 102–133.

14. Hills, *King James Version Defended*, 2. Emphasis in original.

15. James Barr, *Fundamentalism* (Philadelphia: Westminster, 1978), 85–89. See also Harriet Harris's helpful summary and critique of Barr's argument in *Fundamentalism and Evangelicals* (Oxford: Clarendon, 1998), ch. 2. King James Only adherents, then, do not so much criticize the practice of textual criticism, which most often plays a central role in their arguments for the superiority of the King James, as they criticize the destructive influence on it of modern presuppositions and techniques.

16. Even Wilbur Pickering cannot outright deny the role this theological presupposition plays in his attempt "to let the evidence tell its own story," despite his eagerness to escape the charges of circularity leveled against earlier proponents, most prominently Hills. Pickering, *Identity of the New Testament Text*, 153.

17. Hills, for instance, argues that the problem with modern textual criticism goes back to the late seventeenth century when deists and unbelievers decided, for apologetic reasons, to weigh each religion starting on neutral ground and using only "the light of reason." Hills, *King James Version Defended*, 83–84.

18. Interview with Paul Brown, Stonemill Baptist Church, February 23, 2011.

19. Samuel C. Gipp, *The Answer Book* (Northfield: Daystar, 1989), 28–29.

20. Samuel C. Gipp, *Gipp's Understandable History of the Bible* (Miamitown: Daystar, 2004), 14.

21. Interview with Paul Brown, Stonemill Baptist Church, February 23, 2011.

22. See Gipp, *Answer Book*, 58.

23. See, for example, Ruckman, *Christian's Handbook of Manuscript Evidence*, esp. 128–139.

24. Hills, *King James Version Defended*, 107, 209–210.

25. Hills, *King James Version Defended*, 3, 223.

26. Hills, *King James Version Defended*, 130.

27. Molly Worthen, *Apostles of Reason: The Crisis of Authority in American Evangelicalism* (New York: Oxford, 2014), 261.

28. Cornelius Van Til, *The Defense of the Faith*, 2nd ed. rev. and abridged (Philadelphia: Presbyterian and Reformed, 1963), 77.

29. Interview with Matthew Tabor, Kiefaber Community Baptist Church, July 31, 2012.

30. Paul Brown: "[modern text critics] are basing all of what they believe on a philosophy called naturalism. In other words, everything can be explained from the natural experience." Interview with Paul Brown, Stonemill Baptist Church, February 23, 2011. Or, consider the explanation given by Matthew Tabor: "[we] are trying to use man's ideas of understanding certain concepts and questioning manuscripts and coming to a conclusion. You're not taking the manuscripts at [their] best and saying, 'Okay, let the manuscripts . . . unfold for [themselves].'" Interview with Matthew Tabor, Kiefaber Community Baptist Church, July 31, 2012.

31. Zane Hodges, "The Greek Text of the King James Version," in *Which Bible?*, ed. David Otis Fuller, 5th ed. (Grand Rapids: Grand Rapids International, 1975), 35–36.

32. Alfred Martin, "A Critical Examination of the Westcott-Hort Textual Theory," in Fuller, *Which Bible?*, 160.

33. Hills, *King James Version Defended*, 29–86.

34. Interview with Paul Brown, Stonemill Baptist Church, February 23, 2011. One of the pamphlets handed out at Lowes Baptist Fellowship illustrates this point vividly. On the front cover, a cartoonish figure feverishly cuts out of the King James Bible words that, we can only assume, he finds offensive or simply unbelievable. That this illustration so strikingly reflects representations of Thomas Jefferson's act of slicing entire verses and passages out of the Bible highlights the similarity of the two programs in the mind of King James Only adherents. That is, *both* higher and lower criticism stem from the Enlightenment's worshipping of human reason. Terry Watkins, *New International PerVersion* (Pinson, AL: Dial-the-Truth, n.d.). That greater evangelicalism has failed to realize this and its implications for Christian faith is the driving force behind much of the work of Theodore Letis. See, esp., his "B. B. Warfield, Common-Sense Philosophy and Biblical Criticism," *American Presbyterians* 69 (Fall 1991): 175–190.

35. The more moderate Kiefaber Community Church hesitated to draw such strong judgments, insisting that the doctrine of the priesthood of all believers suggests that claims and accusations of this nature are inappropriate for Christians. Displaying an irenicism and ecumenism rare among King James Only advocates, David Brothers emphasized that he tries not to judge others' motives, preferring instead to accept that they have honestly weighed the evidence even if they have come to a conclusion different from his own. "I believe people can be sincere in their beliefs and differ from mine, and I don't believe that they're necessarily anti-God or anti the Bible or whatever. They've looked at the research and they've done their own, and they've come to that position and that's fine. I can accept that and go on." In our conversations together, David clearly struggled with the label "King James Onlyism," though he did not want to renounce it either. Interview with David Brothers, Kiefaber Community Baptist Church, July 16, 2012.

36. Interview with George Robertson, Lowes Baptist Fellowship, August 2, 2012.

37. Thuesen, *In Discordance with the Scriptures*, 41–66.

38. J. I. Packer, *"Fundamentalism" and the Word of God* (Grand Rapids: Eerdmans, 1985), 50, 140, 141. See also J. I. Packer, *Beyond the Battle for the Bible* (Wheaton: Crossway, 1980), 18–19.

39. For a detailed telling of the RSV controversy and evangelicalism's various responses, see Thuesen, *In Discordance with the Scriptures*.

40. Brian Malley, *How the Bible Works: An Anthropological Study of Evangelical Biblicism* (Walnut Creek: AltaMira, 2004), 87.

41. Of course, if this is true, then evangelicals—King James Only or otherwise—are not really biblicists at all, at least not in the term's typical usage as referring to Christians who are continuously shaped and formed by the Bible alone. The direction of influence appears, in large measure, to be precisely the opposite.

42. Grant Wacker, "The Demise of Biblical Civilization," in *The Bible in America: Essays in Cultural History*, ed. Nathan Hatch and Mark A. Noll (New York: Oxford, 1982), 127.

43. John W. O'Malley, *Four Cultures of the West* (Cambridge, MA: Harvard University Press, 2004), 6–10.

44. O'Malley, *Four Cultures of the West*, 12.

45. David J. O'Brien, *From the Heart of the American Church* (Maryknoll: Orbis, 1994), 113.

46. See, in particular, the enlightening study by Wilfred Cantwell Smith, *Faith and Belief* (Princeton: Princeton University Press, 1979).

CHAPTER 14

1. For the advertisement's script and a report on the campaign, see Brooks Advertising, Inc., "The Living Bible—Mother Jr. (30 seconds)," folder 18, box 6, Kenneth Taylor Papers (SC-12), Wheaton College Special Collections, Buswell Library, Wheaton, Illinois. For the marketing strategist's remarks about the advertisement, see D. Keith Stonehocker, "Market Research and the Living Bible," *Christian Communications Spectrum* (winter 1975): 7–9, included in "Notes Regarding the Living Bible manuscripts (Roger Phillips)," folder 14, box 6, Kenneth Taylor Papers. On notions of Christian womanhood, see R. Marie Griffith, *God's Daughters: Evangelical Women and the Power of Submission* (Berkeley: University of California Press, 1997), e.g., 172–176. On evangelical media's emphasis on the moral and spiritual discipline of children, see Heather Hendershot, *Shaking the World for Jesus: Media and Conservative Evangelical Culture* (Chicago: University of Chicago Press, 2004), 34–45.

2. On the growth of commercial Bible production and consumption before 1870 and the transformation of Bibles into fashionable commodities, see Colleen McDannell, *Material Christianity: Religion and Popular Culture in America* (New Haven: Yale University Press, 1995), 71–101.

3. McDannell, *Material Christianity*, 101; on "consumer society," see Kathryn Lofton, *Oprah: The Gospel of an Icon* (Berkeley: University of California Press, 2011), 21.

4. As Julie Ingersoll notes, "products marketed to conservative Christians can give us a sense of the way in which evangelical material culture reflects the American Protestant movement's gendered nature." Julie Ingersoll, *Evangelical Christian Women: War Stories in the Gender Battles* (New York: New York University Press, 2003), quote on 120.

5. Paul C. Gutjahr, *An American Bible: A History of the Good Book in the United States* (Stanford: Stanford University Press, 1999); McDannell, *Material Christianity*, chap. 3; Seth Perry, "'What the Public Expect': Consumer Authority and the Marketing of Bibles, 1770–1850," *American Periodicals: A Journal of History, Criticism, and Bibliography* 24, no. 2 (2014): 128–144.

6. Peter Johannes Thuesen, *In Discordance with the Scriptures: American Protestant Battles over Translating the Bible* (New York: Oxford University Press, 1999), quotes on 10 and 148.

7. Susan Friend Harding, *The Book of Jerry Falwell: Fundamentalist Language and Politics* (Princeton, N.J.: Princeton University Press, 2000), esp. chap. 2.

8. Harding, *Book of Jerry Falwell*, 28, 39.

9. See, for example, B. M. Pietsch, *Dispensational Modernism* (New York: Oxford University Press, 2015), chap. 7.

10. Edwin McDowell, "Paraphrase of the Bible a Big Seller," *New York Times*, March 27, 1985, C19.

11. Peter Johannes Thuesen, *In Discordance with the Scriptures: American Protestant Battles over Translating the Bible* (New York: Oxford University Press, 1999), 46–50, 82.

12. Thuesen, *In Discordance with the Scriptures*, 70.

13. J. P. M. Walsh, "Contemporary English Translations of Scripture," *Theological Studies* 50, no. 2 (June 1989): 336–358, esp. 337.

14. Tessa Whitehouse, "The Family Expositor, the Doddridge Circle and the Booksellers," *Library: The Transactions of the Bibliographical Society* 11, no. 3 (2010): 321–344; see 324 for its publication history in England; on the date 1807, see Seth Perry, "The Endless Making of Many Books: Bibles and Religious Authority in America, 1780–1850" (Ph.D. diss., University of Chicago, 2013), 118.

15. Philip Doddridge, *The Family Expositor: Or, A Paraphrase and Version of the New Testament; with Critical Notes, and a Practical Improvement of Each Section* (Charlestown, Mass.: S. Etheridge, 1807). See the preface and "Directions for Reading the Family Expositor."

16. On Doddridge's esteemed reputation among the English Dissenting community before 1760, see Whitehouse, "Family Expositor," esp. 339–340.

17. Edward L. Greenstein, "Theories of Modern Bible Translation," *Prooftexts* 3, no. 1 (January 1, 1983): 9–39. 17.

18. Edgar J. Goodspeed, *The New Testament: An American Translation* (Chicago: University of Chicago Press, 1923), v.

19. R. Bryan Bademan, "'Monkeying with the Bible': Edgar J. Goodspeed's American Translation," *Religion and American Culture: A Journal of Interpretation* 16, no. 1 (January 1, 2006): 55–93, quote on 70.

20. Bademan, "'Monkeying with the Bible,'" 74.

21. Robert Galveston Bratcher, "One Bible in Many Translations," *Interpretation* 32, no. 2 (April 1978): 115–129; see 128–129.

22. Harold Myra, "Ken Taylor: God's Voice in the Vernacular," *Christianity Today*, October 5, 1979, 18–22, quote on 20.

23. In addition to Today's English Version, for example, see *The Twentieth Century New Testament: A Translation into Modern English* (New York: Fleming H. Revell, 1923), a translation from Greek that English translators designed to "enable Englishmen to read the most important part of the Bible in that form of their own language which they themselves use" (1).

24. "The Family behind 'Living Prophecies,'" *Today*, May 15, 1966, 2–3, esp. 3, included in "Ken Taylor—Articles concerning Taylor and the Living Bible," folder 12, box 6, Kenneth Taylor Papers.

25. James E. Ruark, *The House of Zondervan*, 2nd ed. (Grand Rapids, Mich.: Zondervan, 2006), 87.

26. Kenneth Nathaniel Taylor and Virginia J. Muir, *My Life: A Guided Tour: The Autobiography of Kenneth N. Taylor* (Wheaton, Ill.: Tyndale House, 1991), 216.

27. Don Michel, "Miracle of the Living Bible," *Saturday Evening Post* 247 (April 1975): 58–59, 88, 114; quote on 59. "Return of the Post," *Time* 97, no. 24 (June 14, 1971): 94.

28. Founded by the dispensationalist Bible teacher Lewis Sperry Chafer (1871–1952), for example, Dallas Theological Seminary grew out of the Bible conference movement that Chafer helped develop in the South, where Chafer modeled a style of fundamentalism more moderate than what ministers like J. Frank Norris had championed. Chafer was a friend of Taylor's father, who reportedly once warned Taylor and his brother: "'Unless you fellows get into the Word of God and get it into your lives, you'll never amount to much as Christians.'" B. Dwain Waldrep, "Lewis Sperry Chafer and the Roots of Nondenominational Fundamentalism in the South," *Journal of Southern History* 73, no. 4 (November 1, 2007): 807–836, esp. 812–816; quotation from Taylor and Muir, *My Life*, 210.

29. Don Michel, "Miracle of the Living Bible," *Saturday Evening Post* 247 (April 1975): 58–59, 88, 114.

30. Taylor and Muir, *My Life*, 122–123.

31. George M. Marsden, *Reforming Fundamentalism: Fuller Seminary and the New Evangelicalism* (Grand Rapids, Mich.: Eerdmans, 1987), e.g., 146.

32. Timothy Gloege, *Guaranteed Pure: The Moody Bible Institute, Business, and the Making of Modern Evangelicalism* (Chapel Hill, N.C.: University of North Carolina Press, 2015), e.g., 4–6.

33. Bethany Moreton, *To Serve God and Wal-Mart: The Making of Christian Free Enterprise* (Cambridge, Mass: Harvard University Press, 2009), 87–89.

34. "Family behind 'Living Prophecies,'" 2–3.

35. Myra, "Ken Taylor," 20.

36. Jonathan R. Laing, "The Living Bible Lives and Sells and Makes Kenneth Taylor Happy: His Colloquial Version Succeeds Despite Much Competition," *Wall Street Journal*, March 1, 1974, 1.

37. Keith Hunt and Gladys M. Hunt, *For Christ and the University: The Story of Intervarsity Christian Fellowship-USA, 1940–1990* (Downers Grove, Ill.: InterVarsity Press, 1992), 114.

38. Taylor and Muir, *My Life*, 207.

39. Taylor and Muir, *My Life*, 208–216.

40. D. Keith Stonehocker, "The Living Bible: A Market Research Survey, Sept. 1972," folder 18, box 6, Kenneth Taylor Papers.

41. Tyndale House Publishers, "Their future lies in your hands," advertisement, n.d., folder 23, box 6, Kenneth Taylor Papers.

42. See, for example, Gillian Frank, "'The Civil Rights of Parents': Race and Conservative Politics in Anita Bryant's Campaign against Gay Rights in 1970s Florida," *Journal of the History of Sexuality* 22, no. 1 (2013): 126–160, esp. 128; on Victorian evangelicals, urban reform, and domestic discipline, see McDannell, *Material Christianity*, 83, and Colleen McDannell, *The Christian Home in Victorian America, 1840–1900*, Religion in North America (Bloomington: Indiana University Press, 1986), chap. 1.

43. Eileen Luhr, *Witnessing Suburbia: Conservatives and Christian Youth Culture* (Berkeley: University of California Press, 2009), 69–71.

44. Moreton, *To Serve God and Wal-Mart*, 89–91.

45. Charles B. Williams, *The New Testament: A Translation in the Language of the People* (Chicago: Moody Press, 1950).

46. Taylor and Muir, *My Life*, 174–176.

47. Taylor and Muir, *My Life*, 161–162, 172–173.

48. John Bass and Robert DeVries, *The Christian Book Store* (Homewood, Ill.: Christian Booksellers Association, 1968). The same year that he helped coauthor this book, DeVries left his position as editor-in-chief of Moody Press and became Zondervan's director of publications. "Zondervan Appoints New Director of Publications," *Bookstore Journal*, September 1968, 22.

49. Sid Zullinger, "My Eighteen Years as a Salesmen to the Christian Booksellers," *Bookstore Journal*, September 1968, 10–11.

50. Book Industry Study Group, *Reading in America 1978: Selected Findings of the Book Industry Study Group's 1978 Study of American Book-Reading and Book-Buying Habits and Discussions of Those Findings at the Library of Congress on October 25 and 26, 1978* (Washington, D.C.: Library of Congress, 1979), 35; John P. Dessauer, Paul D. Doebler, and Hendrik Edelman, eds., *Christian Book Publishing and Distribution in the United States and Canada* (Tempe, Ariz.: CBA/ECPA/PCPA Joint Research Project, 1987), 127.

51. Taylor and Muir, *My Life*, 227–235, 242–244.

52. Paul Mouw, "Can You Really Trust a Paraphrase?," *Bookstore Journal*, March 1975, 16–17.

53. Myra, "Ken Taylor," 19.

54. Perry, "'What the Public Expect," 137–139.

55. Tyndale House Publishers, "Year after Year the Living Bible Remains the People's Choice," advertisement, *Christianity Today*, October 5, 1979, 54.

CHAPTER 15

1. Sarah Moore Grimké, *Letters on the Equality of the Sexes and the Condition of Woman* (Boston: Isaac Knapp, 1838), letters 4.23–24; 1.4–5; 3.20–21.

2. Grimké, *Letters on Equality*, letters 2.11–12; 14.102; 1.7.

3. Lucretia Mott, "Uses and Abuses of the Bible," address to the Cherry St. Meeting, Philadelphia, November 4, 1849, in *Lucretia Mott: Her Complete Speeches and Sermons*, ed. Dana Greene (New York: Mellen, 1980), 125.

4. Mott, Speech to a women's rights conference, Cleveland, 1853, in Greene, *Lucretia Mott*, 151.

5. Frances Willard, *The Defense of Women's Rights to Ordination in the Methodist Episcopal Church (Woman in the Pulpit)* (1888), ed. Carolyn De Swarte Gifford (New York: Garland, 1987), 33.

6. Willard, *Woman in the Pulpit*, 20, 27–28, 35–37, 31–32.

7. *Salem (OH) Anti-Slavery Bugle*, June 21, 1851. A better known version of this speech that is often titled "Ar'n't I a Woman" or "Ain't I a Woman?" is based on a later version, written in southern dialect by Frances Gage. The version printed here, recorded by Marius Robinson, is earlier and considered more accurate.

8. Rosalyn Terborg-Penn, "African American Women and the Woman Suffrage Movement," in *One Woman, One Vote*, ed. Marjorie Spruill Wheeler (Troutdale, OR: New Sage Press, 1995), 138–140.

9. Terborg-Penn, "African American Women and Suffrage," 148–149.

10. Julyanne Dodson, *Engendering Church: Women, Power, and the AME Church* (Lanham, MD: Rowman and Littlefield, 2002), 90–97.

11. Elizabeth Cady Stanton, *The Woman's Bible* (1895–98; reprint, Mineola, NY: Dover, 2002), 2:208–209.

12. Matilda Joslyn Gage, *Woman, Church, and State* (Chicago: C. H. Kerr, 1893), 44–47, openlibrary.org, accessed July 3, 2015.

13. Cady Stanton, *Woman's Bible*, 1:40.

14. Cady Stanton, *Woman's Bible*, 2:113.

15. Elizabeth Cady Stanton, Susan B. Anthony, and Matilda Joslyn Gage, eds., *History of Woman Suffrage* (1881; reprint, New York: Arno Press, 1969), 1:165–167.

16. Ida Husted Harper, *The Life and Work of Susan B. Anthony*, vol. 1 (Indianapolis: Bowen and Merrill, 1899), 77, www.gutenberg.org, accessed July 3, 2015.

17. Cady Stanton, *Woman's Bible*, 1:12.

18. Elizabeth Cady Stanton, *Eighty Years and More* (1898; Charleston, SC: Bibliobazaar, 2006) 56.

19. Willard, *Woman in the Pulpit*, 50.

20. Cady Stanton, Anthony, and Gage, *History of Woman Suffrage*, 1:89.

21. *Anti-Suffrage Essays by Massachusetts Women* (Boston: J. H. Haien, 1916), 122, www.gutenberg.org, accessed July 3, 2015.

22. Horace Bushnell, *Women's Suffrage: The Reform against Nature* (New York: Charles Scribner, 1869), 73–77.

23. "Gibbons Supports 'Antis,'" *New York Times*, April 30, 1913.

24. Kate Millett, *Sexual Politics* (1970; reprint, Urbana: University of Illinois Press, 2000), 51–54.

25. Betty Friedan, *The Feminine Mystique* (1963; reprint, New York: Norton, 1997), 166–174.

26. *In Memory of Her: A Feminist Theological Reconstruction of Christian Origins* (New York: Crossroad, 1983).

27. Elizabeth Schüssler Fiorenza, *Searching the Scriptures: A Feminist Introduction* (New York: Crossroad, 1993), and *Searching the Scriptures: A Feminist Commentary* (New York: Crossroad, 1997).

28. Judith Plaskow, *Standing Again at Sinai: Judaism from a Feminist Perspective* (San Francisco: Harper, 1991).

29. Rosemary Radford Ruether, *Sexism and God-Talk: Toward a Feminist Theology* (Boston: Beacon, 1983).

30. Carol Newsom, Sharon Ringe, and Jacqueline Lapsley, eds., *The Women's Bible Commentary* (1992; reprint, Louisville, KY: Westminster John Knox, 2012).

31. Sasha Bronner, "Why Gloria Steinem Says She and Jennifer Anniston Are in 'Deep Sh*t,'" *Huffington Post*, February 11, 2014.

CHAPTER 16

1. Stephen Stein, "America's Bibles: Canon, Commentary, and Community," *Church History* 64, no. 2 (June 1995), 184.

2. *Orthodox Study Bible* (Nashville: Thomas Nelson, 2008), xii.

3. Jack Sparks, "The Making of an Orthodox Study Bible," *Again* 15, no. 3 (September 1992), 19.

4. Theron Mathis, "The Orthodox Study Bible (A Guest Review)," http://web.archive.org/web/20100827151902/http://homepage.mac.com/rmansfield/thislamp/files/20080227_orthodox_study_bible.html, accessed July 7, 2014.

5. Peter J. Thuesen, *In Discordance with the Scriptures: American Protestant Battles over Translating the Bible* (Oxford: Oxford University Press, 1999), 4.

6. Daniel Lieuwen, "Who Decides? Unraveling the Mystery of the Old Testament Canon," *Again* 23, no. 3 (July–September 2001), 8–10.

7. Chad Hatfield, "Three Perspectives on the New Orthodox Study Bible," *Again* 30, no. 2 (April 2008), 17.

8. Hatfield, "Three Perspectives," 17.

9. Patrick Henry Reardon, "Susannah: The Lost Heroine of the Old Testament," *Again* 23, no. 3 (July–September 2001), 16–19.

10. Felix Culpa, "The Orthodox Study Bible: My Turn, I," http://ishmaelite.blogspot.com/2008/03/orthodox-study-bible-my-turn-i.html, accessed August 24, 2014.

11. Archimandrite Ephrem Lash, "The Orthodox Study Bible—A Review," *Sourozh* 54 (November 1993).

12. "Christophoros," comment on Monachos.net (online forum), March 27, 2008, http://www.monachos.net/conversation/topic/1525-orthodox-study-bible-complete-edition/page-4, accessed August 24, 2014.

13. Kevin P. Edgecomb, "Orthodox Study Bible Redux," http://www.bombaxo.com/blog/orthodox-study-bible-redux/, accessed August 24, 2014.

14. Christopher D. Hall, "The Orthodox Study Bible: First Impressions," http://christopherdhall.blogspot.com/2008/06/orthodox-study-bible-first-impressions.html, accessed August 24, 2014.

15. Esteban Vazquez, "The Orthodox Study Bible: My Turn, I," http://ishmaelite.blogspot.com/2008/03/orthodox-study-bible-my-turn-i.html, accessed August 24, 2014.

16. Kevin P. Edgecomb, "Two Septuagints," http://www.bombaxo.com/blog/two-septuagints/, accessed August 24, 2014.

17. Esteban Vazquez, "Neufeld on the Orthodox Study Bible," http://voxstefani.wordpress.com/2009/01/21/neufeld-on-the-orthodox-study-bible/, accessed August 24, 2014.

18. Edgecomb, "Two Septuagints."

19. Culpa, "Orthodox Study Bible."

20. Felix Culpa, "The Orthodox Study Bible's Audio Equivalent," http://ishmaelite.blogspot.com/2008/04/orthodox-study-bibles-audio-equivalent.html, accessed August 24, 2014.

21. Edgecomb, "Orthodox Study Bible Redux."

22. Culpa, "Orthodox Study Bible."

23. Culpa, "Orthodox Study Bible."

CHAPTER 17

1. Edwin Gaustad, "The Bible and American Protestantism," in *Altered Landscapes: Christianity in America, 1935–1985*, ed. David Lotz (Grand Rapids: Eerdmans, 1985), 209–225.

2. James Turner Johnson, introduction to *The Bible in American Law, Politics, and Political Rhetoric*, ed. James Turner Johnson (Philadelphia: Fortress Press, 1985), 5.

3. It is nearly impossible to calculate the number of Bibles sold annually in the United States. However, "a conservative estimate" was that Americans purchased some 25 million Bibles in 2005; Daniel Radosh, "The Good Book Business: Why Publishers Love the Bible," *New Yorker*, December 18, 2006, accessed June 11, 2014, www.newyorker.com/archive/2006/12/18/061218fa_fact1.

4. The American Bible Society's report *The State of the Bible, 2013* reports that 88 percent of adults surveyed in 2013 reported that their household owned a Bible, down from 92 percent who reported so in 1993. *The State of the Bible, 2013*, American Bible Society, 12, accessed June 11, 2014, www.americanbible.org/uploads/content/State%20of%20the%20Bible%20Report%202013.pdf.

5. The American Bible Society's report *The State of the Bible, 2013* reported that the median number of Bibles per household was 3.5 Bibles. *The State of the Bible, 2013*, American Bible Society, 12, accessed June 11, 2014, www.americanbible.org/uploads/content/State%20of%20the%20Bible%20Report%202013.pdf.

6. This was the finding of a Harris Poll conducted in 2014, the same result as was obtained in 2008 when the question was last asked. Michael Timmer, "The Bible Is the US's Most Popular Book," accessed June 11, 2014, www.christianitytoday.com/article/the.bible.is.the%20uss.most.popular.book/http://www.christiantoday.com/article/the.bible.is.the.uss.most.popular.book/37118.htm.

7. Nathan Hatch and Mark A. Noll, eds., *The Bible in America: Essays in Cultural History* (New York: Oxford University Press, 1982).

8. Mark A. Noll, David Bebbington, and George Rawlyk, eds., *Evangelicalism: Comparative Studies of Popular Protestantism in North America, the British Isles, and Beyond, 1700–1900* (New York: Oxford University Press, 1994).

9. Nathan Hatch, *The Democratization of American Christianity* (New Haven: Yale University Press, 1989).

10. Nathan Hatch, "The Christian Movement and the Demand for a Theology of the People," *Journal of American History* 67 (1980): 545–567; George Marsden, "Everyone's Own Interpreter?: The Bible, Science, and Authority in Mid-nineteenth-century America," in Hatch and Noll, *Bible in America: Essays in Cultural History*, 79–100.

11. See chapter 1.

12. Diana Eck, *A New Religious America: How a "Christian Country" Has Become the World's Most Religiously Diverse Nation* (San Francisco: Harper One, 2002).

13. "Nones on the Rise," Pew Research Religion and Public Life Project, October 9, 2012, accessed July 1, 2014, http://www.pewforum.org/2012/10/09/nones-on-the-rise/.

14. Pippa Norris and Ronald Inglehart, *Sacred and Secular: Religion and Politics Worldwide* (New York: Cambridge University Press, 2004); Pierre Brechon, "Cross-national Comparisons of Individual Religiosity," in *The Sage Handbook of the Sociology of Religion*, ed. James Beckford and N. J. Demerath III (Los Angeles: Sage, 2007), 463–489.

15. For example, there may be a higher percentage of evangelical Protestants present within American life than in other countries, with evangelicals being more inclined to read the Bible than those of other Christian faith traditions.

16. Unfortunately, questions tapping views of biblical authority in national surveys are quite varied. Because question wording shapes one's findings, there is "a need for a standard operationalization and understanding of Bible views in research so that findings of different studies are more comparable to one another." Aaron Franzen and Jenna Griebel, "Understanding a Cultural Identity: The Confluence of Education, Politics, and Religion within the American Concept of Biblical Literalism," *Sociology of Religion* 74 (2013): 538.

17. All inerrantists hold the Bible to be infallible, but not all who hold the Bible to be infallible are inerrantists; all literalists are inerrantists, but not all inerrantists are literalists. While such nuances of difference in views of biblical authority may escape the awareness of some "Bible believers," it is nevertheless likely that these differences in perspective on biblical authority are related to whether one views the Bible to be (1) the actual word of God or (2) the inspired word of God. See, for example, Ted Jelen, "Biblical Literalism and Inerrancy: Does the Difference Make a Difference?," *Sociological Analysis* 49 (1989): 421–429; Ted Jelen, Clyde Wilcox, and Corwin E. Smidt, "Biblical Literalism and Inerrancy: A Methodological Investigation," *Sociological Analysis* 51 (1990): 307–313; and Lyman Kellstedt and Corwin E. Smidt, "Doctrinal Beliefs and Political Behavior: Views of the Bible," in *Rediscovering the Religious Factor in American Politics*, ed. David Leege and Lyman Kellstedt (Armonk, NY: M. E. Sharpe, 1993), 177–198.

18. Scholars have analyzed views of biblical authority primarily as an independent variable, seeing the extent to which such views shape responses to other social, moral, and political questions. Scholars have spent far less effort seeking to analyze views of biblical authority as a dependent variable, seeing what factors may shape such differences in biblical authority among highly religious people. There is some evidence to suggest that responses to biblical authority questions may not be "literally" true in that many respondents may choose the inerrancy response simply as a means to reveal their identity as strong "Bible believers" in comparison to those who take weaker views of biblical authority. In other words, responses to such questions may be more a reflection of projecting group boundaries (in-group v. out-groups) than the expression of some particular doctrinal position related to biblical authority. Franzen and Griebel, "Understanding a Cultural Identity."

19. Aaron Franzen, "Reading the Bible in America: The Moral and Political Attitude Effect," *Review of Religious Research* 55 (2013): 393–411.

20. Franzen, "Reading the Bible in America," 394.

21. Using the second wave (2007) of the Baylor Religious Survey, Franzen reports that 42 percent of those who reported reading the Bible "multiple times per week" were not biblical literalists and that 59 percent of those who read the Bible on nearly a weekly basis did not hold literalist views. Franzen, "Reading the Bible in America," 400.

22. As far as I am aware, this is the most recent cross-national survey in which American responses related to biblical authority can be compared to responses found in multiple other Western societies. The International Social Survey Programme, 2008, contained the same question related to the nature of biblical authority, but very few countries chose to include it in their national survey.

23. In addition, different survey organizations use different sampling techniques. As a result, there are "house effects" as well, which also influence the results obtained. For an example of "house effects" related to frequency of reported levels of church attendance, see Corwin E. Smidt, Kevin denDulk, James Penning, Stephen Monsma, and Douglas Koopman,

Pews, Prayers & Participation: Religion & Civic Responsibility in America (Washington, DC: Georgetown University Press, 2008), table 2.2.

24. The response options provided in Bible reading questions, particularly at the lower levels of frequency (e.g., less than monthly, occasionally, rarely or never, never, do not read the Bible, etc.) shape findings related to the relative infrequency with which Americans read the Bible. For example, in table 17.3, the combination of rarely/never as the lowest response option reveals that 41 percent of Americans reported that they rarely or never read the Bible. However, when the response option is limited to "never" then approximately 25 percent of Americans or less report that they never read the Bible.

25. It does appear, however, that the National Surveys of Religion and Politics conducted in 1996 and 2012 tend to capture a somewhat higher percentage of daily Bible readers, though the percentages of those who report that they never read the Bible in these two surveys are comparable to the percentages found in other surveys who report that they "do not read the Bible."

26. Moreover, this pattern of continuity in religious practices among Americans across the past several decades is not limited to Bible reading, as the percentage of Americans who report weekly church attendance has not declined over the past three decades either. For example, slightly more than 40 percent of Americans reported in 1981 that they attended religious services on a weekly basis, and this percentage has remained stable since then—a pattern that stands in contrast to the generally declining percentage of weekly churchgoers found among Canadians and members of other European societies (see table 17.5). However, it is also true that the percentage of Americans who report that they rarely, if ever, go to church has increased over the same period of time.

27. C. Kirk Hadaway and Mark Chaves, "What the Polls Don't Show: A Closer Look at U.S. Church Attendance," *American Sociological Review* 58 (1993): 741–752; C. Kirk Hadaway and Penny Long Marler, "Overreporting Church Attendance in America: Evidence That Demands the Same Verdict," *American Sociological Review* 63 (1998): 122–130; Robert D. Woodberry, "When Surveys Lie and People Tell the Truth: How Surveys Oversample Church Attenders," *American Sociological Review* 63 (1998): 119–122; C. Kirk Hadaway and Penny Long Marler, "How Many Americans Attend Worship Each Week? An Alternative Approach to Measurement," *Journal for the Scientific Study of Religion* 44 (2005): 307–322; Stanley Presser and Mark Chaves, "Is Religious Service Attendance Declining?," *Journal for the Scientific Study of Religion* 46 (2007): 137–145; and, Maurizio Rossi and Ettore Scappini, "Church Attendance, Problems of Measurement, and Interpreting Indicators: A Study of Religious Practices in the United States, 1975–2010," *Journal for the Scientific Study of Religion* 53 (2014): 249–267.

28. Dennis Hoover, Michael Martinez, Samuel Reimer, and Kenneth Wald, "Evangelicalism Meets the Continental Divide: Moral and Economic Conservatism in the United States and Canada," *Political Research Quarterly* 55 (2002): 354.

29. For example, the data from the God and Society in North America Survey reveal that the percentage of Catholics in Canada was 33 percent, while the percentage of Catholics in the United States was 23 percent.

30. For example, using the Sixth National Survey of Religion and Politics (2012), the percentage of evangelical Protestants who reported daily Bible reading was 39 percent, while the corresponding figures for mainline Protestants and Roman Catholics were 16 percent and 12 percent, respectively.

31. Using the God and Society in North America data, the percentage of evangelical Protestants who strongly agreed that "the Bible is the inspired word of God" was 85 percent, while the corresponding percentages for mainline Protestants and Roman Catholics were 51

percent and 49 percent, respectively. Though the percentages differed slightly between Canada and the United States, evangelicals, regardless of country analyzed, far outranked both mainline Protestants or Catholics in their assessments of biblical authority.

32. Will Herberg, *Protestant-Catholic-Jew* (Garden City, NY: Doubleday, 1955); Robert Bellah, "Civil Religion in America," in *American Civil Religion*, ed. Russell Richey and Donald Jones (New York: Harper and Row, 1974), 21–44; and Seymour Martin Lipset, *Continental Divide* (New York: Routledge, 1990).

33. Samuel Reimer, "A Look at Cultural Effects in Religiosity: A Comparison between the United States and Canada," *Journal for the Scientific Study of Religion* 34 (1995): 445–457.

34. Moreover, as people choose to use the same media for different purposes, they bring different social backgrounds and experiences to the same text or program and, as a result, may draw different interpretations from the same content that they read, hear, or see.

35. Robert Wuthnow, ed., *"I Come Away Stronger": How Small Groups Are Shaping American Religion* (Grand Rapids: Eerdmans, 1994); Jody Shapiro Davie, *Women in the Presence: Constructing Community and Seeking Spirituality in Mainline Protestantism* (Philadelphia: University of Pennsylvania Press, 1995); Brian Malley, *How the Bible Works: An Anthropological Study of Evangelical Biblicism* (Walnut Creek, CA: Alta Mira Press, 2004); and James S. Bielo, *Words upon the Word: An Ethnography of Evangelical Group Bible Study* (New York: New York University Press, 2009).

36. Based on the narratives provided by his respondents, Ronald delineates four different models related to ways respondents used biblical texts in their lives: appropriative, therapeutic, educational, and devotional. Emily Ronald, "More Than 'Alone with the Bible': Reconceptualizing Religious Reading," *Sociology of Religion* 73 (2012): 323–344.

37. Ronald, "More Than 'Alone with the Bible.'"

38. Technically, mean scores are affected by extreme scores and do not reveal the actual frequency distribution. However, when one cross-tabulates religious tradition with the relative frequency of responses given to each of the nine purposes posed, one finds that the percentage of "not at all" responses is greater among Catholics than among the religiously unaffiliated for learning "about abortion or homosexuality."

CHAPTER 18

1. For a more extensive survey of children's Bibles from throughout U.S. history, see Russell W. Dalton, *Children's Bibles in America: A Reception History of the Story of Noah's Ark in U.S. Children's Bibles* (London: Bloomsbury T & T Clark, 2015).

2. Leonard S. Marcus, *Minders of Make-Believe* (Boston: Houghton Mifflin, 2008), 298–311.

3. Thomas S. Giles, "Pick a Bible—Any Bible," *Christianity Today* (October 26, 1992), 27.

4. Shannon Maughan, "In the Kids' Corner," *Publishers Weekly* 246.41 (October 11, 1999), 46.

5. LaVonne Neff, "Bible Stories: Facing a Floodtide," *Publishers Weekly* 248.42 (October 15, 2001), 38.

6. See John Locke, *Some Thoughts Concerning Education* (London, 1693), 187, and Ronald Goldman, *Readiness for Religion: A Basis for Developmental Religious Education* (New York: Seabury Press, 1965), 71.

7. Some earlier children's Bibles were produced for younger children, such as Gertrude Smith, *Baby Bible Stories* (Philadelphia: Henry Altemus, 1904), Elisabeth Robinson Scovil, *Wee Folks Stories from the Old Testament: In Words of One Syllable* (Philadelphia: Henry Altemus, 1920), Rosamund D. Ginther, *Bible Stories for the Cradle Roll*, vols. 1–5 (Nashville: Southern

Publishing Association, 1933) and Lenore Cohen, *Bible Tales for Very Young Children* (Cincinnati: Union of American Hebrew Congregations, 1934), but even these tended to be written for elementary age children and not preschoolers.

8. Steven Mintz, *Huck's Raft: A History of American Childhood* (Cambridge, Mass.: Harvard University Press, 2004), 19.

9. John Howard, *Scripture History for the Young* (New York: Virtue, Yorston & Co, Publishers, 1863), 192.

10. Faith Latimer, *Dear Old Stories Told Once More* (New York: American Tract Society, 1877), 100.

11. Samuel G. Goodrich, *Peter Parley's Book of Bible Stories* (Boston: Lilly, Wait, and Co., 1834), 19, and Lucy Barton, *Bible Letters for Children* (London: John Souter, 1831), 11.

12. V. Gilbert Beers, *The Toddler's Bible*, ill. Carole Boerke (Colorado Springs: Cook Communications Ministry, 1992); V. Gilbert Beers, *The Preschooler's Bible*, ill. Teresa Walsh (Colorado Springs: Cook Communications Ministry, 1994); Robin Currie, *The Baby Bible Storybook*, ill. Cindy Adams (Eastbourne, UK: Chariot Books, 1994); Carolyn Nabors Baker and Cindy Helms, *The Beginners Bible for Toddlers*, ill. Danny Brooks Dalby (Dallas: Word, 1995); *Baby's First Bible*, ill. Colin and Moira Maclean (Pleasantville, N.Y.: Reader's Digest Books, 1996); *Baby's Bible*, ill. Mandy Stanley (Cincinnati: Standard, 2003); *Baby Blessings Baby's Bible* (Norwalk, Conn.: Standard, 2004); Diane Stortz, *The Sweetest Story Bible for Toddlers*, ill. Sheila Bailey (Grand Rapids, Mich.: Zondervan, 2010); *Baby's First Bible* (Lutherville, MD: Anno Domini, 2012); *The Big Picture Interactive Bible Stories for Toddlers from the Old Testament* (Nashville: B & H, 2014).

13. To list just a few of the many examples of children's Bibles that emphasize the theme of God keeping children safe: Karyn Henly, *The Beginner's Bible: Timeless Children's Stories*, ill. Dennas Davis (Sisters, Ore.: Questar, 1989), 35; Diane Stortz and Greg Holder, *My Pals Storybook*, ill. Jodie McCallum (Cincinnati: Standard, 1996), 10; Pat Alexander, *My First Bible*, ill. Leon Baxter (Intercourse, Pa.: Good Books, 2002), 37; Mack Thomas, *The First Step Bible* (Sisters, Ore.: Gold 'n Honey Books, 1994), 37; *Touch-and-See Bible*, ill. Eileen Hine (Cincinnati: Standard, 2004), n.p.; Connie Morgan Wade and Diane Stortz, *Rhyme Time Bible Stories: Noah's Ark*, ill. Laura Ovresat (Cincinnati: Standard, 2012), n.p.; Tracy L. Harrast, *My Baby and Me Story Bible*, ill. Gloria Oostema (Grand Rapids, Mich.: Zondervan, 1995), 12; Sally Lloyd-Jones, *Tiny Bear's Bible*, ill. Igor Oleynikov (Grand Rapids, Mich.: Zondervan, 2007), n.p.

14. For an extensive exploration of this theme, see Dalton, *Children's Bibles in America*, 45–118.

15. *Jesus and the Miracle of the Loaves and Fishes* (Omaha: LynnLee Toys, 2001).

16. Sally Lloyd-Jones, *Tiny Bear's Bible* (Grand Rapids, Mich.: ZonderKids, 2007), n.p.

17. Lloyd-Jones, *Tiny Bear's Bible*, n.p.

18. P. J. Lyons, *Little Lion's Bible*, ill. Melanie Mitchell (Grand Rapids, Mich.: Zondervan, 2011).

19. P. J. Lyons, *Little Bunny's Bible* (Grand Rapids, Mich.: Zondervan, 2011).

20. P. J. Lyons, *Little Chick's Bible* (Grand Rapids, Mich.: Zondervan, 2011).

21. Christian Smith with Melinda Lundquist, *Soul Searching: The Religious and Spiritual Lives of American Teenagers* (Oxford: Oxford University Press, 2005), 162–170.

22. Gillian Avery, *Behold the Child: American Children and Their Books 1621–1922* (London: Bodley Head, 1994), 65.

23. *Mother's True Stories* (Boston: Crosby, Nichols, and Company for the Sunday School Society, 1858), Mary Stewart, *Tell Me a True Story* (New York: Fleming H. Revell, 1909).

24. Christine Harder Tangvald, *The Big Big Big Boat, and Other Bible Stories about Obedience* (Elgin, Ill.: Chariot Books, 1993), 11.

25. Susan Elizabeth Beck, *God Loves Me Bible*, ill. Gloria Oostema (Grand Rapids, Mich.: Zondervan, 1993), 11.

26. Mack Thomas, *The First Step Bible* (Sisters, Ore.: Gold 'n Honey Books, 1994), 17.

27. Mack Thomas, *First Step Bible*, 34–35.

28. V. Gilbert Beers, *The Preschooler's Bible*, ill. Teresa Walsh (Colorado Springs: Cook Communications Ministry, 1994), 34–35.

29. Mary Hollingsworth, *My Very First Book of Bible Heroes*, ill. Rick Incrocci (Nashville: Thomas Nelson, 1993), 39.

30. *The Beginner's Bible: All Aboard with Noah!* (Grand Rapids, Mich.: Zondervan, 2009).

31. Selina Hastings, *The Children's Illustrated Bible*, ill. Eric Thomas (New York: Dorling Kindersley, 1994); Marie-Helene Delval, *Reader's Digest Bible for Children*, ill. Ulises Wensell (Pleasantville, N.Y.: Reader's Digest Young Families, 1995).

32. As Nikki Bado-Fralick and Rebecca Sachs Norris note, Americans are obsessed with having fun, even to the point that they feel compelled to market the most somber and serious acts of religious expression as fun and enjoyable activities. See Nikki Bado-Fralick and Rebecca Sachs Norris, *Toying with God: The World of Religious Games and Dolls* (Waco, Tex.: Baylor University Press, 2010), 107–136.

33. I make no claim that my research has been exhaustive, but I have read well over 500 versions of the story of Noah's ark in children's Bibles published in the United States. This article is informed by research partially funded through a Lilly Theological Research Expense Grant distributed by the Association of Theological Schools that allowed me to travel to the American Antiquarian Society in Worcester, Massachusetts, and the Library of Congress in Washington, D.C., and review many children's Bibles.

34. Mary Hollingsworth, *Bumper the Dinosaur Bible Stories*, ill. Rick Incrocci (Colorado Springs: Chariot Family, 1996), n.p.

35. Hollingsworth, *Bumper the Dinosaur Bible Stories*, n.p.

36. "Master Books," http://www.nlpg.com/about-master-books/, accessed June 11, 2014.

37. Gloria Clanin, *In the Days of Noah*, ill. Earl and Bonita Snellenberger (Green Forest, Ariz.: Master Books, 1996), 28, 29, 31, and 32.

38. Ken Ham, *Dinosaurs of Eden: A Biblical Journey through Time*, ill. Earl and Bonita Snellenberger (Green Forest, Ariz.: Master Books, 2001), 23, 26, 133, 40–41, 42.

39. Ken Ham, *The True Account of Adam & Eve*, ill. Bill Looney (Green Forest, Ariz.: Master Books, 2012), 11.

40. Ham, *True Account of Adam & Eve*, 16.

41. Tom Dooley, *The True Story of Noah's Ark*, ill. Bill Looney (Green Forest, Ariz.: Master Books, 2003), 17.

42. Dooley, *The True Story of Noah's Ark*, 30–31.

43. For an interesting case study related to the issue as it played out at Cedarville University, see Kevin Mungons, "Case Study: Teaching Adam," at http://baptistbulletin.org/the-baptist-bulletin-magazine/novdec-13/case-study-teaching-adam-2/, accessed July 20, 2015.

44. For more, see Stephen Prothero, *American Jesus: How the Son of God Became a National Icon* (New York: Farrar, Straus and Giroux, 2003), 3–16.

45. For example, *Scripture History, or Short Sketches of Characters from the Old Testament* (New York: Mahlon Day, 1829) and Mary Sherwood, *Scripture Prints, with explanations in the form of familiar dialogues* (New York: Pendleton and Hill, 1832).

46. See, for example, *Sunday evenings; or, An easy introduction to the reading of the Bible* (New-York: J. & J. Harper, 1832), 27–39; T. H. Gallaudet, *Scripture Biography for the Young, with Critical Illustrations and Practical Remarks,* vol. 1, *Adam to Jacob* (New York: American Tract Society, 1838), 62–69; Favell Lee Mortimer, *Scripture Facts in Simple Language* ([United States]: The American Tract Society, [1848]), 2–8; Mrs. Grive, *Half hours with the Bible; or, The Children's Scripture Story-Book* (New York: McLoughlin Brothers, [1867]), 20–22; Alvan Bond, *Young People's Illustrated Bible History* (Norwich, Conn.: Henry Bill Publishing Company, 1878), 28–29; Carolyn Hadley, *From Eden to Babylon: Stories of the Prophets Priests and Kings of the Old Testament* (New York: McLoughlin Brothers [c. 1890]), 15; J. L. Sooy, *Bible Talks with Children: The Scriptures Simplified for the Little Folk* (New York: Union Publishing House, 1889), 16–18.

47. See, for example, Ethel Hudson, *Bible Heroes: For Use in the Junior B.Y.P.U.* (Nashville: Sunday School Board of the Southern Baptist Convention, 1926) and Ruth Hogue Bobb, *A Bible Highway: Charted for Boys and Girls* (Chicago: International Child Evangelism Fellowship, 1941).

48. Sally Lloyd-Jones, *The Jesus Storybook Bible: Every Story Whispers His Name* (Grand Rapids, Mich.: ZonderKids, 2007), back cover.

49. Lloyd-Jones, *Jesus Storybook Bible*, 54.

50. http://gospelstoryforkids.com/portfolio/gospel-story-bible-2/, accessed on June 26, 2013.

51. Marty Machowski, *The Gospel Story Bible: Discovering Jesus in the Old and New Testaments* (Greensboro, N.C.: New Growth Press, 2011), 17, 18, 55, 68.

52. Rondi DeBoer and Christine Tangvald, *My Favorite Bible* (Grand Rapids, Mich.: Baker, 2011), i. Bold type in the original.

53. Sarah Young, *Jesus Calling Bible Storybook*, ill. Carolin Farias (Nashville: Thomas Nelson, 2012), n.p., 16, 21.

54. See, for example, David Helm, *The Big Picture Story Bible*, ill. Gail Schoonmaker (Wheaton, Ill.: Crossway Books, 2004), Rondi DeBoer and Christine Tangvald, *My Favorite Bible* (Grand Rapids, Mich.: Baker, 2011), and *The Big Picture Interactive Bible Storybook* (Nashville: B & H, 2013).

55. For more, see Osayimwense Osa, ed., *The All-White World of Children's Books and African American Children's Literature* (Trenton, N.J.: African World Press, 1995).

56. R. A. Morrisey, *Bible History of the Negro* (Nashville: National Baptist Publishing Board, 1915) and Morrisey, *Colored People in Bible History* (Hammond, Ind.: W. B. Conkey, 1925).

57. Betty Smith Foley, *Bible Chillun* (Philadelphia: Dorrance, 1939).

58. Lorenz Graham, *How God Fix Jonah*, ill. Ashley Bryan (Honesdale, Pa.: Boyds Mills Press, 1946; reprint, 1974).

59. Ruth B. Bottigheimer, *The Bible for Children: From the Age of Gutenberg to the Present* (New Haven: Yale University Press, 1996), 47.

60. *Minders of Make-Believe*, 298–311.

61. Patricia and Fredrick McKissack, *Let My People Go: Bible Stories Told by a Freeman of Color*, ill. James E. Ransome (New York: Atheneum Books for Young Readers, 1998), vii.

62. *Children of Color Storybook Bible with Stories from the International Children's Bible,* ill. Victor Hogan (Nashville: Thomas Nelson, 2001), vii.

63. *My Holy Bible for African-American Children* (Grand Rapids, Mich.: Zondervan, 2009).

64. See the helpful extended examinations of how children's Bible texts and illustrations treat "otherness" in Bible stories in the essays in Caroline Vander Stichele and Hugh S. Pyper,

eds., *Text, Image, and Otherness in Children's Bibles: What is in the Picture?* (Atlanta: Society of Biblical Literature, 2012).

65. See, for example, Alice Bach and J. Cheryl Exum, *Moses' Ark*, ill. Leo and Diane Dillon (New York: Delacorte Press, 1989); *Holy Bible: Children's Illustrated Edition: Contemporary English Version* (New York: American Bible Society, 2000); and Desmond Tutu, *Children of God Storybook Bible* (Grand Rapids, Mich.: ZonderKids, 2010).

66. James Dobson, *Bringing Up Girls* (Carol Spring, Ill.: Tyndale House, 2010), 13.

67. James Dobson, *Bringing Up Boys* (Carol Spring, Ill.: Tyndale House, 2001), 6.

68. Harvey Albert Snyder, *Boys of the Bible* (Philadelphia: John C. Winston, 1929). Note that even in this case the books were originally published in a combined volume as Harvey Albert Snyder, *Boys and Girls of the Bible* (Philadelphia: W. E. Scull, 1911).

69. Robin Currie, *The Baby Bible Storybook for Boys*, ill. Gonstaza Basaluzzo (Colorado Springs: David C. Cook, 2008), and Robin Currie, *The Baby Bible Storybook for Girls*, ill. Gonstaza Basaluzzo (Colorado Springs: David C. Cook, 2008).

70. Carolyn Larsen, *Little Girls Bible Storybook for Mothers and Daughters*, ill. Caron Turk (Grand Rapids, Mich.: Baker Book House, 1998), 32, 62, 66, and 298. The popularity of the book inspired a spinoff of sorts, Carolyn Larsen's *Little Girls Bible Storybook for Fathers and Daughters*, ill. Caron Turk (Grand Rapids, Mich.: Baker Book House, 2014).

71. Larsen, *Little Girls Bible Storybook for Fathers and Daughters*, 29, 32.

72. Carolyn Larsen, *Little Boys Bible Storybook for Fathers and Sons* (Grand Rapids, Mich.: Baker, 2001). See also Carolyn Larsen, *Little Boys Bible Storybook for Mothers and Sons* (Grand Rapids, Mich.: Baker, 2014).

73. Larsen, *Little Boys Bible Storybook for Fathers and Sons*, 31–33.

74. *Revolve 2008: The Complete New Testament* (Nashville: Thomas Nelson, 2007).

75. *Refuel: The Complete New Testament* (Nashville: Thomas Nelson, Inc., 2008).

76. *Shiny Sequin Bible Holy Bible* (International Children's Bible) (New York: Tommy Nelson, 2011).

77. "Sequin Bible—Pink," Thomas Nelson, http://www.thomasnelson.com/sequin-bible-pink.html, accessed April 25, 2014.

78. *Compact Kids Bible: Green Camo* (New York: Thomas Nelson, 2007).

79. "Compact Kids Bible: Green Camo," Thomas Nelson, http://www.thomasnelson.com/compact-kids-bible-1.html, accessed April 25, 2014.

80. *The Girls Life Application Bible* (Carol Stream, Ill.: Tyndale House, 2006).

81. *The Guys Life Application Bible* (Carol Stream, Ill.: Tyndale House, 2006).

82. *FaiThGirLz! Bible* (NIV) (Grand Rapids, Mich.: Zondervan, 2011).

83. *NIV Boys Bible* (Grand Rapids, Mich.: Zondervan, 2011).

84. Sheila Walsh, *God's Mighty Warrior Devotional Bible* (Nashville: Thomas Nelson, 2012).

85. Thomas Nelson, "*God's Mighty Warrior Devotional Bible*," http://www.thomasnelson.com/god-s-mighty-warrior-devotional-bible, accessed July 30, 2015.

86. Sheila Walsh, *God's Little Princess Devotional Bible* (Nashville: Thomas Nelson, 2012).

87. Thomas Nelson, "*God's Little Princess Devotional Bible*," http://www.thomasnelson.com/god-s-little-princess-devotional-bible, accessed July 30, 2015.

88. Sheila Walsh, *The Princess in Me Storybook Bible* (Nashville: Thomas Nelson, 2008); Andy Holmes, *My Princess Bible*, ill. Sergey Eiliseev (Carol Stream, Ill.: Tyndale House, 2010); *The Precious Princess Bible* (NIrV) (Grand Rapids, Mich.: ZonderKidz, 2010); "Precious Princess Bible NIrV," Zondervan, http://www.zondervan.com/precious-princess-bible-nirv-1.html, accessed April 25, 2014; *The Princess Bible*, New King James Version (Nashville: Thomas Nelson,

2008); *My Beautiful Princess Bible* (NLT) (Carol Stream, Ill.: Tyndale House, 2012); *Princess Bible Tiara Edition* (Carol Stream, Ill.: Tyndale House, 2012); Sheila Walsh, *Sweet Dreams Princess: God's Little Princess Bedtime Bible Stories, Devotions, and Prayers* (Thomas Nelson, 2008), and Walsh, *God's Little Princess Holy Bible* (NKJV) (Nashville: Thomas Nelson, 2014); Fiona Boon, *My Princess Bible Purse* (Nashville: Thomas Nelson, 2012); Sheri Rose Shepherd and Shelley Dieterichs, *Bible Stories for His Beautiful Princess* (Carol Stream, Ill.: Tyndale House, 2014); *The Princess in Me Storybook Bible* (Nashville: Thomas Nelson, 2008); Jean Kavich Bloom, *Bible Promises for God's Precious Princess* (Grand Rapids, Mich.: ZonderKids, 2013); Sheri Rose Shepherd, *Bible Stories for His Beautiful Princess* (Carol Stream, Ill.: Tyndale House, 2014).

89. Carolyn Larsen, *Princess Stories: Real Bible Stories of God's Princesses* (Carol Stream, Ill.: Tyndale House, 2011), 1.

90. See, for example, Peggy Orenstein, *Cinderella Ate My Daughter: Dispatches from the Front Lines of the New Girlie-Girl Culture* (New York: Harper, 2011) and Rebecca Hains, *The Princess Problem: Guiding Our Girls through the Princess-Obsessed Years* (Naperville, Ill.: Sourcebooks, 2014).

91. For a further discussion of this phenomenon, see Russell W. Dalton, "Meek and Mild: American Children's Bibles' Stories of Jesus as a Boy," *Religious Education* 109.1 (2014): 49–53.

CHAPTER 19

1. See chapter 1.

2. Therapeutic religion characterizes the views studied by Chris Smith and Melina Lundquist Denton in *Soul Searching: The Religious and Spiritual Lives of American Teenagers* (reprint, Oxford: Oxford University Press, 2009).

3. The Barna Group, "American Bible Society, State of the Bible, 2013," http://www .americanbible.org/uploads/content/State%20of%20the%20Bible%20Report%202013.pdf. Note some of the related findings: (1) "Nearly half of Americans (47%) strongly agree that the Bible contains everything a person needs to know to live a meaningful life" (p. 8); (2) "Relatively few adults believe the Bible can only be correctly interpreted by people who have years of intense training in theology (8% strongly agree)—suggesting that most adults believe it to be accessible to the common person" (p. 8); (3) "The King James version of the Bible continues to be the version most Bible readers read most often" (p. 17).

4. Pew Research Center for the People and the Press and Pew Forum on Religion and Public Life, "Many Americans Uneasy with Mix of Religion and Politics," http://www.pewforum .org/2006/08/24/many-americans-uneasy-with-mix-of-religion-and-politics/.

5. Alec Gallup and Wendy W. Simmons, "Six in Ten Americans Read Bible at Least Occasionally," October 20, 2000, http://www.gallup.com/poll/2416/six-ten-americans-read-bible-least-occasionally.aspx.

6. Barna Research, "Beliefs Held by Americans in Regard to the Bible," http://www .bibleteachingnotes.com/templates/mobile/default.asp?id=29183&fetch=7872.

7. Martin Marty, "America's Iconic Book," in *Humanizing America's Iconic Book: Society of Biblical Literature Centennial Addresses 1080*, ed. Gene M. Tucker and Douglas A. Knight, Biblical Scholarship in North America 6 (Chico: Scholars Press, 1982), 1–23.

8. *Public Opinion* 14 (January 7, 1893), 333.

9. Marty, "America's Iconic Book," 2.

10. Most recently, see Jacques Berlinerblau, "The Bible in the Presidential Elections of 2012, 2008, 2004, and the Collapse of American Secularism," in *The Bible in the Public Square: Its Enduring Influence in American Life*, ed. Mark A. Chancey, Carol Meyers, and Eric M. Meyers, Biblical Scholarship in North America 27 (Atlanta: SBL Press, 2014), 15–36. See also Elisabeth Schüssler

Fiorenza, "A Republic of Many Voices: Biblical Studies in the Twenty-First Century," in *Foster Biblical Scholarship: Essays in Honor of Kent Harold Richards*, ed. Frank Ritchel Ames and Charles William Miller, Biblical Scholarship in North America 24 (Atlanta: SBL Press, 2010), 137–159.

11. Marty, "America's Iconic Book," 3.

12. Zachary Elkins, Tom Ginsburg, and James Melton, *The Endurance of National Constitutions* (Cambridge: Cambridge University Press, 2009); Comparative Constitutions Project, http://comparativeconstitutionsproject.org/; data on constitutions at http://comparativeconstitutionsproject.org/ccp-rankings/ and http://comparativeconstitutionsproject.org/chronology/.

13. Thomas Jefferson to James Madison, September 6, 1789; Thomas Jefferson to Samuel Kercheval, July 12, 1816, http://www.let.rug.nl/usa/presidents/thomas-jefferson/letters-of-thomas-jefferson.

14. Michael Kammen, *A Machine that Would Go of Itself: The Constitution in American Culture* (New York: Knopf, 1986). For another helpful study, see Daniel Lessard Levin, *Representing Popular Sovereignty: The Constitution in American Political Culture* (Albany: State University of New York Press, 1999).

15. Kammen, *Machine*, xiii.

16. Kammen, *Machine*, 22. In 1936, Edward S. Corwin described how the Constitution became a national symbol between 1789 and 1860 and efforts in the 1930s from such organizations as the Liberty League were to prevent change. "The Constitution as Instrument and as Symbol," *American Political Science Review* 30 (1936), 1071–1085.

17. Thomas Jefferson to Samuel Kercheval, July 12, 1816. See also Louis Michael Seidman, *On Constitutional Disobedience* (Oxford: Oxford University Press, 2012), 7; and Donald S. Lutz, "Thinking about Constitutionalism at the Start of the Twenty-First Century," *Publius* 30.4 (2000), 115.

18. Kammen, *Machine*, 47.

19. James M. Beck, *The Constitution of the United States—Yesterday, Today and Tomorrow* (New York: George H. Doran, 1924), 268. See discussion throughout Kammen, *Machine*, especially 4, 83–84, 220. Kammen notes this illiteracy extended to legislators and lawyers: "In 1927 the chairman of that committee [the American Bar Association's Committee on American Citizenship] carried the condemnation one step farther: 'The law schools are turning out thousands of lawyers every year who know nothing of the Constitution'" (*Machine*, 230).

20. William Hickey, *The Constitution of the United States of America* (Washington, D.C.: J. and G. S. Gideon, 1846). See Kammen, *Machine*, 80.

21. To name only a few, see Johnathan O'Neill, *Originalism in American Law and Politics: A Constitutional History* (Baltimore: Johns Hopkins University Press, 2005); Steven G. Calabresi, ed., *Originalism: A Quarter-Century of Debate* (Washington, D.C.: Regnery, 2007); Sanford Levinson, *Constitutional Faith*, rev. ed. (Princeton: Princeton University Press, 2012); Ilya Somin, "The Origins of Originalism," *Washington Post*, January 21, 2014, http://www.washingtonpost.com/news/volokh-conspiracy/wp/2014/01/21/the-origins-of-originalism/.

22. Jack M. Balkin, "Why Are Americans Originalists?," Yale Law School, Public Law Research Paper no. 492, http://papers.ssrn.com/sol3/papers.cfm?abstract_id=2379587, also published in *Law, Society and Community: Socio-Legal Essays in Honour of Roger Cotterrell*, ed. Richard Nobles and David Schiff (Surrey, England: Ashgate, 2014), 309–326.

23. Balkin, "Why Are Americans Originalists?," 1.

24. Championed by New Evangelicalism. See Eric Pellish, "A More Perfect Union: New Evangelical Politics and Constitutional Originalism in Post-war America" (B.A. thesis, Department of Religious Studies, Case Western Reserve University, 2013), written under Timothy Beal.

25. Balkin, "Why Are Americans Originalists?," 7–8.

26. Both O'Neill (*Originalism in American Law and Politics*) and Somin ("Origins of Originalism").

27. Somin, "Origins of Originalism."

28. Balkin, too, makes the distinction, describing them as thin and thick versions of original meaning. A thin version of originalism is consistent with the position of "living Constitution," since it would not be controversial to first interpret the Constitution in its historic, linguistic, and social context. A thin originalism would get as close as possible to the historical context of the constitutional framers and might "engage in constitutional construction," whereby they "build out the Constitution by creating doctrines that, in their view, best realize the Constitution's words in their own times." The Constitution then is a framework, "leaving to each generation the duty of building out and implementing the Constitution's text and principles in their own time" ("Why Are Americans Originalists?," 4).

29. Balkin, "Why Are Americans Originalists?," 1.

30. Balkin, "Why Are Americans Originalists?," 4–5. Citing Robert H. Bork, "Original Intent: The Only Legitimate Basis for Constitutional Decision Making," *Judges Journal* 26.3 (1987): 13–17.

31. Balkin, "Why Are Americans Originalists?," 2.

32. Balkin, "Why Are Americans Originalists?," 7.

33. Balkin, "Why Are Americans Originalists?," 24. See also Levinson, *Constitutional Faith*.

34. Balkin, "Why Are Americans Originalists?," 11.

35. See Pellish, "More Perfect Union."

36. Balkin, "Why Are Americans Originalists?," 21–22. See also Levinson, *Constitutional Faith*, and Jack M. Balkin, *Constitutional Redemption: Political Faith in an Unjust World* (Cambridge, Mass.: Harvard University Press, 2011).

37. Jaroslav Pelikan, *Interpreting the Bible and the Constitution* (New Haven: Yale University Press, 2004), 101. It should be noted that this is a different issue from how the Bible and the Constitution have used broadly similar interpretative methods. On this, see Pelikan, *Interpreting the Bible and the Constitution*; also Henry L. Chambers, Jr., "Biblical Interpretation, Constitutional Interpretation, and Ignoring Text," *Maryland Law Review* 69.1 (January 2009), http://digitalcommons.law.umaryland.edu/mlr/vol69/iss1/10.

38. Of course, it is only a segment or type of biblical scholarship that has as its goal interpreting the Bible for modernity. On the problems inherent in this enterprise and the humanistic discipline's subtle sympathies, service, and struggles with faith traditions, see Philip R. Davies, *Whose Bible Is It Anyway?*, 2nd ed. (London: T. and T. Clark, 2004); Hector Avalos, *The End of Biblical Studies* (Amherst, N.Y.: Prometheus Books, 2007); Jacques Berlinerblau, *The Secular Bible: Why Nonbelievers Must Take Religion Seriously* (Cambridge: Cambridge University Press, 2005).

39. Saul Cornell, "The People's Constitution vs. The Lawyer's Constitution: Popular Constitutionalism and the Original Debate over Originalism," *Yale Journal of Law and the Humanities* 23.2, article 2 (2011), 306.

40. George F. Parker, *Recollections of Grover Cleveland* (New York: Century, 1909), 382.

41. Diana L. Eck, *A New Religious America: How a "Christian Country" Has Become the World's Most Religiously Diverse Nation* (San Francisco: HarperSanFrancisco, 2001).

42. Pew Research Center's Forum on Religion and Public Life, "The Future of the Global Muslim Population," January 27, 2011, http://www.pewforum.org/2011/01/27/the-future-of-the-global-muslim-population/.

43. Numbers are hard to come by, since the U.S. Census does not collect data on religious affiliation. Most have relied on the Pew 2008 U.S. Religious Landscape Survey, http://religions

.pewforum.org/pdf/report-religious-landscape-study-full.pdf. Based on interviews with more than 35,000 Americans aged eighteen and older, this study finds that "religious affiliation in the U.S. is both very diverse and extremely fluid."

44. Jennifer Harper, "Nashville's New Nickname: 'Little Kurdistan,'" *Washington Times*, February 23, 2013, http://www.washingtontimes.com/blog/watercooler/2013/feb/23/nashvilles-new-nick-name-little-kurdistan/.

45. Similarly, Clarkston, Georgia, which sits just outside Atlanta, is called the "Ellis Island of the South." It was designated a refugee resettlement by the U.S. State Department and now has fifty languages spoken in 1.1 square miles, making it one of the most culturally and religiously diverse populations in the United States.

46. "The Future of World Religions: Population Growth Projections, 2010–2050," April 2, 2015, http://www.pewforum.org/2015/04/02/religious-projections-2010-2050/.

47. Timothy K. Beal, "The White Supremacist Bible and the Phineas Priesthood," in *Sanctified Aggression: Legacies of Biblical and Post Biblical Vocabularies of Violence*, ed. Jonneke Bekkenkamp and Yvonne Sherwood (London: T & T Clark, 2003), 120–131. The Aryan Nations calls itself the "Church of Jesus Christ—Christian."

48. The term is the title for white supremacist terrorists. See the apparent source of the title in Richard Kelly Hoskins, *Vigilantes of Christendom: The Story of the Phineas Priesthood* (Lynchburg: Virginia Publishing Company, 1990).

49. Beal, "White Supremacist Bible," 124.

50. Beal, "White Supremacist Bible," 130.

51. I have argued elsewhere that the Bible consistently exhibits themes of compromise and respect for diversity within a community: "Compromise as a Biblical Value," in *The Bible in Political Debate: What Does It Really Say?*, ed. Frances Flannery and Rodney A. Werline (London: Bloomsbury T. & T. Clark, 2016), 183–195. See also Timothy Beal, *Rise and Fall of the Bible: The Unexpected History of an Accidental Book* (Boston: Houghton Mifflin Harcourt, 2011).

52. "Local Authorities Use a Whisper Campaign to Round Up Gay Men in Northern Nigeria," produced by Carol Hills, *The World*, PRI, February 7, 2014, http://www.pri.org/stories/2014-02-07/local-authorities-use-whisper-campaign-round-gay-men-northern-nigeria.

53. Goldie Blumenstyk, "Eboo Patel Has a Dream," *Chronicle of Higher Education*, April 29, 2013, http://chronicle.com/article/Eboo-Patel-Has-a-Dream/138847/.

54. Pew Forum survey report, "Many Americans Uneasy with Mix of Religion and Politics," released August 24, 2006, http://www.pewforum.org/2006/08/24/many-americans-uneasy-with-mix-of-religion-and-politics/#2).

55. Barna Group, "American Bible Society, The State of the Bible, 2013: A Study of U.S. Adults," 2013, http://www.americanbible.org/uploads/content/State%20of%20the%20Bible%20Report%20 2013.pdf. Note, too, the survey released in 2014 by Barna/ABS, http://www.americanbible.org/uploads/content/state-of-the-bible-data-analysis-american-bible-society-2014.pdf.

56. Consider the established dynamic explored by Harold Berman: "The principal affirmation is that law and religion are two different but interrelated aspects of social experience—in all societies, but especially in Western society, and still more especially in American society today." *The Interaction of Law and Religion* (Nashville: Abingdon Press, 1974), 11.

57. Jamal Greene, Nathaniel Persily, and Stephen Ansolabehere, "Profiling Originalism," *Columbia Law Review* 111 (2011): 356–418 (see especially 370–373).

58. Kammen notes (*Machine*, 72) that "by the mid-nineteenth century, the term 'constitutional' used as an adjective had become a convenient camouflage for...political expediency. A symbolic modifier could be utilized as a spurious legitimizer. America, the land

where politicians kept 'Constitution' poised on their palettes." Consider the use of the word "biblical" in the culture war debates, as in "the biblical view of marriage."

59. Peter J. Smith and Robert W. Tuttle, "Biblical Literalism and Constitutional Originalism," *Notre Dame Law Review* 86.2 (2011), 693.

60. E. D. Hirsch made this same claim in 1987 in *Cultural Literacy: What Every American Needs to Know* (New York: Vintage, 1987), which he followed up with his voluminous (with James Trefil and Joseph F. Kett) *Dictionary of Cultural Literacy: What Every American Needs to Know* (Boston: Houghton Mifflin, 1988). The first section of his dictionary is "The Bible." More recently, see Stephen Prothero, *Religious Literacy: What Every American Needs to Know—and Doesn't* (New York: HarperOne, 2008). Another is Berlinerblau, *Secular Bible*. Most recently, see Timothy Beal, *Biblical Literacy: The Essential Bible Stories Everyone Needs to Know* (New York: HarperOne, 2010).

61. As chapter 1 notes, "Clergy devoted to teaching parishioners about Christian scripture and how to apply it to their lives often find an audience quick to revere the Bible but slow to read it for themselves—at least in a fashion beyond reading into it what they want it to say." Compare this to the 1887 remark by the Unitarian minister Moncure Conway: "people have little more difficulty in reading their prepossessions into a constitution than sects have in finding their several creeds in the Bible"; Moncure D. Conway, "Unpublished Draft of a National Constitution by Edmund Randolph found among the papers of George Mason," *Scribner's Magazine* 2 (September 1887), 319–320).

62. "Teaching the Constitution in the Schools," *New York Commercial*, May 25, 1923, cited in Kammen, *Machine*, 231.

63. No topic better embodies this issue than the First Amendment and the challenges to teaching about the Bible and religion in public school. See most recently Charles C. Haynes, "Battling over the Bible in Public Schools: Is Common Ground Possible?," and Mark A. Chancey, "Public School Bible Courses in Historical Perspective: North Carolina as a Case Study," both in Chancey et al., *Bible in the Public Square*, 181–192 and 193–214, respectively.

64. In the popular mind, as chapter 1 tells us, the Bible is a simple document that can be read simply, literally, without note or commentary. It has been reinforced by a long tradition of reading Scripture and the Constitution in American life. It wasn't just a late-nineteenth-century reaction to evolution and so-called Higher Criticism that fueled Fundamentalism and Evangelicalism. The American Bible Society was founded in 1816 with an explicit mission to encourage a wider circulation of the Holy Scriptures "without note or comment," a phrase repeatedly appearing in American Bible Society annual reports; see, e.g., *Twenty-fifth Annual Report of the American Bible Society, presented 13 May 1841* (New York: Daniel Fanshaw, 1841), 88, 107, 108, 109, and 112. On Americans' predilection for a "biblical"/originalist identity that has been reinforced by the rhetoric of returning to founding principles and values, see Sacvan Bercovitch, *The American Jeremiad* (Madison: University of Wisconsin Press, 1978).

65. To use Berlinerblau's phrase; and see his "Bible in the Presidential Elections of 2012, 2008, 2004," 15–36.

66. Stanley Fish, "One University under God?," *Chronicle of Higher Education*, January 7, 2005, http://chronicle.com/jobs/2005/01/2005010701c.htm.

67. Sites accessed August 15, 2016: http://berkleycenter.georgetown.edu/rfp; http://hds.harvard.edu/faculty-research/programs-and-centers/religious-literacy-project; http://www.pluralism.org/.

CHAPTER 20

1. Barna Group, "The State of the Bible, 2014," http://www.americanbible.org/uploads/content/state-of-the-bible-data-analysis-american-bible-society-2014.pdf, accessed August 4, 2014.

2. Ziming Liu, "Reading Behavior in the Digital Environment," in *Paper to Digital: Documents in the Information Age* (Westport, Conn.: Libraries Unlimited, 2008), 53–70.

3. Liu, "Reading Behavior," 57, 58.

4. Liu, "Reading Behavior," 62.

5. Alan Jacobs, "Christianity and the Future of the Book," *New Atlantis* (fall 2011), http://www.thenewatlantis.com/publications/christianity-and-the-future-of-the-book, accessed August 4, 2014.

6. Heidi A. Campbell, "Introduction: The Rise of the Study of Digital Religion," in *Digital Religion: Understanding Religious Practice in New Media Worlds* (New York: Routledge, 2013), 1–22.

CHAPTER 21

1. Theological Commons, http://commons.ptsem.edu/.

2. Blue Letter Bible, https://www.blueletterbible.org/lang/lexicon/lexicon.cfm?strongs=H930.

3. Accordance, http://www.accordancebible.com/Opening-And-Amplifying-In-Accordance-10.

4. Accordance offers *Calvin's Commentaries* as well as his *Institutes of the Christian Religion*, and one can purchase access to the John Piper Sermon Manuscript Library, with thirteen hundred sermon manuscripts covering thirty years of Piper's ministry, for only $40.

5. John 14:6 is number 3, behind only John 3:16 and John 1:1.

CHAPTER 22

1. Jessica L. Collet and Omar Lizardo, "A Power-Control Theory of Gender and Religiosity," *Journal for the Scientific Study of Religion* 48, no. 2 (2009): 213–231, doi: 10.1111/j.1468-5906.2009.01441.x, quote from p. 213.

2. Collet and Lizardo, "Power-Control Theory."

3. Sergej Flere, "Gender and Religious Orientation," *Social Compass* 54 (2007): 239–253.

4. Alan Miller and Rodney Stark, "Gender and Religiousness: Can Socialization Explanations Be Saved?" *American Journal of Sociology* 107, no. 6 (2002): 1399–1423.

5. Collet and Lizardo, "Power-Control Theory."

6. John P. Hoffmann and John P. Bartkowski, "Gender, Religious Tradition and Biblical Literalism," *Social Forces* 86, no. 3 (2008): 1245–1272.

7. Hoffmann and Bartkowski, "Gender, Religious Tradition and Biblical Literalism," 1251.

8. Gordon W. Allport and J. Michael Ross, "Personal Religious Orientation and Prejudice," *Journal of Personality and Social Psychology* 5, no. 4 (1967): 432–443.

9. Allport and Ross, "Personal Religious Orientation and Prejudice," 434.

10. Richard L. Gorsuch and Susan E. McPherson, "Intrinsic/Extrinsic Measurement: I/E-Revised and Single-Item Scales," *Journal for the Scientific Study of Religion* 28, no. 3 (1989): 352.

11. Paul D. Sullins, "Gender and Religion: Deconstructing Universality, Constructing Complexity," *American Journal of Sociology* 112, no. 3 (2006): 838–880.

12. Analyses were weighted using the General Social Survey weighting variable for 2010. See General Social Survey, "Release Notes for the GSS 2010 Merged Data," October 2011, http://gss.norc.org/documents/other/ReleaseNotesfortheGSS2010MergedData1.pdf.

13. Sarah McGeown et al., "Gender Differences in Reading Motivation: Does Sex or Gender Identity Provide a Better Account?," *Journal of Research in Reading* 35, no. 3 (2012): 328–336.

14. Leslie J. Francis and Gemma Penny, "Gender Differences in Religion," in *Religion, Personality, and Social Behavior*, ed. Vassilis Saroglou (New York: Psychology Press, 2014), 313–337.

15. Cassandra E. Simon, Martha Crowther, and Hyoun-Kyoung Higgerson, "The Stage-Specific Role of Spirituality among African-American Christian Women throughout the Breast Cancer Experience," *Cultural Diversity and Ethnic Minority Psychology* (2007): 26–34.

16. Paul A. Djupe, Ananda E. Sokhey, and Christopher P. Gilbert, "Present but Not Accounted For? Gender Differences in Civic Resource Acquisition," *American Journal of Political Science* 31, no. 4 (2007): 906–920.

17. Mary E. Bendyna and Celinda C. Lake, "Gender and Voting in the 1992 Presidential Election," in *Year of the Woman: Myths and Realities,* ed. Elizabeth Adell Cook et al. (Boulder: Westview Press, 1994).

18. Michael R. Alvarez and John Brehm, "American Ambivalence towards Abortion Policy Development of a Heteroskedastic Probit Model of Competing Values," *American Journal of Political Science* (1995): 1055–1082.

19. Sidney Verba, Kay Lehman Schlozman, and Henry E. Brady, *Voice and Equality: Civic Voluntarism in American Politics* (Cambridge, MA: Harvard University Press, 1995).

20. Jean B. Elshtain, *Public Man, Private Woman: Women in Social and Political Thought* (Princeton: Princeton University Press, 1981).

21. Sullins, "Gender and Religion."

22. Brian Steensland, Jerry Z. Park, Mark D. Rengerus, Lynn D. Robinson, W. Bradford Wilcox, and Robert D. Woodberry, "The Measure of American Religion: Toward Improving the State of the Art," *Social Forces* 79, no. 1 (2000): 291–324.

23. Because more individuals indicated "not at all" as the extent to which they read the Bible for these political reasons, the poverty/war and abortion/homosexuality variables displayed skewness > 1. I took the natural log of each and reran the models; results remained the same.

24. David C. Leege, "Catholics and the Civic Order: Parish Participation, Politics, and Civic Participation," *Review of Politics* 50 (1988): 704–736.

25. Pearson's chi-square tests were administered to each dichotomous variable with gender, all resulting in p values > 0.10.

26. Hoffmann and Bartkowski, "Gender, Religious Tradition and Biblical Literalism."

27. Djupe, "Present but Not Accounted For."

CHAPTER 23

1. C. Smith, R. Faris, and M. L. Denon, "Mapping American Adolescent Subjective Religiosity and Attitudes of Alienation toward Religion: A Research Report," *Sociology of Religion* 64, no. 1 (2003): 111–133; L. G. DeHaan, J. E. Yonker, and C. Affholter, "More Than Enjoying the Sunset: Conceptualization and Measurement of Religiosity for Adolescents and Emerging Adults and Its Implications for Developmental Inquiry," *Journal of Psychology and Christianity* 30, no. 3 (2011): 184–195; S. A. Desmond, K. H. Morgan, and G. Kikuchi, "Religious

Development: How (and Why) Does Religiosity Change from Adolescence to Young Adulthood?," *Sociological Perspectives* 53, no. 2 (2010): 247–270.

2. DeHaan, Yonker, and Affholter, "More Than Enjoying the Sunset."

3. J. J. Arnett and L. A. Jensen, "A Congregation of One: Individualized Religious Beliefs among Emerging Adults," *Journal of Adolescent Research* 17, no. 5 (2002): 451–467.

4. J. C. Meister, and K. Willyerd, "Mentoring Millennials," *Harvard Business Review* 88, no. 5 (2010): 68–72.

5. Arnett and Jensen, "Congregation," 474.

6. Arnett and Jensen, "Congregation," 463.

7. J. Farrell, "The Young and the Restless? The Liberalization of Young Evangelicals," *Journal for the Scientific Study of Religion* 50, no. 3 (2011): 517–532.

8. Pew Forum on Religion and Public Life, *U.S. Religious Landscape Survey: Religious Affiliation: Diverse and Dynamic* (Washington, DC: Pew Research Center, 2008), http://religions .pewforum.org/pdf/report-religious-landscape-study-full.pdf, accessed April 20, 2014.

9. C. Smith and P. Snell, *Souls in Transition: The Religious and Spiritual Lives of Emerging Adults* (Oxford: Oxford University Press, 2009), 116.

10. Pew Forum on Religion and Public Life, *U.S. Religious Landscape Survey*.

11. R. Turner, "The Real Self: From Institution to Impulse," *American Journal of Sociology* 81, no. 5 (1976): 990, 1012.

12. P. Vannini and A. Franzese, "The Authenticity of Self: Conceptualization, Personal Experience, and Practice," *Sociology Compass* 2, no. 5 (2008): 1624.

13. L. E. Lassiter, *The Chicago Guide to Collaborative Ethnography* (Chicago: University of Chicago Press, 2005).

14. M. Q. Patton, *Qualitative Evaluation and Research Methods*, 3rd ed. (Thousand Oaks, CA: Sage, 2002).

15. Patton, *Qualitative Evaluation*.

16. This research was conducted under exempt status at the University of Georgia (project # STUDY00000263).

17. Smith and Snell, *Souls*, 291.

18. Smith and Snell, *Souls*, 290.

19. Turner, "Real."

20. R. H. Turner and J. Schutte, "The True Self Method for Studying the Self-Conception," *Symbolic Interaction* 4, no. 1 (1981): 1–20.

21. Turner and Schutte, "True Self Method," 18.

CHAPTER 24

1. "The Translators to the Readers," in *King James Bible* (London: Robert Barker, 1611), 11; a good overview of the creation of the KJV can be found in Adam Nicolson, *God's Secretaries: The Making of the King James Bible* (New York: HarperCollins, 2003).

2. Gordon Campbell, *Bible: The Story of the King James Version* (New York: Oxford University Press, 2010), 79–82.

3. Paul C. Gutjahr, *An American Bible: A History of the Good Book in the United States 1777–1880* (Stanford, CA: Stanford University Press, 1999), 193.

4. Gutjahr, *American Bible*, 193–194.

5. Margaret Hills, *The English Bible in America* (New York: American Bible Society, 1962), 295.

6. Kenneth Cmiel, *Democratic Eloquence: The Fight over Popular Speech in Nineteenth-Century America* (New York: Morrow, 1990), 216–217.

7. Cmiel, *Democratic Eloquence,* 219.

8. Hills, *English Bible,* 332.

9. Peter J. Thuesen, *In Discordance with the Scriptures: American Protestant Battles over Translating the Bible* (New York: Oxford University Press, 1999), 90.

10. Thuesen, *In Discordance with the Scriptures,* 88.

11. Herbert Gordon May, *Our English Bible in the Making: The Word of Life in Living Language* (Philadelphia: Westminster Press, 1952), 53.

12. Bruce M. Metzger, *The Bible in Translation: Ancient and English Versions* (Grand Rapids, MI: Baker Academic Books, 2001), 167.

13. Metzger, *Bible in Translation,* 168.

14. Folder "Historical Essays TEV—Secondary Material," RG 53, box 2; "Historical Essay, Studies 10–15," manuscript, American Bible Society Archives, Philadelphia, 2, 12.

15. The best discussion of this controversy is found in Thuesen, *In Discordance with the Scriptures,* 93–119.

16. Metzger, *Bible in Translation,* 120.

17. Metzger, *Bible in Translation,* 139–140.

18. Richard Kevin Barnard, *God's Word in Our Language: The Story of the New International Version* (Colorado Springs: International Bible Society, 1989), 180.

19. Daniel Radosh, "The Good Book Business," *New Yorker,* December 18, 2006, 56.

20. Paul C. Gutjahr, "From Monarchy to Democracy: The Dethroning of the King James Bible in the United States," in Hannibal Hamlin and Norman W. Jones, eds., *The King James Bible after 400 Years* (New York: Cambridge University Press, 2010), 164–178.

21. James Deetz, *In Small Things Forgotten: The Archaeology of Early American Life* (New York: Anchor Books, 1977), 88.

22. For the enduring conservative trend of publishing Bibles in leather, see Gutjahr, *American Bible,* 191.

23. The best history of Gideons International is written by one of its former presidents: M. A. Henderson, *Sowers of the Word: A 95-Year History of the Gideons International, 1899–1994* (Nashville: Gideons International, 1995). Statistics on the organization's domestic and international scripture distribution are regularly updated on its website, www.gideons.org.

24. Paul C. Gutjahr, "Sacred Texts in the United States," *Book History* 4 (2001): 351.

25. Richard Behar, "The Thriving Cult of Greed and Power," *Time,* May 6, 1991, 55–56.

CHAPTER 25

1. James S. Bielo, *Words upon the Word: An Ethnography of Evangelical Group Bible Study* (New York: New York University Press, 2009).

2. Nancy T. Ammerman, *Bible Believers: Fundamentalists in the Modern World* (New Brunswick: Rutgers University Press, 1987); Melinda B. Wagner, *God's Schools: Choice and Compromise in American Society* (New Brunswick: Rutgers University Press, 1990); David Harrington Watt, *Bible-Carrying Christians: Conservative Protestants and Social Power* (Oxford: Oxford University Press, 2002).

3. Kathleen Boone, *The Bible Tells Them So: The Discourse of Protestant Fundamentalism* (Albany: State University of New York Press, 1989); Susan F. Harding, *The Book of Jerry Falwell: Fundamentalist Language and Politics* (Princeton: Princeton University Press, 2000); Peter

Stromberg, *Language and Self-Transformation: A Study of the Christian Conversion Narrative* (Cambridge: Cambridge University Press, 1993); Jeff Todd Titon, *Powerhouse for God: Speech, Chant and Song in an Appalachian Baptist Church* (Austin: University of Texas Press, 1988).

4. John Bartkowski, "Beyond Biblical Literalism and Inerrancy: Conservative Protestants and the Hermeneutic Interpretation of Scripture," *Sociology of Religion* 57 (1996): 259–272; Brian Malley, *How the Bible Works: An Anthropological Study of Evangelical Biblicism* (Walnut Creek: AltaMira Press, 2004).

5. See chapter 1.

6. Colleen McDannell, *Material Christianity: Religion and Popular Culture in America* (New Haven: Yale University Press, 1995); Tim K. Beal, *Roadside Religion: In Search of the Sacred, the Strange, and the Substance of Faith* (Boston: Beacon Press, 2005).

7. The methodological details of this fieldwork are unconventional in several ways. I was not granted complete open access to the team's creative labor. I had to arrange each fieldwork visit weeks ahead of time with the team. Throughout the forty-three months of fieldwork, planned visits were canceled or rescheduled by the team on numerous occasions, often with little advanced notice. Ultimately, I logged around 125 hours at the design studio. During this time, my primary forms of data collection were observing and interviewing the artists while they worked at their cubicles and recording team meetings. When possible, I would audio-record my informal interviewing with the artists at their desks. Because the design studio was filled with concept art and other material culture items, I relied heavily on fieldwork photography (with a cache of more than 750 jpeg images). I also audio-recorded semistructured interviews with each team member. The Ark Encounter website was an additional data source, in particular the project blog that provided publicity-oriented updates on the team's progress and arguments in support of creationist historical claims. I supplemented this fieldwork with observations at the Creation Museum on numerous visits, observations at other Answers in Genesis events (e.g., the much publicized Ken Ham–Bill Nye debate in February 2014), and observations at other evangelical museum and entertainment sites (e.g., The Holy Land Experience in Orlando, Florida).

8. See Peter Stromberg, *Caught in Play: How Entertainment Works on You* (Stanford: Stanford University Press, 2009) for a discussion of immersion.

9. See chapter 1.

10. Malley, *How the Bible Works*; see also Bielo, *Words upon the Word*.

11. Vincent Crapanzano, *Serving the Word: Literalism in America from the Pulpit to the Bench* (New York: New Press, 2000), 2–3.

12. Crapanzano, *Serving the Word*, x.

13. See Matthew Engelke, *God's Agents: Biblical Publicity in Contemporary England* (Berkeley: University of California Press, 2013), for an extended discussion of ethnographies of cultural production.

14. Genesis 6:14–16, NIV.

15. Janet Brown, "Noah's Flood, the Ark, and the Shaping of Early Modern Natural History," in *When Science and Christianity Meet* (Chicago: University of Chicago Press, 2003), 111–112.

16. Norman Cohn, *Noah's Flood: The Genesis Story in Western Thought* (New Haven: Yale University Press, 1996).

17. Brown, "Noah's Flood," 116.

18. Larry Eskridge, "A Sign for an Unbelieving Age: Evangelicals and the Search for Noah's Ark," in *Evangelicals and Science in Historical Perspective* (Oxford: Oxford University Press, 1999), 244–263.

19. Richard Bauman, *A World of Others' Words: Cross-cultural Perspectives on Intertextuality* (London: Blackwell, 2004), 4.

20. Richard Bauman and Charles Briggs, "Genre, Intertextuality, and Social Power," *Journal of Linguistic Anthropology* 2 (1992): 149.

21. Mark J. P. Wolf, *Building Imaginary Worlds: The Theory and History of Subcreation* (London: Routledge, 2012): 155.

22. Michael Saler, *As If: Modern Enchantment and the Literary Prehistory of Virtual Reality* (Oxford: Oxford University Press, 2012): 67.

23. Genesis 6:13, NIV.

24. See Brook Wilensky-Lanford, *Paradise Lust: Searching for the Garden of Eden* (New York: Grove Press, 2011), for examples of realist maps of Eden.

25. Bauman and Briggs, "Genre, Intertextuality, and Social Power," 147.

CHAPTER 26

1. J. Mark Bertrand, *Back on Murder* (Minneapolis: Bethany, 2010), 71.

2. Bertrand, *Back on Murder*, 73.

3. The complete list: Bertrand, *Back on Murder*; Candice Calvert, *Trauma Plan* (Carol Stream, IL: Tyndale, 2012); Colleen Coble, *Storm Warning* (Lakewood Ranch, FL: Spencerhill, 2013); Brandilyn Collins, *Deceit* (Grand Rapids, MI: Zondervan, 2010); Mary Connealy, *Out of Control* (Minneapolis: Bethany, 2011); Lynette Eason, *Too Close to Home* (Grand Rapids, MI: Revel, 2010); Chris Farby, *Every Waking Moment* (Carol Stream, IL: Tyndale, 2013); Ann H. Gabhart, *Love Comes Home* (Grand Rapids, MI: Revel, 2014); Katie Ganshert, *A Broken Kind of Beautiful* (Colorado Springs: Waterbrook, 2014); Shawn Grady, *Through the Fire* (Minneapolis: Bethany, 2009); Lisa Harris, *Dangerous Passage* (Grand Rapids, MI: Revel, 2013); Kristen Heitzmann, *Secrets* (Minneapolis: Bethany, 2004); Rachel Hauck, *Georgia on Her Mind* (New York: Steeple Hill, 2006); Denise Hunter, *Dancing with Fireflies* (Nashville: Thomas Nelson, 2014); Karen Kingsbury, *Fifteen Minutes* (New York: Howard, 2014); Creston Mapes, *Nobody* (Colorado Springs: Multnomah, 2007); Richard L. Mabry, *Code Blue* (Nashville: Abingdon, 2010); Aimee Martin, *Forever Home* (San Angelo, TX: Mercy Books, 2014); Lorena McCourtney, *Invisible* (Grand Rapids, MI: Revel, 2004); Meg Moseley, *A Stillness of Chimes* (Colorado Springs: Multnomah, 2014); Christa Parrish, *Stones for Bread* (Nashville: Thomas Nelson, 2013); Tracie Peterson and James Scott Bell, *City of Angels* (Woodland Hills, CA: Compendium, 2012); Allison Pittman, *All for a Song* (Carol Stream, IL: Tyndale, 2013); Francine Rivers, *Bridge to Haven* (Carol Stream, IL: Tyndale, 2014); Joel C. Rosenberg, *Damascus Countdown* (Carol Stream, IL.: Tyndale, 2013); Jake Smith, *Wish* (Carol Stream, IL: Tyndale, 2014); Randy Singer, *The Last Plea Bargain* (Carol Stream, IL: Tyndale, 2012); Janice Thompson, *Fools Rush In* (Grand Rapids, MI: Revel, 2009); Lenora Worth, *An April Bride* (Grand Rapids, MI: Zondervan, 2014); Susan May Warren, *Take a Chance on Me* (Carol Stream, IL: Tyndale, 2013); Alice J. Wisler, *Rain Song* (Bloomington, MN: Bethany, 2008); Nicole Young, *Love Me If You Must* (Grand Rapids, MI: Revel, 2012); William Paul Young, *Cross Roads* (New York: Hatchette, 2012).

4. Gregory Smith et al, "America's Changing Religious Landscape," Pew Research Center, May 12, 2015, http://www.pewforum.org/files/2015/05/RLS-05-08-full-report.pdf; Steven P. Miller, *The Age of Evangelicalism: America's Born-Again Years* (Oxford: Oxford University Press, 2014), 7.

5. David Bebbington, *Evangelicalism in Modern Britain* (Abingdon, England: Routledge, 2002), 3.

6. Some works that have informed my own thinking on this point include Mark Noll, *Between Faith and Scholarship: Evangelicals, Scholarship and the Bible in America* (Vancouver: Regent College, 1986); George M. Marsden, *Reforming Fundamentalism: Fuller Seminary and the New Evangelicalism* (Grand Rapids, MI: Eerdmans, 1987); Peter J. Thuesen, *In Discordance with the Scriptures: American Protestant Battles over Translating the Scriptures* (Oxford: Oxford University Press, 1999); Molly Worthen, *Apostles of Reason: The Crisis of Authority in American Evangelicalism* (Oxford: Oxford University Press, 2014); and Timothy E. W. Gloege, *Guaranteed Pure: The Moody Bible Institute, Business and the Making of Modern Evangelicalism* (Chapel Hill: University of North Carolina Press, 2015).

7. Harold Lindsell, *The Battle for the Bible* (Grand Rapids, MI: Zondervan, 1978). For an update, see G. K. Beale, *The Erosion of Inerrancy in Evangelicalism: Responding to New Challenges to Biblical Authority* (Wheaton, IL: Crossway, 2008). Compare Peter Enns, *The Bible Tells Me So: Why Defending Scripture Has Made Us Unable to Read It* (New York: HarperOne, 2014).

8. Gregory Alan Thornbury, *Recovering Classic Evangelicalism: Applying the Wisdom and Vision of Carl F. H. Henry* (Wheaton, IL: Crossway, 2013), 125, 118.

9. Tanya Luhrmann, *When God Talks Back: Understanding the American Evangelical Relationship with God* (New York: Knopf, 2012), 5, 58–59, 89.

10. James S. Bielo, *Words upon the Word: An Ethnography of Evangelical Group Bible Study* (New York: New York University Press, 2009), 12.

11. Charles Taylor, *A Secular Age* (Cambridge, MA: Harvard University Press, 2007), 173.

12. Taylor, *Secular Age*, 172.

13. Some excellent studies of evangelical novels include Amy Frykholm, *Rapture Culture: Left Behind in Evangelical America* (Oxford: Oxford University Press, 2004); Lynn S. Neal, *Romancing God: Evangelical Women and Inspirational Fiction* (Chapel Hill: University of North Carolina Press, 2006); and Valerie Weaver-Zercher, *Thrill of the Chaste: The Allure of Amish Romance Novels* (Baltimore: John Hopkins University Press, 2013).

14. Most notably, this survey does not include evangelical novels set in the cultural context of the Amish faith traditions or evangelical historical fiction, despite the popularity of those genres. Speculative fiction, supernatural horror, and similar genres were also excluded. Analysis of how the Bible is imagined in those forms of fiction would need to be done separately.

15. James Wood, *The Broken Estate: Essays on Literature and Belief* (New York: Picador, 2000), xxi.

16. Wolfgang Iser, *The Fictive and the Imaginary* (Baltimore: John Hopkins University Press, 1993), 16.

17. Karen Kingsbury, Francine Rivers, and William Paul Young.

18. Frykholm, *Rapture Culture*, 53.

19. Calvert, *Trauma Plan*, 21.

20. Singer, *Last Plea Bargain*, 95; Farby, *Every Waking Moment*, 152.

21. Moseley, *Stillness*, 191.

22. Peterson and Bell, *City of Angels*, 14–18, 126, 131, 234–235.

23. Thompson, *Fools*, 202.

24. Kingsbury, *Fifteen Minutes*, 107.

25. Rivers, *Bridge*, 442.

26. McCourtney, *Invisible*, 158.

27. Mabry, *Code Blue*, 207.

28. Eason, *Too Close*, 62.

29. Wisler, *Rain Song*, 149.

30. Wisler, *Rain Song*, 25.

31. Young, *Cross Roads*, 163.

32. Young, *Cross Roads*, 167.

33. Peterson and Bell, *City of Angels*, 279.

34. Peterson and Bell, *City of Angels*, 281.

35. Mapes, *Nobody*, loc. 1151.

36. Mapes, *Nobody*, loc. 4302.

37. See: Grady, *Through the Fire*, loc. 1803; Eason, *Too Close*, 64.

38. Farby, *Every Waking Moment*, 154.

39. Farby, *Every Waking Moment*, 345.

40. Ganshert, *Broken Kind of Beautiful*, 184.

41. Rivers, *Bridge*, 364.

42. Pittman, *All for a Song*, 200.

43. Collins, *Deceit*, 186.

44. Smith, *Wish*, 278.

45. Harris, *Dangerous Passage*, 261.

46. Harris, *Dangerous Passage*, 264.

47. Kingsbury, *Fifteen Minutes*.

48. Ganshert, *Broken Kind of Beautiful*, 162.

49. Thompson, *Fools*, 202.

50. Eason, *Too Close*, 205.

51. In 2015, 88 percent of households reported owning a Bible. Thirteen percent reported buying a Bible in the past year. Forty-eight percent said they owned four or more Bibles. "State of the Bible 2015," Barna Group, February 2015, http://www.americanbible.org/uploads/content/State_of_the_Bible_2015_report.pdf.

52. See chapter 1.

53. See chapter 1.

54. For a study of the market for evangelical fiction, see Daniel Silliman, "Publishers and Profit Motives: The Economic History of 'Left Behind,'" in *Religion and the Marketplace in the United States,* ed. Jan Stievermann, Philip Goff, and Detlef Junker (Oxford: Oxford University Press, 2014), 165–188.

CHAPTER 27

1. Knight quoted in Larry Yust, *Salvation Mountain: The Art of Leonard Knight* (Los Angeles: New Leaf Press, 1998), 21.

2. Leonard Knight, communication with author, June 2009, in author's possession.

3. Knight quoted in Yust, *Salvation Mountain,* 25.

4. Charlie LeDuff, "Parked in the Desert, Waiting Out the Winter of Life," *New York Times,* December 17, 2004.

5. *Into the Wild* (DVD), dir. Sean Penn, Square 1 Productions, 2008.

6. Throughout this essay I've replicated the messages as they are painted on the mountain rather than standardizing capitalization or punctuation.

7. Quoted in Yust, *Salvation Mountain,* 29.

8. Marilyn Dunn, *The Emergence of Monasticism: From the Desert Fathers to the Early Middle Ages* (Oxford: Blackwell, 2000), 19–20.

9. In February 2014 Leonard Knight died. Since that time, visitors to Salvation Mountain are left more or less to interpret the space for themselves. His absence and the loss of his storytelling have changed the way people experience Salvation Mountain.

10. Leonard Knight, communication with author, June 2009, in author's possession.

11. Emphasis mine.

12. Leonard Knight, communication with author, June 2009, in author's possession.

13. Quoted in Yust, *Salvation Mountain,* 79.

14. Brain Annett, correspondence with author, June 19, 2011.

15. Diana Sainz, "Salvation Mountain—A Unique Surprise," February 16, 2010. Entry for http://dianasainz.wordpress.com/2010/02/16/salvationmountain/, accessed July 24, 2011.

16. William T. Vollmann, *Imperial* (New York: Viking Press, 2009), 1033.

17. David Morgan, *Religion and Material Culture* (London: Routledge, 2010), 7–11.

18. David Morgan, *The Embodied Eye: Religious Visual Culture and the Social Life of Feeling* (Berkeley: University of California Press, 2012), 111, 166.

19. Morgan, *Religion and Material Culture,* 59–70.

20. Person 19, interviewed June 7, 2011.

21. Morgan has an interesting discussion of sensory hierarchies and the way they might support particular ideologies. See Morgan, *Embodied Eye,* 161–165.

22. Mindy Munro, correspondence with author, July 15, 2011.

23. Cindy Holleman, correspondence with author, July 14, 2011.

24. Sainz, "Salvation Mountain—A Unique Surprise."

CHAPTER 28

1. Amy O'Leary, "In the Beginning Was the Word: Now the Word Is on an App," *New York Times,* July 26, 2013. As of July 31, 2014, the count on the YouVerse website was 969 versions in 667 languages, with over 148 million downloads. https://www.youversion.com, July 31, 2014.

2. Ted Olsen, "The Bible in the Original Geek," *Christianity Today,* March 2014, 28–35.

3. See Cathleen Falsani, "The 'Terror' of *Noah*: How Darren Aronofsky Interprets the Bible," *Atlantic,* March 26, 2014; and Brook Wilensky-Lanford, "Flood of Idiocy: What Religious Zealots Don't Understand about *Noah,*" *New Republic,* April 21, 2014, 7–8.

4. Social Security Administration, "Popular Baby Names: Top Names of the 2000s," https://www.ssa.gov/oact/babynames/decades/names2000s.html, accessed August 15, 2016.

5. Daniel Radosh, "The Good Book Business," *New Yorker,* December 18, 2006.

6. *EPA v. Eme Homer City Generation, L.P.,* 572 U.S. [p. 3 of preliminary Supreme Court Record] (2014).

7. D. Paul Monteiro, Associate Director, White House Office of Pubic Engagement, "Remarks by the President at the National Prayer Breakfast" (email memo), February 2, 2012.

8. Ralph Reed, as quoted in David Nakamura and Michelle Boorstein, "At Prayer Breakfast and with Birth-Control Decision, Obama Riles Religious Conservatives," *Washington Post,* February 3, 2012, http://www.washingtonpost.com/local/at-prayer-breakfast-and-with-birth-control-decision-obama-riles-religious-conservatives/2012/02/02/gIQAgy1blQ_story.html accessed February 4, 2012; Peter Wehner, remarks contributed to *Commentary* (email), February 3, 2012.

9. For the Pryor commercial, see https://www.youtube.com/watch?v=-o6D9cPTFgo, accessed August 15, 2016. See also Frank Bruni, "The Bible as Bludgeon," *New York Times,* Sunday Review, December 7, 2013.

10. Brief for United States Conference of Catholic Bishops; National Association of Evangelicals; The Church of Jesus Christ of Latter-day Saints; The Ethics & Religious Liberty Commission of the Southern Baptist Convention; and the Lutheran Church-Missouri Synod as Amici Curiae Supporting Defendants-Appellants, *Baskin v. Bogan*, 7th Cir., case no. 14-2386 (pending), filed July 22, 2014 (p. 6).

11. See Sandra Reimer, "Bible Engagement in Canada: Confidence, Conversation, and Community," *Christian Week*, July 2014, 16.

12. See http://www.in.gov/core/city_county_facts.html; http://www.whateveristrue.com/heritage/biblenames.htm; http://en.wikipedia.org/wiki/Biblical_toponyms_in_the_United_States#Eden (all accessed July 31, 2014).

13. See David Paul Nord, *Faith in Reading: Religious Publishing and the Birth of Mass Media in America* (New York: Oxford University Press, 2004); Paul C. Gutjahr, *An American Bible: A History of the Good Book in the United States, 1777–1880* (Stanford: Stanford University Press, 1999); Peter J. Thuesen, *In Discordance with the Scriptures: American Protestant Battles over Translating the Bible* (New York: Oxford University Press, 1999).

14. James Cardinal Gibbons, *The Faith of Our Fathers: A Plain Exposition and Vindication of the Church Founded by Our Lord Jesus Christ* (1876) (Charlotte, NC: TAN Books, from the 112th edition, n.d.), 80, 67.

15. That center is directed by a convert from Protestantism, Scott Hahn; see Hahn, *Scripture Matters: Essays on Reading the Bible from the Heart of the Church* (Steubenville, OH: Emmaus Road, 2003).

16. For example, Sarah Eekhoff Zylstra, "The Most Popular and Fastest Growing Bible Translation Isn't What You Think It Is," Gleanings, Christianity Today online, March 13, 2014, http://www.christianitytoday.com/gleanings/2014/march/most-popular-and-fastest-growing-bible-translation-niv-kjv.html, accessed August 4, 2014.

17. Margaret Hills, *English Bible in America: A Bibliography of Editions . . . 1777–1957* (New York: American Bible Society, 1962); and for foreign language Bibles, *The National Union Catalog, Pre-1956 Imprints* (Chicago: American Library Association, 1980), vols. 53 and 54.

18. Cindy Crosby, "Not Your Mother's Bible," *Publisher's Weekly*, October 30, 2006.

19. These pioneering works were David Brion Davis, *The Problem of Slavery in Western Culture* (Ithaca: Cornell University Press, 1966); Eugene D. Genovese, *Roll, Jordan, Roll: The World the Slaves Made* (New York: Pantheon, 1974); Albert J. Raboteau, *Slave Religion: The "Invisible Institution" in the Antebellum South* (New York: Oxford University Press, 1978).

20. *An Evening Thought: Salvation by Christ, with Penetential Cries: Composed by Jupiter Hammon, a Negro belonging to Mr. Lloyd of Queen's-Village, on Long-Island, the 25th of December, 1760* (n.p., 1760), Evans no. 49079. Carefully annotated reprintings of this broadside are found in *Phyllis Wheatley: Complete Writings*, ed. Vincent Carretta (New York: Penguin, 2011), 202–204; and Carretta, ed., *Unchained Voices: An Anthology of Black Authors in the English-speaking World of the Eighteenth Century* (Lexington: University Press of Kentucky, 1996), 26–28.

21. "Glory be to God on High" began a 1739 hymn by Charles Wesley, which was widely known in the colonies as number 63 in George Whitefield, *A Collection of Hymns for Social Worship* (London: William Strahan, 1753), 52–53, which paraphrased the *Gloria in Excelsis* from the Book of Common Prayer, which was itself a paraphrase of the angelic song recorded in Luke 2:14.

22. John Coffey, *Exodus and Deliverance: Deliverance Politics from John Calvin to Martin Luther King, Jr.* (New York: Oxford University Press, 2014), 100.

23. Albert Raboteau, "African Americans, Exodus, and the American Israel," *African American Religion: Interpretive Essays in History and Culture*, ed. Paul E. Johnson (reprint, ed. David Hackett; Berkeley: University of California Press, 1994), 84.

24. David Walker, *Appeal...to the Coloured Citizens of the World, but in Particular and Very Expressly, to Those of the United States of America*, ed. Charles M. Wiltse (New York: Hill and Wang, 1965), 14, 66, 59.

25. Martin Luther King, Jr., *I Have a Dream: Writings and Speeches That Changed the World*, ed. James Melvin Washington (San Francisco: HarperSanFrancisco, 1992), 102–106.

26. *New Testament with Psalms and Proverbs*, New Revised Standard Version (Cambridge: Cambridge University Press, 1989), ix.

Figures are indicated by "f" following page numbers. For references to the Scriptures, see the separate Scriptural Index.